Revisiting Gramsci's *Notebooks*

Historical Materialism Book Series

The Historical Materialism Book Series is a major publishing initiative of the radical left. The capitalist crisis of the twenty-first century has been met by a resurgence of interest in critical Marxist theory. At the same time, the publishing institutions committed to Marxism have contracted markedly since the high point of the 1970s. The Historical Materialism Book Series is dedicated to addressing this situation by making available important works of Marxist theory. The aim of the series is to publish important theoretical contributions as the basis for vigorous intellectual debate and exchange on the left.

The peer-reviewed series publishes original monographs, translated texts, and reprints of classics across the bounds of academic disciplinary agendas and across the divisions of the left. The series is particularly concerned to encourage the internationalization of Marxist debate and aims to translate significant studies from beyond the English-speaking world.

For a full list of titles in the Historical Materialism Book Series
available in paperback from Haymarket Books, visit:
https://www.haymarketbooks.org/series_collections/1-historical-materialism

Revisiting Gramsci's
Notebooks

Edited by
Francesca Antonini
Aaron Bernstein
Lorenzo Fusaro
Robert Jackson

Haymarket Books
Chicago, IL

First published in 2019 by Brill Academic Publishers, The Netherlands
© 2019 Koninklijke Brill NV, Leiden, The Netherlands

Published in paperback in 2020 by
Haymarket Books
P.O. Box 180165
Chicago, IL 60618
773-583-7884
www.haymarketbooks.org

ISBN: 978-1-64259-343-3

Distributed to the trade in the US through Consortium Book Sales and
Distribution (www.cbsd.com) and internationally through Ingram
Publisher Services International (www.ingramcontent.com).

This book was published with the generous support of Lannan
Foundation and Wallace Action Fund.

Special discounts are available for bulk purchases by organizations and
institutions. Please call 773-583-7884 or email info@haymarketbooks.org
for more information.

Cover design by Jamie Kerry and Ragina Johnson.

Printed in the United States.

10 9 8 7 6 5 4 3 2 1

Library of Congress Cataloging-in-Publication data is available.

In memory of Joseph Buttigieg,
who opened many Gramscian pathways

∵

Contents

PART 3
Gramsci and the Marxian Legacy

PART 4
Subalternity between Pre-modernity and Modernity

PART 5
Postcolonial and Anthropological Approaches

Foreword

Anne Showstack Sassoon

Recently, after many years of studying Gramsci's writings in different editions and formats, in both English and Italian, I had the opportunity to view a display of the original *Prison Notebooks* for the first time. To say that I was dumbfounded would be an understatement. The beauty of the tiny handwriting, the small size of the actual notebooks, the range of subjects and comments spread across the display cases in dim light to protect the restored pages was overwhelming. It made me think of the generations of scholars who have dedicated their lives to making Gramsci's work accessible to wider audiences, in different languages, across the world. The fact that I viewed these amazing documents with a Gramsci scholar early in his career made the experience all the more meaningful.

As a no longer young student of Gramsci, it gives me the greatest pleasure to know that Gramsci's writings continue to provide the basis of original, highly interesting work by early-career scholars across the globe. That is why this book is so useful. Beyond the work of individuals, a collection like this offers a substantive basis for the nurturing of a community of thinkers, whatever generation they might be. It creates the possibility to open up new conversations. This volume is a rich contribution by a predominantly new generation of Gramsci researchers to the development of Anglophone and international studies. Based on rigorous textual analysis the contributors provide innovative insights into Gramsci's own work, and give scope for reflection on the complexities and contradictions of rapidly changing contemporary national and international realities.

Gramsci's writings are the product of a 'laboratory' in which the very struggle for survival, both personally and politically, provided the impetus for tenacious devotion to intellectual investigation of difficult questions. Both by force of circumstance in a prison cell constrained by harsh restrictions and because of the political and the historical and indeed psychological necessity to grapple with complex, novel historical phenomena, Gramsci was forced to push the boundaries of given categories and language, writing in several notebooks at a time, developing and revising categories all within a project that he set out at the very beginning of his incarceration. It was a period of defeat, setbacks and both personal and political isolation. His response was to read and write as best he could while trying somehow or other to remain in contact with contemporary political reality, with his family, and with those who gave him support, notably the

Cambridge Italian academic in exile, Piero Sraffa, and Gramsci's sister-in-law, Tatiana Schucht, who remained in Italy.

At the same time, the resulting notebooks to this day provide a 'laboratory' for those of us who read him and attempt to make use of what he has to offer in very different contexts and with very different aims. Their incompleteness invites by example both creativity and rigour. They cross the boundaries that have arisen historically between academic disciplines to provide the basis for cross-fertilisation and new fusions that better adhere to the needs of analysing an ever and always rapidly changing contemporary reality. Going beyond textual analysis, Gramsci invites us to work with the material to understand better the difficult questions of our own times and to seek innovative responses. His is both a scientific laboratory and, perhaps, an artist's studio.

As the introduction states, and many of the contributions illustrate, crucial to Gramsci's approach is the need to investigate the threads that connect past and present at all levels of society, from institutional constructs to social practices to the ideas we all hold as intellectuals and as women and men of the street. Recognition of these complexities provides a basis for a strategic analysis of the present. There is no homogeneity, but there are ineluctable threads linking what we are given from the past and the future. This future is something to be constructed. As Marx wrote, human beings make their own history but not in conditions of their choosing. Gramsci's historical perspective is in fact derived from a commitment to understand better the harsh realities of his own time in order to contribute to laying the conceptual and political basis for overcoming the constraints of the present which is in turn the precondition for imagining and creating a better future.

We are therefore indeed fortunate to have new generations of scholars who recognise in Gramsci's writings their capacity to inspire innovative enquiries. This collection is able to build on the philological advances in Gramsci research which have been made over recent decades, predominantly in Italy, and on the opening of Soviet archives after 1989. It benefits from global perspectives. The contributions transcend not only continental but academic boundaries within academia. The cross-fertilisation of ideas across generations, disciplines and continents is reflected in the individual essays and enables them to throw light on neglected aspects of Gramsci's thought.

It is not necessary to go through the litany of contemporary political and social problems confronting countries and peoples across the globe to recognise that new ways of thinking and new insights are necessary for progressive solutions. These go well beyond the realities that Gramsci confronted. We must not exaggerate the negative in a superficial comparison with the 1920s and

1930s. This would only undermine optimism of the will. Nor must negativity obscure the progressive potential within contemporary change, hard as it may be to find. At the same time, pessimism of the intellect tells us that equally we must take nothing for granted. Gramsci is, of course, but one source for renewing our theory and practice. Yet we would be foolish to overlook what he has to offer. And we should be grateful to new generations and veterans of many years like those represented in this volume who continue to contribute to Gramsci studies.

London
December 2017

Acknowledgements

It would not have been possible to put together this book without encouragement and support from many people.

We would like to thank, first of all, the scholars who took part in the London conference from which this book arises, and especially those who helped us to organise it concretely (in particular Alex Loftus, Stathis Kouvelakis and Alex Callinicos). Thanks also to the contributors of this volume, who accepted to be part of this project and worked with passion on their own papers. We are also grateful to Fabio Frosini, Giuseppe Cospito, Giancarlo Schirru and Derek Boothman, for having helped us in reviewing and improving the chapters through their comments, as well as to the late Joseph A. Buttigieg, who first agreed to write the forward, and to Anne Showstack Sassoon, who generously accepted to substitute for him.

Thanks are also due to Danny Hayward (Historical Materialism Book Series) and to the staff of the Social Science section of Brill Academic Publishers: they have been very patient with us and supported us in the different phases of the work.

A special thanks to Peter D. Thomas: as Gramscian scholar, he first encouraged us to publish this book and, as co-editor of the Historical Materialism Book Series, he made it possible.

The Editors
October 2017

Note on the Text

All references in this volume to Gramsci's *Prison Notebooks* follow the internationally established standard of notebook number, followed by number of note, followed by page number. This standard is based on the Italian critical edition of the *Quaderni del carcere* edited by Valentino Gerratana (Turin: Einaudi, 1975) and on its reprints. For instance, Q3, § 76, 353 indicates Notebook 3, note 76, page 353.

As to the English editions, we refer to the critical edition by Joseph A. Buttigieg, that includes Notebooks 1–8 or we quote from the available English anthologies. If necessary, we provide our own translations.

Notes on Contributors

Francesca Antonini
is postdoctoral fellow at the Lichtenberg-Kolleg (Georg-August-Universität Göttingen, Germany). Previously she held research positions at the LabEX CoMod (Université de Lyon)-UMR 5206 Triangle (ENS de Lyon), France and at the Fondazione Luigi Einaudi (Turin, Italy). She received a PhD in the History of Philosophy from the University of Pavia in 2015. Besides Gramsci's thought, her research interests include the history of Italian political thought, the history of Marxism and Communism, and European intellectual history. She has published on Marx, Gramsci and Italian fascism. Her first monograph, on the concepts of Caesarism and Bonapartism in Antonio Gramsci's works, is forthcoming with Brill (Historical Materialism Book Series).

Aaron Bernstein
obtained a PhD in European Studies from King's College London in 2016, with a dissertation comparing Gramsci's re-reading of Marx's thought as a philosophy of praxis with Marx's own critique of philosophy. Aside from Gramsci's thought, his research interests include Marxist theory, European intellectual history, and social and political theory. He is currently turning his PhD dissertation into a book.

Derek Boothman
has translated into English two anthologies of Gramsci's writings, *Further Selections from the Prison Notebooks* (University of Minnesota Press, 1995) and, recently, an edition of the pre-prison letters (*A Great and Terrible World* (Haymarket Books, 2014)). He has written extensively on Gramsci in English and Italian, including a book on Gramsci's concept of translatability, now being updated for publication in English. He is a member of the Italian section of the International Gramsci Society, and has contributed to the Society's *Dizionario gramsciano* (Carocci, 2009) and the earlier volume *Le parole di Gramsci* (Carocci, 2004). He is the current editor of the online *International Gramsci Journal*.

Watcharabon Buddharaksa
completed his PhD in Politics at the University of York, UK, in 2014. He is an Assistant Professor in Politics at the Department of Political Science and Public Administration, Faculty of Social Sciences, Naresuan University, Thailand. He has published extensively on Gramscian theories, Thai political eco-

nomy, and Open Marxism. He is the author of *A Survey of Antonio Gramsci's Political Thought* published by Sommadhi in 2014 (in Thai) and co-edited *On Theories of Political Science and Public Administration* (Naresuan University Press, 2016). He serves on the Editorial Board of the *Journal of Social Sciences, Naresuan University* (JSSNU).

Takahiro Chino

is a Lecturer at Waseda University, Tokyo. After obtaining a PhD from University College London, he was appointed a Max Weber Fellow at the European University Institute, and a Postdoctoral Fellow at the Japan Society for the Promotion of Science. He is now transforming his PhD thesis on Gramsci into a monograph.

Riccardo Ciavolella

is an anthropologist of the CNRS at the Institute of Anthropology of the EHESS, Paris, where he teaches Political Anthropology. His research enquires into the way in which popular and subaltern groups engage in politics and how they can become a political subject. His work merges epistemological reflections on the entanglements between anthropology and Gramscian theories with more empirical ethnographic research among marginalised groups in Africa and Europe on subaltern politics in contemporary societies. His recent works include a book on the history and theories of Political Anthropology (*Introduction à l'anthropologie politique*, with E. Wittersheim (De Boeck Supérieur, 2016), an article on the translation of Gramsci's concepts in present-day urban Africa 'Gramsci and the African *Città futura*', *Antipode*, 2016, and an essay on the experience of anthropologist Ernesto De Martino during the Resistance movement and how this oriented his reading of Gramsci's *Notebooks* 'L'intellettuale e il popolo dalla crisi morale al riscatto socialista', *Nostos*, 2016.

Carmine Conelli

holds a PhD in International Studies at the University of Naples "L'Orientale" and he is a member of the Centre for Gender and Postcolonial Studies (CSPG) at the same University. His research interests cover Southern Italian history and sociology, postcolonial and cultural studies, Subaltern studies, decolonial theory and critical race studies. He has published some essays concerning a postcolonial interpretation of the Italian Southern Question, which has been also the main theme of his doctoral research. He is the co-editor of the book *Genealogie della modernità. Teoria radicale e critica postcoloniale* (Meltemi, 2017).

Anthony Crézégut

graduated from the Political institute (Sciences-po) of Paris, *Agrégé* in History and holds a scholarship from the Ecole française de Rome and Casa Velazquez of Madrid. He is working on a PhD thesis dealing with the reception of Gramsci in France, and through it the construction of an intellectual Marxism and the constitution, and later decomposition, of a left-wing *intelligentsia* in France from the late 1940s to the early 1980s. Among his recent contributions: 'Althusser, étrange lecteur de Gramsci. Lire «Le marxisme n'est pas un historicisme»: 1965–2015' (in *Décalages*, 2016).

Valentina Cuppi

graduated in Philosophical Science at the University of Bologna with a thesis entitled 'Between Education and Instruction: Hegemony in the Writings of Antonio Gramsci'. After some periods of research at the University of Campinas (UNICAMP) in Brazil, the National Autonomous University of Mexico (UNAM), and the University of Buenos Aires (UBA) in Argentina, she obtained a PhD in Political Science with a dissertation in 'Europe and the Americas: Constitutions, Doctrines and Political Institutions' conducted at the University of Bologna, which studied the reception of Gramsci's thoughts in Latin America.

Yohann Douet

is a PhD student in France, at the University of West Paris (Paris-Ouest Nanterre). His main research fields are Marxism, Philosophy of the Social Sciences, and Philosophy of History. In his thesis, he studies Gramsci's notion of history, through his conception of periodisation and the ways in which he conceives of epochs and historical breaks. He has also published articles engaging with the work of Althusser, Poulantzas, Laclau, Mouffe, E.P. Thompson, and Meiksins Wood. He is a member of the editorial committee of the French review Contretemps.web, and co-organises the seminar 'Lectures de Marx' at the ENS Paris.

Anne Freeland

is a PhD candidate in the Department of Latin American and Iberian Cultures and the Institute for Comparative Literature and Society at Columbia University, where she has just completed a dissertation on Gramscian theory in Latin America. She has published articles in the *Journal of Latin American Cultural Studies* and *A Contracorriente*, and her translation of René Zavaleta Mercado's *Towards a History of the National-Popular in Bolivia* is forthcoming from Seagull Books. She teaches at Marymount Manhattan College's campus at Bedford Hills Correctional Facility.

Fabio Frosini

is a lecturer in the History of Philosophy at the University of Urbino. He has been a member of the Scientific Committee of the Fondazione Istituto Gramsci (Rome) since 2008 and of the Board of the International Gramsci Society Italia since 2001. His research interests include Renaissance philosophy and culture, Marxist thought, and the history of political philosophy. His most recent books include *Da Gramsci a Marx. Ideologia, verità e politica* (DeriveApprodi, 2009), *La religione dell'uomo moderno. Verità e politica nei* Quaderni del carcere *di Antonio Gramsci* (Carocci, 2010), *Vita, tempo e linguaggio (1508–1510). L Lettura Vinciana* (Giunti, 2011), and *Maquiavel o revolucionário* (Ideias & Letras, 2016).

Lorenzo Fusaro

holds a PhD in International Political Economy from King's College London and is Associate Professor at the Universidad Autónoma Metropolitana, Mexico, where he teaches Political Economy and conducts research on a project titled 'Great Powers: Revolutions, Uneven Development and the Making of the World Order'. His publications include: *Crises and Hegemonic Transitions: From Gramsci's* Quaderni *to the Contemporary World Economy* (Brill, 2019); *The Prison Notebooks. The Macat Library* (Routledge, 2017, with J. Xidias and A. Fabry); and 'Why China is Different: Hegemony, Revolutions and the Rise of Contender States', (*Research in Political Economy*, 2017).

Robert Jackson

is Lecturer in Politics at Manchester Metropolitan University. He has published in *Science & Society*, the *International Gramsci Journal*, and *Gramsciana: Rivista internazionale di studi su Antonio Gramsci*. He was co-organiser of the *Past & Present* international Gramsci conference at King's College London, and participated in the *Ghilarza Summer Schools 2014/2016*. He is interested in the concept of 'mummification' and the language of life and death in Gramsci. His chapters 'Antonio Gramsci: Persons, Subjectivity and the Political' and 'Violence and Civilization: Gramsci, Machiavelli, and Sorel' appear respectively in the volumes *Subjectivity and the Political: Contemporary Perspectives* (Routledge, 2017) and *The Meanings of Violence: From Critical Theory to Biopolitics* (Routledge, 2018).

Alex Loftus

is a Reader in Political Ecology in the Department of Geography at King's College London. He is the author of *Everyday Environmentalism: Creating an Urban Political Ecology* (University of Minnesota Press, 2012) and co-editor of *Gram-*

sci: Space, Nature, Politics (Wiley-Blackwell, 2012). His research seeks to build on the philosophy of praxis in order to make sense of the politics of urban environments.

Susi Meret

is Associate Professor at the Department of Culture and Global Studies, Aalborg University (AAU), Denmark. She is affiliated with the research group CoMID, Center for the Studies of Migration and Diversity. She coordinated the research network on Nordic Populism and participated in various projects dealing with the emergence and consolidation of radical right-wing populism in Denmark and in Europe. Since 2014 she has actively participated in and researched the refugee-led movements and their struggles for rights, empowerment, and recognition in Germany, Denmark, and Italy.

Sebastian Neubauer

studied Political Science with a focus on Political Theory and the History of Political Thought, as well as Middle East studies at the Free University Berlin and at Northwestern University. He is currently working on a doctoral dissertation at the Free University Berlin and École Normale Supérieure on Louis Althusser, early modern political thought and the formation of postmodern theory.

Alessio Panichi

graduated in philosophy from the University of Pisa and obtained his PhD from the National Institute for Renaissance Studies (Florence). He is currently a graduate student in the Department of German and Romance Languages and Literatures, Johns Hopkins University (Baltimore). His research activity focuses on the history of political thought, particularly on some seventeenth- and twentieth-century writers, such as Tommaso Campanella, Kaspar Schoppe, Norberto Bobbio, and Luigi Firpo. He is the author of a book concerning Campanella's political thinking (*Il volto fragile del potere. Religione e politica nel pensiero di Tommaso Campanella*, ETS, 2015), as well as several essays.

Ingo Pohn-Lauggas

is a Literary and Cultural Studies scholar at the University of Vienna. He is a member of the editorial board of *Das Argument – Journal for Philosophy and Social Sciences* and of the *Historical-Critical Dictionary of Marxism* (HKWM). His publications focus on literary and cultural theory, as well as the work of Antonio Gramsci, e.g. a monograph on Aesthetics and Hegemony in the work of Gramsci and Raymond Williams (Löcker Verlag, 2013). Pohn-Lauggas is editor of the German edition of Gramsci's writings on Literature and Culture (Argument, 2012) and co-editor of the *Selected Writings of Stuart Hall* (Vol. 5: Populism, Hegemony, Globalization – Argument, 2014).

Roberto Roccu

is Senior Lecturer in International Political Economy in the Department of European and International Studies at King's College London. He works in the tradition of critical International Political Economy, and his research interests include social theory, the political economy of reforms and revolutions in the Middle East and North Africa, neoliberalism and financialisation in the Global South, Gramsci and more generally historical materialism. He is the author of *The Political Economy of the Egyptian Revolution* (Palgrave Macmillan, 2013), and his work has appeared in peer-reviewed journals such as *Journal of Common Market Studies, International Relations, Mediterranean Politics, Capital & Class*, and more.

Bruno Settis

holds a Master's degree in History from the University of Pisa and is currently a PhD student at the Scuola Normale Superiore in Pisa and the Centre d'Histoire de Sciences Po in Paris. He is the author of *Fordismi. Storia politica della produzione di massa* (Il Mulino, 2016).

Anne Showstack Sassoon

studied at the University of California, Berkeley, the University of Padua, and the London School of Economics. She taught at Kingston University, Kingston upon Thames, and Birkbeck, University of London and has been a visiting professor at Carleton University (Canada); Aalborg University (Denmark); L'Orientale (Napoli, Italy), and lectured elsewhere in Europe, the US, and Mexico. Her books include *Gramsci's Politics* (Croom Helm, 1980) and *Gramsci and Contemporary Politics* (Routledge, 2000), and edited collections, *Approaches to Gramsci* (Writers and Readers, 1982) and *Women and the State* (Hutchinson, 1987). Her books and articles have been translated into Spanish, German, Italian, French, Finnish, Portuguese, Swedish, Hungarian, and Turkish and made into a talking book in Norway. She lives in London, UK.

Alen Sućeska

graduated with a degree in Philosophy and Sociology from the University of Zagreb in 2011. He finished his PhD in Philosophy at the Goethe Universität in Frankfurt in 2015, with a dissertation entitled 'Hegemonic Language: Towards a Historical-Materialist Theory of Language'. He currently holds a postdoctoral position at the Department for Political Sciences at the University of Vienna. His main interests are state theory, theories of ideology, philosophy of language, and political theory.

Peter D. Thomas
is Senior Lecturer in Politics and History at Brunel University. He is the author of *The Gramscian Moment: Philosophy, Hegemony and Marxism* (Brill, 2009), and co-editor of *Encountering Althusser: Politics and Materialism in Contemporary Radical Thought* (Bloomsbury, 2012), and *In Marx's Laboratory: Critical Interpretations of the* Grundrisse (Brill, 2013). He serves on the editorial boards of *Historical Materialism*, the *International Gramsci Journal*, and the *Historical Materialism Book Series*, the Board of Directors of *Gramsciana: Rivista internazionale di studi su Antonio Gramsci*, and the International Scientific Committee of the *Ghilarza Summer School*.

Nicolas Vandeviver
is a postdoctoral researcher at Ghent University. Trained in Classics (2011) and Comparative Modern Literature (2012), he obtained a PhD in Literary Studies (2017) at Ghent University. In 2017–18 he was a Fulbright Visiting Scholar and Postdoctoral Fellow of the Belgian American Educational Foundation at Columbia University. He has taught and published on North American literary theory, existentialism and its legacies, and postcolonial studies. His forthcoming book *Edward Said and the Authority of Literary Criticism* (Palgrave Macmillan) reconstructs the literary critical milieu from which Said emerged in order to demonstrate how he sought to turn literary criticism into a form of political intervention.

Marta Natalia Wróblewska
holds MA degrees in Philosophy and Applied Linguistics from the University of Warsaw (Poland). She is currently a PhD candidate at the University of Warwick, working on a dissertation in the field of Applied Linguistics. Her main area of research is academic discourse and evaluation.

Introduction: Gramsci Past and Present

Francesca Antonini, Aaron Bernstein, Lorenzo Fusaro and Robert Jackson

The legacy of the Italian theorist Antonio Gramsci (1891–1937) has been widely acknowledged as one of the most significant intellectual contributions of the twentieth century. A crucial element in Gramsci's perspective is his profound sense of the manifold connections between the past and the present. This nexus between explication of the past and strategic analysis of the present is characteristic of the originality of Gramsci's approach. The heading 'Past and Present' is used by Gramsci as an instrument in the organisation and development of his thought, and it constitutes one of the most prominent themes in the *Prison Notebooks*.[1]

On a more general level, Gramsci's ability to dialectically combine seemingly opposed elements in a relationship of unity-distinction (i.e. civil society and the state, structure and superstructure, the spatial elements of historicism, or vice versa the multiple temporalities going across political space) illuminates the capacity of his thought to stimulate critical renewals in various domains of thought. Further investigation of this critical project reveals the aspect of reciprocal 'translatability' that Gramsci identifies between different facets of the knowledge of reality as philosophy, politics and economics. In other words, it brings into relief the idea of a 'homogeneous circle',[2] that is, the constitution of Gramsci's conception of the world and its relation to history, understood as a unitary and dynamic process.

This framework was explored by a two-day international conference held at King's College London and organised by a group of young Gramscian scholars (*Past and Present: Philosophy, Politics and History in the Thought of Antonio Gramsci*, 18–19 June 2015). The conference brought together 45 scholars from 16 countries. The present volume represents a selection of chapters developed from the presentations of the participants. It contains 25 distinctive contributions representing a growing global network of Gramscian thinkers ranging from early-career researchers to experienced scholars.

Strongly focused on the research carried out by early-career participants of the London conference, the principal aim of the book is to give voice to a new

---

1 On this topic, cf. the entry *Passato e presente* by Fabio Frosini in Liguori and Voza 2009, pp. 626–8.

2 Q4, § 46, p. 472; Gramsci 1971a, p. 403.

generation of scholars working on Gramscian themes. Taking its cue from the methodology of the best outputs of recent Gramscian scholarship, the essays collected here offer an innovative and fresh insight into Gramsci's thought. They also illuminate the promising trajectories of future Gramscian research projects.

While originating from different points of view, our collective intention is to investigate in the broadest sense the rich potentialities of the theme 'Past and Present'. We aim to explore this framework by analysing the conceptual laboratory of Gramsci's historical-political narration, as well as his endeavour to theorise the unity of theory and practice. More broadly, we aspire to study the way in which Gramsci's historical perspective intermingles with his engaged concern for the future of a 'great and terrible' world,[3] in a critical sense of what might today be called 'global history'.

In fact, the investigation of Gramsci's thought cannot be separated, as Peter Thomas affirms, from the awareness of living in a 'Gramscian moment'.[4] This volume represents a collection of new research on Gramsci at a point in time when his thought has increased in influence and become diffused across a broad spectrum of disciplines. In the last decades, Gramscian notions have spread through philosophy to history and geography, through cultural theory and subaltern studies, to international relations, linguistics, critical legal studies and beyond.[5] It is exciting evidence of the enduring capacity of Gramsci's thought to generate and nurture innovative inquiries across diverse themes. The chapters of this book engage with on-going debates in these different fields of study and aim to offer a key to interpret their most recent trends.

The novelty of the collection lies not only in its content but also in the methodology it applies. In light of the widespread and heterogeneous deployments of Gramscian ideas, it seems apt and necessary to return to the texts themselves: Gramsci's pre-prison and his prison writings, both the *Prison Notebooks* and the *Letters from Prison*.[6] We are convinced that a rigorous textual ana-

---

3   This is an expression from Rudyard Kipling adopted by Gramsci in letters to his wife Jul'ka; see Gramsci 2014a.

4   Thomas 2009a.

5   Gramscian scholarship has been undergoing a new season of publications, including recent edited collections assessing the contemporary relevance of his thought, such as Green 2011a and McNally 2015. A number of volumes have also explored and applied his thought in diverse fields, such as migration studies (Agustín and Jørgensen 2016), critical theory (Kreps 2015), geography (Ekers et al. 2013), subaltern studies (Zene 2013), postcolonial theory (Srivastava and Bhattacharya 2012), linguistics and translation studies (Ives and Lacorte 2010), and education (Mayo 2010).

6   The critical edition currently available in English is Gramsci 1992–2007. The first three

lysis is the unavoidable condition for a deeper understanding of his work and, consequently, for a fruitful interaction between Gramscian concepts and other theoretical and historical frameworks.

In this respect, the book capitalises on the philological tradition of studying Gramsci that has flourished in recent decades, especially in Italy. As Fabio Frosini notes in his survey of the development of Gramscian scholarship over the last fifty years,[7] the publication first of the critical edition of the *Prison Notebooks* edited by Valentino Gerratana (1975), and then of Gianni Francioni's *L'officina gramsciana* [*The Gramscian Laboratory*] (1984),[8] has affirmed a new approach towards the study of Gramsci's work. While Gramsci's writings have been subjected at times to a process of systematic re-ordering that obscured the dialectical emergence of his ideas, they are increasingly read as texts characterised by a constitutive incompleteness, for both external and internal reasons.[9] Consequently, they require the type of careful diachronic and philological approach that has been developed and refined in recent years, thanks both to individual contributions,[10] and collective initiatives,[11] which have culminated in the ongoing publication of the new critical 'National edition' of Gramsci's works.[12]

---

volumes of the English critical edition of the *Notebooks*, edited by Joseph Buttigieg, currently provide up to Notebook 8. The most widely available anthologies of the *Notebooks* in English are Gramsci 1971a and 1995.

7 Frosini 2008b. See also Vacca 2011.

8 See Francioni 1984 on the structure of the notebooks. This text also contains a strong criticism of Perry Anderson's article 'The Antinomies of Antonio Gramsci' (Anderson 1976). Despite this extensive criticism, Anderson's article remains one of the most influential readings of Gramsci in the Anglophone world. For a detailed account in English, see Thomas 2009a, pp. 41–83. Anderson has recently republished this text as a book with a new Preface, which all too briefly undertakes a condensed explanation of these criticisms (see Anderson 2017).

9 These reasons relating to, respectively, his confinement in prison and his open methodology, see Thomas 2009a, pp. 85–131, in particular p. 126 ff.

10 Some of these contributions are now available in English, such as Cospito 2016 [2011], and Liguori 2015b [2006].

11 These collective initiatives include the ongoing seminars organised by the *International Gramsci Society Italia* in Rome. The first cycle of this seminar (2000–03) was held on the lexicon of the *Prison Notebooks*, and its results published in Frosini and Liguori 2004. The second cycle (2004–06) was also focused on some key Gramscian categories, while the third, on the history of the *Notebooks*, is ongoing (2012–present). Two of the most significant initiatives, in different formats, have been the *Dizionario gramsciano* (Liguori and Voza 2009), and the *Ghilarza Summer Schools* 2014 and 2016, residential courses of advanced study on the thought of Gramsci for early career researchers.

12 An *Edizione nazionale* (National Edition) of the work of Antonio Gramsci is currently in preparation in Italian (see Frosini 2008b, and the special issue of *Studi Storici* (4, 2011)). In

The volume represents a timely encounter of diverse interpretations of Gramsci's ideas with a philological reading of his work. As a longer-term goal, we aim to promote an engagement with the recent achievements of Italian Gramsci scholarship in order to develop a deeper appreciation of and dialogue with them. In the past, studies of Gramsci, especially in the Anglophone world, have lacked the resources to engage fully with the process of development of Gramsci's writings.[13] In contrast, we are now working towards an assessment of the more subtle 'rhythms' of Gramsci's thought.

Furthermore, the book attempts to transcend existing national and 'continental' boundaries within academia, gathering scholars from thirteen different nationalities and from across the globe. In this sense, the volume aims to contribute to the concrete construction of a 'global' Gramscian community that relies on common methodological achievements.

Finally, this philological approach does not imply a dismissal of contemporary readings of Gramsci; on the contrary, it draws attention to neglected aspects of his thought and sheds a new, meaningful light on pressing issues of our historical conjuncture, as many of the contributors here amply demonstrate. This testifies to the status of Gramsci's work as a modern 'classic', capable of being 'contemporary' in different times.[14]

The structure of the volume is divided into the following eight sections: *Global Gramsci: Gramscian Geographies*; *Language and Translation*; *Gramsci and the Marxian Legacy*; *Subalternity between Pre-modernity and Modernity*; *Postcolonial and Anthropological Approaches*; *Culture, Ideology, Religion*; *Historical Capitalism and World History*; *Readings of Gramsci*.

Global Gramsci: Gramscian Geographies contends, on the one hand, that Gramsci's thought makes an important contribution to extant discussions within critical geography and presents the Italian author as a geographical historical materialist (Loftus). On the other hand, Roccu and Buddharaksa deploy Gramsci's writings to comprehend contemporary political and economic developments in Egypt and Thailand.

The section on *Language and Translation* focuses on Gramsci's distinguished analysis of language, sketching a fascinating structural parallel with his concept of ideology (Boothman), and emphasising how the Gramscian conception of

---

addition, an 'anastatic' version of the *Notebooks*, which reproduces the Notebooks in photographic form, has been published under the editorship of Gianni Francioni (Gramsci 2009).

13   On this point, see Thomas 2009a.

14   See Thomas 2009a, p. 130, as well as Frosini 2008b, p. 670.

language as a social and historical process contrasts with positivist currents in linguistics (Sućeska). Finally, Wróblewska examines the translations of Gramsci's texts from the point of view of his own complex theory of translation and translatability.

The section *Gramsci and the Marxian* legacy addresses the relation between Marx and Gramsci from a philosophical point of view, thereby addressing Gramsci's distinctive conception of revolution (Frosini), and points to some of the distinctive aspects of Gramsci's reformulation of Marx's thought as a philosophy of praxis (Bernstein). Furthermore, Antonini discusses the crucial role that historical analogy plays for the two authors.

The fourth section, *Subalternity between Pre-modernity and Modernity*, casts new light on the concept of the 'subaltern', interpreting the latter as exploited and as included, albeit 'passively', within hegemonic power structures (Thomas). While Freeland provides the reader with a combined analysis of Gramsci's categories of subalternity and the national-popular, Meret takes Gramsci's writings as a point of departure for analysing the pressing issues of space, mobility, migrant struggles, and subalternity.

In close thematic connection, the following section (*Postcolonial and Anthropological Approaches*) newly interprets the 'Southern question', taking account of recent insights into Gramsci's understanding of subaltern groups (Conelli). The latter are also chosen as a point of departure for Vandeviver, who makes the claim that Gramsci's conception of subalternity enables a fresh interpretation of Edward Said's *Orientalism*, as opposed to common readings based on Foucault. On the other hand, Ciavolella assesses the influence of Gramsci's ideas on anthropology and on the development of a 'popular politics'.

The section on *Culture, Ideology, Religion* opens with Gramsci's critique of the Catholic Church, highlighting how it differs from that of Benedetto Croce, and is developed from the failures of the latter (Chino). The chapter by Pohn-Lauggas discusses aesthetics, politics and Gramsci's substantive engagement with literature, showing how the latter should be taken into consideration in order better to grasp Gramsci's heterogeneous notes entitled 'Past and Present'. Finally, Jackson argues for the significance of a rarely studied concept in the Gramscian lexicon, the mummification of culture, and its critical function in overcoming the enduring influence of the 'living dead'.

The seventh section, *Historical Capitalism and World History*, stresses the novel contribution that a return to Gramsci's writings makes for our understanding of the transition from feudalism to capitalism, highlighting the dialectical relation between structure and superstructures (Douet). By pointing to Gramsci's state-centric analysis within the *Notebooks*, Fusaro comprehends international relations in a way that strongly contrasts with established neo-Gramscian analyses. Moreover, Settis's contribution casts new light on the Gramscian concept of 'Fordism'.

The final section, *Readings of Gramsci*, collects four essays that analyse the interpretations of Gramsci's thought that have been offered in the second half of the twentieth century in Italy, Latin America and France. While Panichi provides a critical discussion of the interpretation of Gramsci advanced by Norberto Bobbio, Cuppi focuses on the readings by José Maria Aricó, Juan Carlos Portantiero and Carlos Nelson Coutinho. The last two contributions, based on original archival research, illuminate respectively the diffusion of Gramsci's work in France (Crézégut) and its reception by Althusser (Neubauer).

To conclude, the book offers a window onto the ongoing development of a new generation of Gramscian scholars traversing diverse national contexts. Furthermore, it provides a distinctive approach aimed at drawing out the elements of coherence across these new projects and situating them, not as a series of individual elaborations, but within the ambit of a coordinated and collective international project.

PART 1

Global Gramsci: Gramscian Geographies

∴

CHAPTER 1

Gramsci as a Historical Geographical Materialist

Alex Loftus

1   Introduction

Exposed to the vicissitudes of uneven geographical development from an early age, Antonio Gramsci was deeply sensitive to the profoundly unequal spatialities of capitalist processes, as well as to the influence of geography on political alliances, solidarities and common sense. It is therefore unsurprising that several scholars have, in recent years, noted Gramsci's perceptiveness to the ways in which space, uneven development and geography matter. For Edward Said, Gramsci 'created in his work an essentially geographical, territorial apprehension of human history and society'.[1] In Jessop's opinion, Gramsci should be considered a 'spatial theorist';[2] and in Ekers et al. a range of authors elucidate the implicit (in which Gramsci mobilises a spatial or ecological understanding albeit not in name) and explicit (in which Gramsci discusses spatial relations directly) geographical contributions of the Sardinian, a project that the editors hope will enable a reinvigorated historical geographical materialism.[3] In this chapter, I will explore Gramsci's geographies a little further while also considering the surprising lack of dialogue between a spatialised Marxism – or what is sometimes termed a historical geographical materialism – and Gramsci's philosophy of praxis.

Most closely associated with the writings of David Harvey, historical geographical materialism refers to a range of approaches through which scholars have sought to spatialise historical materialism, emphasising the ways in which systems of accumulation are historically and spatially specific, as well as the ways in which space is crucial for the production and reproduction of capitalist social relations. Such approaches have extended Marx's critique of political economy through demonstrating the ways in which space is an active moment in differing modes of production. At the same time, historical geographical materialists have sought to understand the territorial and environmental configurations that result from differing modes of production and

---

1   Said 2001a, p. 464.
2   Jessop 2005.
3   Ekers et al. 2013.

reproduction. The vast majority of this work has drawn directly from Marx even if, more recently, the work of Henri Lefebvre has also figured prominently. Harvey's own fidelity to Marx rather than Marxism is noted in his quip that he spent much of the 1970s reading *Capital* and not *Reading Capital*. If this focus on Marx has generated a wonderfully rich reinterpretation of Marx's critique of political economy, it has not necessarily fostered the same breadth of engagement. Notably, Gramsci's philosophy of praxis has rarely been as central to a spatialised Marxism as one might expect. Thus, if Thomas is right to argue that Gramsci's development of the Marxist tradition 'as a philosophy of praxis represents one of the great "paths untaken" of both twentieth-century Marxism and philosophy'[4] the missed opportunity is equally as great for historical geographical materialism, which appears wilful in the neglect of Gramsci's spatial historicism for its own practice. Following my discussion of this curious paradox, I will make a case for why a future dialogue would be beneficial for the further development of both the philosophy of praxis (as developed by Gramsci) and of historical geographical materialism.

2   Gramsci's Spatial Historicism

It is now widely accepted that Gramsci's philosophy of praxis was acutely aware of a range of geographical processes. As Kipfer demonstrates, this spatial understanding in no sense undermines or competes with Gramsci's 'absolute historicism'. Considering some of the attempts to 'defend' Gramsci's historicism against Althusser's critique, Kipfer notes the tendency to reproduce an unhelpful distinction between the spatial and the temporal. Thus, in Cox's attempt to recuperate Gramsci's historicism, Kipfer suggests, time is collapsed into diachrony with space associated with synchrony and stasis. At the other end of the spectrum, Said's recognition of Gramsci's geographical apprehension of history risks positing a dualism between time and space, as is most evident in Said's critique of Lukács in which Gramsci comes to stand for space as opposed to an evolutionary and unfolding conception of time. Similarly Ed Soja's long-standing critique of 'historicism' appears to reproduce a dualism of space *or* time. Even sympathetic attempts to draw out Gramsci's spatialised understandings thereby risk undermining the specificity of Gramsci's 'historicism'.

---

4   Thomas 2015.

In contrast, Kipfer argues:

> Rather than counterposing time, history, and diachrony to space, geography, and synchrony, Gramsci analysed historical situations as a confluence of multiple, spatially mediated temporal rhythms ... In fact, to emphasize that spatial differentiation and temporal nuance were both at the heart of Gramsci's historicism is another way of underlining his self-reflexive, anti-dogmatic conception of Marxism as philosophy of praxis.[5]

Some of the influences that might have pushed Gramsci to consider spatial and geographical relations can be found in his biography as well as in his early education. John Berger writes: 'I believe this island [Sardinia] gave him or inspired in him his special sense of time'.[6] It would also appear to have inspired a sensitivity to the uneven development of Italy and a sense of the power of the folkloric and the religious within the lives of geographically disparate social groups.[7] Moving from Sardinia to Turin, Gramsci studied under the renowned linguist Matteo Bartoli. In his first year, the former studied Geography before going on to work closely with Bartoli, taking notes and transcribing his mentor's course in Glottology. Carlucci summarises the main contributions of Bartoli, indicating some of the influence of these geographical studies. He notes, in particular, Bartoli's emphasis on areal and spatial linguistics, which meant focusing considerable attention on the geographical relations through which languages transform.[8] Beyond this, 'Bartoli's geographically oriented version of linguistic research acquainted Gramsci with crucial questions concerning diversity'.[9] Although there is a risk in overemphasising the influence of Gramsci's linguistic studies or of overstating claims to Gramsci's formal status as a linguist, recent research has demonstrated how linguistic influences were one of several on the philosophy of praxis. Geography remained important to Gramsci and, when imprisoned in Ustica on the island of Sicily, he taught geography as one of several subjects to his fellow prisoners. Jessop is, nevertheless, right to caution that considering Gramsci's study of 'Geography' in disciplinary terms makes little sense in the context of the 'pre-disciplinary traditions of Italian philosophy'.[10] Instead, an *implicit* geographical perspective,

---

5   Kipfer 2013, p. 86.
6   Berger 2013, p. 7.
7   For more on Gramsci's Sardinian background see Davidson 1977 and Fiori 1990.
8   Carlucci 2013a, p. 205.
9   Ibid.
10 Jessop 2005.

present within Gramsci's understanding of the patterns of economic, political and social change at global, national and local scales, can be found through much of his writing.

These influences come through most strongly in the last essay that Gramsci penned before his incarceration. Although only available in draft form, *Some Aspects of the Southern Question* provides insights into the difficulties of – as well as the possibilities for – forging political alliances across the geographically disparate Italy of the early twentieth century.[11] Peasants and industrial workers were naturalised as political foes within this landscape; the political strategy of the Italian Socialist Party merely played into such a strategy through a promotion of 'southernist literature', a move that, as Short notes, Gramsci views as akin to what would later be termed Orientalism.[12] Given the problematic assumptions underlying such a perspective, Gramsci is explicit in his rejection of environmentally determinist representations of the Southern peasantry. He writes

> It is well known what kind of ideology has been disseminated in myriad ways among the masses in the North, by the propagandists of the bourgeoisie: the South is the ball and chain which prevents the social development of Italy from progressing more rapidly; the Southerners are biologically inferior beings, semi-barbarians or total barbarians, by natural destiny; if the South is backward, the fault does not lie with the capitalist system or with any historical cause, but with Nature, which has made the Southerners lazy, incapable, criminal and barbaric – only tempering this harsh fate with the purely individual explosion of a few great geniuses, like isolated palm-trees in an arid and barren desert.[13]

Against such a deterministic assessment, Gramsci considers the production of space and identity as further moments within the uneven geographical development of the emerging state of Italy. Furthermore, he emphasises the role of intellectuals within the production of space, showing how such individuals serve to consolidate a view of the South, thereby pointing to the need for a new stratum of individuals who might be able to make explicit the basis for a fundamentally different class alliance.

Earlier in the same essay Gramsci refers to an event in which a tannery worker from Sardinia meets a fellow Sardinian serving as a soldier in the Sas-

---

11   Gramsci 1990.
12   Short 2013.
13   Gramsci 1990, p. 444.

sari brigades, and sent to Turin to suppress the strikes taking place within the city. The meeting serves to disrupt the soldier's declared mission – to 'shoot the gentry who are on strike' – and, through encountering a fellow Sardinian who appears so radically different from those whom he assumes make up the industrial labour force, a new geography of solidarity is made possible. Arguing that numerous examples of such encounters can be found during the strikes of August 1917, Gramsci writes that they 'illuminated, for an instant, brains which had never thought in that way, and which remained marked by them radically modified'.[14] For Featherstone, Gramsci's interest in this passage lies in the making of solidarities and their relation to the production of space.[15]

Just as the production of place and identity can be used in Orientalist fashion to construct the 'backwardness' of the South, as opposed to the 'natural' leadership of the north, so Gramsci emphasises how in Kipfer's words, claims to urbanity and rurality are moments in hegemonic struggle.[16] Again, as with the Southern Question, Gramsci seeks to destabilise such claims through demonstrating the historical and social specificity of the city-country relationship; as well as the manner in which the transformation of the city-country relationship might become part of the struggle for communist hegemony.[17]

Gramsci's consideration of spatiality clearly works at a range of different scales. Indeed, as Morton demonstrates, spatial relations are central to the expanded conception of passive revolution developed in the *Quaderni*; and this understanding of comparative international relations also comes through strongly in the co-authored *Lyons Theses* of the Communist Party of Italy.[18] The *Lyons Theses* focus quite directly on anti-colonial and anti-imperial questions and suggest the ways in which Gramsci was considering multiple spatialities from the city to the world system.

3   Historical Geographical Materialism

If Gramsci's spatial historicism now needs no further justification, its powerful presence within the Notebooks, as well as within Gramsci's pre-prison writings, only makes it more perverse that Marxist scholars who emphasise the importance of space have tended to pay such scant attention to the philosophy of

14   Gramsci 1990, p. 448.
15   Featherstone 2013.
16   Kipfer 2013.
17   Kipfer 2013.
18   Morton 2007a.

praxis. It seems necessary to consider, if only briefly, why this relative lack of dialogue might have come about. Part of the reason must lie in Harvey's own trailblazing re-interpretation of Marx. Indeed, although gaining much more attention after the so-called spatial turn in the social sciences, historical geographical materialism can most easily be traced back to David Harvey's path-breaking text 'Social Justice and the City', in which he struggles to develop an adequate foundation for interpreting the profound inequalities within the contemporary city. Moving from what were initially liberal formulations, Harvey turns to a historical materialist approach, in order to make sense of how the city (and urban processes) serve to stabilise a particular mode of production. Latterly, he considers how 'the city may also be the locus of the accumulated contradictions and therefore the likely birthplace of a new mode of production'.[19] In subsequent works, most notably *Limits to Capital*, Harvey deepens and expands this analysis to develop an understanding of the circulation of capital through the built environment, emphasising the ways in which capital as value in motion produces specific spatial and territorial configurations while relying on the development of a complex credit system for its continued reproduction. In *Justice, Nature and the Geography of Difference* Harvey goes the furthest in fleshing out the principles of this historical geographical materialism, placing particular emphasis on a dialectical approach that pays attention to how 'spatial and ecological differences are not only constituted by but constitutive of ... socio-ecological and political economic processes'.[20]

A sophisticated historical materialist approach has subsequently developed that is attendant to geographical difference and to social and spatial relations. In the work of Smith, the ecological and the spatial come to be integrated within a theory that places particular emphasis on 'the production of nature' as one moment within the production of space: under a capitalist system of accumulation the production of space remains a deeply uneven process, producing profound inequalities at the urban, regional, national and global scales.[21] Smith's is, again, a rich reconstruction of Marx's method, which, as with Harvey, appears to rely very little on broader debates in Marxism. For Storper and Walker, such an approach enables an understanding of the complex relations between technological change, the organisational and political foundations of industrialisation and the emergence of uneven geographical development.[22] Building on the work of Smith, Harvey and Haraway, Erik Swyngedouw has

---

19   Harvey 1973, p. 203.
20   Harvey 1996, p. 6.
21   Smith 1984.
22   Storper and Walker 1989.

developed the environmental implications of historical geographical materialism, interpreting the city as a hybrid or cyborg that can be reduced neither to the social nor the natural.[23] From the 1970s, and gathering pace from the 1990s onwards, such work has benefitted from fruitful dialogues with the translated and untranslated works of Henri Lefebvre.[24] For Kipfer, Lefebvre's writings on the production of space cannot be divorced from the French sociologist's own reading of Gramsci. Explorations of this influence are sporadic and fleeting but can be found in Kipfer, Elden, and Crézégut.[25] Nevertheless, in spite of his own spatial historicism, engagements with Gramsci by geographers, urban theorists and others concerned with spatial relations have been few and far between.[26] The most sustained engagements have come in Gillian Hart's[27] critical ethnographic work in South Africa and Stefan Kipfer's exploration of Gramsci's spatial historicism – in the case of Kipfer and Hart, these explorations have often been in dialogue with the work of both Lefebvre and Fanon. Most recently Hart has developed the philosophy of praxis in considering the trajectories of South African politics, caught as it is between the twin poles of a globalising denationalisation, and a populist emergence of new nationalisms.[28]

The fact that these rare engagements with Gramsci have been so rich only adds to the surprise that readings of Gramsci as a historical *geographical* materialist have been exceptions within an overarching political economic reading of the spatialities of capitalism. If a fidelity to Marx as opposed to Marxism – as in the case of Harvey – might partly explain this neglect, perhaps another explanation lies in the fact that while Harvey was reading *Capital* and not *Reading Capital* the important critique of Gramsci within the latter was exerting a profound influence across the social sciences and humanities. Indeed, the enduring legacy of what Tosel refers to as 'the last great debate of Marxist philosophy' has been profound, albeit almost entirely unacknowledged.[29] While Gramsci emerged as the apparent victor in this debate, paradoxically the Althusserian critique has given birth to a range of approaches that play a far more central role in influencing Marxist philosophy and – indirectly – shaping the spatial turn.

---

23   Swyngedouw 1996.
24   Lefebvre 1974; Lefebvre 1991; Merrifield 2002; Elden and Brenner 2009.
25   Kipfer 2008; Elden 2004, p. 219; see also the chapter by Anthony Crézégut in this volume.
26   For a summary, which also serves as the introduction to the first edited collection on Gramsci and space, see Ekers and Loftus 2013.
27   Hart 2002; Hart 2014.
28   Hart 2014.
29   Tosel 1995, p. 9.

Thus, historical geographical materialists as well as critical geographers, planners and urban theorists have almost entirely neglected Gramscian insights – while generally accepting a 'soft' Gramscianism – to the impoverishment of both.

Thomas writes:

> Gramscian 'agency' has enjoyed a very different fate from that of Althusserian 'structure'. While the latter was, for a long period, almost anathema for the reigning academic research programmes, the former became something of a shibboleth for left-wing theory. Arguably, Gramsci suffered the backhanded compliment accorded to every classic: more often referenced than actually read, his very ubiquity ensured a lack of in-depth research.[30]

The irony, Thomas goes on to note, lies in the fact that this soft Gramscianism, based as it is on a *lack* of engagement with Gramsci, has achieved a 'certain weak form of theoretical hegemony'. Importantly, if Gramsci is to be reconsidered as a historical geographical materialist, such a reconsideration needs to go well beyond the earlier soft Gramscianism. Instead, thinking through Gramsci's spatial historicism or historical geographical materialism must, necessarily, be part of a thorough engagement with the philosophy of praxis. In many ways the vibrant debates over the last few decades that have occurred around Gramsci in Italy and Germany – and now in the Anglophone world too – provide a moment of opportunity for reconsidering this relationship (the edited collection by Ekers et al. is a far more extensive attempt to do the same).[31]

4   The Philosophy of Praxis

Several authors have now made a convincing case that the philosophy of praxis is neither a substitute nor a codeword for Marxism.[32] Instead, as Thomas has shown, the philosophy of praxis must be understood as Gramsci's distinctive interpretation and development of Marx. In reconstructing this philosophy of praxis Thomas develops a philological reading of its 'three component parts':

---

30   Thomas 2009a, p. 12.
31   Ekers et al. 2013.
32   Haug 2000; Thomas 2009a; Green 2011c.

absolute 'historicism', absolute immanence and absolute humanism.[33] Each
of these component parts, if taken on a purely semantic level, poses particular problems for contemporary theorisations of space, place and nature.[34]
Thus, historicism smacks of an understanding rooted in the historical process as a smooth narrative of progress and is often taken as the antithesis
of a more nuanced spatialised understanding;[35] humanism, as for much contemporary social theory and philosophy has been critiqued for its assumption of a sovereign human subject. Immanence, although faring better through
recent interest in Spinozan approaches, seems unlikely to fit with any coherent approach that boasts its humanism and historicism. Nevertheless, within
Thomas's detailed reconstruction and contextualisation of these three component parts it becomes clear how the philosophy of praxis might influence
and shape a renewed historical geographical materialism.

Contrasting Gramsci's 'absolute historicism' with that of Croce, Thomas
charts Gramsci's developing understanding through Notebook 4 to the first
appearance (and one of only three) of the term 'absolute historicism' in Notebook 8. Considering the discussion within the special notebooks (10 and 11) in
greater depth, Thomas shows how absolute historicism comes to be defined
against both Bukharin's crude materialism and Croce's own development of
'absolute historicism'. As in Kipfer's approach, he demonstrates the utter failure of Althusser's critique to hit its target given the clear sense in which
Gramsci articulates an understanding of 'the non-contemporaneity' of the
present. This 'incoherent present' is made up of the 'multiple, spatially mediated temporal rhythms' referred to in Kipfer's account.[36] Thus, an 'absolute
historicism' as Gramsci articulated it already appears to entail a spatial historicism. Albeit only fleetingly, Thomas appears to acknowledge such a co-
dependence:

> The *Prison Notebooks* are replete with concrete historical studies and the-
> oretical reflections demonstrating and taking theoretical cognisance of
> the temporal and spatial 'dislocations' that characterise the distinctive
> nature of modern historical experience.[37]

---

33   Thomas 2009a, p. xxiii; Gramsci Q11, § 27 (Gramsci 1971a, p. 465).
34   Importantly, these partly stem from what has been a more profound engagement with the
      well-founded although entirely misdirected criticisms that Althusser levelled at Gramsci.
35   Soja 1989.
36   Kipfer 2013, p. 86.
37   Thomas 2009a, p. 283.

Such temporal and spatial dislocations are present in both Gramsci's under-standing of 'the person' as well as his observations on language.[38]

In sharpening this absolute historicism, Gramsci turns his critique to Buk-harin's crude materialism and, in particular, the latter's summary dismissal of any questions concerning the reality of the external world. For Bukharin

> the question of the existence of the external world is categorically super-fluous, since the reply is already evident, since the external world is 'given', just as practice itself is 'given'.

The question for Gramsci is of much more interest than Bukharin allows. He goes on to ask why it is that the world appears as objectively given. Against the metaphysical conception of materialism put forward by Bukharin, Gramsci's 'absolute historicism' suggests the possibility of an understanding of one's role in shaping reality. The historical constitution of the present – dislocated and non-contemporaneous though it is – as well as the mutability of the present is elaborated through a historical materialism. Thus Gramsci's 'absolute his-toricism' appears to entail an understanding of what Smith would later refer to as the production of nature.[39] Nevertheless, elaborating such a perspective requires a broader understanding of the philosophy of praxis.

Although the sources for Gramsci's philosophy of praxis are many, ranging across his linguistic studies with Bartoli, the Sardinian's reading of Labriola and the sustained development of a critique of Benedetto Croce, Marx's *Theses on Feuerbach* stand out as one of the most influential texts on the *Prison Note-books*.[40] Having translated the *Theses* early in Notebook 7, the language and the concerns of these alluring notes are carried through the notebooks penned during what Thomas refers to as Gramsci's *annus mirabilis* of 1932, clearly influ-encing both Gramsci's spatial historicism and his overall development of the philosophy of praxis.

Marx's turn to 'sensuous activity', to 'human activity as objective activity', and his emphasising of the 'significance of "revolutionary"', of "practical-critical", activity' is flagged up in Thesis I and forms the basis for both Gramsci's own philosophy of praxis and for his critique of crude understandings of mater-ialism. Pondering Bukharin's simplistic dismissal of the question surrounding the so-called reality of the external world, Gramsci notes how dualistic under-standings of humans and the external world have their roots in a religious

38   Gramsci Q11, § 12 (Gramsci 1971a, p. 324); Q11, § 24 (Gramsci 1971a, pp. 450–2).
39   Smith 1984.
40   Thomas 2015.

worldview. Rather than a necessary badge to be worn by the progressive thinker who defends truth against solipsistic subjectivism, Gramsci sees a fixed and unchanging belief in the so-called reality of the external world as *potentially* reactionary. He draws here from the *Theses on Feuerbach* very directly. Elsewhere, Gramsci's development of a dialectical pedagogy draws from Thesis III, in which Marx argues against crude materialism's assumption that context is all that matters in the shaping of the human subject, claiming instead that 'it is essential to educate the educator'. And Gramsci's conceptualisation of 'the person'[41] draws very directly from Marx's dismissal of a fixed unchanging and abstract human essence in Thesis VI. In a wonderful synthesis and supersession of several of the themes of the *Theses*, Gramsci writes, in Notebook 10, that:

> So one could say that each one of us changes himself, modifies himself to the extent that he changes and modifies the complex relations of which he is the hub. In this sense the real philosopher is, and cannot be other than, the politician, the active man who modifies the environment, understanding by environment the *ensemble* of relations which each of us enters to take part in. If one's own individuality is the *ensemble* of these relations, to create one's personality means to acquire consciousness of them and to modify one's own personality means to modify the *ensemble* of these relations.[42]

Even if profoundly influenced by the *Theses on Feuerbach*, claiming that the philosophy of praxis is simply an adoption of the ideas laid out within these brief notes would be to fall prey to the same error as claiming that the philosophy of praxis is merely a codeword for Marxism. Instead, as Thomas notes, Gramsci extends, enriches and develops the reading within the *Theses*.

All this has profound implications for historical geographical materialism. First, as several scholars have recently noted, as radical geography has begun to confront the epochal claims made around the Anthropocene, as well as developing Lefebvre's claims of the complete urbanisation of society, there has been a move towards a more abstract theorising.

The Anthropocene refers to the new geological epoch in which many scientists now argue we find ourselves. This epoch is defined by the influence of humans: an era – as the term implies – that should be viewed as the age of the human. Nevertheless, to frame 'humanity' in such sweeping terms neglects the

---

41   For the most detailed discussion of Gramsci's notion of the person see Thomas 2009a.
42   Gramsci Q10 II, § 54 (Gramsci 1971a, p. 352).

classed, raced and gendered social groups through which relations with nature are established.[43] Similarly the claim that society is now completely urbanised occludes the historically specific ways in which rural-urban relations continue to be produced and reproduced. Such claims often rely on a dismissal of the role of practice and everyday life for their idiographic basis.

Responding to such dismissals, Buckley and Strauss therefore call for renewed attention to praxis and everyday life through both feminist thought and practice, and through Lefebvre's own writings on difference and everyday life.[44] In Gramsci's work one finds an approach that is patiently attentive to a theorising that emerges from the practice of everyday life, that is open to a range of different determinants, and, as I will conclude, that finds within the fragmented world of common sense a kernel of good sense.

Second, one of the key contributions of radical geography has been in theorising the production of space and nature, most often seen in the work of Harvey, Lefebvre, and Smith (although Buckley and Strauss make a very good case that framing the 'canon' in this manner overlooks feminist contributions).[45] As argued at the outset of this paper, Gramsci was deeply attentive to the uneven development of Italy, and, in his critique of Bukharin, he also demonstrated an interest in the mutually co-determining relationship between people and the so-called external world. In short, an understanding of the production of space and nature is implied throughout the philosophy of praxis and throughout Gramsci's extension of this method to understand the uneven development of Italy and Southern Europe.

Third, Gramsci turns our attention to the contradictory, disparate and composite conceptions of the world through which individuals make sense of their relations to others and to the external world. Having laid out one of the most brilliant understandings of the key role that urbanisation plays in the ongoing production and reproduction of capitalism as a system of accumulation, David Harvey contemplates some of the roads not taken within his work, writing that:

> We should never forget, however, that though labour power is a commodity the labourer is not. And though capitalists may view them as 'hands' possessed of stomachs 'like some lowly creature on the sea-shore', as Dickens once put it, the labourers themselves are human beings possessed of

---

43   For recent critiques see Moore 2015; Bonneuil and Fressoz 2016; Swyngedouw 2015.
44   Buckley and Strauss 2016.
45   Harvey 1982; Lefebvre 1991; Smith 1984.

all manner of sentiments, hopes and fears, struggling to fashion a life for themselves that contains at least minimal satisfactions.[46]

One cannot help but feel that Harvey is urging himself to explore what Thomas elsewhere refers to as 'one of the great "paths untaken" of both twentieth-century Marxism and philosophy'. Historical geographical materialism more broadly has generally failed to take this path and, in so doing, has often neglected opportunities to engage more thoroughly with the lived life of the labourer. In the present moment, rather than pitching its analysis at planetary and epochal abstractions, I would argue that it would more fruitfully develop a philosophy of praxis as simultaneously a spatial historicism.

5   Conclusion: Gramsci as a Historical Geographical Materialist

Gramsci's philosophy of praxis develops a form of spatial historicism that is patiently attentive to the situated practices through which social groups make histories and geographies, albeit not under conditions of their own choosing. The context in which Gramsci lived prior to his incarceration, along with his educational background in a spatialised understanding of linguistics, all led to a developing concern with uneven geographies at a range of spatial scales. Challenging the 'naturalisation' of space, within pre-prison writings such as *Some Aspects of the Southern Question*, as well as more widely in the *Prison Notebooks*, Gramsci emphasises how claims to space, and claims to what are historically specific sets of social relations, foster or hinder political alliances and perpetuate unequal power relations. History and geography are thus woven together in what Kipfer refers to as a spatial historicism.

There is much to be gained from a sustained dialogue between a spatialised Marxism and the revitalisation of interest in Gramsci's philosophy of praxis. For Kipfer, the philosophy of praxis *is* a spatial historicism: engaging with this claim enables a fuller appreciation of the spatial concerns that animated Gramsci's carceral research, as well as a new set of influences on radical geographical thought.[47] In particular, such a dialogue will enable a fuller appreciation of the critique of political economy as one of several moments within a broader approach that also pays due attention to the lived life of the labourer – to the sentiments, hopes and fears embedded within the struggle to fashion a life in

---

46   Harvey 1982, p. 447.
47   Kipfer 2013.

this contemporary moment. One particularly rich example can be found in the work of Kipfer and Hart whose efforts to 'translate' Gramsci's writings for the current conjuncture move between the philological engagements drawn out so richly within this collection and concrete engagements with emerging forms of populism in South Africa, and, more recently, in India.[48] Other examples abound and together these suggest rich possibilities for a future dialogue over Gramsci's historical geographical materialism.

---

48   Kipfer and Hart 2013; Hart 2015.

Neoliberalism as Passive Revolution? Insights from the Egyptian Experience

Roberto Roccu

Like every 'complex historical upheaval', and even more in light of its role in reviving the hope of radical transformations, the Egyptian revolution should be addressed taking into account not only the specific conjuncture, domestic and global, within which it emerged, but also and especially long-term trends related to the constitution and transformation of the Egyptian social formation since the Free Officers' coup. Starting from this consideration, this contribution discusses from a Gramscian perspective to what extent the undoubted neoliberalisation experienced by the Egyptian political economy can be understood as a passive revolution.

Starting from the different uses of passive revolution in the *Prison Notebooks*, the first section of this chapter proposes a definition of passive revolution around four key criteria. The second section provides an overview of the extent to which the Egyptian political economy has been transformed, and its direction, starting from Sadat's *infitah* policy, but paying more sustained attention to the policies implemented in the wake of the Economic Reform and Structural Adjustment Program signed under the auspices of international financial institutions (IFIS) in 1991. Building on the first two parts, the third section discusses to what extent the four criteria identified as characteristic of passive revolution capture the nature and effects of the neoliberal turn in Egypt. It is suggested that two of the stabilising effects of passive revolution, the consolidation of the grip on power of dominant classes and the weakening and dismemberment of the emerging subaltern bloc, clearly did not occur in the Egyptian case, as demonstrated by the 2011 revolution. Thus, in line with recent literature assessing the nature of the neoliberal era,[1] the conclusion suggests that the broader process of economic restructuring occurring in Egypt since the late 1980s is better understood as a counter-reformation. It is within this context that we should locate revolutionary and counterrevolutionary dynamics affecting contemporary Egypt.

---

1 See especially Coutinho 2007.

Two clarifications on the core terms of this discussion are necessary before we proceed further. On the one hand, and very much in line with Gramsci's own understanding, passive revolution is taken here as 'a criterion of interpretation',[2] thus hopefully avoiding the temptation of 'making what is a principle of research and interpretation into a "historical cause"'.[3] In contrast with existing literature interpreting passive revolution as a *portmanteau* concept,[4] the concept is understood here as more directly related to a strategy available to dominant classes within very specific relations of political forces. While the structuring role of class relations is thus retained, through this move it becomes possible to shift back the emphasis of passive revolution on the forms of agency that are deployed, on the part of both dominant and subordinate classes, within historically specific circumstances.

On the other hand, Gramsci's considerations on the nature and form of *laissez faire* are of great help in developing an adequate definition of neoliberalism. Both these processes are usually understood as an affirmation of market forces *vis-à-vis* the powers of public intervention. However, such an understanding is based on the fallacious assumption that there is an ontological distinction between politics and economics, which has instead more of a methodological and analytical nature. Exactly like *laissez faire*, neoliberalism 'is a form of state "regulation", introduced and maintained by legislative and coercive means. It is a deliberate policy, conscious of its own ends, and not the spontaneous, automatic expression of economic facts'.[5] David Harvey is certainly correct when suggesting that the aim of the neoliberal project is the restoration or reconstitution of capitalist class power, combined with a rebalancing in intra-capitalist relations that gives pre-eminence to financial capital.[6] At the same time, Gramsci's eminently anti-instrumentalist approach to social phenomena demands that we investigate what are the specific practical tendencies through which this theoretical programme is concretised, and that make neoliberalism different from previous attempts to establish, maintain or strengthen capitalist class power, including the classical liberal one that attracted Gramsci's interest. When assessing the multifarious forms taken by 'really existing neoliberalism',[7] one can identify a set of common policy trends,

---

2   Gramsci 1971a, p. 114, Q15 § 62.
3   Morton 2007a, p. 67.
4   Morton 2007a, p. 68.
5   Gramsci 1971a, p. 160, Q13 §18.
6   Harvey 2005, pp. 31–6.
7   Cahill 2014, pp. 14–31.

including privatisation,[8] marketisation/commodification,[9] deregulation,[10] financialisation,[11] and state-led regressive redistribution.[12] Crucially, all of these measures demand an active and activist state, also in the crafting of market-creating and market-conforming regulations in areas that had hitherto been regulated differently.[13]

1 Between Structure and Conjuncture: Recasting Passive Revolution[14]

In the *Prison Notebooks*, Gramsci uses the compound expression 'passive revolution' with reference to three different historical moments, and with a slightly but constantly expanding meaning. Firstly, passive revolution is invoked to understand concomitant processes of state formation and transitions into capitalist modernity in Europe during the second half of the nineteenth century, with specific emphasis on Italian Risorgimento but also sporadic references to German unification.[15] Secondly, and moving into Gramsci's present, passive revolution is presented as a helpful interpretive lens for understanding

---

8   Privatisation as one of the staple policies in the various instantiations of the neoliberal template is very much accepted throughout the literature. On how this entails a reconfiguration of our relationship with nature, see Mansfield 2008.

9   Scholars from a Marxist tradition, such as Harvey (2005, pp. 160–1), tend to prefer the latter term to the former, but both point towards the increasing pervasiveness of market-coordinated exchanges in spheres of social activity that had been largely decommodified during the era of welfare capitalism, including for instance education and health care (see Esping-Andersen 1990).

10   This involves the rolling back of forms of protection and regulation in a range of areas, from labour markets to the environment to the financial sector. For one of the earliest case studies on deregulation in the US, see Derthick and Quirk 1985.

11   The importance of this set of policies is acknowledged by scholars from a range of different persuasions that are not necessarily attracted by broader processes of neoliberalisation. See for instance Epstein 2005, Krippner 2005 and 2011, Lapavitsas 2013. Within neoliberalism, financialisation plays the essential role of tilting intra-capitalist relations in favour of financial capital. See Harvey 2005, pp. 161–2.

12   Usually, but not exclusively, in the form of regressive tax policies. See Harvey 2005, pp. 163–5.

13   With respect to deregulation in the US financial sector, for instance, the argument has been convincingly made that this process has significantly increased the scope for the action of Federal authorities, and especially the Federal Reserve. See especially Konings 2011, p. 135.

14   This section draws on Roccu 2017.

15   On passive revolution and Risorgimento, see Gramsci 1971a, pp. 57–9, Q19 § 24, and pp. 105–14, Q15 § 59, Q15 § 17, Q15 § 11, Q15 § 62. On the German case, see Gramsci 1971a, pp. 18–19, Q12 § 1, and p. 118, Q10I § 0.

Italian Fascism, thus extending the concept in two directions. Historically, pass-ive revolution is now suggested to potentially apply to 'every epoch character-ised by complex historical upheavals'.[16] Conceptually, we are certainly not deal-ing anymore with a transition into capitalism, but rather with transformations that 'accentuate the "plan of production" element ..., without however touching or at least not going beyond the regulation and control of individual and group appropriation'.[17] Thirdly, passive revolution is mentioned in more fleeting and speculative terms at the start of the notebook on *Americanism and Fordism*, with Gramsci setting out to explore whether these processes 'can determine a gradual evolution of the same type as the "passive revolution" examined else-where'.[18] Thus, Americanism and Fordism appear more as a potential cause, rather than an instance, of passive revolution. In this case, we are even more directly than with fascism referring to a transition within the capitalist mode of production, deriving 'from an inherent necessity to achieve the organisation of a planned economy'.[19]

While these historical and conceptual extensions are undoubtedly of great relevance, and not entirely unproblematic,[20] the contention here is that pass-ive revolution retains a conceptual core, and one that can be fruitfully deployed to research contemporary processes. This starts to emerge if passive revolution is evaluated in counterpoint to Gramsci's best-known concept, hegemony. The latter has a much stronger structural grounding in 'the decisive function exer-cised by the leading group in the decisive nucleus of economic activity'.[21] In Gramsci's terminology, hegemony is an 'organic' concept, rooted in production relations but also encompassing political and civil society, thus allowing the dominant class to be seen as also leading other classes and creating the condi-tions for a harmonious development of structure and superstructure. Passive revolution, as extensively discussed below, occurs when the dominant class fails to lead, while subordinate classes are on their own part unable to mount a credible hegemonic challenge. Thus, passive revolution is crucially dependent on a specific balance of political forces, and is thus a strategy available to the dominant class and that is predominantly situated in political society.[22] In rela-tion to Gramsci's thoughts on periodisation, passive revolution is one of the key

---

16   Gramsci 1971a, p. 114, Q15 §62.
17   Gramsci 1971a, p. 120, Q10I §9.
18   Gramsci 1971a, pp. 279–80, Q22 §1.
19   Gramsci 1971a, p. 279, Q22 §1.
20   For a discussion on whether passive revolution has been subject to conceptual overstretch,
      both in Gramsci's own writings and in its revival in critical International Political Eco-
      nomy, see Callinicos 2010.
21   Gramsci 1971a, p. 161, Q13 §18.
22   See especially Gramsci 1971a, p. 107, Q15 §17.

strategies for prolonging the duration of an epoch *durare*. On its own, however, it is unable to establish a new historical epoch *fare epoca*.[23] At the same time, and in light of its foundations in a given equilibrium of political and politico-military forces, passive revolution has a more durable nature than the specific tactics, such as *trasformismo*,[24] which are deployed by the dominant groups to disarticulate, fragment and decapitate an emerging subaltern bloc. This is not to imply a predetermined hierarchy among these concepts, which are instead to be understood in relational terms. Thus, a passive revolution is not entirely devoid of hegemonic elements, although these are not necessarily to be found in the dominant class,[25] and *trasformismo* may well be necessary for the success of passive revolution.[26] Indeed, in its ability to synthesise organically many of the innovations that Gramsci brings to historical materialism, passive revolution should be seen as a central concept in Gramsci's political theory and praxis.[27]

Based on these considerations, four elements characterising passive revolution in its different uses in the *Prison Notebooks* are particularly relevant within the scope of this study. The first element relates to Gramsci's awareness of the specific international coordinates that are necessary for a passive revolution to occur. He develops this line of argument in two different directions. On the one hand, exogenous developments, with respect to both forces and relations of production, compel social formations to initiate a transition with the potential of bringing about some form of developmental catch-up. This transition might be from a non-capitalist to a capitalist mode of production, as in the case of Italian Risorgimento, but also a transition between different regimes of accumulation within the same mode of production, as it happened with the intensification of the planned component through corporatist arrangements in fascist Italy and with the diffusion and internationalisation of Fordism. Thus, echoing Trotsky's seminal theoretical development, passive revolution is predicated on 'the whip of external necessity',[28] providing substance to Burawoy's

---

23   Gramsci 1975, Q14 § 76. See also Thomas 2009a, pp. 152–3.
24   Gramsci 1971a, p. 58, Q19 § 24, and p. 109, Q15 § 11.
25   Gramsci 1971a, pp. 104–5, Q15 § 59.
26   Gramsci 1975, pp. 386–8, Q3 § 19.
27   See for instance Kanoussi and Mena 1985, and Voza 2004.
28   Trotsky 2007, p. 5. As for Gramsci, in his journalistic activity prior to his arrest, he repeatedly referred to uneven development, stating for instance that 'capitalism is a world historical phenomenon and its uneven development means that individual nations cannot be at the same level of development at the same time' (see 1964, p. 391). However, in the *Prison Notebooks* there is no explicit reference to this expression.

claim that '[w]here Trotsky's horizons stop, Gramsci's begin'.[29] On the other hand, references to the importance of the politico-military equilibrium and to the dissemination of specific ideologies across different social formations suggest that the conditioning role of the international also encompasses super-structures.[30]

These international transformations might make restructuring necessary, but do not determine whether the latter takes a passive revolutionary form. Hence, the international is better conceived as a necessary but not sufficient condition for passive revolution. All the other three elements present in Gram-sci's use of passive revolution depend on the very specific relation of political forces anticipated earlier, characterised by a dominant class that fails to be hegemonic and subaltern classes that lack 'the degree of homogeneity, self-awareness and organisation' required for successfully challenging the domin-ant class.[31] This situation is often presented by Gramsci in Hegelian terms, with the limitations of the thesis that do not prevent it from achieving

> ... its full development, up to the point where it would even succeed in incorporating a part of the antithesis itself – in order, that is, not to allow itself to be 'transcended' in the dialectical opposition ... it is precisely in this that the passive revolution or revolution/restoration consists.[32]

As the dominant class is not hegemonic, and thus cannot rely entirely on civil society for the production of consent, the first specifically political charac-teristic of passive revolution is its heavy reliance on state power as the main instrument through which it is carried out. This is obviously most visible in how passive revolution is deployed with reference to the Italian Risorgimento, where the economic transition towards capitalism and the political transition towards a unitary state occur simultaneously. Here, Gramsci refers explicitly to 'the function of Piedmont' as 'that of a ruling class', which had to step up and lead the processes of state formation in light of the absence of 'a homogenous ruling class'.[33] While the centrality of the state is most apparent in the notes on Risorgimento, the necessity of state action is visible also in the move towards

---

29   Burawoy 1989, p. 793. In his work on state formation and transformation in modern Mex-
      ico, Adam Morton has articulated more systematically the relation between uneven and
      combined development and passive revolution. See Morton 2011, p. 4 and pp. 99–102.
30   See especially Gramsci 1971a, pp. 175–6, Q13 §2, and pp. 181–2, Q13 §17.
31   Gramsci 1971a, p. 181, Q13 §17.
32   Gramsci 1971a, p. 110, Q15 §11.
33   Gramsci 1971a, p. 104, Q15 §59.

the 'intermediate economy' of corporatism in Fascist Italy,[34] as well as in what Gramsci expects to be the transformations imposed on Europe by the establishment of Fordist methods, and the attendant ideology of Americanism, in the US.

Another characteristic that stems from the specific relation of political forces that make passive revolution possible is already included in the compound term itself, as this is a process aiming to render the subaltern classes 'passive'.[35] In this regard, Gramsci is on the one hand adamant that the inability of the antithesis to similarly develop its potential to the fullest crucially depends on its own limitations, as it is 'uncertain, hesitant, internally weak'.[36] The critique of Mazzini's leadership and more generally of the political strategy followed by the Action Party during Risorgimento is perhaps the best illustration of this focus.[37] On the other hand, however, Gramsci's attention to specific techniques of state power, and especially to *trasformismo*, points towards the ways in which the dominant class acts in order to prevent the constitution of a subaltern bloc. Indeed, the capillary work through which individuals but also entire groups belonging to subaltern forces are co-opted and thus absorbed into the ruling bloc effectively amounts to their decapitation and dismemberment, often followed by centrifugal processes that inevitably weaken subaltern classes.

After accounting for the 'passive', it is in the hitherto neglected revolutionary element that we find the final key feature of passive revolution. As aptly put by Callinicos, passive revolution is a process though which 'revolution-inducing strains are displaced and at least partly fulfilled'.[38] Thus, passive revolution entails a progressive dimension, in that there is at least some measure of satisfaction, however limited or distorted, of the demands raised by the embryonic subaltern bloc. From a classical Marxian perspective, all the three instances of passive revolution analysed or simply adumbrated in the *Prison Notebooks* imply an advancement of productive forces, albeit one that is contained within existing relations of production. While this certainly means greater exploitation, once should not forget that 'for Gramsci, the development of capital is equal to the development of the proletariat',[39] thus deepening contradictions and creating greater possibilities for struggle. This rejection of a linear

---

34   Gramsci 2007a, p. 378, Q8 § 236.
35   For a recent discussion of demobilisation as one of the key goals of passive revolution, with specific reference to Latin America, see Modonesi 2014.
36   Gramsci 1971b, p. 343.
37   Gramsci 1971a, p. 108, Q15 § 11.
38   Callinicos 2010, p. 498.
39   Baratta 2004, p. 33, my translation.

conception of progress, towards a multifaceted and essentially dialectical one, is especially visible in Gramsci's repeated pairing of passive revolution with Quinet's 'revolution-restoration'. Following from this, Gramsci demonstrates an ability of addressing transformations that, while progressive and indeed partly because of this, fall short of a transition between modes of production and succeed in defusing revolutionary demands. This is nowhere clearer than in the following quote, where the extent of the transformations achieved by passive revolution is made explicit and linked to its international preconditions, thus allowing our discussion of passive revolution to come full circle:

> But the complex problem arises of the relation of internal forces in the country in question, of the relation of international forces, of the country's geo-political position. In reality, the drive towards *revolutionary renewal* may be initiated by the pressing needs of a given country, in given circumstances, and you get the revolutionary explosion in France, victorious internationally as well. But the drive for *renewal* may be caused by the combination of progressive forces which in themselves are scanty and inadequate though with immense potential, since they represent their country's future, with an international situation favourable to their expansion and victory.[40]

2   Neoliberalism in Egypt: A Very Short History

Both the magnitude and the trajectory of the transformations undergone by the Egyptian economy during the long phase of neoliberal globalisation can be better appreciated when placed in adequate historical context. This is especially the case since Egypt is arguably the country that did not call itself socialist or communist that went furthest in terms of state presence in the economy. This was achieved through two waves of nationalisations carried out under Nasser, the first in 1956 focusing on assets held by foreigners in the wake of the Suez Canal crisis, and the second in 1960–61 targeting the local capitalist class, broadly opposed to Nasser's state-centred developmentalist project. Much like in other postcolonial late developers, the state had to take on the function of collective capitalist, able to mobilise the resources necessary for modernising the national economy. Combined with land reform on the countryside, this strategy was geared towards dismantling the 'half-per-cent society'

---

40   Gramsci 1971a, p. 116, Q10II § 61, emphasis added.

of landowners and *comprador* bourgeoisie of the colonial era, replacing it with a state capitalist class, which revolved around the army but expanded significantly in the shape of a large public sector. Importantly, for rhetorical but also practical reasons, the populist social contract underpinning Nasser's rule gave a much more central role to industrial workers and peasants. In this regard, De Smet's characterisation of this phase as one of 'progressive Caesarism', based on the consent of broad layers of the population, and providing benefits to subordinate classes, albeit in a highly regimented and paternalistic form, is a very accurate one.[41] Both these elements – the centrality of the state in the economy and the different composition of the bloc supporting its modernising project – are to be kept in mind, as they will have significant repercussions on the nature and form of the reforms undertaken first under Sadat and then under Mubarak.

The political economy of Sadat's Egypt was characterised by two main shifts. On the one hand, Law 43 of 1974 opened Egypt up to foreign investment, through the so-called *infitah* policies, entailing the creation of special economic zones and the attempt to establish a framework aimed at allowing Arab petrodollars, Western technologies and Egyptian labour to interact productively making Egypt a regional powerhouse.[42] Importantly, this economic strategy was accompanied by the effective 'engineering' of an indigenous private capitalist class, albeit one largely dependent on the state.[43] On the other hand, the Camp David accord in 1978 altered Egypt's geopolitical positioning, away from the leadership of the Non-Aligned Movement, which had given it the possibility of extracting rents from both superpowers, to becoming one of the main US allies in the Middle East. These two transformations represent a major shift from Nasser's state-dominated developmentalism. However, it is difficult to find more than the germs of a neoliberal turn in Sadat's policies. Such germs are in fact also difficult to be seen in the first years of Mubarak's presidency, with the 1980s being characterised as the decade of 'dilatory reform'.[44] Nevertheless, the re-emergence of private capital, foreign and local, however mediated by and subordinated to the state, and Egypt's insertion in the circuit of US-led imperialism created the preconditions for the broader neoliberal turn of the early 1990s.[45] Importantly, with the disintegration of the Soviet bloc, Egypt's key geopolitical position, as the North African linchpin of the broader US strategy in the Middle East, has paid dividends giving Egypt much greater

---

41   De Smet 2016, pp. 154–8.
42   Cooper 1982, p. 91.
43   Ayubi 1995, pp. 351–2.
44   Richards 1991.
45   For an early diagnosis of these developments, see Zaalouk 1989.

leverage than most developing countries *vis-à-vis* IFIs. Given the centrality of international compulsion to the definition of passive revolution provided above, this is another point worth keeping in mind when assessing the neoliberalisation of the Egyptian economy.

Being perceived by Egypt's key policymakers as a moment of 'reckoning',[46] the fiscal crisis of the late 1980s forced the state to give into the IMF's pressures towards the implementation of a structural adjustment programme. While this was signed in 1991, when the privatisation law was also enacted Law 203 of 1991, 1992 is arguably the year bearing the most distinctive signs of the neoliberal turn, embodied in two consecutive pieces of legislation. Law 95 of 1992 relaunched the Egyptian stock exchange, which had been in a long period of 'deep sleep'.[47] Combined with moves towards capital account liberalisation, this bill signalled the start of a period of increasing state support towards the banking sector, estimated by the IMF to amount to a fiscal subsidy of about 10 percent of GDP by 1996/97.[48] On the other hand, the new tenancy law 96 of 1992 put the nail in the coffin of the Nasserist social pact, creating the conditions for a 'counter-revolution' in the countryside in favour of large landowners.[49] By the full implementation of the law in 1997, almost one million peasants were evicted and more than 700,000 jobs lost.[50]

By the late 1990s, the Egyptian government was widely portrayed as a success story of structural adjustment.[51] A combination of debt forgiveness agreed with Paris Club creditors, fiscal restraint and extensive privatisations put state finances back on track,[52] although foreign direct investment did not take off as expected. The impetus for reforms withered around the turn of the century, partly due to the shockwaves of the East Asian financial crisis hitting the Egyptian shores, and partly because of a major fracture within the dominant groups embattling the ruling National Democratic Party (NDP). This pitted the various fractions of the state capitalist class, once again under the army leadership, generally in favour of a gradualist approach to reform and the preservation of

---

46   Amin 1995, p. 16.
47   Roll 2010, p. 352.
48   International Monetary Fund 1997, p. 35.
49   See especially Saad 2002.
50   Mitchell 2002, p. 265.
51   *The Economist* went so far as to call Egypt 'the IMF's model pupil' in a March 1999 issue.
52   The first two elements are linked, in that debt cancellation on the part of Paris Club creditors was essential for Egypt achieving a dramatic reduction in its budget deficit. See Ikram 2006, p. 67. In 1998, an IMF report ranked Egypt fourth in terms of privatisation proceeds as a share of GDP. See International Monetary Fund 1998, p. 52.

specific red lines,[53] against a rising private capitalist class, coalescing around Mubarak's son Gamal, with much stronger links to transnational capital and a more clearly neoliberal outlook. The latter's victory within the NDP in the 2002 party congress was followed by major changes within the political personnel at both party and cabinet level, with the marginalisation of the more tradi-tionally statist ministries.[54] This in turn produced the conditions for a drastic acceleration in reforms, with a new wave of privatisations now affecting sectors previously considered off-limits, including cement, oil refineries and banks. A new central banking law was followed by three World Bank-sponsored finan-cial sector reforms programmes, resulting in an increasing financialisation of the Egyptian economy, although a highly skewed one.[55] While a comprehens-ive tax reform proved impossible, a set of incremental measures broadened the tax base through a General Sales Tax, lowered the corporate tax, and created tax holidays for companies operating in the Special Economic Zones. Addi-tionally, the introduction of temporary contracts in 2003 was the first major step towards the deregulation of labour markets, oriented by the World Bank's *Doing Business Report*, which under the indicator 'Rigidity of employment' includes pretty much any form of labour protection, from minimum wage to working hours limits, as an obstacle for greater investment.[56]

From this overview, it is not difficult to infer that neoliberalism as a policy regime increasingly permeated Egypt before the 2011 revolution, as all of the trends outlined earlier as characteristic of neoliberalism had, to a varying extent, transformed the Egyptian political economy. At the same time, such transformation also preserved remarkably Egyptian features, often discussed in the literature to highlight how limited the substance of reforms was.[57] For

---

53   These red lines were specifically related to the preservation of a manufacturing sector dir-ectly in the hands of the army and not engaged in military production, and largely off the book. This has been estimated to account for a portion of the Egyptian economy ranging between 15 and 30 percent. For a seminal account on this issue, see Springborg 1989. For details on contemporary developments, see Marshall and Stacher 2012 and Abul-Magd 2016.

54   For a detailed discussion of the changing power relations in favour especially of the Min-istry of Trade and Industry, and weakening the Ministry of Planning, see Soliman 2011, pp. 131–5.

55   While total stock market capitalisation increased by more than 700 percent only in the period between 2001 and 2007, seven families and their respective business conglomer-ates accounted for about one fifth of this capitalisation. See Roccu 2013, p. 64. With respect to the banking sector, 0.19 percent of clients accounted for about 51 percent of the total credit extended to the private sector, with about 30 corporations receiving nearly 40 per-cent of total credit supply. See Osman 2010, pp. 115–16.

56   Hanieh 2013, pp. 53–4.

57   See especially Kienle 2003, Schlumberger 2008 and Wurzel 2009.

instance, while significant transformations have occurred with respect to public sector ownership in the manufacturing as well as the banking sector,[58]
it is difficult to maintain that the state is not anymore a major actor in the
Egyptian economy. However, more than showing the lack of substantial economic transformations, this element points towards the analytical limitations
of approaches studying neoliberalism through the state-market dichotomy.
While certainly still central to the Egyptian economy, it is undeniable that
the state has undergone a process of restructuring, rescaling and repurposing.
Indeed,

> [n]eoliberal reform in Egypt did not at all entail a 'retreat' of the state
> from the 'economic field', but a redirection of state power and resources
> towards an increased accretion of rents via an aggressive policy of dispos-
> session, which only benefitted global capital and a small clique within the
> Egyptian ruling classes.[59]

The enduring economic functions of the state in this instance are perhaps best
illustrated with reference to agriculture. While facilitating accumulation using
the iron fist against peasants protesting against the new tenancy law, the Egyptian state did not hesitate to intervene in the liberalised fertiliser market in
the mid-1990s during a dramatic crisis of undersupply, with a specialised bank
restarting public sector provision.[60] Rather than as a limit to accumulation on
neoliberal terms, this intervention is better seen as an attempt at coupling the
accumulation and the legitimation function invested upon the state in a phase
in which sustained repression revealed the complete unravelling of the Nasserist hegemony.

Despite this and other seemingly idiosyncratic articulations, the restructuring brought about by reforms in the Egyptian social formation suggest that
also the aim of neoliberalism as a class project had been achieved. On the
one hand, the position of capital had been strengthened significantly *vis-à-vis*
labour, bringing to an end the populist social pact while enabling accumulation in a variety of ways. On the other hand, the greater role taken on by finance
with respect to profit realisation significantly increased foreign capital access
to the Egyptian economy, in turn tilting relations within the dominant classes
in favour of the more outward-oriented section of private capital. As a result
of these transformations, extensive reliance on state power had succeeded in

---

58   Roccu 2013, pp. 43–9.
59   De Smet 2016, p. 179.
60   Bush 1999, pp. 68–9.

'upgrading' the Egyptian economy for it to better meet the demands of accumulation on a global scale, thus restructuring the economy under conditions of decayed hegemony without having to transform political and social relations. Can this process be understood as a passive revolution? Mubarak's overthrow in 2011 on the back of an 'active' revolution would seem to suggest that it cannot, but this is a question worth addressing in detail, and will be at the heart of the following section.

3   Before and after the 2011 Revolution: Neoliberal Restructuring
       without Passive Revolution?

The hypothesis that neoliberalism might take the political form of a passive revolution in late developing countries, particularly subject to the vagaries of uneven and combined development because of their economic and political subordination, has been advanced perhaps most forcefully by Adam Morton.[61] This is predicated on Gramsci's quip on one of the key points made by Marx in his *Preface* to *A Contribution to the Critique of Political Economy*, namely that '[a]t a certain point of development, the material productive forces of society come into conflict with the existing relations of production ... From forms of development of the productive forces these relations turn into their fetters'.[62] In acknowledgement of the resilience and adaptability of capitalism, Gramsci suggests that 'a social form "always" has marginal possibilities for further development and organisational improvement, and in particular can count on the relative weakness of the rival progressive force as a result of its specific character and way of life'.[63] Within this discussion, Morton proposes passive revolution as a criterion for interpreting how, in contexts characterised by concomitantly late state formation and capitalist development, the further development imposed by uneven and combined development does not translate into a radical rupture in social relations. On a more empirical level, Morton suggests that passive revolution can present itself in two different ways: as a revolution from above, and as 'a revolutionary form of political transformation ... pressed into a conservative project of restoration'.[64] However, the earlier discussion of Gramsci's uses of passive revolution in the *Prison Notebooks* suggests that what Morton sees as two 'alternate' meanings are instead necessarily inter-

---

61   See especially Morton 2007b, 2010, 2011.
62   Marx 1987b [1859], p. 263.
63   Gramsci 1971a, p. 222.
64   Morton 2011, p. 39.

twined in Gramsci, who would see a passive revolution when a restructuring from above becomes instrumental to the weakening of an emerging subaltern bloc through the partial fulfilment and displacement of its demands.[65]

This discussion on whether processes of neoliberalisation can be understood as passive revolutions has received some attention also with reference to Egypt. A position very similar to Morton's was originally espoused by Brecht De Smet, with neoliberal reforms presented as 'an offensive passive revolution',[66] compared and contrasted with passive revolutionary waves that had characterised state formation in Egypt since the 1952 Free Officers' coup. A debate ensued on *Jadaliyya*,[67] where Joel Beinin, arguably the foremost historian of the Egyptian labour movement, takes issue with De Smet's suggestion that 'the meaning of passive revolution is nearly interchangeable with that of "reformism"'.[68] As it links this definition to what he perceives as De Smet's 'teleological understanding of the historical process',[69] Beinin hints at the risk of considering every major reform a passive revolution that inevitably delays the simultaneous social and political emancipation that can only be achieved through permanent revolution.[70] In light of this disagreement, it might make sense to provide a more systematic discussion based on the key features of passive revolution outlined above, while at the same time paying attention to some dynamics of both the 'active revolution' of 2011 and its turbulent aftermath.

Starting from the international preconditions of passive revolution, the importance of the 'whip of external necessity' pushing Egypt towards restructuring, and one of a neoliberal type, cannot be underestimated. The transformations in the global production structure ushered in by the much greater mobility enjoyed by capital since the 1970s have produced an intensification of uneven development,[71] which in turn makes the pursuit of national pathways to development much more arduous, increasing significantly the pressure on poorer countries to reform. In this respect, restructuring presents itself in Egypt as an externally induced process. At the same time, mechanistic tendencies ought to be resisted in this respect, as there were significant forms of agency at work in the Egyptian case. Two of them are perhaps more relevant here.

---

65   Callinicos 2010, p. 498.
66   De Smet 2014a, p. 27.
67   See De Smet 2014b and 2014c and Beinin 2014a and 2014b.
68   De Smet 2014a, p. 17.
69   Beinin 2014a.
70   For a more detailed discussion of the immanent relation between social and political emancipation as the kernel of permanent revolution, see De Smet 2016, pp. 33–6.
71   See especially Kiely 2007, pp. 424–34. With respect to how this affected the Middle East, see especially Achcar 2013, pp. 7–75.

On the one hand, specificities in the politico-military equilibrium emphasised by Gramsci, related to Egypt's key geostrategic position in the Middle East, meant that IFIs who had been usually pursuing rather aggressively the Washington Consensus template elsewhere were more lenient and flexible towards Egypt.[72] On the other hand, agency matters also with respect to which specific discursive and ideological articulation became dominant in Egypt. Here, the 'new thinking' (*fikr al-jadid*) put forward by business and technocratic components within the NDP was essential in portraying export-led growth based on a thorough opening of the economy as the only way for breaking with the debt dependency that cyclically threatened fiscal sustainability.[73] The combination of these elements helps us understand why restructuring in Egypt occurs on essentially neoliberal lines, but also how uneven development is combined through different modalities and temporalities afforded by agency. This combination also shines through in the way neoliberal reforms restructure the Egyptian social formation as a whole, and within it the relation between classes and class fractions.

The central role of the state in the neoliberal turn is arguably the element that emerges most clearly from the earlier discussion. Very much along the lines of Gramsci's understanding of passive revolution, this was predicated on the limitations of both dominant and subaltern classes. Through the piecemeal transformations undertaken under Sadat, the former had been broadened to include a state-dependent private capitalist fraction as a 'junior partner' to the army-led state capitalist component.[74] However, this failure to deliver on the developmental objectives at the heart of the Nasserist social pact meant that this broadening of the ruling bloc did not bolster the hegemonic potential of the dominant classes in Egyptian society. For their own part, while cyclically producing bursts of 'sporadic and incoherent rebelliousness',[75] subaltern classes failed to mount a meaningful challenge to the *status quo*, largely because of widespread repression, but also because they had been 'uncertain, hesitant, internally weak', to use Gramsci's own words.

Within this context, dominant classes made extensive use of state instruments to tilt relations of political force in their favour while restructuring

---

72   See especially Momani 2005 on IMF-Egypt relations.

73   See Roccu 2013, pp. 74–93.

74   Ayubi 1995, p. 352.

75   Gramsci 2007a, p. 252. The 'bread riots' of 1977 and the Helwan strikes of 1989 are perhaps the most visible examples of these forms of popular resistance. On the former seen from a comparative perspective, see Sadiki 2000. On the latter and its relation with labour mobilisation after the 2011 revolution, see Makram-Ebeid 2015.

the economy to meet the requirements of global capital accumulation. This also occurred through *trasformismo*, for instance through the co-optation and control of trade unions, but was also directly inscribed within the institutional set-up in such a way as to limit the avenues through which subaltern concerns could be legitimately raised.[76] Through the neoliberal turn, another private capitalist component enters into the ruling bloc, still tightly linked to the regime, but also with much stronger ties with global capital. This has two important repercussions within the ruling bloc. On the one hand, the rise of this component is not entirely dependent on the regime itself, as it had happened with the *infitah* bourgeoisie. On the other hand, as neoliberal policies empower this component *vis-à-vis* other groups within the ruling bloc, this fraction has a strong interest in accelerating economic reforms, which is exactly what occurred after the 'change of the guard' within the ruling party.[77] This in turn increasingly antagonised the state capitalist component. Thus, if passive revolution is expected to consolidate the position of the dominant classes, these destabilising effects of neoliberal reforms within the ruling bloc appear at odds with the concept.

The very occurrence of a popular uprising leading to the fall of an autocrat who had been in power for nearly three decades suggests that another of the expected effects of passive revolution – the passivity of subaltern forces – had not been achieved either.[78] However, one might still want to consider the hypothesis that the neoliberal turn represented a failed passive revolution,[79] for instance pointing towards the attempts at combining economic liberalisation with limited political opening in the 1990s.[80] Yet, to be helpful as a criterion of interpretation, passive revolution should not only meet the subjective intent of the dominant classes aiming to undertake it, but also the objective outcomes produced within the social formation.

Finally, it is difficult to maintain that a process entailing the partial fulfilment and displacement of popular demands occurs if such demands have risen to the point of turning into a political revolution. In light of the widespread de-industrialisation, and the role played by various forms of rents in

---

76   This point very much mirrors one of Poulantzas' key contributions to state theory, and one with a distinctly Gramscian lineage, which defines the state as 'the material condensation of a given relationship of forces', see Poulantzas 1978, p. 73.

77   On intra-regime dynamics, see especially Kandil 2012, pp. 200–20.

78   On the dynamics of mobilisation leading to the 2011 revolution, see especially Abdel-Rahman 2015. On the specific role of working classes, see Alexander and Bassiouny 2014.

79   See for instance De Smet 2016, p. 226.

80   See especially Kienle 2001 and Kassem 2004.

the 'successful' phase of capital accumulation in Egypt, even the 'progress-ive' objective dimension of the further development of forces of production does not appear to have been met to any significant degree. On a more sub-jective level, the extent to which *trasformismo*, both 'molecular' and 'of entire groups',[81] has occurred did not really amount to a decapitation and dismem-berment of the emerging subaltern bloc. Particularly throughout the 2000s, repression was the main instrument through which these objectives were pur-sued.

A more interesting question, but one that can only be touched cursorily in this contribution, and on which definite conclusions are certainly premature, is whether the post-2011 period might provide better foundations for a success-ful passive revolution.[82] The pivotal role taken by the Supreme Council of the Armed Forces immediately after Mubarak's oust appears exactly to capture 'how a revolutionary form of political transformation is pressed into a con-servative project of restoration'.[83] The partial fulfilment of popular demands through the prosecution of Mubarak, his sons and several associates, fair and open parliamentary and presidential elections in 2011 and 2012, as well as some populist economic measures following Morsi's overthrow would all seem to conform to a passive revolutionary template, especially as these measures pre-vented regime change to expand into a social revolution. However, widening fractures within the ruling bloc, showcased at regular intervals in the post-revolutionary period, dispel this hypothesis and indeed point towards the fra-gility of the new regime. Most importantly, the continued reliance on raw repression and fear, from Maspero to Raba'a,[84] suggest that the current phase is much better understood as a full-fledged counterrevolution.

4 Conclusion

In times of 'complex historical upheaval' such as the ones Egypt is going through, Gramsci's work certainly provides profound insights. Perhaps even more than at specific concepts, it is at Gramsci's method that researchers

---

81 Gramsci 1971a, p. 58 f., Q8 § 36.
82 For a similar argument with respect to the Morsi presidency and the position of the Muslim Brotherhood vis-à-vis both dominant and subaltern classes, see Tuğal 2012.
83 Morton 2011, p. 39.
84 These are the two largest massacres to have occurred since the 2011 revolution. The former, in October of the same year, saw the death of 28 people, mostly Copts. The latter resulted in the death of at least 600 Muslim Brotherhood supporters who had gathered around two major mosques following Morsi's overthrow in July 2013.

should be looking more. For it is only through the philosophy of praxis underpinning the Gramscian conceptual constellation that we can grasp the relational, and thus adaptable, nature of concepts deployed in different historical
and geographical circumstances.[85] Defined in terms of 'absolute secularisa-
tion and earthliness of thought',[86] the philosophy of praxis demands that we
examine social relations from a perspective that is immanent to the historical
process, thus accounting for its elements of global universality as well as for
its local peculiarities. It is from this methodological standpoint that one can
fully appreciate the preconditions of the Egyptian revolution as well as its subsequent developments, the structural constraints limiting its potential and the
forms of agency, deployed and not, that can be mobilised to fulfil such potential.

The undoubted usefulness of a Gramscian method, however, does not necessarily entail that all of Gramsci's concepts are relevant at all times. For instance,
passive revolution can certainly help us better account for the consolidation of
an independent state in Egypt under Nasser, as well as the modernisation of
its economic foundations, particularly as this was a process that advanced the
position of subaltern classes, albeit in a deflected and distorted form. Two elements from the Egyptian experience with neoliberalism since the late 1980s
might recall passive revolutionary processes as understood by Gramsci. On the
one hand, economic restructuring was effectively necessitated by the intensification of uneven development in the neoliberal era. On the other hand,
the central role played by the state in carving the Egyptian way to neoliberalism, and the many peculiarities characterising it, can also be understood in
terms of a sensitivity to a specific balance of political forces within the country. However, this contribution suggests that it is exactly by looking in more
detail at this component that reference to passive revolution for interpreting
the neoliberal turn in Egypt does not appear to be warranted. If passive revolution is expected to restructure socioeconomic relations while consolidating the
grip on power on the part of the dominant classes, the major fractures that
reforms created among various components of the ruling bloc, and that still
reverberate making the post-revolutionary regime particularly fragile, render
a reference to passive revolution somewhat problematic. Similarly, a passive
revolution renders subordinate classes passive by partially fulfilling and dis-
placing their demands. In the turn towards neoliberalism in Egypt, one would
struggle to find ways in which demands advanced by subaltern forces were met

---

85   See especially Thomas 2015.
86   Gramsci 1971a, p. 465, Q11 § 27.

to any significant extent. Even more importantly, the passivity of the masses was not achieved, and indeed neoliberal reforms, in their specifically Egyptian instantiation, actually established some of the key preconditions for the 2011 revolution.

The current phase is probably better understood as a counterrevolution, which follows an 'active' revolution, although perhaps one that in time we will come to consider a failed one. As aptly put by Wu Ming, 'counterrevolution is not the opposite of a revolution; counterrevolution is a revolution against the revolution'.[87] In the Egyptian case, the counterrevolution epitomised by Morsi's removal from power in July 2013, but with roots to be found in the management of the immediate aftermath of Mubarak's fall, is inserted within a broader process of neoliberal restructuring of the economy, and of social relations more broadly. From a Gramscian perspective, this might be understood as a 'counter-reformation'. While usually referred to the Catholic Church's reaction to Protestant Reformation when used in the *Prison Notebooks*, through reference to Gramsci's relational method and to his philosophy of praxis, counter-reformation can help us navigate the contradictory processes of neoliberalisation in peripheral social formations. In the specific Egyptian case, reference to counter-reformation could help us understand the neoliberal turn as a rolling back of the achievements that the Nasserist era, for all its limitations, had meant for subaltern classes. Simultaneously, as counter-reformation is 'not a homogenous bloc, but a substantial, if not formal, combination of old and new',[88] this concept would also account for the adaptation and transformation of the Egyptian social formation in a direction that would allow for its combination in a regressive form with the intensified uneven development of the neoliberal era.

---

87   Wu Ming 2014, p. 110.
88   Gramsci 1975, p. 2292, Q25 § 7.

CHAPTER 3

The Old Is Dying and the New Cannot Be Born: 'Past and Present' of Thailand's Organic Crisis

Watcharabon Buddharaksa

1 Introduction*

Contemporary political crises in the past decade and the present are traditionally conceived of as crises of political morality. For example, the conservative social forces[1] within the Thai state considered ex-Prime Minister Thaksin Shinawatra[2] and his social and political allies as a major threat to the nation only because of their lack of political integrity. This chapter contests this *political 'common sense'* perspective and argues against a conservative conception of the world and that the crisis of the Thai state, in fact, is an organic, and also ongoing crisis. This *'organic crisis'* view has been constituted for several structural reasons and should be discussed in relation to both areas of political economy and social ideology of the past history of the Thai state. The structural crisis in Thailand should be viewed as what Gramsci calls a crisis of hegemony where *the old is dying and the new cannot be born.* This situation

---

* This chapter was first presented at the *'Past and Present: Philosophy, Politics, History in the Thought of Antonio Gramsci'* International Conference at King's College London in June 2015 and received financial support from Naresuan University and the University's Faculty of Social Sciences. I would like to thank the organising committee of the conference, Anne Showstack Sassoon (a chair on my panel), Peter Thomas, and Derek Boothman for their moral support while we met at the conference. I also thank Werner Bonefeld for his comments on earlier drafts of this chapter and the anonymous reviewers for their helpful and constructive feedback.

1 In this chapter I use the term 'social forces' as overlapping with other terms such as social classes and social groups, and conceived of them as a broader concept of class in a Weberian sense. And by the 'conservative social forces' I mean mostly the Yellow Shirts Movement (emerging in 2005) and the People's Democratic Reform Committee. For definitions of the Yellow and the Red Shirts, see notes 33 and 35 below.

2 An ex-Prime Minister of Thailand between 2001 and 2006 who had won two landslide victories in both 2001 and 2005 general elections in Thailand. He was ousted from power by the military coup in 2006. Since then he has not returned to political power; however, he had significant influence on his three political proxies, Samak Sundaravej, Somchai Wongsawat (Thaksin's brother-in-law), and Yingluck Shinawatra (Thaksin's sister).

has three crucial features of crisis ridden value: social and economic disparity, overwhelming roles of royalism and nationalism, and harsh applications of *lèse majesté* laws. To overcome the political common sense view of Thaksin held by the Thai rightists, and to restore long term social and political orders of the Thai state, it is necessary to bring these three fundamental problems to the fore and critically examine, discuss, and debate them. In short, while it might not be an absolute way to achieve a more just and fairer society for the Thai state, thinking in a *'Gramscian way'* is crucial as a first step to critique the Thai version of common sense and to imagine, with hope, for long term solutions to the organic crisis of the Thai state.

The chapter will begin with Gramscian theories and their application to Thai politics[3] focusing on the notions of common sense and crisis of authority. The second section explains the crisis-ridden features of *'the past'* of Thai politics. These distinct characteristics of the Thai state should be seen as, what Gramsci has referred to as, the old is dying. The third section deals with *the uncertain 'present'* of Thailand's organic crisis, what Gramsci refers to as, the new cannot be born. Lastly, *the future* of Thai politics will be discussed in the conclusion.

2   Gramscian Theories and Thai Politics

For a decade, Thailand's political conflicts have been perceived as a result of political corruption of the evil Thaksin government and its successors.[4] In order to contest this conservative perception of the world, this chapter employs Gramscian theories of common sense and crisis of authority as a major framework to examine Thailand's crises.

2.1   *Common Sense*

According to Gramsci, *'common sense'* (*senso comune*)[5] is the *'philosophy of nonphilosophers'*, or in other words, the *'conception of the world'* that is uncritically

---

3   Gramscian political theory has seldomly been applied to the analysis of Thai politics due to several reasons (see note 73 below). Employing a Gramscian perspective to grasp the politics of social transition of the Thai state could overcome the determinist explanation of social change and reveal the more complicated interrelations of social forces in both political economy and ideological terrains of the Thai historical bloc. In addition, the Gramscian framework can deal with social actors – which this work considers as social forces/social groups – and the balance of class forces in terms of both economic class interests and ideological-cultural practices.

4   See for example Manager 2014; Dailynews 2015.

5   While the term 'common sense' has been used widely in Gramscian scholarship worldwide,

absorbed by the various social and cultural environments in which the moral individuality of the average man is developed.[6] In analysing ways of thinking and acting, Gramsci uses a variety of terms and many of these are overlapping, as is the case with *'philosophy', 'ideology', 'conception of the world', 'mode of thought, action', and 'world view'*. All of these terms refer to the general way of thinking and acting which determines the specificity of a social class, social group, or historical formation.[7]

Common sense is the conception of the world that is established by the ruling class in order to secure *'class interests'* and control subaltern worldviews.[8] This process of building common sense perspectives operates through the function of intellect in the sphere of civil society. The vital point is, according to Gramsci, that in order to become autonomous and be able to change the existing social relations, the subaltern/subordinate groups need to *'develop a new conception of the world'* that is not dependent on ruling class ideology.[9] To overcome common sense, the subaltern needs to replace it with what Gramsci called *'good sense'* (*buon senso*)[10] or a new conception of the world raised by the autonomy of subaltern classes in order to raise the intellectual level of the people.[11] In addition, Thomas succinctly offers definition of *senso comune* (common sense) as 'Perhaps it is useful "practically" to distinguish philosophy from senso comune in order better to indicate the passage from one moment to the other: in philosophy the features of individual elaboration of thought are the most salient; in senso comune, on the other hand, it is the diffuse, uncoordinated features of a generic form of thought common to a particular period and a particular popular environment'.[12]

For the Thai version of common sense, from late 2005 until the present, the conservative social forces in the country uncritically perceived that Thailand had reached the pinnacle of crisis, leading to two coups d'état within

---

Peter Thomas argues that the translation of the term from Italian to English is not entirely congruent with what Gramsci means in Italian. Thomas argues that using this term as an original 'senso comune' is more appropriate (see Thomas 2009a, p. 16 n. 61).

6   Gramsci 1971a, p. 419, Q11 §13.

7   Robinson 2005, p. 473; see more discussion on Gramsci's common sense in Liguori 2009b; Liguori 2015b, pp. 85–110; on Gramsci's conception of the world, see Wainwright 2013.

8   Bocock 1986, p. 46; Green 2006, pp. 284–300; Green 2011c.

9   Robinson 2005, p. 473.

10   However, it should be noted here that good sense does not directly replace any given common sense. Good sense already exists in an episodic and disrupted form in each society, but must be elaborated in a new common sense.

11   Gramsci 1971a, p. 340, Q11 §12; Greaves 2009, p. 172; Green 2006.

12   Thomas 2009a, p. 377.

eight years and a significant number of deaths, because of the proclaimed wicked Thaksin government and its followers.[13] This passive mode of thought has prevailed over Thai politics and, at the same time, marginalised those who were opposed to this common sense view as a threat to the state[14] and had to be detained under the Martial Law. Labelling Thailand's crisis as a result of a wicked Thaksin and its allies is useful for the Thai ruling elites. As long as this common sense exists, it conceals more genuine features of the crisis of the Thai state which are addressed in the second and third sections below.

2.2   Crisis of Authority

One of the most significant political concepts of Gramsci is that he sees the relationship of each social force in any given society from a *'dialectical perspective'*. Hegemony of the dominant social class and a given historical bloc[15] do not always last forever. Nevertheless, hegemony and historical bloc could be in a situation called *'crisis'* – challenged by other subaltern social groups – and the replacement of hegemonic position could take place at any point. Gramsci himself uses the term 'crisis' interchangeably with *organic crisis, crisis of hegemony, crisis of historical bloc,* and *crisis of authority*.[16] Gramsci provides a general idea about the crisis of authority as shown in the passage below:

> In every country the process is different, although the content is the same. And the content is the crisis of the ruling class's hegemony, which occurs either because the ruling class has failed in some major political undertaking for which it has requested, or forcibly extracted, the consent of the broad masses (war, for example), or because huge masses (especially of peasants and petit-bourgeois intellectuals) have passed suddenly from a state of political passivity to a certain activity, and put forward demands which taken together, albeit not organically formulated, add up

---

13   Nation TV 2015.

14   By means of being a threat to the state in Thailand is similar to being a threat to the monarchy. For a broad picture of the politics of sacredness of the Thai monarchy, see Marshall 2014.

15   It should be noted here that the term 'bloc' was used by Gramsci in two major ways: first, as a 'historical bloc' when he means the concrete totality formed by the articulation of the material base and the politico-ideological superstructure; second, as a 'social bloc' or an alliance of social classes under a given regime, see Coutinho 2013, p. 97, n. 12. In this chapter, I use the term historical bloc in the second sense as similar to the state.

16   Salamini 1981, p. 59.

to a revolution. A 'crisis of authority' is spoken of: this is precisely the crisis of hegemony, or general crisis of the state.[17]

Following Gramsci, the crisis of authority could take place in two ways. *Firstly*, the ruling class can lose the consensus of their power over other social groups, and *secondly*, rather than being a weak class, the subaltern/subordinate social groups can overcome political passivity and begin to articulate their own demands to the ruling class.[18] In addition, Salamini[19] argues that organic crisis in Gramsci's perspective occurs as a result of contradictions which accumulate over time within a specific historical bloc, offsetting the institutionalised equilibrium of forces.

Moreover, Gramsci offers an important idea that is beneficial for understanding contemporary Thai politics in the passage below:

> The 'crisis of authority' – if the ruling class has lost its consensus, i.e. is no longer 'leading' but only 'dominant', exercising coercive force alone, this means precisely that the great masses have become detached from their traditional ideologies, and no longer believe what they used to believe previously, etc. The crisis precisely in the fact that *the old is dying and the new cannot be born*; in this interregnum a great variety of morbid symptoms appear.[20]

The *'crisis of authority'*, in other words the crisis of hegemony and historical bloc, occurs when the common sense that dominated the subaltern is no longer working. It is a situation in which the subaltern social forces under the leading and organising roles of the intellectuals of each social force could challenge the existing conception of the world. Nonetheless, as Gramsci writes *'the old is dying and the new cannot be born'*; the situation of hegemonic crisis is a circumstance of the society in which confusion occurs because there is no obvious hegemonic position among social forces during the time of crisis.

This Gramscian notion of crisis of authority is crucial.[21] In this chapter, I hold that political crises in Thailand since 2005 were not only crises of political mor-

---

17   Gramsci 1971a, p. 210, Q13 § 23*.
18   Reed 2012.
19   Salamini 1981, p. 59.
20   Gramsci 1971a, pp. 275–6, Q3 § 34, emphasis added.
21   And it is distinct from other theories of crisis as it does not privilege one aspect of society over another as the unit of analysis. Rather, Gramsci's conception of organic crisis looks

ality that emerge only through wicked governments. Conflicts of the Thai state in the recent decade, I argue, should be seen in the organic, or structural, sense. Political common sense which was constructed and held as dominant by the Thai ruling classes had concealed the true features of Thailand's crisis. The following sections will unravel what, indeed, lies beneath the surface of crisis of morality of the Thai state.

3   Considering 'the Past': The Old Is Dying

Political crises in Thailand since 2005 led the country to have had six governments for both civilian and military administrations, two military coups in 2006[22] and 2014,[23] and a number of street fights. From the conservative polit-

---

at the whole as a configuration of a balance of social forces. Analysing Thai political crisis through a Gramscian perspective offers a comprehensive, historically based, and critical account of the past, present, and future of the Thai state.

22   The coup in 2006 took place, as the coup maker claimed, in order to prevent political violence that might happen via the clash between the Yellow and the Red Shirts movements at that time. The so-called 'good coup' or the popularly supported coup could be seen as a 'royalist-backed' action which was extraordinary and distinct from a Western democratic point of view. The coup in 2006 was a chance for the old social elites to interfere in various aspects of Thai politics. The junta attempted to establish a new 'political rule' to prevent the emergence of an extra-strong government comparable to the previous Thaksin government. The return to power of the Thai army since 2006 has continued until the present even though the country had some short period of civilian governments between 2007 and 2014.

23   The coup in 2014 happened as a consequence of the mass protest in late 2013. The demonstration in early November 2013, initially, emerged from the leading roles of the middle-class social groups led by many academic institutions in Bangkok to protest against Pua Thai Party's attempt to launch the draft of the Amnesty bill. The middle-class social forces in Bangkok believe that this law, to some extent, might clear the corruption cases of the former Thaksin government. However, the demonstration was transformed to be anti-Pua Thai and anti-Thaksinism in late November 2013 under the name of the 'People's Democratic Reform Committee' (PDRC). The PDRC was led by Suthep Tuagsuban, a former politician and executive of the Democrat Party and the PAD (the Yellow Shirts). The movements and occupations of bureaucratic offices in Bangkok led the Pua Thai government to dissolve the Parliament on 9 December 2013 and announce a new general election to be held on 2 February 2014. However, the Democrat Party boycotted this general election and the Election Commission could not peacefully hold the election in some areas of the country, especially in the South (a major political stronghold of the Democrat Party and the PDRC). The PDRC supporters obstructed the state officials from facilitating the election which eventually led to the annulment by the Constitutional Court as they ordered that the 2 February election was illegitimate. Up to May 2014, the political situation in Thailand was uncertain and in a deadlock since the Constitutional Court recently ordered the

ical common sense were the result of the wicked Thaksin government and its allies. Nevertheless, following Gramscian notions of crisis of hegemony, this chapter argues that crisis of the Thai state, in fact, contained three distinct features: that *political economy, political ideology, and the juridico-political* contributed to the crisis.

3.1   *Political Economy: Increasing of Social Disparity*

Structure (political economy)[24] and Superstructure (culture, ideology) form a historical bloc, as Gramsci once argued.[25] The crisis-ridden features of the Thai state manifest the underlying troubles of Thailand in both political economy and ideological terrains. In terms of political economy, political struggles in the last decade in Thailand revealed the crucial character of capitalist development in Thailand that has increased '*social disparity*'.

Thailand's modern economic development can be dated back to the 1950s, which represented a milestone of modern capitalist development. Thai political economy and political ideology in the 1950s had created the condition of '*subalternity*' in which subaltern social groups were excluded from the pool of political power and social wealth and suppressed by dominant social groups.[26] Economic and social inequalities resulted from the US-led economic policies developed in the 1950s that mainly concentrated on industrialisation, but ignored other economic sectors, especially the rural poor and also lacked any concentration on improving the living conditions of the people. The inequalities in income distribution in Thailand are clearly indicated by the World Bank's GINI index.[27] The index represented the picture of uneven development of modern Thai political economy since the 1950s and this information is helpful

---

caretaker Prime Minister to step down on 7 May 2014 as she had abused power by transferring the head of National Security Commission in 2011. All these events led the Thai army to conduct the coup once again on 22 May 2014. On the 2014 military coup, see Hewison 2015; for a profound account of politics of social relations a decade prior to the coup in 2014, see Buddharaksa 2014a.

24   Economic matters, in the first few decades of reception of Gramsci in the English-speaking world, have been ignored by most Gramscian scholars. However, Krätke and Thomas 2011 point out that Gramsci himself never ignored the importance of the relations of production in the sphere of what Marx called the structure. For other comments on the issue of Gramsci's contribution to political economy, see, for example, an American Sociologist Michael Burawoy 2003.

25   Gramsci 1971a, pp. 366, 377, Q10 §12, Q7 §21.

26   See Buddharaksa 2014a, pp. 70–9; Buddharaksa 2014b, pp. 134–40.

27   Thailand had 47.86 in 1992, 40.02 in 2009, and the most recent data indicates that Thailand had 39.4 in 2013, see World Bank GINI Index (World Bank Estimate). These GINI index figures are double those of a country with good income distribution.

in order to make sense of those who struggle against the military government because economic policies had been changed and uncertain.

The constant feature of social disparities in the Thai historical bloc since the late 1950s have been delivered through the economic crisis in 1997. This crisis led to the reconfiguration of political power in the Thai state. The Thai Rak Thai (TRT) party,[28] which benefited from the new 1997 constitution, entered into politics and offered new hope for Thai social forces in the post-1997 crisis era. However, as I argue in this chapter, the TRT government and the rise of the so-called 'Thaksinism'[29] had little impact in improving structural conditions that could have resolved the problem of social disparity over the long term such as the launching of a land reform act, improvements to the tax system, and enhancing labour productivity.[30] Thaksinism in fact provided some concrete benefits to the rural peasants and labourers such as the implementation of a low-cost health care scheme and offering micro-credit to local communities. Nevertheless, the Thaksin government – as a coalition of capitalist factions – did not structurally change to a progressive tax system that includes inheritance and land taxes or address the matter of land reform for the rural poor. Rather, as a capitalist faction, Thaksinism emerged under a strong state[31] in order to guarantee a free and peaceful market for investors at both domestic and international levels. This meant that the Thai historical bloc under the catalytic role of Thaksinism during the transition period of 2001 to 2006 still retained the problem of social disparity as was the case beforehand.

While Thaksinism was transforming the old historical bloc[32] that carried the feature of social disparity to become an alternative Thaksin-led bloc, it

---

28   The Thai Rak Thai party (TRT), formed in 1998, was a pioneer in Thai politics in terms of offering a set of concrete innovative social policies to Thai people. However, from the anti-TRT point of view, they blamed TRT's social policies as financially irresponsible and populist. Once the Thaksin government was ousted by the coup in 2006, the TRT was disbanded by the Constitutional Court due to the controversial case of election fraud relating to the general election of 2 April 2006. This judgement also banned the 111 core members of the TRT party from politics. Nevertheless, the TRT had formed an alliance with the 'People's Power Party' in 2007 and transformed once again in 2008 as 'Pua Thai Party'.

29   Using the term 'Thaksinism' (Thaksin regime), derived from Thatcherism in the UK. However, those who pioneered employing this term in Thai politics are Kasian 2006 and Pitch 2004.

30   Lauridsen 2009.

31   On the idea of free economy and the strong state, see Bonefeld 2010, 2012, 2014.

32   This study perceived the old historical bloc as the Thai state since the modern economic development in the 1950s as a point of departure until the collapse of economic crisis in 1997. After the crisis, this study holds it as a transition period and it has yet to complete its transition.

failed to offer benefits to all social groups within the state. Thaksinism was resisted by some other capitalist factions and, more specifically, the middle class and some of the working class who later formed themselves as a Yellow Shirt social group.[33] During the transition period of the Thai state which began when the Thaksin government came to power in 2001 the crisis-ridden character of the Thai state projected that social disparity was in a process of change that could have led to either better or worse scenarios.[34] However, the project of the Thaksin-led alternative historical bloc could not be completed as the other 'crisis' of the Thai state took place with the military coup in 2006. During the three-years of the post-coup period the incomplete transition of the historical bloc eventually led to the organic crisis/crisis of authority of the state presently still in existence. It remains the case that no Thai governments have dealt with the matter of social disparity over the long run.

In addition, as part of the social disparity problem, the matter of poverty has been understood to be the main reason behind the uprising of the Red Shirts[35]

---

33   The Yellow Shirt movement was a combination of various social forces – ranging from the Thai middle class, labour union, old social elites, such as military and royal families, and capitalist fractions – who shared a basic idea of fighting against Thaksinism as it is a corrupted regime. This chapter argues that they were political actors who attached themselves to the conservative ideology; in other words, the royalist-nationalist ideology. This social force claimed that the Thaksin government challenged the royal hegemony of the Thai monarchy and should be thrown out of political power. Therefore, the Yellow Shirts movement attempted in many ways to create a condition that led to the coup d'état which finally succeeded in September 2006.

34   By 'better' I mean the Thaksin government could transform the Thai political economy in the direction of the Western standard so that social and economic gaps in the country could have been reduced relative to the previous decades. And for the 'worse' scenario, I mean that Thaksin could have brought the country to another economic crisis due to lack of government expenditure discipline, meaning that social and economic gaps in Thailand could worsen.

35   To consider who exactly the Red Shirts are and what they represent, it is necessary to consider both political economy and ideological instances. The Red Shirts forces do not constitute a unified social group. Rather, it is composed of many social classes and combines both the rich and the poor in the Weberian sense of income categorisation. This is similar to the Yellow Shirts as it is a social bloc that is comprised of 'broad social alliances' of social forces that are able to continually expand and dwindle in terms of its alliances. However, it could be seen that even though the Red Shirts were constituted by different socio-economic classes, they did share some 'economic incentives' that were lost after the collapse of the Thaksin government by the conservative military coup in 2006. This chapter argues that the Red Shirts had been confronting the dominant royalist-nationalist political ideology of the Thai state by challenging the existence of the monarchy in the modern world and demanded a genuine liberal democracy.

subaltern social forces, who were understood by the Thai ruling and middle classes as those who were politically ignorant and supported the Thaksin government only because of vote-buying, over the past few years. However, it should be seen that poverty – more specifically absolute poverty – is not a major issue for Thailand's economic development in recent years. Many studies have showed that the Red Shirts protestors are not the rural poor in the absolute sense as was the case in the early 1950s. However, they could be seen as a 'new' type of social group; the 'new lower middle class'.[36] Walker[37] argues that this new social group in rural Thailand should be seen as the 'middle-income peasants' who are no longer poor in the absolute sense. Nevertheless, they enjoy consumer comforts similarly to the urban middle class and urban workers because they benefitted from the improvement in rural standards of living. Moreover, these middle income peasants are part of a diversified economy rather than relying on subsistence cultivation as was the case in the past. In contemporary rural Thailand agriculture remains important but peasant livelihoods are no longer predominantly agricultural livelihoods. They are no longer just farmers[38] as traditionally perceived by the Thai middle class. This coincides with what Sopranzetti[39] argues; the gap between city and countryside in Thailand has been decreasing due to connections created by rural immigrants who are working in urban areas. Rural people who have the chance to live and work in urban and industrial cities seem to experience a sense of inequality between the two societies. These 'urbanised villagers' transmitted the sense of humbleness that is a product of the social disparity of the Thai state to their rural families and peers.[40]

In short, Thailand's old historical bloc (1950s–early 2000s) concealed the problem of social inequality and carried the 'tendency' towards the clash between the dominant and the subaltern social forces in order to adjust these uneven social relations. The constructed political common sense of humbleness of the oppressed social groups in the Thai state eventually erupted following the post-2006 military coup as most of the rural poor attempted to struggle in order to defend Thaksinism – a regime that advanced their concrete interests – and led to the formation of the Red Shirts movement.

---

36   Apichat 2007; 2011; 2013a, pp. 14–35.; 2013b.
37   Walker 2012.
38   Walker 2012, p. 8.
39   Sopranzetti 2012.
40   Naruemon and McCargo 2011.

3.2   *Political Ideology: The Overwhelming Role of Royalism-Nationalism*
The organic crisis of the Thai state in the recent decade also manifested the
very crucial unseen 'ideological problem' of the Thai state. It is argued here
that the profound troubles within Thai politics in the terrain of superstructure
have been due to the overwhelming role of royalism-nationalism ideology in
Thai politics. Royalism and nationalism do not naturally take place to regulate
social forces. Rather, it has been a struggle that the Thai social elites constructed in order to preserve their own interests. The dominant political ideology
of Thailand coheres the monarchy and the nation in all spheres of social and
political life.[41]

The Thai monarchy had been weakened in its power and significance by
the 1932 revolution.[42] It was not until the coup d'état of 1957 that Field Marshall Sarit Thanarat, the coup leader, brought the monarchy back to its place.[43]
After five decades of the revitalisation of power the monarchy has been a
moral-political centre of the state and actively involved in Thai politics at times
of national crises in 1976, 1992, and 1997.[44] Thai royalism-nationalism works
along with other political ideologies such as liberalism and authoritarianism
and is highly reflexive to the political situation in each historical period. In
the late 1970s, royalism-nationalism was employed by the royalists against the
longstanding authoritarianism of the Thai military along with the rise of student liberalism. While the country was suffering from economic crisis in 1997,
royalism-nationalism was maintained and employed as a factor of social cohesion at the time of crisis by the King himself. However, the military coups
in 2006 and 2014 employed royalism-nationalism as a major ideological tool
against Thaksin and Yingluck governments respectively. And this ideology itself
has been constructed as a standard conception of the world for being morally
good (respect to the king and the nation). This implies that there is no place for
alternative modes of thought in the Thai state as people will definitely not be
perceived as being good citizens.

---

41   Jory 2003.
42   The absolutist regime of King Prachadhipok (Rama VII) was overthrown by the People's
      Party (Khana Ratsadon), a combined group of young blood civilians and military, on
      24 June 1932. The revolution was the crucial point of departure for the new era in modern
      Thai politics which was entirely different from the ancient regime as the supreme power
      no longer belonged to the absolute monarchy, but rested with ordinary people. However,
      Thailand did not transform itself to become a republic after the 1932 revolution; instead,
      the People's Party invited King Prachadhipok to be the king under the first ever Consti-
      tution of Siam in December 1932. At present, King Bhumibol is the King Rama IX of the
      Chakri Dynasty.
43   Thak 2007; see also Thongchai 2014.
44   Dressel 2010; Handley 2006; Ji 2007, 2010.

King Bhumibol took his chance to be the moral leader of the nation during the time of crisis in 1997 and cohered social forces in the Thai historical bloc through his proposed notion of the *'Sufficiency Economy Philosophy'*[45] (henceforth, SEP) expounded in his annual royal birthday speech on 4 December 1997.[46] SEP has played crucial roles in the Thai state since then and has dominated the spheres of life over Thai subalterns. It is argued here that along with the King's political interventions in 1973 and 1992 as a conflict trouble-shooter, the King's political action in late 1997 was also vital to emphasise his royal power as the moral leader of the country.[47] The SEP in 1997 can be seen as the confirmation of the extraordinary power of the King and the significance of 'royalism' also significantly increased after the crisis in 1997.

At the time of the crisis in 1997, the SEP was highly respected in the country as an alternative economic development strategy for the country in contrast to orthodox neoliberal projects.[48] However, it should be noted here that the conception of SEP itself is not an anti-capitalist idea, rather it is a practicing guide of how to live consistently with the bourgeois ideology.[49] The SEP has been emphasised as a 'hegemonic common sense' for social forces, communities, business firms, and bureaucratic authorities in Thailand's historical bloc to fol-

---

45   The King's notion of the SEP is derived from the work of E.F. Schumacher's 'Small is Beautiful' combined with Buddhist beliefs on the medium way and self-sufficiency in consumption.

46   In the King's birthday speech of 4 December 1997 he proposes his idea to the public as follows:

> Sufficiency Economy is a philosophy that guides the livelihood and behaviour of people at all levels, from the family to the community to the country, on matters concerning national development and administration. It calls for a 'middle way' to be observed, especially in pursuing economic development in keeping with the world of globalization. Sufficiency means moderation and reasonableness, including the need to build a reasonable immune system against shocks from the outside or from the inside. Intelligence, attentiveness, and extreme care should be used to ensure that all plans and every step of their implementation are based on knowledge. At the same time, we must build up the spiritual foundation of all people in the nation, especially state officials, scholars, and business people at all levels, so they are conscious of moral integrity and honesty and they strive for the appropriate wisdom to live life with forbearance, diligence, self-awareness, intelligence, and attentiveness. In this way we can hope to maintain balance and be ready to cope with rapid physical, social, environmental, and cultural changes from the outside world (quoted in Medhi 2003).

47   McCargo 2005.

48   Chambers 2013, pp. 86–8.

49   Unger 2009.

low the king's proposed ideas. The SEP has even been taught in the primary curriculum for Thai pupils and published in various forms such as comics provided by the Thailand National Identity Board in order to gain wider support from people in every social strata.[50]

In addition, the SEP has functioned as one of the major hegemonic tools that the conservative social forces have employed to configure social relations in Thailand from 1997 to the present, except for the short period of five years under the TRT government. Thaksinism ignored the King's SEP and implemented its own neoliberal policies; therefore after the military coup in 2006 the junta brought the SEP back and used it as a major ideological tool against Thaksinism. Then since 2006 the SEP has been insisted upon as a moral framework for the junta government and the successor Democrat government between 2008[51] and 2011. Both treated it as a superior concept to the so-called 'Thaksin's populist policies'.

The concept of SEP has been widely accepted and accommodated in various spheres in the Thai historical bloc during the post-1997 era.[52] However, this concept has been met with some criticism from scholars, as, *firstly*, it is only political rhetoric of the social elites and not applicable in real life, and it has been used as an ideological tool against political opposition. Following the crisis in 1997 the King proposed the concept of SEP as a new path for Thai society, economy, and even culture. Based on Buddhist philosophy and moral principles, the SEP aims to create a new type of economic man who lives moderately, is not greedy, and is not over exploitative. However, these principles are difficult to implement in real life under social relations of neoliberalism.

---

50   Isager and Ivarsson 2010, p. 232. The Thailand National Identity Board was formed in 2006 as a department under the Prime Minister's Office. It can be argued here that operations of this board aim to ideologically dominate Thai society in terms of setting up a standard conception of the world on the basis of: the Nation, the Religion, and the Monarchy. Bureaucratic organisations throughout the country have to follow ideological frameworks launched by this board.

51   In the year 2008, many countries had been affected by global economic crisis; however, it is argued here that the organic crisis of the Thai state since late 2005 has mainly been driven by political and ideological matters along with economic conflicts as a form of imbalance of class interests among social forces in the Thai historical bloc. This chapter does not deny the theoretical stance of neo-Gramscianism in IPE on the connection between global capitalism and internal politics. Nevertheless, as the influence of the global economy did not significantly affect the politics of the balancing and rebalancing of class forces in the Thai historical bloc since late 2005, this chapter does not take the 2008 crisis, or crisis of neoliberalism on the world scale, into account.

52   Apichai et al. 2006, 2009.

Isager and Ivarsson[53] argue that the SEP is only political rhetoric that is crucial in order to strengthen the 'moral fibre' of the nation rather than elevate people's material living conditions.

Secondly, the concept of SEP did not improve the concrete living conditions of the poor and other social forces as is evident in that poverty and income gaps in Thailand still exist and worsen every year.[54] However, scholars believe that another aspect of the SEP is that it can be inferred that it is an attempt by the royalist and capitalist social classes to keep the rural majority poor and happy.[55] *Lastly*, the massive bureaucratic budget spent on a number of projects entitled 'following the King's concept of SEP' has never been questioned. Specifically, the Royal Project Foundation, which was established in order to administer any projects initiated by the King, spent huge amounts of money on projects under the SEP framework without any declaration on the budget.[56]

In short, the SEP has been challenged as only political rhetoric or a campaign in order to build hegemony to configure social relations over social forces in the state. The maintenance of the SEP by the King and the conservative social groups created a regime in which moral leadership is attached to the King, the monarchy, and the royalism-nationalism ideology rather than the state and ordinary people. The over-involvement of the royalist-nationalist ideology employed by the monarchy and conservative social forces in modern Thai politics could not take place without the enforcement of legal power through the application of the lèse majesté laws, as shown below.

3.3   *Juridico-political: Harsh Applications of Lèse Majesté Laws*

Thailand's crises, this chapter argues, did not come to the fore only because of corrupt politicians. As shown in the earlier sections, Thailand has been facing a situation that can be described as, in a Gramscian sense, an organic crisis. The country failed to cope with the problem of social and economic inequality and also has been dominated by royalist-nationalist ideology. This section reveals the third crisis-ridden feature of Thailand's organic crisis seen as the harsh application of the '*lèse majesté laws*' and the problem of political prisoners in Thailand. Working mutually with the royalist-nationalist ideology, the juridico-political apparatus of the Thai state upholds the laws that mostly charge the political opposition as disloyal to the monarchy and have been employed against the freedom of speech of Thai social forces.

---

53   Isager and Ivarsson 2010.
54   Unger 2009, p. 154.
55   Unger 2009, p. 145.
56   Walker 2010, p. 260.

The lèse majesté law and the Computer Crime Act served this authoritarian objective highly effectively in the past few years through and beyond the crisis of 2010. Considering the number of cases where individuals have been charged with insulting the monarchy, there was a sharp increase after the 2006 military coup and there have been more than 500 cases since 2011[57] and more than 400 cases in 2015.[58] This can be taken to imply that the royalist-nationalist ideology has been crucial during the time of intense conflict and that the monarchy has been employed as a political weapon more in that period compared to previous decades of Thai politics.

Thailand's lèse majesté law has appeared in various forms over the last century since the emergence of a modern legal system. There are three vital stages in the development of lèse majesté laws in Thailand including: the lèse majesté law in the pre-1932 revolution period; lèse majesté law after the regime change; and lèse majesté law after the 1950s. *Firstly*, the lèse majesté appeared in several forms in the absolute monarchy of Siam. The 1900 edict was the first lèse majesté law, which at that time was created in order to protect the reputation of the royalty and the King's officials. Injuring the reputation of the King could lead to three years imprisonment. Then in 1908 the lèse majesté law was expanded in its scope to include the royal family and punishment was increased to seven years imprisonment for defamation of the King and three years for other members of the royal family.[59]

The *second* stage in the development of Thai lèse majesté laws took place after the 1932 revolution. The overthrow of the absolute monarchy eventually led to some changes to the law itself. In 1934, the criminal code was revised under the implementation of the first democratic constitution in late 1932. This law allowed people to express criticisms of the state and punishment was set at a maximum of seven years.[60] However, the most important stage of the lèse majesté law in Thailand is the period from the 1950s onward. In 1957 there was a major revision of the Thai criminal code. The result of this revision led to the current form of the lèse majesté law in Thailand which appeared in 'article 112' that provided special coverage only for the King, Queen, heir apparent, and regent. However, the punishment remained the same.[61] The *third* stage, which is the most crucial step in the development of lèse majesté law in Thailand, took place just after the student massacre at Tham-

---

57   Janya 2011.
58   Prachatai 2015.
59   Somchai and Streckfuss 2008; Streckfuss 2010, pp. 124–5.
60   Streckfuss 2011, p. 98.
61   Streckfuss 2011, p. 103.

masat University on 6 October 1979. A coup d'état had been conducted on the same day and the putschists launched the Coup order No. 41 in order to increase the punishment under all defamation-based laws. This led to a massive increase in punishment for those who insulted the King and royal family to a minimum of three and a maximum of 15 years imprisonment.[62] This lèse majesté law remains the same and functions very effectively the same presently.

In addition, along with the active application of article 112 of the criminal code, there is an emergence of the new coup d'état heritage, the Computer Crime Act of 2007, which addresses the very large number of lèse majesté crimes on the internet.[63] In fact, the Computer Crime Act itself does not contain any clause specifically on crimes towards the monarchy. The law originally covers the security matters of the state. Nevertheless, Thai state officials see the criticisms of any aspects related to the monarchy, whether or not it is for academic reasons, as the first priority of national security. The Computer Act had forced the termination of a very high number of websites related to any criticism of the monarchy with more than 80,000 sites closed between 2007 and 2011[64] and even significantly increased to more than 100,000 sites down after the coup in 2014.[65] The genuine ideological content underlying the 2010 political turmoil, this chapter argues, is the overwhelming employment of the royalist-nationalist ideology along with the harsh application of the state's juridico-political apparatus via the lèse majesté law. This resulted in a significant rise in the number of political prisoners who have been charged with crimes against the monarchy in recent years.

In short, this section has contested Thailand's political common sense – the idea that wicked politicians are the only cause of the country's crises. In contrast, I have addressed the three major crisis-ridden features of the Thai state – increasing social disparity, the overwhelming influence of the royalist-nationalist ideology, and harsh applications of the lèse majesté laws. These underlying problems have been created since the modern development of Thai politics from the late 1950s and have been transmitted through many decades. The transition that began following the economic crisis in 1997 has been accelerated under Thaksinism between 2001 and 2005. Eventually, it led to the eruption of all the latent conflicts in Thailand that were brought to the fore and appeared as the confrontations between the conservative Yellow Shirt and the

---

62   Streckfuss 2011, p. 105.
63   Sawatri 2011, pp. 54–61.
64   Sawatri 2012, p. 137.
65   TCIJ 14 April 2014.

more liberal Red Shirt movements. The peak of crisis in 2010 resulted in hundreds of deaths and in protests against Yingluck government and led to another military coup in May 2014.

4   The 'Present' and Its Uncertainty: The New Cannot Be Born

In his *Prison Notebooks*, Gramsci once described the notion of 'organic crisis' as a historical situation in which *'the old is dying, but the new cannot be born'*.[66] What is dying in the Thai historical bloc is the erosion of the sacredness of royalism-nationalism that centres on the monarchy, the growing demands of the subaltern for a fairer economy, and the increasing demand for protecting human rights and human dignity. In this situation, conservative social forces attempt to escape from the organic situation of the crisis of authority by enforcing the aggressive lèse majesté law towards the constructed 'otherness' who possess different ideologies and worldviews. In Gramscian theory, the area of 'political society', in which the state could operate its coercive practices, has a dialectical relationship with another theoretical terrain which is 'civil society' where hegemony is more crucial than force.[67] Therefore, any political practices that might be operated in political society are definitely resonant with civil society at the same time.[68] In the case of Thai politics, the forceful application of the juridico-political apparatus via the lèse majesté law has contributed to the politics within civil society in which there exists a growing number of debates and greater critical awareness through several social institutions.

In recent years, several Thai subaltern social groups seemed to realise that the overwhelming social roles of the monarchy and its ideological hegemonic projects along with the application of the lèse majesté law are genuine obstruc-

---

66   Gramsci 1971a, pp. 275–6, Q3 §34.
67   See state and civil society in Gramsci 1971a; Liguori 2015b.
68   One should note here the dialectical relationship on the terrains of political-civil societies is Gramsci's 'totalitarian approach' (he never uses the term 'totalitarianism', only the adjective 'totalitarian'). Gramsci employs this methodological approach throughout his prison notebooks to describe the attempt by a State or a party to fill every space in the political as well as the cultural sphere, i.e. to establish a totalising 'conception of the world' (the preferred one of the ruling class) and consequently to banish any alternative worldviews. In the case of Thailand, the ruling elites have been constructing a totalising conception of the world via a number of repressive state apparatuses and ideological hegemony (see note 72 below). On this matter see, for instance, Gramsci 1971a, pp. 157–8, Q15 §6; Gramsci 1971a, pp. 147–9, Q15 §4; Gramsci 1971a, pp. 264–5, Q6 §136.

tions to reaching the so-called liberal democracy.[69] Political regimes that could not provide spaces for minorities and that restrict freedom of speech represent a kind of authoritarianism even though they possess the legal form of democracy through constitutions and elections. At this stage, some critical social groups in Thailand – who can reveal to the public the roles of the royalist-nationalist ideology and uncover the roles of the monarchy as an anti-democratic force – have been incrementally rising up. For instance, the Nitirat group (the enlightened jurists), a group of critical legal scholars at Thammasat University, plays a leading role in constructing critical awareness towards the existing role of the monarchy and the lèse majesté law since 2010. Moreover, some leftist academic communities such as Fah Deaw Kan journal (the Same Sky), Midnight University, and the alternative media of Prachatai Online also risk themselves by offering rare political spaces for the publication of critical writings.[70] However, it should be noted here that these movements are only tiny sectors of a whole civil society within the Thai state. Further, these movements do not have an effect upon social forces to a great extent because of the structural limitations of the lèse majesté laws, which are even tougher after the coup in May 2014.[71] Therefore, this situation could be seen as one where *'the new'* or, what I call, the alternative/critical/challenging social forces which have been growing, are still neither mature nor critical enough[72] to contest the tradi-

---

69   For a discussion of Thai liberalism, see Connors 2012.

70   Chuwas 2011.

71   The Thai army has been calling those who have public criticisms of the junta to be brainwashed under their so-called 'attitude adjustment programme'. This programme is a method employed by Thailand's ruling military junta to neutralise its critics and opponents. Those 'invited' for attitude adjustment are detained without charge and interrogated, with settings ranging from vacation to detention-like facilities. Treatment ranges from effusive politeness to terse language; from being kept in a military camp where you can walk around and play sports to being detained in a small room with no vista to the world, depending on your learning curve toward the attitude adjustment process (see Pravit 2015). Unfortunately, there are no certain data to confirm the number of people who have been called since the coup, and the junta continue to operate this programme.

72   The alternative/critical/challenging social forces in Thailand are not mature enough to change Thai political economy for two reasons. On the one hand, political-legal constraints serve to limit their social and political actions. The constraints have appeared in various forms such as the lèse majesté laws of the Criminal Code, Computer Crime Act, Martial Law, and also Article 44 of the 2014 interim constitution that grants the Prime Minister absolute power. On the other hand, several Thai social groups could not think beyond the dominant conception of the world due to the lack of critical education in the Thai educational system. The reason behind this absence of critical studies in Thailand can be attributed to the strong influence of the authoritarian regime and the overwhelming role of royalism (and also its legal applications). The Thai state has perpetuated a

tional mode of thought/conception of the world; they are also not sufficient to construct a whole new democratic historical bloc at this historical stage. This means that the organic crisis of the Thai state is an ongoing process that cannot be solved in a short period of time and will require years to address effectively so as to reconstruct a new type of social relation in the Thai state.

5   Conclusion: The Future(?)

Gramsci noted that a crisis of authority is apparent in societies when 'the old is dying and the new cannot be born; in this interregnum a great variety of morbid symptoms appear'.[73] After a decade of political conflicts within the Thai state since late 2005, social and political uncertainties ended up as the morbid regime of authoritarian government which rules the country by fostering extreme nationalism and royalism. After so many years of the authoritarian regime, the sides of the Red and Yellow shirts have emerged as answers to this situation, but in fact both movements have failed to improve living conditions. The failure to improve the condition of people's lives, the inability to learn to live with a variety of political ideologies, and the infringement of human dignity are the real troubles of the Thai state.

Because of the complicated nature and history of Thailand's organic crisis as discussed in this chapter, it must be concluded that the future of the Thai state is not an easy topic to consider or project. This is further complicated because the prevailing sentiment is that the Thai crisis of authority is considered a myth, when in reality it is a real factor which needs to be addressed. Thailand's brighter future needs structural change and long-term attempts to reconstruct and achieve a stronger and fairer political and civil society. However, this chapter argues that the Thai state should, at least, urgently deal with the three major crisis-ridden features as shown above. Creating fairness in the opportunities for Thai subaltern social groups in terms of both social dignity and inclusive economic development is crucial. Apart from that, the hegemonic royalism-nationalism should be changed to imagine a new political ideology

---

mode of thinking in which obedience to the ruler, like the monarchy and authoritarian military government, is normal and criticising their political roles risks one being charged under lèse majesté and other laws. Therefore, it is difficult for radicals and the left in Thai academia to publish critical social and political studies even for an academic audience. Allowing radical theories to be applied in these political circumstances can aid the political resistance of several social forces. Official suppression of dissenting views is the reason why the critical and challenging social forces have barely taken root in Thailand.

73   Gramsci 1971a, pp. 275–6, Q3 § 34.

that provides places for ordinary human dignity and social welfare. In addition, the harsh application and existence of the lèse majesté laws should be revised and legally changed.

To make all these suggestions possible, the Thai historical bloc needs a strong state to achieve a fairer political economy, secure social security, and protect human rights. At the same time, to struggle against the hegemonic ideology, the subalterns need to play leading roles, as do intellectuals in various forms such as by becoming individual public figures or via political parties, civil society organisations, among others. Stakeholders need to be involved in providing critical education and lifelong adult education to raise critical awareness of social forces. Constructing a critical conception of the world is a long-term project. However, it is an essential requirement in order to overcome the existing political 'common sense' that has dominated Thai society. Failure to do so will mean that it will not be possible to achieve a 'more' democratic and a fairer society as the subalterns have imagined.

PART 2

Language and Translation

∴

CHAPTER 4

Gramsci: Structure of Language, Structure of Ideology

Derek Boothman

The history of every language is the history of those who spoke or speak
it, and the history of languages is the history of the human mind.

from the *Zibaldone* of GIACOMO LEOPARDI, entry of 31 July 1822[1]

∴

1 Introduction

Sometimes important sources and aspects of Gramsci's thought seem either
hidden even from him and are implicit, or at least left unsaid. Such seems partially the case with the use Gramsci makes of Marx's theses on Feuerbach for
his concept of man/humanity. Here we argue that Gramsci's appreciation of
the structure, development and use of language, or rather languages, stemming
from his university linguistics training, has its parallel in these same aspects
of his highly individual concept of ideologies, as emerges in the *Prison Notebooks* two decades further on; here also, this linkage is never quite fully explicit.
The glottology (comparative historical linguistics) course that he followed and
then transcribed at the request of his professor,[2] Matteo Bartoli, dealt to a great
extent with the historical development of languages, spilling over into what
Bartoli later called an 'areal linguistics' approach; in both of these, the social
aspects of language are quite strongly in evidence. Bartoli drew attention to a
marked 'layered', or stratified, structure of language, present in all languages

---

1 Quoted by Tullio De Mauro 1979, p. 115.
2 At the time of writing, Gramsci's transcription is unpublished, but it has been prepared for
imminent publication by Giancarlo Schirru. My thanks go to the president and director of the
Fondazione Istituto Gramsci for permission to consult and quote from Gramsci's handwritten

and which his course dealt with especially in regard to Latin, the neo-Latin languages and those of the Balkans. Intuitively, given the fact that ideology in its explicit form is expressed by linguistic (or, more generally, semiotic) means, one might expect the language-ideology nexus in Gramsci to assume very particular forms. Indeed, in Gramsci's model of ideologies, the notion of 'stratification' plays a key role, attested to when he speaks, for example, of the 'layers of sediment deposited by old ideologies'[3] or, in the first notebook of all where, in the cultural sphere, 'diverse ideological strata are variously combined'.[4] Language has a history and presents not so much a single conception of the world as various 'conceptions of the world' – a notion that partially coincides with that of 'ideology' – and thus *is* also history, indeed a sedimented history.[5] We now proceed to sketch out some of the nexuses, similarities and homologies between the developments and structures of ideology and language.

2   Gramsci's Concepts of Ideology[6]

That similarities exist in Gramsci between the structures of language and ideology should not come as a surprise, given the intimate link in his thinking between language and culture, and the role this latter plays in ideology. And neither should one be surprised if the language-ideology link is of a different nature in him as compared with many other Marxists. Indeed it is well known to the point of being a truism that his approach towards and concepts of ideology are quite, and at times radically, different from those of other Marxists: this sometimes includes Marx himself, with Engels, then Lenin and, just slightly later, Lukács, whose 'imputed consciousness' idea seems indeed far distant from the concepts that Gramsci went on to develop.

The concept of ideology as a false consciousness, as a distorted vision of reality, has been common in the thinking of Marxists, at least from when (1932) Marx and Engels's *German Ideology* first came fairly fully into circulation.[7] And, as a reinforcement of what became the 'vulgate', towards the end of his life Engels did write of 'false consciousness' in a letter to Franz Mehring, adding

---

3   Q5, § 131; Gramsci 1996b, p. 384.
4   Q1, § 43; Gramsci 1992, p. 129.
5   Lecercle 2006, p. 158.
6   An authoritative treatment of Gramsci's concept of ideology is given by Guido Liguori (2004, pp. 131–49) and in the same author's entry *Ideologia* in Liguori 2009c, pp. 399–403.
7   The content of this incomplete set of manuscripts was almost certainly unknown to Gramsci; one part was published by Rjazanov in 1926, then what was claimed to be the full extent of the manuscripts appeared, under Adoratskij's name as editor, in 1932.

a rider, however, saying that ideologies can and often do have an 'effect upon history'.[8] While Gramsci often uses 'ideology' in a negative sense, the 'false consciousness' concept is, at most, in the background in the *Notebooks*. As one of his main reference points, on a number of occasions he refers explicitly to the view expressed by Marx in the 1859 *Preface*, namely that during a period of 'material upheaval', 'ideological forms' are 'the terrain on which men become conscious of' the conflict between 'the economic conditions of production' and the 'juridical, political, religious, artistic or philosophical forms' and hence allow people to 'resolve' that conflict. This is a literal English translation of Gramsci's own Italian translation of the relevant part of the *Preface*, as it appears in Notebook 7.[9] In the *German Ideology*, Marx states that the 'ideas of the ruling class are in every epoch the ruling ideas', and in certain circumstances there is a struggle for what, in translation, he calls 'dominance', resulting in a separation of powers. There, a fact sometimes overlooked, he also draws attention to the presence of revolutionary ideas opposed to ruling class ideas, presupposed by the existence of a revolutionary class.[10] At this point we are near what Gramsci calls a 'struggle between two hegemonies'.[11]

Again in Notebook 7, Gramsci takes up a similar theme when speaking of the 'solidity of popular beliefs', here paraphrasing Marx's observation that 'a popular conviction often has as much energy as a material force', which he follows up with the famous formulation that material forces are the content and ideology the form of the historical bloc;[12] elsewhere, he refers to the extent 'to which superstructures react upon the structure',[13] indicating that ideologies can influence material conditions.

Guido Liguori notes that a positive theory of ideology, regarding all social groups, is for Gramsci a 'conception of the world' and the 'locus of constitution of collective subjectivity',[14] around which there may develop a war of position and the struggle for hegemony that runs through the whole of society. But there is also another, very important sense of ideology that is found in Gramsci, namely 'popular ideology', and it is perhaps here that the link-up with languages (in the sense of models of their structure, shape and development) is most evident.

---

8   Engels, letter to Mehring of 14 July 1893, https://www.marxists.org/archive/marx/works/1893/letters/93_07_14.htm, trans. Dona Torr.
9   Q11, § 29; Gramsci 1971a, p. 459, which also gives Antonio Labriola's version of this passage.
10   Marx and Engels 1976a [1846], pp. 59–60.
11   Q8, § 227; Gramsci 2007a, p. 373; see also Q11§12; Gramsci 1971a, p. 333.
12   Q7, § 21: Gramsci 2007a, p. 172.
13   Q13, § 2; Gramsci 1971a, p. 176.
14   Liguori 2009c, p. 401.

As said, Gramsci seems to stop short of an explicit linkage between language and ideology, although it underlies what he wrote. In tracing the notion of ideology to French materialism, he refers to Destutt de Tracy's *Eléments d'Idéologie, originally published in* 1801–15, and its more complete Italian version which appeared shortly afterwards (1819). Stemming from Destutt's work we have, as Gramsci observes, two senses of ideology, an original 'science of ideas', which included questions of grammar and language, and the now more usual 'system of ideas'. The distinction between 'science' and 'system' comes across fairly explicitly in Notebook 11, where Gramsci observes that Bukharin remains trapped in 'Ideology', and that term 'in the philosophy of praxis implicitly contains a negative value judgment', and that same 'philosophy of praxis represents a clear supersession [of Ideology] and, indeed, historically contraposes itself to Ideology'; at this point Gramsci tends towards the opinion that, methodologically, the philosophy of praxis is at least closer to a 'science' than to a 'system' of ideas. The negatively-connotated type of ideology, Gramsci continues, must be analysed historically 'as a superstructure'.[15]

Liguori observes that Gramsci's concept of ideology may be reconstructed only by taking into consideration other terms he uses in the *Notebooks* such as 'conception of the world, philosophy, conformism, religion, faith, common sense, folklore etc.';[16] all these terms are correlated and may be *partially* superposed one on another so that, indeed, in one place Gramsci himself glosses 'popular ideology' as 'common sense'.[17] To these terms Liguori adds conformism and also language (*linguaggio*),[18] which in Gramsci's outlook does in fact 'contain the elements of a conception of the world'. And, as this same paragraph states earlier, 'when one's conception of the world is not critical and coherent but disjointed and episodic, one belongs simultaneously to a multiplicity of mass human groups (*uomini-massa*)'.[19] Some of the elements of the list indicated by Liguori obviously correspond either to what Gramsci himself calls 'ideology in the pejorative sense' of the term, meaning 'a dogmatic system of eternal and absolute truths',[20] or to the ideology of 'groups or small groups characterized by their own ideological and psychological impulses'.[21]

---

15   Q11, § 63; Gramsci 1971a, pp. 375–6; cf. also the first draft Q4§35 in Gramsci 1996b, pp. 174–5.

16   Liguori 2004a, pp. 139–40.

17   Q16§27.

18   Liguori 2004a, p. 144. In this context 'linguaggio' may be understood as 'discourse'.

19   Q11, § 12, Notes III and I; Gramsci 1971a, pp. 325 and 324 respectively.

20   Q11, § 62; Gramsci 1971a, p. 407.

21   Q1, § 43; Gramsci 1992, p. 128.

Summing up, among other things, ideology – as noted above – is for Gramsci the locus of the constitution of collective subjectivity, it is the 'terrain on which men move' according to a semi-geological metaphor of Liguori's,[22] and is one way in which the individual may take part, often syncretically, in different world views.

3   Gramsci's University Linguistics Studies

At the University of Turin, Gramsci followed the two-part course in glottology held by Matteo Bartoli. The first part dealt with the development of Latin, and was followed by a study of the Balkan languages (see below). For a fuller, but compatible and well-established treatment of Latin than that contained in Bartoli's lecture notes, I have here relied on an authoritative study by Giacomo Devoto[23] who, at the time Gramsci was imprisoned, was a younger generation linguist, mentioned quite approvingly in the *Notebooks*. A first thing to be noted about the approaches that characterise both Bartoli and Devoto is the notion of centres of linguistic irradiation, which are responsible for spreading some standard form of language that is adopted by a community. Bartoli on one occasion even uses the word 'hegemony' for such centres, while 'prestige' occurs in Devoto. 'Irradiation' ('irradiazione') is used surprisingly frequently by Devoto, but Gramsci makes a rather sparing use of the word, which occurs just eight times in the whole of the *Notebooks*. On two occasions (a first draft text and its redrafted one), it is used to refer to the ideas current in eighteenth- and nineteenth-century France, but then it famously occurs in the last notebook (Q29, on grammar) to pose the question of what the national 'centres of irradiation' are for *linguistic* innovation. In Gramsci's earlier monographic notebook on Machiavelli, irradiation is similarly used, but in the context of the spread of ideology to challenge the notion that ideas and opinions are 'spontaneously "born" in each individual brain' and to assert, instead, that there are instead centres of 'formation, of irradiation, of dissemination, of persuasion' that may consist of a 'group of men, or a single individual even which has developed them and presented them in the political form of current reality'.[24] We have then a first example of a link-up between ways in which both language and ideology function.

---

22   Liguori 2004a, p. 147.

23   Devoto 1974.

24   Q13, § 30; Gramsci 1971a, pp. 192–3.

Bartoli's treatment of the historical evolution of Latin bordered on, and indeed at times passed over into, what would later be called sociolinguistics. Like another linguist mentioned approvingly in the *Notebooks*, Graziadio Isaia Ascoli, Bartoli's general approach paid great attention to linguistic stratifications, to the substrata – often of quite different origins – in languages. They may be, for example, residuals left after military conquest or may be due to the confluence of peoples and cultures, including those of class; examples cited by Bartoli and Devoto include the Osco-Umbrian and Etruscan substrata in Latin and its successors; later on, from the North, there were Celtic, Gallic ('Gallo-Roman' in Bartoli's terminology) or Iberian influences, which it may be better to class as superstrata.[25] Again here, there is a very clear parallel with the functioning and structures of ideology. As regards the language-ideology nexus, three languages in the Balkans – Albanian, Romanian and Bulgarian – stand out in Bartoli's treatment but, for reasons of space, discussion here will be limited to just Albanian among the Balkan languages; ancient and modern Greek, together with other languages, such as Italian and English, are here mentioned just in passing.

Due to the particular structure of Albanian and its nature as an isolated branch of the Indo-European family, in Bartoli's view a descendant of ancient Illyrian,[26] it is useful to take this language as a starting point. After a brief comment on some of its salient features, we move on to where there is thought to be a useful analogy with Gramsci's concepts of ideology.

The name itself 'Albania' has the root 'Alb', regarding whose meaning[27] there is some doubt but, in the opinion of some linguists, it cannot be judged as separate from the name 'Alp', the meaning being a 'high place' or possibly even, according to Bartoli, a mountain; according to Devoto, 'alba/alpa' has the fundamental meaning of '[a] stone'.[28] No more than 400 words of the original stratum of the language survive in modern Albanian,[29] and some linguists put the number at only around half of this (200–250). Then, as regards another Balkan region, 'Dan' or in the more ancient form 'Den', is stated possibly to have the same root as 'Delm' meaning 'sheep' in Albanian – hence the neighbouring Delmatia and then Dalmatia,[30] and therefore a rugged place for sheep. This may

---

25   Timpanaro 1969, pp. 246–7; and Bartoli 1912–13, Part 2, p. 85.
26   Cf. There are not 'many agreements between the Illyrian lexis and Albanian but they are very precise' (Tagliavini 1965, Chapter 2, Section 2).
27   Bartoli 1912–13, Part 2, p. 32.
28   Devoto 1974, p. 33.
29   Bartoli 1912–13, Part 2, p. 122.
30   Bartoli 1912–13, Part 2, p. 29; also Tagliavini 1965, Chapter 2, Section 2.

be compared with Italy, whose name, Bartoli states, is etymologically linked to 'vitulus' (in modern Italian 'vitello') meaning a calf; 'Italy' is thus a fertile place, suitable for cattle. In cases such as these, the original words become totally del-exicalised, their initial meaning and significance being forgotten, just as is often the case in ideology.

Structurally, on top of the substratum of the original Albanian – Illyrian as the local 'variant' of the Ario- or Indo-European family – there came many other influences as linguistic superstrata, which now, at distance of centur-ies and millennia, themselves appear as substrata of modern Albanian. This highly stratified nature of the language is illustrated by Bartoli's identification, on top of the Illyrian, of traces and importations of Latin and neo-Latin lan-guages, Greek both ancient and modern, Slav languages, Turkish and Arabic, an observation echoed by Gramsci[31] nearly twenty years after he had followed Bartoli's course. Greek and Slav show up in the two main dialects, the Greek-influenced Tosk in the South, and the more Slav-influenced Gheg in the North; in the middle is Elbasan, considered 'purer' and more beautiful by Bartoli, since it has conserved more of the features of the 'original' language. And Bartoli does not hesitate to point to one important reason for all these influences, namely the fact that crossing Albania is the important via Egnatia,[32] the main consular road from the Adriatic across to Thessalonica, and from then on to Constantinople. The road served as an important link for travellers, bringing linguistic influences in the wake of trade, between the Roman Empires of the East and West; the road continued to function through the Crusades and on to the building of the railways. There is, then, every historical reason why Albania was a melting-pot for various linguistic influences.[33]

The sedimentary stratification of the Albanian language, left by the differ-ent ethnic groupings, is marked to the extreme, a feature which emerges quite clearly from Gramsci's transcription of his professor's course. This sedimenta-tion may be compared with comments in the *Prison Notebooks* regarding the presence of 'previous ideological currents, each of which "may" have left a sediment in various combinations with preceding or subsequent sediments',[34] lines which are copied in Q24§4 with the sole modifications that 'preceding' is replaced by 'of the past' and, much more importantly, the past participle 'com-

---

31   Q3§156; Gramsci 1996b, p. 127.

32   Bartoli 1912–13, Part 2, p. 10.

33   Bartoli 1912–13, Part 2, p. 33.

34   Q1, §43; Gramsci 1992, p. 129. I have replaced Buttigieg's 'deposit' with the more literal translation 'sediment', more akin to ideological and linguistic 'stratification' and 'sedi-mentation' dealt with here.

bined' (in Buttigieg's translation 'in various combinations') becomes 'combining'. The final version thus puts the emphasis on ideological processes actually taking place at the present time which combine with those of the past and also *possibly* slightly shifts the emphasis from 'preceding' ideologies (maybe no longer valid) to those 'of the past', maybe still with us especially in the form of metaphorical 'sediments'. This repeats, more or less exactly but unknowingly, what the British social and cultural anthropologist Edward Burnett Tylor called 'survivals', namely 'processes, customs, and opinions, and so forth, which have been carried on by force of habit into a new state of society different from that in which they had their original home, and they thus remain as proofs and examples of an older condition of culture out of which a newer has been evolved'.[35]

4   Disappearance and Reappearance: Change and Evolution

It is a truism that some words, such as place names and often, especially, names of rivers, are exceptionally conservative, with only minor modifications apparent across the centuries. And words may unexpectedly appear even in countries other than those of their origin. The Scandinavian root 'lek-' ('play') reappears for example in Lancashire dialect as 'to lake', with the same meaning ('laking at cards') or, as used more metaphorically and sardonically in the days of the cotton industry, to be at home or 'on short time' because of a lack of orders at the factory, e.g. 'we're laking this week'. Again quoting Lancashire dialect, 'hoo', pronounced like 'who', is not a relative or interrogative personal pronoun, but the third person feminine singular 'she' (Old Frisian 'hoo' and Old English 'heo'), remaining unchanged in form and meaning from modern English's ancestor, Old Frisian. Other influences, Germanic and Scandinavian, too numerous to begin to list here are also present in much of Northern and Eastern England.

Often, of great importance for cultural and ideological reasons, words that were once current disappear only to reappear later after centuries of disuse (at least by some social classes), like river currents in a Karst region that also disappear and then reappear elsewhere.[36] Some words seemingly disappear in the

---

35   Tylor 1920, p. 16.
36   Bartoli deals with a geological conundrum of this type. A current on the coast of Cephalonia suddenly disappears underground; only in the 1950s was it demonstrated that it re-emerged through a natural underground conduit elsewhere along the coastline. Whether Bartoli, as elsewhere, was describing the Balkan terrain or metaphorically illustrating an aspect of language is not clear.

current of time, lost in the speech of some social classes, then appear at considerable lengths of time, having survived in the oral speech of subaltern groups. As the poet Hugh MacDiarmid says:

> And rejoice over how κάμνω found in Homer
> In the sense of 'make' survived in popular speech
> For 3000 years, though it did not get into books.[37]

Plautus (late third to early second centuries B.C.E.) used *canutus* (modern Italian *canuto*, meaning 'white-haired' or 'white-bearded' and metaphorically, by extension, 'wise'), a word which then reappeared in written form only in the sixth century C.E. In other cases, 'a series of words' survived only in manuscripts in libraries to be then re-exhumed and 'returned to the spoken language', i.e. at the time of the humanists.[38] This may be linked with Gramsci's line of reasoning[39] regarding one serious scholar's refusal to recognise that 'Middle Latin' and what he termed 'humanistic or philosophical Latin' are 'really two languages because they express two conceptions of the world that, in a sense, are antithetical': in other words, although the two languages are near-congruent, in Gramsci's view they are different because they express two different outlooks in the sense of being 'historically organic ideologies ... necessary to a given structure'.[40]

Often a word may remain in a recognisable form, but this time its meaning changes, occasionally fairly radically but usually logically, in passing from one language or type of discourse to another. Gramsci explicitly cites examples – 'dis-aster' and 'dis-grace' – of what many, but not all, linguists call a 'dead metaphor', again a process of delexicalisation, here linked to astrology and religion respectively. But there are other types of radical but logical change. In pre-industrial cultures in several languages there is a close link between 'cattle' and 'wealth'. Pliny the Elder could relate how 'Servius was the first king who stamped the copper [money] with the images of sheep and oxen'.[41] One of Gramsci's university textbooks, by an author mentioned in what for Gramsci are approving tones in the *Notebooks*, illustrates the sort of etymological link that may be found. English, for example, incorporated the Norman French *catel*

---

37   MacDiarmid 1967, p. 404.
38   Devoto 1974, pp. 128 and 167–8 respectively.
39   Q5, § 123; Gramsci 1996b, p. 370.
40   Q7, § 19; Gramsci 2007a, p. 171.
41   Marx 1987a [1857–58], p. 187. Pliny the Elder, *Historia naturalis* I.18, c.3; 'Servius rex ovium boumque effigie primus aes signavit', quoted in Marx's *Grundrisse*.

(central Old French *chatel*) to become on the one hand 'cattle' and on the other 'chattels' or goods, i.e. wealth. Other times, a process of linguistic evolution may put a word denoting one of these things back into the language with the meaning of the other. This happened with the Anglo-Saxon *feoh*, 'cattle', which then came to mean a sum of money, a *fee*; and, in the opposite direction, *scribl* (from the Latin *scrupulum*), a 'coin' in old Welsh, became the twelfth-century Welsh *ysgrubl* with the meaning of 'cattle, beast of burden'. Or again, a term may be taken from common everyday language, given another meaning, and put back into circulation with its original meaning often suppressed and forgotten. The Latin *fenum* originally meant 'the product', but then for agricultural producers it took on the more restricted meaning of 'hay' (modern Italian form: *fieno*), while in ancient Greece, the term for goods in general ($\tau\alpha\,\chi\tau\eta\mu\alpha\tau\alpha$) began to be used by the peasantry for their cattle.[42]

Gramsci sums up analogous processes by saying that a culture, especially a new one, 'coins brand-new words or absorbs them from other languages as loan-words giving them a precise meaning', often 'depriving them of the ideological "halo" they possessed in the original language'.[43] He in fact concludes this passage by referring to the new lease of life taken on by the word 'imminent', not because it became obsolete and was then resuscitated, but because in Marx its 'ideological' and semantic meaning shifted from the presence and operation of the deity in the universe to a purely secular 'this-worldliness', in the sense of Marxism as a philosophy of praxis that represents the opening of philosophy to the real world.[44]

As with language, so – very often – with ideology. What, one may ask, are examples of the evolution of ideology? For the purpose of illustration, we may take two cases, one from the *Notebooks* themselves and another from an external source. A subject with strong ideological connotations that is introduced in the very first notebook, and then continues through to some of his very last ones, is that of Jacobinism. In a key paragraph of the first notebook Gramsci defines the original Jacobins as a 'particular party in the French Revolution which conceived of the revolution in a particular way' and who were characterised by 'extreme energy and resolve', due to the 'merits of that program and that method' of theirs. He goes on to say however that 'in political language' the two aspects of Jacobinism had been split, and the name had come to represent a 'politician who was energetic and resolute because fanatic-

---

42   Bréal 1983 [1900][1], pp. 117 and 109.
43   Q11, § 24; Gramsci 1971a, p. 452.
44   Frosini 2009b, p. 409.

ally convinced of the thaumaturgical power of his ideas'.[45] The original Jacobins were not abstract ('astratti') even though, after a passage of time, their language now seems so: 'their language, their ideology reflected perfectly the needs of the time in keeping with French traditions and culture' where that language and ideology are, a little later, termed 'ultra-realistic'.[46] But the use here of the word 'abstract' indicates an ideological transition from the political projects of the original Jacobins, based among other things on the 'unity of town and country' – the 'relations between city and countryside',[47] which was to become a hallmark of Gramsci's policies for Italy[48] – to an empty shell. The ideological passage is summed up where Gramsci writes that the notion of Jacobinism became 'detached, as almost always happens, from the conditions of place and time, and reduced to formulas, and became something different, a larva, empty and inert words',[49] while, later on, he writes of the 'utopian character of mummified Jacobin ideologies'[50] and then, with reference to the same period, this latter-day Jacobinism is characterised 'very wretchedly, by the radical-socialists of Herriot and Daladier'.[51]

From outside the *Notebooks*, a classic case of complex ideological shifts is tarantism, the apparent bite of a tarantula spider. In the south-eastern Italian region of Puglia, part of the ancient Magna Graecia, this was the subject of a famous study carried out in 1959 by a team headed by Ernesto De Martino,[52] a well-known ethnologist influenced by Gramsci's writings; there is also a similar example at Ossi in Gramsci's native Sardinia, of which presumably he was aware. The attack takes place prevalently in June and, in the overwhelming majority of cases, the victim is female, with the cure involving a frenetic dance (i.e. a musical exorcism) and an entire ritual, now connected with Saints Peter and in particular Paul. The phenomenon is (relatively) modern, but a parallel with the ritualistic cure dating to much earlier times is drawn by De Martino when he quotes a German scholar, Robert Eisler (1922–23), on Orphic-Dionysiac thought in Christian antiquity. Phenomena similar to tarantism are also found even earlier in ancient Greece and mentioned, among other places, in fragments of Aeschylus, the 'symptoms' being described in Pliny's

---

45   Q1, § 44; Gramsci 1992, pp. 140–1; recopied in Q19, § 24, Gramsci 1971a, p. 66.

46   Q1, § 44 and Q1, § 48; Gramsci 1992, pp. 147 and 158 respectively.

47   Q8, § 35; Gramsci 2007a, p. 256.

48   Gramsci 2014a, p. 240 and cf. p. 171.

49   Q13, § 37, referring to the France of the 1920s.

50   Q16, § 9; Gramsci 1971a, p. 399.

51   Q19, § 24; Gramsci 1971a, p. 63.

52   De Martino 1961, cf. here pp. 216–17 and 404–5.

Natural History,[53] with a scorpion or a horsefly being the culprit rather than a tarantula. Another parallel is that in Puglia, only the local inhabitants are prone to being bitten, while Pliny narrates that the bite of the scorpion at Latmus (South-West Turkey) is fatal only to the native inhabitants, outsiders not being so susceptible; again, in both places and times, the bite is lethal only to women and girls.[54] Ideology, like the examples of words quoted previously, goes underground, perhaps even disappearing for a time – except for the local community – and then resurfaces centuries later, perhaps in another place relatively distant from, but connected with its origins (a metaphorically Karstic process), and with Paul and Peter replacing figures from Greek mythology.

It may be, as a hypothesis, that in the local community women and girls tended to work where insects of the above types were more common; and certainly, convulsive movements – like those typical of the exorcistic and prolonged tarantella dance associated with tarantism – produce endogenous morphines which 'reduce the body's sensitivity to pain – as "natural painkillers" they produce a sense of euphoria', a feature of shamanic (and similar) healing.[55] Ideological phenomena may sometimes, or often, therefore fit into a reality framework. And for Gramsci, at least some types of ideology, as expressed in the superstructures of a society, do have their basis in reality: 'the complex and discordant [interlinear variant: contradictory] *ensemble* of the superstructures is the reflection of the *ensemble* of the social relations of production'.[56]

5   Linguistic and Ideological Innovation

As seen in the above example, analogously to lexical items, ideology may also go underground and then reappear; but just how does innovation come about in the two fields? Gramsci is explicit about this in language. In a very interesting paragraph, he concludes that 'innovations are not individual' and that, while the 'jargons of various professions' innovate molecularly, 'innovations occur through the interference of different cultures' and a new class coming to power innovates *en masse*.[57] One striking example of this is of course Nor-

---

53   De Martino 1961, pp. 221 and 405 respectively.
54   Pliny, *Hist. Nat*, op. cit. Book XI.
55   Harvey and Wallis 2007, p. 61.
56   Q8, §182; Gramsci 1971a, p. 366.
57   Q6, §71; Gramsci 1985, pp. 177–8.

man England, which eventually modified radically the whole English language of all classes. But what was possibly uppermost in Gramsci's mind was the young Soviet Union, the language policies advocated by Lenin in particular, and their connected educational proposals put forward, among others, by his wife N.K. Krupskaja. Some ideologically-loaded terms were difficult to explain to the Russian peasantry and subject to consistent distortion and misunderstanding by them, examples being common words such as democracy, republic and others with a neo-Latin rather than Slav root.[58] Such problems were typical during a period of great linguistic innovation accompanied by a mass literacy campaign, in which the worker correspondents' movement played an inestimable role.[59]

The massive influx of Italian words into English in Shakespearean times is another striking illustration of a hegemonic culture, here that of the Renaissance, that innovates and renews another language. And much earlier, Christianity also spread words, expressing hegemonic concepts and ideology, into many languages.[60] At the lexical level, there were influxes of new words often from Greek – the lingua franca of the Christian colonies of the Pauline letters – into Latin, passing from there into other languages. Some of the incoming words became officialised and institutionalised, such as the one for 'church' – *ekklesia*, the root of 'ecclesiastic' in English, the Welsh 'eglwys' and the Italian 'chiesa'. Initially meaning the community of the faithful, and still understood as such by radical Catholics and in particular by the adherents of liberation theology, this term was taken over by the Christian hierarchy with the connotation of the church as an Institution. Again we see an ideological struggle over a word and what lies behind it; analogously, on several occasions, Gramsci draws attention to social and ideological struggles waged by radical religious movements analogous to, or based on, primitive Christianity (Gandhi, perhaps Tolstoy, certainly Davide Lazzaretti 'the prophet of Monte Amiata', shot down when his movement was threatening to establish Christ's kingdom on Earth), and often opposed by either the hierarchy or by the political, but not always necessarily religious, right.[61] There is, in short, as both Gramsci and his slightly younger contemporary V.N. Vološinov (see below) argued, an ideological struggle over words and the ideological connotations that different social groups attach to them.

---

58   Cf. Carlucci 2013a, pp. 105–8 and Brandist 2005, pp. 78–9.
59   Cf. various articles from these sources in *L'Ordine Nuovo*; see also Gramsci 2014a, pp. 187 and 277.
60   Cf. Devoto 1974, pp. 150–2.
61   Q13, §37: cf. the excerpt in Gramsci 1995, p. 93.

But are there variations on this theme in Gramsci, perhaps backed up independently by other evidence? In Q13§17, he writes that an 'ideology, born in a more developed country, is disseminated into less developed countries, impinging on the local interplay of combinations'.[62] Here, the ideological aspect is in evidence, but the basic idea seems once again to come from Bartoli, particularly his comments on Rome. Among these, we read that linguistic influences depend on 'the power of a people as regards both culture and wealth; [Rome ...] destroyed the ancient nationalities and the ancient languages and imposed her own hegemony on all the activities of the spirit'.[63] Then, despite the 'resolute difference of linguistic structures between Etruscan and Latin', and the long-lasting autonomy of the 'two traditions, not only linguistic but also socio-cultural', a number of institutional words from Etruria were introduced into Rome through the 'prestige of Etruscan civilization, [which] above all in the sixth century B.C.E., coordinated cultural life in central Italy', and through the growth of a flourishing culture and economy 'that irradiated from Etruria and affected Rome and its hinterland'. Devoto cites, among other things, important terms such as 'populus', and also personal name structures, which entered this early phase of Latin;[64] additionally Augusto Ancillotti has just recently added other words pertinent to political and institutional life – 'atrium' being one example – to the list of Latin words originating from Etruscan.[65] Numerically the influx was small, at what Gramsci calls the 'molecular' linguistic level,[66] but at the level of the city-State institutions, of great importance. These linguistic influences have remained, becoming part not only of ancient Roman culture, but of a wider European culture and civilisation. Interestingly however Rome's linguistic 'irradiation' during Republican times stopped 'on the frontiers of Etruria',[67] the advanced Etruscan civilisation being robust enough at least to protect itself and not *initially* be overrun by a mightier power. Thus we have a militarily superior power (Rome) for a long time undergoing the political and cultural, and in some sectors linguistic, hegemony of a militarily weaker one (Etruria).

One language, culture, or ideology – sometimes of a more 'primitive' people – may indeed supplant another. Bartoli notes that the Germanic peoples who invaded the Roman Empire of the West, certainly 'were to a great extent ab-

---

62   Q13, § 17; Gramsci 1971a, p. 182; cf. first draft in Gramsci 1996b, p. 180.
63   Bartoli 1912–13, Part 2, p. 47.
64   Devoto 1974, pp. 197, 144, 52 and 77 respectively.
65   Personal communication; in course of publication.
66   Q6, § 71: Gramsci 2007a, p. 178.
67   Devoto 1974, p. 215.

sorbed by the indigenous peoples and Romanized (in Italy, in France, in the Iberian peninsula etc.) but beyond the Alps and along the Rhine ... they kept their language, and even imposed it on the Romans; so in the same way in the Balkan peninsula one part of the Slavs were Graecized but ... a great part of them succeeded in maintaining their own language'.[68] There is here a striking parallel with a note of Gramsci's on the fall of Rome, then considered an enigma by many historians. Its history 'is to be sought in the development of the "barbarian" populations', yet 'no one wants to admit that the decisive forces of world history were not then within the Roman Empire (primitive though they were)'.[69] It may be objected that this is not quite dealing with cultures and ideologies, which is true only if we are looking for a direct link; ideologies do however come into the question through the society itself of the 'barbarian', more 'primitive' peoples. What emerges in a more direct fashion is an analogous situation in the Reformation, where ideologies are indeed replaced through renovation. The classic examples in Europe are the sixteenth-century Lutheran Reformation and the eighteenth-century French politico-philosophical ones. The former, together with Calvinism, 'created a vast popular-national movement through which their influence spread: only in later periods did they create a higher culture' while France 'experienced a great popular reformation in the eighteenth century with the Enlightenment, Voltairianism, and the Encyclopaedia. This reformation preceded and accompanied the Revolution of 1789. It really was a matter here of a great intellectual and moral reformation of the French people, more complete than the German Lutheran Reformation, because it also embraced the great peasant masses in the countryside, and had a distinct secular basis and attempt to replace religion with a completely secular ideology'.[70]

Where for once Bartoli seems to stop short at a socio-linguistic level, and perhaps uncharacteristically Devoto goes further, is in the latter's statement that 'a language may be abandoned to a drift caused by the unleashing of internal forces, independently of any mixing process, as happened with Latin in the early Republican era'.[71] Is there a parallel to this ideologically? Consciousness seems a case in point, on which Gramsci is apparently close, but not necessarily identical, to Lenin, whose thesis is that full knowledge/consciousness of a situation can only come from outside the working class. This in my view is not to be understood in the sense handed down in some sort of vulgate that elements

---

68   Bartoli 1912–13, Part 2, p. 53.
69   Q15, §5; Gramsci 1995, p. 223.
70   Q16, §9; Gramsci 1971a, p. 394.
71   Devoto 1974, p. 144.

extraneous to the working class ('intellectuals', the Party, the Party leadership or whoever) bring in that consciousness; instead a knowledge of an entire socio-politico-economic situation is needed, not merely one limited to immediate circumstances. An ideological equivalent to the 'unleashing of internal forces' lay notably for Gramsci, but not only him, in the movement of the 'Red Years' in Turin immediately after World War I, in which the workers' 'element of "spontaneity" was not neglected, much less disdained'.[72] Here Gramsci's intellectuals, both of the 'traditional' type and those 'organic' to the proletariat were necessary.

6   Ideology and Language: A Final Word

Drawing out the implications of what Gramsci writes on language and on ideology, one sees that crucial aspects of the two function in a like manner and, it may be said, are homologous. There is at times an astonishing congruence between Gramsci and Vološinov,[73] who neatly condenses Gramsci's link between a word or phrase and their ideological associations into his notion of the linguistic 'sign' and its ideological 'theme' – the object of the sign having 'two faces, like Janus', each bearing its different, conflicting theme.[74] Earlier, Bréal – in terms that one might more expect to read in an avowed Marxist – noted that 'every social class ... seeks to bend ... general [linguistic] terms to its own use; concrete linguistic usage, in its turn, will then give them back with the imprint of the ideas and functions of those classes'.[75] For Vološinov, for Bréal and for Gramsci, words are constructs between people organised socially, and are often ideologically loaded. Vološinov calls this the 'social multiaccentuality' of his linguistic-ideological sign: terms may be used with different ideological connotations. Gramsci then goes further than the other two, generalising this into different conceptions of the world, with conservatives attempting to stabilise a *previous* ideology, through the agency of their 'traditional intellectuals'. While language in Gramsci presents and may even contain conceptions of the world and their 'complex and discordant' superstructures, Vološinov writes that the linguistic sign represents the inter-

---

72   Q3, § 48; Gramsci 1996b, p. 50.
73   Gramsci's son Giuliano, in conversation with the present author, said he did not know of any contact between the two men; in any case, Vološinov's involvement in the language-ideology nexus was still in the future during Gramsci's period in Russia.
74   Vološinov 1973, pp. 22–3.
75   Bréal 1900, pp. 108–9, translation modified.

section of 'differently oriented social interests', not merely reflecting mechanically but 'refract[ing]' social existence.[76] From different starting points, the two thinkers then converge: ideology and language are the two sides of the same coin.

76   Vološinov 1973, pp. 135–6, 68 and 23 respectively.

CHAPTER 5

Hegemonic Language: The Politics of Linguistic Phenomena

Alen Sućeska

1   Introduction

Ever since Franco Lo Piparo published his book *Lingua, Intellettuali, Egemonia in Gramsci*[1] [*Language, Intellectuals, Hegemony in Gramsci*], there has been a slow but steady rise in the interest in Gramsci's thoughts on language in his *Prison Notebooks*, first in Italy, as was to be expected, but since the 1990s also in the Anglophone world. This has resulted in a series of very innovative and inspiring papers, books and discussions in the last twenty years or so, which showed that Gramsci's views on language offer a unique social and historical perspective whose roots are to be found in his political views and convictions.[2] It is precisely in this sense that Gramsci does not write about language as a linguist, but as a revolutionary and a politician. He conceives of language as a social and historical phenomenon, which should be discussed within the framework of the modern capitalist state and its hegemonic apparatuses. Through such theoretical approach, language is shown to participate in the production of the various ideological effects of this apparatus, namely, what is central to Gramsci, in the production of consent and, effectively, the subalternity of the masses. These themes have been brilliantly discussed by several authors, such as Craig Brandist, Peter Ives, Jean-Jacques Lecercle and David McNally,[3] among others.

I wish to propose a further development of the topic of language in Gramsci, namely, to link language to his concept of the person (*la persona* in Italian), a theoretical move which I believe is justified by Gramsci's linking, already present in the *Prison Notebooks*, of language and 'common sense'. Language

---

1   Lo Piparo 1979. A shorter text in English which summarizes Lo Piparo's views from his book can be found in Lo Piparo 2010.

2   Contrary to Lo Piparo, who claimed that Gramsci was primarily a linguist, not a Marxist. It is slightly ironic that perhaps precisely because of such a controversial thesis, Lo Piparo caused a flourishing of *Marxist* discussions on language in Gramsci's *Prison Notebooks*.

3   Brandist 1996a, 1996b; Ives 2004a, 2004b; Lecercle 2009; McNally 2001.

does not indicate merely how a person thinks and feels; it also indicates, on a more general level than that of the individual, through its socially dominant form, the standard or national language, the dominant form of thinking and feeling, and that, in return, indicates the dominant type of personality being socially 'produced' through various social, economic, historic and ideological incentives and limitations within the existing social relations. None of this would make any sense, however, without Gramsci's concepts of hegemony and the integral state, because it is primarily a matter of *politics* that such processes occur in the first place. Therefore, it is essential to understand these fundamental concepts in order to trace Gramsci's trajectory from developing Lenin's notion of hegemony into a complex concept,[4] through advancing Marx's points on man in the *Theses on Feuerbach* to a more complex notion of 'the person', to developing, amongst many other noteworthy things, a new approach to language.

Bringing these concepts into a relationship should, in my opinion, prove quite fruitful, not merely in the 'purely scholastic' field of Gramscian studies or the theoretical field of Marxism, but also in the field of politics and political struggle in contemporary societies. In doing so and bearing the potential ultimate political benefit of this discussion in mind, we also remain faithful to Gramsci's intentions – which permeate the entirety of the *Prison Notebooks* – of understanding the contemporary world in order to be better prepared to change it (or, at least, to start from ascertaining why it does not change in any progressive direction).

2   Introducing Language into Politics and Politics into Language

> ... the integral state is not, in the first instance, a normative proposition, a theoretical abstraction to which reality is expected to adjust. Rather, it is a theoretical intervention into a determinate political conjuncture.[5]

2.1   *The Integral State*

Gramsci's concepts of hegemony and the integral state have been developed as a result of his analysis of the changes of the form of political rule in the nineteenth century, changes which have, since then, established themselves as a dominant form of political practice of the new ruling class: the bourgeoisie.

---

4   On this, as well as Gramsci's relationship to Lenin, see Thomas 2010, Part 6.2.3., pp. 228–32.
5   Thomas 2010, p. 140.

The revolutions and nationalist movements that swept through Europe from the French Revolution up to the unification of Italy and Germany in 1871[6] represented the social and political changes that corresponded to the changes in the mode of production. The transition from feudalism to capitalism, which had arguably begun centuries ago in the economic sphere, was followed by the overthrowing of the feudal ruling classes and the consolidation of the new, capitalist ruling classes.[7] In order to legitimise itself as a new leading political force, the bourgeoisie had to denounce the former form of rule dominant in feudalism, namely, direct political domination through violence. What was necessary was 'a new "consensual" political practice distinct from mere coercion'.[8]

Thus, what the bourgeoisie did in order to appear fundamentally different from the aristocracy was to claim it was introducing an 'open society', where all are nominally equal before the law and have, in principle, the same chances for success and for climbing the social ladder. It is with this purpose in mind that the state gradually changes its form in order to be able to produce consent precisely in this way. Gramsci writes:

> The revolution which the bourgeois class has brought into the conception of law, and hence into the function of the State, consists especially in the will to conform ... The previous ruling classes were essentially conservative in the sense that they did not tend to construct an organic passage from the other classes into their own, i.e. to enlarge their class sphere 'technically' and ideologically: their conception was that of the closed caste. The bourgeois class poses itself as an organism in continuous move-

---

6   I do not wish to suggest that this was somehow a historically homogeneous period, or, even worse, that all its events were of a purely teleological character. On the contrary, as all periods of history, it was full of tendencies and counter-tendencies, social, economic and political, as was evidenced, for example, by various progressive nationalisms and revolutions in 1848 or the Paris Commune in 1871. However, the period did ultimately end with the consolidation of the bourgeoisie as a new ruling class.

7   In Marx's words: 'At a certain stage of development, the material productive forces of society come into conflict with the existing relations of production or – this merely expresses the same thing in legal terms – with the property relations within the framework of which they have operated hitherto. From forms of development of the productive forces these relations turn into their fetters. Then begins an era of social revolution. The changes in the economic foundation lead sooner or later to the transformation of the whole immense superstructure'. Marx 1987b [1859], p. 263. It should be pointed out that this was an important text often used by Gramsci, as he not only referred to it explicitly multiple times, but also translated it in Notebook 7 of the *Prison Notebooks*.

8   Thomas 2010, p. 144.

ment, capable of absorbing the entire society, assimilating it to its own cultural and economic level. The entire function of the State has been transformed; the State has become an 'educator', etc.[9]

This is what constitutes what Peter Thomas terms the bourgeois revolution of the political, contained in the fact that '[i]n principle, (bourgeois) freedom and its consummation in the state is open to all'.[10] Of course, this was a gradual historical process of learning and adapting, not only because such a fundamental change in political practice of an entire class does not happen overnight, but also because it was not something that was easy to accept: after all, is a class truly the ruling class if it accepts and integrates members of other classes into its ranks? But, as Eric Hobsbawm writes, by the 1870s, 'the rulers of the advanced states of Europe, with more or less reluctance, were beginning to recognise not only that "democracy", i.e. a parliamentary constitution based on a wide suffrage, was inevitable, but also that it would probably be a nuisance but politically harmless'.[11] Indeed, not only was it politically harmless, but highly beneficial in the long run.

The new form of the state was the dialectical unity of 'two major superstructural "levels": the one that can be called "civil society", that is the ensemble of organisms commonly called "private", and that of "political society" or "the State". These two levels correspond on the one hand to the function of "hegemony" which the dominant group exercises throughout society and on the other hand to that of "direct domination" or command exercised through the State and "juridicial" government'.[12] The reason why the integral state is a *dialectical unity* of these two 'levels' is that they reinforce each other: civil society (the sphere of civil institutions, social movements, political parties) legitimises the Weberian 'monopoly on violence' of political society, while political society (the sphere of the army, the courts and the repressive apparatus in general) ensures that in times of crisis, the production of consent within civil society can go on uninterrupted. As Thomas notes, it is the use of force within political society, though, that is the 'decisive factor' in this relationship. 'Civil society

---

9   Gramsci 2012b, p. 260 (Q8, § 2). All the references to the English translations of Gramsci's *Prison Notebooks* will be accompanied with a reference, in parentheses, to the Italian edition of the *Notebooks*, edited by Valentino Gerratana (see Gramsci 1975), where Q denotes the number of the notebook, while § denotes the number of the note within the notebook.

10   Thomas 2010, p. 144.

11   Hobsbawm 2013, p. 15.

12   Gramsci 2012b, p. 12 (Q12, § 1). In a different notebook, Gramsci writes 'that one might say that State = political society + civil society, in other words hegemony protected by the armour of coercion'. Gramsci 2012b, p. 263 (Q6, § 88).

is the terrain upon which social classes compete for social and political leadership or hegemony over other social classes. Such hegemony is guaranteed, however, "in the last instance", by capture of the legal monopoly of violence embodied in the institutions of political society'.[13] Thus, the integral state, in an almost century-long process, had become 'a network of social relations for the production of consent'.[14]

2.2   Hegemony and 'Common Sense'

Arriving at the ins and outs of hegemony is where we also arrive at language in politics. Hegemony is not simply a state of affairs; it does not represent a certain state of class-dominance which, once achieved, remains unchanged and static until a sudden messianic-like social rupture would break it. What makes hegemony a complex concept is precisely the fact that it denotes a continual process of political integration, of constant adapting to new social phenomena, groups and movements.[15] Hegemony needs to be constantly reaffirmed and reasserted, and any opposition to it that is not integrated into it has to be eliminated (which is where the institutions of political society come into play, if ideological and political elimination are not effective). Because of this, hegemony is only possible thanks to a huge hegemonic apparatus and an army of traditional intellectuals[16] whose labour utilises this apparatus. It is this combination of a hegemonic apparatus and an army of traditional intellectuals that produces consent: ideas, beliefs, values and practices which are made dominant and which support existing social relations. That explains why Gramsci

---

13   Thomas 2010, p. 137.
14   Thomas 2010, p. 143.
15   This is the reason why I believe Raymond Williams came closest to fully grasping the meaning and value of Gramsci's concept in the first couple of decades after the publication of the *Prison Notebooks*, since he emphasised precisely these characteristics of hegemony. For further reading, see Williams 1977.
16   'Every social group, coming into existence on the original terrain of an essential function in the world of economic production, creates together with itself, organically, one or more strata of intellectuals which give it homogeneity and an awareness of its own function not only in the economic but also in the social and political fields'. Gramsci 2012b, p. 5 (Q12, §1). We cannot delve deeper into the very important topic of intellectuals here, but for the purposes of this text, we shall elaborate on the difference between traditional and organic intellectuals. Essentially, all intellectuals are 'organic' in the sense described above, but the intellectuals of the ruling classes, through an '*esprit de corps*', as Gramsci says, perceive themselves as autonomous and independent of the class of their origin. These are thus termed 'traditional intellectuals', while the 'organic intellectuals' are the intellectuals of the subaltern classes which are conscious of their class origin and affirm this origin in their practice as members of their class.

defines hegemony as 'intellectual and moral leadership':[17] the phrase 'being led to believe something' has an almost literal meaning here. Furthermore, because it is conceived in such a way, hegemony is a profoundly *material* concept[18] – it always refers back to its material source in society, namely, the institutions of the hegemonic apparatus and its labourers, the traditional intellectuals. Gramsci emphasises this when he writes that 'ideas and opinions are not spontaneously "born" in each individual brain: they have had a centre of formation, of irradiation, of dissemination, of persuasion – a group of men, or a single individual even, which has developed them and presented them in the political form of current reality'.[19]

Language plays an essential role in hegemony, that is, the production of consent, for several reasons, some of which are more, some less obvious. Firstly, it is hardly conceivable how ideas could be expressed, and therefore disseminated at all, without using language in some form. Secondly, if we analyse what the hegemonic apparatus, or the 'centres of irradiation', comprises, we move beyond the seeming triviality of the link between ideas and language: the education system; the media, from the television, through the newspaper and the radio, to the Internet; cultural institutions, like cinemas, theatres, museums, and so on; popular literature; and so on and so forth.[20] In all of these social institutions and the corresponding practices within them, an *institutionalised* and *systematised* form of language appears: the standard or national language. This is significant because national language is not only a grammatical system, but also an ideological one, in the sense that it ascribes specific values and meanings to specific words or sentences, or even that it prescribes certain ways of speaking. Thirdly and finally, in the rise of hegemony as a new form of political practice, that is, the formation of the integral state in the nineteenth century, which we briefly described above, national language was of significant importance. Without it, neither the various national unifications in

---

17   Gramsci 2012b, p. 57 (Q19, § 24).

18   Cf. Rehmann 2013, pp. 117–46.

19   Gramsci 2012b, pp. 192–3 (Q13, § 30).

20   That these are some of the potential elements of the 'centres of irradiation' is hinted at by Gramsci in one of his notes in the *Prison Notebooks*, titled 'Sources of Diffusion of Linguistic Innovations in the Tradition and of a National Linguistic Conformism in the Broad National Masses'. The note begins by an immediate list, which is as follows: '1) [t]he education system; 2) the newspaper; 3) artistic writers and popular writers; 4) the theatre and sound films; 5) radio; 6) public meetings of all kinds, including religious ones; 7) the relations of "conversation" between the more educated and the less educated strata of the population ...; 8) the local dialects, understood in various senses'. Gramsci 2012a, p. 183 (Q29, § 3).

nineteenth-century Europe, nor the establishment of bourgeois hegemony in general, and thus the consolidation of the bourgeoisie as the new ruling class, would be possible.[21]

In the struggle for hegemony between competing classes, the stakes are high: what is in question is not only political domination, but also the dominant way of thinking and feeling, a dominant world view. In bourgeois hegemony, Gramsci terms this dominant world view 'common sense' (*senso comune*).[22] The term denotes something quite opposite to the identical English language idiom: 'common sense' is a fragmented, incoherent and contradictory world view, which significantly limits critical thought. 'Common sense' changes with the times, but its effects never change.

> Common sense is not a single unique conception, identical in time and space. It is the 'folklore' of philosophy, and, like folklore, it takes countless different forms. Its most fundamental characteristic is that it is a conception which, even in the brain of one individual, is fragmentary, incoherent and inconsequential, in conformity with the social and cultural position of those masses whose philosophy it is.[23]

Thus, essentially, it is by (re)producing 'common sense' and maintaining its dominance as a mode of thought that civil society (in other words, the combined labour of traditional intellectuals within the hegemonic apparatus) is producing consent. Maintaining a grip over the dominant form of language is essential for achieving this political goal.

---

21   Indeed, language was part and parcel of all nineteenth-century nationalist projects in Europe. Of course, like the nation itself, national language had to be invented. The 'terrain' for the formation of national language was already there when the national revolutions in Europe started, as it was 'merely' a question of choosing the most prestigious dialect, i.e. the one that dominated others either politically, economically, culturally, or, in most cases, in all of those ways at once. This was easier in some countries than in others, such as France compared to Italy (whose linguistic unification remained a problem for so long that even Gramsci discussed it as a contemporary issue in his time). For a very intriguing explanation of how this process occurred in France, see Bourdieu 2012, pp. 46–8.

22   This is not to imply that common sense is a *single, unitary* worldview. As will be seen in the quote just below, as well as in the later sections, 'common sense' is composed of various elements, both from the past and the present, both from present social classes and past ones which do not exist anymore. However, since the bourgeoisie utilises this peculiar ideological 'collage' for the preservation of the *status quo*, it does not change the fact that 'common sense' is made and maintained as the dominant mode of thought.

23   Gramsci 2012b, p. 419 (Q11, § 13).

2.3   Language as Means of Social Production

Which bring us to one of our central points: language is not merely a *means* of transferring information from an abstract 'sender' to an equally abstract 'receiver', as modern communication studies would have it; it is also a *means of social production*, as Raymond Williams convincingly argued in his works.[24] The class which, in a general sense, controls the dominant form of language – national language – through the various elements of its hegemonic apparatus, also controls one of the primary means of social production. Although one cannot find such formulations explicitly in Gramsci's *Prison Notebooks*, it is quite easy to locate notes where an understanding of language as something *more* than just a simple linguistic medium is evident. In one of his most brilliant notes, translated under the heading 'The Study of Philosophy', Gramsci defines language as 'a totality of determined notions and concepts and not just of words grammatically devoid of content'; then again, a bit further, he writes that 'in "language", there is contained a specific conception of the world'.[25] This is a concept of language completely different to the one present in the dominant current of modern linguistics, but even to that of Ferdinand de Saussure, its founder.[26] The point is that Gramsci completely switches emphasis: instead of the static and synchronic structure of language abstracted from society in Saussure's *langue*, Gramsci is interested precisely in those *diachronic* linguistic phenomena which are *inextricably* linked to society, which Saussure banishes from 'the science of language'[27] – namely, a 'conception of the world'; a 'totality of determined notions and concepts'.[28] In short, in the *Prison Notebooks* Gramsci discusses language as a politician and, ultimately, as a revolutionary, not as a linguist.

---

24   Williams 2005, pp. 51–5.
25   Gramsci 2012b, p. 323 (Q11, §12).
26   For very instructive criticisms of Saussure, but also the dominant currents of linguistics, precisely from a social and historical standpoint, see Bourdieu 2012, p. 33; Ives 2004b, pp. 12–32; Lecercle 2009, pp. 1–44; McNally 2001, pp. 45–78.
27   Saussure 1959, pp. 15–20.
28   This is why I disagree with Alessandro Carlucci's thesis that there are significant similarities between Saussure's and Gramsci's understanding of language. I believe the set of notes translated as 'The Study of Philosophy' alone provides enough evidence to the contrary, and, indeed, that one of Gramsci's most noteworthy contributions to a Marxist conception of language in his *Prison Notebooks* is precisely that he indirectly *distanced himself* from classic linguistics. Carlucci's thesis can be found in his otherwise brilliant book, which was a significant contribution to clarifying some other misconceptions within the topic of 'Gramsci and languages': Carlucci 2013a, pp. 70–89.

3   From 'Common Sense' to 'Good Sense'

> If it is true that every language contains the elements of a conception of
> the world and of a culture, it could also be true that from anyone's lan-
> guage one can assess the greater or lesser complexity of his conceptions
> of the world.[29]

If we conceive of language as Gramsci did, which is politically, as a profoundly
social and historical phenomenon, we enter into an entirely different mode of
thought from that of linguistics, one which imposes new insights upon us. As
a means of social production in bourgeois hegemony, language participates in
the production of 'common sense', a fragmented and uncritical consciousness,
as well as in maintaining it as a dominant mode of thought amongst the masses.
The political effect of this is that, in classical Marxist terms, although the subaltern[30] masses share a common general interest through their class position,
and although their unification would be the beginning of the end of their subalternity, they uphold a form of consciousness which is in contradiction with
those social facts and, what is perhaps most significant, they appear to do so
willingly. Gramsci manages to explain this peculiar and paradoxical state of
affairs by introducing, as analytical categories, two 'distinct consciousnesses',
one 'practical' and present in the activity of the masses, that is, in the reality of
their subaltern social position, and the other which is 'exterior' to them and in
opposition to the practical one, but which they nonetheless claim to follow.

> The active man-in-the-mass has a practical activity, but has no clear theor-
> etical consciousness of his practical activity, which nonetheless involves
> understanding the world in so far as it transforms it. His theoretical con-
> sciousness can indeed be historically in opposition to his activity. One
> might almost say that he has two theoretical consciousnesses (or one con-
> tradictory consciousness): one which is implicit in his activity and which
> in reality unites him with all his fellow-workers in the practical transform-

---

29   Gramsci 2012b, p. 325 (Q11, § 12).
30   'Subaltern classes are subject to the initiatives of the dominant class, even when they rebel;
      they are in a state of anxious defense' (Q3, § 14, cited according to Green 2002). As Green
      notes, Gramsci differentiates between various 'stages' of subalternity, according to various
      levels of political organisation the subaltern group possesses. However, the various subal-
      tern classes always share a common interest, regardless of the 'level' of their subalternity,
      which is the seizure and gradual abolition of the state, and it is primarily this that I refer
      to when I talk of subaltern classes in this text. For a broader discussion of the concept of
      'the subaltern', see Green 2002.

ation of the real world; and one, superficially explicit or verbal, which he has inherited from the past and uncritically absorbed. But this verbal conception is not without consequences. It holds together a specific social group, it influences moral conduct and the direction of will, with varying efficacity but often powerfully enough to produce a situation in which the contradictory state of consciousness does not permit of any action, any decision or any choice, and produces a condition of moral and political passivity.[31]

Thus, the effect of 'common sense' is a 'condition of moral and political passivity', a condition shared among the masses, which permits no truly autonomous action, decision or choice. In political terms, this is subordination. What is particularly significant for us is the fact that Gramsci characterises the second type of consciousness as a *verbal* one, which indicates that this 'consciousness' is expressed in language. Furthermore, the 'man-in-the-mass' has 'inherited' this consciousness from the past and has uncritically absorbed it – precisely this is 'common sense'. In short, the second, verbal form of consciousness is 'common sense', which was imposed upon the masses in the past and in the present – indicating this is a *historical process* – not in the active sense that some external social group forced the masses to do so, but in a passive one (inherited, absorbed).

But 'common sense' is not equal or even analogous to the concept of 'false consciousness'. Lukács's 'false consciousness' oversimplifies the entire process which precedes the condition of passivity in the masses and it abstracts from the various social institutions, agents and practices which were necessary in order to achieve this in the first place. As Jan Rehmann writes, in Lukács, 'integration into bourgeois society appeared to follow automatically from commodity-fetishism and its "radiation", without requiring ideological powers, hegemonic apparatuses, ideologues, ideological practices and rituals'.[32] Furthermore, 'false consciousness' excludes all the 'alternative' practices which hegemony can tolerate or integrate into itself without endangering the existing power relations in society, as well as truly 'oppositional' ones (to use another distinction made by Raymond Williams),[33] which always offer potential for revolutionary change. In the same note from the *Prison Notebooks*, Gramsci explicitly rejects such a reading of his 'two consciousnesses':

---

31   Gramsci 2012b, p. 333 (Q11, §12).
32   Rehmann 2013, p. 80.
33   Williams 2005, pp. 41–2.

[t]his contrast between thought and action, i.e. the co-existence of two conceptions of the world, one affirmed in words and the other displayed in effective action, *is not simply a product of self-deception*. Self-deception can be an adequate explanation for a few individuals taken separately, or even for groups of a certain size, but it is not adequate when the contrast occurs in the life of the great masses. In these cases the contrast between thought and action cannot but be the expression of profounder contrasts of a social historical order. It signifies that the social group in question may indeed have its own conception of the world, even if only embryonic; a conception which manifests itself in action, but occasionally and in flashes – when, that is, the group is acting as an organic totality. But this same group has, for reasons of submission and intellectual subordination, adopted a conception which is not its own but is borrowed from another group; and it affirms this conception verbally and believes itself to be following it, because this is the conception which it follows in 'normal times' – that is when its conduct is not independent and autonomous, but submissive and subordinate.[34]

Thus, what we have in Gramsci is the acknowledgment that, yes, the state of affairs in 'normal' circumstances of bourgeois hegemony is grim, as the masses find themselves in a condition of 'moral and political passivity'; however, we know, both logically and historically, how such a state of affairs was achieved and how it is being maintained (the institutions of the hegemonic apparatus + the practices of traditional intellectuals), as well as that this passivity is not somehow 'absolute', but that an 'embryo' of a different world view which signals a world of revolutionised social relations exists and is present in the masses. This is a much more 'productive' conception compared to that of 'false consciousness', both in the theoretical and the political sense, as it both directs us towards revolutionary potential in the masses, and, at the same time, allows us to understand how such potential is being repressed.[35]

---

34   Gramsci 2012b, pp. 326–7 (Q11, §12). My emphasis.
35   Likewise, as Marcus Green and Peter Ives point out, 'common sense' is not a matter of the 'stupidity' of the masses (an argument most common among cynical liberals): 'the contradictory nature of common sense is not the product of some sort of intellectual or psychological deficiency on the part of the masses. Rather, the contradictory nature of common sense is largely defined by the contradictory nature of the ensemble of social relations, economic exploitation and the various exclusions they produce and reproduce'. Green and Ives 2010, p. 304. What is, perhaps, missing from this otherwise excellent observation is the historically contradictory nature of 'common sense', that is, the fact that certain notions or modes of thought did make sense in the past, but do not make any

The authentic, embryonic world view is what Gramsci terms 'good sense' (*buon senso*),[36] as opposed to 'common sense'. But the one does not *negate* the other; 'good sense' is 'the healthy nucleus that exists in "common sense"',[37] although 'common sense' dominates and thus determines the form of consciousness:

> When one's conception of the world is not critical and coherent but disjointed and episodic, one belongs simultaneously to a multiplicity of mass human groups. The personality is strangely composite: it contains Stone Age elements and principles of a more advanced science, prejudices from all past phases of history at the local level and intuitions of a future philosophy which will be that of a human race united the world over.[38]

The uncanny coexistence of the two 'senses' is again affirmed: on the one side, we have the disjointed and episodic 'common sense' (Stone Age elements; prejudices from all past phases of history), while on the other, we have an implicitly critical and coherent 'good sense' (principles of a more advanced science; intuitions of a future philosophy).[39] It is the social and ideological domination of 'common sense' itself that is preventing 'good sense' from emerging and developing into something more than an 'embryo'.

4   The Person

In acquiring one's conception of the world one always belongs to a particular grouping which is that of all the social elements which share the same mode of thinking and acting. We are all conformists of some conform-

---

sense in the present. This is best expressed precisely in the historicity of language: 'language is at the same time a living thing and a museum of fossils of life and civilisations'. Gramsci 2012b, p. 450 (Q11, §28).

36   It has to be noted that 'good sense' does not have a singular or clear meaning in the *Prison Notebooks*, as Gramsci often uses the term with different and conflicting meanings. The analysis that follows in this section of the text tries to offer one attempt at interpreting 'good sense' in line with the general trajectory of Gramsci's thought.

37   Gramsci 2012b, p. 328 (Q11, §12).

38   Gramsci 2012b, p. 324 (Q11, §12).

39   Jan Rehmann introduces a perfect metaphor for 'common sense': 'Gramsci's common sense could be compared to a quarry consisting of several layers of different geographical periods deposited upon each other. These "layers" are the raw materials to be processed and transformed by ideological apparatuses and ideologues'. Rehmann 2013, p. 128.

ism or the other, always man-in-the-mass or collective man. The question is this: of what historical type is the conformism, the mass humanity to which one belongs?[40]

4.1   'Characters' and 'Masks' in Fractured Time

When Gramsci discusses the question 'what is man?', continuing and developing the arguments of Marx's *Theses on Feuerbach*, he ends up writing one of the most beautiful segments of the *Prison Notebooks*. Like Marx, Gramsci rejects the 'Feuerbachian' notion that man has an essence at all. It is Marx's sixth thesis that is Gramsci's starting point: 'the human essence is no abstraction inherent in each single individual. In its reality it is the ensemble of social relations'.[41] Paraphrasing the thesis, Gramsci comments:

> That 'human nature' is the 'complex of social relations' is the most satis-
> factory answer, because it includes the idea of becoming (man 'becomes',
> he changes continuously with the changing of social relations) and be-
> cause it denies 'man in general'. Indeed social relations are expressed by
> various groups of men which each presuppose the others and whose unity
> is dialectical, not formal. Man is aristocratic in so far as man is a serf, etc.[42]

It is for this reason that Gramsci rejects the term 'subject', and uses the term 'person' instead. The term subject etymologically implies a unitary, self-conscious and definitive individual (who is, again etymologically, indivisible), which is obviously contradictory to a *process of becoming* Gramsci refers to. At the same time, this is also the reason why the term 'person' makes perfect sense: in its etymological roots traceable back to Stoicism, 'the person is a category of analysis less focused upon the interiority of a consciousness as constitutive of identity, than with the imposition (and passive or active acceptance) of an "exterior" network of social relations that create the terrain of social action and therefore social identity'.[43]

Contrary to the implication of its etymology, the individual is then not at all indivisible; she is in fact ridden with various social roles – 'masks' or 'characters' – which she constantly strives to balance, to bring into an equilibrium, but never fully succeeds in doing so. 'Gramsci posits the non-identity of the individual in a series of temporal dislocations that they (or rather, more often,

---

40   Gramsci 2012b, p. 324 (Q11, § 12).
41   Marx 1976a [1845], p. 4.
42   Gramsci 2012b, p. 355 (Q7, § 35).
43   Thomas 2010, p. 398.

the juridico-political apparatus) only sometimes manage to unify in an uneasy *modus vivendi*. He emphasises the various social roles played by any particular individual, in an ensemble of social roles, as related but distinct "persons".[44] Such a concept of the person is inextricably linked to Gramsci's concept of the 'non-contemporaneity' of the present.[45] 'For Gramsci, the present is necessarily non-identical with itself, composed of numerous "times" that do not coincide but encounter each other with mutual incomprehension'.[46] This is a simple consequence of social practices having each their own temporality, so the present, composed of these temporalities, is necessarily fractured. This can be seen, for example, 'in the relations between urban centres and rural peripheries'[47] – life evolves at a different pace in the village than in the city. It is not only perceived differently, it is also *lived* differently, in concrete practice. Furthermore, '[o]n an international level, the hegemonic relationships between different nations consign some social formations to the past "times" of others'.[48] This can be evidenced in the uneven development in which certain nations find themselves, which is not, of course, an effect of any essential characteristic of a specific nation or people or geographic region (the 'backwardness' of the East deployed from an occidental perspective being the most common example), but is a consequence of differing historical experiences.

Such an understanding of the present, with an emphasis on its both synchronically and diachronically fractured, non-contemporaneous character, is one of the essential links between language and the concept of the person. The reason is that the 'non-contemporaneity of the present in Gramsci is a function and symptomatic index of the struggle between classes. The present, as the time of class struggle, is necessarily and essentially "out of joint", fractured by the differential times of different class projects'.[49] Such a structure of the present, with class struggle as its cause, is something we can easily locate in

---

44   Thomas 2010, p. 398.

45   As Daniel Bensaïd points out, the first steps towards this insight were made by Marx, who broke with the unitary Hegelian conception of linear time and has multiplied it 'according to the plural rhythms and cycles of a broken political temporality' (Bensaïd 2009, p. 71). This broken temporality is expressed primarily in the functioning and movement of capital, but is also characteristic of all aspects of modern society (in good part as a result of the effects capital has on social relations). Bensaïd elaborates on the economic aspects of this broken temporality by dissecting capital's contradictory way of organising social time (see Bensaïd 2009, pp. 71–81).

46   Thomas 2010, p. 283.

47   Thomas 2010, p. 285.

48   Ibid.

49   Ibid.

language. Language is the 'sediment' of past social histories, of which some pre-vailed and are thus still present in the words we use, while others perished and if they are present in language at all, they are present as anachronisms. Besides, as Gramsci writes, language is inherently metaphorical, and it is precisely there that it is easiest to trace this fractured character of the present:

> The whole of language is a continuous process of metaphor, and the his-tory of semantics is an aspect of the history of culture; language is at the same time a living thing and a museum of fossils of life and civilisations. When I use the word 'disaster' no one can accuse me of believing in astro-logy, and when I say 'by Jove!' no one can assume that I am a worshipper of pagan divinities. These expressions are however a proof that modern civilisation is also a development of paganism and astrology.[50]

Thus, language not only *expresses* social time, but, since it is subject to the laws of non-contemporaneity, possesses an equally *fractured* character as the person. Just as the person is the hub of the contradictory ensemble of social relations which it finds itself in, language reveals layers of often conflicting his-torical experiences coexisting next to each other. The various 'masks' a person is trying to unify are expressed in the various languages this person speaks: she will speak differently as a mother, differently as a worker, differently amongst members of her class and members of a higher (or lower) class. And if this person belongs to the subaltern classes, her language(s) will express this sub-alternity in the form of fractured 'common sense'.

4.2 'What Is Man?'

If we follow this line of argument, the answer to the question 'what is man?' is always a historically relative one. In bourgeois hegemony it is not a very bright one: determined by 'common sense', mankind is only a glimpse of what it could be and, governed by a fragmented, incoherent and uncritical consciousness, its fate is determined by fetishes which mankind created in the first place (such as the capitalist market),[51] and, accordingly, it is such a type of personality and

---

50   Gramsci 2012b, p. 450 (Q11, § 24). '"Dis-aster" refers to an unfavourable conjunction of the stars'. Gramsci 2012b, p. 452, footnote 99 (Q11, § 24).

51   Although not explicitly about market fetishism, Gramsci does write about fetishism in general in the *Prison Notebooks*: 'since a deterministic and mechanical conception of his-tory has wide currency ..., single individuals (seeing that, despite their non-intervention, something nonetheless happens) are led to think that in actual fact there exists above them a phantom entity, the abstraction of the collective organism, a species of autonom-

of 'man-in-the-mass' that will prevail. Although the masses share a common interest thanks to their subaltern class position in society, they are *led* to believe and perceive otherwise, and end up being divided and often in conflict with each other. The abolition of this state of affairs means that mankind should transition from 'common sense' to 'good sense', which would imply precisely 'overcoming bestial and elemental passions through a conception of necessity which gives a conscious direction to one's activity. This is the healthy nucleus that exists in "common sense", the part of it which can be called "good sense" and which deserves to be made more unitary and coherent'.[52] A transition from the dominance of a passive type of personality (determined by 'common sense') to an emergence of an active, critical and revolutionary type of personality (determined by 'good sense').

It is the task of the organic intellectuals of the various subaltern classes to locate 'good sense' and stimulate its development. Perhaps a good starting point could be the simple demand for a decent life which every person possesses – having access to food, shelter, healthcare, education and so on. These very simple, but very basic human impulses, present in every one of us, can be and often are directed in a wrong direction, whereby other members of the subaltern classes are blamed, and we thus have racism, nationalism, sexism, xenophobia, Islamophobia and similar phenomena. All of these signify the prevalence of 'common sense' over 'good sense'. Overcoming these 'bestial and elemental passions' would then consist in recognising that hatred towards other groups will not only solve nothing, but is also unjustified. A further step would be recognising the structural (social, political and historical) reasons why a person's own class, as well as other subaltern classes, find themselves in such an inhumane social position. This would develop a 'conception of necessity' which would at the same time offer the potential for 'a conscious direction in one's activity' in the recognition of the fact that only by unifying with similar social classes can a subaltern class try to end its subordination and exploitation. Fighting these social phenomena means also fighting the divisive language that is their means of production – a hegemonic language.[53] Thus, fighting hegemonic

---

ous divinity that thinks, not with the head of a specific being, yet nevertheless thinks, that moves, not with the real legs of a person, yet still moves, and so on'. Gramsci 1995, p. 15 (Q15, §13).

52 Gramsci 2012b, p. 328 (Q11, §12).

53 Hopefully, it is clear by now that such a claim would not ascribe any 'essential' value-characteristics to language, but only historical ones – which is exactly the merit of Gramsci's approach to language. Language is not oppressive or revolutionary by itself. It only has such a *function* under certain historical conditions and as an effect of certain social practices.

language requires the development of an alternative hegemonic language, a 'language of the subaltern',[54] an effective 'conquering' of the means of social production.

4.3   Towards Political and Cultural-Linguistic Unification

Of course, this also does not mean arguing for a 'linguistic emancipation', or anything similar which might sound like it came out of the twentieth-century philosophies of the 'linguistic turn'. Creating a language of the subaltern is only possible as part of a much wider alternative hegemonic political project, whose goal is the ultimate political unification of the subaltern masses. What I believe can be extrapolated as Gramsci's 'point' in regards to such a project, and what I tried to show in this paper, is that language bears an important role in it, and should not be neglected in helping us understand why people think and act the way they do, and how understanding language as a social phenomenon can help us change this. As Gramsci writes, 'every cultural current creates a language of its own, i.e. it participates in the general development of a determinate national language, introducing new terms, giving a new content to terms already in use, creating metaphors, using historical names to facilitate the understanding and judgement of specific contemporary situations, etc., etc.'.[55]

In other words, just as is the case with intellectuals,[56] every social group creates its own language 'organically' as well, but the subaltern classes can utilise their consciousness of this fact to give this process some direction and purpose. That is the reason why Gramsci argued for a new and organic 'national language', one that would aim to resolve the frictions between the subaltern classes, instead of multiplying and strengthening them: '[i]nstead of trying to impose a normative grammar on people, ... it would be more ethical and more pragmatic to develop a normative grammar that did not have to manage these various frictions but instead was itself the product of their resolution'.[57]

The concepts of normative and spontaneous grammar are introduced by Gramsci in Notebook 29: spontaneous grammar is '"immanent" in language itself, by which one speaks "according to grammar" without knowing it',[58] that is to say, one speaks in accordance to the forms of speech one has internalised;

---

54   These are not Gramsci's words, but I believe they are in Gramsci's spirit.
55   Gramsci 2012a, p. 414 (Q24, §3). Also, in another note: 'one might say that every social group has a "language" of its own'. Gramsci 2012a, p. 120 (Q6, §62).
56   See footnote 16.
57   Ives 2004a, p. 51.
58   Gramsci 2012a, p. 180 (Q29, §2).

normative grammar, on the other hand, 'is made up of the reciprocal "censorship" expressed in such questions as "What did you mean to say?", "What do you mean?", "Make yourself clearer", etc., and in mimicry and teasing. This whole complex of actions and reactions come together to create a grammatical conformism, to establish "norms" or judgements of correctness or incorrectness'. In other words, national language is normative grammar, because normative grammar 'always presupposes a "choice", a cultural tendency, and is thus always an act of national-cultural politics'.[59] A cultural-linguistic unification would therefore mean a formation of a new normative grammar based on resolving frictions between the subaltern classes by overcoming the parochialism of spontaneous grammar, since someone who only speaks according to spontaneous grammar, in other words, dialect, 'necessarily has an intuition of the world which is more or less limited and provincial, which is fossilized and anachronistic' and '[h]is interests will be limited, more or less corporate or economistic, not universal'.[60] This makes spontaneous grammar clearly related to the incoherence and fragmented nature of 'common sense' and the person dominated by it, which is why cultural-linguistic unification is an essential part of political unification of the subaltern classes.

Naturally, such a process is extremely complicated and its outcome cannot be predicted, only – in the spirit of Gramsci's note on prediction[61] – fought for, lest we wish to end up in a new type of social engineering error. As Gramsci explains, since this process

> occurs through a whole complex of molecular processes, it helps to be aware of the entire process as a whole in order to be able to intervene actively in it with the best possible results. One need not consider this intervention as 'decisive' and imagine that the ends proposed will be all reached in detail, i.e. that one will obtain a *specific* [*determinata*] unified language. One will obtain a *unified language* [*lingua unitaria*], if it is a necessity, and the organized intervention will speed up the already existing process. What this language will be, one cannot foresee or establish: in any case, if this intervention is 'rational', it will be organically tied to tradition, and this is of no small importance in the economy of culture.[62]

---

59   Gramsci 2012a, p. 182 (Q29, §2).
60   Gramsci 2012b, p. 325 (Q11, §12). This does not mean that Gramsci considered dialects unimportant or in any way 'harmful'. For a more detailed discussion on Gramsci's relation to dialects, see Carlucci 2013a, p. 11.
61   'Prediction and Perspective', Gramsci 2012b, pp. 169–72 (Q13, §13 and Q13, §14).
62   Gramsci 2012a, p. 183 (Q29, §3). Gramsci's emphasis.

Such a unified language of the subaltern is what is essential in making 'good sense' 'more unitary and coherent' and directing it towards solidarity, action and a revolutionary world-view. It is in the workings of this future language (and the political practices of the subaltern classes which it will be a part of) that revolutionary knowledge is created and spread, thereby confirming what Christine Buci-Glucksmann termed the gnoseology of politics: 'philosophical positions have their effects in all practices, and ... all practices contain know-ledge effects – a dual dialectic, in other words'.[63] It is precisely within the frames of this dialectic that Gramsci discusses language and aims to show how the dia-lectic itself can be used both by reactionary and progressive social forces. Thus, perceiving language politically enables us to better understand this dialectic, as well as utilise it for progressive social goals and for creating a new, revolu-tionary type of person.

---

63   Buci-Glucksmann 1980, p. 349.

CHAPTER 6

Translations of the *Prison Notebooks* into Polish: A Gramscian Analysis

Marta Natalia Wróblewska

1   Introduction

Antonio Gramsci investigated productively a wide range of topics pertaining to the domains of politics, philosophy and culture, making his mark on the development of the respective disciplines. For many decades, however, his observations on language and translation were largely overlooked in Gramscian scholarship. This began to change with the publication of Franco Lo Piparo's pioneering book,[1] Sen's influential article linking Gramsci's insights on the nature of language to the theory of the later Wittgenstein[2] (topic later taken up again by Lo Piparo[3]), and monographs exploring the role of language and translation in Gramsci's biography[4] as well as investigating in more detail the topic of language and translation in Gramsci's theory.[5]

Currently Gramsci's writings are a point of reference not only for researchers in the fields of Philosophy, Political Science or Italian Studies, but also those investigating topics in Cultural Studies (e.g. in the tradition of Stuart Hall's Birmingham School), Discourse Analysis (particularly in the neo-Gramscian strand advanced by Laclau and Mouffe), Postcolonial Studies (in the thought of Gayatri Spivak and others) as well as in Translation Studies. Within this last field it has been argued that Gramsci could be considered the founding father of the cultural translation strand.[6] Through his influence on Wittgenstein (via Piero Sraffa) Gramsci's thought would have stimulated the entire linguistic turn within the social sciences and humanities, giving rise to a context- and culture-conscious understanding of the construction of language and meaning.

---

1   Lo Piparo 1979.
2   Sen 2003.
3   Lo Piparo 2014.
4   Boothman 2004; Carlucci 2013a.
5   Ives 2004a; Ives and Lacorte 2010.
6   Wagner 2011.

In this chapter I build on the existing research on translation theory in Gramsci's thought and attempt to apply his own method to a practical endeavour – an analysis of translations of the *Prison Notebooks* existing to date in Poland. I will start with an overview of the meanings of 'translation' in Gramsci, based on the relevant fragments of the *Prison Notebooks* and in reference to research carried out to date. I will later analyse the same fragments of the *Notebooks* in their Polish translation (contrasting them with the Italian original). The aim of this exercise is to verify whether Gramsci's concepts of translation can be productively applied to interpret concrete choices of his Polish translators and editors in different historical periods. The structure of the argument is thus circular – we depart from Gramsci's writings on translation in order to re-examine the Polish translations of the *Prison Notebooks* and verify if Gramsci's ideas on translation apply to the translations of his own texts. The chapter will close with a final remark on the role of Gramsci's theory in contemporary intellectual and political life in Poland and with a few thoughts on possible editorial projects which could enhance it.

When quoting the *Prison Notebooks* in the Italian original I always cite Garratana's critical edition.[7] For most citations I provide the number of notebook and paragraph as well as traditional bibliographic data. In the section dedicated to the analysis of translations I provide the Italian and Polish version, as well as the English 'word for word' translation of the latter. Standard English translations of the quoted fragments, along with extensive comments of the translators can be found in *Selections from the Prison Notebooks*[8] (for Q10II§44, Q10a§48, Q11§12, Q11§65) and *Further Selections from the Prison Notebooks*[9] (Q11§45–Q11§50).

2   Gramsci on Translation

Philology, alongside philosophy, was the subject of Gramsci's university studies at the University of Turin and it remained his passion throughout the years spent in prison. The philosopher's interest in problems related to language finds its reflection in the amount of space he dedicated to them in his writings. Though scholars usually speak of the philosopher's 29 prison notebooks, he actually began 33. The four that are so often omitted are those dedicated

---

7   Gramsci 1975.
8   Gramsci 1999.
9   Gramsci 2001b.

to translation exercises. The most famous translations carried out by Gramsci are his adaptations of the Brothers Grimm fairy tales, now published in book form.[10]

The topic of translation is an object of systematic analysis in Notebook 11, in the section entitled 'On the translatability of philosophical and scientific languages', but mentions of translation as practice or theoretical concept also appear scattered in other sections of the *Notebooks* as well as in Gramsci's letters.

When approaching the topic of translation in Gramsci's theory, one should always bear in mind that he does not use the term in just one way. Gramsci does not offer a definition of the term 'translation' in the *Notebooks*; the term is also missing from the index of Garratana's edition. Below I present three different meanings which can be attributed to the term 'translation' in Gramsci's theory: 1) transferring from one language to another; 2) transferring from one paradigm to another and 3) translating from theory into practice. At the end, I separately introduce the notion of 'translatability' (which in the *Notebooks* is discussed jointly with 'translation'). I find this classification useful for my analysis, but it is far from being the only possible one – for instance Frosini, following Boothman, writes of the 'weak' and 'strong' understanding of 'translation'.[11] The grouping of topics advanced here should be read as an effort to systematise Gramsci's fragmentary writings for the purpose of the analysis presented in the second section of this study. It has to be kept in mind however that the three described types of translation are not mutually exclusive; on the contrary, they overlap and can be understood as different dimensions of one activity.

The first, intuitively understandable, meaning of 'translation' is connected to the practical act of transferring meaning from one language to another. Importantly, for Gramsci translation is never just rendering words or sentences in a different language, but always mediating between entire cultures. In a letter in which the philosopher encouraged his wife, Julca, to become a translator from Italian to Russian, he identified distinctive characteristics of a good translator:

> A qualified translator should be able not only to translate literally, but also to translate the conceptual terms of a specific national culture into the terms of another national culture, that is such a translator should have a critical knowledge of two civilizations and be able to acquaint one with

---

10   Gramsci 2008b.

11   Frosini 2003b. For a useful overview of uses of 'translation' and 'translatability' in the *Prison Notebooks* see: Boothman 2010; Gaboardi 2015, pp. 98–105.

the other by using the historically determined language of the civilization to which he supplies the informative material.[12]

When speaking of translation between languages, Gramsci often puts the name of the language in quotation marks – probably to indicate that it stands for a larger reality than just the linguistic one. When in Q1§44 he makes a remark on Giuseppe Ferrari who was unable to translate 'French' into 'Italian'[13] – he is clearly not speaking of an inability to translate from one language into another due to lack of skill or inconsistency between two languages, but rather of a difficulty linked to differing national experiences and realities. This is also the case for the often quoted fragment (Q11§46) in which Gramsci repeats the words of Lenin: 'we have not been able to "translate" our language into those of Europe'.[14] The main difficulty related to translation stems from the fact that languages were formed in the course of historical processes, which differed on the material, and economic level, as well as on the level of theoretical reflection.

The second understanding of 'translation' in Gramsci is connected to transmitting from one paradigm into another. The term is used in this manner for instance in the theorist's much-quoted ironical remark (Q11§45) on the peculiar language of philosophers and scientists who tend to use their own 'Esperanto' and who believe 'everything that is not expressed in their language is a delirium, a prejudice, a superstition'.[15] We can find a practical example of this sort of translation in one of Gramsci's own translations – namely the Brothers Grimm fairy tales in which references to Christian faith were eliminated while the narratives were transferred into the background of the translator's native Sardinian countryside.[16]

If we look at Gramsci's theoretical remarks on translation understood as mediating between paradigms we will see that also on this level the term can take on various meanings. Firstly, it can signify translation between cultures on different levels of development or shaped by different ideologies – e.g. in Q1§44 (as noted above) Gramsci writes about Ferrari's inability to translate from the languages of a politically more advanced country to the language of the less advanced one; similarly, in Q11§48 he repeats after Marx a remark on the possibility of translation between Proudhon's political language and

12   Gramsci 1994, p. 207.
13   Gramsci 1999, p. 225.
14   Gramsci 2001b, pp. 450–1.
15   Gramsci 2001b, p. 447.
16   See Borghese 2010, pp. 148–55.

that of classic German philosophy.[17] Secondly – translation can refer to uncovering and productively exploiting parallels between different methodological approaches in one scientific discipline. Still in Q11§48, Gramsci quotes fragments of an open letter of Luigi Einaudi which mentions Vailati's ability to translate between geometry and algebra, between hedonism and Kantian morals, between normative and applied economics, and Loria's capacity of expressing an economic argument using the 'language' of Adam Smith, Ricardo, Marx, etc.[18] Finally, translation can occur between different scientific approaches – in Q11§65 Gramsci argues that on a basic theoretical level 'translation' must be possible in the triad philosophy-politics-economy;[19] similarly, in Q13§13 he asks whether 'Machiavelli's essentially political language can be translated into economic terms, and to which economic system it could be reduced'.[20]

The last meaning of 'translation' in Gramsci applies to translating between theory and practice, that is – translating speculative philosophy into a philosophy of praxis (where praxis has a dual nature that includes both theory *and* practice). As typical of Marxist thinkers, Gramsci was not interested in pure theory, but wished to apply theory to political reality – philosophy of praxis was to unite both theoretical thought and practical applications. In Q7§35 Gramsci writes:

> [We] arrive also at the equality of, or the equation between, 'philosophy and politics', thought and action, that is, at a philosophy of praxis. Everything is political, even philosophy or philosophies ... and the only 'philosophy' is history in action, that is, life itself.[21]

The relationship between thought and practice can thus be conceptualized in terms of translation. Naturally, this understanding is closely connected to the previous step – translating between paradigms. A theory must first be expressed in a 'language' adequate to the given historical moment (conditioned by the material conditions of production, or, in terms of classical Marxism, by the material base[22]), before it can become a point of reference for polit-

---

17   Gramsci 2001b, p. 451.
18   Gramsci 2001b, p. 452.
19   Gramsci 1999, p. 745.
20   Gramsci 1999, p. 346.
21   Gramsci 1999, p. 676.
22   Importantly, Gramsci's understanding of the relationship between material conditions of production (base) and elements of superstructure, such as ideology, is far from deterministic. In fact, contrary to frequent misconceptions, it was not so even for Marx himself. A fuller discussion of Gramsci's approach to the problem is outside the scope of this text. For a discussion of base and superstructure in Marx see Harman 1998, pp. 7–54.

ical action. Gramsci reflects on the relationship between practice and the-oretical ideas in Q9§63, where he writes that all philosophies are born not from former philosophies but from real social developments. He concludes that:

> every truth, even if it is universal and even if it can be expressed by an abstract formula of a mathematical kind (for the sake of theoreticians) owes its effectiveness to its being expressed in the language appropriate to the specific concrete circumstances. If it cannot be expressed in specific terms, it is a Byzantine and scholastic abstraction, good only for phrase mongers to toy with.[23]

If the evolution of speculative philosophy into philosophy of praxis can be con-sidered the ultimate scope of Gramsci's project of social emancipation, we see that this 'type of translation' must necessarily be based on the two previous steps – the translation of notions and ideas specific for a given source reality into a given target reality (which will often be connected to a translation of a particular text between two languages). The question that suggests itself at this stage is the following: what are the conditions of translation? This ques-tion brings us to the issue of 'translatability'.

In addressing the issue of whether translation (understood in any and all of the above ways) is possible and to what degree, Gramsci builds on the above-mentioned division between structure and superstructure.

On the possibility of 'translation' the theorist writes these lines (Q11§47):

> Translatability presupposes that a given stage of civilisation has a 'basic-ally' identical cultural expression, even if its language is historically differ-ent, being determined by the particular tradition of each national culture and each philosophical system, by the prevalence of an intellectual or practical activity etc.[24]

Certain stages of different civilisations will have a similar, or virtually identical, cultural expression, though the 'language' in which it is expressed might vary depending on the tradition of each nation. Translation between such cul-tures, including theory and political ideas, is thus feasible – one cannot be reduced to the other, however, as Gramsci notes (Q11§48): 'this translatabil-

---

23   Gramsci 1999, pp. 437–8.
24   Gramsci 2001b, p. 451.

ity is not "perfect" in every respect, even in important ones ... but it is so in its "basic" essentials'.[25] Would translation be possible between two cultures at radically different stages of development? This issue is addressed in Q11§47:

> Thus it is to be seen whether one can translate between expressions of different stages of civilisation, in so far as each of these stages is a moment of the development of another, one thus mutually integrating the other, or whether a given expression may be translated using the terms of a previous stage of the same civilisation, a previous stage which however is more comprehensible than the given language etc.[26]

Hence, for a socially-aware translator, who would attempt a translation in Gramsci's terms, the primary point of reference should be the similarity of the base of two cultures – in the present moment or between the present phase of one culture and the past phase of another. In order to properly understand the text and render its sense the translator must reach out through layers of superstructure to the base of social relations which underlie the original text, and then find its equivalent in the reality of the target language. In Gramsci's theory the act of translating is never a direct transition from one natural language into another, it is always mediated through the reality of both societies. The process of analysing the structure of both languages and societies, from the superstructure to the base (and the other way round) in their particular historical form makes translation a historical act which 'moves increasingly away from the mathematical scheme and arrives at historical judgment or a judgment of taste' (Q16§21).[27]

Finally, we might add that Gramsci attributed an intrinsic, *organic*, quality of translatability to Marxism, or philosophy of praxis. He conceived it not as a finished theory, but as one in permanent development, which makes it possible to *translate* the concepts of both past and contemporary philosophies into those of Marxism. Marx's theory, according to Gramsci, will one day be superseded and incorporated (i.e. translated) into a new paradigm expressed in a novel *linguaggio*, where the concept of freedom will replace the notion of necessity (Q7§33).[28] According to Carl Marzani this approach makes Gram-

---

25   Gramsci 2001b, pp. 453–4.
26   Gramsci 2001b, p. 451.
27   Gramsci 1985, pp. 384–5.
28   Gramsci 1999, pp. 711–13.

sci's theory worthy of the name 'open Marxism' (in fact, this is the title Marzani gave to his selection of Gramsci's texts)[29] and in Derek Boothman's view it puts his thought in direct opposition to the closed system of Marxism-Leninism.[30]

3   Gramsci in Translation (into Polish)

There are two partial Polish translations of Gramsci's *Notebooks*, neither of which carries the title *Prison Notebooks*. The first edition, entitled *Pisma wybrane (Selected Writings)*, was published in 1961 in two volumes. It is a compilation of Gramsci's writings based on Platone's edition *Opere di Antonio Gramsci*. It features selected fragments from volumes 2–7 (which contained selections from the *Notebooks*) and volume 9 (articles published in the magazine *Ordine Nuovo*), as well as selected letters (volume 1) and an essay on the Southern Question. Volumes 8 and 10–12 of Platone's edition were published in 1958 and 1969–71 respectively – too late to be included in the Polish translation.

In the first Polish edition the numbers of paragraphs and notebooks are not marked (not even in the table of contents as in the respective Italian edition), which gives the text an illusion of uniformity (however the original character of the *Notebooks* is explained in the Introduction). Otherwise, the edition follows quite closely the choices of the Italian editors – reproducing the dictionary of Gramsci's 'codes', following the differences in font sizes, etc. The first volume opens with an essay 'The relevance of the thought and life of Antonio Gramsci', by Palmiro Togliatti, at that time the leader of the Communist Party of Italy, and unofficial co-editor of the first Italian edition.

At the moment when the first Polish edition of the *Notebooks* was published, Poland was a communist state with a developed 'ideological' policy of publishing – numerous translations of oeuvres of Marxist authors were commissioned with prominent specialists and published with great care by national publishing houses. This enabled a very early (1950) publication of Gramsci's *Letters from Prison* prepared by prestigious left-wing literary publisher Czytelnik.[31] The Polish edition of the *Notebooks* was also one of the first to appear in the world – selections from the text were published earlier only in Serbo-Croatian (1951), Spanish (1958) and Russian (1959). The *Notebooks* were pub-

---

29   Marzani 1957b; Gramsci 1957b.
30   Boothman 2010, p. 130.
31   Gramsci 1950.

lished by Książka i Wiedza, a publishing house with leftist traditions dating back to the pre-war period, in a prestigious at the time series 'Biblioteka myśli socjalistycznej' ('Library of Socialist Thought'), as the fifth book to appear in the series. The fragments were selected by Ludovico Tulli, translator of Polish literature into Italian, and advised on by specialists from the Gramsci Institute in Rome. The translation was entrusted to distinguished translator Barbara Sieroszewska and the support of several leading Polish intellectuals for the enterprise is acknowledged in the foreword.

The second Polish edition, published in 1991, and based on Gerratana's critical edition (1975), is entitled *Zeszyty filozoficzne* (*Philosophical Notebooks*)[32] – the title is due to the profile of the publication, which focuses on philosophical questions in the *Notebooks*. It was published in another prestigious series: 'Biblioteka Klasyków Filozofii PWN' ('Library of the Classics of Philosophy of the Polish National Scientific Publishers'). It includes the translation of entire Notebooks 10 and 11 plus miscellaneous notes. The major difference between the two editions lies in the organisation of the text, which, in the second edition, finally follows the structure given to it by Gramsci, i.e. it is divided into separate, numbered paragraphs and not merged into one seemingly uniform text. The editor of the second Polish edition, Sław Krzemień-Ojak (author of one of the two existing monographs on Gramsci in Polish) deemed that the first translation was accurate enough to be reprinted thirty years after its first publication. For this reason, the paragraphs translated earlier by Sieroszewska were included in the new edition with only minimal amendments. The fragments published for the first time were translated by Joanna Szymanowska.

A comparison of the two Polish editions allows for observation of the publisher's (slowly) evolving approach to the role of translators. Sieroszewska's name figures only on the fourth page of the 1961 edition in tiny letters, together with the names of three editors, and she is not mentioned in the introduction of the book, nor are any issues connected to translation. In the 1991 edition, the translator has been 'promoted' to the third page, below the title and the author's name, where she figures together with the editor and the translator of the remaining parts of the *Notebooks* – Joanna Szymanowska.

In Translation Studies, the topic of the visibility of the translator has been one of the foci of the discussion on the nature and purpose of translation – a development later labelled as 'the cultural turn in Translation Studies'. From this point of view, the visual change in signalising the role of the translator in

---

32   Gramsci 1991.

the Polish editions of Gramsci's *Notebooks* can be perceived as a step toward valorising the role of the translator. And yet, the solution adopted in the 1991 edition remains hardly satisfactory, as the reader has no way of knowing which paragraph was translated by which of the two translators (if not by comparing the two editions). Similarly, they will not learn how exactly the editor blended into one integral text two different translations carried out at a thirty-year interval. In the 'Editor's Note' in the second edition, we find no explanations as to possible alignments, changes in terminology, amendments made to the first version due to new interpretations, etc. Thus, the material work of the two female translators remains almost invisible.

As mentioned in the introduction to this chapter, the fragments of the Polish editions which will be studied here in detail are the core ones dedicated by Gramsci to translation, namely Q11§12 (up to note 4), Q11§45–Q11§50 as well as Q10a§44, Q10a§48 and Q11§65. Additionally, I look at Q11§56, comparing the translation of the terms 'buon senso' and 'senso comune' which figure in the previously mentioned paragraphs. These fragments have not been selected as the most important or most difficult to translate, but simply as an interesting sample and as an exercise in succinctness – to test a theory looking precisely at the text which describes it.

In Platone's edition, the above-mentioned fragments, save Q11§65 and Q11§56, appear in the first chapter ('Avviamento allo studio della filosofia e del materialismo storico') of the second volume ('Il materialismo storico e la filosofia di Benedetto Croce' – 1952). Paragraphs Q11§46–Q11§49 are the ones originally entitled by Gramsci 'Translatability of Scientific and Philosophical Languages'; Q11§45, dealing with philosophical Esperanto, precedes them directly, while Q11§12 opens the entire chapter (in the first edition entitled 'Alcuni punti preliminari di riferimento'), offering a general framework of investigations. As for the paragraphs from Notebook 10, these were placed by the editors in the middle of the chapter, bundled together under the title 'Il linguaggio, le lingue, il senso comune' ('Language, languages and common sense'). Q11§65 ('Filosofia – Politica – Economia') was positioned already in the next section, but starts with a reflection on the mutual translatability of the triad philosophy-politics-economics and carries a remark 'see previous notes on translatability'.[33] Q11§56 ('Buon senso e senso comune') was placed by the editors in a different volume altogether – "Passato e presente" (1951). In Gerratana's edi-

---

33   Gramsci 1952, Q10§44, pp. 25–26; Q10§48, pp. 25 (first point of Paragraph Q10§48 merged into the beginning of Q10§44); Q11 §12 (up to note 4), pp. 3–5; Q11§45–Q11§50, pp. 61–70; Gramsci 2008a: Q11n§65, p. 141; Q11§56, p. 143.

tion the analysed fragments appear in volume II – as parts of Notebook 10 (1932–35) – 'La filosofia di Benedetto Croce' and Notebook 11 – 'Introduzione allo studio della filosofia' (1932–33).[34]

The paragraphs I analyse, being situated at the end of Notebook 10 and in Notebook 11, are present in both Polish editions. Only very few differences can be found between the paragraphs published in the two Polish editions – these are connected to minor amendments in the second edition of the Italian text. For example, Gramsci's note on the necessity of verifying a piece of information which closes Q11§48 was restored in both second editions – the Italian and the Polish one which followed it.[35] Apart from such changes, in the second Polish edition some original Italian terms have been added in parenthesis, e.g. 'linguaggio' in Q10§44.[36] Unfortunately, the Italian terms were not introduced in a consistent manner.

In conclusion, though there are two Polish editions of the *Notebooks*, one published thirty years after the other, we can effectively speak of a single translation – executed by Sieroszewska and later seamlessly complemented by Szymanowska. The only differences are minor editorial ones and even these can be usually attributed to alterations in the source text, and not to changes in the style or policy of translating, shifts in the interpretation of particular Gramscian notions etc. When quoting the Polish translation in this text, I refer to the second edition.

A closer look at the selected fragments of the Polish translation of the *Notebooks* will enable an examination of its specific features. Interestingly, there are quite a few issues regarding the translation of two terms crucial for the paragraphs in question, namely: 'language' and 'translation'. The Polish translators are not the only ones to have tackled the difficult task of rendering the difference between 'linguaggio' and 'lingua' and finding a suitable equivalent for the Italian 'tradurre' – already Carl Marzani, one of the first English translators of Gramsci commented on this problem.[37]

The title of the Paragraph Q10§44 'Il linguaggio, le lingue, il senso comune' ('Language, languages and common sense') – is rendered in Polish as 'Język, języki, zdrowy rozsądek'.[38] A reader unacquainted with Polish language might assume that in Polish there exists just one word for the two Italian terms 'lin-

---

34 Gramsci 1975, Q10§44, pp. 1330–2; Q10§48, pp. 1334–8; Q11§12 (up to note 4), pp. 1375–8; Q11§45–Q11§50, pp. 1466–76; Q11§56, p. 1482; Q11§65, pp. 1492–3.
35 Gramsci 1975, p. 1470; Gramsci 1991, p. 334.
36 Gramsci 1991, p. 158.
37 Marzani 1957b, pp. 59–60.
38 Gramsci 1991, pp. 158–61.

guaggio' and 'lingua', namely – 'język'. However, this is not the case, which is evident even in a subsequent paragraph of the translation where 'concezione del linguaggio di Vailati' ('Vailati's concept of language') is translated as 'koncepcja mowy'. Until the end of this paragraph, 'linguaggio' is consistently rendered as 'mowa' (literally 'speech'), which is a good, but unfortunately inconsistent choice.

In Q11§46–Q11§48[39] we encounter another of the mentioned terminological issues – should Gramsci's 'tradurre' ('to translate') be rendered as 'tłumaczyć' or 'przekładać'? In Polish there are two verbs for the action of translating, and they both happen to have another figurative meaning: in the case of the first word, 'to explain', and in the case of the second, 'to transfer, transpose'. When rendering Gramsci's 'tradurre', the translator must make a conscious choice between two possible tactics. In the first they would use both terms, giving separate meanings to each of them – for example by distinguishing between the literal and the metaphorical uses (and ideally explaining the choice in a footnote). In the second approach they would choose one of the verbs and use it consistently as an equivalent of the single term from the original. The second of the mentioned terms ('przekładać') seems an ideal equivalent of 'tradurre' – in fact it is used most commonly in Polish in two contexts – translating from language to language, and 'putting theory into practice' ('przełożyć teorię na praktykę'), which carries exactly the connotations a translator would be looking for.

Sieroszewska uses the verb 'przekładać' in the title of the Section v – 'Przekładalność języków naukowych i filozoficznych'[40] – ('Translatability of scientific and philosophical languages'),[41] and later in Q11§46 – 'nie umieliśmy 'przełożyć' naszego języka na języki europejskie' ('we have not been able to "translate" our language into those of Europe').[42] Two lines later however, in Q11§47, she switches to the other verb – 'tłumaczyć' – 'wzajemna przetłumaczalność różnych języków filozoficznych i naukowych' ('Translability of Scientific Languages'[43]). In total, in Paragraphs § 46–§49 forms derived from 'tłumaczyć' appear nine times and forms derived from 'przekładać' – five times. The equivalent use of these two terms without any logical pattern deprives the term of its theoretical charge and blurs the entire issue of translatability. This difficulty is even present in Gramsci's oft-cited rhetorical question (Q11§48): 'ma

---

39   Gramsci 1991, pp. 330–4.
40   Gramsci 1991, p. 330.
41   Gramsci 2001b, p. 450.
42   Gramsci 2001b, p. 451.
43   Ibid.

quale lingua è esattamente traducibile in un'altra? quale singola parola è tra-ducibile esattamente in un'altra lingua?' ('but what language is exactly trans-latable into another? what single word is exactly translatable into another language?').[44] In the Polish version we read 'jakiż jednak język daje się dokład-nie *przełożyć* na inny, który pojedynczy wyraz da się dokładnie *przetłumaczyć* na inny język?'[45] (emphasis mine). One Italian word 'tradurre' was translated in two different ways within just one sentence, and in a context where it is quite obvious that Gramsci is referring to the act of translating from language to language. Clearly in this case stylistic reasons took precedence over accur-acy.

In Q11§48[46] we encounter another mistranslation which further blurs the question of translation in Gramsci. In a fragment already quoted above, Gram-sci writes that translation is possible 'in its basic essentials' ('lo è nel «fondo» essenziale'). We could expect a slight difference between the two Polish edi-tions, as the position of the quotation mark was changed in the respective Italian originals. Surprisingly, however, in both Polish editions the entire phrase is ... missing! (in the 1991 edition it would have appeared on p. 333). It is diffi-cult to say whether deleting this line was a conscious decision of the translators (perhaps it was deemed redundant?) or a simple mistake in copying, which went unnoticed by the editors of both editions.

If we needed further proof of the rather free approach of the translators and editors to the issue of translation in Gramsci's thought, we should take a look at the Polish version of Q11§65, where the fragment on the mutual translatab-ility of philosophy, politics and economy is significantly simplified.[47] Where Gramsci writes of 'convertibilità da una all'altra, traduzione reciproca' ('con-vertibility from one to the other, reciprocal translation'[48]) in the Polish version we find 'wzajemna przetłumaczalność każdego z tych elementów' ('mutual translatability of both these elements'). Two Italian terms ('convertibilità' and 'traduzione') are rendered by just one Polish term ('przetłumaczalność') and 'translation' is turned into 'translatability'.

These seemingly small mistranslations in paragraphs connected to language unfortunately contribute to a misrepresentation of the problem of transla-tion in Gramsci in the eyes of the Polish reader. Firstly, the verb 'to trans-late' ('tradurre') is rendered using two different words ('przekładać' and 'tłu-

---

44   Gramsci 2001b, pp. 453–4.
45   Gramsci 1991, p. 333.
46   Gramsci 1991, pp. 331–4.
47   Gramsci 1991, p. 361.
48   Gramsci 1999, p. 745.

maczyć'), which makes it unrecognisable as a single term of Gramsci's theory. Secondly, the problem of translating between different paradigms is misrepresented (as we have seen on the example of Paragraphs Q11§48 and Q11§65) and thirdly, Gramsci's conclusion on the conditions of translatability is erased altogether. Unfortunately, 'translation' is not the only Gramscian notion which is not rendered precisely in the Polish edition.

In the paragraphs investigated in this chapter, discrepancies occur also in the case of other terms. I have already looked at the heading of paragraph Q10§44 – 'Il linguaggio, le lingue, il senso comune' ('Language, languages, common sense'),[49] focusing on the rendering of terms 'linguaggio' and 'lingua'. Other questions arise when we look at the translation of the term 'senso comune', and the term with which it is often paired – 'buon senso'. In order to determine whether these two terms were correctly translated into Polish, we should closely consider their meaning in the original text.

It is perhaps not immediately self-evident that these two terms have different meanings at all – for instance in Q10§48 Gramsci writes of 'il senso commune o buon senso' ('common sense or good sense'), which could suggest they are synonyms. On the other hand, he distinguishes between the two for instance in Q11§56 where he quotes a fragment from Manzoni's 'The Betrothed' in which the two terms are juxtaposed – 'good sense existed but it was kept hidden for fear of common sense',[50] or in Q11§12, note 4, where he directly opposes 'good sense' to 'common sense' – '(p)hilosophy is criticism and the superseding of religion and "common sense". In this sense it coincides with "good" as opposed to "common" sense'.[51] In this last fragment 'good sense' is associated with philosophy, criticism and superseding of religion, while 'common sense' would be a set of unconsciously held beliefs.

Though the differentiation between 'common' and 'good sense' might seem a trifling matter to a casual reader, for Gramscian scholars the two terms have come to be understood as opposed to one another, or aspects of two superseding phases of social development.[52] Both from the point of view of Gramscian scholarship and good practice in the field of translation, the two terms should be rendered consistently in two different ways. It is not so in the Polish edition of the *Notebooks*. The table below shows the different renderings of the two terms in different paragraphs of the Polish edition.

---

49   Gramsci 1991, p. 158.
50   Manzoni 1956, p. 446, cited in Gramsci 2001b, p. 736.
51   Gramsci 1999, p. 630.
52   For further comment see Hoare and Nowell-Smith's comments in Gramsci 1999, pp. 626, 630.

Paragraph, page	Original Italian term	Polish translation	Literal English translation of the Polish term	Comment
Q10§44	il senso comune	zdrowy rozsądek	sane sense	–
Q11§12	1) il senso comune 2) il buon senso	1) potoczny rozsądek 2) zdrowy rozum	1) common sense 2) sane mind	An endnote (in both editions) contains the original terms.
Q11§56	1) il senso comune 2) il buon senso	1) potoczny rozsądek 2) 'zdrowy rozsądek'	1) common sense 2) sane sense	The original terms are given in brackets, the term for 'buon senso' is taken in inverted commas, which is not the case in the original.

As we can see, the term 'senso comune' has been rendered in two different ways ('zdrowy rozsądek', 'potoczny rozsądek') and so has the term 'buon senso' ('zdrowy rozum', 'zdrowy rozsądek'). The fact that the terms overlap and contain different variations of the same words adds to the confusion (even as a native speaker of Polish I needed to draw up the table above to keep track of the different terms). These inconsistencies are probably due to the fact that the translators put stylistics over accuracy and perhaps perceived these notions as literary terms rather than notions of Gramsci's theory.

A final observation on the translation of 'senso comune' and 'buon senso': when rendering in Polish a fragment from Manzoni's 'The Betrothed' cited by Gramsci in Q11§56, Sieroszewska is actually quoting ... her own translation of the novel from 1958! And hence the translation of these two notions was simply transferred from an earlier text which initially had nothing to do with Gramsci and his theory. While following this earlier translation is a legitimate choice, the readers would have profited from a clearer explanation of the use of these terms rather than having to accept the vagueness of the notions appearing in the Polish translation of the *Prison Notebooks*.

In closing the analysis of the Polish translation of selected paragraphs from the *Prison Notebooks*, I will draw the reader's attention to just two more curious renderings of Gramscian terms. In Q11§12, note 1, we encounter the term 'uomo-massa' (the original phrase is 'si è sempre uomini-massa o uomini-collettivi'[53]) – problematic also in the English editions, where it was rendered as 'collective man' (the whole phrase being 'one is always as it were a "col-

---

53   Gramsci 1975, p. 1376.

lective man", a person within a social group') (Marzani's translation[54]), 'man-mass' ('man-mass or man-collective') (Marks' translation[55]), 'man-in-the-mass' ('man-in-the-mass or collective man') (Hoare and Nowell-Smith's translation[56]), Gramsci, and finally 'Man as Mass' in Boothman's rendering of Q7§12.[57]

In the Polish translation – the entire phrase reads 'jesteśmy zawsze masą ludzką, czyli ludźmi żyjącymi w gromadzie'[58] ('we are always a human mass or people living in a flock'). 'Uomo-massa' was translated as 'masa ludzka' (literally 'human mass') and 'uomo-collettivo' as 'people living in a flock'. This is not a fortunate translation since, unlike all the English translations, the Polish rendering – 'masa ludzka' – refers to a collective (*a mass*) rather than an imagined, hypothetical collective person (as does the original 'uomo-collettivo'). Other than evoking in the reader's mind associations with Ortega y Gasset's writings, this translation also creates a stylistic problem a few lines later when Gramsci writes that 'man belongs simultaneously to a multiplicity of men-masses' (Marks' translation).[59] In the Polish translation we read '[człowiek] należy jednocześnie do wielu grup masy ludzkiej'[60] (literally 'one belongs simultaneously to several groups of human mass'), which sounds awkard ('human mass' suggests an image of something too big to become part of further groups).

This is one of the points where the existing translation reads as a bit too stiff and perhaps outdated (e.g. the word 'gromada' – 'flock'). Interestingly, a better translation of 'uomo-massa' – 'człowiek zbiorowy' (literally 'collective human') – was proposed already in 1962 in an essay on Gramsci by Jerzy Szacki,[61] but was not taken up by the editor of the second Polish edition. The diverse existing English translations of the term 'uomo-collettivo' testify to a continuous reflection on Gramsci's thought and suggest different superseding or competing interpretations. The continuous use of the same, albeit imperfect, rendering of the term in Polish suggests in turn a lack of deeper engagement with existing scholarship and to a certain 'fossilisation' of the language of Gramscian theory.

Finally, in Q11§49[62] we find another inconsistency – 'tranquilla teoria', a term which appears three times in the paragraph, is translated into Polish twice as 'spokojna teoria' ('tranquil theory') and once as 'pokojowa teoria' ('peaceful the-

---

54   Gramsci 1957b, p. 17.
55   Gramsci 1957a, p. 59.
56   Gramsci 1999, p. 627.
57   Gramsci 2001b, p. 415.
58   Gramsci 1991, p. 212.
59   Gramsci 1957a, p. 59.
60   Gramsci 1991, p. 212.
61   Szacki 1962.
62   Gramsci 1991, pp. 334–7.

ory'). The first choice is clearly better since what Gramsci has in mind is not a *pacifist* theory but a theory which is tranquil, dormant as opposed to one which is effective, as his philosophy of praxis.

Even this brief analysis of selected fragments of Gramsci's texts in their Polish rendering shows the shortcomings of the existing translation(s). The imperfection of the existing Polish editions should not, in my opinion, be attributed to lack of competence or good will on the side of the translators or editors. Considering how soon after the publication of Platone's edition of the *Prison Notebooks* the first Polish edition appeared, and what the material conditions of translation and related research at the time were, the volumes strike the reader even today as meticulously translated and edited and remain a valuable source. The second edition is equally correct, though in very close reading one discovers inconsistencies and errors, some of which could have been avoided.

To most readers the translation infelicities discussed above, and similar ones, will be of little, if any, importance. However, the heated discussions concerning the Italian editions of the *Notebooks* and their various English translations show that for Gramscian scholars even minor terminological shifts (see for instance the numerous existing translations of 'uomo-massa') can have profound consequences for the understanding of Gramsci's theory. I believe it is precisely the lack of wider-scale engagement with Gramsci's thought that is to blame for the shortcomings of the Polish editions of the *Prison Notebooks*. After all, translations are not produced in isolation, but are 'made up of other texts' – they draw on a language and understanding developed in previous essays, commentaries, lectures, discussions.

The authors of the Polish translations of the *Prison Notebooks* are recognised specialists in the field of Italian literature – Sieroszewska is known for her translations of Italo Calvino, Carlo Manzoni (as mentioned before) and other 'classics', while Szymanowska is an established researcher in Italian Studies. However, neither of them appears to be a specialist in the field of Marxism, or philosophy in general, in contrast to the authors of the English-language versions who are all avid readers and recognised commentators of Gramsci's thought. The English editions of the *Notebooks* all feature introductions and commentaries from the translators, which is not the case in the Polish editions, where the translators remain largely 'invisible'. In the Polish editions it is the editors who play the role of experts of Gramsci's thought. Clearly though, it is difficult for one person – especially studying Gramsci in relative isolation – to be an expert on all the areas covered in the *Notebooks*. For example, Krzemień-Ojak's monograph[63] on Gramsci presents the theor-

---

63   Krzemień-Ojak 1983.

ist's views on politics, culture and aesthetics, while the topic of language is not even mentioned. This might suggest that the paragraphs focusing on translation were not among the most important ones in the eyes of the editor. Perhaps it is due to this fact that the rigour of their translation leaves much to be desired. This remark should not be read as a critique of the Polish editors or translators – indeed, the topic of language in Gramscian studies truly came to the fore only after the publication of both Polish translations of the *Notebooks*, perhaps in a most visible manner with Sen's article highlighting the connection between Gramsci's theory of language and the philosophy of the later Wittgenstein.[64]

4   Conclusions and Final Remarks

The aim of translating and publishing books is to make texts accessible to the public in a language which can be understood and, ideally, taken up in ongoing discussions. Otherwise, this activity could be called, in Gramsci's words (Q9§63), 'a scholastic abstraction, good only for the phrase-mongers to toy with'.[65] The *Prison Notebooks* have stimulated debates worldwide not only in academic circles, but also among the wider public, including activists, intellectuals and workers. But could Gramsci's oeuvre become a point of reference for societal debates in Poland in the form in which it exists today? Having analysed the translation(s) of Gramsci's work into Polish, we can attempt to answer this question. Though the fragments analysed here were only selected ones, and indeed perhaps not the ones most crucial for understanding Gramsci's political message, they do illustrate the translators' and editors' approach to the publication and point to challenges in comprehension which a Polish reader could face.

    In the Polish intellectual panorama Gramsci remains predominantly a historical intellectual figure, 'a classic' rather than a voice in ongoing philosophical and political discussions. The existing translations of the *Prison Notebooks* seem to reinforce such an approach – the first edition casts him as a classic of Marxist thought, the second as a classic philosopher *tout court*. This framing of Gramsci's work seems to be a conscious choice on the part of the editors – in the introduction to the second Polish edition we read that although Gramsci's work has been a topic of intellectual reflection worldwide for decades, recent interest in his work has diminished as:

---

64   Sen 2003.
65   Gramsci 1999, p. 438.

everything has been published, every detail of his biography has been studied, all historical material exhausted, all possible variants of inter-pretation tried out ... and while for decades [Gramsci] has been part of the living tradition, he has now been shifted to the area of respected leg-acy ... This is how we present him in the current edition.[66]

Historically, in the times of People's Poland Gramsci's thought was taken up by authors such as Jerzy Szacki or Zygmunt Bauman, as a more 'human' altern-ative to rigid, dogmatic Marxism (Bauman explicitly states that reading the *Prison Notebooks* – probably in the Polish edition from 1961 – had a major influ-ence on his life and shaped many of his ideas, starting with his first book).[67] It is in this period that the only two book-length positions on Gramsci in Pol-ish were published. Paweł Śpiewak's work from 1977 is the closest we have in Polish to a 'Gramsci reader' – it is a book composed in equal parts of an access-ible introduction to key concepts in Gramsci (focused around nodes: history, politics, revolution and ideology) and a selection of texts in their Polish trans-lation (all following the edition from 1961). Krzemień-Ojak's 1983 monograph in turn is composed of four parts: Gramsci's biography and three sections focus-ing on philosophy, theory of culture and aesthetics in his theory. Apart from these books there are a few dozen articles in academic journals on Gramsci's thought, mainly focusing on historical and political issues, seldom interacting with Gramsci as a philosopher whose thought could have any relevance to cur-rent debates. Little has been written in Polish on Gramsci's insights on popular culture, not to mention language and translation. After the Polish economic transformation (1989), interest in Gramsci's thought only diminished – in the not so wide panorama of left-wing theory it was postmodernists who came to the fore, and if Gramsci was at all present in theoretical reflection in the last two and a half decades, it has mainly been in a mediated form – through the works of Althusser, Laclau and Mouffe, etc.

In analysing the fate of Gramsci's thought in Poland, we cannot pass over the historical circumstances that condition it. A turning point is, of course, the economic transformation which saw a strong neoliberal political discourse pervading economy, politics and education. All theory associated with 'the pre-vious regime' became suspicious and was largely scrapped from university edu-cation programmes. In consequence, academic traditions of Marxist thought were abandoned, and scholars often hastily concealed traces of engagement with left-wing thought from their resumes. Perhaps this shift could also explain

---

66   Krzemień-Ojak in Gramsci 1991, pp. xxxvi–xxxvii.
67   See Bauman 1992, p. 206.

the tone of the introduction to the second edition of the *Prison Notebooks* – probably commissioned still under the communist regime but published already two years after the transformation.

In today's Poland, a large majority of the young generation supports right-wing political parties and movements, which often capitalise on a strong and crude anti-communist component. According to one of the common hypotheses, this tendency can be attributed to the fact that the young do not know any other 'language' in which to voice their dissatisfaction and express a social critique apart from the radical right-wing nationalist and xenophobic one.[68] At the same time, left-wing movements find themselves without a common symbolic framework: postmodern currents, popular in academia, are still perceived by the wider public as overly complex and abstract, while classics of Marxism are figures associated with the previous system (and hence totalitarianism, oppression etc). Currently, even left-leaning Polish political movements shy away from associations with Marxist thinkers, in order to avoid creating an image of a 'radical', communist movement.

Could we conceive of Gramsci's 'open Marxism' becoming a point of reference in political and ideological debates and struggles over hegemony in today's Poland? Though the current historical conditions do not seem favourable, a lack of contemporary publications on Gramsci's thought certainly further hinders the enterprise of reintroducing his voice into the intellectual debate. If we were to propose a strategy for bringing back Gramsci's thought to Poland, not just on a historical level, but as a valuable voice on matters which remain of importance, we could express such a plan in terms of Gramsci's theory of translation.

Building on the classification of levels of translation presented in the first part of this chapter, the following steps could be taken: 1) on the level of translating language – a new, accurate, and well-researched edition of some of Gramsci's writings would be necessary; 2) on the level of translating paradigms – a critical introduction or commentary would help clarify Gramsci's concepts, express them in a language relevant for the stage of societal development in which Poland finds itself and relate such reflections to current political problems (such as the rise of the hegemonic nationalist discourse and the role of popular culture in reinforcing it); 3) on the level of translating theory into practice – such a readable, critical edition could help create an accessible, yet conceptually sophisticated language of social critique which would constitute a valuable tool in the contemporary struggle over hegemony in Poland.

---

68   See for instance Kozłowski 2015.

In considering the 'translation' of Gramsci's thought into Polish we should thus think more broadly than just about the material translation of his texts – in which case we could just gladly state, following Krzemień-Ojak, that 'everything has been published'. Rather, we should reflect on *how* these texts have been translated, whether their language is still understandable and relevant in the context of the current stage of societal development and how they could be rendered differently (perhaps better) today. Finally, and crucially, we should ask how Gramsci's philosophy can be translated into a *philosophy of praxis*. Even on the material level, a new translation of the *Prison Notebooks* could be more than just a typical scholarly hardback edition. It could draw on the possibilities offered by technology and knowledge built up by several online projects dedicated to Gramsci (such as the excellent *Quaderni del Carcere Online* and *Gramsci Project*) as well as new trends in editing, perhaps becoming a multi-modal publication, an open-access e-book with an online forum for debates or perhaps even a comic book (Kate Evans's excellent illustrated biography of Rosa Luxemburg has paved the way). For Gramsci's voice on contemporary issues to be heard in contemporary language, his thoughts would have to be translated on all three of the above-described levels.

PART 3

Gramsci and the Marxian Legacy

∴

CHAPTER 7

Time and Revolution in Gramsci's *Prison Notebooks*

Fabio Frosini

1   Past and Present

One can say, as a first approximation, that for Gramsci 'past' and 'present' coincide respectively with 'history' and 'politics':[1] the past is past history and the 'historiography' that recounts it; while the present is politics 'in action' – the real clash of organised forces – and, at the same time, it is the strategic reflection that helps these forces to 'assume positions' within this clash, and to prevail. But historiography is also a political act, a political intervention in the present, inasmuch as it critically interprets the present as an outcome of a determinate past; and political practice is also a form of reflection on the struggle, inasmuch as it criticises the projects of other political forces and strategically elaborates its own.

In short, from a Gramscian perspective it is impossible to separate the 'subjective' aspect from the 'objective' of the times 'past' and 'present': the objectivity of past events is reflected in the subjectivity of historiographical intervention, and the subjectivity of strategic elaboration is incorporated in the objectivity of the struggle unfolding. Real events and ideas of these events are two interlinked aspects; yet not in a static way, but functional: the victories (or defeats) of the past reaffirm themselves in the present thanks to historical accounts, while the conflicting critical and strategic elaborations realised by the forces in struggle help these to 'resolve' the conflict in one or another direction.

The reciprocal or mutual *immanence* of 'events' and 'ideas of these events' is not an evident fact; on the contrary, it is the result of the central philosophical nucleus of Gramsci's thought.[2] Gramsci calls this nucleus the 'unity of theory and of practice'. To be precise: the version of the unity of theory and practice that Gramsci places at the centre of the renewal of Marxism, defined by him as the 'philosophy of praxis', is that which he calls 'translatability of languages'.

---

1   In this chapter I summarise the arguments set out in more detail in Frosini 2009.
2   For a thorough exposition of the notion of immanence in Gramsci's thought see Badaloni 1988, pp. 15–44, Thomas 2009a, ch. 8, and Frosini 2010a, ch. 2.

This theory is a particular development of the Gramscian theory of ideologies. To ideologies, affirms Gramsci, should be assigned a gnoseological and not merely psychological or moral value.[3] Ideologies, in other words, are the terrain on which the knowledge of truth occurs. But given that these are always both instruments of social and political organisation, and interpretations of reality, their functioning is simultaneously of a theoretical-cognitive and practical-organisational character: they are at the same time universal (as they are functional to the knowledge of the truth) and partial (as they are instruments of domination at the service of a social class). Declaring ideologies as the *only* point of access to truth, Gramsci also establishes that there does not exist an 'interpretation' that is not *also*, in some way, a 'transformation' of reality; and, at the same time, he makes it impossible to distinguish *in absolute terms* between partiality and universality, practical commitment and knowledge of the 'truth'.

The distinction will then be between ideologies that, organising social forces and interpreting the 'position' occupied by these in the conflict with other social forces, succeed in prevailing over the others; and ideologies that, incapable of organically 'connecting' interpretation (theory) and organisation (practice), consign the social forces they represent to a subaltern position. The distinction lies in short in the degree of 'power', which coincides with the 'truth': it will not be a qualitative type (in the sense of truth/error), but 'quantitative' (in the sense of the different degrees of capacity to organise practical reality and, in this way, to produce a new reality).[4]

This equalisation of 'truth' and 'power' and this conception of 'ideology' as 'practical power' can appear heterodox from a Marxist point of view. In reality Gramsci draws it from a contextual reading – highly original, it is true – of the *Theses on Feuerbach* with the *Poverty of Philosophy*. In this way, the thesis, according to which 'man must prove the truth, i.e., the reality and power, the this-worldliness of his thinking in practice' ('In der Praxis muß der Mensch die Wahrheit, i.e. Wirklichkeit und Macht, Diesseitigkeit seines Denkens beweisen', thesis 2)[5] is linked by Gramsci to the way in which, in the *Poverty of Philosophy*, Marx considers the practical power of the political economy of Ricardo.[6]

---

3   See below, footnote 30.

4   On this point see more extensively Frosini 2009, pp. 108–20. See also Frosini 2014.

5   Marx 1976a [1845], p. 3; for the original text see Marx 1958 [1845], p. 5.

6   The idea that the philosophy of praxis, formulated in the *Theses on Feuerbach*, finds a coherent development in *The Poverty of Philosophy*, is clearly affirmed by Gramsci: 'The Poverty of Philosophy ... contains fundamental statements concerning the relationship between the structure and the superstructures, and concerning the concept of dialectics specific to historical materialism. From a theoretical point of view, *The Poverty of Philosophy* can be seen as the application and development of the *Theses on Feuerbach*, whereas *The Holy Family* is

The latter, thanks to a precise idea of 'laws' as those which occur *only given certain premises or conditions* (his method of 'let's suppose that')[7] expresses a precise political project, consisting in the occurrence of conditions given by the affirmation of the bourgeoisie as the dominant class. In other words: Ricardo demonstrates the way in which a series of scientific regularities 'springs' from a terrain of political struggle. It is important to stress the relevance – for several reasons – of this reference to Ricardo and to classical political economy. It testifies to the presence, in Gramsci's *Prison Notebooks*, of a genuine interest in the method of economic science, the notion of economic law, abstraction, etc., and, in connection with all this, Marx's *Capital* as a 'critical' turning point in the development of this method.[8] But at the same time the reference to Ricardo's method cannot be confined, for Gramsci, to the terrain of the development of a scientific approach to the 'anatomy' of civil society. Much more than that, as Gramsci writes on 30 May 1932 to his sister-in-law Tatiana Schucht, it has to be asked whether

> Ricardo has been important to the history of philosophy besides the history of economics, in which he's certainly a figure of primary importance ... And can one say that Ricardo helped to direct the early theoreticians of the philosophy of praxis toward going beyond Hegelian philosophy and toward constructing their new historicism, purified of every trace of speculative logic?[9]

In a text written at the same time, Gramsci states that Ricardo has to be considered as 'one of the points of departure of Marx's and Engels's philosophical

---

an intermediate and still vague phase, as one can see from the passages referring to Proudhon and especially to French materialism' (Notebook 4, § 38; Gramsci 1975, pp. 461–2; Gramsci 1996b, p. 185).

7   Gramsci's source, in this respect, is Gide-Rist 1926, pp. 161 and 556.

8   For an exhaustive account of Gramsci's ideas on political economy see Thomas 2009a, pp. 347–62.

9   Gramsci and Schucht 1997, p. 1015 (letter to Tatiana Schucht of 30 May 1932). It is noteworthy that the letters sent by Gramsci to Tatiana Schucht were regularly copied and forwarded by her to the economist Piero Sraffa, who was a covert member of the Italian Communist Party and an influential economist working in Cambridge with John Maynard Keynes. Sraffa, in turn, transcribed the letters and forwarded them to the leadership of the PCd'I in Paris and Moscow. Regarding this background, one can say that in this letter Gramsci is making known to his Party his original interpretation of Marxism as a peculiar form of 'immanenticism': a question whose relevance cannot be overestimated in an age of rigid materialist orthodoxy. For an up-to-date account of this clandestine 'channel of communication' between Gramsci and his Party, and for an assessment of its political significance, see Vacca 2012.

experiences that led to the development of historical materialism'.[10] To sum up, a new interpretation of the link between truth and power goes hand in hand, in Gramsci's *Notebooks*, with a reassessment of the philosophical significance of classical political economy for the development of Marx's approach. What is implied here is that the emphasis on the unity of theory and praxis does not result in an indiscriminate abandonment of the idea of a regularity and rationality in history, just as it does not lead to the reduction of 'truth' and 'universality' to mere 'effects' of a balance of forces.

2   Translatability

The reason for the impossibility of reducing the intertwining of truth and power to nothing but the product of a balance of forces, lies in the theory of translatability, in which we can identify the most innovative and original contribution given by Gramsci to Marxist theory.

It is impossible to reconstruct here the theory of translatability in all of its facets and the history of its genesis in the *Prison Notebooks*.[11] We will therefore limit ourselves to giving a brief outline of it, stressing the overall results to which it leads.

Put succinctly, one can say that the theory of translatability establishes that any 'theoretical' position cannot *really* (i.e. concretely, effectively) be understood, if it is not 'considered' from the point of view of its 'practical' implications, and vice versa, that no 'practical' position can be understood, if one does not 'extract' the 'theory' which is present in it. Theory and practice are united not insofar as they are parallel or identical, but insofar as they are mutually 'translatable': theory is *inside* practice, and practice is *inside* theory. Or better: one sees the *true* meaning of theory only if one translates theory in practice, and vice versa.

This formulation can appear abstract. In reality, nothing could be further from that. An example taken from the *Prison Notebooks* will be sufficient to show it. This example is crucial, because it is precisely on its basis that Gramsci develops the theory of translatability. It concerns the great alternative between France and Germany in the Europe of the age of the Revolution and the Res-

---

10   Notebook 8, §128; Gramsci 1975, p. 1019; English trans. Gramsci 2007a, p. 309.

11   For an accurate account of the theory of translatability in both its aspects – systematic and genetic – see Boothman 2004. See also Frosini 2010a, pp. 167–78 and 2010b, and Lacorte 2010 and 2012.

toration. German philosophy and French politics, Gramsci notes,[12] are two distinct languages – respectively 'theoretical' and 'practical' – which in appearance are wholly opposites and not in communication with one another. But this is true, only if they come to be considered in themselves, as if they were complete and self-sufficient phenomena, that have *within themselves* the criteria to be understood. In reality, national history is incomprehensible if it gets separated from international history, or better: the national 'moment' acquires its true significance (that is its meaning of 'truth-power' in the sense of Marx) only if it comes to be seen as a 'national/international nexus'.[13] The 'nation'

---

12   See Notebook 1, § 44; Gramsci 1975, p. 51; English trans. Gramsci 1992, p. 147; Notebook 1, § 151; Gramsci 1975, p. 134; English trans. Gramsci 1992, p. 231; Notebook 3, § 48; Gramsci 1975, p. 331; English trans. Gramsci 1996b, p. 51; Notebook 4, § 3; Gramsci 1975, p. 423; English trans. Gramsci 1996b, p. 143; Notebook 4, § 42; Gramsci 1975, pp. 467–8; English trans. Gramsci 1996b, p. 192; Notebook 8, § 208; Gramsci 1975, p. 1066; English trans. Gramsci 2007a, p. 355.

13   The most definite and clear enunciation of the relevance of this nexus for the notion of hegemony, and therefore for the whole of the philosophy of praxis, is probably Notebook 14, § 68, where Gramsci comments on a text published by Stalin in 1925 ('Questions and answers. Speech Delivered at the Sverdlov University, June 9, 1925', see Stalin 1954 [1925], pp. 158–214) and republished in Italian translation in the party newspaper *l'Unità* between 20 February and 5 March 1926 (see Paggi 1984, pp. 350–1). Although in the *Notebooks* Gramsci dates it erroneously to 'September 1927', it is to this text that he is undoubtedly referring (see Grigor'eva 1995, p. 114n): 'It deals with certain key problems of the science and art of politics. The problem which seems to me to need further elaboration is the following: how, according to the philosophy of praxis (in its political manifestation) – in the formulation of its founder but particularly in the clarification of its most recent great theoretician – the international situation should be considered in its national aspect. In reality, the "national" relation is the result of an "original", unique (in a certain sense) combination, which needs to be understood and conceived in this originality and uniqueness if one wishes to dominate it and lead it. To be sure, the line of development is towards internationalism, but the point of departure is "national". It is from this point of departure that one must begin. Yet the perspective is international and cannot be otherwise. Consequently, it is necessary to study accurately the combination of national forces that the international class will have to lead and develop, in accordance with the international perspective and directives. The leading class is in fact only such if it accurately interprets this combination, of which it is itself a component and precisely as such is able to give the movement a certain direction, within certain perspectives. In my opinion, the fundamental disagreement between Leone Davidovici [i.e. Trotsky] and Bessarione [i.e. Stalin] as interpreter of the majority movement is on this point. The accusations of nationalism are inept if they refer to the nucleus of the question. If one studies the majoritarians' struggle from 1902 up to 1917, one sees that its originality consists in purging internationalism of every vague and purely ideological (in a pejorative sense) element, to give it a realistic political content. It is in the concept of hegemony that those exigencies which are national in character are knotted together' (Gramsci 1975, pp. 1728–9; English trans. Gramsci 1971a, pp. 240–1).

in relation to the international context, exactly as the individual compared to society, are 'nodal points', whose identity and autonomy (which are not denied by Gramsci) derive from a work of translation; they are in other words the effect of a praxis and not an initial 'given', a contingent (historical) result and not an ontological characteristic.

In this sense, French politics and German philosophy, as 'national' expressions that characterise in an original and unmistakable way France and Germany between Revolution and Restoration, acquire their real meaning only if they are translated into their 'opposite'. Thus, in Jacobin politics there is implicitly contained a 'philosophy'. Gramsci recognises the subsequent developments of this philosophy in the great historical experiences of 1848 and 1917, respectively in the 'slogan', launched by Marx, of 'revolution in permanence',[14] and in the theory and practice of 'hegemony' developed by Lenin.[15] Vice versa, in German classical philosophy there is contained a politics, that consists in the theoretical comprehension of the meaning of the Revolution, a comprehension that realises, at the same time, its speculative translation, i.e. an 'absorption' of the practical effects of the Revolution within the frameworks of liberal civilisation and the state. This opposite 'translation' with respect to Jacobinism, not of practice into theory but of theory into practice, is, as will be seen later, that which Gramsci at a certain point calls 'passive revolution'.[16]

3   'Personality' and 'Human Reality'

Translatability is, as has been seen, a development of the thesis of Marx, according to which the truth and power of thought are demonstrated in praxis. Translatability in other words renders comprehensible how the unity of truth and power is concretely realised, without truth getting reduced to power nor vice versa, that power becomes a mere expression of truth. This 'equilibrium', this 'dialectic' between the two moments of universality and particularity explains the way in which Gramsci interprets the relation, which I recalled at the beginning, between subjective time and objective time: the relation between subjective intervention, i.e. the element of politics in action, and that of the identification of the real conditions, i.e. the narration of history.

---

14   See Notebook 1, § 44; Gramsci 1975, p. 53; English trans. Gramsci 1992, p. 150; Notebook
      8, § 52; Gramsci 1975, pp. 972–3; Gramsci 2007a, p. 267; Notebook 9, § 133; Gramsci 1975,
      p. 1195.
15   See Notebook 10 I, § 12; Gramsci 1975, p. 1235.
16   See Kanoussi 2000, pp. 66–81, Thomas 2006, Burgio 2009, pp. 127–50.

Between subjective time and objective time there is not, according to Gramsci, a real separation; they are 'abstractions' made within a single reality. For the philosophy of praxis, between the sphere of the individual and that of society (and the state) there does not exist a substantial disparity; rather: resuming a tradition of thought that goes back to Machiavelli and, passing through Bruno and Spinoza, arrives at Hegel and Marx, Gramsci rejects any notion of an 'internal' experience (purely individual), that could be separated from external expression, from the concrete practice of the individual, that are always already social practice and in some sense 'political'.

This concept emerges in a text of Notebook 9 (§ 99), belonging to the section on the *Risorgimento*: 'The national personality (like the individual personality) is an abstraction if it is conceived outside the international (and social) nexus. National personality expresses a "distinction" of the international complex, therefore it is linked to international relations'.[17]

This is a very complex text, which I will try to analyse by points:

a) the word 'personality' indicates the unmistakable composition that constitutes the person and which is much more than the mere individual: the person is not serial, but has a structure, an individual and unique structure in the last instance.

b) The term 'personality' is used to designate the nation exactly like the individual, in the sense that the individual with respect to society is a person exactly like the nation with respect to international relations.

c) If one separates the nation from the 'international nexus', or the individual from the 'social nexus', one falls into 'abstractions' without meaning.

d) This structural connection of the 'person' with the 'nexus' does not nullify the uniqueness of the 'person'; on the contrary, it is its foundation; in fact, it is on the basis of this connection that the 'distinction' is produced.

e) It follows that only by recognising the primacy of the 'nexus' and of the 'complex' in relation to the individual elements that constitute it, will these elements be recognised in their originality and real, authentic uniqueness. In other words: 'relations' precede the 'distinct', they constitute it as 'distinct', i.e. as an *autonomous* element.

f) There is not a real difference between the individual moment and collective or national moment; on the contrary, the original 'personality' is

---

17   Gramsci 1975, p. 1161.

produced at all levels, individual and collective, but can be recognised only if one abandons the point of view according to which the individual precedes society.

g)   But Gramsci also implicitly criticises the opposite idea, that society precedes the individual: the term 'distinct' is an index, written by Gramsci in quotes to signal a specific, technical usage.[18] The reference is evidently to the Crocean theory of 'distincts', according to which the unity of reality does not nullify its constitutive elements, but on the contrary exists as a unity of these elements only thanks to the independence and autonomy of each of these. Hence, Gramsci is opposed to the holistic approach developed by the actualism of Gentile.

Against Gentile, Gramsci uses 'distinction'; but, thinking the latter as an aspect that *gets produced* by the 'nexus' or 'complex', outside of which it is a mere 'abstraction', he redefines the Crocean concept in a materialistic way. This double distancing leads to conceiving the 'singularity' of the elements of reality as, on the one hand real and effective, but on the other as transitory products of a complex of relations, which the elements 'express'. Individual and collective, also like active and passive, are not opposed, but necessarily imply each other.

The idea that the philosophy of praxis is born as a complete rupture with the traditional alternative of materialism and idealism, is enunciated by Gramsci in relation to the *Theses on Feuerbach*, in which he – following Engels – identifies the 'brilliant germ' of the new philosophical position of Marx.[19] Also in the passage of Notebook 9 just discussed, on national and individual 'personality', the double critique of individualism and holism is justified with an implicit, but very clear, reference to thesis 6 on Feuerbach, in which the same word recurs – *abstraction (Abstraktum)* – also used by him in the text of Notebook 9: 'But human reality is not an *abstraction* immanent in the single individual. In its reality it is the ensemble of the social relations' (in Gramsci's own translation of the sixth thesis: 'Ma la realtà umana non è un'astrazione immanente nel singolo individuo. Nella sua realtà è l'insieme dei rapporti sociali').[20]

---

18   On this point see Guzzone (2017).

19   'Es sind Notizen für spätere Ausarbeitung, rasch hingeschrieben, aber unschätzbar als das erste Dokument, worin der geniale Keim der neuen Weltanschauung niedergelegt ist' (Engels 1962 [1888], p. 264). And see Notebook 4, § 3; Gramsci 1975, p. 424; English trans. Gramsci 1996b, p. 144.

20   Gramsci's translation in Gramsci 2007b, p. 744. See Marx 1976a [1845], p. 4; for the original text see Marx 1958 [1845], p. 6.

4   Present Time and Hegemony

The past-present nexus therefore signifies, when not understood in an abstract way, that a series of 'elements' that compose a determinate 'personality' – whether individual, collective or national – are *reorganised* on the basis of a determinate project. This reorganisation coincides with that which Gramsci – referring to the experience of the individual – calls 'adherence to the present'. The present, he writes, is not only a 'surpassing' of the past, but is, specifically, its '*criticism*'. This criticism must also be a criticism of 'that part of ourselves' which corresponds to the past. It is necessary in short 'to have an exact consciousness of this real critique and to give it not only a theoretical, but *political* expression. In other words we must be more adherent to the present, which we ourselves have contributed to creating, having consciousness of the past and its continuation (and reliving)'.[21] The past-present nexus poses in short a problem of contemporaneity (or anachronism).

However, this problem of the *political articulation* of the past/present nexus exists for Gramsci, as has been seen, on both the individual and collective plane. The single human being, the political party, the entire nation: the political necessity to 'adhere to the present' makes itself felt on all these levels. Only by organically connecting actual practice to past history, and vice versa, does it become possible to be 'contemporary'. However, this does not mean making a given element coincide with a presumed 'course of history'. Just the opposite: the 'course of history' is none other than the 'effect of necessity' produced on the national and international plane by a given hegemonic articulation, and this latter, in turn, is the result of the capacity that a determinate national class possesses to realise coherent 'translations', i.e. capable of 'universalising' its own ideology, organising the national/international nexus to its own advantage.

Consequently, 'present time' can be defined as the intertwining of hegemonic practices, an intertwining that realises itself in distinct ways at the personal/individual, local, national and international level. Therefore, present time is never a unitary fact, but, structurally, it is the contingent unitary effect – on different spatial levels – of a plurality of relations always in movement, and which only temporarily acquire a certain stability.[22] It also follows that,

---

21   Notebook 1, § 156; Gramsci 1975, p. 137; English trans. Gramsci 1992, p. 234 (translation modified).

22   In this sense it can be said that Gramsci draws on Marx's sixth thesis on Feuerbach, with a particular emphasis on the anti-metaphysical implications contained in the use of the French 'ensemble' instead of 'totality' (*das Ganze, Totalität*). On the notion of 'ensemble'

when Gramsci (in the just quoted passage from Notebook 1 concerning the 'adherence' to the present time) affirms the necessity to criticise politically the past/present nexus, he is not referring to an adjustment to a 'present' understood as a unitary, absolute and static space. He thinks, instead, of a hegemonic kind of intervention, thanks to which the relation between the 'complex' of relations and a determinate 'distinct', that expresses this nexus, comes to be *rearticulated* in a manner to render this 'distinct' less dependent on the complex, and therefore much more capable of contributing to determining the balance of forces in the overall context.

The mere 'flow' of time does not 'decide' the changes that can occur in its interior. Time, inasmuch as it is a bearer of a determinate meaning or significance, is always incorporated in a series of spatial (geographical) determinations, that in turn result from the way in which the various hegemonic articulations mutually and reciprocally dispose themselves.[23] Therefore one can really speak of 'past' and 'present' (i.e. of genuinely temporally distinct dimensions), only if one is in the presence of a, real or possible, *modification* of the relations among the elements that one finds in this time/space (or pluralised time).

5   The 'Two Principles of Historical Materialism'

The modification, real or possible, of the relations between the elements of space-time corresponds to that which Marx, in the *Preface* to *A Contribution to the Critique of Political Economy*, calls 'an era of social revolution'.[24] It arises, Marx maintains, at the moment in which the 'social relations' within which the 'productive forces' were hitherto developed, turn (*umschlagen*) from 'forms of development' into their 'fetters'.[25]

It is in this moment, and only in this, that the question of a 'revolution' of the entire society is posed: each 'stage' (*Stufe*) of development of the nexus between productive forces and relations of production must have reached its limit, and it is at that point that the alternative between the 'past' and the 'present' is concretely posed: 'Mankind thus – concludes Marx – inevitably sets itself only such tasks as it is able to solve'.[26]

---

see Luporini 1967, pp. lxxxiii–lxxxiv, Luporini 1974, pp. 382–4, Balibar 2007 [1993], pp. 30–2, Macherey 2008, pp. 150–60, Frosini 2009, pp. 50–1, Balibar 2014.

23   See Frosini 2013a.

24   See Marx 1987b [1859], p. 263; for the original text see Marx 1961 [1859], p. 9.

25   Ibid.

26   Ibid.

Marx therefore postulates two distinct 'times': one of development and one of crisis. In the time of development one has the quantitative expansion of a given structure constituted by a certain relation between productive forces and relations of production; in the time of crisis one has the qualitative reorganisation of these elements in a new structure, in the sense that new relations of production 'replace' the old, but these must *already* be formed within the old society. The role of politics is circumscribed to periods of crisis. Here also, however, politics performs a function of *support* to those relations that 'already' must have been formed within the old society, and this formation is a 'natural' process exactly like that of the development of the productive forces.

The property relations change, therefore, only as a consequence of the change of the relations of production. Or put differently: the same *swerve* from 'development' to 'crisis' is an element *internal* to 'development'. Consequently, the modification between the elements of space-time is also an expression of the logic of continuity. On this basis, the relation between 'past' and 'present' is dominated by the 'past'. And it is this, i.e. the material base of society, that produces in its interior the 'conditions', and the 'tasks' corresponding to these. In short, the clear distinction between development and crisis postulated by Marx, resolves itself in an 'absorption' of the crisis within development, in the sense that the crisis is explained departing from development, but one cannot say the converse: development is not comprehensible departing from crisis.

Now, if we return to the initial question, namely the past/present nexus as the key for understanding the relation between time and revolution, we must recognise the profound distance between the *Preface* to *A Contribution to the Critique of Political Economy* and the approach of Gramsci. And yet this is precisely one of the texts to which he appeals with increasing conviction in order to delineate the contours of his 'return to Marx'[27] and, on this basis, to define the 'philosophy of praxis'. This attention can be considered a strategic choice, dictated by the fact that the *Preface* was commonly considered as the distillate of historical materialism, and was therefore read in a deterministic and economistic key.

The point of attack of Gramsci is precisely the nexus between the 'maturation' of 'conditions' in the womb of the 'old' society, and the 'tasks' that are born from and depend on this 'maturation', in which we have recognised the foundation of the primacy of 'development' over 'crisis'. In the *Preface* this nexus is

---

27   On Gramsci's 'return to Marx' see Izzo 2009, pp. 23–74.

presented as that between a *premise* (the 'conditions') and a *consequence* (the 'tasks'). In connecting the two moments, Marx in fact uses the adverb *daher*, '*that's why ...*'.[28]

It is on this point that Gramsci intervenes, transforming the gap between premise and consequence into an organic interlacing between 'two principles' which it is necessary to *mediate dialectically*.[29] Gramsci conceives the relation between conditions and consequences, or between material premise and political initiative, as a pair of opposites that return to some form of dialectical unity. This idea is justified by his approach to Marxism: according to Gramsci Marxism is born, as has been seen, with the *Theses on Feuerbach*, as a dismissal of the speculative alternative between materialism and idealism and, therefore, of the same idea of a 'speculative' philosophy. The primacy of real 'conditions' on political 'praxis' is, from this point of view, inadequate to express Marx's theoretical revolution, and risks throwing Marxism backwards, towards the old forms of reductionism and anti-dialectical dichotomies. The intertwining of 'truth' and 'power', the conception of ideologies as jointly the site of knowledge and practical transformation,[30] in the end the theory of translatability: these ele-

---

28   'Eine Gesellschaftsformation geht nie unter, bevor alle Produktivkräfte entwickelt sind, für die sie weit genug ist, und neue höhere Produktionsverhältnisse treten nie an die Stelle, bevor die materiellen Existenzbedingungen derselben im Schoß der alten Gesellschaft selbst ausgebrütet worden sind. *Daher* stellt sich die Menschheit immer nur Aufgaben, die sie lösen kann ...' (Marx 1961 [1859], p. 9, my emphasis).

29   This difference was noted and commented upon by Gerratana 1997, pp. 83–118 (see esp. pp. 109–12).

30   This conception of ideologies as the terrain where both true knowledge and action take place is drawn by Gramsci from another passage in the 1859 *Preface*, where Marx observes that 'in studying such transformations [i.e. the "era of social revolution"] it is always necessary to distinguish between the material transformation of the economic conditions of production, which can be determined with the precision of natural science, and the legal, political, religious, artistic or philosophic – in short, ideological forms *in which men become conscious of this conflict and fight it out*' (Marx 1987b [1859], p. 263, my emphasis). The last remark is a quite secondary and incidental one, since Marx focuses on the *difference* between the scientific investigation of the transformation of society, and the ideological representation of them, rather on the function played by the ideologies. In contrast, Gramsci makes this remark the basis for his own notion of the 'gnoseological' function of the ideological superstructures, as he states explicitly in Notebook 4, § 37: 'When dealing with the question of the "objectivity" of knowledge from the point of view of historical materialism, the point of departure should be the affirmation by Marx (a well-known passage in the introduction to *A Contribution to the Critique of Political Economy*) that "men become conscious (of this conflict) on the ideological level" of juridical, political, religious, artistic or philosophical forms. *But is this consciousness limited solely to the conflict between the material forces of production and the relations of production – as Marx's text literally states – or does it apply to all consciousness, that is, to all knowledge?* This is the

ments, that constitute the Marxism of Gramsci, prevent the detachment, if not by abstraction, of the objective side from the subjective.

6 'Permanent Revolution' and 'Passive Revolution'

The truth-power of the 'two principles' of historical materialism will only result from their mediation. On this point, Gramsci makes two apparently inconsistent affirmations. The first dates to October of 1930, and is resumed, in the second draft, in 1932.[31] In its first version, Gramsci affirms: 'In the meantime, one might say that the dialectical mediation between the two principles of historical materialism mentioned at the beginning of this note is the concept of permanent revolution.'[32] The second affirmation dates to April–May of 1933:

> The concept of 'passive revolution' must be rigorously derived from the two fundamental principles of political science: 1. that no social formation disappears as long as the productive forces which have developed within it still find room for further forward movement; 2. that a society does not set itself tasks for whose solution the necessary conditions have not already been incubated, etc. It goes without saying that these principles must first be developed critically in all their implications, and purged of every residue of mechanism and fatalism. They must therefore be referred back to the description of the three fundamental moments into which a 'situation' or an equilibrium of forces can be distinguished, with the greatest possible stress on the second moment (equilibrium of political forces), and especially on the third moment (politico-military equilibrium).[33]

---

problem which can be worked out with the whole ensemble of the philosophical theory of the value of ideological superstructures' (Gramsci 1975, p. 455; English trans. Gramsci 1996b, p. 177).

31 For the dating of texts in the *Prison Notebooks*, I rely on Cospito 2011b, pp. 896–904.

32 Notebook 4, § 38; Gramsci 1975, pp. 456–7; English trans. Gramsci 1996b, p. 179. The second version contains a few variations which are not secondary and unimportant: 'In the meantime, one might say that the dialectical mediation between the two methodological principles of historical materialism mentioned at the beginning of this note can be sought in the historical-political formula of permanent revolution' (Notebook 13, § 17; Gramsci 1975, p. 1582).

33 Notebook 15, § 17; Gramsci 1975, p. 1774; English trans. Gramsci 1971a, pp. 106–7.

The two texts date back to different moments of elaboration in the *Prison Notebooks* and partly reflect distinct preoccupations: the first belongs to a crucial moment in the development of the concept of hegemony, while the second is one of the points of arrival in the reflection on the concept of 'passive revolution'. These belong, however, to the same fundamental problematic, as is apparent not only from the common reference to Marx's *Preface*, but also from the fact that passive revolution is a *type of hegemony*.[34] Finally, in the text of Notebook 4, immediately after the passage I cited, Gramsci elaborates for the first time that notion of 'relations of forces',[35] which in the text of Notebook 15 is recalled as the conceptual framework that permits a non-fatalistic or mechanistic understanding of the two 'principles' of the *Preface*.

Hegemonic processes, relations of forces, theory of history: herein lies the common horizon of these two notes. There exists however a trait that clearly distinguishes them. In one case Gramsci speaks of 'dialectical mediation' of the two principles, while in the second he speaks of a 'rigorous deduction'. In essence: if the nexus between past and present (between 'conditions' and 'political action') is dialectically mediated, one has the concept of 'permanent

---

34   This point is constantly misinterpreted in the literature. As a matter of fact, Gramscian scholars tend regularly to *oppose* 'hegemony' (which in turn is reduced to its early Jacobin version) to 'passive revolution' (understood as a repressive socio-political innovation, or 'revolution from above'). The truth is, on the contrary, that neither bourgeois hegemony can be confined to its original 'progressive' and democratic form of the French Revolution, nor is a passive revolution *only* a form of 'restoration'. The most important case of 'passive revolution' taken into account in the *Notebooks* is Italian fascism. This, Gramsci writes, can be considered as 'a new "liberalism" under modern conditions', that is, as an innovative replica of nineteenth-century 'liberalism' (Notebook 8, § 236; Gramsci 1975, pp. 1088–9; English trans. Gramsci 2007a, p. 378). This text can be dated to April 1932. But already in February–March 1930, Gramsci writes a note on what he calls 'Jacobinism (of content)' as distinguished from the early Jacobinism. This new kind of Jacobinism, he writes, 'found its formal perfection in the parliamentary regime which, in the period of the greatest abundance of "private" energies in society, brought about the hegemony of the urban class over the whole population in the Hegelian form of government with permanently organized consent (with the organization being left to private initiative and thus having a moral or ethical character since it was, in one way or another, a "voluntary" consent)' (Notebook 1, § 48; Gramsci 1975, p. 58; English trans. Gramsci 1992, p. 155). Here we have a vivid description of what Gramsci will call 'war of position', as the kind of struggle carried out by the bourgeoisie in the nineteenth century. And in Notebook 8, § 236, he refers to just this point when he writes: 'Thus one might say that, in the previous historical cycle, the French Revolution was a "war of movement," whereas the liberal epoch of the 19th century was a long war of position' (Gramsci 1975, p. 1089; English trans. Gramsci 2007a, p. 378). The 'long war of position', that is the 'Jacobinism (of content)' as a historical development of bourgeois hegemony, is now called passive revolution.

35   Cf. Notebook 4, § 38; Gramsci 1975, pp. 457–9; English trans. Gramsci 1996b, pp. 180–2.

revolution', while if from this same nexus one carries out a simple 'deduction', that which results is 'passive revolution'. In fact, in the same Notebook 15, in a text of June–July 1933, significantly entitled *Past and Present. First epilogue*, Gramsci again recalls that: 'It would seem that the theory of passive revolution is a necessary critical corollary to the *Introduction to the Critique of political economy*'.[36]

What exactly does 'necessary critical corollary' mean? A corollary is a 'consequence'. Therefore, we are confronted here by a clear and precise warning on the part of Gramsci: the way in which the past/present nexus is presented in the *Preface, per se*, propels one to think history as a process of molecular accumulation, that *by definition* always assigns a preponderant role to the 'past'. Historical innovation 'springs' from an internal dynamic of the already dominant elements. This happens because, if 'past' and 'present' – i.e. theory and practice, history and politics – are not understood in their *dialectical unity*, history tends to appear as an objective flux, in which the only political action is that of those who, wanting to 'revolutionise' the existing conditions, have to choose: either they act on the basis of these, or they will be confined to an unrealistic subjectivism.

Herein lies therefore the 'necessity' of that 'corollary', and the 'critical' character of this consequence of the theory of Marx. That consequence must be drawn, and in other words the 'theory of passive revolution' *must be developed*, in order to demonstrate the *risks* of that way of understanding history. And that is, in the terms of Gramsci, to show that, so long as the 'two principles' of the *Preface* are treated *separately*, the first will have the upper hand and the 'present' will be the continuation of the past. Passive revolution arises, in fact, when (as has been seen above regarding Germany and France) the 'translation', i.e. the unity of philosophy and politics, is realised departing from philosophy; i.e. when a class of intellectuals succeeds in 'absorbing' within its own discourse the political dimension of the class struggle, rendering possible a development devoid of deep and profound trauma and real innovation.

But, in its own way, passive revolution is also a 'translation', that is a form of the unity of theory and practice, i.e. in the last instance, of hegemony. Herein lies the *proximity* between 'passive revolution' and 'revolution in permanence'. The latter emerges, as Gramsci writes, when the struggle and the practices of insubordination of the dominated classes are unified in a 'hegemony', i.e. when it is understood – at the price of bloody struggles and of many defeats – that the subalterns can escape from their condition, only when they will have learned

---

36   Notebook 15, § 62; Gramsci 1975, p. 1827; English trans. Gramsci 1971a, p. 114.

to realise, *from their point of view*, the 'translation' of theory and practice. *From their point of view*: i.e. departing from practice, that is as a process of real, political unification of their mentality in a coherent praxis. This development is not absent from Marx's *Preface*, on the condition that the two 'principles' are mediated dialectically. From the dialectical mediation of the two principles, in other words, arises the capacity, which only thanks to the organic intellectuals and to the 'modern prince' is made possible, to rethink the past as political struggle and the present as the site of the constitution of truth-power.

Both revolution in permanence and passive revolution are therefore forms of hegemony. But it matters whether the translation occurs *departing from theory* or *departing from practice*. Departing from theory leads inevitably to the production of the representation of a unitary time, whose own unfolding brings forth the 'revolution'. This risk is present in Marx, not incidentally, at the moment of the defeat and diminishing of the whole proletarian front. The 'laws' of political economy, like the 'laws' of history, are the crystallisations of hegemonic processes, but they 'express' these processes from the point of view of theory, not of practice.

The reference to Ricardo's 'philosophical' relevance for the formulation of Marx's 'philosophy of praxis' must be read in this sense. In Ricardo, Gramsci is saying, Marx could find a vivid example of a 'theory' that is *at the same time* characterised by the partiality proper to a hegemonic force and by the universality of an 'objective' apprehension of the development of society.[37] In this coalescence of commitment and impartiality Marx could find at the same time the seeds of his new 'philosophy of praxis' and the temptation to indulge in a mechanistic interpretation of economic laws. What is at stake is then the ability to hold together these two sides, avoiding both the risk of falling back into an idea of praxis as something *opposed* to circumstances, and that of committing to the impersonal 'laws' of history the realisation of our will.

---

37   See the definition of the 'fatalist economists' as 'the historians of this epoch, [who] have no other mission than that of showing how wealth is acquired in bourgeois production relations, of formulating these relations into categories, into laws, and of showing how superior these laws, these categories, are for the production of wealth to the laws and categories of feudal society' (Marx 1976b [1847], p. 176).

CHAPTER 8

From Marx's *Diesseitigkeit* to Gramsci's *terrestrità assoluta*

Aaron Bernstein

1   Introduction

Antonio Gramsci's reformulation of Marxism as a 'philosophy of praxis' in the *Prison Notebooks* has been subjected to diverse interpretations. During the early years of its reception, following the publication of a thematic edition of the *Prison Notebooks* in the late 1940s and early 1950s, the term was often thought to be a mere synonym or camouflage for 'Marxism', 'historical materialism', or 'Marxism-Leninism', a circumlocution designed to evade the prison censorship, and which signalled Gramsci's adherence to the orthodox Marxism of the Third International.[1] In contrast, other interpretations understood the term 'philosophy of praxis' as indicative of Gramsci's subversion, whether intentional or not, of 'true' Marxism, due to the influence of Italian neo-idealism, Hegelianism, or even the subjective idealism of Fichte and Schelling, on his thought.[2] However, more recent scholarship, with the help of the 1975 publication in Italian of the critical edition of the *Prison Notebooks* under the editorship of Valentino Gerratana,[3] and not long after, the important research of Gianni Francioni,[4] has established that this locution, whose emergence and progressive formation in the *Prison Notebooks* can be philologically traced, in fact represents a distinctive conception of Marxism and its unique philosophical status.[5]

---

1   Cf. Felice Platone's commentary on the postwar thematic edition of the *Prison Notebooks*, Gramsci 1948–51. Wolfgang Fritz Haug has critically examined these positions in Haug 1999 and 2000.

2   For different variants of this position, cf. Althusser and Balibar 1970, Riechers 1970, and more recently Vanzulli 2013.

3   Gramsci 1975, which provided scholars with access, for the first time, to the *Prison Notebooks* in the original form in which they were written.

4   Francioni 1984.

5   Cf. Liguori 2006, Frosini 2003a, Frosini 2004a, Frosini 2008a, Liguori and Voza (eds) 2009, Thomas 2010, and Haug 1999, 2000, and 2001.

Nevertheless, despite these gains, the existing literature on this topic has not thoroughly studied the centrality of Marx as arguably the most important point of reference for Gramsci's development of the concept of the philosophy of praxis.[6] The emergence and progressive elaboration of this concept in the *Prison Notebooks*, which cannot be found in Gramsci's pre-prison writings, is in fact indissolubly intertwined with a curious 'rediscovery' of Marx and his philosophical significance, one which not only involves a drastic shift in Gramsci's understanding and evaluation of Marx's thought in relation to his earlier views, but also in his understanding of philosophy. In contrast to Gramsci's youthful conception, according to which Marx was philosophically without value, and his thinking tainted by positivism, a view that led the young Gramsci to filter Marx's thought through the mediation of neo-Hegelian categories,[7] in prison Gramsci comes to see Marx as the founder of a wholly independent and original conception of the world, a new philosophy which not only supersedes all prior philosophical thought, but fundamentally redefines the entire nature of philosophy itself. Consequently, accurately understanding Gramsci's reinterpretation of Marx in prison is indispensable for an understanding of his broader concept of the philosophy of praxis.[8]

This chapter seeks to examine the nature and significance of Gramsci's reformulation of Marxism as a philosophy of praxis, specifically as this depends on a unique re-reading of Marx, and whose centre of gravity lies in the 'Theses on Feuerbach'.[9] I argue that the locus of this conception lies in Gramsci's re-elaboration of Marx's affirmation of the this-worldliness (*Diesseitigkeit*) of thought that demonstrates its truth, reality and power, in practice into the terms of an 'absolute immanence', or an 'absolute worldliness or earthliness' of thought, the consequence of which is a sophisticated understanding of the dynamics of knowing and interpreting within political struggles which highlights the necessarily partial nature of political truths. Marx's proposal of the unity of theory and practice in the 'Theses' becomes, in Gramsci's philosophy of praxis, the actual partial standpoint, or 'visual angle' from which Marxist theory grasps both itself as a mode of theorising and knowing from a specific position

---

6   The recent research of Fabio Frosini constitutes the major exception. Cf. Frosini 2001, 2004a, 2009, and 2011. Thomas 2010 also contains suggestive insights in this regard.

7   See in particular Gramsci 1982, p. 514, Gramsci 1984, pp. 348–9, Izzo 2011, p. 81. On Gramsci's early idealism, see Basile 2011, pp. 117–28.

8   Giasi 2011 provides insights regarding the specific Marxian texts to which Gramsci had access in prison.

9   Henceforth, referred to simply as the 'Theses'.

and point of view inside the struggle, as well as the theoretical discourses and representations of its antagonists.

2 A Philosophy of the Act (Praxis) in the Profane Sense: Gramsci, Labriola, and Gentile

The commencement of Notebook 4, in May 1930, signals emphatically Gramsci's 'return to Marx'.[10] The fourth notebook, the first of a bloc of notebooks bearing the title 'Notes on Philosophy. Materialism and Idealism', represents the start of an extended meditation concerning the nature, meaning, and significance of Marx's thought, one which is explicitly philosophical and pursued continuously over the course of Notebooks 7 and 8 (the second and third series respectively, of 'Notes on Philosophy. Materialism and Idealism').[11] From the outset, this enterprise is structured around a determinate plan, namely, that

> The essential part of historical materialism ... of Marxism consists in its surpassing of the old philosophies and also in its way of conceiving philosophy – and this is what must be systematically demonstrated and developed. In the realm of theory, Marxism is not to be confused with or reduced to any other philosophy; it is original not only because it surpasses previous philosophies but also, and above all, because it opens up a completely new road: in other words, it renews from top to bottom the whole way of conceiving philosophy.[12]

Gramsci further specifies that 'this new construction of his (Marx), this new philosophy', which leads to 'the overthrow of the question of philosophy from its traditional position ... the death of philosophy in the traditional sense', 'is already clearly evident in the theses on Feuerbach'.[13]

---

10 Buci-Glucksmann 1980, p. 21; Frosini 2001, p. 33.
11 Chronologically extending from May 1930–May 1932.
12 Q4, §11, pp. 432–3.
13 Q1, §132, p. 119, Q4, §3, p. 424. Requested in a letter to Tatiana Schucht dated 24 March 1930, Gramsci received and translated Engels's edited version of the 'Theses' sometime during the period from March to November 1930, and which chronologically corresponds to the composition of the first series of 'Notes on Philosophy' (Notebook 4). See Frosini 2004a, p. 99.

According to Gramsci, the essential core of Marx's theory lies in the super-session of all previous philosophical thought, in particular the classic opposition between traditional philosophical materialism and idealism, on the basis of an original philosophical construction achieved by Marx in his 'Theses', i.e. a new and original conception of the world implicit in, but never systematically expounded by Marx himself.[14] By identifying the 'Theses' as the foundation of a new philosophical construction, Gramsci is in fact conducting a belated intervention into a crucial debate that took place in Italy at the turn of the century over how to understand Marx, taking the side of Antonio Labriola against Giovanni Gentile, the former's interpretation of Marx's thought as a philosophy of praxis against the latter's dualistic, speculative idealist misinterpretation, especially of the 'Theses', which Gentile exploited as the central text in order to philosophically decapitate Marxism.[15]

This is evident in Gramsci's earliest suggestion (Autumn 1930) of a potential reworking of historical materialism along the lines of a philosophy of praxis:

> neither idealistic nor materialistic 'monism', neither 'Matter' nor 'Spirit', but rather *'historical materialism'*, that is to say, concrete human activity (history): namely activity concerning a certain organised 'matter' (material forces of production) and the 'nature' transformed by man. Philosophy of the act (praxis), not of the 'pure act' but rather of the 'impure' – that is, the real – act, in the profane sense of the word.[16]

Here, Gramsci is tacitly challenging Gentile's earlier interpretation of Marx's 'Theses', the edited Engelsian version of which he was the first to translate into Italian in 1899. According to Gentile's idealist misinterpretation,[17] Marx was supposedly attempting to synthesise praxis and activity, conceived speculatively as that of thought, with material reality, understood in traditional philosophical terms as the metaphysics of matter.[18] It follows that Marx's attempt to correct metaphysical materialism by re-conceptualising matter in dynamic movement as a result of subjective human praxis, and thus, to move from

---

14   Q4, §1, pp. 419–20, Q4, §3, p. 424, Q4, §39, p. 465.

15   On this Italian debate over Marx, see De Giovanni 1983, pp. 3–25.

16   Q4, §37, p. 455.

17   A misinterpretation aided by a mistranslation of some parts of the 'Theses'. Cf. the first thesis, in which (in Engels's edited version), 'thing [*Gegenstand*]', was replaced with 'the term of thought', Gentile 2014, p. 116. Similarly, Marx's 'objective [*gegenständliche*] activity', was explained as activity that creates or produces the sensible object, Gentile 2014, p. 121.

18   Gentile 2014, pp. 126–9, 225, 232.

a static metaphysics of matter to a *historical* materialism, is utterly incoherent, and the very notion of a 'historical materialism', an oxymoron.[19] Gentile thus argued that Marx's philosophy of praxis was traversed by an insurmountable contradiction between form (praxis) and content (matter), the concept of praxis as developed by philosophical idealism and the attempt to apply this to sensuous reality. On this basis, he concluded that Marx's philosophical construction, the true character of which was contained in the 'Theses', relapsed into a platonic metaphysical dualism between thought and reality, the spiritual praxis of the subject and material reality, the subject and object of knowledge, idealism and materialism.[20] Gentile's re-reading of the 'Theses' served as the basis for the later elaboration of his own philosophy of spirit as the pure act (which Gramsci here explicitly criticises), conceived by the former as the only coherent solution to the dyadic metaphysical opposition between thought and reality, subject and object, in which the activity of thought itself constitutes reality, thus forming the foundation of objective truth and knowledge. The metaphysics of transcendence was therefore, purportedly overcome in his 'actual idealism', a veritable absolute immanence securing the identity of thought and reality in the action of the former.[21]

In other words, at stake in the above passage is not only the philosophical significance of Marx's 'Theses', but also that of the concept of immanence, a novel non-metaphysical re-conceptualisation of which Gramsci had repeatedly asserted lay at the basis of Marx's new concept of philosophy,[22] and in this connection, Gramsci is undoubtedly defending Labriola against Gentile. Without explicitly referring to the 'Theses', Labriola, in *Socialism and Philosophy* (1898),[23] defended the philosophical autonomy and specificity of Marx's historical materialism as a 'philosophy of praxis'[24] which transcends all

---

19   For Gentile, matter in historical movement would seize to be matter, Gentile 2014, p. 229.

20   Gentile 2014, pp. 120, 223, 225, 229, 231–3. Thus, Gentile understood Marx's eleventh thesis as a demand for philosophers, by purely intellectual and spiritual means to transform a material world with which this spiritual and philosophical praxis was fundamentally incompatible, Gentile 2014, p. 231.

21   Gentile 1987, pp. 14–21, Gentile 1923, pp. 31–71, 246–7. This idea was obviously tacitly presupposed in his earlier critique of Marx, providing Gentile with the opportunity to plant the seeds for his later, mature philosophy. Cf. Salina, Introduction to Gentile 2014, p. 5; Frosini 2004a, p. 98.

22   Cf. Q4, §11, p. 433 and Q4, §17, p. 438. On the concept of immanence in Western thought, cf. Yovel 1989; Frosini 2004b, p. 2; Thomas 2010, pp. 320–2.

23   Gramsci did not have this text in prison, but he had previously owned a copy, and had most certainly read it. See Buttigieg's 'Notes' in Gramsci 1992, p. 441.

24   It was Labriola who coined this term.

previous forms of philosophical materialism and idealism.[25] It does so on the basis of a non-idealist concept of praxis, understood as human work, labour, and material production. It is the historically variable social relations in which labour and production are organised that provides the framework within which humans relate to their material and social environment.[26] This in turn generated a conception of all thought and relations of knowledge as historically constituted on the basis of material, social, and practical life, and in which the specificity of Marx's thought as a 'philosophy of praxis' lay in its status as a thought-form radically opposed to all forms of metaphysics and speculative transcendence, both that of traditional philosophical idealism and materialism, i.e. a new philosophy wholly 'immanent' in the non-metaphysical sense to the reality about which it philosophises, insofar as Marx's theory consciously and critically recognises its own concrete foundations in the historical, material, social, and political practices that form its basis and which it strives to comprehend in order to transform.[27]

In the above passage (Q4, §37), Gramsci defends Labriola's earlier philosophical positions, thus affirming exactly what Gentile had denied; indeed, Marx's thought could be considered a philosophy of the act (praxis), but not in Gentile's sense as a contradictory attempt to synthesise subjective praxis, thinkable only within the terms of spiritual and intellectual activity, with a material reality, conceivable only in traditional philosophical terms as a static, ahistorical metaphysics of matter. On the contrary, following Labriola, the concept of praxis sketched in the 'Theses' must be grasped in non-idealist terms as 'concrete human activity', 'that is, the real act, in the profane sense of the word'. It is human practical activity, i.e. work, labour, and material production that constitutes 'the dialectical mediation', the 'active union between man and nature',[28] and on the basis of which the 'dualism between man and nature' can be rejected.[29] It follows that Marx's theory cannot be 'confused with vulgar materialism or with the metaphysics of "matter" which is bound to be eternal and absolute'.[30] The 'theses on Feuerbach' demonstrate how 'Marx had gone beyond the

---

25   Labriola 1912, pp. 14, 23, 60–2, 84. See also Labriola 1908, pp. 98–9.

26   Labriola 1908, pp. 64, 120–1, 160, and Labriola 1912, pp. 43, 84–5.

27   Labriola 1908, p. 170, and Labriola 1912, pp. 42–3, 60–2, 109. On the concept of immanence in Labriola, cf. Thomas 2010, pp. 342–3.

28   Q4, §47, p. 473. Gramsci correctly translated Marx's phrase 'sensuous human activity, practice [Praxis]' (*sinnlich menschliche Tätigkeit*) as 'attività sensibile umana, praxis', Gramsci 2007b, p. 743.

29   Q4, §43, p. 469.

30   Q4, §40, p. 466.

philosophical position of vulgar materialism',[31] criticising the prior materialist philosophical tradition for its static and ahistorical conception of material reality in purely objective terms, without reference to a subject, i.e. 'human sensible activity' or 'praxis' that actively transforms it.[32] Rather, Marx's thought is quite literally a '*historical materialism*', a conception of the material world insofar as it is historically and socially transformed through concrete human labour and the production process, 'as a *human relation*', or to the extent that it becomes 'an "economic factor" of production', incorporated in a historically determinate ensemble of social and class relations, as Labriola had already argued.[33] Neither a transcendent metaphysics of 'matter', nor the transcendence of an ideal spirit, reality has been redefined in the non-metaphysical terms of human praxis, as the historically variable social relations in which human beings organise labour and the production process, actively transforming nature in order to meet needs.[34] Consequently, human thought only emerges within the framework of human historical, social, and practical development.[35]

Understood from this perspective, it becomes clear that Gramsci's sudden interest in the 'Theses', as well as his attempt to go back to Engels's original version in order to extract his own translation, had a precise strategic function and significance, namely, that of confuting Gentile's re-reading in order to demonstrate that it is in reality, 'Labriola's philosophical views', i.e. 'his formulation of the philosophical question' which needs to be resumed and developed, and ultimately, 'should be made to prevail',[36] and on the basis of which Gramsci could critically intervene in the contemporary debates over the philosophical status of Marxism, uprooting the double revision to which the Marxism of his

---

31   Q5, § 39, p. 572, written just after Q4, § 37.

32   Gramsci 2007b, p. 743. Notice here that Gramsci correctly translated Gegenstand as 'the object', in contrast to Gentile's idealistic reduction of it to a 'term of thought', Gentile 2014, p. 116. Nor, in Gramsci's translation of the 'Theses', do we find anything even remotely resembling Gentile's idealist explication of 'objective [gegenständliche] activity', as activity that creates or produces the sensible object, Gentile 2014, p. 121. See Gramsci 2007b, pp. 743–5.

33   Q4, § 25, p. 444.

34   Q4, § 32, p. 451, Q4, § 37, p. 455.

35   Q4, § 41, p. 467.

36   Q3, § 31, p. 309, Q4, § 3, p. 422. Gramsci would have been reminded of this debate between Labriola and Gentile over Marx's so-called philosophy of praxis by Croce's direct reference to it in *Materialismo storico ed economia marxistica*, a text which Gramsci had with him from the beginning of his stay in Turi, and in which Croce explicitly referred to the 'Theses', Labriola's *Socialism and Philosophy*, and Gentile's *La Filosofia di Marx*, Croce 1900, p. 153. Later in the *Prison Notebooks*, Gramsci will explicitly reference these statements by Croce, and in a highly significant context, as we will see.

time had been subjected, between a traditional philosophical materialism on the one hand, and its syncretic fusion with idealist philosophical currents on the other.[37] Not only has Gramsci undermined Gentile's dualistic and 'spiritualised' interpretation of the 'Theses', he has also undercut the latter's proposed 'solution' to Marx's alleged dualism, namely, his idealist philosophy of spirit as the 'pure act' as purportedly the only true absolute immanence, but in reality, a merely speculative identification of thought and being through the purely intellectual and spiritual 'activity' of the subject positing itself in the form of an object. Contrary to the 'method of immanence' in Gentile's 'actual idealism', Marx's theory does not think 'the absolute concreteness of the real in the action of thought'.[38] Conversely, it is a theory that thinks its own concreteness in the 'impure', 'profane' practical world that forms its basis, consciously and critically recognising itself as *part* of the historical, social, and practical world it strives to understand in order to transform.[39]

Hence, despite Gramsci's puzzling failure to 'explicitly refer to Labriola's contributions in his discussion of Marx's new concept of immanence',[40] there is an organic interconnection between Gramsci's simultaneous desire to resurrect Labriola's earlier philosophical positions, establish the 'Theses' as the central nucleus of a new philosophy that supersedes traditional philosophical materialism and idealism, and his repeated assertion that a novel non-metaphysical concept of immanence lay at the basis of Marx's new philosophy. For it was Labriola who had already positioned a novel, non-metaphysical concept of immanence at the heart of the distinctive specificity of Marx's so-called 'philosophy of praxis', as a theory which is not 'transcendent' (literally 'from or beyond'), but instead recognises its own concrete formation and insertion within a historically determinate network of social and practical relations. For Labriola, this meant that Marx's philosophy of praxis was a self-conscious mode of knowing and comprehending the antagonistic social world 'from within' it (literally 'immanently') from a particular social and practical position, or as Labriola himself put it, 'in our social group and from the point of view which we occupy in it',[41] thus a philosophy that consciously identifies itself with and presupposes the particular standpoint, or *visual angle*, of the proletariat.[42]

---

37   Q3, §31, pp. 308–9.
38   Gentile 1923, pp. 246–7.
39   Q4, §45, p. 471, Q4, §40, p. 465.
40   Thomas 2010, pp. 341–2.
41   Labriola 1912, pp. 46–7.
42   Labriola repeatedly stressed the partiality of Marx's philosophy as a conception of the world of the proletariat. Cf. Labriola 1912, pp. 31, 40–1, 51, 75, 81, 201. On this point, see Frosini 2004b, pp. 3–4.

It is precisely this conception of Marx's thought as a *partial* mode of understanding the antagonistic social world 'from within', i.e. immanently, that Gramsci will proceed to develop, explicitly drawing out these connections between Marx's 'Theses', and the necessity, following Labriola, of re-elaborating them as a philosophy of praxis in connection with a new, non-metaphysical concept of immanence. For now, however, we can say that Gramsci's initial 'return to Marx' in Notebook 4 finds its underlying coherence in Labriola's framework of historical materialism as a philosophy of praxis, and in which, as Frosini argues, Labriola's sketch of a non-metaphysical conception of immanence as the concreteness, or 'earthly' status, of human thought, together with a non-idealist concept of praxis, are decisive, paving the way for an understanding of the concrete 'unity of subject and object, and therefore a theoretical space departing from which the same problem of the dualism of consciousness and the world loses meaning', and with it, the metaphysical dualism between materialism and idealism.[43]

3   The 'Worldly' Basis of Thought and Knowledge

Given the repudiation of philosophical idealism and materialism, understood as transcendent metaphysical hypostatisations, i.e. given that there is no underlying substance constitutive of reality that can function as ontological guarantee or metaphysical foundation for the truth-status of theories and propositions, how then to understand the concepts of truth and knowledge?

Not coincidently, it is in the same note, Q4, §37, discussed in the previous section, in which Gramsci rejected the traditional philosophical dualism between materialism and idealism in favour of a concrete and historical conception of reality understood in relation to human material and social practices, and the concomitant conception of thought as historically circumscribed within determinate social and practical relations, that he also confronts the problem of knowledge, claiming that 'When dealing with the question of the "objectivity" of knowledge from the point of view of historical materialism, the point of departure should be the affirmation ... that "men become conscious (of this conflict) on the ideological level" of juridical, political, religious, artistic, or philosophical forms', and proceeds to aver that the various ideological forms are coterminous and identifiable with all consciousness and, therefore, all know-

---

43   Frosini 2001, pp. 43–5.

ledge.[44] In contradistinction to Marx's more restricted sense of ideology in the 1859 Preface, Gramsci widens the scope of its meaning in what Guido Liguori calls a 'dilated' re-reading of the 1859 Preface in which, as Gramsci suggests, *all* forms of human consciousness have an ideological, and hence, political status. This interpretation, as Liguori posits, establishes 'the possibility of a *positive* conception of ideology. Marxism, thus, becomes an ideology among the others', having as its aim or purpose making a class 'become conscious', in particular, the proletariat.[45]

Even more significantly, Gramsci explicitly attributes a gnoseological validity to the ideological terrain: 'Marx's assertion – that men become conscious of economic conflicts on the terrain of ideology – has a gnoseological and not psychological or moral value'.[46] As Frosini argues, 'Gramsci is reading the Preface on the basis of the *Theses on Feuerbach*, the concept of *ideology* on the basis of the reformulation of the question of *truth* in terms of praxis'.[47] Speaking of the 'the question of the "objectivity" of knowledge from the point of view of historical materialism', Gramsci's reference point was clearly Marx's second thesis, in which the latter claimed that '[t]he question whether objective truth can be attributed to human thinking is not a question of theory but is a practical question. Man must prove the truth, i.e. the reality and power, the this-worldliness [*Diesseitigkeit*] of his thinking in practice'.[48] This is further corroborated by the language employed in the immediately following note in which, referencing the 1859 Preface, Gramsci had written that the social and political forces struggling to supersede a structure wracked by crises and contradictions, seek 'to demonstrate (in the final analysis through their own triumph)' by various ideological means the necessity for its historical supersession.[49] This usage of the word 'demonstrate' corresponds exactly to Gramsci's translation of the second thesis at the beginning of Notebook 7, in which Marx's phrase 'must prove' (in Engels's edited version) was rendered as 'deve dimostrare'.[50]

---

44   Q4, § 37, pp. 454–5.
45   Liguori 2004a, pp. 134, 137.
46   Q4, § 38, pp. 464–5.
47   Frosini 2009c, p. 34. The peculiarity of this attempt to read two texts in harmony with one another that were composed in radically disparate periods in Marx's intellectual development can be readily conceded. But that Gramsci did so is not at all surprising considering he received the two texts together in the same anthology in 1930.
48   Marx 1976a [1845], p. 6. I quote Engels's version, since it was this to which Gramsci had access.
49   Q4, § 38, 455–6.
50   Gramsci 2007b, p. 743.

Marx's second thesis becomes, in Gramsci's re-reading, the theoretical nucleus for a reconstitution of the traditional categories of truth and knowledge *within* the space of ideology; the entire terrain of human consciousness and knowledge is politically and ideologically overdetermined, with the consequence that there is no longer any fundamental, qualitative distinction between truth and falsity, ideological and non-ideological (or scientific), but rather, quantitative distinctions between different modes of consciousness according to their varying degrees of practical political power (truth) *within* the ideological terrain. Truth and knowledge are identified with their varying degrees of practical efficacy on the ideological terrain of political struggle, and in the last analysis, with hegemony.[51]

This dilated, gnoseological conception of the ideological-superstructural forms as constituting the common and necessary terrain both of consciousness and knowledge,[52] is undergirded by Gramsci's construal of 'the ensemble of the social relations' propounded by Marx in the sixth thesis on Feuerbach, an affirmation that becomes 'the centre of gravity' of Gramsci's reading.[53] The latter is explicitly conceived as a terrain of struggle and conflict, a historical and dialectical network of class contradictions and antagonisms. Hence, not simply the 'nature' of human beings, but indeed social reality itself, are constituted and understood within the historical framework of social contradictions and conflicts.[54] Gramsci has fused Marx's sixth and fourth theses, i.e. the conception of human nature in terms of the historical ensemble of social relations with Marx's characterisation of the latter in terms of its 'inner strife and intrinsic contradictoriness'.[55]

It is precisely the historical ensemble of social and practical relations, grasped as a political terrain of hegemonic class struggle, which constitutes the concrete ground, i.e. the 'worldly' or 'earthly' site of all thought and knowledge, (*la base mondana*) as Gramsci translated the 'secular' or 'earthly' from Marx's fourth thesis on Feuerbach,[56] in short, the 'impure', 'profane' practical world on which, as Gramsci suggested, Marx's philosophy must base itself.[57] It is because human thought and knowledge are formed within historically

---

51   Q4, §38, pp. 464–5.
52   Liguori 2004a, p. 138.
53   Frosini 2004a, p. 100.
54   Q7, §35, pp. 884–5.
55   Marx 1976a [1845], pp. 7–8. Gramsci translated this as the 'self-laceration' and 'inner contradiction' traversing the social world, Gramsci 2007b, p. 744.
56   Ibid.
57   Q4, §37, p. 455.

determinate relations of social and political struggle that Gramsci can outline a perspective in which human thought and knowledge necessarily have an
ideological and therefore, political status.

4   The Philosophy of Praxis as an Absolute Immanence, an Absolute Worldliness and Earthliness of Thought

The apprehension of reality and human beings themselves as historically and
politically constituted within a contradictory field of social struggle, and therefore, that of the terrain of human thought and knowledge as constituting an
antagonistic and contradictory field,[58] provides the conceptual framework for
the re-elaboration of the nature of philosophy itself, analysed historically and
politically as the expressions of the internal class contradictions of society. 'All
hitherto-existing philosophy', Gramsci writes, 'has been the product and the
expression of the inner contradictions of society'.[59] It follows that the historicity of philosophy is dialectical, a terrain of conflict between a multiplicity of
competing philosophical systems and conceptions of the world.[60]
    Within this framework, 'historical materialism' is distinguished by the fact
that it 'conceives of itself as a transitory phase in philosophical thought'. As
a philosophy, 'it is the full consciousness of contradictions, the consciousness
wherein the philosopher himself, understood both as an individual and as a
social group, not only understands contradictions but posits himself as an element of the contradiction and raises this element to a principle of politics
and action'.[61] Again, this is an implicit reference to the fourth thesis, in which
Marx wrote that the fact of religious self-estrangement must 'be explained by
the inner strife and intrinsic contradictoriness' characteristic of the 'secular' or
'earthly' world, and that 'The latter must itself, therefore, first be understood in
its contradiction and then, by the removal of the contradiction, revolutionised
in practice', in short, 'criticised in theory and transformed in practice'.[62] Also
implicit here is Marx's second thesis; the 'inner strife and intrinsic contradictoriness' characteristic of the 'secular' or 'earthly' basis of thought, as previously
indicated, was translated by Gramsci as the 'worldly' or 'earthly' basis (*la base*

---

58   Q8, § 182, p. 1051.
59   Q4, § 45, p. 471. This is a clear reference to Marx's fourth thesis, the 'inner contradictions' of
        society corresponding to Gramsci's translation of the fourth thesis, Gramsci 2007b, p. 744.
60   Q4, § 45, p. 471, Q10, II, § 41 (i), p. 1299.
61   Q4, § 45, pp. 471–2.
62   Marx 1976a [1845], p. 7.

mondana), hence, directly linked to Gramsci's translation of Marx's term *Diesseitigkeit* – i.e. the 'this-worldliness' of thought which concretely proves its truth in practice, which the former rendered directly (*il carattere terreno*) – i.e. the 'worldly' or 'earthly' character of truth linked to practical power.[63]

To reiterate, in a world founded on contradiction and conflict, all thought and knowledge are ideological (political). However, as Liguori correctly states, 'not all ideologies are equal'.[64] As an ideology or philosophy, Marxism does not respond to the struggles and cleavages of social reality by placing itself in a transcendent position from which it claims to represent the impartial interests of all humanity; it does not construct images of unity in place of the strife constitutive of reality. Rather, it takes the terrain of struggle and contradiction as its analytical point of departure, recognising its own 'earthly' or 'worldly' basis in the antagonistic social world, as a concrete mode of interpreting and understanding the antagonistic social world 'from within' it, that is, necessarily within the political field of social conflicts, and from a particular ideological standpoint assumed within it.[65] In short, it is conscious of (rather than seeking to deny) its own partiality as a theory, form of knowing and understanding from a particular class standpoint within the struggle itself, a 'philosophy of the act (praxis)' in the 'real', 'profane sense'.[66]

This concrete sense of immanence as a mode of theorising and knowing practically and politically from a particular standpoint situated within the class struggle, still only implicit in the fall of 1930, is lurking underneath the first appearance, in its exact form, of the locution 'philosophy of praxis'. Gramsci argues that Machiavelli 'articulated a conception of the world that could also be called "philosophy of praxis" ... in that it does not recognise transcendental or immanent (in the metaphysical sense) elements but is based entirely on the

---

63   Gramsci 2007b, p. 743. As suggested earlier, Gramsci's return to Marx's 'Theses' involves a strategic, linguistic battle against Gentile's reading and translation. Rather than the 'worldly' or 'earthly' basis of thought (*la base mondana*), Gentile translated this as 'substrate' (*sostrato*) in an attempt to force Marx into a materialist metaphysical essentialism. Additionally, instead of the 'worldly' or 'earthly' character of truth (*il carattere terreno*), he strangely translated Marx's *Diesseitigkeit* as the 'positivity' (*la positività*) of thought, Gentile 2014, pp. 117–18.

64   Liguori 2004a, p. 138.

65   'The philosopher ... cannot evade the present terrain of contradictions', 'even historical materialism is an expression of historical contradictions'. As a philosophy, 'it is the full consciousness of contradictions, the consciousness wherein the philosopher himself, understood both as an individual and as a social group, not only understands contradictions but posits himself as an element of the contradiction and raises this element to a principle of politics and action', Q4, § 45, pp. 471–2.

66   Q4, § 37, p. 455.

concrete action of men, who out of historical necessity works and transforms reality'.[67] According to Gramsci, Machiavelli was, like Marx, a theoretician 'of militant politics, of action'.[68] He did not speculatively envisage a utopian, ideal state of affairs, but composed books of 'immediate political action' linked to the analysis of the concrete political situation.[69] He did so, moreover, from the standpoint of a particular class, and with a view towards the concrete trans- formation of reality.[70] As Gramsci later wrote, Machiavelli 'is not merely a sci- entist: he is a partisan, a man of powerful passions, an active politician, who wishes to create new relations of forces'. Accordingly, he based his thought on 'effective reality' (*realtà effettuale*), that is, the concrete terrain of 'a relation of forces in continuous movement and change of equilibrium'.[71] As Thomas stresses, in 'the moment of politics', there is the demonstration of 'the *necessary particularism or partiality* of a knowledge and intellectual practice that has dis- pensed with any "transcendental elements" and bases itself entirely upon the "concrete action" of "man" in history'.[72] Machiavelli thus provided a model for a conception of the world as a 'philosophy of praxis', fundamentally opposed to the metaphysics of transcendence and immanence (in the metaphysical sense), Gramsci tacitly suggesting a link between Machiavelli, as a theorist and philosopher of the effective reality of relations of forces from a particular stand- point within it, and a concrete, non-metaphysical conception of immanence.

The second appearance of the phrase 'philosophy of praxis' appears in the crucial Q7, § 35, as a concluding formulation to Gramsci's argument that human nature is the ensemble of social relations, understood as a concrete terrain of class struggle:

> Thus one arrives also at the equality of, or the equation between, 'philo- sophy and politics,' thought and action, that is, at a philosophy of praxis. Everything is political, even philosophy or philosophies (see the notes on the character of ideologies), and the only 'philosophy' is history in action, life itself.[73]

---

67   Q5, § 127, p. 657, written in November–December 1930, significantly just after the previ- ously discussed Q4, § 45 (October–November 1930), and Q4, § 37 (September–October 1930).

68   Q4, § 10, p. 432.

69   Q5, § 127, p. 657.

70   Machiavelli wrote from the standpoint of 'those who are not in the know', i.e. 'The revolu- tionary class of the time, the Italian people and nation', just as Marx had addressed his thought to a specific class, Q4, § 8, p. 431.

71   Q13, § 16, pp. 1577–8.

72   Thomas 2010, p. 426.

73   Q7, § 35, p. 886.

The connection between Gramsci's re-reading of the sixth and fourth theses, i.e. the understanding of human reality as the 'worldly' terrain of class struggle, and consequently, that of all thought and knowledge in ideological and political terms as the foundation for the re-elaboration of philosophy itself as politically and ideologically overdetermined, is explicitly brought together. In accordance with Gramsci's re-reading of the second thesis, the truth, i.e. reality and power (*il carattere terreno*) of *all* philosophy is not transcendent, but instead finds its 'earthly' ground in the terrain of political struggle, hence on a *continuum* with ideology, distinguishable from the latter only according to its degree of effectiveness from the standpoint of hegemony.[74] The philosophy of praxis not only critically 'translates' all philosophy, even in its speculative form, into the concrete terms of its practical power as a hegemonic conception of the world,[75] but also critically rethinks its own philosophical status departing from the political struggle, as a philosophy or conception of the world of a class that seeks to establish its own hegemonic state.[76]

Gramsci pursues this enterprise in Notebook 8, in the third series of 'Notes on Philosophy'. In a note entitled 'Philosophy of praxis',[77] Gramsci disputes Croce's interpretation of Marx's eleventh thesis on Feuerbach, according to which 'one cannot speak of Marx as a philosopher and therefore one cannot speak of a Marxist philosophy since what Marx proposed was, precisely, to turn philosophy upside down – not just Hegel's philosophy but philosophy as a whole – and to replace philosophising with practical activity', noting the inconsistency of Croce who earlier had explicitly recognised 'that Antonio Labriola was justified in pointing out the need to construct a "philosophy of praxis" on the basis of Marxism'.[78] Instead of signifying a repudiation of all philosophy

---

74   In Notebook 10, this issues in a general redefinition of all philosophy as the hegemony or 'catharsis' of a fundamental social class, distinguishable from ideology in quantitative, rather than qualitative terms, Q10, I, §10, p. 1231, Q10, II, §6, p. 1244. See Liguori 2004a, p. 146; Frosini 2003a, p. 91; Frosini 2008a, pp. 730–1.

75   See Q4, §45, pp. 471–2, in which Gramsci registered the political and ideological effects of the unitary concepts of speculative philosophy, and Q7, §35, pp. 883–6, in which the same speculative philosophical concepts were grasped in terms of their practical functioning in the concrete world of politics, the integral state, and hegemonic struggle between classes. As Gramsci would later write, the philosophy of praxis reduces 'all speculative philosophies to "politics", to a moment of historic-political life; the philosophy of praxis conceives the reality of human relations of knowledge as an element of political "hegemony"', Q10, II, §6 (iv), p. 1245.

76   Q7, §33, pp. 881–2, Q7, §35, p. 886.

77   Q8, §198. This is the first appearance of the term in the third series.

78   Q8, §198, p. 1060. Croce had written that from the standpoint of the doctrine of knowledge according to Marx, 'one might speak with Labriola of historical materialism as a

in favour of revolutionary political praxis, Gramsci contends that Marx's eleventh thesis was meant to indicate 'that philosophy must become "politics" or "practice" in order for it to continue to be philosophy', in other words, 'the unity of theory and practice'.[79] The link between Marx's 'Theses', and the necessity, following Labriola, of re-elaborating Marxism as a philosophy of praxis has now become explicit. In particular the eleventh thesis is identified as the substrate for the re-elaboration of Marx's theory as a 'philosophy of praxis', i.e. the theoretical basis in Marx for the equation between 'philosophy and politics', thought and action, that is, a philosophy of praxis that Gramsci averred in Q7, § 35.[80]

Furthermore, at this juncture in Gramsci's prison research, we have a concrete sense of what this equalisation of thought and action, philosophy and politics, signifies. 'A philosophy of praxis', as he argues in the next appearance of the term after Q8, § 198, must 'present itself as a critique of "common sense" (but only after it has based itself on common sense in order to show that "everyone" is a philosopher and that the point is not to introduce a totally new form of knowledge into "everyone's" individual life but to revitalise an already existing activity and make it "critical")'.[81] The philosophy of praxis is (implicitly) the 'immanent' critique of common sense, i.e. that philosophy which does not attempt to present itself as transcendent to the practical struggles it seeks to comprehend, but contrarily, self-consciously has 'as its point of departure an analysis and a critique of the philosophy of common sense, the philosophy of nonphilosophers', one in which, 'in the course of elaborating a superior and scientifically coherent form of thought, it never fails to remain in contact with the "simple" and even finds in such contacts the source of the issues that need to be studied and resolved'.[82]

As in the earlier appearances of the term, implicit in the concept of Marxism as a 'philosophy of praxis' lies the notion of a distinctive form of theorising and knowing practically and politically from a particular class standpoint within the field of struggle itself. From the early thesis of historical materialism as a

---

philosophy of praxis ... as a particular way of conceiving and resolving ... the problem of thought and being', explicitly referring to the 'Theses', Labriola's *Socialism and Philosophy*, and Gentile's *La Filosofia di Marx*, Croce 1900, p. 153.

79   Q8, § 208, p. 1066.

80   Significantly, after Q8, § 198, the term 'philosophy of praxis' reappears with greater frequency in the notes of Notebook 8, before systematically replacing 'historical materialism' and 'Marxism' in Notebooks 10 and 11.

81   Q8, § 220, p. 1080.

82   Q8, § 173, pp. 1045–6, Q8, § 213, pp. 1070–1. On this point, see Thomas 2010, p. 377.

'philosophy of the act (praxis)' in the profane sense, in which, as a theory, it does not deny the reality of struggle, but instead takes this struggle as its analytical point of departure, consciously seeing itself as an element within it, and thus, as a partial mode of theorising within the struggle (fall 1930), this conception reappeared in reference to Machiavelli, and in clear connection with an alternative, non-metaphysical concept of immanence, Gramsci arguing that the latter repudiated all elements of transcendence, basing his theory on the concrete terrain of political struggle, and this, moreover, as a partisan, i.e. an active man of politics and passions (winter 1930). In 1931, this idea found a formulation in the thesis of 'the equality of, or the equation between, "philosophy and politics," thought and action, that is, at a philosophy of praxis', as the delineation of a conception that rethinks philosophy in a concrete way departing from politics, in short, the concrete unity of theory and practice, philosophy and politics understood within the framework of hegemony, as a philosophical conception of the world of a determinate social class that wants to found a state. Now, in early 1932, Gramsci concretises this idea in the conception of a philosophy of praxis that takes the form of a critique of common sense, organically basing itself on the life and thought of the popular masses in order to give coherent form and expression to their historically vital needs and interests. Hence, it represents a form of theorising and knowing practically and politically within the arena of hegemonic struggle itself, more precisely in an active, reciprocal pedagogical relation with the life and consciousness of the popular classes which form its concrete basis and which, as a philosophy whose function is to become a conception of the world of the masses, it strives to coherently articulate.

In the significantly expanded second draft of Q8, § 198, in which the eleventh thesis on Feuerbach was identified as the theoretical basis in Marx for the reelaboration of Marxism as a philosophy of praxis, Gramsci now explicitly links his understanding of the eleventh thesis with the second. Confronting again Croce's allegedly erroneous conception of the eleventh thesis as a rejection of all philosophy in favour of revolutionary praxis, and reaffirming the need 'to construct a philosophy of praxis posed by Antonio Labriola', Gramsci contends 'is one not instead dealing with the demand, in the face of the "scholastic", purely theoretical or contemplative philosophy, of the revindication of a philosophy that produces a corresponding ethic, a realizing will and that, in the last analysis identifies itself with these? The XI thesis ... (represents) the energetic affirmation of a unity between theory and practice', adding that this 'is only the assertion of the "historicity" of philosophy made in terms of an absolute immanence, of an "absolute worldliness" ... it has deduced from mere contemplation an active will capable of transforming the world and in this practical

activity there is also contained the "knowledge" that it is only rather in practical activity that there lies "real knowledge" and not "scholasticism".[83]

The eleventh thesis, as the energetic affirmation of the unity of theory
and practice, philosophy and politics, that is, a philosophy of praxis, must be
grasped as an 'absolute immanence', i.e. an 'absolute worldliness'. The new non-
metaphysical concept of immanence is then directly related to Marx's stress on
the need for a thought that practically and politically demonstrates its truth,
reality and power, its this-worldliness [*Diesseitigkeit*]. 'Absolute immanence'
is used as a synonym for 'absolute worldliness' [*terrestrità assoluta*], directly
recalling Gramsci's translation of Marx's *Diesseitigkeit* as *il carattere terreno* –
i.e. the 'worldly' or 'earthly' character of truth linked to practical power.[84] As
he reaffirmed in Notebook 11, the philosophy of praxis represents 'the absolute
worldliness and earthliness' of thought [*la mondanizzazione e terrestrità assoluta del pensiero*], and 'It is along this line that one must trace the thread of
the new conception of the world'.[85] '*Mondanizzazione*' thus implicitly recalls
Gramsci's translation of the fourth thesis, the 'inner strife and intrinsic contradictoriness' characteristic of the 'secular' or 'earthly' basis of thought that
Gramsci translated as the 'worldly' or 'earthly' basis (*la base mondana*).[86] In
fact, in the C-text of the crucial Q4, § 45, in which Gramsci suggested a concrete mode of interpreting and understanding the antagonistic social world
'from within' it, that is necessarily inside the field of social conflicts, and from
a particular political and ideological standpoint assumed within it ('the consciousness wherein the philosopher himself, understood both as an individual
and as a social group, not only understands contradictions but posits himself as
an element of the contradiction and raises this element to a principle of politics and action'[87]), he now makes the stronger claim that philosophy 'raises this
element to a principle of knowledge and therefore of action',[88] i.e. the identification of knowledge and action, philosophy and politics, truth and praxis (the
philosophy of praxis). Finally, one can note that two notes later, in the C-text of
Q4, § 37 in which Gramsci first suggested that Marxism should be reconstructed
as a 'philosophy of the act (praxis) ... in the profane sense' (also as we will recall,
the same note in which he had first presented the dilated, gnoseological reformulation of ideology), Gramsci now adds 'in the "worldly" sense' – 'philosophy

---

83   Q10, II, § 31 (i), pp. 1270–1 (June–August 1932).
84   Gramsci 2007b, p. 743.
85   Q11, § 27, p. 1437 (July–August 1932).
86   Gramsci 2007b, p. 744.
87   Q4, § 45, pp. 471–2.
88   Q11, § 62, p. 1487 (August-the end of 1932).

of the act (praxis, development) ... in the most profane and worldly [*mondano*] sense of the word', thus linking this to Marx's second and fourth theses, and to the status of the philosophy of praxis as an 'absolute immanence', an 'absolute worldliness and earthliness of thought'.[89]

In other words, what had been implicit since Notebook 4 and in the earlier appearances of the term 'philosophy of praxis' has now become explicit; as a philosophy of praxis, Marx's theory is not transcendent in relation to the concrete reality it seeks to comprehend, nor is it immanent in reality in the speculative idealist sense. Rather it is immanent to the reality about which it philosophises in the concrete, non-metaphysical sense that it self-consciously recognises its own earthly or worldly basis (*la base mondana*), i.e. its concrete conditions of emergence within a historically determinate terrain of social, political, and ideological struggle. It therefore does not set itself above the terrain of class struggle and contradictions, but conceives itself as a theory necessarily traversed and overdetermined by the class contradictions by which historical reality is lacerated. It seeks to grasp the terrain of social, political, and ideological struggle from within it (immanently), and hence is a form of interpreting, understanding, and knowing practically and politically inside the very terrain of struggle it seeks to coherently elaborate and theorise. It thus constitutes a form of knowing and understanding from a necessarily *partial* standpoint within the terrain of struggle itself, as a philosophy or conception of the world which works to coincide and identify itself with the specific needs, problems, and ways of life and seeing the world of the working masses. In short, the truth, reality, and power of the philosophy of praxis lies in this distinctive form of knowing.[90]

---

89   Q11, §64, p. 1492.
90   Frosini 2004a, pp. 108–9; Frosini 2009, p.104.

CHAPTER 9

Interpreting the Present from the Past: Gramsci, Marx and the Historical Analogy

Francesca Antonini

1   Introduction[1]

From his early writings onwards, Antonio Gramsci was fascinated by historical parallels. In the pre-prison articles comparisons between different historical epochs are used as interpretative tools and as instruments of sharp criticism.[2] In both cases, their scope is clear, insofar as they strengthen Gramsci's attempt to define the strategy of the workers' movement in the troubled Italian context of the first decades of the twentieth century.

After his imprisonment, however, the situation changed. If Gramsci's strong political engagement does not fade away, the outlook he adopts in the *Prison Notebooks* is different. In this framework, historical parallels are seen and used in a new, problematic perspective, shaped by Gramsci's attempt at 'doing something *für ewig*', as he wrote in a famous letter to his sister-in-law Tatiana.[3]

The aim of this chapter is to illustrate the Gramscian notion of historical analogy and to show its heuristic potential. After a general introduction to Gramsci's way of reasoning in the *Prison Notebooks*, I will focus on historical comparisons as such. To demonstrate their fundamental role in Gramsci's framework, I will take as a case study a challenging historico-political category, the one of Caesarism. Gramsci's account of Caesarism will be contextualised within the discussion on the theme between the nineteenth and the twentieth centuries and it will be analysed in the framework of the *Prison Notebooks*. On this basis, I will investigate the connection between this approach and the Marxian legacy, as it emerges from his historical works. In conclusion, some

---

1   I wish to thank Aaron Bernstein, Giuseppe Cospito, Fabio Frosini and Robert Jackson for their useful comments.

2   It should be noted that the use of comparison as a heuristic tool was common in late nineteenth-century to early twentieth-century debates. Historical analogies have been deployed by, among others, Engels, Sorel and Croce. The latter's thought deeply influenced Gramsci's own views.

3   Gramsci 1979, p. 79. On this issue see in particular Mastroianni 2003, pp. 225–7. Francese 2009, although more recent, is quite superficial.

general observations on Gramsci's original conception of history and on the relationship between past and present are formulated.

2   The Role of Historical Analogy in Gramsci's Thought

2.1   'Cuvier's Little Bone'

One of the most striking images used by Gramsci to reflect on methodological issues is the one of Cuvier's little bone.[4] First suggested in Q1, §26, this reference to the French palaeontologist has to be interpreted in the light of his investigation of what Gramsci calls Lorianism, 'a category invented by Gramsci as a device that enabled him to group certain types of Italian intellectuals together',[5] and to condemn their narrow-minded way of thinking. In this very short paragraph Gramsci hints at the figure of the Italian criminologist Cesare Lombroso, a model of Lorianist behaviour, who affirmed that a criminal attitude can be deduced from physical features. Thanks to its elliptic triple reference (Cuvier, Loria, Lombroso), Q1, §26 acquires a specific, deep methodological meaning. In short, when Gramsci says that 'from the little bone of a mouse sometimes a sea serpent was reconstructed', he is warning against undue inferences and generalisations.[6] Together with his strong refusal of positivism, this is a core element of the *Prison Notebooks*.

This image returns in a more developed form in Q14, §29, and after that in Q28, §3. While in the latter occurrence the Gramscian criticism of sociology is formulated along the lines of Q1, §26, in Notebook 14 the metaphor of the little bone is used in a different sense. In the first place, Gramsci assimilates Cuvier's principle to the principle of correlation, and, at a broader extent, to the use of analogy. On this basis, he reflects on the application of Cuvier's principle in the field of social sciences, wondering whether 'the principle of correlation is useful, exact and fruitful in sociology, beyond the metaphor'.[7] His positive answer sounds quite surprising if we consider the above-mentioned criticisms. In §29, although always cautious, Gramsci recognises that elaborating general trends from affinities between single episodes could be useful,

---

4   Cf. Buttigieg 1990, p. 61.

5   Buttigieg 1992, p. 43. This formula is inspired by the economist Achille Loria (1857–1943); Lorianism is also the subject of the previous and of the following notes (§§ 25 and 27).

6   Q1, § 26, p. 22; Gramsci 1992, Vol. 1, p. 116. Cf. Buttigieg 1990, pp. 62 *et passim*. On this point see also Q11, § 52, where Gramsci writes: 'Even the law of large numbers, although very useful as a model of comparison, cannot be assumed as the "law" of historical events' (Gramsci 1971a, p. 412).

7   Q14, § 29, p. 1687.

especially when dealing with present-day issues, since it reinforces, and sometimes supplies, political action: 'However, it is different in the case of political
action and that of the principle of correlation (like the one of analogy) applied
to the predictable, to the construction of possible hypotheses and perspectives'.[8]

From this point of view, the stress on the forecasting element that features
the historical parallels is particularly important, in contrast to the decontextu-
alised and careless use of analogies made by 'lorianist' intellectuals.

In Q14, §29 Cuvier's principle is generalised and, at the same time, inextricably linked with specific historical and political coordinates. This histor-
icisation and politicisation is exactly what makes possible Gramsci's critical
appreciation of the principle of correlation, i.e. of analogy. Comparisons are
no longer conceived of as absolute truths but as working hypotheses, that can
be fruitfully adopted to investigate political reality. Thus, this note opens up a
meaningful perspective on the Gramscian conception of historical comparisons, seen as a precious instrument of historical comprehension and political
strategy.[9]

2.2   *Abstract Models and Concrete Examples*

As has been shown, in Gramsci's conception of history, theoretical reflections
and the investigation of concrete case-studies are complementary aspects of
his analysis.[10] On the one hand, to become an effective interpretative tool, every
abstract scheme must be adapted to a specific social and political context. On
the other hand, history is not a collection of unique, unrelated episodes; every
case has its specific features, but it is necessary to locate the similarities and to
elaborate a common background to analyse them.[11] What matters, for Gramsci,
is therefore to trace the meaning of 'historical necessity'.[12] That means formu-

---

8   Q14, §29, p. 1687.

9   See Burgio 2014, pp. 125–38, who stresses (to a certain extent maybe excessively) also
     Gramsci's political target. Here and in the following pages, I use both 'comparison' and
     'analogy'; it is clear, however, that the comparison is only made possible by the identific-
     ation of an analogy, which means by the existence of similar patterns. On this point, see
     Burgio 2016.

10   For an analysis of Gramsci's account of history, see Burgio 2014.

11   See Burgio 2014, pp. 125–38.

12   For the use of the expression 'historical necessity' (*necessità storica*), see as an example
     Q3, §18 or Q8, §233; on this point see Burgio 2016, pp. 78–80. See also the entry on *Neces-
     sità* by Fabio Frosini in Liguori and Voza 2009, pp. 583–5. As Cacciatore noted (in his entry
     for '*Storicismo*' in Liguori and Voza 2009, p. 816), 'historical necessity' has to be understood
     here 'in a "concrete-historical" sense'.

lating 'practical criteria of historical and political interpretation', or, in other words, to approximate the 'generic hypothesis' to 'concrete historical reality'.[13]

Significantly, Gramsci never talks in a positive sense about laws of history, but of 'criteria' in the *Prison Notebooks*: he uses the expression 'laws of history' only on a few occasions and always in a negative sense.[14] As to the expression 'practical criteria', this is an oxymoron, since it qualifies an abstract element (a criterion) as 'practical'; however, given Gramsci's methodological statements, its meaning is clear.[15] Furthermore, the polemical weight embedded in this expression has to be noticed. This combination of both theoretical and historical elements reveals the intent to distinguish himself from the abstract and ahistorical approach of the vulgar Marxists, notably from Bukharin's conception of historical materialism.[16]

2.3   *The Power of Analogy*

In this framework, the fundamental role of analogy stands out. Gramsci is a master in creating surprising and often illuminating parallels: terms of comparison could be either political events, social attitudes, single historical figures or even ideologies and philosophies (a survey of the different types of comparisons established by Gramsci could have been much longer, though). As to the analogies of the *Prison Notebooks* we could mention for instance the ones between: the medieval crisis and the modern crisis (cf. Q6, §10); the protestant Reformation, the French Revolution and Marxism; the passive revolutions of the nineteenth century and the transformations of the twentieth century (cf. Q15, §59).[17] As Burgio observes, Gramsci's analogical judgements rely at

---

13   Q4, §66, p. 511; Gramsci 1996b, p. 240; Q13, §27, p. 1621; Gramsci 1971a, p. 221.

14   Cf. Q4, §25 and Q11, §30, where he investigated the status of scientific knowledge by discarding some prejudices about it – I quote from the second version of the note (Gramsci 1971a, p. 467): 'Nor, again, can it be held that the laws of a given natural science are identical with the laws of history'. On Gramsci and science, see Antonini 2014.

15   As Burgio noticed, a forerunner of this formula could have been represented by the expression 'practical scheme' used by Gramsci in some pre-prison articles (see Burgio 2014, pp. 137–8). However, Gramsci never uses this expression in the *Prison Notebooks*, where the term 'scheme' is always conceived of as highly normative and therefore negative – he qualifies it as 'sociological' (Q1, §130; Q7, §15; Q9, §133; Q13, §27), 'abstract' (Q3, §48; Q11, §52) or 'general' (Q9, §136).

16   On this point, see Frosini 2013b, p. 2. It is noteworthy that, when describing his attitude towards history as a quest for 'practical criteria' of interpretation, Gramsci echoes (by reassessing) Croce's definition of historical materialism as a mere collection of historiographic criteria, not as an independent theoretical position, a self-standing philosophy.

17   For an (albeit incomplete) survey of the historical comparisons drawn by Gramsci, see

least partly on his reading of Marx's 1859 *Preface*, which is itself based on the assumption of the comparability between the processes of crisis in the different epochs.[18]

From a certain point of view we could also argue that there is a 'family resemblance' between Gramsci's use of analogies and the category of translatability – if we understand comparison in the broadest sense, the most famous and striking Gramscian parallel is probably the one established between French political thought and German philosophy, already evoked by Marx in the *Holy Family*.[19]

Strictly speaking, historical analogies are drawn by Gramsci between specific situations and figures that allow him to highlight their common features and to elaborate long-standing political categories. In this respect, Gramsci mostly compares events that took place in different epochs, in order to point out their paradigmatic features. The capacity to link non-contemporaneous events constitutes the principal strength of historical analogies, since connecting past and present is essential to understand the historical narrative and, ultimately, to intervene successfully in the political dynamic.

Nevertheless, Gramsci is conscious of the risks connected to the use of analogies and he repeatedly warns against a carefree and naive use of historical parallels.[20] This is the reason why, for instance, in a famous note on the subaltern groups (Q3, §18, later reassessed in Q25, §4) Gramsci condemns the comparison made by Ettore Ciccotti between the ancient and medieval system and the modern one:[21]

Burgio 2016, pp. 84 ff. It should be noted, however, that Burgio does not engage with a critical discussion of the analogy embedded in the concept of Caesarism, despite recognising its importance (Burgio 2016, p. 99).

18   See Burgio 2016, p. 81 *et passim*.

19   Cf. for instance Q1, § 44, that introduces the topic of 'translatability', one of Gramsci's core concepts (on this category, see Frosini 2010b, pp. 171–86; but see the entire Part II of Ives-Lacorte 2010). The category of translatability and that of historical analogy are partially overlapping but they do not have to be confused. Both of them establish a relationship between a closer or 'internal' element (politics, praxis, etc.) and a more distant or 'external' one. However, while translatability is a form of critical reduction, analogy provides Gramsci with a practical criterion of action.

20   On the use of historical analogies, especially with political purposes, see Canfora 2010; with regard to Gramsci, see Burgio 2016. Generally speaking, it should be noted that analogies imply not only underlying affinities between two distinct events or figures, but also an awareness of the differences between them. The richness (and the ambiguity) of analogies lies in this status of identity and non-identity at the same time.

21   Ettore Ciccotti (1863–1939) was an Italian historian and politician.

the method of 'analogy' affirmed and theorised by Ciccotti could give some 'circumstantial' results ... Another research criterion should be taken into account to show the dangers embedded in the method of historical analogy as a key of interpretation: in the ancient and medieval state both the territorial-political centralisation and the social centralisation (and the latter depends on the former) were minimal.[22]

Despite this warning (strictly connected to the polemical context of Gramsci's discussion), Gramsci's judgement on historical analogy as a whole is positive. Not by chance in Q15, §11, a key paragraph for his political theory, he affirms: 'since similar situations almost always arise in every historical development, one should see if it is not possible to draw from this some general principle of political science and art'.[23]

3   The Caesarist Model between Marx and Gramsci

3.1   *Caesarism as Historical Analogy*

Gramsci's observations show their validity to the highest degree if we take into account the category of Caesarism. Generally speaking, this concept describes a situation in which a charismatic figure emerges and establishes a form of autocratic government, usually supported by reactionary forces. This category arises in the description of the middle of the nineteenth century and explicitly refers to the new-born French Second Empire of Napoleon III. However, the roots of this phenomenon should be sought far earlier, as the very name suggests: the eponymous hero of the category is the Roman *dictator* Julius Caesar. Historical analogy lies therefore at the origin of this political concept and it displays its essential character.

The history of Caesarism is well-documented and I cannot repeat it here.[24] A milestone in this framework is represented by Marx's historical masterpiece, *The Eighteenth Brumaire of Louis Bonaparte*. Here, however, Marx rejects the concept of Caesarism and adopts the one of Bonapartism, because, as

---

22   Q25, §4, pp. 2286–7.

23   Q15, §11, p. 1767; Gramsci 1971a, p. 109. On the meaning of historical analogies in Machiavelli, a well-known model for Gramsci's political reflections, see Ruggiero 2015.

24   On the history of the category of Caesarism, see in particular Cervelli 1996. See also Mangoni 1979, Groh 1979, Baehr and Richter 2004, and Richter 2005 that analyses this concept within its semantic field, i.e. with cognate concepts such as Bonapartism or Dictatorship.

he affirms, the economic and social situation of antiquity cannot be compared with modern capitalist society.[25] This strong refusal notwithstanding, the 'methodological tool' of analogy also plays a crucial role in Marx. The opening of *The Eighteenth Brumaire* is famous: 'Hegel remarks somewhere that all facts and personages of great importance in world history occur, as it were, twice. He forgot to add: the first time as tragedy, the second as farce'.[26]

Although Marx is making a historical parallel, the comparison is explicitly problematised because of the different characterisation of the occurrences (either as tragedy or as farce).[27] Furthermore, the very same title is the result of an (implicit) historical comparison: Marx is aware that the 'Eighteenth Brumaire' is properly the successful *coup d'état* of Napoleon Bonaparte (Napoleon I) in 1799, but he applies consciously this definition to the *putsch* of his nephew in 1851.

Despite Marx's discarding of the category of Caesarism and, paradoxically, thanks to the popularity of Marx's *Eighteenth Brumaire*, the concept of Caesarism had a great success and was used by many thinkers from the left as well as from the right. After Marx, the category of Caesarism was applied to a large number of different historical and political scenarios. New categories inspired by the concept of Caesarism were created: Bismarckism, Boulangism, etc. The result is an intricate and fascinating 'play of mirrors', where the previous applications influence the most recent ones, by renewing continuously the historical analogy that represents the core of the concept.

3.2   *Gramsci and the Caesarist Tradition*

In this scenario, the Gramscian theory of Caesarism is by far the most sophisticated and richest one. His reading stands out because of his capacity to take into account previous elaborations, and especially the Marxian one, as well as to reuse them in an original way to interpret his troubled times. Marx's *Eighteenth Brumaire* is indeed one of Gramsci's main sources from the 1920s onwards, and it becomes even more important after his imprisonment, as demonstrated

---

25   See Marx 1985 [1869], p. 57 (it is the *Preface* to the second edition of the *Eighteenth Brumaire*, 1869): 'I hope that my work will contribute towards eliminating the school-taught phrase now current, particularly in Germany, of so-called Caesarism. In this superficial historical analogy the main point is forgotten, namely, that in ancient Rome the class struggle took place only within a privileged minority, between the free rich and the free poor, while the great productive mass of the population, the slaves, formed the purely passive pedestal for these combatants'. On Marx's discarding of the concept of Caesarism, see also Bravo 2003.

26   Marx 1979 [1852], p. 103.

27   See also Tomba 2013, pp. 35–59.

by the number of notes that rely on it, directly or indirectly. As I have argued elsewhere, Gramsci's uninterrupted 'dialogue' with Marx's historical works represents a *Leitmotiv* of his thought.[28]

As to the connection between Caesarism and historical analogy in the *Prison Notebooks*, it is noteworthy that, at an early stage of his reflections, Gramsci mentions the opening of the *Eighteenth Brumaire* with the opposition between tragedy and farce, although stressing mostly the Hegelian origin of this image (Q3, § 51).[29] By evoking this parallel Gramsci seems to warn against an oversimplified use of the historical analogy. Caution is particularly necessary when dealing with Caesarism, since this concept, as well as it cognate category of Bonapartism, was precociously misinterpreted.

Establishing a parallel between contemporary Caesarist phenomena and their ancient or modern forerunners is therefore not an immediate operation for Gramsci, who does not trust superficial applications of the category of Caesarism. That emerges clearly, for example, from Q17, § 21, which contains a strong rejection of Napoleon III's Caesarism, as well as a criticism of its renewal by the author of an article on Julius Caesar in the journal *Nuova Antologia* of September 1933.[30] Gramsci's suspiciousness could be traced also in the notes explicitly dedicated to the construction of his own theory of Caesarism: in Q13, § 27, for instance, he talks about 'a generic hypothesis, a sociological schema (convenient for the art of politics)' and describes Caesarism as a 'polemical-ideological formula, and not a canon of historical interpretation'.[31] Nevertheless I disagree with those that read these expressions as a 'definite discarding of the concept of Caesarism'.[32] On my part, I think that this caution does not imply a dismissal of the category, but instead a warning against a misuse of it – the repeated stress on this point is due to the particularly troubled history of the category.

---

28   Direct references are contained in Q3, § 51, Q7, § 24, Q9, § 133, Q13, §§ 23 and 27. Many other notes refer however indirectly to this work by Marx. For an analysis of Gramsci's readings of the *Eighteenth Brumaire* and for an overview of his Marxian sources before and after his imprisonment, see my forthcoming book (Antonini forthcoming).

29   It is interesting that in the following texts (§§ 52 and 53) he quotes also from Marx's *The Holy Family*, showing that this cluster of notes is moulded by a 'Marxian' spirit.

30   See Q17, § 21, p. 1924: 'the theory of Caesarism that is now predominant (cf. the discourse of Emilio Bodrero *The Humanity of Julius Caesar*, in the "Nuova Antologia" of 16 September 1933) was introduced into political language by Napoleon III, who was not a big historian or philosopher or theoretician of politics. It is certain that in Roman history the figure of Caesar was featured not only or not principally by "Caesarism" in this strict sense'.

31   See Q13, § 27, pp. 1621 and 1619; Gramsci 1971a, pp. 220 and 221.

32   Cospito 2011a, p. 289.

In other words, Gramsci's methodological concern about keeping together the abstract elements and the concrete ones, the theoretical paradigm and the analysis of single case studies re-emerges here, as shown above.[33] As a matter of fact, far from rejecting *in toto* the category of Caesarism, Gramsci affirms that:

> none of these observations is absolute; at various moments of history and in various countries they have widely differing significance ... These observations must not be conceived of as rigid schemata, but merely as practical criteria of historical and political interpretation.[34]

4   Caesarism in the *Prison Notebooks*

4.1   *Two Notes from Notebook 13*

But what is Caesarism exactly, according to Gramsci? The concept of Caesarism is an important category in the Gramscian conception of politics and history; closely linked to more famous concepts such as 'passive revolution', 'hegemony', 'organic crisis' and 'war of position', it represents a model of authoritarian-dictatorial regime.[35] In what follows I will focus on how this concept is moulded by historical comparisons. For this purpose, I will concentrate on two notes from the 'special' Notebook 13 on Machiavelli's politics, § 23 and § 27. Although written in a relatively late phase of Gramsci's work (October–November 1933), they represent a crucial passage in the elaboration of the concept of Caesarism.[36]

Q13, § 23, in particular, gathers many texts from the 'miscellaneous' Notebooks 4, 7, and 9, but it is much more than the simple sum of its parts: the single elements find in this second version a deeper sense; textual variants and new observations significantly enrich the general meaning. As Gramsci clearly

---

33   That also means that not every example of political leadership can be classified as Caesarist and, vice versa, that Caesarism does not imply necessarily the presence of a strong leader.

34   Q13, § 23, pp. 1605 and 1610; Gramsci 1971a, pp. 212 and 217.

35   On the Gramscian theory of Caesarism, see Fontana 2004 (however, his reconstruction is simplified and, from a certain point of view, wrong). Hints to the Caesarist issue are contained also in Roberts 2011. As to the secondary literature in Italian, see in particular Mangoni 1979, De Felice 1977, and more recently Burgio 2014. For a critical discussion of the bibliography, and for a fresh analysis of Gramsci's theory of Caesarism, see Antonini forthcoming.

36   For the most recent chronology, see Cospito 2011b.

states in the title (*Observations on Certain Aspects of the Structure of Political Parties in Periods of Organic Crisis*), the topic of the note is how political parties behave in the context of 'organic crisis' or 'crisis of hegemony' (he is clearly referring to his own times).[37] If a new order does not emerge and the crisis does not find a solution, then a charismatic figure, a Caesar, arises. The emergence of this leader is usually prepared by a reinforcement of the conservative forces within society and the state, notably the civil and military bureaucracy. In this framework, Gramsci reflects on the differences between Bonapartist-Caesarist phenomena and pure military governments.

This note is marked by frequent historical comparisons. The first one is represented by the quotation of *The Eighteenth Brumaire* by Marx.[38] Thanks to this hint he is evoking not only a theoretical paradigm of interpretation, but also the historical context to which Marx refers – he is establishing therefore also a very synthetic comparison between mid-nineteenth-century France and Europe in the postwar period. The second one involves the references to Greece and Spain as examples of pure military regimes based on brutal coercion, while authentic Caesarism is based on a form of consensus.[39] The third and more articulated historical comparison is strictly connected to Gramsci's methodological concerns. Here he writes:

> these observations [on Caesarism] must not be conceived of as rigid schemata, but merely as practical criteria of historical and political interpretation. In concrete analyses of real events, the historical forms are individualised and can almost be called "unique". Caesar represents a very different combination of real circumstances from that represented by Napoleon I, as does Primo de Rivera from that of Zivkovic, etc.[40]

---

37   On Gramsci's conception of the 'organic crisis', see the entry by Lelio La Porta in Liguori and Voza 2009, pp. 180–2 and Thomas 2009a, *passim*.

38   Q13, § 23. In the first version of this part of Q13, § 23 (Q4, § 69) the reference to the *Eighteenth Brumaire* is missing.

39   See Q13, § 23, p. 1608; Gramsci 1971a, p. 215: 'this series of observations is indispensable for any really profound analysis of the specific political form usually termed Caesarism or Bonapartism – to distinguish it from other forms in which the technical-military element as such predominates, in conformations perhaps still more visible and exclusive. Spain and Greece offer two typical examples, with both similar and dissimilar characteristics'.

40   Q13, § 23, p. 1610; Gramsci 1971a, p. 217. Primo de Rivera was dictator of Spain between 1923 and 1930, with the support of the monarchy. Petar Živković was Yugoslavia's prime minister between 1929 and 1932, and the instrument of King Alexander's dictatorial rule during those years.

Here Gramsci establishes an illuminating multiple comparison between different forms of Caesarism: Caesar versus Napoleon I, Primo de Rivera versus Živković, but also Caesar/Napoleon I versus Primo de Rivera/Zivkovic. Given that all these political phenomena show common features that allow them to be classified as Caesarist, the emphasis put by Gramsci on the differences between them stands out. From the methodological point of view, this stress on the specificity of single cases allows Gramsci to explore the variety of the general category of Caesarism and to discover its essential richness.

4.2   *The Taxonomy of Caesarism*

In § 27 this pivotal role of analogy is even clearer. This paragraph is the result of the combination of §§ 133 and 136 from Notebook 9 and contains an elaborated classification of the different types of Caesarism. The note opens with the expression of Gramsci's desire to 'compile a catalogue of the historical events which have culminated in a great "heroic" personality'.[41] This declaration is followed by a famous definition of Caesarism:

> when the progressive force A struggles with the reactionary force B, not only may A defeat B or B defeat A, but it may happen that neither A nor B defeats the other – that they bleed each other mutually and then a third force C intervenes from outside, subjugating what is left of both A and B.[42]

As he adds later, however, 'it is possible to render the hypothesis ever more concrete, to carry it to an ever greater degree of approximation to concrete historical reality, and this can be achieved by defining certain fundamental elements'.[43]

These statements illuminate Gramsci's articulation of the category of Caesarism and his use of historical comparisons. As in § 23, analogy brings him to stress both affinities and dissimilarities. As to the concrete examples suggested by Gramsci to explain the different alternatives on the field, he uses a limited number of historical cases, with slight changes (especially when dealing with contemporary phenomena). The result is a multifaceted description of the historical situations taken into account, portrayed from different points of view according to the different variables.

---

41   Q13, § 27, p. 1619; Gramsci 1971a, p. 219.
42   Q13, § 27, p. 1619; Gramsci 1971a, p. 219.
43   Q13, § 27, p. 1621; Gramsci 1971a, p. 221.

In addition to this, in § 27 historical comparisons are combined with the use of antithetic conceptual couples. The first one is the famous opposition between *progressive* and *regressive* Caesarisms. As he writes, 'Caesarism is progressive when its intervention helps the progressive force to triumph', regressive, when its intervention helps the reactionary one.[44] Examples of progressive Caesarism are Caesar and Napoleon I, instances of regressive Caesarism Napoleon III and Bismarck.[45] After this we have the opposition of *modern* and *pre-modern* Caesarisms, where, in Gramsci's view, the watershed between modernity and pre-modernity is represented by the defeat of the French Commune in 1871 (note that he refrains from using the category of contemporaneity). Pre-modern Caesarism, like Caesar and Napoleon I, usually takes place thanks to a military *coup d'état*, while the modern one is the result of a longer process of reorganisation of the state supported by bureaucratic apparatuses. Then Gramsci focuses on the types of crisis that have led to Caesarist episodes – *organic* or *contingent* – and on the *qualitative* or *quantitative* dimension of these solutions. Again, while Napoleon's Caesarism stands out from a 'real' crisis and is 'absolutely' progressive, the regime of his nephew was 'brought about by a "momentary" political deficiency of the traditional dominant force' and it is 'merely ... quantitative'.[46] The conceptual articulation ends here, but we could argue that Gramsci did not consider it as definitive: as a matter of fact this note is more a sketch than a concluded text, much like the *Prison Notebooks* as a whole.[47]

In short, the original combination of these two dialectical strategies (the use of historical analogies and of opposing conceptual couples) makes Gramsci's

---

44   Q13, § 27, p. 1619; Gramsci 1971a, p. 219.

45   In short, the Caesarist solutions applied by Caesar and Napoleon I are qualified as positive insofar as they made possible the transition from one type of state to another. Although Gramsci does not engage with a detailed description of the different historical contexts, we could argue that the progressive force supported by Caesar can be identified with the groups (*populares*, people from the roman provinces), which increased their economic and political weight in the delicate phase of the decline of the republic and the birth of the empire (for a careful account of Caesar's 'democratic dictatorship', see Canfora 1999). More precise could be the identification of the progressive force supported by Napoleon Bonaparte with the bourgeoisie – see in this framework the famous definition of the 'long' French Revolution as a 'bourgeois revolution'. Napoleon III and Bismarck, contrarily, did not introduce substantial changes in the state and therefore their political action is backward-looking.

46   Q13, § 27, p. 1621; Gramsci 1971a, p. 221.

47   Some textual hints suggest this interpretation: see the passage where Gramsci says that 'A Caesarist solution can exist even without a Caesar, without any great, "heroic" and representative personality. The parliamentary system has also provided a mechanism for such compromise solutions' (Q13, § 27, p. 1619; Gramsci 1971a, p. 220).

interpretation of the category of Caesarism extremely powerful and allows him to display the potential of the concept.

4.3   Interpreting the Present from the Past

Although he mostly refers to past cases of Caesarism (especially Caesar, Napoleon I and Napoleon III), it is clear that Gramsci looks at the present when he reflects on the nature and on the characteristics of Caesarist regimes.

A crucial point of reference in Gramsci's comparative analysis is represented by the authoritarian governments of his time, fascist Italy and the USSR. On the one hand, the comprehension of the mechanisms that rule these opposite but somehow similar regimes are the final terms and objects of his investigation. On the other hand, the troubled historico-political situation in which Gramsci lives strongly influences his own conception of Caesarism and represents the context in which he develops his analysis of the category. Some references to these historical experiences make clear this connection. For instance, Gramsci mentions openly in Q13, § 27 the 'Caesarist' attitude of fascism before 1926 and Mussolini's charismatic character. As to Soviet Russia, allusions to its Caesarist features can be found in notes on 'statolatry' as well as in texts on so-called 'black parliamentarism' – both these issues are connected to the Caesarist phenomenon, and describe (although not explicitly) the ambiguously authoritarian outcomes of Russian socialism.[48]

Gramsci's more general analysis of the features of contemporary Caesarism is also extremely significant. Indeed, Caesarism contributes to clarifying the 'democratic-bureaucratic' essence of modernity.[49] It sheds light on the totalitarian character of twentieth-century regimes and on the new type of hegemony required by them.[50] Particularly remarkable are Gramsci's observations on the transformation within the state and within the state apparatuses, that unfolds some of the most significant political reflections of the *Prison Notebooks* – I

---

48   See Q8, §130 and Q14, §§ 74–6. The issues raised here are complicated and cannot be investigated in detail; see Antonini forthcoming.

49   On the description of contemporary regimes as 'democratic-bureaucratic', see for instance Q12, §1. Illuminating in this respect are Frosini 2016a, Frosini 2016b, and the already quoted Frosini 2017.

50   Gramsci's account of totalitarian politics is not to be confused with the concept of totalitarianism elaborated in the aftermath of the Second World War. In Gramsci's view, the term totalitarian denotes simply a 'conception of the world' that does not allow the existence of contemporary, concurrent ideologies – see Antonini 2016 for a critical discussion of the relationship between the categories of Caesarism and Totalitarianism. A rather unconvincing entry for '*Totalitario*' by Renato Caputo can be found in Liguori and Voza 2009, pp. 851–3.

refer here in particular to the observations on bureaucracy and police (conceived of in the broadest sense) as key elements of the Caesarist solution.[51] These issues are not easy to interpret and I cannot analyse them here; however, it is important to mention them to show how deeply past and present are intermingled in Gramsci's view. Moreover, that proves how far-reaching the historical analogy represented by the category of Caesarism is.

5 Gramsci between Tradition and Innovation

5.1 *Marx, Gramsci and* The Eighteenth Brumaire

This is, roughly speaking, Gramsci's articulation of the category of Caesarism. In this last section, I would like to focus briefly on the relationship between Gramsci and his main source – Marx's *Eighteenth Brumaire* – with regard to the category of Caesarism. Actually, I think that his 'dialogue' with Marx has a long-lasting effect on Gramsci and it contributes significantly to stimulating his reflections on Caesarism, both from a substantial and from a formal point of view. With regard to the content, many elements of Gramsci's analysis are in fact inspired by Marx: the description of the bureaucracy; the distinction between the 'real' and the 'legal'; the centrality of the figure of Louis Napoleon; etc.[52] What is more important in the framework of our analysis, however, is Marx's influence on Gramsci's methodology.

As I showed before, the Marxian account is problematic, since it refuses the historical analogy represented by the concept of Caesarism but, at the same time, Marx employs other historical comparisons himself in order to show the affinities and differences between Napoleon III and his uncle and, broadly speaking, between the Revolution of 1848 and the Great Revolution of 1789 and its aftermath. As for Gramsci, he shares Marx's polemical refusal of the vulgar formulation of Caesarism. However, his reply is more than simple polemics. He reacts by explicitly reinventing and reassessing the category of Caesarism and, in a broader sense, the instrument of historical comparison. To sum up, I would argue that Gramsci deepens Marx's legacy and he gives back to analogy its profound heuristic value.

Moreover, Gramsci's reassessment of Caesarism seems to take cue from Marx's very style of 'comparative' analysis. It is likely that the Gramscian model of reasoning was influenced by Marx insofar as it is focused on stressing the

---

51   See Antonini forthcoming, *passim.*
52   See again Antonini forthcoming, *passim.*

differences between similar historical events. I would suggest that the opposition between tragedy and farce depicted in the opening of Marx's work as
well as other conceptual couples (explicitly or implicitly) evoked in the *Eighteenth Brumaire* could have stimulated somehow Gramsci's reassessment of the
principle of historical comparison, especially in relation to the category of
Caesarism.[53] Exemplary in this respect is Gramsci's sophisticated articulation
of the Caesarist phenomenon – cf. the already mentioned distinction between
progressive and regressive Caesarism as well as the other ones deployed by
Gramsci (modern or pre-modern, systematic or transitory, qualitative or quantitative).

5.2   *Analogy, History and Historicism*

To sum up, Gramsci's reflection on Caesarism is composite and many-sided and
it offers a meaningful insight into his conception of historical comparisons.
For its part, analogy displays itself as a pivot of the *Prison Notebooks* and the
evaluation of its role allows us to reach a deeper comprehension of Gramsci's
historical understanding.

History, in Gramsci's view, cannot be separated from philosophy and politics, and it constitutes with them what we could define, *mutatis mutandis*, as a
'homogeneous circle'.[54] In this perspective, on the one hand, the connection
between past and present made possible by the analogy opens up challenging
new theoretical scenarios, thanks to the emergence of historical paradigms and
to the possibility of drawing a wider historical narrative.[55] On the other hand, as
already shown at the outset, these comparisons reveal clear political features,
insofar as 'history interests us for "political" reasons' and the past history is the
'the basis of present and future history'.[56]

The issues analysed here can then be placed within the context of Gramsci's
'integral history' and, on a more general level, within his 'absolute historicism',
as the more comprehensive framework of Gramsci's thought.[57] In conclusion,
it is only in this context that the importance of historical analogies stands out,
in particular the analogy represented by the concept of Caesarism.

---

53   It is not irrelevant to notice that Gramsci's train of thought often relies on the use of oppos-
     ite conceptual couples, by revealing, *mutatis mutandis*, a 'dilemmatic' or 'binary' way of
     reasoning – the relationship between Gramsci's dialectical thinking and his use of ana-
     logy is also a challenging topic, that deserves to be investigated.
54   See Q11, §65, p. 1492; Gramsci 1971a, p. 403.
55   On Gramsci's conception of history and on the relationship between history and philo-
     sophy in the Italian tradition (notably Croce and Gentile), see the entry *Storia* by Fabio
     Frosini in Liguori and Voza 2009, pp. 807–11 and Frosini 2011–12.
56   Q14, §63, p. 1723; Q4, §25, p. 444; Gramsci 1996b, p. 165.
57   See the entry on '*Storicismo*' by Giuseppe Cacciatore, in Liguori and Voza 2009, pp. 814–18.

PART 4

Subalternity between Pre-modernity and Modernity

∵

CHAPTER 10

We Good Subalterns

Peter D. Thomas

In the 'Preface' to *Beyond Good and Evil* (subtitled *Prelude to a Philosophy of the Future*), Nietzsche famously wrote that

> the struggle against Plato ... has created a magnificent tension of spirit in Europe, the likes of which the earth has never known: with such a tension in our bow we can now shoot at the furthest goals. Granted, the European experiences this tension as a crisis or state of need; and twice already there have been attempts, in a grand fashion, to unbend the bow, once through Jesuitism, and the second time through the democratic Enlightenment ... But we, who are neither Jesuits nor democrats, nor even German enough, we *good Europeans* and free, *very* free spirits – we still have it, the whole need of spirit and the whole tension of its bow! And perhaps the arrow too, the task, and – who knows? the *goal* ...[1]

According to a certain composite image of popular interpretations, the figure of the subaltern derived from Gramsci's *Prison Notebooks* represents all that such 'good Europeans' are not. The subaltern lacks that magnificent tension of spirit that incessantly pushes free spirits towards 'progress' and a transvaluation of all values. The crisis of the European is oriented to the future and its imposing goals; the subaltern, on the other hand, remains submerged in the muck of ages, if not a residue of the past then not entirely at home in the present. While 'good Europeans' are subject to the hegemonic logic of modern state construction, the subaltern lies before or beyond it, in some indeterminate zone of affect. The subaltern, that is, constitutively lies at the 'limit' of representation,[2] understood in the senses both of *Vertretung* and of *Darstellung* (as suggested by Spivak in her influential text 'Can the Subaltern Speak'?).[3] As such, the sub-

---

1   Nietzsche 2002, pp. 2–3.

2   'The subaltern is necessarily the absolute limit of the place where history is narrativized into logic' (Spivak 1988a, p. 207).

3   Spivak 1988a; see also Spivak 1985. Morris 2010 provides an account of the various iterations of this influential text. For a recent example of its continuing productivity as a paradigm of research, see Olsen 2015. Arguably the most consequential elaboration of Spivak's approach

altern is understood as a variant of modern political thought's dream (or is it a nightmare?) of its repressed foundation, from the rebellious multitude that menaced the emergence of sovereignty at its dawn to the shadowy figure of *homo sacer* called upon to preside over its postmodern twilight. The supposedly unrepresentable subaltern is thus ultimately represented as the literal incarnation of the principle of exclusion as the foundation of the political, and of political modernity as such.

A cursory glance at the *Prison Notebooks* would seem to confirm this characterisation of the subaltern as an ahistorical remainder not yet entirely caught up in the march of historical progress. For instance, Gramsci's special notebook on this topic, Notebook 25, is entitled 'On the Margins of History (History of subaltern social groups)' [*Ai margini della storia (storia dei gruppi sociali subalterni)*]. It contains a wide range of historical examples, ranging from ancient Rome to Medieval Europe to post-Risorgimento Italy, seemingly grouped together in an indifferent order. It has therefore seemed to more than one reader that Gramsci attempted to develop a transhistorical concept of the subaltern, of the night in which all subalterns are subalterns.[4] It was this reading that allowed the notion of subalternity to appear to be particularly relevant to colonial and postcolonial contexts, offering a transhistorical vocabulary that seemed to escape the 'historicist', 'teleological', or 'Eurocentric' prejudices common to most theories of modernity and modernisation. It was also the apparently generic nature of Gramsci's explorations that made them so amenable to their subsequent diffusion into a wide range of disciplinary and national traditions in the forms of the various subaltern studies, from the original interventions into South Asian historiography of the subaltern studies collective to the literary, sociological, anthropological and theoretical accents that have marked subaltern studies' translation into Latin America, Central and East Asia, the Middle East, the USA and Ireland.[5]

In this chapter, I will argue that a closer study of the development of the notion of subaltern classes or social groups in the *Prison Notebooks* provides us with a very different perspective on the political constitution of the specific

---

to the theme of subalternity, despite other differences between them, was in Chakrabarty 2000.

4   A representative example of this type of reading can be found in Young 1990 and particularly Young 2012.

5   Among the numerous attempts to translate subaltern studies into other national, linguistic and cultural contexts, see Lloyd 1993, Beverley 1999, Mignolo 2000, Rodríguez and López 2001, Atabaki 2008, Cronin 2008, Pandey 2010, and Rabasa 2010. For reflections on the original subaltern studies collective's initiatives, see Chakrabarty 2002, pp. 3–19. For overviews of the field's international development, see Chaturvedi 2000 and particularly Ludden 2001.

experience of subalternity that for Gramsci characterises political modernity. This notion of the subaltern is not defined by its exclusion from the construction of modern state power in the particular bourgeois hegemonic project that Gramsci comes to nominate as 'passive revolution'.[6] Rather than excluded, the subaltern social groups for Gramsci are integrally 'included', or 'actively integrated', in the hegemonic relations of the bourgeois integral state.[7] This inclusion or integration, however, should not be thought in terms of an incorporation within the modern state-form of elements previously located 'outside' it. Rather, inclusion here should be understood in terms of something closer to an active sense of its etymological origins, as an 'enclosing'. Subaltern social groups are enclosed within the relations of the integral state, and it is precisely this 'enclosure' that constitutes them as distinctively modern subaltern social groups. They are conceived not as a sociological entity endowed with a prior history that remains determining if not determinant, but as constituted solely within and by the novel political relationality that exists only within political modernity. Whatever the origins of their members in so-called 'pre-modernity', subaltern social groups *qua* subaltern social groups only exist as such within the dialectical relations of civil and political society, or in other words, with the hegemonic relations of force that structure the bourgeois integral state. In a strict sense, they are produced by it. Rather than exclusion, inclusion or even 'inclusive exclusion', it might therefore be more appropriate to speak of the 'constitution' of subaltern social groups.[8] Subalternity in this sense is a function of the process of material constitution of the modern state itself, understood not as a 'machine' of regulation, administration and rationalisation (in a Weberian sense), but in terms of a distinctively modern political relationality and rationality. Rather than an exceptional or marginal case, whether conceived as originary raw material for a project of 'exodus' (such as promoted by contemporary radical political ontologies), or the unjustly wronged and oppressed that motivates the liberal tradition's expansionary project of integration into the benefits of citizenship and its system of enabling rights, subaltern-

---

6 There now exists an extensive literature on the concept of 'passive revolution' much of it conflicting with other interpretations. For a recent philological and contextual interpretation, see Di Meo 2014.

7 See Francioni and Frosini 2009, p. 209.

8 For Agamben, 'the juridico-political order has the structure of an inclusion of what is simultaneously pushed outside' and the 'relation of exception' is the 'extreme form of relation by which something is included solely through its exclusion' (Agamben 1998, p. 18). For Gramsci, on the other hand, the 'inclusion' or 'constitution' of subaltern social groups in the modern state is substantive and non-exclusionary; on the contrary, it functions by means of their activation and mobilisation, albeit in passive forms.

ity for Gramsci is all too quotidian and central; it describes the basic structuring conditions of political modernity in all of its contradictory forms.

My concern here is not to take up a partisan position in the recent polemics and critiques of the ostensibly anti-enlightenment or anti-universalist stances of subaltern studies;[9] the plurality of its international development and articulations, and the conflicts that have traversed it from within, have given rise to a variety of tendencies that cannot easily be reduced to a coherent or consistent paradigm.[10] Nor am I concerned to condemn Guha, Spivak or many others for their supposed philological 'misunderstandings', or more generously, their 'creative readings'. It was and remains the great merit of what might now be regarded as the 'classical subaltern studies' of the collective gathered around Guha to have directed attention to the importance of this concept in the *Prison Notebooks*, which had been largely though not entirely neglected by Gramsci scholars before them.[11] Early 'subalternists', basing themselves upon a creative reading of the partial English translation of Gramsci's carceral writings from 1971, *Selections from the Prison Notebooks*, thereby opened up rich new fields of research, including but by no means limited to the now almost 'canonical' exploration of the subaltern's 'incapacity'.[12] The research agendas and pro-

---

9   Chibber 2013 stimulated the most recent controversies, though similar critiques can also be found in Kaiwar 2014 and, earlier, Chaturvedi 2000 and Brennan 2001a.

10   Guha's original appropriation of the notion of subalternity from Gramsci, for instance, arguably contains a more nuanced version of its structuring, collective dynamics of relations between elites and subalterns than the one that became common under the influence of Spivak's famous intervention, focused upon the phenomenological or even existential dimensions of the singular figure of the subaltern. See Guha's contributions to the early volumes of *Subaltern Studies* (Guha 1982–99) and particularly Guha 1997.

11   For instance, an Italian discussion of subaltern classes and related concepts, particularly the 'popular' occurred in the late 1940s and early 1950s, involving, amongst others, De Martino, Luporini, Fortini and Cirese, but failed to find a wider international audience at the time. See Pasquinelli 1977 and Cirese 1973, and for a commentary, Liguori 2011 and 2015. Interestingly, this debate was initiated (with an essay by De Martino in 1948) before the publication of those of Gramsci's *Prison Notebooks* that contained the notes on 'subaltern social classes' (in the volume on the Risorgimento in the thematic Platone-Togliatti edition, published in 1949), and did not cite Gramsci's specific notes on subaltern classes even after they became available (although Gramsci was widely quoted in these discussions in relation to other themes, including 'folklore'). This anomaly suggests that there was an independent tradition of subaltern theorising in Italian social and political thought prior to and independent of Gramsci, a tradition that is still to be reconstructed fully and its impact on Gramsci assessed.

12   I am referring here to the proliferation of studies entitled with variations of Spivak's famous question, now so extensive as to constitute almost a particular 'genre' or even 'subdiscipline' of critical inquiry.

jects produced by the transnationalisation of the notion of subalternity (from India to Latin America to Ireland and beyond) now effectively constitute their own distinct paradigm of research, separate from – and increasingly citing less frequently – the suggestive studies in the *Prison Notebooks* that had initially inspired them.[13]

However, one of the less noted legacies of the Subaltern Studies collective is also the inspiration that it has provided to new initiatives in the field of Gramscian philology,[14] as well as, particularly more recently, renewed engagements with the relevance of Gramsci's concepts for contemporary political analysis.[15] Benefitting from recent philological and historical-contextual advances in our knowledge of his work, and an integral Italian critical edition of his texts, this scholarship has highlighted the extent to which Gramsci offers a much more expansive understanding of forms of subalternity. Rather than unrepresentable, subaltern social groups in the *Prison Notebooks* are depicted as the product of elaborate representative and self-representative strategies; rather than being unable to speak, Gramsci's historical and cultural analyses emphasise the extent to which the subaltern continually makes its voice heard in contradictory and complex cultural, social and political forms, in both 'postcolonial' and 'metropolitan' realities; rather than a figure of socio-economic and political exclusion, the subaltern for Gramsci represents a complex process of inclusion in the forms of the modern nation-state; rather than opposed to the figure of the citizen, the political theory developed in the *Prison Notebooks* suggests that the subaltern should instead be comprehended as a specific form in which the contradictions of modern citizenship are most intensely realised. It is in the spirit of this season of studies that I will now attempt to present an outline of the emergence of the concept of subaltern classes in the early *Prison Notebooks*, in order to argue that they contain *in nuce* a distinctive and novel theory of political modernity.

---

13   Although Gramsci's name was and continues to be invoked as a type of 'founding father' of subaltern studies, detailed engagement with his actual texts was relatively limited at the origins of subaltern studies, and is even less present in most recent work within the field (including most critiques of it). In the first volume of *Subaltern Studies*, Gramsci in general and his comments on subaltern classes in particular are rarely cited except in Guha's contributions, and even in these there is little sustained textual analysis. See, e.g., Guha 1982, pp. vii, 8.

14   Buttigieg 1999 and his entry in Liguori and Voza 2009, pp. 826–30, Green 2002 and 2011, Baratta 2007, Frosini 2010a, Modonesi 2010.

15   Nilsen and Roy 2015, Crehan 2016.

1   Subalternity in the *Prison Notebooks*

Explicit terms from the semantic field of subalternity can be found in Gramsci's
pre-prison writings, though their occurrence is relatively rare. In those cases,
we mostly confront a generic usage of the term, derived from the metaphoric
deployment of originally military terminology. Such a generic usage is maintained also in some passages in the *Prison Notebooks*, particularly in the early
phases of its development.[16] 'Subaltern classes' or 'subaltern social groups' is
not a topic in Gramsci's initial work plan at the beginning of the first notebook or in letters from this period.[17] Those plans do, however, include themes
that seem to represent a continuation and deepening of Gramsci's theoretical
research project immediately prior to imprisonment in 1926, embodied in the
unfinished text *On The Southern Question* [*Alcuni temi della quistione meridionale*]. In retrospect, if such a problematic perspective can be permitted, we
can now see this latter text as constituting an important phase in Gramsci's
research on themes, such as disaggregation, amorphousness, lack of conscious
or self-direction, which he will only much later group together and systematically develop under the rubric of 'subaltern classes' and related terms. The
term 'subaltern classes' itself, however, does not appear in *Some Aspects of the
Southern Question*.[18] As Buttigieg has argued, that fact that the subaltern social
groups later constitute the subtitle of a special notebook (from 1934–35) suggests that Gramsci himself only slowly became aware of the importance of this
topic for his overall project.[19] If the concept of subalternity is already at work in
Gramsci's texts in his pre-carceral or even early carceral writings, it does so in a
hidden way – 'hidden' not only from the fascist censors, but also from Gramsci
himself.

The first appearance of the term 'subaltern social classes' (importantly, in
the plural) occurs in the title of a note written in early June 1930, 'History of the

---

16   See, for instance, Q1, § 43, p. 37, § 48, p. 60 and § 54, p. 67 written in February–March 1930.
      Dates of individual notes are given according to the chronology established in Francioni
      1984, and the revisions contained in the appendix to Cospito 2011b. 'A texts' refer to Gram-
      sci's first drafts; 'C texts' to revised notes; while 'B texts' exist in a single version.

17   See Francioni and Frosini 2009.

18   Spivak's repeated assertion that *Some Aspects of the Southern Question* is the most signi-
      ficant text for understanding Gramsci's conception of subalternity (see 1988, p. 283 and
      2005, p. 47) could thus only be valid by presupposing the presence of a concept without
      its designating word – an interpretative strategy that, beyond its risks of anachronism and
      idealism, obscures the genuine innovations represented by Gramsci's deliberate choice of
      a new vocabulary during the development of the *Prison Notebooks* project.

19   Liguori and Voza 2009, entry *Subalterno, subalterni* by J.A. Buttigieg, p. 826.

dominant class and history of the subaltern classes' [*Storia della classe domin-ante e storia delle classi subalterne*].[20] In that brief note (which he transcribes in 1934, with significant revisions, under the title 'Methodological criteria'),[21] Gramsci outlines some of the fundamental perspectives that remain determ-ining for all of his research on this theme. He argues that

> The history of the subaltern classes is necessarily disaggregated and epis-odic: there is in the activity of these classes a tendency to unification, even if on provisional levels; but it is the less apparent part that only appears when victory is achieved. The subaltern classes suffer the initi-ative of the dominant class, even when they rebel; they are in a state of alarmed defence. Every trace of autonomous initiative is thus of inestim-able value. At any rate, the monograph is the most adequate form for this history, which requires a great accumulation of partial materials.[22]

The unexpected appearance of the term 'subaltern' here in 1930 is framed by a series of other notes from the same period that explore similar substantive themes, though without deploying this nascent vocabulary. Indeed, two notes earlier, in late May 1930, Gramsci had dedicated an extended consideration to the curious case of the literally 'unarmed prophet' David Lazzaretti (later tran-scribed as the first note in Notebook 25).[23] The term 'subaltern' itself is not used in this 'A text' of 1930 (unlike the corresponding 'C text' from 1934), but in Note-book 3 Gramsci nevertheless begins to develop important themes regarding the need for a concrete analysis of the condition of subaltern social groups, including their overdetermination by the political conjuncture.[24] Crucially, in Notebook 3 Gramsci also poses the problem of the representation of the sub-altern social groups as itself one of the determinant conditions of subalternity. Subaltern social groups are seen as subaltern insofar as they are unable to pro-gress to forms of self-representation through the formation of their own strata

---

20 Q3, §14, pp. 299–300.
21 Q25, §2, pp. 2283–4.
22 Q3, §14, pp. 299–300.
23 Q3 §12, pp. 297–9; Q25, §1, pp. 2279–83.
24 As Gramsci's analysis emphasises, Lazzaretti's popular prophetic movement emerged in the period when the Catholic Church's abstention from 'official' politics in the post-Risorgimento state had released subaltern energies from containment within established political structures. In this sense, Gramsci presents a very different reading of the polit-ical status of this 'subaltern revolt' from Hobsbawm's seemingly independently-developed analysis of the supposedly 'pre-political' dimensions of Lazzaretti's movement. See Hobs-bawm 1959.

of intellectuals, but instead remain represented as objects of contemplation by and for the discourses of the dominant classes. In Notebook 3, Gramsci already posits the centrality of this dimension of the experience and perception of subalternity; Q3 §12 in fact begins with, and is structured by, observations on the modes of representation of Lazzaretti by Italian social theorists from the post-Risorgimento period such as Bulferetti and Verga, and includes a sharp critique of the influence of figures such as Lombroso.

Four notes later, in early June 1930, a crucial methodological stage in the development of Gramsci's research is delineated.[25] He notes here the importance of distinguishing analytically between the conditions of 'pre-modern' and 'modern' subaltern social groups (understood not in ideal-typical terms, but historically, in relation to the forms of the modern state in the wake of the French Revolution, and particularly its later consolidation in processes of passive revolution). Crucially, he also reflects on the limits of the transhistorical analogies implicit in these comparisons. This distinction becomes increasingly important in his discussions of subalternity; by the time of Notebook 25, it has become a central organising perspective, to such an extent that this historical distinction between 'old' and 'new' subalterns could be argued to represent the core dimension of Gramsci's 'mature' concept of subaltern social groups.[26] He argues that

> The modern state abolishes many autonomies of the subaltern classes – it abolishes the state as a federation of classes – but certain forms of the internal life of the subaltern classes are reborn as parties, trade unions, cultural associations. The modern dictatorship abolishes these forms of class autonomy as well, and it tries hard to incorporate them into the activity of the state: in other words, the centralisation of the whole life of the nation in the hands of the dominant class becomes frenetic and all-consuming.[27]

---

25 Q3, §18, pp. 302–3; later transcribed in Q25, §4, p. 2287, which also includes elements of Q3, §16, pp. 301–2.

26 This dimension of Gramsci's conception of the 'modernity' of subaltern social groups, constituted within wholly modern political dynamics, was clearly noted by Guha 1982, particularly p. 4.

27 Q3, §18, p. 303. The C text contains significant revisions: 'The modern state replaces the mechanical bloc of social groups with their subordination to the active hegemony of the leading and dominant group; it thus abolishes some autonomies, which, however, are reborn in another form, as parties, trade unions, cultural associations. The contemporary dictatorships abolish legally also these new forms of autonomy and try hard to incorporate them into the activity of the state: the legal centralisation of the whole life of the nation

'History of the subaltern classes', from August 1930, is undoubtedly Gramsci's most significant analysis of the variegated and gradated nature of the
formation of subaltern social classes and groups.[28] It is both Gramsci's most
extensive presentation of a criterion for research into the history of subaltern
social groups, and also, simultaneously, an outline of a political strategy for the
emergence from subalternity.[29] Such is its importance that it is worth citing
extensively:

> The historical unification of the ruling classes is in the state and their his-
> tory is essentially the history of states and of groups of states. This unity
> has to be concrete, and thus the result of relations between the state and
> civil society. For the subaltern classes unification does not occur: their his-
> tory is intertwined with that of 'civil society', it is a disaggregated fraction
> of it. It is therefore necessary to study: 1) the objective formation of the
> subaltern class through the developments and changes that took place in
> the economic sphere, the extent of their diffusion and their descent from
> other classes that preceded them; 2) their passive or active adherence to
> the dominant political formations; that is, their efforts to influence the
> programs of these formations with demands of their own; 3) the birth
> of new parties of the ruling class to maintain control of the subaltern
> classes; 4) the formations of the subaltern classes themselves, formations
> of a limited and partial character; 5) the political formations that assert
> the autonomy of the subaltern classes, but within the old framework; 6)
> the political formations that assert complete autonomy, etc. The list of
> these phases can be further specified with internal phases or with com-
> binations of different phases.[30]

Having attained to this methodological perspective in the summer of 1930,
Gramsci goes on to discuss themes related to subalternity extensively in his
subsequent notebooks, both explicitly (in over 30 notes written between 1930
and August 1933), and implicitly, in a series of notes on themes that he will
come to call 'indirect sources'.[31] These include utopias and philosophical novels, which are analysed in a novel fashion not in terms of their removal or

---

in the hands of the dominant group becomes "totalitarian" [*totalitario*]' (Q25, § 4, p. 2287).
   For a discussion of the significance of these revisions, see Frosini 2012a, pp. 71–5.
28   Q3, § 90, pp. 372–3, later transcribed in Q25, § 5, pp. 2287–9.
29   See Green 2002 for a discussion of the strategic implications of this note.
30   Q3, § 90, pp. 372–3.
31   See, for an example of the genre, Q25, § 7, pp. 2290–3.

critical distance from the periods in which they were produced, but as expressing, even and especially unconsciously and unintentionally, the experiences
and repressed desires of subaltern social groups. From the margins of Gramsci's
research plans at the beginning of his imprisonment, the theme of subalternity becomes one of the most central lines of research in the most productive
phase of his carceral writings. What are the reasons for this genuine conceptual explosion?

2   Subalterns in the 'Integral State'

My thesis is that the significance of this developing research theme can only
be integrally understood by attending to the context in which it emerges and
is developed, or in other words, its temporal relation to other themes in this
phase of the *Prison Notebooks* project. For Gramsci's research on subaltern
social groups is initiated in the same period in which he begins to develop
his central concepts of the 'integral state' and 'passive revolution'. In a certain
sense, the three concepts function as dialectical counterpoints to each other,
each complementing and extending the lines of research pursued under other
the headings of the others, in a process of conceptual expansion and intensification. On the one hand, subalternity is one of the themes by means of which
Gramsci clarifies for himself the political significance of the concepts of the
integral state and passive revolution; that is, subalternity is conceived as the
concrete political relation that is produced by the historical emergence of the
bourgeois integral state. On the other hand, the concept of the modern state as
an 'integral' state, particularly when complemented by Gramsci's parallel development of the notion of passive revolution as a 'logic' of state development in
the late nineteenth and early twentieth centuries, is one of the ways in which
he clarifies the historical and political structuring dynamics of subalternity.[32]
For reasons of space, I am unable to undertake in this chapter an extensive
discussion of these concepts, or of the many disputes and erroneous readings
to which the first (that is, the integral state), in particular, has been subjected,
from Bobbio to Anderson and beyond to contemporary debates on 'posthegemony'.[33] However, the main coordinates of the novel state theory developed

---

32   Modonesi 2015 explores the mutually constitutive natures of subaltern socio-political rela-
        tions and passive revolutionary processes.
33   Bobbio 1990a, Anderson 1976. For critiques of the Bobbio-Anderson thesis, see Francioni
        1984 and Thomas 2009a. A synthesis of the debate on 'posthegemony' can be found in
        Beasley-Murray 2010.

in the *Prison Notebooks* in its relation to the theme of subalternity need to be briefly outlined, because it is precisely by means of this dialectical relationship that the full novelty of Gramsci's notion of subalternity comes into clearest relief.

Against what were effectively the neo-Kantian revisions of Marxist state theory by dominant currents in both the Second and Third Internationals, in the *Prison Notebooks* Gramsci undertakes both a critique of and a critical return to the rational kernel of the Hegelian theory of the state.[34] Like Hegel (and in opposition to the various caricatures of the state theory of the *Philosophy of Right*, within and outside Marxism), Gramsci insists upon the dialectical, mutually constitutive relations between 'civil society' and what he characterises as 'political society' or 'state'. This expansive conception of the modern state as a political relation enables a more precise analysis of its real extension and efficacy throughout the social formation, as both principle and practice of organisation and regulation, than is possible for instrumentalist conceptions of politics and the state that limit themselves to the apparent institutions of the state apparatus. As Francioni has noted, the central note in the development of this conception, constituting nothing short of a sea-change the redefines Gramsci's entire carceral project dates from October 1930.[35] It represents a point of no return; the dialectical 'identity-distinction between civil society and political society' enables Gramsci to theorise the modern state as a complex socio-political relation of inclusion, rather than in terms of the exclusionary figures that have dominated modern political thought since at least Hobbes.[36] They are relations of integration that are articulated in varying degrees of extension and intensity in different contexts, from the organising and directive instances summarised in the notion of 'political society', to the associative, externally directed practices and supposedly 'non-political' dimensions of social life frequently regarded by the liberal tradition as constituting a genuinely 'civil society'.[37]

---

34 On the struggle between neo-Kantian and Hegelian state theory in the late nineteenth and early twentieth centuries, see Colliot-Thélène 1992.
35 Q4, § 38, pp. 455–65. See Francioni 1984, p. 196.
36 Q8, § 142, written in April 1932.
37 For this reason, Gramsci cannot easily be accommodated either to the debates on civil society inspired by Eurocommunism in the 1970s, or in the reprisals that accompanied so-called 'globalisation' in the 1990s. While Chatterjee (2004, p. 51 and 2011, pp. 145–6) briefly mentions the Gramscian resonance of his deployment of the notion of 'political society' (as opposed to 'civil society'), he does not explore further the connections (and discrepancies) between the two usages. Ultimately, Chatterjee's notion of 'political society' despite its gestures towards Foucault and notions of 'governmentality' arguably ends

Hegemony in this context is conceived as the practice of the material constitution of the type of political power specific to the modern state, traversing both of the great superstructural '"levels"' [*piani*] 'that can be called' '"civil society"', 'that is, the totality of organisms commonly called "private"', and '"political society or state"'.[38] Given Gramsci's problematisation of these terms (placed under what Dario Ragazzini has called a 'philology of the quotation mark'),[39] I have elsewhere argued that it is clarifying to abandon the spatial metaphor and conceive of civil society and political society not as geographical terrains, but as particular forms of imbricated socio-political relationality.[40] In this sense, hegemony represents the synthesis of associative and organising instances, each essential to the relationship, but a synthesis that occurs on the terms of and is directed by only one of those relations, namely, that of political society.

The decisive feature of this complex state theory for comprehending the particular status of the subaltern classes is that they remain entrapped within the relationality proper to civil society; their history, as Gramsci argues, 'is intertwined with that of "civil society", it is a disaggregated fraction of it'.[41] They are unable, *qua* subaltern social groups, to assume the self-directive and directing capacities embodied in the form of the political. In the corresponding C text, Gramsci adds that 'the subaltern classes, by definition, are not unified and cannot unify themselves until they become the "state"'.[42] Civil society, far from being a terrain of freedom beyond the state, as sometimes still suggested by liberals today, is thus the mode of relationality characteristic of the disaggregated subalterns; it is a form of the 'performance' of subalternity, to use a concept promoted by Judith Butler.[43] The subaltern social groups are continually fractured by the interventions of the political society that 'interpellates' them within the state in a specific non-essentialist sense; that is, as

---

up unwittingly reproposing under another name the defining coordinates of 'civil society' precisely as it was conceived by Hegel (and, following him, Gramsci): that is, as a politically overdetermined system for the regulation of needs and as an 'external state' (cf. Hegel 1942, §183). Chatterjee is led into this semantic shift due to the fact that his own concept of 'civil society' remains largely indebted to the liberal rather than Hegelian tradition.

38   Q12, §1, written in May–June 1932. For different arguments regarding Gramsci's distinction between the varying forms of hegemony, see Gerratana 1997, p. 124 ff., Thomas 2009a, pp. 221–8, and Frosini 2015.

39   Ragazzini 2002, p. 17.

40   See Thomas 2009a, particularly pp. 170–3.

41   Q3, §90, p. 372. C text: Q25, §5, p. 2288.

42   Q25, §5, p. 2288.

43   Butler 1990.

a relationship that has always already occurred. They are thereby constituted as subaltern 'raw material' for its directive operations. Rather than outside of or opposed to the 'hegemonic', the 'subaltern' in this sense is integrally and immanently related to it, as simultaneously the presupposition and the product of its operations.

This is the context of the emergence of Gramsci's concept of subaltern social groups and related terms in the early phases of the *Prison Notebooks*. The theoretical and political consequences of this complex semantic field are elaborated in Gramsci's later notebooks, particularly at the moment in which Gramsci attempts to re-organise his lines of research into the 'special notebooks';[44] Notebook 25 inherits this dynamic, even and especially in its incompletion. Any reading of Gramsci's only apparently scattered reflections on subalternity that aspires to produce an historically grounded comprehension of his thought needs to be conducted with this dynamic developmental process in mind. Rather than a mosaic of fragmentary ruminations on subalternity, what instead emerges is a reading of the *Prison Notebooks* as founded on a distinctive theory of political modernity conceived as a new form political relationality, which, far from repressing and excluding subalterns, mobilises and includes them as integral elements in the new systems of political power.

3   Three Figures of the Subaltern

What theoretical and political consequences can be drawn from this reading of the emergence of the semantic field of subalternity in the *Prison Notebooks*? I would like to emphasise three 'figures' or ways in which this reading offers to renew our understanding of the subaltern not as 'residue' of the past or 'limit' of the present, but as a concept directly relevant for the comprehension of contemporary political processes.

First figure: the 'irrepressible subaltern'. Gramsci's concept of subalternity is radically different from the notion that the subaltern almost literally 'incarnates' complete submission and total oppression, in a zone beyond representation. In some of Spivak's more provocative formulations, for instance, the subaltern becomes an almost mystical concept, in a Wittgensteinian sense: the subaltern not only cannot speak, but is also that figure of whom one should not speak, lest one falls into the trap of speaking for the subaltern and thus dominating it. In Spivak's words, '[I]f the subaltern can speak then, thank God, the

---

44   On the different phases of Gramsci's work, see Francioni 2009 and 2016.

subaltern is not a subaltern any more'.[45] Gramsci's emphasis upon the varying degrees of subalternity, or of stages in a process of a potential emergence from the relations of confinement within the subaltern relationality of civil society, provides a more analytically satisfying perspective within which to think the real conditions of possibility of self-liberation of subaltern social groups. The type of subalternity that Gramsci investigates in the *Prison Notebooks* is a hegemonic relation that is specific to the form of bourgeois hegemony consolidated and 'condensed' in the modern state. Subaltern social groups do not simply exist as such, in a supposedly 'pre-political' or even 'natural' dimension before or beyond the state.[46] Rather, they are actively produced within the dialectical relations of the integral state; indeed, they are an active expression and index of its efficacy. Rather than an amorphous mass of the 'oppressed', there are many subalterns, or varying degrees of subalternity, structured by the specific capacities and institutional forms of social groups in civil society and their relation to the organising instances or relations of political society. This insight, alongside Gramsci's analyses of the relations between *senso comune* and *buon senso*, and between ideology and philosophy, as non-qualitative distinctions – that is, situated on a continuum of social and political practices – constitutes the theoretical foundation for hegemony as a method of political work.[47] Were there no degrees of subalternity, were civil society a terrain of total domination rather than a continually renewed hegemonic relation of subordination, hegemony, as the emergence of capacities for self-direction and leadership of previously subaltern social groups, would not be a realistic political strategy.

Second figure: the 'intersectional subaltern'. Subaltern classes or social groups for Gramsci are clearly not, as had frequently been suggested,[48] simply a 'codeword' for the proletariat, whether that latter term is understood either as industrial wage workers, according to Third International orthodoxy, or as a political capacity, according to the young Marx's original appropriation and

---

45   Spivak 1990, p. 158.

46   The critique of the notions of the 'pre-political' and the 'archaic' was one of the central elements of Guha's understanding of the subaltern, though his parallel argument regarding a qualitative distinction between 'metropolitan' and 'colonial forms' of the modern state ('dominance and hegemony' in the former, 'dominance without hegemony' in the latter) did not always allow him to draw the full implications of this insight; for precisely insofar as 'political' subaltern social groups already participate and are constituted within the hegemonic dynamic of political modernity, in however 'compromised', 'deficient' or 'non-ideal typical' a form.

47   See Badaloni 1972.

48   As noted in Green 2011c, p. 97.

transformation of this term.[49] Nor, on the other hand, should Gramsci's development of the semantic field of subalternity be understood as opposed to Marx's analysis of the conditions of constitution of the modern working class movement, as Guido Liguori has emphasised.[50] Gramsci's uneven development in his later notebooks of the notion of subaltern social *groups* (instead of the initially designated *classes*) should similarly be understood not as an indication of an incipient break with Marxism, or a risk of the 'dilution' of Marxist categories of analysis.[51] Rather, it should be read as an acknowledgement, central to the more creative dimensions of the Marxist traditions, of the multiple forms of oppression in modern societies that structure them precisely as class societies (rather than societies organised in estates or castes).[52] Gramsci's notion of 'subaltern social groups' include those groups that the Marxist vulgate traditionally regarded as the working classes, but also goes beyond them, to comprehend the way in which supposedly 'economic' relations are always intimately connected to a wider range of oppressive relations, whether those of gender, ethnicity, regionality, and so forth.[53] In this sense, Gramsci's development of the notion of subalternity can be understood as an enrichment of the political vocabulary of the Marxist tradition. In the light of contemporary debates, it might even be regarded as an early theory of 'intersectionality', albeit one that problematises the juridical figures that characterise much of this field of research today.[54]

Third figure: the 'citizen *sive* subaltern'. Gramsci's theorisation of the process of constitution of subalternity provides a specific focus on subaltern experience in the modern state-form and its institutions of citizenship, not as a supplement to its 'otherness', but as the form within which subalternity is most intensely realised.[55] Subaltern social groups for Gramsci are not simply given

---

49   On the concept of the proletariat as a 'political capacity', see Kouvelakis 2003, p. 350.

50   Liguori 2011.

51   See the detailed analysis of this uneven semantic shift in Liguori 2016.

52   See Zene 2011.

53   This dimension is noted in particular in Crehan 2016. On Gramsci's articulation of race and class in his theorisation of subalternity, see Francioni and Frosini 2009, p. 209 and Green 2011c.

54   For a synthesis of recent debates on intersectionality, see Lutz et al. 2011.

55   Pandey 2006 and 2010 explore the notion of the citizenship as 'supplementary' to the subaltern's (logically if not historically) prior constitution, with the paradoxical figure of the 'subaltern citizen'. Paradoxically, in this formulation 'citizen qualifies subalternity' (2010, p. 4), rather than the reverse. Pandey's concept thus effectively presupposes a 'Spivakian' concept of the subaltern as being constituted prior to hegemonic, political relations (which are only subsequently introduced in the form of citizenship, conceived as 'an indicator of the political quality of all subalternity' (2010, p. 5)). For Gramsci, on

in the sense of a foundation of a political ontology, or as an almost organic constituent (when not destituent) power that might be mobilised against the constituted power of the capitalist state (which seems to be the position still proposed by some strands of Italian post-workerism, in a belated re-inheritance of Sorel).[56] Rather, subalternity for Gramsci is actively produced by the hegemonic relations that constitute the modern state, conceived as a product of the specificity of the bourgeois hegemonic project embodied within passive revolutionary processes. Even more significantly, Gramsci's argues that the modern state depends upon subalternity in order to constitute itself as the state; it must structurally produce and reproduce some social groups as subaltern precisely in order to guarantee its own continuation as a ruling order. The production of subaltern social groups is a central function of all forms of the modern state, whether in the extreme forms of fascist dictatorship or colonial administration, or in the seemingly more benign forms of liberal representative regimes with their systems of political elites and passive citizenries. Insofar as tendentially 'democratic' (that is, 'democratic' not in a procedural or substantive sense, but in the sense of positing the collective of the demos as both object and – even when 'absented' – subject of politics), modern states must include and mobilise increasingly broader strata of their societies in order to maintain their functional legitimacy – even and especially when this inclusion and mobilisation occur in passive forms that immediately neutralise any threat of a 'cathartic' transition from subalternity to hegemonic politics.[57] For this reason, subaltern social groups remain on the 'margins' of history, but are not 'without' or 'outside' history; they are fully present actors on its stage, though reduced to minor and fleeting roles.

In this conception, the subalterns are not comprehended simply as the oppressed or dominated, in an abstract and transhistorical sense; rather, they are actively incorporated in an historically specific system of hegemonic power, in forms of passive citizenship just as much as by practices of pacification.[58]

---

the other hand, 'modern' subalternity does not precede citizenship, but instead coincides with it in a relation of simultaneous constitution.

56   Whatever their other significant differences, Negri and Agamben share this tendency to posit the condition of possibility of emancipatory politics in a pre- or post-political realm. Cf. Negri and Agamben 2014.

57   On the importance of 'catharsis' in the philosophy of praxis, see Q10ii, §6, p. 1244 and Thomas 2008.

58   On the history of the notion of passive citizenship in the French revolutionary process, see Sewell 1988. For reflections on the philosophical status of citizenship, see Balibar 2011.

The ruling classes, in their turn, are not comprehended simply as oppressors or dominators, 'thanks to God', to use again Spivak's metaphor. In Notebook 25, Gramsci argues that

> the historical unity of the ruling classes occurs in the state and their story is essentially the history of states and of groups of states. But we shouldn't think that such unity is purely juridical and political, even if this form of unity has its importance, and not merely a formal importance: the funda-mental historical unity, in its concrete nature, is the result of the organic relations between state or political society and 'civil society'.[59]

Insofar as the historical unity of the ruling classes results from the organic rela-tions between political society and civil society, such unity presupposes just as much as it imposes the production of subalternity. The ruling class needs to produce – and to reproduce continually – subaltern social groups in order to become and to maintain itself as a ruling class. This relational dynamic consti-tutes a fragile and tenuous basis of enduring political power. It is not conceived as autonomous or self-foundational, as many modern theories of sovereignty suggest, from Hobbes to Weber and Schmitt and beyond. Rather, it always remains dependent upon the ongoing subjugation of its interpellated antagon-ist. The condition of the subalterns for Gramsci is thus both index and concrete form of what the Marxist tradition traditionally described as 'class struggle', in the expansive sense highlighted in the opening pages of the *Manifesto of the Communist Party*: namely, not a 'merely' economic condition, but the driving force of epoch-defining historical development.

4 We Good Subalterns

The fate of Gramsci's subalterns is not originally or ultimately to be *excluded*, the condition seen by traditions of political theology as the precondition of modern political order. Far from being *vogelfrei* – to use Marx's description of doubly-free modern wage-labour – or 'bare life' [*vita nuda*] – in Agamben's less poetic formulation – the misfortune of the subalterns consists precisely in the fact that they are *included* integrally in modern state power, as the passive basis of its continuing formal dominance. Subaltern social groups for Gramsci are thus not residual, and the subaltern is not to be found elsewhere, in the past

---

59   Q25, §5, p. 2287.

or on the peripheries of 'modern' social formations. On the contrary, Gramsci's concept of subalternity attempted to describe the fundamental conditions of the most 'advanced' political forms of the modern state: the everyday disaggregated, externally determined lifeworlds that each one of us inhabits, all the while almost convincing ourselves that we are free. In other words, when Gramsci discusses the subaltern, is not speaking about somebody else, but is speaking directly to us; in the word of Horace, much loved by Marx: *De te fabula narratur*. Also we, we good (post) Europeans, are the subalterns.

As Gramsci came to recognise throughout his research, conditions of subalternity are not to be overcome by fiat, or a decision of the will.[60] As structural relations inscribed in the conditions of political life within the bourgeois integral state, they will only be overcome through a patient work of construction of an alternative social order, in which the subaltern social groups progressively become aware of and practice their capacity for self-direction and autonomous initiative: in short, their own hegemonic project. The task of what Gramsci calls the 'integral historian', alert to the richness of energies that constitutes the real but obscured role of the subalterns as the driving material force within the modern state, is to contribute to the preparation and endurance of such a cathartic process.[61]

---

60   Compare Gramsci's original formulations in Q3, §14, pp. 299–300, to the revisions undertaken in Q25, §2, pp. 2283–4.

61   Q25, §2, p. 2284.

CHAPTER 11

Subalternity and the National-Popular: A Brief Genealogy of the Concepts

Anne Freeland

In *Traveling Theory* (1982), Edward Said calls attention to the tendency of concepts that are transported across time and space and re-inscribed in historical and institutional contexts other than those to which they respond at their inception to lose some of their vitality or fossilise as cultural dogma. In a later essay, *Traveling Theory Reconsidered* (1994), he recognises in the earlier text an ideological notion of originality and derivation in which every iteration is necessarily a pale shadow of its true form; in their displacement, theories can also gain critical force, breaking through limitations that constrained their initial formulation. Drawing on this understanding of traveling theory in its double sense, this chapter is conceived as a partial sketch of the Gramscian origin of the concepts of the subaltern and the national-popular from the point of view of a particular endpoint in their trajectories: that of Latin Americanist scholars who take up the terms, including – but also before and after – the North American-based Subaltern Studies Group, who take as their models the South Asian Subaltern Studies group and the work of Gayatri Chakravorty Spivak more than Gramsci's own texts. My intention here is not only to offer new readings of the formulation of the concepts in Gramsci, but to intervene in the growing body of scholarship on their subsequent appropriation by proposing a conception of this legacy that is less focused on finding error, or even productive misreadings, and instead highlights tensions in the Gramscian sources that anticipate future reorientations and even reversals in Gramsci's theoretical architecture.

1   Subalternity

In tracing the history of the category of the subaltern, it should first be noted that the development of a specialised concept of subalternity probably owes much to the decision of Gramsci's translators to use the English cognate for almost every occurrence of the term *subalterno* and its variants, which often might have been more naturally (which is not to say better) translated with another word – subordinate, oppressed, inferior, etc., depending on the context – since the term is in common colloquial use in Italian in a way that it is not in English.[1]

In a passage like that in Notebook 4, §1 – 'Engels is supposed to have been lacking in theoretical skills (or at least occupies a subaltern position in relation to Marx)' – it means simply *inferior*, and the cognate does not convey anything that 'inferior' would not. (I'm quoting from Joseph Buttigieg, but Quintin Hoare and Geoffrey Nowell Smith also use the English 'subaltern'.) In most other cases, however, for example where *classi subalterne* might have read 'lower classes', or 'oppressed classes', or the position of the Catholic Church could have been described as 'subordinate' instead of subaltern, the production of a specific concept through this iteration may well be warranted.

In its narrowest sense, the subaltern is one of inferior rank and therefore takes commands from a superior. This seems to me to be an apt concept-metaphor for the expanded sense, in which subalternity designates instrumentality, a lack of historical personhood and political autonomy, a greater degree of subjection to the laws of historical necessity (Notebook 25, §4). This is continuous with some of the intermediate, narrower figurative uses of the military term, such as Gramsci's description of the intellectuals as carrying out subaltern functions of the dominant class.[2]

If there is a relatively unified concept of subalternity in Gramsci, it is elaborated in Notebook 25, in which prior notes, some of which do not yet contain the term, are compiled and revised under the title 'On the Margins of History (The History of Subaltern Social Groups)'. Much has been written on the sub-

---

1   The Treccani dictionary, for example, gives the following definitions for *subalterno*: 'Che è subordinato, in sottordine e in diretta dipendenza, rispetto ad altri di grado maggiore, o anche, riferito a istituzioni e sfere di attività, rispetto ad altre di livello superiore ... sostantivato, con valore generico, chi è in un grado gerarchico inferiore o alle dipendenze di altri ...'. Vico is cited as an example of the term's use in 'the arts and sciences' 'la Metafisica è la scienza sublime, che ripartisce i certi loro subbietti a tutte le scienze che si dicono "subalterne,"' followed by the more quotidian and only recently outdated sense of an employee or assistant, and, in a usage that carried over into English in the seventeenth century, designating a lower rank in a public or military post. Finally, in 'ethnology, sociology, and culture', the Gramscian sense that has developed in the twentieth century is given: 'la cultura di un popolo che è rimasto a lungo in posizione di dipendenza da una cultura dominante'. The Oxford English Dictionary, by contrast, gives only specialised or 'rare' uses, among them that derived from Gramsci's incorporation, in English translation, into the disciplinary lexicon of cultural studies: 'Now chiefly in critical and cultural theory, esp. post-colonial theory: of or relating to those who are marginalized or oppressed'.
2   Buttigieg sees no significant relationship between these usages (2013, p. 35), and yet chose – again, I think rightly – to maintain the cognate in these instances in his excellent translation.

ject, and so I will limit my remarks to some summary comments on two areas of debate that come up in this literature and that are pertinent to the subsequent uses of the concept in subaltern studies:

1. *Supplementing class.* There is a tendency in Gramscian scholarship to point out a broadening and indeed an increasing vagueness in the concept as it travels through subaltern studies into a more general field of postcolonial theory and cultural studies. While this is obviously and inevitably the case if we are looking for a definition that fits all instances over an ever-proliferating corpus across not only different authors but different disciplines and theoretical orientations, given the flexibility of the concept in Gramsci noted above, I think that the tendency with each of its iterations within the smaller, more easily delimited corpora that constitute the major moments of this development (such as that of the early volumes of the *Subaltern Studies* series edited by Ranajit Guha, that of the Latin Americanist group, and an evolving definition in Spivak's work) is rather toward a greater specificity or precision, which does not necessarily entail a narrowness of scope.[3]

A recurring theme of this debate in reference to Gramsci's own texts has been the philological question of the significance of Gramsci's original terminology in relation to the conventional Marxist analogues, alternately claimed as mere code words to elude the prison censors and as substantial theoretical innovations. The most pertinent here is 'subaltern' in relation to 'proletariat', and then subaltern 'groups' in relation to 'classes'.[4] Both lexical choices seem to be consistent with Gramsci's implicit theorisation of the category. In revising prior notes in Notebook 25, Gramsci almost always changes 'classes' to 'groups', and while 'classes' is sometimes maintained, 'groups' is never changed to 'classes'; in gathering his developing ideas into a more cohesive text organised around the theme of subalternity, it was clear to Gramsci that in most cases

---

3   Buttigieg maintains that 'it is futile to search for or attempt to formulate a precise definition of "subaltern" or "subaltern social groups/classes" as conceived by Gramsci' (2013, p. 36), but he seems to be in the minority. Guido Liguori (see, for example, 2015, p. 130) is representative of the critique of 'culturalist' appropriations of Gramsci, particularly within subaltern studies.

4   Gramscian scholars including Peter Thomas, Buttigieg, and Marcus Green have argued against the assertion that 'subaltern' is a mere code word for 'proletariat', attributed, for example, to Spivak, although it should be noted that when Spivak writes this, she follows it with the remark that 'the word soon cleared a space, as words will, and took on the task of analysing what "proletarian," produced by capital logic, could not cover' (2000, p. 324; she has made the same qualification elsewhere). Green (2002, p. 9) and Buttigieg (2013, p. 36), having dismissed this claim, nonetheless find the censorship argument more persuasive as an explanation for the shift from 'classes' to 'groups' (see also, for example, Buci-Glucksmann 1980, p. 75).

subalternity was not reducible to class.[5] In the subsequent corpus of scholarship that takes up and reworks the concept, it is generally conceived as a
supplement and not, as has been claimed, as a mere substitute for class, or more
precisely, a category in which class is necessarily supplemented and traversed
by other social conditions, and this supplementation of class is already present
in Gramsci, if only implicitly theorised.

This incommensurability with a differential social position defined strictly
by class relations already implicit in Gramsci is thematised in subaltern studies both in terms of methodology (Marxism needs to be supplemented) and in
terms of the social subject itself or object of study (subjects other than the proletariat come into view). In the early work of the South Asian collective, closely
following Gramsci's own lines of inquiry, it is the peasantry, a subject outside
of capital logic in a particular sense because it is the immediate *precapitalist*
antecedent of the proletariat according to the stagist teleology, that occupies
this position; it does so, however, in a way that puts this teleology into question.
Already in the work of the South Asian collective, but more explicitly with the
Latin Americanist group, this category is further complicated – articulated in
its difference not only from the proletariat as the subject of class struggle but
from the logic of struggle as the engine of a historical dialectic defined by class
positionality – through the concept of indigeneity. Guha's famous definition
of the subaltern in the work of the group as 'a name for the general attribute
of subordination in South Asian society whether this is expressed in terms of
class, caste, age, gender and office or in any other way' in his preface to *Selected Subaltern Studies*,[6] while maintaining the breadth of the original concept
(rather than reserving it for an elusive radical alterity or exteriority per the common allegation of critics of subaltern studies), coincides with the transition
of the project into the disciplinary and discursive spheres of cultural studies
and deconstruction, for which the compilation, co-edited with and introduced
by Spivak and with a foreword by Edward Said, marks a kind of threshold.
From this opening to subsume other forms of subordination, the concept does
indeed, in certain contexts within this later corpus, including the work of some
of the Latin Americanists, come not to substitute culture for class as a structuring principle but to mark a rejection of any kind of structural analysis that
assumes a social totality or linear historical progression, stagist or not.

---

5   Green himself argues precisely this point – but without reference to the change in wording
    between Notebook 25 and prior notes – in 'Race, Class, and Religion: Gramsci's Conception
    of Subalternity' (Green 2013).
6   Guha 1988a.

2. *The question of autonomy.* A second (and related) major theme of the dis-puted appropriation of the concept of the subaltern within cultural theory is that of its relation to hegemony and the capacity for autonomous action from a position of subordination. In Gramsci the extent to which subaltern groups act autonomously is equivalent to the extent of their progress in overcoming their subalternity, or 'becoming state', outlined in his famous (but tentative) six-point programme of study laid out in Notebook 25, § 5 (the first draft of which appears in Notebook 3, § 90). The phases that Gramsci identifies are:

> (1) the objective formation of the subaltern groups through the develop-ments and changes that took place in the economic sphere; the extent of their diffusion; and their descent from other classes that preceded them, the mentality, ideology, and objectives of which they retain for a period of time; (2) their passive or active adherence to the dominant political formations; that is, their efforts to influence the programs of these forma-tions with demands of their own and the consequences of these efforts in determining processes of decomposition and renewal or new formations; (3) the birth of new parties of the ruling class to maintain control of the subaltern classes; (4) the formations of the subaltern groups themselves that make demands of a limited and partial nature; (5) the formations that assert the autonomy of the subaltern classes, but within the old frame-work; (6) the formations that assert complete autonomy, etc.[7]

Here, in addition to the substitution of 'classes' in the original version from Notebook 3 in every instance where Gramsci writes 'groups', significant changes include the addition of the final clause of point 1, 'the mentality, ideology, and objectives of which they retain for a period of time', and, at the end of point 2, 'and the consequences of these efforts in determining processes of decomposition and renewal or new formations'. The first addition indicates the persistence of ideological structures, and indeed of an ethico-political regime ('objectives' or 'ends') across different historical moments in the development of the productive forces constitutive of the class/group, that is, across different modes of production. This is consistent with the departure from the category of class, as it suggests components of an evolving political subjectivity that exceed

---

7   Here and below, I have modified Buttigieg's translation of the original version of the note in accordance with Gramsci's revisions in the later notebook, since the Buttigieg translation includes only the first eight notebooks. For all passages from Notebooks 1–, I use Buttigieg's translation; translations of passages from subsequent notebooks, where no earlier version is indicated, are mine alone. Unattributed translations of other authors are also mine.

determination within the class structure. The expansion of point 2 emphasises the force of subaltern demands in shaping emergent formations; the progression that Gramsci is interested in tracking here is not merely a change in relative position, but a substantive alteration of the social formation from below. In both cases the element of continuity in the development of a collective social subject is reinforced in Gramsci's more sustained elaboration of the theme.

In their work on peasant and worker mobilisation, the South Asian Subaltern Studies group stressed the relative autonomy of these groups in their objectives and modes of struggle, sometimes falling into the developmentalist language that assumes a passage from political infancy to mature consciousness, but also modifying the notion of autonomy in the direction that Gramsci himself, as I have argued, suggests in his revisions in Notebook 25, emphasising not just a quantitative measure of initiative but also a qualitative difference with regard to the desires, ethical principles, and episteme that inform subaltern political action in relation to those of the leadership of the nationalist movement. The principal divergence from Gramsci's envisioned methodology lies in that while for Gramsci the study of subaltern groups is framed as fundamentally a study of the process of desubalternisation, taking into account its substantive, ethico-political dimension, in the South Asian Subaltern Studies group's revision of colonial and nationalist historiography the primary focus is on the elements that distinguish these processes from the narrative of political modernisation assumed by both bourgeois historiography and classical Marxism.

Guha's claim that in India there was (or is) an autonomous politics of the subaltern groups – a position shared by other members of the collective – has sometimes been misconstrued as a conception of subalternity as a non-relational condition. Guha takes care to pre-empt such a reading:

> We recognize of course that subordination cannot be understood except as one of the constitutive terms of the binary relationship of which the other is dominance [not hegemony, which will take the place of 'dominance' as subalternity's opposite pole in some of the later subaltern studies work], for 'subaltern groups are always subject to the activity of ruling groups, even when they rebel and rise up'.[8]

The conception of autonomy in the work that Guha is introducing here retains an affinity with the Gramscian idea of a graduated process of autonomisation, as well as with the methodological injunction that every trace of autonomous

---

8   Guha 1988, p. 35. The unattributed (and often cited) sentence is from Notebook 3, § 14, transcribed in Notebook 25, § 2.

action should be studied by the 'integral historian' (Q25, §2; Q3, §14), while marking a shift towards a privileging of action from below as a potential interruption of the logic of historical progression through capitalist modernity, a theoretical bearing that later scholars of subalternity, including the Latin Americanists, will take up and amplify.

Along with the notion that subaltern studies exaggerates the capacity for autonomy on the part of subaltern groups,[9] there is, and for related reasons, although in reference to its later period, a more common, opposite contention that subaltern studies goes too far in denying subaltern agency. The link between the two tendencies lies in the separation of subalternity from the hegemonic order, first as a positive alterity, and then as an absolute exteriority silenced by its discursive incommensurability and therefore conceivable only in negative terms, the ubiquitous stand-in for this position being Spivak's alleged claim that the subaltern cannot speak.[10] Subalternity in Gramsci is

---

9   Massimo Modonesi identifies in Guha (as representative of subaltern studies in general) 'a contradictory essentialization: the subaltern is, by definition, autonomous' (2010, p. 46). This contradiction, for Modonesi, results from Guha's positing of subaltern autonomy without the mediation of Gramsci's six-phase process (2010, p. 45). The autonomy that Guha claims is indeed prior to and not the transcendence of hegemonic control; his assumption of such an autonomous politics does not amount to a Gramscian scheme in which the intermediate steps are skipped, but to a modified conception of the political 'consciousness' or 'unity' of subaltern groups. Modonesi recognises this in his criticism of the 'possible excesses … of postcolonialism', citing Silvia Rivera Cusicanqui and Rossana Barragán's introduction to an anthology essays from the *Subaltern Studies* series in Spanish translation, where a drift toward identity politics that will become a major axis of debate about and within subaltern studies begins to take place.

10   Peter Thomas makes a compelling case for a reading of subalternity as inseparable from Gramsci's theory of the integral state, and therefore as a position that is by definition within modernity and within hegemony (Thomas 2015). His argument provides a counterpoint to some of the readings of subalternity under discussion here in a way that is less straightforward than one might assume at first glance, and that therefore merits some comment. In the first place, being cut off from access the state (Spivak's phrase is slightly different – 'removed from all lines of social mobility' [2012, p. 430, and elsewhere]), or the hegemonic discursive field, is indeed a relation to the state, and a constitutive one, if the state must constitute itself through what it excludes; in the second place, that externality is not necessarily equivalent to absolute oppression, but can mean precisely the opposite, that is, a degree of autonomy, even if this autonomy does not translate into any kind of recognisable agency within the hegemonic sphere of the state. Finally, Spivak insists that no one can claim to be subaltern, because subalternity precludes the ability to make claims intelligible within the dominant discourse; Thomas's assertion that 'we' are the subalterns (2015, p. 92) assumes a different conception of the term, and it is not the same statement that Spivak declares impossible, since here there is no trace of *identity* in the position claimed. In fact, in enlarging the scope of subalternity, Thomas is perhaps mak-

always, at least potentially, a moment of a historical process of collective subject formation that has a hegemonic articulation as its telos. In most of its subsequent iterations it remains a differential position and not a site of radical or absolute difference – as Spivak reminds us, a structural position without identity. But in Gramsci it is not yet, as it will become for the Latin American subalternists and others since the late 1980s, taking up and modifying Spivak's frequently cited definition of the subaltern as 'the absolute limit of the place where history is narrativized into logic',[11] a negativity that can be read as a positive force in its political and epistemological resistance to any hegemonic articulation. For a certain strain of subaltern studies it becomes the position from which to deconstruct the teleology of which in Gramsci it constitutes an initial moment, whatever its content, as itself produced by the hegemony of modernity, or modernity as hegemony, as totalisation.

The 'Founding Statement' of the Latin American Subaltern Studies group contains the different stages of this conceptual development: the history of Latin America is constructed as one of (only partially successful) processes of desubalternisation, starting with the Mexican and then finally the Cuban and Sandinista revolutions, but in the subsequent moments of this history of struggle – with the emergence of *testimonio* in the cultural sphere, for example – the meaning and function of the category shifts to one of a vindication of subalternity as a position from which to deconstruct the collective – national-popular – projects of liberation. The 'Statement' ends with a citation of the final lines from Rigoberta Menchú's testimony edited by Elizabeth Burgos: 'I'm still keeping secret what I think no one should know. Not even anthropologists or intellectuals, no matter how many books they have, can find out all our secrets';[12] the space of subalternity guards some positive content that loses its fetishistic power the moment it is exposed. Not only is the subaltern removed from the teleology of modernity whose embodiment is the state, but this immutable and constitutive removal becomes its positive content, and one with political, cultural, and commercial value.

---

ing a move that has something in common with Spivak's rejection of any vindicatory appropriation of the concept from the site of a particular positive identity by means of its restriction. Likewise, Spivak uses the term in a sense entirely consistent with Thomas's when she talks about the dismantling of the welfare state as a process of resubalternisation.

11   Spivak 1988b, p. 16.
12   Menchú 1984, p. 247.

2   The National-Popular

Gramsci's most substantial notes on the national-popular deal with the cultural sphere, and specifically with the absence of a national-popular literature in Italy. This is connected to the socio-historical development of the country, and of particular interest for Gramsci is its relation to the question of the lack of popular mobilisation in the Risorgimento. Here I consider the significance of the term as articulated in relation to these two interconnected themes, followed by a consideration of other uses of the concept in the notebooks which, taken together, highlight the ambiguities already implicit in the cultural and historical notes: in reference to a national-popular *collective will* as the essence of the modern prince and to the national-popular as integration into the capitalist market.

Notebook 21, titled *Problemi della cultura nazionale italiana: I. Letteratura popolare*, collects revised versions of Gramsci's key notes on the national-popular. Note 5, 'Concetto di "nazionale-popolare",'[13] thematises the concept as one of theoretical import, formulating the problem of the disjunction between the national and the popular in Italy. The note takes as its point of departure an article in the periodical *Critica Fascista* decrying the serial publication in Italian newspapers of nineteenth-century French novels and calling for a more rigorous examination of the underlying social causes of the greater marketability of foreign literature, which, he insists, are not to be found in the judgment of the press, as the *Critica* piece suggests, or in the tastes of its readership, but in the absence of a national intellectual class capable of producing a popular literature:

> why is there no 'national' literature of this type in Italy, if there is a market for it? Note the fact that in many languages 'national' and 'popular' are almost synonymous ... In Italy the term 'national' has a very narrow ideological sense and in any case it does not coincide with 'popular,' because in Italy the intellectuals are distant from the people, that is, from the 'nation,' and they are bound instead to a caste tradition ...

Here Gramsci identifies a double sense of the term *national* analogous to that of *culture* often referenced since the emergence of the disciplinary field of cultural studies, asserting that the 'nation' in Italy was understood as proper to an elite segment of the country, the *cultured* stratum.

---

13   See also Gramsci 1975, Q3, § 63, 'I nipotini di padre Bresciani'.

When Gramsci reiterates the question in the same note, he formulates his answer in terms of hegemony:

> What is the significance of the fact that Italians prefer to read foreign authors? It means that they undergo the intellectual and moral hegemony of foreign intellectuals, that they feel more closely linked to foreign intellectuals than to national ones, that Italy does not have a moral and intellectual national bloc, whether hierarchical or, much less, egalitarian.

The national-popular bloc is constituted through a hegemonic relation, which can be more or less egalitarian, that is, more or less hierarchical. This relation, in its ideal form, is one of identification and education, which alternate in a dialectical process.[14] Gramsci's opposition between an elite and a popular conception of the nation does not imply a positive valorisation of subaltern 'sentiments', culture, or knowledge as they exist, but of the will and capacity to develop these, in a sense, from within, into superior forms.

In a note on Vincenzo Gioberti, an intellectual and political leader of the Risorgimento,[15] the concept of the national-popular, understood as a hegemonic relation, is qualified as 'Jacobin': 'Gioberti, albeit vaguely, has a Jacobin concept of the "popular-national," of political hegemony, that is, of the alliance between the bourgeoisie-intellectuals and the people'.[16] The national-popular (or 'popular-national') relation is again not an equivalence but an alliance, and an asymmetrical one. Note 21 of Notebook 8, on the projected work that Gramsci proposed to call *The Modern Prince* following his reading of Machiavelli as a theorist of hegemony, indicates that the book should have a chapter on Jacobinism. Here he diagnoses the 'successive failures of the attempts to create a national-popular creative will' throughout the history of Italy as the result of

---

14   '[P]opular sentiments are not experienced as those of the authors, nor do the authors have a "national educational" function, that is, they have not taken up and do not take up the task of developing popular sentiments after reliving them and making them their own'. Gramsci 1975, Q21, §5, p. 2114.

15   Notebook 17, §9, '*Argomenti di cultura: Gioberti e il giacobinismo*'. Gramsci cites a passage from Gioberti on the national-popular that resonates strongly with his own formulation, cited above, from Notebook 21: 'A literature cannot be national if it is not popular; because, if it is the vocation of few to create it, its use and enjoyment ought to be universal. Moreover, since it should express common ideas and sentiments and bring to light those feelings that lie latent and confused in the heart of the multitudes, its cultivators must not only look to the benefit of the people but portray its spirit; indeed this is not only the end but also the beginning of a civil literature'.

16   He then qualifies this: 'Jacobin in theory, that is, because in practice he was unable to apply his doctrines'. Gramsci 1975, Q17, §9, pp. 1914–15.

the feudal and fragmented distribution of political power, 'an internal situation that can be called "economic-corporative,"' that is, without the ethico-political articulation that constitutes a collective historical subject capable of acting outside of a logic of simple self-interest or instrumentality. Gramsci writes,

> there never was an effective 'Jacobin' force – precisely the force that creates the national-popular collective will, the foundation of all modern states ... *The Modern Prince* should focus entirely on these two basic points: the formation of a national-popular collective will, of which the modern Prince is the active and operative expression, and intellectual and moral reform.

When Gramsci criticises the regional writers for their 'touristic' and 'paternalistic' gaze, he goes on to say that a more militant nationalism is preferable to this kind of sentimental and essentialising portrayal;[17] in his discussion of the Risorgimento in the same note, he argues that one of the causes of the weakness of the national-popular element in the movement was precisely the myth of an Italian nation that has always existed since ancient Rome. The obstructive, conservative force of such a myth for the critical and creative work of national formation outweighs whatever strategic value it might have in the process of unification.

What each of these points shows is that the distance between the 'national' intellectuals and the 'people' is not a question of authenticity but of alliance, of ethico-political self-positioning. Gramsci emphasises this in his revision of Notebook 3, §63 in Notebook 21, §5; the clauses in italics below are added in the later note: 'The intellectuals do not come from the people, *even if by chance one among them happens be of popular origins* ... They are something detached, cut off from reality – a caste, that is, *and not an articulation, with organic functions, of the people itself*'. Spivak has pointed out – and the passage above confirms – that the organicity of the 'organic' intellectual has to do with organisation rather than essence or identity; an organic intellectual – whether of the dominant class or of the popular, or subaltern, strata – is connected to

---

17   '... regional literature has been essentially folkloric and picturesque: the "regional" population has been seen "paternalistically," from the outside, with a disenchanted, cosmopolitan, touristic spirit in search of strong feelings, authentic in their rawness. From this point of view Enrico Corradini and Pascoli, with their overt and militant nationalism, are preferable insofar as they seek to resolve the traditional literary dualism between the people and the nation, even if they have fallen into other forms of rhetoric and oratory' (Gramsci 1975, Q21, §1, p. 2110).

its class or group not by nature or origin but by function. The national-popular collective will is not pre-given but must be produced.

I will conclude my discussion of the concept of the national-popular developed in Gramsci's notebooks by citing a passage that offers something of a counterpoint to the 'Jacobin concept'. In a note on Fordism, a national-popular – as opposed to merely nationalist – economic policy is one that views the masses as a national *market* rather than as mere 'cattle' (*bestiame*):

> in certain countries where capitalism is still backward and the economic structure consists of a mixture of modern big industry, artisan production, midsize and small-scale agriculture, and large land holdings, the masses of workers and peasants are not considered to be a 'market.' ... There are countries that have nationalism but no national-popular situation – in other words, countries in which the great popular masses are treated like cattle.
>
> Notebook 6, §135

In this passage a 'national-popular situation' is, as in other contexts, connected to the idea of historical subjectification, perhaps of citizenship, figured as humanisation through its opposition to *bestiame*. But the opposition is also, and more explicitly, between a population regarded by the state as cattle and one that is regarded as a *market*. The incorporation of the people as an active element of the social or national body is here coextensive with the consolidation of an advanced capitalist economy. While the 'Jacobin' concept is derived from a bourgeois historical process, the form of articulation, expressed in political rather than economic terms, is assumed to be transferable to a new – socialist – content or ethico-political horizon, and it is this possibility that Gramsci wants to highlight in his elaboration of the concept. The note on Fordism, without negating this transferability, makes clear that a 'national-popular situation' is not necessarily a good thing in itself, and reminds us that its empirically knowable historical form is that of the bourgeois nation-state.

3   Conclusion

We have seen that the category of the national-popular in Gramsci already contains the vanguardist and integrationist structure that will prompt the criticism of the subalternist scholars from within an intellectual culture wary of these aspects, but it always represents a sphere of inclusion rather than exclusion of the subaltern. For Gramsci, the production of a national-popular collective will corresponds to a process of desubalternisation of the popular masses, and even within 'advanced' capitalism, a national-popular state is one in which the masses are no longer 'treated like cattle'. In the appropriation of the terms by the Latin Americanists, following the South Asian group's critique of Indian nationalism, the national-popular comes to name a mode of political organisation that further subalternises those who constitute the necessary outside of any totalising hegemonic articulation, of which the nation is the paradigmatic form. Subalternity, then, can come to designate not a condition to be transcended but a position that in fact represents a certain epistemological privilege, while the national-popular, embodied in the historical nationalist and populist movements of the region, is the erasure of difference, for example, the erasure of indigeneity through the ideologeme of *mestizaje*.

The development of the concept of the national-popular as something that masks and deepens rather than eradicating the condition of subalternity can perhaps be traced to the disjunction between the peasantry and the nation highlighted by the South Asianist scholars.[18] But while the absence or failure of hegemony in colonial India, as posited in Guha's *Dominance without Hegemony* (1997), was a central tenet of the original Subaltern Studies group, the hegemonic projects of Latin American internal colonialism – the various populist and nationalist movements in early to mid-twentieth-century Latin America – if necessarily incomplete, had at their core the expansion of the nation to formally and symbolically include the majority of the people through the construction of mestizo national identities within the cultural and intellectual spheres.[19] The exclusions that operated within these discourses and regimes could no longer be attributed to a lack of national-popular orientation of the dominant classes, but were inherent in the institutionalisation of a unified nation-people itself.

The reversal in the valorisation of the concepts of the national-popular and the subaltern outlined here (or, more broadly, between hegemony – a term more often counterposed to subalternity, with the same implications – and the subaltern) tends to reduce the Gramscian terms to stable and unequivocal positions within a normative politics: the national-popular names the hegemonic regime that is distinguished from pure domination in means only and not in substance within a political culture marked by a broadly conceived postnationalism and even poststatism, while the subaltern marks the incompletion of

---

18   Although in Notebook 6, § 135, cited above, Gramsci explicitly distinguishes between the
      national-popular and nationalism plain and simple.

19   For a critical analysis of this 'national-popular' moment in Latin American politics and
      culture, see Williams 2002.

this regime, the fracture from which its undoing can be precipitated, or at least imagined. We can cull from Gramsci's notebooks an equally normative political project onto which subalternity and the national-popular can be mapped as a starting point prior to the emergence into historical subjecthood and a step on the path to a popular hegemonic project respectively; this framework, however, as I hope my discussion here bears out, does not exhaust Gramsci's theoretical formulation of the concepts. Subaltern groups, always and by definition occupying a position of subordination to be overcome, are not reducible to this position or incapable of an autonomous politics, but actively contribute through their own ideological formation to the construction of new society; a national-popular articulation, as the incorporation of subaltern groups into the nation, on the other hand, can represent an emergence from subalternity into hegemony, into the nation, through a bourgeois mode of citizenry-as-market that only fortifies the existing capitalist regime. Our reading of both concepts and the of larger theoretical constellation in which they are embedded must take into account this equivocality, through which they might serve as figures for any element of a discourse that might be mobilised in the service of a disembodied or transhistorical politics.

CHAPTER 12

What Can We Learn from Gramsci Today? Migrant Subalternity and the Refugee Movements: Perspectives from the Lampedusa in Hamburg

Susi Meret

1   Metropolitan Struggles, Migrant Subalterns

Global metropolitan cities have become vital hubs of trade, movement and profit making, arenas for competition for local and global resources.[1] Within the migrant metropolis,[2] social and economic competition unfold and conflicts, hierarchical structures, inequality and marginalisation are produced and reproduced by the neoliberal system. This happens, for example, through gentrification, which executes a 'creative destruction' needed by capital to maintain control over space, and to grant circulation and further accumulation, particularly in times of crisis.[3] At the same time, the space in the migrant metropolis is inhabited by the struggles for rights in and to the city, giving form and content to anti-systemic movements, involving, among others, asylum seekers, refugees, and migrants.

These groups of citizens are among those to have raised their voices to reclaim their rights,[4] first of all to the city. Regardless of their status, refugees today are increasingly active in social movements; they join in political and social protests, engage in mobilisations and political activities, actively manifesting their 'right to have rights'.[5] In many respects, contemporary refugee-led protests strive to address the need to react politically against neoliberal hegemony. These struggles have triggered new discussions of political strategies and alliances, which address the need of different groups to break free from marginalisation and social and political silencing.[6] In order be heard, refugees act as political subjects and demand social change in contexts, which, for

---

1   See Sassen 1991.
2   See De Genova 2015.
3   See Harvey 1985, 2008.
4   See Monforte 2015 and Nyers 2008.
5   See Arendt 1968, pp. 296–8. See Isin and Nielsen 2008.
6   Gundogdu 2015.

them, are increasingly defined by policies of exclusion, criminalisation and discrimination. This makes contemporary refugee-led mobilisations and activities important moments that lay bare patterns of individual and collective political subjectivation. Furthermore, it prefigures the entrance of new actors intervening with others to imagine and create alternative social and political spaces, modes of community making and alliance building, which are worth being considered.

2   Breaking Fear and Silence: Refugees Voicing the Subalterns'
         Consciousness

Grassroots mobilisations and struggles initiated by refugees since the 1990s echo the efforts made by subaltern groups to get organised, achieve political visibility, and a voice of their own. The Sardinian intellectual and political activist Antonio Gramsci (1891–1937) was the first to show interest in the way the subaltern classes had organised throughout history in the fight to emancipate themselves from their oppressors. For Gramsci, the subalterns' struggle for emancipation follows historical patterns, which can still help illustrate how subalterns organise and fight today.[7] As Green observes:

> Gramsci ... [understands] the subaltern as a historically determined category that exists within particular historical, economic, political, social and cultural contexts. He attempts to understand the process, development and lineage of the subaltern; how they came into existence, how some survived at the margins, and how others succeeded in their ascent from a subordinate social position to a dominant one. In short, he wants to understand how the conditions and relations of the past influence the present and future development of the subaltern's lived experience.[8]

Gramsci's interest in the subalterns was not that of the pure historicist. According to his prison notes, written between 1929–35, his was a profound political preoccupation with growing social and political inequalities in a society which kept some citizens at the margins of history. Gramsci's political and social experiences prompted him to study how networks of solidarity and autonomy can generate locally and eventually spark transversal alliances between groups of subalterns with a collective aim: to transform society. For

---

7   Gramsci 1975, Q25, § 4, pp. 2284–90.
8   Green 2011b, p. 75.

Gramsci, who had migrated from rural, insular Sardinia to industrialised Turin in 1911, this approach sought to address the reasons that had previously prevented the formation of strong social and political ties between the Northern Italian industrial proletariat and the Southern landless labourers. The question for Gramsci was to understand how those at the margins of history and society, controlled by the ruling classes, can achieve a 'class consciousness of themselves'.[9] Gramsci also knew that social and political changes do not come unaided; as Modonesi also observes, subalternity in Gramsci's understanding articulates a process of relationships, awareness and autonomy rather than a social condition, or a given status.[10] The 'degree' of subalternity depends, therefore, on the transformative potential and level of 'consciousness' experienced by the subalterns through the diverse phases of their life experiences. Political subjectivation involves individual and collective self-awareness, education, emancipation, political consciousness, self-organisation, action, and, in particular, it requires the motivation and ability to act collectively. The struggle for emancipation can be seen as a radical and transformative process, starting from individual awareness and eventually developing into collective political acts of antagonism and autonomy. The unification of the struggles, class solidarity and alliances are central themes in Gramsci's writings from the early years of his political activism.[11] Class interests, here, are not only defined by specific relationships of production, but also by how individuals and groups experience and react to or against these conditions.

During the prison years, Gramsci focused specifically on these issues. Reading the prison notes, we are reminded of the conditions for many contemporary undocumented migrants as well as of their fights to obtain rights and recognition. Historically, uprisings against the ruling classes have often emerged locally. They were characterised by spontaneity, geographical dispersal and a lack of coherence and continuity. The ruling classes used these weaknesses to maintain the status-quo and stay in control over these groups. However, in recent times 'new' anti-systemic movements, differentiated along social, ethnic, racial, and gender lines, have revealed an increasing capacity to cross the boundaries of the local and national in order to challenge the system at its core. The internal contradictions of globalised capitalism and its recurrent and profound crises have contributed to the rise and activities of anti-systemic movements worldwide.[12] Yet, the hegemonic crises and the strength

---

9   Q3, §48, p. 328.
10   Modonesi 2014, p. 36.
11   Gramsci 1977, p. 118.
12   Arrighi, Hopkins and Wallerstein 1989.

of the protests have not yet translated into real and enduring social change, although, equally, the concerted attempts of the ruling elites to demobilise and disempower the antagonistic movement have not managed to curb it. If we compare the obvious 'problems of translatability'[13] and the differences between the system of subordination today to the issues in Gramsci's times, contemporary refugee-led movements can be seen to be indicative of the transformative potential of a twenty-first-century social movement,[14] with the capacity to mobilise diverse groups in society against proliferating inequalities.

This chapter aims to illustrate the emergence and development of refugee-led movements in Europe, using the theoretical and methodological approach to subalternity developed by Gramsci, while also drawing on the concrete experience of the refugee-led group *Lampedusa in Hamburg* (LiHH) and other refugee-led groups in Germany on a more general level. From this approach several questions arise: How can the emergence of the refugee movements in Germany be explained? What are their claims and demands? What are the patterns of political subjectivation, alliance formation, solidarity and community building within the *Lampedusa* group and its European counterparts? How, lastly, can these movements be supported and encouraged?

Taking a Gramscian lens to the struggle by today's subalterns for social justice and recognition requires reflecting upon the potential of participatory political activity and research. By that token, individuals and groups in academia, who conduct action research, and who are politically engaged, should strive to support and act in solidarity with the organic articulation of these voices in society. This would include critical reflection as to the role of the research community engaged in the study of social movements.

3   Re-politicising Participatory Action Research

Stuart Hall[15] once observed that Gramsci 'was constantly using theory to illuminate concrete historical cases or political questions; or thinking large concepts in terms of their application to concrete and specific situations'.[16] Gramsci questioned issues that seemed to be part of 'the natural order of the things'

---

13   See Zene 2013.
14   Angela Davis, a Black American political activist, suggested this on 15 May 2015, during her
        Berlin visit (see https://vimeo.com/127986504).
15   Hall 1987, p. 16.
16   Hall 1986, p. x.

and he suggested alternatives for political change and social transformation. Gramsci was, according to Fiori, a restless, open-minded spirit, whose main concern was to:

> ... understand how culture developed, for revolutionary reasons: the ultimately practical significance of theoretical life. He wanted to find out how thinking can lead to actions ... how thoughts can make people's hands move, and how and in what sense ideas themselves may be actions ... In short, like the outstanding pragmatist he was, Gramsci was concerned above all else at this time to understand how ideas become practical forces.[17]

In this sense, Gramsci was an *ante litteram* participatory action researcher and his political engagement and action with the workers were particularly intense and militant during the Turin years. Gramsci's goal was to radically transform the unequal and unjust distribution of power, resources, and rights in society through an inclusive revolutionary process. This entailed the co-construction of knowledge and a self- and collective critical education. It also called for critical reflection in terms of the effects of living in a society driven by the capitalist relationships of production and of power. Gramsci valued education, self-education and mutual education as stepping-stones towards building a collective consciousness, which would prompt solid and coherent political action. In this, he distanced himself from a blind reliance on the workers' revolutionary spontaneity. Gramsci's early article 'Socialism and Culture',[18] expounds, for instance, how political 'consciousness' is acquired by humanity 'only by degree'. He points to the need to create, develop and prepare the revolutionary process by:

> ... an intense labour of criticism, by the diffusion of culture and the spread of ideas amongst masses of men who are at first resistant, and think only of solving their own immediate economic and political problems for themselves [and] who have no ties of solidarity with others in the same condition.[19]

For Gramsci, emancipatory struggles required conscious, 'educated' and well-informed subjects. This involved the development of critical counter-hegemonic approaches to both knowledge and practice, to be achieved collectively.

---

17   Fiori 1970, p. 93.
18   Gramsci 1977, p. 57.
19   Gramsci 1977, p. 12.

My encounter with the refugee-led group 'Lampedusa in Hamburg' (LiHH) created the opportunity to initiate forms of co-participatory and collective action discussed by Gramsci. The study and activity conducted in Germany and elsewhere in Europe over the past years has made clear to me that a researcher's academic approach cannot easily be divided from her personal involvement in the struggles for rights and emancipation. Critical research needs, in this sense, also to be action-oriented, building upon shared construction of knowledge and experience with the members of the movement. It also prompts self-reflection about the approach to activism, both as academics and as bearers of asymmetric socioeconomic relationships of power and of white privileges.

The reflections and notes on the LiHH and on the European refugee movements more broadly laid out in the sections below are based on discussions, talks, interviews, participatory observations as well as field notes collected since November 2013 at demonstrations, seminars, at refugee conferences in Germany (Hamburg in particular) and when travelling together to demonstrations in Calais, Rome, Amsterdam, and Copenhagen.

4   Learning from Our Struggles: Gramsci and the Turin Lessons

When Gramsci arrived in Turin in 1911, he was twenty years old. The Turin years signalled a dramatic turn in his life and influenced his thoughts and writings, also after his imprisonment by the fascists in 1926. In Turin he found a vibrant social and political milieu in a fast growing and industrialised city following the Great War.[20] The political situation in the city had been changed by WWI and animated by the 1917 Russian Revolution. Gramsci met with local communist groups and with anarchist revolutionary milieus. He became involved in the workers' movement, which had become stronger and increasingly organised since Italian unity in 1860 and in particular in the postwar years. In a letter to his wife Julia Schucht in 1924, he wrote:

> [In Turin] I became acquainted with the working class of an industrial city and I understood the real meaning of what I had at first read from Marx out of intellectual curiosity. So it is that I became impassioned with life, the struggle and the working class.[21]

---

20   Fiori 1970, pp. 82–114.
21   Gramsci in Santucci 2010, p. 47.

Turin – the city of the automobile industry and metal workers – or as he wrote in a report to the Comintern in 1920:

> ... Turin attracted the best of the Italian working class ... The development of this city is extremely interesting in relation to Italian history and the history of the Italian proletarian revolution. Thus, the proletariat of Turin became the spiritual leader of the Italian working masses, bound to this city by multifarious ties: family, tradition, history and spiritual ties.[22]

For Gramsci, the only way to achieve social change was by encouraging and supporting an intellectually autonomous, educated, self-empowered, strong and cohesive working class movement. This involved alternative practices of self-education, self-organisation and self-empowerment among the local workers. The aim was to strengthen co-participation and democratic decision-making in and outside the workplace.

In the socialist paper *Avanti!* in *Il Grido del Popolo*, and later in *L'ordine nuovo*, Gramsci formulated and reflected on the workers' 'duty of organising and associating' and on the importance of individual political awareness to create the basis for a future collective strategy and a coherent organisation. This involved, among other things, reflections on the alliances between the vanguard political movement, the party and the trade unions in bestowing the activities and the self-empowerment of the workers' organisations.[23] The wave of work strikes and factory occupations of the so-called Biennio Rosso (The two red years, 1919–20) brought about a period crucial to the development of Gramsci's theories and his reflections about the relationship between theory and praxis. In particular, Gramsci's experiences with the factory councils in Turin were formative; as scholars have observed,[24] the idea of the autonomy of work, where the worker/producer becomes a political and self-empowered subject in the production process, took concrete shape under the organisation and developments of the so-called *councilism*. Self-organisation allowed workers to break free from the 'slavery to which capitalism would have liked to condemn them forever'.[25]

On 3 April 1920, Gramsci wrote in *Avanti!*[26] that 'proletarian Turin' was living its 'week of passion', where 'struggles are spreading over and intensifying and

---

22   *Nel Tempo della Lotta*, p. 128.
23   Gramsci 1977, pp. 92–6.
24   Modonesi 2014, pp. 11–14.
25   Gramsci 1977, p. 90.
26   Gramsci 1964, p. 94.

new fights are preparing, which require new and different tactics than usual, with conflicts ... whose outcomes are still unknown'. The revolutionary energies were concentrated in urban Turin, later expanding to the rest of the country. His writings during this time, clearly show Gramsci's concern about the workers' organisational strategies; a prelude to what he hoped would allow the propagation of the struggles elsewhere in Italy. The wave of factory occupations received full support and encouragement from the group of the *ordinovisti*. They strongly supported the strengthening of the councils, considering them beneficial for both the formation of the communist worker and for the construction of a new solidarity-led society. The council organisation was adopted by the Turin branch of the metal workers' trade union and by local sections of the Italian Socialist Party (PSI). The idea was to convert the factory workshop committees created during the war into assemblies of elected delegates, who would control production. The councils would allow the election of delegates to a ward committee:

> an expression of the whole of the working class living in the ward ... that is legitimate and authoritative, that can enforce a spontaneously delegated discipline that is backed with powers, and can order the immediate and complete cessation of all work throughout the ward.[27]

Organisation at the community level would constitute a political and a social platform, which was later to be adopted by democratic workers' committees in the rest of Italy and inspire similar organisations among the peasantry. As early as 1919, Gramsci wrote about factory workers and landless peasants being the driving forces of the envisioned proletarian revolution.[28]

The industrialists in Turin responded to the factory councils with a lockout. The protests escalated, and armed metal workers, also in Genoa and Milan, occupied factories and began to implement direct workers' control of production. Prime Minister Giovanni Giolitti's government opted for a strategic approach in an attempt to manufacture consent among the opposing parties. This resulted in an agreement in 1920 signed by the government, the PSI as well as the trade unions.

In his writings, Gramsci explains how the factory councils promoted self-organisation, critical education and autonomy to broaden the workers' democratic participation, and to encourage the recruitment and bottom-up engage-

---

27   Gramsci 1977, pp. 79–82.
28   Gramsci 1977, pp. 113–18.

ment at the local level. The factory councils, thus, stimulated both individual and collective 'thought and action', showing the strength and promises of shared thinking in addressing solutions and goals.[29] Gramsci argued that the workers' direct and autonomous participation in the struggle added to their political self- and collective awareness. It also added to the creation of a shared solidarity that could 'produce concrete and constructive action'.[30] The factory councils were seen as the tool to structure and coordinate the workers' spontaneous and revolutionary initiatives, aided by the trade unions and the party. Gramsci wrote that:

> By virtue of its revolutionary spontaneity, the Factory Council tends to spark off the class war at any moment; while the trade union, by virtue of its bureaucratic form, tends to prevent class war from ever breaking out. The relations between the two institutions should be such that a capricious impulse on the part of the Councils could not result in a set-back or defeat for the working class; in other words, the Council should accept and assimilate the discipline of the union. They should also be such that the revolutionary character of the Council exercises an influence over the trade union, and functions as a reagent dissolving the union's bureaucracy and bureaucratism.[31]

These expectations were disappointed and the aftermath of the workers' councils defeat in October 1920 happened at a time, which saw the rise of fascism in Italy. Gramsci urged those who had participated in the movement not to relinquish, but to 'start from the beginning'. This, however, necessitated a deeper reflection about 'the reasons that contributed ... to the recent revolution and its defeat ... reasons which are not to be found in the efforts, talent, faults, mistakes and treacheries of a few leaders, but in the general state of society, in the condition of each distraught nation'.[32]

Gramsci addressed what he deemed a lack of 'revolutionary cohesion', that is to say, a lack of disciplined organisation, of transversal solidarity and collective action within and among the proletarian forces in society. He noted the trade unions' and the PSI's central organs' reluctance to support the workers' self-organised experience with the councils. Their reaction was based on the idea that they had a better knowledge of the needs of the working class

---

29   Gramsci 1977, p. 79.
30   ibid.
31   Gramsci 1977, p. 94.
32   Gramsci 1964, p. 96.

and about how to achieve them. Internal division followed, with the grassroots' movements on the one side and the party and the trade union leaders on the other, which, in turn, allowed the industrialists and the government to defeat the movement.

Gramsci's lessons from *councilism* can help motivate and strengthen the organisation and strategies of present day anti-systemic movements focused on social and political change. In the case of the refugee-led movements, his reflections can tell us something important about self-organisation, autonomous practices and transversal alliances.[33] The process of emergence and formation of (new) political subjectivities goes together with a struggle of self-empowerment and autonomy, which, particularly for the subalterns, is forged through experiences with oppression and subordination, but also encounters the difficulties created by internal conflicts and lack of coherent and common goals.

5   Gramsci on the History, Alliances and Potentials of the Subalterns

Gramsci's 1926 writings on the Southern Question[34] correspond well with his experiences in Turin. In this text Gramsci devoted more attention to what he considered the thorny question of alliances: the opportunities created by transversal solidarity and the process of political subjectivation and emancipation of the subalterns. In the Southern Question, Gramsci departs from an analysis of Italy's geopolitical situation and socioeconomic cleavages which had generated and widened under the process of Italian unification. Gramsci remarked how the historical legacies of the so-called Risorgimento still prevented the realisation of real alternatives to capitalism. But the reasons behind the 'poverty' of the Southern regions were not recognised by the popular masses in the North, he also noted. Northerners did not understand that Italian unification had not happened under equal conditions, but rather under the hegemonic control of the North over the South. In Gramsci's words, the North was a 'tentacular parasite', getting richer at the expense of an impoverished and exploited South. This was a form of internal colonialism explained by the hegemonic narrative on the basis of the 'congenital human barbarity of the Southern man'.[35] This, in turn, fostered stigmatisation and forms of racialisation distinguishing between a 'civic industrialised North' and a 'backward and clientelist South',

---

33   Modonesi 2014, pp. 7–8.
34   See Gramsci 1966.
35   Gramsci 1966, p. 39.

attitudes that continue to thrive to this day in Northern Italy. The economic and socio-political divide grew with the colonial expansion initiated under the Crispi governments (1887–89 and 1889–91), which broadened the hierarchies and inequalities on a wider geopolitical scale. The 'mirage of the African colonies' providing land to the southern peasants was 'a diversionary tactic to avoid having to affect a more equitable redistribution of land in Italy itself'.[36] Yet, the situation of dominance and exploitation in and beyond Italy contrasted with the 'perpetual ferment', which Gramsci observed was generated among the poorest peasants, the dispossessed, and the landless agricultural labourers in the South. Their antagonism and counter-hegemonic reactions were manifest, but their protests and insurrections were, nonetheless, unsuccessful due to their overall lack of cohesiveness, a dispersed and localised dimension, incoherent organisation and insufficient continuity. As a result, the protests often failed to reach beyond the local level.[37] In the Southern Question, Gramsci emphasised the need to overcome these constraints and maintained the necessity for a broader solidarity-based class alliance between the landless peasants in the South and the urbanised working class in the North. The Southern Question discusses, among other things, the difficulties encountered as part of the emancipation of the subalterns, since the values, ideas and opinions of the hegemonic classes permeated all levels of society, politics and culture. 'Organic intellectuals', to use Gramsci's phrasing, play an important role when the aim is to maintain and legitimate the status quo:

> Every social group, coming into existence on the original terrain of an essential function in the world of economic production, creates together with itself, organically, one or more strata of intellectuals which give it homogeneity and an awareness of its own function not only in the economic but also in the social and political fields.[38]

This makes it even more difficult for subalterns to give rise to their own organic intellectuals and to avoid misplaced alliances with society's dominant groups, whose interest it is to prevent dissent and political practices aimed at radical change in that society. Gramsci considered Italian intellectuals to be co-responsible in the production and reproduction of the hegemonic culture. In the Southern Question he wrote of the role of the 'organic intellectuals' who work to keep subaltern groups in a condition of inferiority, passivity and

---

36   Srivastava and Bhattacharya 2012, p. 91.
37   Gramsci 1966, p. 45.
38   Gramsci 1975, Q12, §1, p. 1513.

dependence.[39] Gramsci wrote, furthermore, of the 'intellectual block' – a reactionary force that prevents the realisation of the necessary social and economic transformations, because the existence of this 'block' reinforces, for instance, the paradigm of 'Southern backwardness'[40] and of similarities based on the 'humble peasant'.

6   The Subalterns in the *Prison Notebooks*

In the *Prison Notebooks* (1929–35), Gramsci gradually moved towards the notion of subalternity, which he explicitly mentioned for the first time in note 14 of the third notebook from 1930. Here, he refers to the history of the dominant classes and of the subaltern classes,[41] remarking on the difficulties to unify, which the subaltern groups have faced throughout history. In note 18 of the same notebook, Gramsci discussed a study by historian Ettore Ciccotti about the decline of slavery within the Roman Empire. Gramsci observed that the historically defensive nature of the subalterns can be explained by them being deprived of political autonomy. At the same time, he warned against an uncritical use of historical analogy, when comparing, for example, the conditions of slaves in Ancient Rome to the plight of the plebs during the Middle Ages. The political autonomy of the subalterns, he maintained, was severely curtailed in modern times, particularly with the surge of authoritarian regimes.

> The modern state abolishes many autonomies of the subaltern classes – it abolishes the state as a federation of classes – but certain forms of the internal life of the subaltern classes are reborn as parties, trade unions, cultural associations. The modern dictatorship abolishes these forms of class autonomy as well, and it tries hard to incorporate them into the activity of the state: in other words, the centralisation of the whole life of the nation in the hands of the ruling class becomes frenetic and all-consuming.[42]

In 1934, Gramsci devoted Notebook 25 to the history of subaltern groups. He observed that the history of these groups has been overlooked. Their rebel-

---

39   Gramsci 1966, pp. 45–8.
40   Gramsci 1966, p. 39.
41   Q3, §14, pp. 299–300.
42   Gramsci 1975, Q3, §18, p. 303.

lion, mobilisation, and organisation have been suppressed by the dominant classes, their autonomous leaders criminalised, and their history dismissed as marginal, inconsistent and fanatical as in the case of Lazzarretti's movement in the nineteenth century.[43] Once again, the main obstacle to the political mobilisation of the subaltern groups is deemed to be the internal fragmentation and lack of cohesiveness, which also prevents groups from achieving a deeper political awareness:

> The history of the subaltern classes is necessarily fragmented and episodic. Undoubtedly in the activity of these classes there is a tendency towards unification, albeit in provisional stages, but this is the least conspicuous aspect and it manifests only when victory is secured.[44]

Solidarity for Gramsci is not general unity or homogeneity, rather he referred to a broader alliance among the peasantry, the proletariat and the intellectuals based on mutual solidarity and cooperation that can trigger political and social change.

Gramsci's interest in the history and development of subaltern groups is thus analytical as well as methodological. Green[45] considers Gramsci's intent to be threefold: 1) to produce a methodology of subaltern historiography; 2) to create a history of the subaltern groups that would oppose a history based on the making of the dominant classes and elites and 3) to define a political strategy of transformation based on the subaltern groups' historical development, experience and initiatives. Gramsci saw in the initiative and activity of the subaltern groups features of autonomy, self-organisation, and self-empowerment, which could make socio-political transformations possible through conscious and collective political action. At the same time, he observed the need to encourage and support the resistance by working to strengthen self-organisation, self-empowerment, coherence and continuity within the group, which will then be helpful in the struggle.

Many of the rebellions and protests by refugee-led movements in recent decades have faced similar challenges with regard to spontaneity, scope, and extemporaneity. The initiatives from these groups often arise and develop locally, and in some cases gain momentum, but they also often fail to achieve long-lasting results and recognition. Nevertheless, the refugee movements reveal

---

43   Gramsci 1975, Q25, §1, pp. 2279–83.
44   Gramsci 1975, Q25, §2, p. 2283.
45   Green 2011b, pp. 74–7.

new potentialities in terms of an increasing appeal to the need for self-organisation and to claims that emphasise the right of all migrants to gain a voice,
visibility, recognition and representation in society.

7   From Lampedusa to Hamburg: Patterns of the Rise and Organisation of a Refugee-led Movement

The Lampedusa in Hamburg (LiHH) is a movement that started in early spring
2013 in Hamburg, by self-organised refugees, who had fled war-torn Libya in
2011. More than 50,000 Africans in Libya had to escape the war.[46] Most of the
LiHH members had crossed the perilous stretch of the Mediterranean Sea to
reach Europe and along with many other refugees ended up on the shores
of Lampedusa in Italy – hence the first part of their name – during the Arab
Spring. The Italian government managed the crisis by launching a state-of-
emergency programme known as Emergency North Africa. In February 2013,
the authorities deemed the emergency over, although this left most of the
refugees with no place to stay or economic means of support. Many travelled
further north, hoping to find a better life, and a number of refugees met later
in Hamburg.

The LiHH organised and claimed their 'right to have rights'. These were: the
right to stay ('Here to Stay'), to educate themselves, to work and to be recognised as refugees with documents from another EU country. Their demands
also encompassed a critical approach to the Dublin regulations, which prevent
refugees from moving freely in Europe and require them to stay in the country
of arrival. In 2013 and 2014 they successfully organised a refugee movement of
historical proportions: a high degree of solidarity among citizens of Hamburg,
who participated in demonstrations, organised activities and events, and acted
in solidarity by providing economic support and housing. The group is still supported by an array of advocacy groups, independent trade unions, and cultural
and political associations and groups, as well as by single citizens of Hamburg.[47] Their activities over the years have managed to rouse people, who would
not normally meet or work together. However, the heterogeneity of the support
network and the actors involved have also sparked internal disagreements, particularly regarding the political strategy employed to achieve their goals and
address local and national authorities. In many respects, the challenges experi-

---

46   See Campbell 2013.
47   See Meret and Della Corte 2016.

enced by the LiHH have re-actualised some of the thorny issues, such as who to ally with, group solidarity, and community building, encountered by the subaltern movements mentioned by Gramsci.

8   The German Context

Are refugees given voice and the opportunities to formulate their demands and organise their strategies? Do anti-racist and pro-migrant groups, organisations, networks and parties act with them, or are these allies moved by the belief that they are helping people they perceive as victims? Hamburg's (and Germany's) historically and politically active setting of pro-migrant, anti-racist groups[48] certainly contributed to and encouraged the emergence and the consolidation of a group like the LiHH. However, because of the variety of the activities and the German networks, creating lasting solidarity alliances at the national and European level have proved problematic. Mobilisation and goals have often remained local in scope.[49] There are, of course, a few exceptions, such as the Karawane für die Rechte der Flüchtlinge und MigrantInnen (The Caravan for the Rights of Refugees and Migrants, Karawane) and the VOICE Refugee Forum.[50] Over the past decades, these two groups have fought for the self-organised and empowered movements of non-status migrants. Their activities have prompted refugees to take up the fight for a political voice and representation. The VOICE Refugee Forum (the VOICE) is a result of such efforts and was launched in the 1990s. Karawane is a 'network of individuals, groups and organizations of refugees, migrants and Germans based on anti-imperialism and antiracism, ... engaged in the struggle for socio-political justice, equality and respect for the fundamental human rights of everyone'.[51] The network was founded in the late 1990s in response to the tightening of the German asylum laws and the rising number of racist attacks. Karawane significantly distinguishes itself from other pro-refugee/pro-migrant actors[52] by rejecting the humanitarian and white-European hegemonic and colonial approach. Similarly, the VOICE[53] gave rise in the 1990s to a wave of German based self-organised group of non-status migrants, initially of Nigerian descent. Unlike other Ger-

---

48   See Jakob 2016, and Monforte 2014.
49   Monforte 2014, pp. 52–6.
50   The VOICE 2014.
51   Karawane 2011.
52   See Monforte 2014, pp. 70–104.
53   http://www.thevoiceforum.org/.

man anti-racist groups and pro-migrant advocacy organisations, the VOICE and Karawane highlight the right and necessity of asylum seekers to be active participants in the struggle concerning their own rights, thus setting themselves apart from institutions and pro-migrant groups, which keep migrants in the background, acting and speaking for them instead of with them.[54] The VOICE has run campaigns against detention in German Lagers and against the practice of mandatory residence (*Residenzpflicht*) and confinement. The group encourages practices of self-empowerment and autonomy among asylum seekers, refugees and migrants through meetings, seminars, visits to asylum camps. They also use local media platforms to create and sustain support locally but aim at building links at the national and European level.

The mobilisation triggered by the LiHH from May 2013 to the spring of 2014 added a few new elements to the fight for refugee rights in Germany. In particular, the transnational composition and migration patterns of the group members and their previous experiences in Libya and with the Italian system bestowed the group with diverse experiences to draw from, in their approach to issues of social mobilisation, political organisation and networking. Also, their early contact with German networks that explicitly sustained self-organisation and self-empowerment contributed to further build their political awareness, autonomy and solidarity, both with the group members and with the supporters in Hamburg.

9   'Here to Stay', and Organise

'Here to Stay' is perhaps the group's best and most recognisable slogan and the one which most clearly asserts their goal. The way the LiHH organised was vital to the development and the consolidation of the group in Hamburg, particularly in the movement's inception phase. As Gramsci observed in relation to the Factory Councils, collective decision-making and a cohesive structure at the local level are determinant to sustain and consolidate engagement in the struggles. The LiHH was started on the initiative of a few, whose efforts later concretised into a structured and broader organisation with four main spokespersons in the front, who actively engaged to bring together the Libyan war refugees in Hamburg. The spokespersons dealt with both internal and external communication. Born in different African countries, they shared

---

54   See Jakob 2016.

similar migration patterns, spoke several languages and had a well-established network in their communities. Some already had past experience with political and human rights activism, while others had experiences with informal trade unionism in Libya. The LiHH spokespersons enhanced group visibility and facilitated communication of the group's aims and goals to the wider Hamburg society. Their statements, activities and positions were disseminated and shared on the group homepage and on diverse social media platforms.

The group convened twice a week: once to discuss and coordinate actions and make decisions within the LiHH; and once to debate them with the larger assembly of the Hamburg networks, organisations, advocacy groups, and supporters. The weekly internal meetings were hosted at the St. Pauli headquarters; several of the group members had also been given temporary sleeping places in the building's basement. Local community delegates participated, debriefing the group on discussions carried out ahead of the meeting in the smaller communities around the city. This structure and organisation sought to promote an inclusive and flat decision-making model. This would allow the LiHH spokespeople to communicate to the public on behalf of the majority, while maintaining a close connection with members living in different parts of Hamburg. The LiHH opted from the start for public visibility by organising street actions, demonstrations, and talks, but also by acting as the main referent for the dialogue with citizens and authorities. While the LiHH gained sizeable support at the street level, the group continued to be denied rights and recognition at the institutional level.

LiHH activities involved a process of political subjectivation; they explicitly questioned naturalised and internalised identities, roles, positions, and functions. By occupying and inhabiting public spaces, to which the LiHH members were not entitled, they directly contested the policies of confinement and invisibility imposed on them by their lack of legal status in Germany, and established a political platform and framework of their own. This meant that they could place themselves on the same level as other citizens: entitled to equal rights and recognition.

In May 2013, the LiHH requested a dialogue with the Hamburg authorities.[55] They wanted to know what the Hamburg Senate planned to do about the Libyan refugees living on the city's streets. Hundreds marched with them from the Hamburg Hauptbahnhof to the Rathaus, where the LiHH wanted to meet

---

55   See The Lampedusa in Hamburg, 2013.

with the then SPD mayor Olaf Scholtz. LiHH spokesman Asuquo Udo[56] recollects the surprise at their presence and demands and the spontaneous reaction of a policeman at the Rathaus:

> LiHH: 'We are the Lampedusa in Hamburg and we are here to demand our rights'.

> Policeman: 'Where are your papers? Do you know the German law says you have to stay 500 m from here? We are going to deport all of you!'

> LiHH: 'And what criteria will you use to deport us, mister? We want to see the mayor now!'

Their action was unexpected and although the LiHH never spoke to the mayor, the incident made the group visible and gave them a voice among the citizens of Hamburg. A tent functioned as a 24-hour info point, as a meeting place and as a presidium in the city (still at Steindamm 2), and added further to the LiHH's visibility in the city on a daily basis.

The way the LiHH organised itself played a vital role in giving the group visibility and a clear structure, besides setting a set of aims and goals that could be discussed at the different levels, but primarily among the group members. This seems decisive for the outcome of a movement, especially in the early phases. The way the LiHH organised also ensured decentralisation in the decision-making process, involving local groups in the decisions about which way to go. To paraphrase Gramsci, this organisational structure was well suited to the demands of a coherent 'war of manoeuvre', which defined the group's struggle, particularly in the beginning. However, the movement failed to meet the requirements of the 'war of position',[57] as it showed not to have a fitting strategy for how to proceed, consolidate, and in particular how to exploit the momentum that had been created by the movement by the end of 2013. Nor did the LiHH have a clear strategy as to which role should be assigned to political supporters in the struggle.

---

56   Interview with Asuquo Udo, February 2014.
57   For a clarification about the use of 'war of position' versus 'war of movement' in Gramsci, see Thomas 2009a, pp. 148–50.

10   Building Locally, Linking Globally

Transferring the struggles from the local/urban to the national and the European level requires the development of political opportunities that can support building a broader network of contacts, actions, and activities. This can help counteract what Gramsci saw as the tendency towards fragmentation, isolation and dispersion and the lack of coherent organisation of the subalterns' mobilisations. Also, learning from each other's successes and mistakes can help consolidate a movement's position both within and beyond national borders. This is what Gramsci advocated should be done after the defeat of the workers' movement of the Factory Councils in the 1920s. Solidarity and transversal alliances among different subaltern groups are vital; not as 'instrumental additions', but rather as 'co-constitutive and transformative of these very groups'. Thus for Gramsci, internationalism was 'more than the sum total of national party strategies [and] it involved the production of trans-local and transnational forms of solidarity'. These efforts are constrained and often repressed by the ruling classes in their efforts to divide and conquer. The political emancipation of the subaltern groups becomes manifest only 'once the historical circle is completed'.[58] However, as Gramsci observed, even when subaltern groups are successful, they are in a continuous 'alarmed state of defence'[59] and being in this position means that they might easily succumb to the power exercised by the dominant class. The LiHH experienced this at a relatively early stage. By the end of October 2013, the Federal Senate of Hamburg asked the refugees to accept the German status of *Duldung* (toleration-status), which involves years of waiting for a residence permit under conditions of restricted basic rights, such as moving, studying and working. For LiHH members, additionally, the Senate proposed a new asylum procedure in Germany, remitting the status of refugees that many had obtained from the Italian authorities years prior.

This occurred as the Senate and the bishopric struck an agreement behind the LiHH's back, creating a misplaced alliance in that the LiHH members, who had taken sanctuary in the Church of St. Pauli now felt pressured by the members of the clergy to accept the deal. This divided the group and affected its cohesiveness, resoluteness, and coherence as a resistance movement fighting the system. The agreement between the Senate and the church revealed the role played by the Hamburg clergy as organically constitutive of the bloc of hegemonic elites striving to maintain the status quo.[60]

---

58   Q25, §2, pp. 2283–4.
59   Ibid.
60   Q5, §7; Q20, §3.

For many, the rapid unfolding of events at the end of 2013 set off a phase of decline, both politically and with regard to the street-level mobilisation in Hamburg. But if motivation was fading, the situation sparked reflections about the movement's need to create a closer network of activities and ideas exchange with other groups in Germany and in Europe.

In October 2014, a five-day meeting with socio-cultural and political events celebrated the VOICE twentieth anniversary in Jena, Germany:

> 20 years of active resistance ... in Germany ... a proof that self-organisa-
> tion of the affected persons is the only alternative for the struggle of the
> oppressed ... our aim [is] to fight and end the fear and insecurity of being
> a refugee here in Germany and Europe as a whole.[61]

Representatives of the German refugee movement debated several central issues in Jena. Specific attention was given to discussions about how to unite the struggles, how to deal with the system's strategy to divide and conquer, and how to cope with gender, ethnic and generational differences within the movement. The conference also reinforced the importance of the political aspect as 'the proof of [the refugees'] existence' and of the need for subject-ive and collective political awareness, at the basis of the mobilisation. Other issues such as how to maintain and increase visibility 'above the street level', how to secure commitment from people and engage them on a longer-term basis as well as how to build transversal solidarity and gain political influence were also debated during the meeting. The conference elicited an important debate among representatives of locally organised refugees about how to build a stronger, shared platform. As one of the participants observed: 'We do not need new demonstrations, we need to get stronger now'.[62]

The Jena initiative was followed by the nationwide refugee conference in Hanover on 21–23 August 2015. The Hanover conference confirmed the refugee groups' interest in reaching beyond the local/regional level of the protests, by building closer links with other refugee-led groups in Germany. It also showed the emergence of an organic intellectuality within the movement. The LiHH was among the co-organisers of the Hanover conference, hosted by the Refugee Protest Camp. This was a refugee-led group (mainly Sudan nationals), which occupied the city's Weißekreuzplatz from 2014–16. The Hanover conference showed an increase in the number of active groups of refugees operating in

---

61   The VOICE 2014.
62   Male participant, the VOICE meeting, October 2014, Jena.

different parts of Germany, East and West. It also showed the participants' determination to get together and learn from each other's experiences,[63] despite general feelings of uncertainty and insecurity engendered by restrictive asylum rules and repatriation schemes.

Networking and experience sharing among the various groups at the transnational level was the central theme at a refugee-led conference that followed in Hamburg by the end of February 2016. The Hamburg meeting was labelled as an 'International Conference of Refugees and Migrants', with the goal and the ambition to 'foster a powerful network of refugees and migrants and to create a platform for reflection and learning'.[64] The framing was an appeal to form transversal political alliances and encouraged the creation of new alliance constellations that could also act at the European level. The idea was to support and strengthen demands at the transnational level, which groups, such as the CISPM (International Coalition of Sans-Papiers Migrants and Refugees) are currently working towards.

The Hamburg refugee conference was another step towards a European-wide platform, although it also revealed that many issues should be addressed at the local and national level initially in order to then be able to organise and consolidate the struggle on the transnational level. Among the challenges that re-emerged during the discussions is the issue of alliances and solidarity building. This is made even more acute by policies and practices that encourage the exclusion and marginalisation of refugees (with and without documents), thereby continuing to deny them rights and making them exploitable.

11   Conclusions

What we call a globalised and capitalist world harbours fundamental and growing contradictions at its core, fostering socioeconomic inequalities and conflicts, with forced migration as one of today's most symptomatic effects. Historic and accelerating processes of capitalist accumulation and enlargement that have reached the limits of the world system trigger migrant mobility. The consequences of these developments, including the patterns defined by migration for survival, are permanent and escalating. Contemporary capitalist societ-

---

63   Oranienplatz activist Napuli Paul Langa at the Hanover refugee conference, 22 August 2015: 'We are not learning from our mistakes. People are cheating on us and we are not learning. But we are still here. Maybe not in that big numbers, but still here and we will stay'.

64   LiHH, 2016.

ies continue to respond to the organic crises of the capitalist system by oscillat-
ing between opposing, contradicting and often short-sighted policy measures:
opening/confining, including/excluding, merging/dividing, moving/securing.
The reactions against these conditions materialise in the protests and struggles
prompted by a migratory subalternity. The proliferation of the protests and
of the struggles among the migrant subalterns is triggered by demands of
basic rights, in a context of negated recognition, confinement and marginalisation. The development of these movements since at least the 1990s shows
the increasing efforts made by refugee-led groups to get organised, find their
autonomous leaders (organic intellectuals), create alliances, and coordinate
strategies and programs at the national and transnational levels in order to
overcome their subordination. Yet today's subalterns face challenges that are
similar to those observed by Gramsci, when he studied the rise, organisation
and history of the subaltern classes. Despite their will to help generate a political and social transformation, the activities of the subaltern groups rarely
achieve continuity, political power, and permanent victory. As the LiHH experience illustrates, to some extent the reasons for this include the lack of strategic
direction, coherence and continuity in the various phases which characterise
the struggle. In particular, grassroots movements seem to fail to benefit from
the 'momentum' and the public support achieved through the mobilisation
at the local level. Progress in the struggle entails building upon a critical consciousness based on mutual learning[65] from the movement's positive achievements as well as from their failures, and also on the ability of groups to connect
and understand the power relationships that produce and reproduce subalternity.

---

65   The Silent University 2016, http://thesilentuniversity.org/.

PART 5

Postcolonial and Anthropological Approaches

∵

Back to the South: Revisiting Gramsci's *Southern Question* in the Light of Subaltern Studies

Carmine Conelli

1 Introduction

For decades now, Antonio Gramsci has been one of the most highly regarded political writers read around the world. Different disciplines and fields of study have borrowed ideas and thoughts from his writings, contributing to the international spread of the thought of the Sardinian founder of the Communist Party of Italy. The various uses of Gramsci[1] in areas as geographically and politically different as *Cultural Studies* in England and *Subaltern Studies* in India are testament to his increasing influence on human and social sciences notwithstanding the continually contested philological interpretation of his writings claimed by Gramscian scholars.[2]

Paradoxically, at the same time, in Italy the dissemination of his thought took a very different path. Soon after the publication of the first edition of his *Prison Notebooks* edited by Palmiro Togliatti, Gramsci's *oeuvre* came to be mummified in the mausoleum of the Italian Communist Party. Gramsci was seized by the Party who presented him as a 'thinker and man of action', in order to deal with the tradition of Italian intellectuals from a Communist perspective.[3] The idea was to construct his heritage by presenting him both as a milestone in the history of the party but also as a national antifascist thinker to oppose Croce's hegemony in the Italian social fabric. To follow Paolo Capuzzo and Sandro Mezzadra's argument, it is logical to think that, while Gram-

---

1   Filippini 2011 offers a practical guide to the heterogeneous interpretations of Gramsci around the world, showing how its uses traverse a variety of traditions of thought, including right-wing Republican political strategies in the United States.

2   For instance, the interpretations of the term 'subaltern' as provided by some postcolonial critics have entailed huge philological debates among Gramscian scholars. Compare Green 2002, 2013a; Thomas 2015.

3   Frosini 2008b, pp. 663–4. Introducing the legacy of Gramsci in Italy, the author explains how in dealing with other traditions of thought without putting into question their idealism and historicism, 'Gramsci's thought was thus reduced to a variation of Benedetto Croce's historicism'.

sci's thought in the 1960s provided useful tools for dealing with the radical experiences of those wanting to break with the official communist parties in their own countries, in Italy itself the social movements which wanted to break with communist orthodoxy at home, such as that of Workerism, had to opt for a break with Gramsci himself.[4] Probably due to the very *openness* of Gramscian thought, that, as Ranajit Guha suggests, 'invites and encourages adaptation'[5] to other scenarios, his pioneering interpretation of the *Southern Question* has inspired postcolonial writers around the world interested in the possibilities provided by his *open Marxism* and his 'non-reductive approach to questions concerning the inter-relationship between class and race'[6] mediated by the relevance he assigned to the analysis of the culture of subaltern classes. In this respect, his experience as a young man born and raised in Sardinia was centrally significant and this arguably allows us to speak of him as a *thinker from the South*,[7] as his writings reflect his untimely awareness of the processes of racialisation which constituted the actuality of Italian society.

Many have noted that the relevance which Gramsci assigned to the study of the culture of southern subaltern groups has only been taken seriously in the postwar period by Ernesto De Martino and his team, who, drawing from Gramsci's idea that peasant culture should not be disregarded but rather considered a serious matter of research, conducted several ethno-anthropological investigations in Southern villages anticipating some themes introduced in the social sciences by cultural studies.[8] But if we were to sum up the heritage of Gramscian thought concerning the Southern question, the balance cannot be considered positive. If in the early postwar period, the PCI promoted land occupations in the South – having in mind Gramsci's alliance between southern peasants and northern workers in the new framework of *progressive democracy*,[9] the massive emigration of southern peasants towards northern factories

---

4   Capuzzo and Mezzadra 2012, p. 43.

5   Guha 2011, p. 295.

6   Hall 1996, p. 436.

7   As Young (2012, p. 23) points out: 'Gramsci's interest in colonialism was derived directly from his early life in Sardinia, from his personal experience of the Italian dialectic of colonization and emigration, but was mediated intellectually by his membership of the Comintern and the PCI'. For a further account of the relevance of Gramsci's biographical roots on his political thought on the Risorgimento, see Carlucci 2013b, pp. 131–4.

8   For an account of the relationships between Gramsci and De Martino, see Pizza 2013. Rivera 2007 clarifies the reasons why De Martino could have anticipated some issues later developed by Cultural Studies.

9   Ginsborg 1984, pp. 83–4.

failed to provide the Party with the necessary answers concerning the changing landscapes of the southern countryside.[10] Despite the important publication of the collection of essays *La questione meridionale* (1966), edited by Franco De Felice and Valentino Parlato, Gramsci's ideas about the North-South divide seem to have travelled more around the world than to have contributed to a real updating of the state of the analysis of the Southern Question in the Italian social movements. What I want to propose here is to *travel*, taking account of the lesson provided by Edward Said – for whom theories can circulate from one temporal or geographical situation to another without being rigidified or codified by the pressure of existing circumstances.[11] Here Gramsci, after travelling to Calcutta and Delhi under the direction of the Subaltern Studies collective, can come back to the Italian South, opening up new pathways to explore an original rereading of the Southern Question. During this journey, I will argue that the discourse imposed on the *Mezzogiorno* during the process of the nation-building of the Italian State could be understood within the framework of the *global colonial archive*. Following this line, I will then engage in the fruitful dialogue between Gramsci's account of the Southern Question and its readings by postcolonial critics with the aim of promoting an *epistemological uprooting* of the Southern problem.

2   The Emergence of a Domestic Colonial Archive

From Italian unification in 1861 until today, the *Mezzogiorno* has been persistently marginalised from the Italian national narrative of progress and modernity. Contrasted to the virtuous and modern North – commonly considered the driving force of the Italian economy – the South has been represented as the ball and chain that has impeded Italy's progress to the standard of the rest of Europe because of its inhabitants' natural tendency to laziness, clientelism, criminality, etc. In other words, described through the Western Eurocentric gaze, the South stands as a concept that embodies all the negative characteristics of a binary juxtaposition with the developed and advanced Northern regions of Italy. Over the past few decades, scholars involved in the journal *Meridiana* and in Anglophone Italian Studies departments have challenged this stereotyped and misleading vision of a supposed uniform backwardness

---

10   Compare Biscione 1995, p. 59.
11   Said 2001b, p. 436. In *Traveling Theory Reconsidered*, Said revises his 18-year-old essay *Traveling Theory* where he originally argued that theories travelling to other times and situations can be tamed and lose their original antagonistic power.

of the Southern regions of Italy. Borrowing from Edward Said's *Orientalism* a new idiom to decode the discourse against the South and its inhabitants, these scholars have carried out a remarkable analysis of the role played by stereotypes and representations in shaping the inferior image of the Mezzogiorno during the Italian nation-building process.[12] The construction of a barbarous and picaresque Southern Italy, depicted as poor and backward, had begun between the end of the eighteenth and the beginning of the nineteenth century, through the continuous interaction of stereotypes and prejudices about Southern popular classes amongst the European élites who *travelled* around the South during the so-called *Grand Tour* and the Neapolitan bourgeoisie influenced by Enlightenment values.[13] Marta Petrusewicz, by tracing the birth of the Southern Question back to 1848[14] – when liberal exiles settled in England and Piedmont after failed uprisings against the Bourbon monarchy – shows how the South emerges as a constructed category. The nationalist patriots employed a consistent *orientalistic* cultural archive of representations and prejudices about the South in supporting their demands for the unification of Italy, addressing an anti-southern discourse particularly against southern subalterns' ancestral traditions, which were considered too backward to follow unification, freedom, democracy and progress.[15] However, my argument is that only after 1861 – the period of colonial ventures 'overseas' undertaken by other European powers – when the Piedmont annexed the former territories of the Kingdom of the Two Sicilies, did the Mezzogiorno come to be considered as the *darkest Italy*[16] and the discourse against southerners to acquire racial nuances. If analysed through the prism of *coloniality* provided by the Peruvian sociologist Aníbal Quijano and the decolonial critique, the encounter between the populations of Northern and Southern Italy during the process of unification mirrors the one between Europeans and Indios at the time of Columbus that produced historically new and racially connoted social identities.[17] The

---

12   Compare Petrusewicz 1998, Schneider 1998, Dickie 1999 and Moe 2002.
13   Compare also Gramsci on Goethe and the so-called 'mystery of Naples' (Gramsci 1975, Q22, § 2, p. 2144; English edition 1971, pp. 281–2).
14   Petrusewicz 1998, p. 135.
15   See the statements attributed to the Neapolitan patriot Francesco Trinchera, quoted in Moe 2002, p. 145.
16   See Dickie 1999.
17   According to Quijano, the conquest of the Americas in 1492 and the consequent European control over the Atlantic establishes a model of power, of which a fundamental axis is the social classification of the world's population around the idea of race, a mental construction that expresses the basic experience of colonial domination. In Quijano's words: 'The racial axis has a colonial origin and character, but it has proven to be more durable

process of the nation-building of the Italian state, analysed through this critical lens, reflects the local *translation* of colonial global power, as the Mezzogiorno and its inhabitants are depicted through historicist representations drawn from the global colonial archive, being observed, described and represented as the opposite pole of civilisation and progress, that is to say, of Europe and the Italian nation itself.[18] These representations, disrupting the veil of the homogeneous narrative of the Risorgimento – as the rebirth of the Italian nation from foreign oppression – produced an archive that legitimated, in the name of *modernity*, the representation, conquest and mission of civilising the backward South. Walter Mignolo has distinguished between the concept of Renaissance as 'a rebirth of classical legacies and the constitution of humanistic scholarship for human emancipation' and its darker side as 'the justification of colonial expansion and the emergence of a genealogy that announces the colonial and the postcolonial'.[19] In light of this rebirth can we speak of a darker side of the Risorgimento by investigating the archive of the Italian nation-building process against the grain?

3   Unveiling the Italian *Imagined Community*

In the *Prison Notebooks* Antonio Gramsci exposed the construction of the Italian nation-state and its historical narrative as an élite achievement, providing an incisive analytical category for interpreting class composition during the process of nation-building. What happened was described by the Sardinian intellectual in terms of a *passive revolution*,[20] as the Risorgimento's protagonists, lacking the conditions for complete hegemony over the new nation, involved the established dominant classes in their claims to power, rather than promoting social change. In his reflections, Gramsci argued that Italian uni-

---

and stable than the colonialism in whose matrix it was established. Therefore, the model of power that is globally hegemonic today presupposes an element of coloniality' (2000, p. 533).

18   The identification of Southern Italy as Africa and as non-European is self-evident, for example, in the words written to Cavour by Luigi Carlo Farini, the Chief Administrator of the South in the first months of Piedmontese control there: 'But my friend, what lands are these, Molise and the South! What barbarism! This is not Italy! This is Africa! Compared to these peasants the Bedouins are the pinnacle of civilization. And what misdeeds!' (quoted in Moe 2002, p. 165).

19   Mignolo 1995, p. vii.

20   For the analysis of the overall process of the Risorgimento through the category of 'passive revolution', see Gramsci 1975, Q19, § 24, pp. 2010–34 (Gramsci 1971a, pp. 55–84).

fication was realised by a heroic minority, and could not be felt as a real need by popular masses, whose demands for agrarian reform were crucially ignored. The Italian Risorgimento could thus be easily depicted as the story of a small number of élites who led the masses from foreign subjugation to freedom on the basis of a unified culture. The sentiments of these protagonists dated back to the thirteen century, when a unified literary Italian language was born with Dante's illustrious vernacular.[21] Hence, we can speak of the emergence, in the 1860s, of a new *imagined community*, forged on a remote and forgotten tradition, namely one culturally shaped by reassembling pre-existing models into a nation which appears to have the characteristics of an ethnic community, composed – from time immemorial – of biological and cultural aspects shared by all its members.[22] This is likewise evident in traditional Italian historiography, which, omitting the masses from the national epic, has actually reproduced a linear and progressive vision of Italian history. In Gramsci's own words, the history of the Italian Risorgimento and unification has been told as a 'national biography' or a 'fetishistic history',[23] where mythological and abstract characters such as *Unity, Revolution, Italy* become the protagonists of history and the past is interpreted in the light of the present on the basis of a deterministic linearity, in order to reinforce, in the masses, the elements that constitute national feeling. For instance Benedetto Croce accomplished this function, defending the epic of the Risorgimento and the consequent annexation of the backward South to the modern North, simultaneously blaming the birth and the heritage of the long-standing Southern Question on centuries of foreign maladministration and spoliation that had transformed the South into a *paradise inhabited by devils*.[24] This historiographical representation, as has been illustrated by Gramsci, illustrates the failure of the Italian bourgeoisie to involve the (southern) masses in the new-born national formation. Although, as Adam Morton has recently argued in relation to the circumstances of state-formation processes in Italy, the passive revolution has to be considered also in terms of a spatial metaphor, in particular as an 'emergent spatialisation strategy that structured and shaped state power in Italy'.[25] Since his earlier writings, Gramsci focused his attention on the failure of Italian revolution and its consequences in the post-unification period. In his own words:

---

21 Gramsci 1975, Q6, §78, pp. 745–6.
22 Compare Banti 2000, p. 112.
23 Gramsci 1975, Q9, §106, pp. 1169–70 and Q19, §50, pp. 2069–70.
24 Davis 2006, p. 3.
25 Morton 2013, pp. 48–9.

The compromise whereby unity is preserved ... gives the toiling masses of the South a position analogous to that of a colonial population. The big industry of the North fulfils towards them the function of the capitalist metropolis. The big landowners and even the middle bourgeoisie of the South, for their part, take on the role of those categories in the colonies which ally themselves to the metropolis in order to keep the mass of working people subjugated. Economic exploitation and political oppression thus unite to make of the working people of the South a force continuously mobilized against the state.[26]

By describing the Southern question as a problem of internal colonialism, where the alliance between the Northern industrial bourgeoisie and the Southern rural landowners that kept the peasants of the South of Italy and the Islands subjugated, Gramsci invites us to consider the Southern question as a territorial one and, from this perspective, to establish a programme of worker and peasant government 'that will win large-scale support from the masses'.[27]

4   North and South: Geographies of Power

While his essay *Some aspects of the Southern Question* remained incomplete due to Gramsci's detention in 1926, the author does nonetheless further develop his analysis of southern society in Italy, reasoning on the possibility for the Communist Party to build a 'class alliance between Northern workers and Southern peasants to oust the bourgeoisie from State power'.[28] The essay seems to prefigure themes successively proposed by scholars in the postcolonial field: as Robert Young has recently put it, the originality of Gramsci's interpretation of the Southern Question stands in an 'advanced, preemptively postcolonial understanding for someone on the left in his period'.[29] According to Miguel Mellino, many postcolonial critics have proposed a '*translation* of some of his key concepts in other and specific historical contexts than an analytical or (even) critical continuation of his particular Marxist perspective'.[30] This could be an accurate assumption, considering that Gramsci himself was far from

---

26   Gramsci 1988, p. 144.
27   Gramsci 1994b, pp. 263–4.
28   Gramsci 1994b, p. 315.
29   Young 2012, p. 23.
30   Mellino 2016, p. 58.

being a *Marxist* 'in either doctrinal, orthodox or "religious" sense'.[31] Rather, in David Arnold's words, his attention to consciousness and to the cultural and ideological dimensions of hegemony and subordination provides a basis for a critical understanding and analysis of the subaltern classes and offers a corrective to the tendency towards a deterministic concentration upon societies' economic 'base'.[32]

However, Edward Said, in his *Culture and Imperialism*, claims the relevance of another anomaly in Gramscian's thought that would have been extremely substantial for the unfolding of postcolonial studies. Drawing from Gramsci's latest pre-prison essay, Said illustrates the importance of *space* – what Mezzadra and Capuzzo have redefined as Gramsci's *geographical materialism*[33] – in opposition to the centrality assigned by György Lukács to temporality as the unit of measure of historical transition.[34] If Lukács's theory postulates the convergence of different historical-social experiences into a progressively homogeneous trajectory, Gramsci's analysis, as argued by Stuart Hall, also points the way different modes of production can be *combined* within the same social formation; leading not only to regional specificity and unevenness, but to differential modes of incorporating so-called 'backward' sectors within the social regime of capital. Theoretically, what needs to be noticed is the persistent way in which *these specific*, differentiated forms of 'incorporation' have consistently been associated with the appearance of racist, ethnically segmentary and other similar social features.[35]

This is self-evident in Gramsci's analysis of the endorsement by the Italian Socialist Party of the theories of the positivist school of anthropology that, at the end of nineteenth century, legitimised a scientific theory of southern backwardness on racial lines.

> It is well known what kind of ideology has been disseminated on a vast scale by bourgeois propagandists among the masses in the North: that the South is the ball and chain that is holding back the social development of Italy; that Southerners are biologically inferior beings, semi-barbarians or complete barbarians by natural destiny; that if the South is backward, the fault does not lie with the capitalist system or any other historical cause, but with Nature, which made Southerners lazy, inept, criminal and bar-

---

31   Hall 1996, p. 412.
32   Arnold 1984, pp. 155–6.
33   Capuzzo and Mezzadra 2012, pp. 49–50.
34   Said 1993, p. 49.
35   Hall 1996, p. 437.

baric – only tempering this cruel fate with the purely individual explosion of a few great geniuses, who stand like solitary palm-trees in an arid, barren desert. The Socialist Party was to a great extent the vehicle for this bourgeois ideology within the Northern proletariat. The Socialist Party gave its blessing to all the 'Southernist' literature of the clique of writers who made up the so-called positivist school: men like Ferri, Sergi, Niceforo, Orano and their lesser followers, who repeated the same refrain in different forms. Yet again, 'science' was used to crush the abject and the exploited, but this time it was a science dressed up in Socialist colours and claiming to be the science of the proletariat.[36]

Furthermore, focusing on the relationship between knowledge and power as it results from Gramsci's essay in its racial matrices, the birth of the Southern Question could also be explained as an ideological *dispositif* aiming at the accumulation of information to provide documentary evidence of its backwardness and thus to justify its subordination to the North.[37] *Southernism* could be interpreted in the same manner as Said's *Orientalism*, namely as a branch of social science seeking to explain the South, establishing itself in the academy and in the social fabric. The South becomes literally a career; the behaviour of the *Southernists* is characterised by a constant generation of truths about the South. Similarly to the Saidian Orientalism, *Southernism* has enabled Italian culture to manage and even produce the South ideologically.[38] In this sense, Gramsci is extremely acute when he describes Benedetto Croce and Giustino Fortunato as the most active reactionaries of the whole peninsula; their task is to prevent any insubordination and possible revolutionary action that could lead to a dangerous crisis of the agrarian bloc. In Gramsci's opinion, Croce in particular, 'has detached the radical intellectuals of the South from the peasant masses and made them participate in national and European culture. Through this culture, he has ensured their absorption by the national bourgeoisie and hence by the agrarian bloc'.[39]

Deepening his argument during his prison years, in a memorable passage of his *Notebooks* Gramsci explicitly asserts that the representation of the South as backward and inferior was functional to the reproduction of the progress of the North:

---

36   Gramsci 1994b, pp. 316–17.
37   Compare Capone 1991, p. 128.
38   Said 2003, p. 3.
39   Gramsci 1994b, pp. 333–4.

The poverty of the Mezzogiorno was historically 'inexplicable' for the popular masses in the North; they did not understand that unity had not taken place on a basis of equality, but as hegemony of the North over the Mezzogiorno in a territorial version of the town-country relationship – in other words, that the North concretely was an 'octopus' which enriched itself at the expense of the South, and that its economic-industrial increment was in direct proportion to the impoverishment of the economy and the agriculture of the South. The ordinary man from Northern Italy thought rather that, if the Mezzogiorno made no progress after having been liberated from the fetters which the Bourbon regime placed in the way of a modern development, this meant that the causes of the poverty were not external, to be sought in objective economic and political conditions, but internal, innate in the population of the South – and this all the more since there was a deeply-rooted belief in the great natural wealth of the terrain. There only remained one explanation-the organic incapacity of the inhabitants, their barbarity, their biological inferiority ... In the North there persisted the belief that the Mezzogiorno was a 'ball and chain' for Italy, ... that the modern industrial civilisation of Northern Italy would have made greater progress without this 'ball and chain'.[40]

In other words, reading between the lines of these notes by Gramsci, it could be argued that a machinery of imaginative geography has imposed a negative identity on the South in order to hide the asymmetric relationships of power with the rest of the nation. Re-reading the domestic colonial archive *contrapuntually*, as Edward Said suggests,[41] thus means to take account of the order of discourse which has constantly reproduced the racialisation of the South, and simultaneously of the counter-histories coming from the South which could unmask the existing colonial relationships of power.

5   Gramsci Travelling to India ...

In order to decolonise and dismantle this domestic colonial archive, I will therefore seek to interpret the Southern question through the prism suggested by the Gramscian methodological turn. As Iain Chambers has suggested, exposing the open and dynamic aspects of culture in the redefinition of rela-

---

40   Gramsci 1975, Q19, § 24, pp. 2021–2 (1971a, pp. 71–2).
41   Said 1993, p. 51.

tionships of power, the comprehension of political and cultural struggle should not be understood in the light of the binomial modernity-backwardness, but re-signified through the critical coordinates of hegemony and subalternity.[42] This fundamental insight provided the Indian collective of Subaltern Studies, in their anomalous translation of Gramsci's thought, with the basis for their 'histories from below'. Inspired by the methodological criteria for the *History of the Subaltern Classes*[43] of the Sardinian Marxist, the collective led by Ranajit Guha accepts Gramsci's invitation to seek 'every trace of autonomous initiative by subaltern groups', although disassociating themselves from the same concept of *subaltern groups* that Gramsci had coined analysing Italian society over the final two decades of his short life. Seeking to challenge the elitist historiographies of Indian nationalism proposed by nationalist and colonialist scholars, Subaltern Studies aims to analyse the *politics of the people* as an autonomous domain whose reasons were ignored by the above-mentioned historiographies,[44] rebelling specifically against the idea proposed by Eric Hobsbawm,[45] who maintained that the peasant insurgencies should be seen as *prepolitical*. In other words, Subaltern Studies have offered a historiographical theory for the *politics of the people* in which the historicist bias that characterises Gramsci's conception in relation to the linear path that would have lead the peasants from subalternity to citizenship – heritage of his Marxist concept of class consciousness – disappears.

In *Elementary Aspects of Peasant Insurgency in Colonial India*, Guha aims at overturning this idea, reacting against the notion that peasant revolts are purely spontaneous. According to the founder of Subaltern Studies, recognising the peasant as the author of his own rebellion means to give him a consciousness.[46] On the contrary, for Gramsci there is no room in history for pure spontaneity; a conscious movement has to be organised with a conscious direction and a programme.[47] In order to understand Guha's theorisation of the political consciousness of the peasants, one should take into account the actuality of colonial and postcolonial India, where the nature of the relationships between owners and peasants was explicitly coercive. In this sense, for the peasants, reacting against this relation of power which had subjugated them was a political action that aimed at the destruction of the authority of élites. Furthermore,

---

42   Chambers 2010, p. 8.
43   Gramsci 1975, Q25, §5 and §2 (1971a, pp. 44–51).
44   Compare Guha 1988b, pp. 37–44.
45   Hobsbawm 1965, p. 24.
46   See Guha 1983, p. 4.
47   Gramsci 1975, Q3, §48, pp. 328–32 (1971a, pp. 196–200).

in Guha's opinion, the absence of a programme to replace this authority does not mean that the revolt was pre-political.[48] Conversely, as illustrated by his early essay *Workers and peasants*, Gramsci believed that the peasants were incapable of organising their aspirations and needs collectively and of effectively changing the relations of oppression which they experienced in what he will later refer to as the great *social disintegration* of the South.

> Hence the peasant still has the mentality of a glebe serf: he erupts in violent revolt against the 'gentry' every now and then, but he is incapable of seeing himself as a member of a collectivity (the nation for the landholders, the class for the proletarians), nor can he wage a systematic and permanent campaign designed to alter the economic and political relations of society. Under such conditions, the psychology of the peasants was inscrutable: their real feelings remained occult, entangled and confused in a system of defence against exploitation that was merely individualist, devoid of logical continuity, inspired largely by guile and feigned servility. Class struggle was confused with brigandage, with blackmail, with burning down woods, with the hamstringing of cattle, with the abduction of women and children, with assaults on the town hall – it was a form of elementary terrorism, without long-term or effective consequences.[49]

Rather, for Gramsci, escaping a condition of subalternity entails following a path whereby the dominant hegemonic bloc is overthrown and the subalterns ultimately take the state. As he states in the *Prison Notebooks*, 'subaltern groups are always subject to the activity of ruling groups, even when they rebel and rise up: only "permanent" victory breaks their subordination, and that not immediately'.[50] As I have already outlined, translated into the concrete particular situation of his time, this meant to forge an alliance between the northern workers and southern peasants against the dominant bloc composed of the southern landowners and the northern industrialists. The leading role of this alliance was assigned by Gramsci to the Turin workers' vanguard, that could give a conscious direction to the peasants from the South, emancipating them from the oppression of the rural bourgeoisie. Although Gramsci incorporates the southern peasants – recognising their distinct subjectivity – and, as Nicola Short argues, rejecting the racialisation that marginalised them in the Italian

---

48   Compare Guha 1983, p. 25.
49   Gramsci 1977, pp. 83–4.
50   Gramsci 1975, Q25, § 2, p. 2283 (1971a, p. 55).

social fabric[51] – my contention is that subordinating the peasants to the leadership of the industrial workers, Gramsci's antihistoricist tension – which informs his vision of the relationship between subalternity and hegemony – remains trapped in the same historicist order of discourse that has historically relegated southern peasants (and by extension the entire South), to an IMAGINARY *waiting room of history*[52] – to paraphrase Dipesh Chakrabarty's famous enunciation. As underlined by Mellino:

> differing from Gramsci's perspective, Indian historians seemed to be saying that in order to recover subaltern subjectivities, peasants must remain on (or need to be put back to) the margins of History (of historicism): peasant rebellions cannot be understood in their political, cultural and subjective specificity from within any modern grand narrative (colonial, nationalist, Marxist), for the very reason that these represent tools of knowledge external to their socio-cultural world. It is in this way that the term 'subaltern' is transformed into a signifier, since it does not have to carry the weight of any grand narrative on its shoulders. Subalterns are those on the margins of history: subjects immersed in the autonomous space (which does not mean archaic or traditional) of their own historicity.[53]

This elucidates the different meaning the term 'subaltern' acquires in the Indian translation of Gramsci, who actually considers the subalterns as actively produced inside the dialectical relationships of the integral State.[54] By contrast, Subaltern Studies have probably never been interested in a philological use of the 'subaltern' as sketched by Gramsci. They may have employed this signifier – due to its openness in relation to Eurocentric grand narratives – to represent not the 'amorphous mass of the oppressed', but the autonomous domain of the politics experienced by *people* in colonial and postcolonial India.

Going back to our argument, taking into account the previously mentioned imposition of the discourse of modernity on the South going hand in hand with the colonial-racial framing that marks North-South relationships, I would like to point out that there is no room for an autonomous historical-social space for southern subalterns; to reprise the famous formulation by Gayatri Spivak,[55]

---

51   Short 2013, p. 205.
52   Chakrabarty 2000, p. 8.
53   Mellino 2016, p. 68.
54   Thomas 2015, p. 90. Compare also Green 2002, pp. 3–8.
55   See Spivak 1988a.

the southern 'subalterns cannot speak' if their actual situation is understood under the epistemic lens of Western (colonial) modernity.

6   ... and Back to Southern Italy

Today the South is still perceived and represented through the continuous reproduction of binomial categories of interpretation employed within the social sciences and public opinion (developed/underdeveloped, modern/traditional, productive/lazy, civilised/savage), that have been called upon up to the present as instruments of evaluation and comparison of Southern social and economic standards in relation to the North of Italy. This has been evident during the recent crisis in the Eurozone, where the neoliberal discourse that informs EU politics has ascribed responsibility for the economic recession to the so called PIGS[56] nations, enabling experts to theorise about a *two-speed Europe*, consisting of a vanguard North, and a South (to which Italy belongs) which gets left behind. In the meantime, the Italian scenario constitutes a particular framework in which the blame for the economic slow-down is shifted to its southern regions: during the crisis, a wide range of familiar stereotypes and prejudices were reactivated and the image of a lazy and idle Southern Italy is reiterated anew.

Bringing Gramsci back home after his *travel* to India guided by the historians of Subaltern Studies, therefore finally interrupts this empty and homogeneous narrative which has historically characterised the social sciences, imposing on the South the grammar of progress and development. Recently, several scholars have followed this illegitimate Gramscian turn, employing new categories drawing particularly from Partha Chatterjee's theorisation of *political society*[57] in order to give a new interpretation of the struggles of rural day labourers in the South of Europe[58] and of social movements in contemporary Southern Italy.[59] The reappropriation of a Southern Italian subjectivity is at stake here. Its articulation is only possible by thinking beyond what Raewyn Connell[60]

---

56   The acronym for Portugal, Italy, Greece and Spain. According to the neoliberal discourse, these nations are characterised by common 'bad habits' such as corruption, clientelism, maladministration, laziness and wasteful spending. In actuality, the crisis mainly afflicts the PIGS countries, as they are obliged to dismantle their welfare state systems.

57   Chatterjee 2004.

58   See Caruso 2015.

59   Compare Orizzonti Meridiani 2014.

60   See Connell 2007.

describes as the inherent *northerness* which pervades the historicist narrative of the social sciences, which actually relegates the South to the margins of Italian national history. Furthermore, a dialogue with other *Souths* would allow a repositioning of the Mezzogiorno in a global cartography which calls into question the traditional historical and geographical coordinates – as, for example, the study of history as solely the history of nation-states – and invites an analysis of the Southern Question, within the frame of the *global souths*: those places that, through an act of epistemic violence, are considered in terms of lacks and absences in relation to the progress and the development of the 'north' and the West. It seems crucial to reopen and unravel the domestic colonial archive through the *toolbox* provided by this renewed and unexpected Gramsci, in order to grasp and challenge the embeddedness of the discourse on Southern's inferiority in the Italian unconscious.

CHAPTER 14

Resisting Orientalism: Gramsci and Foucault in Counterpoint

Nicolas Vandeviver

1   Introduction

In the introduction to *Orientalism*, Edward Said famously indicates that throughout his work he will be employing Michel Foucault's notion of *discourse*. This is necessary, he argues, because

> without examining Orientalism as *a discourse* one cannot possibly understand the enormously systematic discipline by which European culture was able to manage – and even produce – the Orient politically, sociologically, militarily, ideologically, scientifically, and imaginatively during the post-Enlightenment period.[1]

This particular citation has caused critics to regard the Foucauldian intertext in *Orientalism* as its primary theoretical underpinning, even though Said's work also explicitly engages with the work of Antonio Gramsci. The further impact of this theoretical bias meant that Foucault's insights on the workings of texts, discourse, and the operations of power became the central methodological toolbox in the emerging field of postcolonial theory and colonial discourse analysis.[2] But Said's formulation of Orientalism as a discourse and his use of that notion throughout his seminal text have also generated intense critical activity with regards to his work.[3] Generally speaking, Said's critics commonly seem to take for granted that because of his explicit indebtedness to Foucault's notion of discourse, his conceptualisation and analysis of power must be similarly Foucauldian.[4] Adopting such a Foucauldian stance on power means dismissing the individual human subject and its intentions, and transferring agency

---

1 Said 1978, p. 3.
2 Young 1990, pp. 10–11; O'Hanlon and Washbrook 1992; Loomba 2005, p. 49; Nichols 2010, p. 120.
3 Young 2001, p. 186.
4 Ahmad 1992, p. 165; Bhatnagar 1986; Clifford 1988, pp. 255–64; Emig 2012; Gandhi 1998, pp. 74 ff.; Loomba 2005, pp. 42–3; Ochoa 2006; Teti 2014; Young 2001, p. 387.

to antihumanist institutional wills and repressive but nevertheless productive systems.[5] Regardless of the accuracy of the interpretation, this view of power is frequently interpreted by critics, including the later Said, as one that is grim. It is a conceptualisation in which power is seen as nomothetic, unstoppable in the growth of its domination and ultimately irresistible because it exhausts all human activity, dismisses individual human agency, and empties out resistance as well as the production of counter-discursive knowledge.[6] Because Said allegedly conceptualises power in this Foucauldian way, critics have charged him with being trapped within the framework of Orientalism and even perpetuating that framework by denying the possibility of agency and resistance on the part of the colonised.[7] In short, *Orientalism* is said to lack a theory of resistance (in the same way that Foucault's work is said to do).[8] Is this truly the case though?

Taking one of these commentaries as a starting point, I want to address the problem of resistance in *Orientalism*. This chapter presents a detailed analysis of *Orientalism*'s conceptualisation of power and agency that shows how Said relies on Foucault's notion of discourse and the function of texts, but supplements these insights with Gramsci's theory of hegemony to conceptualise culture, agency and power. I argue for a contrapuntal reading of *Orientalism* that places it in a combined Foucauldian *and* Gramscian light that does not take these intertexts to be conflicting, irreconcilable or mutually undermining – as the majority of Said's critics have done – but regards them as complimentary. In doing so, my reading draws upon Said's conceptualisation of the crucial notion of counterpoint.[9] Even though the term *counter* in *counterpoint* is ostensibly a term of opposition, contrapuntal criticism's goal is not the separation and exclusion of ultimately polarised lines of thought but rather their inclusion into a mixed, hybrid form of thinking.[10] A contrapuntal reading, as Jonathan Arac has stressed, is therefore not aggressive and dichotomous, but loving and joining.[11] This is crucial because conceptualising Orientalism as a discourse *and* as the product of hegemony in counterpoint allows us to understand not only the

---

5   Foucault 1976, pp. 121–5.

6   Baudrillard 1977, pp. 45–50; Mills 2003, pp. 123 ff.; Said 1992, pp. 239–40, and 2000a, p. 47.

7   These are precisely the defining characteristics of Orientalism's reductive vision of human history that robs Orientals of agency and the production of knowledge. It takes for granted that the Orient requires and even insists upon Occidental rule (Said 1978, p. 34).

8   Clifford 1988, p. 263; Ahmad 1992, pp. 159–219.

9   See Said 1993, pp. 59–60.

10   Said 1993, p. 15.

11   Arac 1998, p. 57.

workings of Orientalism, but also to reevaluate the possibility of resistance to Orientalism by highlighting the agency of intellectuals that Said believed in.

2   Orientalism as a Discourse

In a defining commentary on *Orientalism*, James Clifford admired the book for its pioneering attempt to apply a Foucauldian paradigm to the study of imperialism. However, he ultimately finds Said's use of discourse analysis flawed and theoretically inconsistent.[12] The problem with *Orientalism*, according to Clifford, is that Said's attempt to carry out an anti-humanist Foucauldian discourse analysis of the archive of Orientalism with the attendant deterministic vision on human agency is marred by an incompatible humanist belief in the power of individual authors.[13] This becomes clear in the introduction to *Orientalism*, Clifford argues,[14] in which Said clearly avows his indebtedness to Foucault whilst simultaneously distancing himself from the French thinker:

> I do believe in the determining imprint of individual writers upon the otherwise anonymous collective body of texts constituting a discursive formation like Orientalism … Foucault believes that in general the individual text or author counts for very little; empirically, in the case of Orientalism (and perhaps nowhere else) I find this not to be so. Accordingly my analyses employ close textual readings whose goal is to reveal the dialectic between individual text or writer and the complex collective formation to which his work is a contribution.[15]

It is precisely this humanist belief in individual human intention and the imprint of individual authors that Clifford finds incompatible with Said's use of discourse analysis derived from Foucault, who was of course a radical critic of humanism and developed the notion of discourse initially as a means of getting away from a philosophy centred on the human subject.[16] Such a philosophy presupposes a priori unifying anthropological and psychological categories

---

12   Clifford 1988, pp. 255–64.
13   Clifford 1988, pp. 262 ff. This criticism, which boils down to the argument that Said's analyses undermine themselves because they are too humanist and hence 'not Foucauldian enough' has often been voiced by critics (see Hart 2000, p. 74).
14   Clifford 1988, p. 269.
15   Said 1978, pp. 23 ff.
16   Foucault 1969, pp. 22 ff.

and, usually foregrounds books, oeuvres, and authorial subjects in cultural analyses.[17] Discourse analysis, on the other hand, desubjectifies and removes the
entire field of psychology. It no longer regards authors as individuals with particular experiences, but considers them to be functions or labels attached to
discursive statements.[18] To be clear, this does not mean that the notion of the
author is banished altogether from Foucault's analyses; it does, however, entail
thinking of authors transcendentally as a purely ontological principle of a text
without taking recourse to personalised, psycho-biographical terms to explain
any form of textuality.[19] As such, Foucault does not employ any close readings
of particular statements but focuses on the conglomerate formation of discursive statements.

Said has adopted a contrapuntal approach to cultural analysis, which follows Foucault in thinking of texts not merely as expressions of ideas but also as
worldly and material in ways that vary according to genres and historical periods.[20] Yet unlike Foucault, Said does not dismiss the authority of individuals
and, consequently, pays attention to both discursive *and* personal statements.
This becomes clear in the methodological devices Said develops for studying
what he calls authority. On the one hand, he uses the term *strategic formation*
to describe the ensemble of relationships of an individual text with other texts
as well as the way in which these analysable textual formations acquire unity,
mass, strength and thus authority in the culture at large. Said analyses both the
(discursive) relations of such textual formations to other textual formations
and the (non-discursive) relations to audiences, institutions and the Orient
itself.[21] On the other hand, he uses the term *strategic location* to denote the
way in which a particular author in a text positions himself with regards to
the Oriental material he describes. Said focuses on the prior knowledge an
author relies on and refers to, the motifs he uses, the images he conjures up,
and the voice he adopts.[22] *Strategic formation* causes Said to read literature
not as an isolated cultural practice but as a medium of representation connected to political tracts, journalistic articles, travel books, religious treatises, and
philosophical studies. It also seems to explain what Said means by describing
Orientalism *as a discourse* and conceptually mirrors Foucault's description of
the regularities of discourse and the formation of strategies in *L'Archéologie du*

---

17   Foucault 1969, pp. 31–3.
18   Foucault 1994.
19   Burke 1998, p. 107.
20   Said 1978, p. 23.
21   Said 1978, p. 20.
22   Ibid.

savoir.[23] Yet the term *strategic location* is a clear sign that Said departs from Foucault by showing interest in authors not as passive labels attached to discursive statements, but as active subjects with individual intentions, experiences, and contributions who actively position themselves vis-à-vis an anonymous collective formation.[24] The term implies that individuals maintain the authority over their texts and, equally importantly, are ultimately responsible for the choices they make and the (perhaps unintended) results of those choices.

Said's application of discourse analysis differs from Foucault's in that Said holds on to individual intentionality as an explanatory category of the mechanisms of power articulated in discourse. Even though Said, like Foucault, is interested in the circulatory network in which power produces knowledge and knowledge imposes power on the Oriental, he approaches these networks from a different perspective. Even if Foucault argues that power is intentional and has certain goals, he does not take that to mean that power is the result of an individual's choices or decisions.[25] An explanation of the effects of power cannot be found at the level of individual intentionality given that all human volition is constituted by structures of discourse. Ultimately, Foucault is not interested in the statements of individuals, but focuses instead on the relations of statements in a field and the underlying *dispositif* – the enabling rules of discourse and its underpinning interests.[26] For Said, on the other hand, power is something one possesses – something Foucault deems impossible –[27] with an intention or will to use, exploit or abuse these power relations.[28] Orientalism, Said writes, is not simply a discourse but also 'a certain *will* or *intention* to understand, in some cases to control, manipulate, even to incorporate, what is a manifestly different (or alternative and novel) world'.[29]

While for some critics this may at first sight be nothing more than Said's adaptation of Foucault's anonymous *will-to-know* for his own work,[30] Said's

---

23 Foucault 1969, pp. 41, 87–91. Discourse analysis has a threefold focus: first, it studies the internal formative relations between statements, next, the relations between different groups of statements thus established (discursive formations) and, finally, the relations between these groups of statements and events of a different kind (technical, economic, social, political) (Foucault 1969, p. 41).

24 A prefiguration of this crucial term to think authority in the context of a pre-existing and at first sight even overwhelming tradition of writing can be found in the concepts of *beginning* and *intention* which Said had developed earlier in *Beginnings* (Said 1975).

25 Foucault 1976, p. 125.

26 Foucault 1976, p. 16.

27 Foucault 1976, p. 122.

28 Racevskis 2005, p. 92.

29 Said 1978, p. 12.

30 Mills 2003, p. 71.

analyses also seek to take into account those forces that drive individuals, such as profit, ambition, ideas, and even the sheer love of power,[31] as well as explicitly treat the historical phenomenon of Orientalism as a form of 'willed human work'.[32]

Critics reading *Orientalism* in a Foucauldian light have argued that Said's interpretation of discourse analysis is the result of a somewhat careless and unmeditated reading of Foucault.[33] I, however, want to argue that Said's focus on personal statements in addition to discursive statements and his belief in the power of individuals are precisely well thought-out critical responses to Foucault that explicitly draw upon Gramsci's theories and insights on power, agency and culture. In doing so, I am not the first to draw attention to this Gramscian intertext in *Orientalism*.[34] It is by now a commonly held view that the influence of Gramsci on postcolonial studies is precisely due to *Orientalism* and the Subaltern Studies Group of the early 1980s.[35] But although these allusions are well known, most critics downplay Gramsci's importance as the stamp of Foucault on *Orientalism* is time and again highlighted as the work's single most important theoretical influence.[36]

Timothy Brennan is perhaps the staunchest advocate of recognising the importance of the Gramscian intertext in *Orientalism*. In fact, he has argued multiple times that even though Foucault's theories are important for Said's early works – *Beginnings*[37] most notably – they hardly have anything to do with the argument made in *Orientalism*.[38] *Orientalism*, Brennan feels, should therefore not be understood as Foucauldian but as Gramscian, and the central concept of the book to him is not the Foucauldian concept of *discourse* but the Gramscian or Chomskyan notion of *institution*.[39] Although Brennan provides a more than necessary counterweight in the debate about *Orientalism*'s theoretical underpinnings and rightly asks us to pay attention to the Gramscian line of thought in that work, he bends the stick too far and thereby obscures the book's Foucauldian underpinnings. Neil Lazarus does not bend the stick as far, arguing in line with Brennan that although Said *speaks* Foucauldian he

---

31   Said 1983a, p. 222.

32   Said 1978, p. 15.

33   Ahmad 1992, p. 165; Chuaqui 2005, pp. 99–100; Clifford 1988, pp. 271–2; Emig 2012, p. 140.

34   See Brennan 2006 and Hussein 2002.

35   Bhattacharya B. 2012, p. 83.

36   Clifford 1988, pp. 255–64; Kennedy 2000, p. 25; Loomba 2005, pp. 42–3; Niyogi 2006, p. 135; Racevskis 2005; Young 2001, p. 387.

37   Said 1975.

38   Brennan 1992, 2000, and 2001b.

39   Brennan 2006, p. 123.

clearly does not *think* Foucauldian. As such, Lazarus argues, we should translate Said's notion of *discourse* into something resembling Raymond Williams's notion of *hegemony*, which he sets out in Gramscian terms in *Marxism and Literature*.[40] I think both wrongfully construct a one-sided, Gramscian Said. As I have already stressed, Orientalism should be analysed as a discourse in the Foucauldian sense of the word and is even marked by the same disciplinary vision that characterises the punitive discourse that Foucault analyses in *Surveiller et punir*.[41] By this, I mean that it orders, synchronises, categorises, makes intelligible, and essentialises because 'it presumes that the whole Orient can be seen panoptically'.[42] For reasons of space and focus, I cannot develop this argument any further here. Suffice to say, however, that one should not obscure the explicitly Foucauldian underpinnings of *Orientalism*. Instead of stressing the primacy of one intertext over the other or trying to bring Said's analyses into line with either a Foucauldian or a Gramscian orthodoxy,[43] I propose a contrapuntal reading of *Orientalism* that places it in a complementary Foucauldian and Gramscian light that does not grant either of the two the upper hand. In order to do justice to Said's approach to secular criticism, we have to consider Orientalism as both a discourse *and* as the product of hegemony. Allow me to argue why.

3   ... and as the Product of Hegemony

In an essay that came out of a recurring National Endowment for the Humanities summer seminar at Columbia University that he taught from 1977 to 1979, Said balances Foucault's conceptualisation of the function of texts against Derrida's. In the essay, he explicitly favours the former's for its ability to not only show the internal workings of texts but also their worldly affiliations with 'institutions, offices, agencies, classes, academies, corporations, groups, guilds, ideologically defined parties and professions'.[44] Yet despite its worldliness, Said finds Foucault's theory ultimately inadequate as a means of dealing with historical change precisely because it does not pay attention to individual statements:

---

40   Williams 1977; Lazarus 2011, pp. 192–3.

41   Foucault 1975.

42   Said 1978, p. 240.

43   The phrase is Lazarus's. Although he is right to point out that this is precisely what *Orientalism*'s Foucauldian critics have done (Lazarus 2011, p. 189), its Gramscian critics have also tried to reconcile Said's 'heterodox' criticism with a canonical version of Gramsci – whatever that may be, given the unsystematic nature of Gramsci's writings.

44   Said 1983a, p. 212.

Foucault's thesis is that individual statements, or the chances that individual authors *can* make individual statements, are not really likely. Over and above every opportunity for saying something, there stands a regularising collectivity that Foucault has called a discourse, itself governed by the archive … Though obviously anxious to avoid vulgar determinism in explaining the workings of the social order, he pretty much ignores the whole category of *intention*.[45]

According to Said, Foucault conceptualises discourse as something that dominates and even overwhelms subjects.[46] As I have already discussed, Said believes that individuals *can* make personal statements and contribute to (and thus potentially oppose) a collective discursive formation such as Orientalism. Even though he is positive on the whole about Foucault's view of the function of texts,[47] Said finds it lacking in terms of context and ultimately, therefore, ahistorical. According to him, the study of the workings of texts can only achieve fullness in its historically contextual mode, which means broadening the historical context to include, amongst all other worldly affiliations, the human intentionality that produces these texts.[48]

By disregarding human intentionality, Foucault imagines power as too sterile and irresistible and, Said was to say in an interview in 1992, 'ultimately becomes the scribe of domination'.[49] In this sense, Said, who is politically committed,[50] feels uneasy about Foucault's rather disinterested stance from the operations of power, and criticises him for leaving out oppositional forces and thereby lapsing into political quietism –[51] a criticism that was also often voiced in

---

45   Said 1983a, p. 186, emphasis added.
46   See Foucault 1970, p. xiv.
47   What Said admires in Foucault's theory of the function of texts is the idea that 'the text is part of a network of power whose textual form is a purposeful obscuring of power beneath textuality and knowledge' (Said 1983a, p. 184). It is the role of the critic to make visible once again this connection and to challenge 'the culture and its apparently sovereign powers of intellectual activity' (Said 1983a, pp. 184–5).
48   Bhattacharya N., Kaul, Loomba and Said 2004; Brennan 2005; Christopher 2005, p. 118.
49   Said 1992, p. 239.
50   Said became politically active in 1967 in response to the Arab-Israeli conflict of June. He published his first political essay on the representation of Arabs in 1970 (Said 1970) and became an independent member of the Palestinian National Council in 1977.
51   Said was later to clash with Foucault on precisely this matter, arguing that Foucault never thinks about power from the perspective of opposition, rather from its actualisation: 'Foucault's imagination of power is largely *with* rather than *against* it … [H]is interest in domination was critical but not finally as contestatory or as oppositional as on the surface it seems to be. This translates into the paradox that Foucault's imagination of power was by

France by Jean-Paul Sartre, Simone de Beauvoir, and other critics of the left.[52]
'What one misses in Foucault', Said goes on to write,

> is something resembling Gramsci's analyses of hegemony, historical
> blocks, ensembles of relationship done from the perspective of an en-
> gaged political worker for whom the fascinated description of exercised
> power is never substitute from trying to change power relationships with-
> in society.[53]

To supplement Foucault's conceptualisation of the workings of texts and in
lieu of what he considers to be flawed ideas on power and agency – both with
regards to authors and the critic – Said favours Gramsci's ideas on hegemony
as a means of conceptualising culture, agency, and power relations, both in the
essay and in *Orientalism*:

> ideas, cultures, and histories cannot seriously be understood or studied
> without their force, or more precisely their configurations of power, also
> being studied. To believe that the Orient was created – or, as I call it,
> 'Orientalized' – and to believe that such things happen simply as a neces-
> sity of the imagination, is to be disingenuous. The relationship between
> Occident and Orient is a relationship of power, of domination, of varying
> degrees of a complex *hegemony*.[54]

Apart from restating that Orientalist discourse is driven by an intention – both
on the level of the collective and the individual –[55] Said argues that the relationship of power that informs Orientalism and that is perpetuated by Orientalist
discourse should be seen as a form of cultural leadership, or what Gramsci has
identified as *hegemony*. 'Culture, of course', Said goes on to specify,

---

his analysis of power to reveal its injustice and cruelty, but by his theorization to let it go
on more or less unchecked' (Said 2000a, p. 242).

52   See Eribon 2011, pp. 276–80. In an interview, Sartre polemically called Foucault's air of
neutrality and his precedence of structures the final bulwark of the bourgeoisie against
Marxism (Sartre 1966). Although distinctly less sympathetic to Marxism, Said shares many
criticisms of Foucault with Sartre – perhaps a residue of his Sartre-inspired existential-
phenomenological work on Joseph Conrad (Said 1966). These analogies fall outside the
scope of this chapter.

53   Said 1983a, pp. 221–2.

54   Said 1978, p. 5, emphasis added.

55   Hussein 2002, p. 240.

is to be found operating within civil society, where the influence of ideas, of institutions, and of other persons works not through domination but by what Gramsci calls consent ... It is hegemony, or rather the result of cultural hegemony at work, that gives Orientalism the durability and strength I have been speaking about so far.[56]

To be clear from the outset, in my discussion of the Gramscian notion of *hegemony* I am aligning myself with Peter Thomas's understanding of it. Contrary to Perry Anderson's widespread antinomian view in which hegemony (consent) and domination (coercion) are seen as qualitatively distinct and oppositional forms of power,[57] Thomas argues that one should see them

> as strategically differentiated forms of a unitary political power: hegemony is the form of political power exercised over those classes in close proximity to the leading group, while domination is exerted over those opposing it.[58]

The unfolding of power, Thomas argues, happens through the winning of consent of included classes and coercion against excluded others.[59] In a dialectical integrated process, hegemony both prepares for a future domination and secures that achieved dominance: consent always appears in tandem with a certain degree of coercion.[60] Not only is Thomas's understanding, to my mind, closer to Gramsci's conceptualisation of power relations as the dual nature of Machiavelli's Centaur 'half-animal and half-human ... levels of force and consent, authority and hegemony, violence and civilisation',[61] it also closely fits Said's description of how Orientalism helped first to unfold and later maintain European-Atlantic dominance over the Orient. Historically speaking, Said finds it remarkable that in the Orient 'very little consent is to be found'.[62] Orientalism's relationship of power is unitary in that non-Orientals hold onto power and speak for Orientals, who are excluded from the right of self-representation and held in check through a series of colonial institutions (military, legislative, judiciary, administrative, educational, religious, academic, imaginative).

---

56   Said 1978, p. 7.
57   Anderson 1979, pp. 20–1.
58   Thomas 2009a, p. 163.
59   Thomas 2009a, pp. 162–3.
60   Thomas 2009a, pp. 163–4.
61   Gramsci 1971a, p. 170.
62   Said 1978, p. 6.

The relative strength between the Occident and the Orient allowed the former to dominate the latter and enabled the formation of Orientalism as a Western discourse to support that dominance in the culture at home and prepare for colonial interference abroad;[63] subsequently, from Napoleon's invasion of Egypt in 1798 to the present, one is able to see the manufacturing of consent of the Oriental population by both Western and Eastern intellectuals alike.[64] Orientalism, to put it in Gramsci's words, can thus be seen as a power relation of 'hegemony protected by the armour of coercion'.[65]

The conceptualisation of Orientalism as a discourse *and* as the product of hegemony at the same time is crucial in two ways.[66] First, Gramsci's term

---

63   Ibid.

64   Said 1978, pp. 81–2, 322–3.

65   Gramsci 1971a, p. 263.

66   There are very few studies that consider Foucault's and Gramsci's understanding of power together. Though some critics forcefully reject the possibility of combining the work of the two thinkers, I am on firm ground with the few critics who suggest that the two oeuvres should be considered complementary and that the selective combination of their insights supplements the inevitable flaws or theoretical blind spots in either theory (Cocks 1989, p. 26; Ekers and Loftus 2008; Hardt and Negri 2000; Kreps 2015; Laclau and Mouffe 1985; Radhakrishnan 1990; Torfing 1999). Chantal Mouffe was one of the first to argue that Gramsci and Foucault approach many of the same theoretical concerns and that the former's understanding of hegemony can be reconciled with the latter's notion of discourse (Mouffe 1979). Mouffe draws upon Gramsci's insights that the struggle for hegemony happens in civil society during a war of position (see Gramsci 2007a, p. 267) to reconceptualise hegemony as a discursive phenomenon (Torfing 1999, p. 14). According to her, social conflict is a struggle over meaning that is being fought at the ideological level by intellectuals of opposing blocs through the constant disarticulation and re-articulation of discourses (Mouffe 1979, pp. 185–6). The struggle ends when one bloc has successfully disarticulated the opposing bloc's discourse and has rearticulated certain key discursive elements in ideological terms of its own (Mouffe 1979, p. 198; see also Laclau and Mouffe 1985). Moreover, I find myself strengthened in combining the ideas of Gramsci and Foucault by the work of Michael Ekers and Alex Loftus on the political ecology of water. They too combine both writers' ideas and stress that Foucault's understanding of power has antecedents in Gramsci's work on hegemony and the integral state (Ekers and Loftus 2008, pp. 702–3). In their view, Foucault's micropolitical theory of power follows up on Gramsci's insights on hegemony and the consolidation of power from the public sphere of the state right down to the intimacies of everyday life, such as privative initiatives, the thought of intellectuals and the modern home (Gramsci 1971a, pp. 5–13, 55 ff., n. 5, 258). While Foucault did not deny the existence of the state in the Gramscian sense and even explicitly acknowledged that relations of power and the regimes of truth operate within broader, macropolitical forms of hegemony (Foucault 2000, p. 133), he thought it necessary to decentre power and take as a starting point the intricate, dispersed micropractices of modern power that were hitherto being obscured in analyses that focused too much on the apparently sovereign power of the state and its apparatus (Foucault 1976, pp. 116–18).

hegemony allows Said to think not only of culture in terms of determining yet productive constraints – an idea one also finds in Foucault's cultural analyses –[67] but allows him to do so without dismissing the individual agency of subjects and blurring the individuality of authors.[68] After all, Gramsci argues that although there are forces of dominance and subordination at work in history that are independent of human will – the refractory social forces such as a city's population or the number of firms, for instance –, these forces serve as the conditions on which a society can transform and certainly do not rule out human intention or overwhelm willed human work.[69] *Hegemony* is a sensitive analytical term that takes into account the constraints affecting subjects while simultaneously acknowledging the active role these subordinate subjects play in the operations of power.[70] The dominant class, Gramsci writes, does not merely coerce its power upon subaltern classes, 'but manages to win the active consent over those over whom it rules'.[71] An analysis of power relations must therefore study both the historical conditions in which men live and that shape their subjectivity *and* study the will and initiative of these men in reaction to these conditions.[72] It is clear from Gramsci's writings that conscious and willful actions of men are, after all, the prime motors of history.[73] Gramsci's theory of hegemony enables Said to pay attention to personal statements in addition to discursive statements, and to conceptualise Orientalism

> as a dynamic exchange between individual authors and the large political concerns shaped by the three great empires – British, French, American – in whose intellectual and imaginative territory the writing was produced.[74]

The second important consequence of Said's use of the term hegemony is that it tackles the criticism of allowing no alternative to Orientalism. Even though Said avows that he has paid insufficient attention to developing such an alternative,[75] change is always possible in a hegemonic analysis simply because a hegemonic social form can never exhaust all human behaviour, energy, or

---

67   See Foucault 1976, pp. 123–4.
68   Said 1978, p. 9.
69   Gramsci 1971a, pp. 180–1; Williams 1977, p. 108.
70   Gramsci 1971a, pp. 265–6; Jones 2006, p. 41.
71   Gramsci 1971a, p. 244.
72   Gramsci 1971a, pp. 125–33, 244.
73   Gramsci 1971a, p. 130; Daldal 2014, p. 151; Thomas 2009a, p. 156.
74   Said 1978, pp. 14–15.
75   Said 1978, p. 325.

intention.[76] There are always significant forms of human practice that happen against or outside the dominating hegemonic social order and, Said was to write later in a way that balanced Gramsci's insights with Foucault's, 'this is obviously what makes change possible, limits power in Foucault's sense, and hobbles the theory of that power'.[77] Every social form has the possibility further to develop into a new or alternate form, however marginal that development may be.[78] In effect, a social form can only ever be partially and temporarily fixed, never fully. For if such absolute fixity would exist in the social world, there would be nothing to hegemonise and it would simply be considered domination.[79] This insight guarantees the possible emergence of new forces which can then, in turn, become hegemonic and forms the basis for Raymond Williams's elaboration of historical change in terms of dynamic interrelations between residual, dominant, and emergent forces. In this theory, these emergent forces are representative to areas of human behaviour which are neglected, repressed, or even unrecognised by the dominant hegemonic order.[80] These new forces can become dominant and topple the hegemonic discourse of Orientalism, for instance, through meaningful and willed human action, led by intellectuals.

Gramsci attributes an important role to intellectuals in the dissemination of hegemony and the manufacturing of consent, as well as in the production of a counter-hegemony.[81] They are responsible for the elaboration of ideology through culture and are ultimately capable of realising moral and intellectual reform at the level of civil society.[82] Said stresses the importance of intellectuals as agents in the practice of Orientalism too, albeit in a negative way. He describes Orientalism as a form of '*intellectual authority* over the Orient within Western culture'[83] in which he distinguishes both 'the historical authority' – Orientalism as a discursive formation – and 'the personal authorities' –[84] the personal statements of Orientalist scholars. Intellectuals are in no way free-floating individuals and must be considered in relation to the precise historical structures in which they function as intellectuals.[85] But even within these struc-

---

76   Williams 1977, p. 125.
77   Said 1983c, p. 247.
78   Gramsci 1971a, p. 222.
79   Laclau and Mouffe 1985, p. 134.
80   Williams 1977, pp. 122–3.
81   Gramsci 1971a, pp. 9–14; Mouffe 1979, p. 187; Holub 1992, p. 6.
82   Gramsci 1971a, pp. 12, 60–1.
83   Said 1978, p. 19, emphasis added.
84   Said 1978, p. 20.
85   Gramsci 1971a, p. 9; Jones 2006, p. 82.

tures, they are still producers of objects, ideas, texts and, particularly in the case of Orientalism, representations posing as 'truth'.[86] This raises some critical questions:

> How do ideas acquire authority, 'normality,' and even the status of 'natural' truth? What is the role of the intellectual? Is he there to validate the culture and state of which he is a part? What importance must he give to an independent critical consciousness, an *oppositional* critical consciousness?[87]

Despite Orientalism's functioning as a discourse, Said's term *strategic location*, as I have already indicated, implies that individuals must position themselves in relation to the existing discourse of Orientalism. However, because they ultimately hold on to authority, they can therefore be held accountable for their statements and actions when they contribute to the Orientalist discourse, solidify its insights, and perpetuate its structures.[88] In that respect, Said indicts scholars like William Jones or Bernard Lewis for upholding a textual attitude[89] towards the Oriental material they describe as a means of subduing the infinite variety of the Middle-East to an essentialised representation, which then serves as a validation for the imperial subordination of its peoples.[90] Even though they would consider their scholarly work to be impartial and detached from the political concerns of their time, it is actually saturated, Said believes, by political significance and ultimately validates the operations of imperial power.[91] As a result, Orientalists like Jones and Lewis cease to function as critical intellectuals and instead become 'experts of legitimation'[92] of the hegemonic discourse of Orientalism. In order to remain critical, intellectuals need to be aware of

---

86   See Said 1978, p. 21.

87   Said 1978, pp. 325–6.

88   Said 1978, p. 130. Brennan has recently argued that Said's use of discourse differs from Foucault's in that the former's 'does not preclude the idea of guilty agents of power, people with agendas and privileged interests, constituencies of active belief and policy, or the basic *injustice* of the operation that we should oppose on the grounds of human dignity' (Brennan 2013, pp. 18–19).

89   A textbook example of such an attitude is the view that is ridiculed by Voltaire in *Candide* or by Cervantes in *Don Quixote*. This view, according to Said, is a common human failure of preferring 'the schematic authority of a text to the disorientations of direct encounters with the human' (Said 1978, p. 93).

90   Said 1978, pp. 77–8, 315–21.

91   Said 1978, pp. 9–11.

92   Said 1983b, p. 172.

their worldly circumstances and their political function in civil society and remain oppositional to the workings of power in political society.[93]

Said's indictment of Orientalists is inspired by Gramsci's division of the intelligentsia into traditional and organic intellectuals. Whereas an organic intellectual is connected to an emergent social group and is aware of his or her everyday function in the economic, social and political fields,[94] a traditional intellectual misrecognises himself or herself as being severed from the social group of which he or she is a part and does not consider his or her workings to be of everyday political relevance.[95] These latter intellectuals 'represent an historical continuity uninterrupted even by the most complicated and radical changes in political and social forms'[96] and mistakenly consider themselves as 'independent', autonomous, endowed with a character of their own.[97] Said's critical intellectual is an organic intellectual who pays careful attention to his or her own worldliness as well as the worldliness of his or her study object. He or she is actively involved in society and constantly struggles to change minds.[98] Such an intellectual is needed in service of proper humanistic scholarship and emancipatory democracy in order to combat the hegemonic discourse of Orientalism that is perpetuated by traditional intellectuals such as Jones and Lewis, who rely so much on *idées reçues* that they become blind to the differentialities of the Middle-East and its peoples.[99]

Orientalism, on the other hand, does not perpetuate the hegemonic framework it analyses, but actively tries to combat that hegemonic discourse by critically analysing it in the past and present in order to undermine its overwhelmingly powerful consent.[100] In the introduction to *Orientalism*, Said invokes Gramsci's idea of self-consciousness as the starting point for every critical analysis:

---

93   Ashcroft and Said 2004, p. 100.

94   Gramsci 1971a, p. 5.

95   Jones, 2006, pp. 87–8.

96   Gramsci 1971a, p. 7.

97   Gramsci 1971a, p. 8.

98   Said 1994, p. 4.

99   See Said 1978, p. 94, and 1994, p. 89.

100   The loss of active consent causes, what Gramsci calls, a crisis of authority in which the dominant class has lost its cultural leadership and exercises coercive force alone. This means that the subaltern classes 'have become detached from their traditional ideologies, and no longer believe what they used to believe previously' (Gramsci 1971a, p. 276). Coercion alone, without the accompanying consent, cannot ultimately prevent emergent ideologies from rising up, mobilising people, and eventually becoming dominant (Gramsci 1971a, pp. 275–6).

> The starting-point of critical elaboration is the consciousness of what one really is, and is 'knowing thyself' as a product of the historical process to date, which has deposited in you an infinity of traces, without leaving an inventory ... [T]herefore it is imperative at the outset to compile such an inventory.[101]

Because every human subject is the product of an ensemble of relations,[102] the critic has to ascertain what these relations are and compile an inventory of them before her or she can change them for the better. Only when the material conditions are recognised, inventoried, and analysed is the active subject able to transform reality through willed and meaningful counter-hegemonic action.[103] *Orientalism* is Said's conscious attempt at compiling such an inventory of himself as an 'Oriental' in order to challenge the hegemony of Orientalism and, to use Raymond Williams's words in *Culture and Society*,[104] contribute to 'unlearning ... the inherent dominative mode'.[105] After all, acquiring consciousness of the complex relations of which a subject is the hub already modifies these relations. 'In this sense', Gramsci continues, 'knowledge is power'.[106] That powerful agency stems from Said's analysis of Orientalism as a discourse,

---

101   Gramsci quoted in Said 1978, p. 25.

102   Gramsci 1971a, pp. 352–3.

103   Bobbio 1979, pp. 34–5. According to Said, it is the function of the critical intellectual to invent a better and more just social and political order, not in the romantic sense in which something is created 'from scratch' but 'from the known historical and social facts' (Said 2004, p. 140) and then promoting it as a reality.

104   Williams 1958.

105   Williams quoted in Said 1978, p. 28.

106   Gramsci 1971a, p. 353. Gramsci uses this aphorism to argue that even the slightest knowledge of the ensemble of relations – both genetically in the movement of their formation and synchronically at a given period as a system – leads to a better understanding of one's own environment and subjectivity. This understanding is a source of agency for individuals because it is the basis for modifying this ensemble of relations and thus one's subjectivity. In this way, an individual is able to shape power (Gramsci 1971a, pp. 352–3). While there is a great deal of resonance and continuity between Gramsci's and Foucault's understanding of power, one can discern a crucial difference at this point. Gramsci's notions of knowledge and power differ from Foucault's in that Gramsci believes man to be the *subject* of knowledge and thus an agent or locus of power (Gramsci 1971a, pp. 351–3). Foucault, on the other hand, dispenses these ideas and considers man to be the *object* of knowledge that is produced by impersonal, diffuse, and abstract relations of power (Foucault 1975, p. 32). Being conscious of one's subjectivity and the relations of power that produce this subjectivity – insofar as this would even be possible according to Foucault – is never enough to change them and does not generate agency for individuals (see Daldal 2014, pp. 166–7).

his subsequent rejection of humanism-as-history by exposing the excrescences of humanism, and the insight that the production of knowledge and the operations of power can only be studied together in their full, imaginative, economic, social, and political context.[107]

But although Gramsci believes in the agency of individual intellectuals to change society, a lone intellectual is limited in his or her strength. A willful action only becomes meaningful when it is the organic will of a class or a group of people and, then, through strength in numbers, acquires the potential to be truly radical.[108] In order to successfully combat a hegemony it is vital to link one's own concerns to the politico-social concerns of others and to make clear that one's own sufferings and experiences are connected to those of many.[109] This is precisely what Said sees as his intellectual vocation:

> The intellectual's representations – what he or she represents and how those ideas are represented to an audience – are always tied to and ought to remain an organic part of an ongoing experience in society: of the poor, the disadvantaged, the voiceless, the unrepresented, the powerless.[110]

Recognition of human suffering is a crucial step, but insufficient in and of itself. Individual suffering must be universalised and linked to other peoples' sufferings.[111] As a result, Said goes to great pains to stress that Orientalism is not just an isolated academic problem but representative of a significant problem in human experience, identity formation, and the representation of other cultures.[112] Orientalism's failure is an intellectual as much as a human one, because in its opposition to a world region that it considered irreconcilably alien, Orientalism dehumanised that region and its inhabitants and thereby, Said writes, 'failed to identify with human experience, failed also to see it as human experience'.[113] Intellectuals in the postcolonial world must learn from Orientalism's fatal mistakes and realise that though every experience is highly subjective, it is at the same time historical and secular and can thus be understood through proper historical and secular scholarship.[114] In the conclusion to *Orientalism*,

---

107   Said 1978, p. 27.
108   Gramsci 1971a, p. 353.
109   Gramsci 1971a, p. 221.
110   Said 1994, p. 84.
111   Said 1994, p. 33.
112   Said 1978, pp. 325–6; see also Said 1979 and 1981.
113   Said 1978, p. 328.
114   Said 1986, pp. 55–6. Recently, Baidik Bhattacharya has pointed out the analogies between Said's secular criticism and Gramsci's secular humanism (Bhattacharya B. 2012, pp. 92–3).

Said links the challenge of his work to the various decolonisation movements worldwide, expressing their common goals:

> The worldwide hegemony of Orientalism and all it stands for can now be challenged, if we can benefit properly from the general twentieth-century rise to political and historical awareness of so many of the earth's peoples. If this book has any future use, it will be as a modest contribution to that challenge.[115]

Orientalism is organically tied to the struggle for the political, historical, and imaginative emancipation of (formerly) colonised peoples. As such, it is an act of resistance to the very framework it describes and contributes to the forma-tion of a counter-hegemonic discourse.

His argument is convincing but we should not forget the formative influence of the philo-logy of Erich Auerbach and the thought of Giambattista Vico on Said's secular criticism.

115   Said 1978, p. 328.

CHAPTER 15

The Changing Meanings of People's Politics: Gramsci and Anthropology from Subaltern Classes to Contemporary Struggles

Riccardo Ciavolella

1 Introduction

Since their first appearance in political, intellectual and scientific circles, Gramsci's writings and theories have been recurrently referenced in anthropology and other close disciplines studying popular forms of culture and politics.[1] Anthropological uses of Gramsci's notions and approach have taken place at different moments and in different contexts: firstly, in the Italian postwar period; in the 1960s' Third-Worldist social sciences; in postcolonial and cultural studies and poststructuralist theories from the 1980s; and more recently, in international debates on social movements and popular uprisings in a globalised world. Despite their heterogeneity, all these meetings of anthropologists with Gramsci's theories come at times and in contexts which have raised similar questions to radical intellectuals concerning popular forms of politics. These questions refer to two different types of *translation* which Gramsci thought about: how to *translate* popular forms of rebellion – traditionally expressed in cultural manifestations, religious heterodoxy, folklore, or purely 'defensive' actions – into a popular movement of emancipation; and how to *translate* the disaggregated subjectivities of subaltern and popular groups – from the working class to the peasantry, from European subaltern groups to the oppressed peoples of the colonised world – into a common and organised political subject, a *collective will*. The recurrent need to refer to Gramsci to treat these questions proves the plasticity or even the actual *translatability* of Gramsci's approach throughout epochs and contexts. But as Gramsci himself argued, in these processes of translation there is inevitably something that gets lost;

---

1 This article is based on research carried out as a Visiting Scholar at the *École française de Rome*, in the framework of a larger scientific programme on anthropology and Gramsci of the Fondazione Istituto Gramsci of Rome, the EHESS in Paris, the *École française de Rome* and the International Association Ernesto de Martino.

especially in the context of a social science, such as anthropology, where Gramsci's theories often have been cited with weak reference to his actual "rhythm of thought in development". Thus, the connexion between anthropology and Gramsci in studying popular politics deserves a recurrent *aggiornamento* or readjustment in replacing anthropologists' uses of Gramsci in the light of a more philological understanding of his thought.

This chapter starts by highlighting the interest for anthropologists in reading Gramsci's notes and ideas on popular politics. It then retraces the different ways in which his ideas on that issue have been of inspiration for political anthropologists. Firstly, it describes the way in which Gramsci was introduced to Italian anthropology in the postwar period, in a time when the spirit of the Liberation informed the discovery of the cultural worlds of 'the people' and when intellectuals aspired to make of it a protagonist on the political scene of the new Italian Republic. The chapter then switches to the European level, where anthropology first met Gramsci, in association with social history, at the end of the 1950s for the study of subaltern classes, especially rural groups not yet completely incorporated into state and capital modernity and colonised peoples struggling for their independence. Thirdly, I show the critical, but also partial, use of Gramsci's concepts in the poststructuralist anthropology of resistance and of peasant societies in postcolonial worlds. And finally, I reflect on the possibilities and limits of 'translating' Gramsci today for understanding popular politics, with a brief discussion of Ernesto Laclau's concept of populism and the influence of anthropologist Peter Worsley's work in order to wonder about the *translatability* of Gramscian methodology in the anthropology of contemporary political subjects.

2   Popular Politics and the Subaltern Political Subject

In both his prison writings, Gramsci engaged in a socio-historical analysis of subaltern and popular politics.[2] His purpose was not simply descriptive, but political. He wanted to grasp onto the potentialities of these popular forms of politics for producing a 'people' as an active political subject. This required a sort of *catharsis*;[3] the formation of a 'people', in a revolutionary and not in a bourgeois sense, requires that subaltern groups move up from their social *economic-corporative stage*, determined by their material and historical condi-

---

2   See in particular Q3, Q11 and Q25.
3   Q10 I §§ 6–7, Q10 II § 10, see also Thomas 2009b.

tions, to an *ethico-political* one of *collective will* and action.[4] This was seen as a hard task, requiring the articulation of very different subaltern groups, like the peasantry and urban proletariat, which are all but a uniform and specific 'class' and are rather socially fragmented and disaggregated.

Gramsci clearly aimed at re-politicising the representation of people's actions, practices, cultures and *conceptions of the world.*[5] In particular, his non-mechanical historicism allowed him to elude any positivistic representation of popular groups and in particular their folklorisation as survivors – positive or negative – of a non-historical world, as was the case in Italian anthropology and sociology at the time.[6] But 'popular culture' could not be reduced to a mere aggregate of disparate forms of cultural expression by subaltern and marginal groups in the sense of *folklore.*[7] Intended as a potential common culture of all subaltern groups, popular culture, grounded on a new common sense, was a political objective: a key factor in the process of modernisation of the Italian nation-state in a bourgeois system, and eventually in the process of constituting a new hegemony. For Gramsci, such a cultural hegemony, to be conquered in the domain of civil society and through a war of position, was a preliminary step to obtaining political hegemony. In that perspective, Gramsci was deeply critical of the bourgeois notion of 'the people': even when they intended to 'go to the people', 'populist' bourgeois intellectuals were in reality detaching themselves from real people.[8] Their aesthetic appreciation of popular folklore allowed for the deepening, rather than for the bridging, of the gap between upper and lower classes.[9] At the same time, for Gramsci there was another possible way to think of the people: this aggregation of all the subaltern groups could also be seen as a cultural and social site for the emergence of the 'people-nation',[10] a common ground for the potential blossoming of a new popular political subject with a common culture or sense and a collective will. The first point to keep in mind about Gramsci is this: on one side, he strongly criticised any 'populist' representation of popular classes; on the other, he interrogated their potentialities for emerging as a political subject.

---

4   Q13.
5   Q3 § 48.
6   Q1 § 27, Q25 § 8, see also Ciavolella (forthcoming).
7   Q27.
8   Q1 § 119, Q19 § 28 and Q21 § 5.
9   Q11 § 67.
10   Q21 § 5.

This historicist perspective on popular culture broadly resonates with those parts of the *Notebooks* where Gramsci inquired into the possibilities for subaltern groups to engage into an 'autonomous political initiative', in particular in Q25, where Gramsci laid out the basis for the study of all stages of politicisation and of 'the history of subaltern groups'. One of the greatest problems for Gramsci was their social fragmentation: their uneven integration into the historical process of modernity was an obstacle to the creation of a 'people' as a collective political subject. For Guido Liguori,[11] subaltern groups differ in the way in which they can be actors of historical transformations, with groups such as peripheral peasantries being 'marginal', and others more 'advanced', namely the urban proletariat. The latter should be the true driving force of subaltern political initiatives and thus assume a leading role for all the subaltern groups. The interpretation of subalternity as divided in different categories grounds on a specific reading of the history of subaltern groups in terms of differences in their integration or autonomy *vis-à-vis* the state. Actually, in Q5 § 4, Gramsci operates a distinction between subaltern groups in relation to different historical State forms. In the ancient or medieval state, he argued, subaltern groups had a 'certain autonomy' from the point of view of political and cultural institutions and of social organisation. On the contrary, in the modern state, subordination to dominant classes is so deep and overwhelming that it abolishes any autonomy of subaltern groups.

Despite this distinction, we know that, when referring to contemporary subaltern groups, Gramsci refused a sociological typology of subalternity and rather preferred to understand it from a dynamic and dialectical perspective. As Peter Thomas has recently argued,[12] in the context of modern hegemonies, it is not possible to understand subalternity as a site outside a historical relationship with the centre of power. Gramsci precisely considered subalternity as a relation of power: 'the subaltern are always subject to the political initiative of dominant classes'.[13] Interested in those subaltern groups that where coeval to him and that were brought into the process of encapsulation into the modernity of state and capital, the distinction between marginal and central subaltern groups in history became not an issue of distinction, but a matter of degree in the historical possibilities of engaging into an 'autonomous political initiative' for transforming society *inside* power relations and the battlefield of hegemony.[14] Different subaltern groups can have different historical roles in

---

11   Liguori 2015c.
12   Thomas 2015.
13   Q3 § 14.
14   Q25.

the process of emancipation, some being more 'advanced' in acquiring political consciousness. But the issue at stake for Gramsci is to understand how these different groups, with different backgrounds and political potentialities, can become allies and articulate into a common project, a collective will and a common political action.

It is from this perspective that we can engage in crossing Gramscian theory on subalternity with political anthropology. This is possible because the latter has historically inquired into the historical subjectivities of 'marginal' subaltern subjects, from marginalised peasants to colonised urban dwellers, who were increasingly integrated into modern states, colonial or postcolonial domination and the capitalist world-system, but who were also – as those radical intellectuals hoped – engaged in a process of emancipation. As for Gramsci, the issue at stake for these anthropologists was the political potentiality of subaltern and popular forms of resistance.

3   The Progressivism of Popular Culture in Italian Anthropology

Ernesto de Martino is known as the main Italian anthropologist of the postwar period for engaging in the study of religious practices and beliefs of peasant societies as an expression of their historical subjectivity. From a certain perspective, politics as an object of study was very far from de Martino's analysis. But this ethnology of religion and popular culture was in reality an intellectual effort to affirm the historical dignity and *presence* of rural and especially – but not only as we will see – southern subaltern groups in history against discourses and visions of cultural and socio-political elites. Thus, de Martino was fuelled by a political ambition of intellectually translating subaltern people's aspirations for emancipation, and contributed to the broader movement of radical intellectuals, such as Carlo Levi or Rocco Scotellaro, aiming to renew the Southern question in the postwar moment.

In 1949, Gramsci's *Prison Notebooks*, published in the Platone and Togliatti edition, won over de Martino, at that time a Crocean historian of religions. Gramsci became the main influence on the new direction that de Martino's work was embarking on. In the same year, with his article *Intorno ad una storia del mondo popolare subalterno* ('About a history of the subaltern popular world'), published in the journal *Società*,[15] de Martino became one of the first anthropologists worldwide to make two dramatic steps towards an anthropo-

---

15   De Martino 1949.

logy engaged in the emancipation of what he had come to call the 'subaltern popular worlds'. This article opens with strongly denouncing any collusion of anthropologists with imperial initiatives. It is worth recalling that de Martino was doing this, some 10 years before other attempts were made within the traditional anthropological circles of big colonial powers, like the UK and France,[16] and 30 years before postcolonial critiques of anthropology. The first paragraph of the article reads:

> The attitude of the 'European-Western civilisation' towards the cultural forms of the subaltern popular world, that is of the colonial peoples and of the labouring and peasant proletariat of hegemonic nations, reflects in the rawest way the needs, the interests and the parallel humanistic limitation of the dominant class, the bourgeoisie.[17]

This critical outlook to the cultural and ideological attitude of bourgeois dominant classes did not symmetrically invert the opposition between the West and the rest. It rather reversed a cultural opposition based on Eurocentrism in a socio-political opposition between dominant classes of the bourgeoisie and all the subjects of the subaltern popular world. De Martino was implicitly associating colonised peoples with all the labouring and peasant classes beyond any cultural or political border. He then called for anthropology to replace the current visions of Western civilisations, aiming to make the discipline a science of and for the emancipation of the oppressed.

In order to undertake that project of turning the world upside down, de Martino engaged in the debate about *folklore* or popular culture, which the bourgeois world saw as a conservative survival of archaic cultural forms having no historical relevance. In contrast, de Martino tried to detect the potentialities of *folklore* in becoming a *progressive* driving force for social transformation. This opened a large debate during the 1950s among the Italian Left about *demology* (in Italy, 'the study of the people', or popular culture, as it came to be known) and its political and ideological implications. The study of folklore expressed a strong duplicity: some refused it on the basis of the irrational primitivism that had fuelled Nazis' ideology, while others, like de Martino, tried to redeem it as the 'conception of the world' of subaltern groups, and to reorient it as the basis for a new culture of popular emancipation.

---

16   Asad 1973, Copans 1975.
17   De Martino 1949, p. 411, my translation.

This debate had Gramsci and his 'observations on folklore' at its core.[18] Gramsci was certainly interested in folklore as a 'conception of the world', and more broadly, he was interested in subaltern cultures as embryonic manifestations of marginal people's rebelliousness against cultural and political hegemony. But as Italian anthropologists have later recognised,[19] Gramsci also formulated, at the same time, a sharp political criticism of folklore as a disorganised conception of the world unable to support a new popular culture of emancipation, and of popular culture and resistance as unable to transform society. As a Marxist and a political activist, Gramsci thought that only a more structured political consciousness and organisation could transform and then emancipate subaltern cultures: while in 'a state of anxious defence', people are 'subject to the initiatives of the dominant classes, even when they rebel'.[20] Actually, Gramsci opened to the possibility that elementary forms of resistance can be something more than mere passive resistance, or in his own words, a mere 'fact'. They may not, however, be enough for emancipation, unless these molecular forms are brought 'to the surface' by active political engagement for the transformation of historical blocs connecting economy and culture. Thus, Gramsci made the anthropologists face a dilemma in interpreting folklore, between (a) a populist insistence on a people's capacity to express its cultural autonomy and creativity as a way of resisting dominant culture and (b) a historicist invitation to politically go beyond those embryonic popular forms of cultural rebelliousness.

Italian anthropologists tried to resolve these ambiguities by insisting on popular culture as permeated by an 'operating force' (*forza operante*). This idea was developed by Vittorio Lanternari in response to the critique of folklore studies made by Giovanni Giarrizzo,[21] who argued that their interpretation of Gramsci suggested an artificial and ahistorical division of society between official and popular cultures. The same idea was in reality already developed by de Martino with the notion of 'progressive folklore'.[22] He advanced this notion at the beginning of the 1950s, thanks to his reading of Gramsci and of the Soviet ethnologists who interpreted folklore as a transformative popular contribution to revolution. But it is worth noting that de Martino started to think about 'progressive folklore' some years before, in relation not to his readings but to his political experiences. In 1944, he left Rome as a displaced person

---

18   Q27.
19   De Martino 1951c, 1992, Cirese 1973.
20   Q3, §14.
21   Lanternari 1954, Giarrizzo 1954.
22   De Martino 1951b, 1951c.

and went to rural northern Italy (Romagna region) where he engaged in the Resistance activities as a political ideologist. He then realised the power of popular contestation in popular songs, histories, and resistance activities. In the years following the war, he gained political experience with the Socialist Federation in Bari and Lecce, where he met peasants and herders, with their 'human forgotten histories', but with whom he intended to participate toward the 'foundation of a better world'.[23] Then, around 1950, de Martino went back to Romagna with a research project on the traces of political antagonism and the spirit of emancipation in popular imaginaries, songs, discourses and stories. These were considered 'folklorist manifestations in a direct relationship with the popular experiences of social subjectivation (*soggezione sociale*), of protest, of rebellion, of struggle or even of victorious emancipation'.[24] His experience in Romagna, while starting to deconstruct his idea about a geographical limitation of the 'Southern question' and of popular culture, was a key moment in the theorising of popular culture of workers and peasants as able to graft onto an emerging cultural commitment of popular groups for the transformation of society, in that case thanks to the social and cultural activities of the Resistance and then of the Communist Party.

De Martino was strongly criticised by the Italian Communist Party for his ideas about folklore and popular culture as tools of emancipation. In the Left and inside the Communist Party, such approaches received several critiques. Interested in the same issue of popular culture, but preferring to focus on the culture of proletarians, in journals like *Il Politecnico* or *l'Avanti!*, many intellectuals denounced the risk of ethnology and folklore studies. Franco Fortini criticised demology as a primitivist science of irrationality.[25] Mario Alicata and Cesare Luporini appropriated Gramsci's more modernist side and his criticism of any traditionalism about popular culture, in order to recall the mission of the working class, and not of marginal subaltern groups, as the most advanced political subject in the revolutionary process of modern postwar Italy.[26] In 1965, all the intellectuals working on popular cultures were criticised by Alberto Asor Rosa as 'populist' and 'Gramscianist' who, 'while going towards the people and before coming to it, transforms it into a myth'.[27] That, quite paradoxically, is strikingly similar to the criticism Gramsci himself made of bourgeois intellectuals.

---

23   De Martino 1953, pp. 318–22.
24   De Martino 1951a, pp. 251–4.
25   Fortini 1950.
26   Alicata 1954, Luporini 1950a and 1950b.
27   Asor Rosa 1988 [1965], p. 134.

In fact, Italian Gramscian anthropologists like de Martino, but also Vittorio Lanternari, were following Gramsci to partly disconnect the notion of the 'subaltern' from that of the working class, while studying the way in which peripheral populations were entering modernity and becoming political subjects. As we have seen, well before the anthropological self-analysis of the 1970s and 1980s, De Martino already criticised the link between ethnological naturalism, bourgeois society and colonial imperialism. De Martino and Lanternari, in a way, anticipated many of the issues discussed by postcolonial anthropology and criticism and made of the Italian Southern Question a sort of paradigm to understand the Third-World. Their reflections on peasant societies in rural Italy could then be enlarged to all the subaltern groups of the world, and especially to Third-World and colonised societies, as Lanternari explicitly did.[28] Lanternari, in particular, was able to connect the Demartinian school of religious studies of Italian popular groups with anti-colonial and Third-Worldist Francophone and Anglophone political anthropologists working on similar issues since his first work on *The Religions of the Oppressed*,[29] published in Italian in 1960. This book received a widespread response in international discussions, being translated into French in 1962 by Robert Paris (who will become the French translator of Gramsci's Notebooks, too) for the anti-colonialist publisher F. Maspero, and in English in 1963, and drew the attention of Eric Hobsbawm, who wrote a preface. This was only one example, deserving of analysis, of a latent triangulation, on an international level, between Gramsci's legacy in Italian ethnology and history of religions, international political anthropology and social history of the 1950s and 1960s.

4   Anthropology and Social History on Millennial Movements and Popular Resistance

In the 1950s, some British and French political anthropologists were reflecting on the ways in which colonial populations were entering modern politics and the world-system and facing cultural and social transformations such as cultural syncretism, industrialisation, proletarisation and urbanisation. This was the case in particular of some scholars and their disciples of the Manchester school, notably Max Gluckman, and Georges Balandier in Paris. As in the case of Italian anthropology, which nevertheless remained relatively unknown

---

28   Lanternari 1972 and 1974.
29   Lanternari 1963.

in the international debate until the 1960s, particular attention was given to popular cultures and especially to religious expressions, such as millennial and prophetic movements. These were analysed as expressions of political subjectivity of colonised peoples entering history, and as forms of political resistance of oppressed peoples to domination, exploitation and acculturation, involving issues like popular utopias, expectations of social or cultural apocalypse and/or regeneration, rituals of rebellion, and the emergence of charismatic religious leaders with roles that could be defined as 'political'.

At the end of the 1950s, Max Gluckman was working on the rebellion of the Mau Mau in Kenya as a local form of emerging anticolonial movement, while colonial authorities still interpreted their ritualised or uncontrolled expressions of popular anger as the legacy of 'tribal' cultures. In the context of the new anthropological interpretation of popular cultural movements as essentially political and anti-colonial, Gluckman organised a seminar in Manchester in 1956 on popular social movements in a comparative perspective starting from what he was studying in Africa. Contributors and discussants were, among others, historian Norman Cohn who was preparing a book on Revolutionary millenarianism and mystical anarchists in the Middle Age; anthropologist Peter Worsley, who was working on the *cargo cults* in colonial Melanesia as a cultural and religious reaction to both colonial domination and integration into the world capitalist wage labour system; and historian Eric Hobsbawm, who was interested in pre-industrial (*archaic*) forms of social movements in Europe, from social banditry and mafia to luddism, through millennial movements.[30] Among other cases, Hobsbawm analysed the religious and political experience of Davide Lazzaretti, the initiator of a millennial movement during the Italian Risorgimento mixing Christianity with republican values and utopias, which Gramsci had already discussed in Q25 as an example of a subaltern movement in history. Lazzaretti was first mentioned to Hobsbawm in 1952 by Ambrogio Donini, a Marxist historian of religions and first president of the Gramsci Institute.

Worsley and Hobsbawm in particular shared a common view on popular cultural movements: they considered these, in a way, as an imperfect anticipation of a more conscious political movement that will later emerge among the disinherited. Referring to millennial movements of the Middle Age, Cohn's position on that issue was slightly different. He posited that millennial movements were not the expression of subordinate peoples' despair, since there was

---

30   Cohn 1957, Worsley 1957, Hobsbawm 1959.

no direct connection between movements and social conditions.[31] For Worsley and Hobsbawm, on the contrary, millennial movements, at least at the dawn of modernity, prefigure a cultural rebellion of the oppressed, which took form in religious terms. As such, these movements were bound to evaporate and then give way to more secular political movements. In that sense, Worsley talked of the new Melanesian *cargo cults* as a form of *proto-nationalism*, that is cultural and religious movements which clearly manifest political antagonism to domination, but which are nevertheless unable to turn into proper 'secular' movements of liberation. They only constitute their anticipation in time, as long as nationalist liberation movements, of the secular type, are inevitably emerging in parallel. In a similar manner, Hobsbawm talked of popular rebellions, like the one of Lazzaretti, as *pre-political*, that is as 'archaic forms of social movements' which are inevitably replaced, in political modernity, by mass and class revolutionary politics. In his preface to the second edition of *The Trumpet Shall Sound*,[32] Worsley reminded readers that Hobsbawm and himself were usually 'cited as deserving of criticism' on the issue of the historical substitution of millennial movements by secular movements. That was the case of George Shepperson, an Africanist historian who became a reference for the study of African struggles for independence and for the African and Negro liberation movements, but who nevertheless criticised Worsley and Hobsbawm on that point by opposing their position to the more prudent one of Cohn.[33]

Worsley was one of the first to comment in English on Gramsci's *Letters*, but he only comes to engage deeply with Gramsci's ideas in the 1990s to discuss the uneven distribution of knowledge in different societies.[34] At the end of the 1950s, Hobsbawm was engaging rather directly with Gramsci. In 1960, one year after the publication of *Primitive Rebels*, Hobsbawm wrote in Italian, from a Gramscian perspective, the article *Per lo studio delle classi subalterne* ('For the Study of Subaltern Classes').[35] The article shows many affinities with de Martino's article of 1949. Published in the same journal *Società*, the main topic was very similar, as the titles attest. And in a similar manner, Hobsbawm called for a convergence of the anthropology of popular and subaltern movements (like that of Gluckman and Worsley) and Gramscian theory, through social history. Nevertheless, it is surprising to see that Hobsbawm did not make any reference

---

31   Cohn 1962, pp. 37–8.
32   Worsley 1967, p. xlii.
33   Shepperson 1962.
34   Worsley 1997.
35   Hobsbawm 1960.

to De Martino's work, as Carlo Ginzburg has recently noticed.[36] It is important to stress that, in the article, Hobsbawm insisted on the historicism of Gramsci to emancipate political anthropology from any persisting naturalism and structural-functionalism.

As in the case of the Italian discussion about folklore, the international encountering of political anthropology and social history, on the subject of popular religious and political movements in the subaltern worlds, ended up with dilemmas on how to avoid romanticised visions while still considering subaltern cultures as possible grounds for a politics of emancipation and, at the same time, on how avoiding modernist visions seeing them as irrational or, at least, imperfect forms of popular politics. These dilemmas finally referred to another one, that between naturalism and historicism in analysing popular culture and politics. Worsley and Hobsbawm gave the dilemma a response that was slightly, but significantly, different from that of the 'progressive folklore' or the 'operating force' of de Martino and Lanternari, insisting more on the idea of a real popular progressive politics as a complete *catharsis* from religious and folkloric social movements.

The solution given to those dilemmas, especially by Hobsbawm, has had a dramatic impact on the way in which Gramsci's theories on popular resistance and folklore were considered in the ensuing decades, especially in peasant studies, where the anthropology of subalternity first concentrated. Actually, since the late 1970s, anthropologists or subaltern scholars have strongly criticised Hobsbawm and his notion of the *prepolitical*. For James C. Scott, the main reference in the anthropology of resistance and peasant studies,[37] the notion of the 'pre-political' would implicitly express a teleological representation of popular social movements as something anticipating a modern Marxist political initiative, while still lacking a more structured political consciousness. In a similar manner, for Ranajit Guha, founder of *Subaltern Studies*, the notion would thus deny any capacity of subaltern groups to be actively and consciously involved in their practices of resistance to power or even in the process of nation-making during colonial times.[38] This criticism of Hobsbawm's notion was justified, but it had some consequences on the way in which these authors interpreted Gramsci. Both Scott and Guha considered that the teleological and Eurocentric vision of Hobsbawm came from his reading of Gramsci and of Marxism in general. We know that, for Gramsci, 'spontaneous' popular and

---

36   Ginzburg 2013, pp. ix–x.
37   Scott 1985.
38   Guha 1997.

subaltern political action without 'conscious leadership' (*direzione consape-vole*) was only a form of subversion (*sovversivismo*) – a 'negative' and 'defensive' form of rebellion manifesting itself through 'a series of denials' and a 'generic' anger towards the powerful[39] – which was unable to turn into a revolutionary politics for the emancipation of the masses and the formation of a 'people'. This was an idea that historians and anthropologists of resistance could hardly accept. Guha,[40] for example, while still considering Gramsci a topical refer-ence, has eluded or even criticised Gramsci's call for the subaltern to acquire a higher level of political consciousness and organisation as an elitist and ped-agogical attitude towards subaltern groups. They have rather preferred to study the emergence of anti-hegemonic discourses in different subaltern groups by relying only on his interpretation of resistance as denials.

From the 1970s, with the diffusion of Gramscian writings in the international Anglophone production of knowledge, anthropology has made use of Gram-sci in a way that approximates that of E.P. Thompson. In the introduction to *Customs in Common*,[41] the social historian makes reference to Gramsci and the idea of double consciousness to describe the way in which people may manifest conformity with the dominant ideology, but at the same time have a different common sense 'derived from the shared experience of exploitation' with fel-low workers and neighbours. Interestingly enough, Thompson developed this idea in an intervention at a Conference of Indian Historians in 1976,[42] where he called for a convergence, through social history, of political anthropology and Gramscian theory, an attempt very similar to that of Hobsbawm of 1960. For Thompson, however, Gramsci was useful to anthropologists not for his histor-icist vision, but rather for understanding hegemony as a social drama, in Victor Turner's sense.[43] That is where consensus may be publicly manifested in pub-lic spaces controlled by the powerful, but where dissent may emerge in private social sites.

In the 1980s and '90s, political anthropology of popular resistance made par-tial and contradictory uses of Gramsci's ideas. Several Anglophone anthropo-logists have read him in 'poststructuralist' terms, artificially reducing his ideas to the debates on structure versus agency and coercion versus consent.[44] For

---

39   Q3, p. 323.
40   Guha 1999, p. 4.
41   Thompson 1991, p. 11.
42   Thompson 1977.
43   Turner 1974.
44   Schwartzmantel 2009, Kurtz 1996.

Kate Crehan,[45] these readings of Gramsci by anthropologists, as in the case of Comaroff and Comaroff,[46] have given a 'light' interpretation of Gramsci's theory of hegemony, considering it analogous to Bourdieu's *doxa*: a cultural uniformity politically imposed by power, neglecting its relation to economic structures and taking for granted the idea of a discursive uniformity between dominant and subaltern groups. More recently, a more precise knowledge of Gramsci in theoretical and even philological terms has allowed anthropology to go beyond these conundrums. For example, Crehan or other Anglophone neo-Gramscian anthropologists working especially on contemporary peasant societies[47] insist on the dialectical way of thinking about hegemony and resistance.

5   Translating the 'People' Today?

In the twenty-first century, the situation is certainly different from that of Gramsci's time and of political anthropologists in the 1960s or 1980s. First of all, we should consider that the meaning of subalternity of Gramsci's time has profoundly changed. Pier Paolo Pasolini, one of the principal heirs of the Italian and Gramscian populist current, nostalgically denounced and prophetically anticipated the 'anthropological transformation' of popular classes through the common sense of consumerism which made difficult any identification of positive folkloric values. Despite this uniformisation through market consumption, current forms of capitalism also produce a high level of fragmentation in society. As Gavin Smith has stressed,[48] capitalism has turned from the expansive hegemony of industrial relationships to the selective integration and exclusion of social groups with finance and rentier capitalism, producing fragmentation and disarticulation between social subjects. As such, current forms of capitalism weaken any attempts for building up bridges between disparate social movements and political subjects.

In reaction to this situation, populism is sometimes an answer given by post-Gramscian thinkers, such as Ernesto Laclau, insofar as it bypasses the problem of difference in popular groups and forms a radical democratic 'people'. The problems affecting radical politics in building up subaltern and popular polit-

---

45   Crehan 2002.
46   Comaroff and Comaroff 1991, pp. 25, 125.
47   Gledhill 2000, pp. 11–12, see also Roseberry 1994 and Smith 2004.
48   Smith 2014.

ical subjects make of the present time a new 'Gramscian moment',[49] even if Gramsci's theories are alternatively taken as a source of inspiration and contrasted.[50] In different manners, radical theories react to this by evoking the potentialities of a politics 'from below', be it through the concepts of 'multitude'[51] or the 'people'.[52] In this situation, both Gramsci and anthropology – though more often the former than the latter – are called into question.

Contemporary social movements, protests, and popular revolutionary or reformist attempts call for real democracy, politics for real people and direct participation, with the idea that people's politics is opposed to the 'caste' of institutional politics and of governing elites, which also resonate, sometimes explicitly, with the ideas of Laclau in their anti-elite discourses of new populist movements. From Laclau's perspective, 'populism' is certainly different from 'people's politics': it can be considered, *from above*, as a form of politics of governing elites or of emerging leaders, which implies political representation as a symbolic mediation between them and the social fabric. Nevertheless, theories on populism stem from reflections about the (non-)existence, *from below*, of an actual political practice of the 'people'. This is what Gramsci and, indeed, anthropologists have constantly tried to grasp and describe. It is widely known that Laclau's reflection on 'populism' is deeply influenced by his reading of Gramsci. But for anthropologists, it is worth recalling that Laclau also drew on his reading of other social scientists, most notably Worsley. Indeed, Worsley was among the first scholars to inquire into the politics of the people in order to theorise the emergence of populism. His anthropological studies on millennial movements brought him to increasingly focus his attention on the Weberian issue of charismatic leadership among those popular and religious experiences. Yet, unlike Weber, Worsley was interested in the historical and social conditions, often defined as 'crisis', that allow for the emergence of new charismatic leaders among the masses. For Worsley, one of the social conditions for the emergence of millennial movements and charismatic leadership was the constitutive fluidity of society, with different social groups sharing a common sentiment of frustration and deprivation, but also being dissolved in a mass whose unity was only affirmed through the movement itself. Worsley pursued his reflections in the 1960s, but the political context of national independence of ancient colonies and of Third-Worldism convinced him to focus his attention on those more 'secular' experiences of popular politics.

---

49   Thomas 2009a.
50   Ciavolella 2015.
51   Hardt and Negri 2004.
52   Laclau 2005.

It is precisely in his study of politics in the *Third World*[53] – a notion which originated in the French debate around Balandier – that Worsley developed his considerations about 'populism'. He later expanded on this in an article,[54] which will be considered by Laclau as the 'main contribution' to the study of populism and a starting point for his reflections on that subject.[55] The shift of interest from millenarism to populism reflects a similar shift in Worsley's attention from the domain of popular movements as socially shared experiences, especially in the domain of religion, to that of populism as a political ideology, or better, as a tool of political ideology in the domain of secular movements. As we have seen, Worsley considered these two types of movements as profoundly different national movements of liberation, one being secular and the ancient millennial movements being destined to become marginalised as minority sects. But for Worsley, a similar process of charismatic leadership and of subject formation is common in the two movements. Actually, 'populism' becomes for Worsley a secular option for national movements of liberation, which cannot rely on a cohesive social force because of the fragmentation of their social basis.

This is a situation from the Third World that for Laclau becomes paradigmatic of any contemporary political situation, especially in post-Marxist times, where the definition of political activity cannot be grounded on the basis of socially determined political subjects like classes. As is widely known in Gramscian philology, Laclau relied on Gramsci, but he did so in a partial way. This was certainly necessary to Laclau in order to make an *aggiornamento* of Gramsci's theory, a new *translation* of his concepts in a different and particular historical situation.[56] But Laclau also risked taking Gramsci out of Marxism: this is unproblematic if it means freeing our reading of society from mechanical and materialistic determinism, as Gramsci himself actually did, but it becomes problematic if we renounce 'connecting' with subaltern groups more than in a simple symbolic, and populist, way. Relying on Piotte,[57] Laclau firstly offered an analysis of the concept of hegemony as articulated at two complementary levels: '(1) The type of relationship that can win popular masses; (2) the class articulation by which the Party organizes its hegemony'.[58] Laclau initially accepted this complementarity, but he progressively insisted on the first issue

---

53   Worsley 1964.
54   Worsley 1969.
55   Laclau 2005, first chapter.
56   Frosini 2012b.
57   Piotte 1970.
58   Laclau 1977, pp. 141–2.

of winning popular masses, while the issue of articulation of classes lost some importance in his eyes as he started to refuse, influenced by poststructuralism, any idea of overdetermination of classes.

In some of the theoretical discussions accompanying contemporary social movements, anthropology has found a role to play, precisely thanks to its traditional capacity to displace the focal point from politics to the political or to 'politics from below'.[59] That is why anthropology has achieved some success today in contemporary social movements. All the more so since anthropological literature and ethnological examples of living and organising society differently have inspired thinking about counter-hegemonic alternatives and other possibilities.[60] In addition, anthropologists feel that they have the tools to avoid intellectual populism by filling up the *empty signifier* of 'the people' with their empirical knowledge of 'real people doing real things', as Sherry Ortner put it.[61] This is thanks to ethnography and participant observation and by capturing the subject's point of view. But anthropology is not immune to the risk of reproducing some of the populist fantasies that Gramsci detested in those exploring people politics.

The recent renewal of Gramscian scholarship, as in the case of Peter Thomas,[62] has fortunately reminded us of the importance of going back to the essence of a Gramscian way of thinking about the possibility of a new collective will, a contemporary 'modern prince', without giving in to postmodern visions of floating subjects and political projects. This is where the anthropology of popular politics can again contribute to the discussion, if the anthropologist wishes to engage, *gramscianamente*, in a political reflection on popular movements and emancipation. As an 'integral historian', the anthropologist usually creates 'monographs' collecting the dispersed 'traces' of the 'history of' particular and specific 'subaltern groups'. But he could also try to understand how to 'connect' with those different subaltern groups, by understanding them in their historical formation, as well as in their political activities. In a way, the practice of ethnography as an existential experience of 'going native' could approximate, in Gramscian terms, the 'sentimental connection' Gramsci talked about when referring to the necessity for an intellectual to unify knowledge, comprehension, and feelings in order to understand people's lives and views.

---

59   Gutkind 1977, Hymes 1974, Bayart et al. 1992.
60   Graeber 2007.
61   Ortner 1995.
62   Thomas 2013a and 2013b.

PART 6

Culture, Ideology, Religion

∴

CHAPTER 16

Religion, Common Sense, and Good Sense in Gramsci

Takahiro Chino

1 Introduction

Gramsci vigorously explored the social functions of religion and in particular the Catholic Church in Italian society since his pre-prison years. Not only does it confirm yet another example of the wide range of interests Gramsci had, but it also shows the utmost importance of this topic which stems from its relationship to his view of civil society and to that of the relationship between the superstructure(s) and the economic base, some of the core ideas in his entire philosophy. In a passage in the *Prison Notebooks*, he claimed:

> I do not think that many people would argue that, once a structure has been changed, all the elements of the corresponding superstructure must of necessity collapse. What happens, instead, is that from an ideology which arose to guide the popular masses ... several elements must survive: natural law itself, which may have declined for the educated classes, is preserved by the Catholic religion and is more alive in the people than one thinks.[1]

Gramsci thus recognised the autonomy of religion working in civil society as a residue of a former economic structure. Even if the existing economic structure collapses, considered Gramsci, it does not necessarily follow that the collapse simultaneously obliterates the corresponding superstructure. Clearly here, the still resilient influence of Catholicism on Italian society is the prime example of the relative autonomy of the superstructure within the given constraints of the economic base.

It has long been discussed whether Gramsci was a theorist of autonomy of superstructure or a more orthodox Marxist. Notably, Jacques Texier criticises Norberto Bobbio for overemphasising the autonomous role of the superstruc-

---

1 Q10II, § 41xii, p. 1322; Gramsci 1995, p. 398.

ture in Gramsci, and endorses the determining role of the economic base over the superstructure. He argues that Gramsci's civil society represents 'the complex of practical and ideological social relations ... which is established and grows up on the base of determined relations of production'.[2] However, it is shown by Gramsci's own arguments on how religion works in the superstructure irrespective of the collapse of the base, as above, that the role of politics, as well as other exercises of human agency, lies in dealing with the remaining superstructural elements such as the Catholic influence on Italian society. This wider implication could attract more interest in Gramsci's view of religion, although to date little attention has been paid to it with only a small number of studies since the 1970s and '80s when some important studies on the subject first emerged.[3]

Previous literature on this topic has not focused on how Gramsci elaborated his own critique of the Church against Benedetto Croce's. As this short piece of work cannot do justice to all aspects of Gramsci's view of religion, I limit myself to focusing on two crucial issues. First, I examine Gramsci's view that Croce critically failed to look at the popularly grounded strength of the Catholic Church. Contrary to Croce's intention, Gramsci asserted, this rather reinforced the Church by maintaining the gap between the intellectuals and masses that had lasted since the Renaissance. Second, I investigate how Gramsci elaborated his own critique of the Catholic Church after observing Croce's misdirected attempt. Looking closely at people's 'common sense', which is unsorted, unsophisticated, and what Croce rejected, Gramsci discerned that it includes 'good sense' as a more appropriate understanding of the world. Showing that good sense could be elaborated from common sense enables Gramsci to propose a programme that goes beyond the longstanding separation between the intellectuals and masses upon which the views of both Croce and the Catholic Church rested. At this juncture, the thrust of Gramsci's critique appears to remedy the division of social groups from which Italian social and political problems emerged.

---

2 Texier 1979, p. 71.

3 As for important works on this topic, see Portelli 1976; La Rocca 1991; and Frosini 2010a. Bruno Desidera's detailed, yet not complete, bibliography on the topic suggests that only a small amount of literature has been added to the list since the 1990s. See Desidera 2005, pp. 299–334, and Chino 2018.

2   The Transformation of the Catholic Church

Before examining Gramsci's criticism of Croce, let us briefly look at how Gramsci analysed the Catholic Church, regarding how it changed itself over time and how it exercised its influence in Gramsci's time.

According to Gramsci, the French Revolution marked the critical event for the Catholic Church, as it triggered secular forces to express their conceptions of the world such as liberalism and socialism. Thus, Catholicism no longer enjoyed its position as the only universal account of the world, and instead was seen to represent only *an* account of the world, competing with other world-views. In Gramsci's words, the Catholic Church thus became a 'party'.[4] This in turn spurred the emergence of three camps within the Church, defined by the degree to which they accepted the fruits of secular and modern thought.[5] Crucially, Jesuitism, occupying a middle position between Integralism as the most conservative group and Modernism the most progressive, was the centre of the Church in Gramsci's time, just as he insisted that 'Jesuitism can be said to be the most recent phase of Catholic Christianity'.[6] Gramsci described Pius XI, the pope in his time, as a 'Jesuit pope' due to his efforts to spread the Church's influence over the Italian masses, and thereby to prevent mass apostasy in modern times.[7]

Along this line, in Gramsci's time, the Lateran Pacts were ratified in 1929, which accompanied the Concordat between the fascist state and the Church. It enabled the Church to enjoy its privilege as the official religion in many respects. First, the Pacts made religious education mandatory not only in primary but also in secondary schools, thereby offering the Church a secular means to penetrate Italy's public educational system. Together with the foundation of the Catholic university in 1921, the Church also forged educational paths to recruit new elements of clergy. Second, the Pacts granted special status to Catholic Action, the so-called 'secular arm of the Church', as the only official religious organisation allowed to act in the secular terrain where no political parties reside in any longer. This arrangement also allowed Catholicism to spread its teachings outside of the Church. All in all, the Lateran Pacts allowed the Church to disseminate Catholic teachings among the Italian masses via secular means.

---

4   Q20, §1, p. 2081; Gramsci 1995, p. 29; Q20, §2, p. 2086; Gramsci 1995, p. 34.
5   For the struggle among these three currents, see, for example, De Rosa 1966; Molony 1977; Atkin and Tallett 2003; Pollard 2008.
6   Q23, §37, p. 2233; Gramsci 1985, p. 311.
7   Q20, §4, p. 2092; Gramsci 1995, p. 81.

The Lateran Pacts were criticised by many intellectuals from various currents, including Benedetto Croce, the greatest liberal and idealist intellectual of the time. Yet, Gramsci considered Croce's critique misdirected. Let us examine Gramsci's critique of Croce in turn.

3   Ironic Outcomes of Croce's Critique

First, I show that the young Gramsci was inspired by the Crocean idea of separating confessional religion and faith. He gradually became aware of Croce's social function to highlight, rather than to remedy, the social boundaries between the intellectuals and masses. The young Gramsci was deeply inspired by Croce's article 'Religion and Peace of Mind', originally published in 1915, in developing his view of religion.[8] In this short article, Croce rejected confessional religions including Catholicism as mythological, and argued that they were not exclusively entitled to the production of faith. By separating faith from religion, he claimed that philosophy can provide a more assured form of faith to people than religion, and aimed to gradually replace religion with philosophy. Gramsci provided a Marxist version of the Crocean account in some of his pre-prison writings. For example, in a short note appended to the reproduction of the famous article 'Revolution against *Capital*' in *Grido del Popolo* in 1918, Gramsci says:

> Nothing can be substituted if innovators do not have something substitutable at their disposal. Religion is a necessity. It is not an error. It represents the primordial and instinctive form of the metaphysical needs of man. The socialists must substitute religion with philosophy. Therefore, they must have a philosophy.[9]

Certainly, Gramsci understood Croce's writing neither in an anti-clericalist sense nor as an attempt to abolish the religious, but as an idealist programme to provide a better form of faith than religion.

In the 'Notes on the Southern Question', however, Gramsci emphasised a different aspect of Croce's philosophy to sever the intellectuals from the masses.

---

8   Croce 1915. Later Croce republished this article in his *Fragments of Ethics* in 1922. The English translation of the *Fragments* includes this article. See Croce 1924b.
9   Gramsci 1982, pp. 21–2 n. 1. This article first appeared in *Avanti!* on 24 December 1917, yet the note referring to Croce's view of religion only appeared in its reproduction in *Grido del Popolo*. The note is omitted in the English translations of this article.

The so-called neo-Protestants or Calvinists have not understood that in Italy, since a mass religious reformation would be impossible given the conditions of modern civilization, the only historically possible reformation has already taken place, with the philosophy of Benedetto Croce. The direction and method of thought have been changed and a new conception of the world has been constructed, transcending Catholicism and every other mythological religion. In this sense, Benedetto Croce has fulfilled an extremely important 'national' function. He has detached the radical intellectuals of the South from the peasant masses and made them participate in national and European culture. Through this culture, he has ensured the absorption of these intellectuals by the national bourgeoisie and hence by the agrarian bloc.[10]

While Gramsci shared the Crocean proposal of creating 'faith' in an immanentist manner, he rejected doing so in a Crocean fashion because the very function of Crocean philosophy was to detach the Southern young intellectuals from the Southern peasantry. All in all, for Gramsci, Croce ignored the masses who had little access to his idealist philosophy and hardly shared a faith in it with him. It is precisely from this perspective that in his prison writings Gramsci carried out a thorough critique of Croce's *prima facie* combative stance to Catholicism.

In the *Prison Notebooks*, Gramsci examined the grounds of the failure of Croce's critique of the Church in order to elaborate his own. In prison Gramsci defined Croce's proposal of replacing religion by philosophy as a 'moral and intellectual reform'.[11] Yet, as already noted in the 'Southern Question' article, Gramsci did not approve of the Crocean way of pursuing it. As explicated in a passage which Gramsci could have used for his planned, but never completed, *Anti-Croce*, he counterposed his proposal to that of Croce.[12]

> For [Croce] religion is a conception of reality, presented in mythological form, together with an ethic that conforms to this conception. Every philosophy, that is to say every conception of the world, in so far as it has become a 'faith', i.e. is considered not as a theoretical activity (the creation of new thought) but as a spur to action (concrete ethico-political activ-

10   Gramsci 1971a, p. 156; 1994b, p. 334.
11   Gramsci 1994a, p. 56.
12   For the phrase 'Anti-Croce' see Q10 I, §11, p. 1234; Gramsci 1995, p. 356. But if we are to compare Croce and Gramsci, we have to be careful not to swallow Gramsci's representation of Croce immediately as adequate. The antidote to this temptation could be found in Bellamy 2001.

ity, the creation of new history) is therefore a religion. Croce is however
very cautious in his relationship to traditional religion ... Although Croce
appears not to want to make any intellectual concession either to religion ... or to any form of mysticism, his attitude is however anything but
militant and combative ... A conception of the world cannot prove itself
worthy of permeating the whole of society and becoming a 'faith' unless
it shows itself capable of substituting previous conceptions and faiths at
all levels of state life ... Moreover, one cannot but emphasise that a faith
that cannot be translated into 'popular' terms shows for this very reason
that it is characteristic of a given social group.[13]

This passage explicates the different conceptions of the shared proposal: while
Croce stressed the supremacy of philosophy over religion in that it could give
a more assured peace of mind, Gramsci focused on whether a certain form of
faith remains only intellectual or becomes a popular one upon which people
rest their actions. For Gramsci, if Croce's proposal cannot become an action-
guiding principle, then it fails to provide a new 'faith'. It was precisely from this
perspective that Gramsci accounted for the ineffectiveness of Croce's harsh criticism of the Catholic Church.

In his *History of Europe in the Nineteenth Century*, Croce harshly criticised
confessional religions such as Catholicism, and doing so made it a new entry for
the Index of Forbidden Books.[14] Croce's critique is that confessional religions
cannot be faith-makers unless they hold external elements such as myth and
legend. He thus praised the supremacy of liberalism as the Religion of Liberty,
which purely consists of immanent development of liberty.[15] However, Gramsci discerned that Croce's ardent support of liberalism appeared inconsistent
due to his ambiguity about liberal Catholicism. In this book, Croce exalted the
first wave of liberal Catholicism during the Risorgimento – Neo-Guelphism – as
an ally to liberalism; however, he did not endorse its second wave in his time –
Modernism – as its ally. This inconsistency probably stems from Modernism's
democratic tendency and Croce's reservation over democracy as potentially
turning into the tyranny of the majority.[16] Croce thus appeared as a *de facto*
anti-modernist, and in practice supported the Jesuits despite his anti-Jesuit
assertions, a 'precious ally of the Jesuits against modernism'.[17] Ironically, there-

---

13   Q10 I, § 5, pp. 1217–18; Gramsci 1995, pp. 338–9.
14   Verucci 2006.
15   Croce 1963, Ch. 1, esp. pp. 18–19.
16   Croce 1963, p. 32.
17   Q10 II, § 41iv, pp. 1304–5; Gramsci 1995, pp. 471–2.

fore, Croce's ideal of jettisoning confessional religions came to back up Catholicism. This irony suggests, Gramsci illustrated, that Croce was in a high-cultural tradition of the Italian intellectuals, who detached themselves from the masses, since the Renaissance.

> Croce is, in essence, anti-confessional ... and for a large group of Italian and European intellectuals his philosophy ... has constituted a real and proper intellectual and moral reform of a 'Renaissance' type. 'To live without religion' (and here without confessional religion is meant) was the pith that Sorel elicited from his reading of Croce ... But Croce has not 'gone to the people', has not wanted to become a 'national' element (just as the Renaissance men were not, unlike the Lutherans and Calvinists), has not wanted to create a group of disciples who ... could popularize his philosophy in his place and try to make it into an educational element right from the primary school state (and thus educational for the simple worker and peasant, that is to say for the simple man in the street). Perhaps this was not possible, but it was worth the trouble of trying to do it, and not having tried is also significant ... How could one destroy religion in the consciousness of the ordinary person without at the same time replacing it? Is it possible in this case only to destroy without creating? It is impossible.[18]

Regardless of whether Croce's proposal of 'living without religion' was intellectually persuasive or not, Catholicism was in fact believed by many, whereby it continued to live among the people. For Gramsci, '[i]t is a prejudice of fossilized intellectuals to believe that a conception of the world can be destroyed by criticisms of a rational kind'.[19] Without understanding how the Church elicited the resilience from its popular background, Croce failed to bridge the two counterposed elements: the Religion of Liberty for the intellectuals on the one hand, and Catholicism for the masses on the other.

All in all, for Gramsci, Croce asserted, only to his fellow intellectuals, that the Church was against the historical development of liberalism, thereby failing to appeal to the masses that underpinned its very strength. In the final analysis, Croce ironically helped reinforce the Church as they have an affinity in maintaining this social separation.

---

18   Q10 II, § 41i, pp. 1294–5; Gramsci 1995, pp. 408–9.
19   Q10 II, § 41i, p. 1292; Gramsci 1995, p. 406.

4   Religion, Common Sense, and Good Sense

As shown in the previous section, Croce failed to grasp the popularly grounded strength of Catholicism. This observation made Gramsci closely examine
ordinary people's unsophisticated and often contradictory view of the world,
namely 'common sense' as a set of various elements stemming from past philosophies and religions.[20] Apart from Croce's intellectualist approach that clearly
distinguished philosophy and common sense, Gramsci considered it possible
to derive from common sense the elements of 'good sense' as a more appropriate account of the world.[21] Rather than condemning common sense because
of its unsophisticated features, Gramsci proposed his alternative that aims to
overcome the underlying dichotomy between the world of philosophy by intellectuals, and the world of common sense by the masses, the dichotomy shared
by both Croce and the Church. From this perspective Gramsci accounted for
the resilience of Catholicism and elaborated his own alternative – the Gramscian version of 'moral and intellectual reform'.

Let us now look closely at Gramsci's analysis of common sense. He discerned
that people's common sense, which underpinned their ways of thinking and
acting, held a large number of elements of a Catholic origin, irrespective of
whether they were aware of it. The prime example of this is people's belief that
the external world is objectively real.

> In fact the belief is of religious origin, even if the man who shares it is
> indifferent to religion. Since all religions have taught and do teach that
> the world, nature, the universe were created by God before the creation
> of man, and therefore man found the world already made, catalogued and
> defined once and for all, this belief has become an iron fact of 'common
> sense' and survives with the same solidity even if religious feeling is dead
> or asleep.[22]

Scientific knowledge is essentially renewable regarding its *a posteriori* nature.
By contrast, argued Gramsci, people derived the objectivity of the world from a
Catholic conception of the world that cannot be altered once settled in people's
common sense, as this conception appears as the truth. At this juncture, intellectualist criticism such as Croce's can hardly address this spontaneous and
infallible nature of common sense.

---

20   Q11, §12, pp. 1375–6; Gramsci 1971a, pp. 323–4.
21   Q11, §12, p. 1378; Gramsci 1971a, pp. 325–6.
22   Q11, §17, p. 1412; Gramsci 1971a, p. 441.

The common sense influenced by Catholicism resulted in people's inability to act coherently, making them act in a contradictory manner to that which they expressed verbally. This contradiction is due to an imposed conception of the world from the intellectuals of other social groups, so Gramsci argues:

> This contrast between thought and action, i.e. the con-existence of two conceptions of the world, one affirmed in words and the other displayed in effective action, is not simply a product of self-deception. Self-deception can be an adequate explanation for a few individuals taken separately ... but it is not adequate when the contrast occurs in the life of great masses. In these cases the contrast between thought and action cannot but be the expression of profounder contrasts of a social historical order. It signifies that the social group in question may indeed have its own conception of the world, even if only embryonic; a conception which manifests itself in action, but occasionally and in flashes – when, that is, the group is acting as an organic totality. But this same group has, for reasons of submission and intellectual subordination, adopted a conception which is not its own but is borrowed from another group; and it affirms this conception verbally and believes itself to be following it, because this is the conception which it follows in 'normal times' – that is when its conduct is not independent and autonomous, but submissive and subordinate.[23]

Gramsci called this contradiction between thought and action 'contradictory consciousness'. One consciousness is 'implicit in his activity and which in reality unites him with all his fellow-collaborators in the practical transformation of the real world', whereas the other one is 'superficially explicit or verbal, which he has inherited from the past and uncritically absorbed'. This contradictory state of consciousness in turn produces 'a condition of moral and political passivity', without permitting him to take any autonomous decision of action.[24] If people's consciousness appears contradictory and thus passive, they can hardly express their concerns. They come to merely repeat what they have taken for granted as common sense.

Without ascribing such passivity to their intellectual dishonesty, Gramsci accounted for a contradictory consciousness as being produced by the exist-

---

23   Q11, §12, p. 1379; Gramsci 1971a, pp. 326–7.
24   Q11, §12, p. 1385; Gramsci 1971a, p. 333 (English translation is amended by TC). On 'contradictory consciousness' see Femia 1981, pp. 35–50; pp. 218–35.

ing equilibrium between the intellectuals and masses, or the higher philosophy and the popular common sense.

> The relation between common sense and the upper level of philosophy
> is assured by 'politics', just as it is politics that assures the relationship
> between the Catholicism of the intellectuals and that of the simple. There
> are, however, fundamental differences between the two cases. That the
> Church has to face up to a problem of the 'simple' means precisely that
> there has been a split in the community of the faithful. This split cannot
> be healed by raising the simple to the level of the intellectuals (the Church
> does not even envisage such a task, which is both ideologically and eco-
> nomically beyond its present capacities), but only by imposing an iron
> discipline on the intellectuals so that they do not exceed certain limits of
> differentiation and so render the split catastrophic and irreparable ... The
> Society of Jesus is the last of the great religious origin ... New orders which
> have grown up since then have very little religious significance but a great
> 'disciplinary' significance for the mass of the faithful. They are, or have
> become, ramifications and tentacles of the Society of Jesus, instruments
> of 'resistance' to preserve political positions that have been gained, not
> forces of renovation and development. Catholicism has become 'Jesuit-
> ism'. Modernism has not created 'religious orders', but a political party –
> Christian Democracy.[25]

Jesuitism cautiously maintained a relationship between the intellectuals and
the masses, the relation that most benefited the Church making the masses
subordinate to their intellectuals' influence. The authority of the Church, therefore, could not be challenged by the masses whose consciousness remained
contradictory and passive. Since common sense *per se* is built upon past ideas,
it often made it impossible to address contemporary problems as the case of
contradictory consciousness reveals. Gramsci holds that:

> [o]ne's conception of the world is a response to certain specific problems
> posed by reality, which are quite specific and 'original' in their immedi-
> ate relevance. How is it possible to consider the present, and quite spe-
> cific present, with a mode of thought elaborated for a past which is often
> remote and superseded?[26]

---

25   Q11, § 12, pp. 1383–4; Gramsci 1971a, pp. 331–2.
26   Q11, § 12, p. 1377; Gramsci 1971a, p. 324.

For the Italian masses, their common sense could not be a clue to address their present problems, as it was largely informed by Catholic conceptions stemming from a remote past.

Gramsci's alternative to contradictory consciousness is to elaborate 'good sense' from the unsorted common sense. Such a Gramscian way of dealing with common sense could be a conservative path in that it seeks to improve the given common sense rather than replacing it with something that idealist philosophers find reasonable. Yet, at the same time, it is a part of radical politics, because what he proposed for elaborating good sense was his version of 'moral and intellectual reform', through which the gap between the intellectuals and masses could be overcome.

> The position of the philosophy of praxis is the antithesis of the Catholic. The philosophy of praxis does not tend to leave the 'simple' in their primitive philosophy of common sense, but rather to lead them to a higher conception of life. If it affirms the need for contact between intellectuals and simple it is not in order to restrict scientific activity and preserve unity at the low level of the masses, but precisely in order to construct an intellectual-moral bloc which can make politically possible the intellectual progress of the mass and not only of small intellectual groups.[27]

Gramsci was thus adamant in remedying the gap between two cultures, high and popular, or philosophy and common sense. Doing so would differentiate Gramsci from Crocean intellectualism on the one hand, and from the Church's enduring reproduction of the contradictory consciousness in their minds on the other. Gramsci insisted that this reform 'corresponds to the nexus Protestant Reformation + French Revolution'.[28] This reform was necessary due to the exclusion of the masses from Italian politics since the Risorgimento. In this respect, Gramsci's 'moral and intellectual reform' aimed to provide the masses with the ethos by which they could constitute a part of new ruling group of the Italian state.

---

27   Q11, §12, pp. 1384–5; Gramsci 1971a, pp. 332–3.
28   Q16, §9, p. 1860; Gramsci 1971a, p. 395.

5   Conclusion

This short chapter has explored Gramsci's critique of Catholicism. First, I have looked at how it was informed by Gramsci's analysis of Croce's misdirected criticism of the Catholic Church. For Gramsci, Croce's critique only appealed to his fellow intellectuals, by contending that the Church was at odds with a liberal ethos. He thereby did not take into account the masses, who had nothing to do with Croce's philosophical discussions. But it was they who supported the Church's authority as their daily common sense was influenced by Catholic teachings. In the final analysis, Croce helped to maintain the gap between the intellectuals and masses that had endured since the Renaissance. Second, I have illustrated how Gramsci developed his own critique of the Catholic Church reflecting on Croce's failure, by particularly looking at common sense as a set of people's ordinary, often unorganised and even contradictory ways of thinking and acting. Rather than rejecting common sense, Gramsci thought it possible to find in it 'good sense' as a more appropriate account of the world. Contrary to Croce's project of exalting idealist liberalism against Catholicism, Gramsci's was to avoid such a dichotomy, since it presumed the underlying social gap between the intellectuals and the masses. Thus, Gramsci did not just criticise the social role of the Catholic Church, but also aimed at remedying the division of social groups in Italian society.

CHAPTER 17

Past and Present: Popular Literature

Ingo Pohn-Lauggas

1   Introduction

Antonio Gramsci makes use of a variety of different categories and headings in order to sort the material in his *Prison Notebooks*. For instance, they contain recurring headings, such as: 'Criteria of Method', the 'History of the Italian Intellectuals', and 'Introduction to the Study of Philosophy'. Gramsci also creates his own categories, such as 'Father Bresciani's Progeny', in order to describe propagandistic trashy literature,[1] or employs neologisms, such as 'Lorianism',[2] to refer to scientific trash as a 'general symptom of cultural decline'.[3] Often, the mere fact that Gramsci assigns certain themes, phenomena or personalities to one of these categories, can be meaningful and very instructive – both about the topic, but also about the category itself. The heading 'Past and Present' is one of these categories, and the way in which Gramsci uses it is exceptionally instructive: it appears almost exclusively in the miscellaneous notebooks, and unlike other categories, the material included under this heading did not lead to a thematic notebook.[4]

The content subsumed in the *Prison Notebooks* under the heading 'Past and Present' is highly heterogeneous, as Gramsci used it to trace – very generally speaking – the relationship between the individual level of experience and historical context. Using this definition, it seems evident that there is hardly anything outside the ambit of the heading 'Past and Present'. Bearing in mind the central importance of Gramsci's investigations of the group of topics that we might call 'the political of literature',[5] it is remarkable that he

---

1   See Paladini Musitelli 2004.
2   See Lauggas 2015a.
3   Q28, § 6, p. 2229.
4   Gramsci wrote in the first years of his imprisonment texts, so-called A-texts, which he later revisited, reworked, amended and reformulated, and partly arranged in thematic notebooks (C-texts). The critical edition (Q) includes the work of both writing phases as well as those texts that are only available in one version (B-texts). For a further explanation, see Buttigieg's *Preface* in Gramsci 2011 (PN – *Prison Notebooks*), Vol. 1, p. xv.
5   Haug 2006, p. 158.

does not connect, with one exception,[6] his studies of popular literature with the heading 'Past and Present'. In this chapter, I will explore the possible reasons for this and attempt to re-think Gramsci's comments on popular literature in the *Prison Notebooks*, and significantly in his prison letters, under the specific perspective that results from the conception of the category of 'Past and Present'.

2   Culture and Literature

In a famous letter from the spring of 1927, Gramsci – after being imprisoned for a few months – outlines his research project and names four areas on which he would like to focus: a history of the intellectuals, a study of comparative linguistics, one of Pirandello's Theatre, as well as an essay on 'cheap novels' and popular literature consumption.[7] 'At bottom', he states, 'if you examine them thoroughly, there is a certain homogeneity among these four subjects: the creative spirit of the people in its diverse stages and degrees of development is in equal measure at their base'.[8] Gramsci's writings on literature are thus closely related to his theory of hegemony and to the question of the intellectuals:

> Two writers can represent (express) the same socio-historical moment, but one can be an artist and the other a mere scribbler. To try to deal with the question just by describing what the two represent or express socially, that is, by summarizing more or less thoroughly the characteristics of a specific socio-historical moment, hardly touches at all upon the artistic problem. All this can be useful and necessary, indeed it certainly is, but in another field: that of political criticism, the criticism of social life, involving the struggle to destroy and to overcome certain feelings and beliefs, certain attitudes toward life and the world. This is not the criticism or the history of art, nor can it be presented as such ... .[9]

It is rather the struggle for a new culture (later, we will return to this). Consequently, Gramsci distinguishes his reflections on (artistic) literature from

---

6   Q3, § 53, pp. 334–5; Gramsci 1985, pp. 345–6; Gramsci 2011, Vol. 2, pp. 54–5. This exception will be explored later in more detail.

7   For an overview, see Paladini Musitelli 2009.

8   Letter to Tatjana Schucht, 19 March 1927; Gramsci 1994a, Vol. 1, p. 84.

9   Q23, § 3, p. 2187; Gramsci 1985, p. 93.

those on 'culture'. Opening the first notebook one finds a work programme comprising sixteen entries, in which the questions of intellectuals and of literature should be treated in separate chapters.[10] In the same way Gramsci distinguishes between culture and art: culture is the place of the social, the political, the ideological, whereas art is the (methodologically) separated place of the aesthetic. This premise results from Gramsci's understanding of what he calls 'the forms of cultural organisation which keep the ideological world in movement'.[11] The two notebooks that carry 'Culture' in their title[12] thus cover a spectrum of topics ranging from the history of mentalities, epistemological, philosophical and economic issues to questions of State theory.

With regard to literature, Gramsci in his analysis brings sociological and aesthetic issues together, as I will show later more precisely, and this connection forms the political core of what he has developed in the field of literature. In his essays on popular literature, Gramsci draws up 'the "catalogue" of the most important questions to be examined and analysed',[13] which ranges from the non-'popularity' of Italian literature, the political character of humanism and the Renaissance to the non-existence of Italian children's literature. The concept of hegemony brings these issues down to the common denominator of the struggle for a 'new culture'. One of the central tasks consists in clarifying which 'type of literary criticism'[14] is suitable to Marxism.[15] Literary criticism here stands for political rather than artistic criticism – what with reference to Francesco De Sanctis is called 'militant criticism' (*critica militante*).[16]

The heading 'Return to De Sanctis' refers to the important literary historian and critic who in 1870–71 published a two-volume *History of Italian Literature*,[17] in which he considers the major works of Italian literature in the context of the social and cultural history of their time.[18] During the Risorgimento this work contributed significantly to the process of the Italian unification in the field of culture. Gramsci thought that the type of literary criticism outlined by De

---

10   Q1, p. 5; Gramsci 2011, Vol. 1, p. 99.
11   Q11, §12, p. 1394; Gramsci 1971a, pp. 341–2.
12   Notebook 16 (1933/34) and 26 (1935). Detailed analyses of the 'Cultural themes' (*Argomenti di cultura*), as these notebooks are entitled, are offered by Wagner 1999 and Baratta 2009.
13   Q21, §1, p. 2108; Gramsci 1985, p. 200.
14   Q23, §3, p. 2188; Gramsci 1985, p. 95.
15   See Haug 2011, p. 133; Musolino 1977.
16   Q23, §3, p. 2188; Gramsci 1985, p. 94.
17   Q23, §1, p. 2185; Gramsci 1985, p. 91. For a discussion, see Buttigieg 2001.
18   See Apweiler 1997.

Sanctis[19] was necessary for the struggle to advance a new culture. He viewed it as a criticism that 'is militant, not "frigidly" aesthetic; it belongs to a period of cultural struggles and contrasts between antagonistic conceptions of life'.[20] This is an important principle. Art is nothing outside the social. Gramsci was one of the connoisseurs of the book market and the magazine landscape of the 1920s and early 1930s, dealing with popular literature, newspapers and serial novels, folklore, mystery and adventure literature; he thus provides us with an excellent training in reflecting on and understanding the interaction between literature and society.

3   Past and Present

If we now face the category 'Past and Present', it seems plausible, as in so many other contexts, to begin with Gramsci's reflections on Marx's *Theses on Feuerbach*.[21] The sixth thesis says that the human being is 'no abstraction inherent in each single individual', but rather 'the ensemble of the social relations'.[22] We may clearly not 'abstract from the historical process' here.[23] In this way we arrive at a core element of the 'definition' of 'Past and Present'. Its conception has – roughly speaking – two complementary sides.[24]

One interpretation is the demand to examine the individual's experience of life for its universal content, and thus to give its presentation an educational value, a 'pedagogical universality',[25] as Gramsci puts it. This moves the biographical process into focus, even Gramsci's own path can be seen from that perspective.[26] His detachment from Sardinia was one element in Gramsci's path towards socialism, i.e. his own 'de-provincialization'.[27] He did not however repudiate his past; 'as a socialist, he discovered new answers to questions he was confronted with in his life in Sardinia', Giuseppe Fiori reports in his biography of Gramsci, 'but, as a Sardinian, he refused to separate the peasant problem from the problem of the socialist revolution'.[28]

---

19   See Guglielmi 1976; Muscetta 1991.
20   Q23, §3, p. 2188; Gramsci 1985, p. 94.
21   Marx 1976a [1845], pp. 3–5.
22   Marx 1976a [1845], p. 4.
23   Ibid.
24   See Liguori and Voza 2009, entry *Passato e presente* by F. Frosini.
25   Q14, §78, p. 1745.
26   See Vacca 2012.
27   Q15, §19, p. 1776.
28   Fiori 1995, p. 110.

In this context of 'de-provincialization', it is interesting to mention a passage from Notebook 15 on Francesco Guicciardini,[29] a contemporary and friend of Niccolò Machiavelli. Gramsci refers to him a number of times in the context of the problem of a 'modern Prince'.[30] However, in the passage that is interesting for the context of this article, the focus is on Guicciardini's work *Ricordi politici e civili* (*Political and Civil Memoirs*), which dates from the early sixteenth century. It is the autobiographical and literary founding text of the genre of moral-political aphorism. Gramsci writes:

> These are 'memoirs' insofar as they do not describe autobiographical events in the strict sense ... but rather civil and moral ... 'experiences' ... which are closely connected to his own life and its events, and which are reflected upon in their universal or national significance. Such a text can be more useful in many ways than autobiographies in the stricter sense, particularly when it refers to living processes that are marked by the constant effort to overcome a backward way of life and thought, as it was precisely for a Sardinian at the beginning of this century ... .[31]

The autobiographical perspective therefore provides general insights. Further, Gramsci remarks:

> If it is true that one of the most pressing necessities of Italian culture was the need to de-provincialize, even in the most progressive and modern urban centres, this process would stand out even more clearly as it was experienced by the 'triple or quadruple provincial', as was certainly a young Sardinian at the beginning of the century.[32]

The importance of such an incidental remark in Gramsci's thought becomes apparent when we relate it to a more famous passage, in which he poses the problem of human nature. Gramsci refers to the sixth of Marx's *Theses on Feuerbach*,[33] and states: 'Man is to be conceived as an historical bloc of purely individual and subjective elements and of mass and objective or mater-

---

29 Francesco Guicciardini (1483–1540), a historian, statesman and one of the most important political writers of the Italian Renaissance.
30 See Q6, § 87, pp. 762–3; Gramsci 1995, pp. 17–18.
31 Q15, § 19, p. 1776.
32 Ibid.
33 Marx 1976a [1845], p. 4.

ial elements with which the individual is in an active relationship'.[34] If we connect this principle with the remark about Guicciardini, and see both trains of thought from the perspective of the task to examine the individual's experience of life for its universal content, we will also recognise in these sentences some key passages for the understanding of the heading of 'Past and Present'.

This leads us to a second interpretation of the heading. It is outlined in its very first appearance in Notebook 1. There, Gramsci not only refers to the present as 'criticism', but also as a 'surpassing' of the past:

> What should be discarded is that which the present has 'intrinsically' criticized and that part of ourselves which corresponds to it. What does this mean? That we must have an exact consciousness of this real criticism and express it not only theoretically but *politically*.[35]

What is to be examined first is how history – understood as a unitary and dynamic process – 'in its dialectic, always in the act of struggle between past and future, becomes a part of the individual's experience'.[36] Second, we should address how individuals struggle to take advantage of this fact for the good of progress: political, practical criticism consciously discards certain surpassed burdens of the past.

Both aspects of this understanding of 'Past and Present' are essential pillars of Gramsci's philosophical architecture, this much is obvious. It is therefore no surprise that the most varied content is collected under this apparently heterogeneous heading. There is, after all, hardly any field that might not be related to the set of problems thus established for 'Past and Present'. All the more surprising, then, that Gramsci does not (with one exception) link his examinations of popular literature to this heading. Investigating the reasons for this makes it once more necessary to return to Gramsci's texts and to read them accurately.[37]

4   Serial Novels

My starting point will be the problem of the national-popular, a category that is often wrongly exclusively related to problems of literature. Giorgio Baratta suspected that this could be also a consequence of the first thematic editions

---

34   Q10.II, § 48, p. 1338; Gramsci 1971a, p. 360.
35   Q1, § 156, p. 137; Gramsci 2011, Vol. 1, p. 234, emphasis in original.
36   Liguori and Voza 2009, p. 627.
37   See Buttigieg 1994; 2002; Wagner 2012.

of the *Prison Notebooks*, which followed the logic of academic disciplinary order rather than the development of Gramsci's thought, causing 'some interpretative blindnesses'.[38] The interest, however, is the interwovenness of socioeconomic and political questions with those of culture and literature, not least for instance the Italian debate, known as *Questione della lingua*,[39] pervading the discussion.[40] This not only shows the scope of Gramsci's thought, but also its constitutively interdisciplinary character. One should not commit the mistake of isolating these questions from each other, but rather sharpen them by connecting them coherently – a coherence that is provided by the concept of hegemony:[41] 'In the light of this concept, literature is finally thought of as a "popular" and "national" problem by systematically elaborating what was already prepared by De Sanctis and by shifting the obvious "connection of problems" to the terrain of the philosophy of praxis'.[42] But, the crucial fact for us consists in this: Gramsci's examinations of the national-popular transgresses the same limits as the heading of 'Past and Present'.

'Many prisoners underrate the prison library', Gramsci writes in 1929 in a letter to his sister-in-law Tatjana Schucht:

> Mostly it is pious texts and third-rate novels. However, I think a political prisoner should extract blood even from a beetroot. The true skill lies in setting one's respective reading a goal and taking notes (if you are allowed to do so).[43]

The questions with which Gramsci approaches these books are very precise:

> Why is this particular kind of literature always the most read and printed one? Which needs does it satisfy? Which expectations does it meet? Which feelings and point of views make this rubbish so successful?[44]

These are problems with regard to aspects of the sociology of literature (what is printed?) and the national-popular (which needs are satisfied?), even before the concept and theory were developed in the *Prison Notebooks*. But at the same

---

38   Baratta 2000, p. 67.
39   Debates on the Italian language from Dante up to the present.
40   See Manacorda 1975.
41   See the different approaches collected in Pala 2014.
42   Sanguineti 2000, p. 202.
43   Letter to Tatjana Schucht, 22 April 1929. Gramsci 1994a, Vol. 1, p. 263 f.
44   Ibid.

time, it is also a problem of aesthetics: What pleases? On the one hand, the aesthetic consequence of the criterion national-popular is revealed, and, on the other hand, the aesthetic becomes politicised.[45]

Gramsci's goal is, amongst others, to fathom out the question of 'why and how a literature is popular',[46] or not. The 'Non-National-Popular Character of Italian Literature' ('Carattere non nazionale-popolare della letteratura italiana') is a separate heading in the *Prison Notebooks*.[47] What is at stake is more than the 'beauty' of a text:

> There must be a specific moral and intellectual content which is the elaborated and finished expression of the deepest aspirations of a given public, of the nation-people in a certain phase of its historical development. Literature must be at one and the same time a current element of civilization and a work of art. Otherwise, instead of artistic literature there will be a preference for serial literature ... .[48]

Distancing himself from Benedetto Croce's aesthetics of immanence and his life's work of grasping beauty and poetry in its pure form,[49] Gramsci subordinates the 'study of the beauty of a work' to 'the study of why it is "read", "popular", "sought after" '.[50] Or, 'in the opposite case', he asks, 'why it does not touch the people and arouse their interest', thus 'showing up the lack of unity in the cultural life of the nation'.[51]

The thematic Notebook 21 (1934–35) is dedicated to 'Popular Literature'. Gramsci strives, amongst other things, for a regular classification and systematic indexing of this field. Under the title 'Various Types of Popular Novel', he organises the novel into categories, such as the 'sentimental type', the traditional 'historical novel' of the Dumas brand, the 'detective novel', the 'gothic' or 'geographical, scientific, adventure novel'.[52] Under the category of popular novels of 'overtly ideologico-political' character, Eugène Sue is mentioned, which is of special interest in the context of this study. Gramsci ascribes to Sue 'demo-

---

45   I have elaborated on this issue in my monograph on aesthetics and politics in Gramsci and
      Raymond Williams (Lauggas 2013).
46   Q21, §4, p. 2113; Gramsci 1985, p. 264.
47   For example, Q14, §14, p. 1669; and Q15, §42, p. 1801; Gramsci 1985, pp. 236–7.
48   Q21, §4, p. 2113; Gramsci 1985, p. 264.
49   See Pohn-Lauggas 2015b.
50   Q23, §51, p. 2247; Gramsci 1985, p. 291.
51   Ibid.
52   Q21, §6, pp. 2120–1; Gramsci 1985, pp. 359–60.

cratic tendencies linked to the ideologies of 1848'.[53] We recall that the category of 'Past and Present' is not generally applied in relation to popular literature. Only once, in Notebook 3, written more than four years prior, is it applied to these questions, and even then it involves Eugène Sue. In the 1840s, Sue was one of the most widely-read authors in France. He is held to have established the genre of the serial novel in newspapers and his *Les Mystères de Paris* (*The Mysteries of Paris*), published in a newspaper from 1842 to 1843, was an extremely successful serial novel. Thus, Sue serves for Gramsci as an example of markedly ideological political scribbling. But, how does this concern the category of 'Past and Present'?

Gramsci regards French feuilleton romanticism as a 'source of culture', which can serve 'to explain certain kinds of behaviour by subaltern intellectuals'.[54] He hints at his own journalistic writings from the 1920s, predating his imprisonment, in which Gramsci had highlighted the influence of feuilleton literature on some aspects of the fascist mentality. Under the pseudonym 'Manalive', in the newspaper *L'Unità* (28 February 1924), Gramsci engages with the 'romantic milieu, in which the fascist mind was formed' and relates this to the serial novel.[55]

> This is the romantic side of the fascist movement ... An unbalanced imagination, a shudder of heroic fury, a psychological restlessness that contain no ideas but only the sentiments that pervade the serial novels of the French romanticism of 1848. ... The historical conjuncture has made it possible for this romanticism to become a 'ruling class' and for all of Italy to become a serial novel.[56]

Recalling the earlier criteria, crudely drawn, under which certain material is gathered under the heading 'Past and Present', we can now note the example of the influence of the 'old' popular novel of Eugène Sue on the mentalities and ideologies of Gramsci's present. This example illustrates a *second* definition of the heading, namely as the conjunction of problems of the absence of criticism, and thus a lack of success in overcoming the past.

---

53   Q21, §6, p. 2120; Gramsci 1985, p. 359.
54   Q3, §53, p. 334; Gramsci 2011, Vol. 2, p. 54.
55   See Gramsci 1975 (Q3, §53, note 1), p. 2596; Gramsci 2011, Vol. 2, pp. 451–2.
56   Gramsci 1971b, pp. 367–9, quoted from Gramsci 2011, Vol. 2, p. 453.

5   National-Popular

Returning to Notebook 21, in which Gramsci is particularly interested in the topic of serial novels,[57] we find that the heading 'Past and Present' is absent. In the 1930s, several Italian daily newspapers printed French nineteenth-century novels in individual episodes, and used just the 'sentimental literature', among others *The Count of Monte Cristo* by Alexandre Dumas, which Gramsci grapples with repeatedly. He believes that the enthusiastic consumption of these serial novels is symptomatic. There was no reason that a contemporary and sophisticated artistic literature might not become popular. Thus, Gramsci gives the Russian novel as an example.[58] It was also conceivable that a popular literature could originate in Italy itself, but neither was the case at that historical moment. It was therefore reasonable for newspapers to look abroad for their supply. As to the reason for this, Gramsci identifies the already-mentioned lack of unity between the world views of the authors and the population. In other words, the emotional landscapes of the latter are foreign to the former:

> The intellectuals do not come from the people ... . They do not feel tied to them (rhetoric apart), they do not know and sense their needs, aspirations and feelings. In relation to the people, they are something detached, without foundation, a caste and not an articulation with organic functions of the people themselves.[59]

The fact that Gramsci continues to reformulate this statement at a number of different points shows its importance with regard to the theory of hegemony. To Italians, their own intellectuals are more foreign than the foreign ones. They are therefore exposed to an external intellectual and moral hegemony. The influence of French historical novels produces a peculiar attachment of the Italian people to French traditions; they are more familiar with Henry IV than with Garibaldi, feel more beholden to the Revolution of 1789 than to the Risorgimento. 'They are interested in a past that is not their own', is Gramsci's for-

---

57   This interest in popular culture is one of the reasons why Gramsci's writings play a pivotal
       role in the later emergence of the discipline of cultural studies (Lauggas 2013; Vacca et al.
       2008). According to Birgit Wagner, the focus on the forms of serial narrative in particular
       can be applied to contemporary forms: 'It will have to be said that by now the import-
       ance of serial narrative has increased exponentially within the audio-visual culture and is
       one of the central aspects of contemporary mass culture. Gramsci provides very original
       considerations for its analysis' (Wagner 2012, p. 9).
58   Q21, § 5, p. 2114; Gramsci 1985, p. 206.
59   Q21, § 5, p. 2117; Gramsci 1985, p. 209.

mulation in Notebook 23 on literary criticism.[60] He goes on, 'They use French metaphors and cultural references in their language and thought etc.; culturally speaking, they are more French than Italian'.[61]

In passing, I would like to mention the name of Francesco Guicciardini, whose *Ricordi politici e civili* served as an illustration for *one* interpretation of 'Past and Present'. Guicciardini also forms part of this context, albeit in a different place. In a short paragraph with the heading 'Non-National-Popular Characteristics of Italian Literature', Gramsci writes about the Italian novel.[62] He says that compared to the French, it was 'more external, narrow-minded, without a national-popular or universal human content'.[63] While 'the Italian' – also according to Guicciardini – only 'studies how to "dominate", how to be stronger, more skilled, more cunning', the French wants to understand, 'in order to influence and obtain an "active and spontaneous consent"'.[64] The key terms of the theory of hegemony in quotation marks are easy to see here, and it is obvious that the absence of the latter 'characteristic' is debilitating in the struggle for hegemony.

In Notebook 21, as we have discussed, Gramsci says that literature 'must be at one and the same time a current element of civilization and a work of art'.[65] In the original, the term translated as civilisation is *civiltà*,[66] a term that is always difficult to translate. Gramsci mostly used it as synonym for culture. This can be seen in paragraph three of Notebook 23 on literary criticism, which I already quoted in the introduction to this chapter. Under the heading 'Art and the Struggle for a New Civilization', Gramsci states 'that a critique of literary civiliz-ation, a struggle to create a new culture [sic], is artistic in the sense that a new art will be born from the new culture'.[67] This translation reflects Gramsci's use of the terms *civiltà* and *cultura* while in the German edition the term *Kultur*

---

60   Q23, §8, p. 2197; Gramsci 1985, p. 216.
61   Q23, §8, pp. 2197–8; Gramsci 1985, p. 216; here I deviate from William Boelhover's transla-
      tion in *Selections from Cultural Writings* and stay closer to the Italian original text, because
      in the former's translation the two questions concerning history and 'cultural identity' –
      so central in this context – are conflated. This does not correspond to Gramsci's statement.
      Boelhover indeed translates: 'Culturally speaking, they are interested in a past that is more
      French than Italian'.
62   Q15, §14, p. 1771. Note that the title is replaced by 'The Italians and the Novel' in Gramsci
      1985, p. 266.
63   Q15, §14, p. 1772; Gramsci 1985, p. 267.
64   Q15, §14, p. 1771; Gramsci 1985, p. 266.
65   Q21, §4, p. 2113; Gramsci 1985, p. 264.
66   Q21, §4, p. 2113.
67   Q23, §3, pp. 2187–8; Gramsci 1985, pp. 93–4.

(culture) is used consistently in these positions.[68] We cannot elaborate upon this very important question at this point, but it may be sufficient to record that *civiltà*, in the quoted literary context, may also be understood as 'lived culture'. *This* meaning of 'culture' indicates the sphere of prevailing discourses, to express it with a later term: it is the central starting point for the 'reaching' of people. Here rests the political core of what the imprisoned communist has developed in the field of literature.[69]

For Gramsci, the theoretician on hegemony, the 'reaching' of people aims at the (political) potential for social change. With this connection, as has become apparent, the aesthetic becomes political, because the sphere of aesthetic quality is crucial for the willingness to be reached at all.[70] So political literary criticism concentrates on the content, but is aware of the meaning of expression. Despite its content, a successful work of art will always have admirers and will be liked: 'The people are "contentist", but if the popular content is expressed by great artists, these will be preferred'.[71] When Gramsci initially negotiates culture and art, content and form, moral and aesthetic values, equally and evidently separately, in a second step, of course, he is 'contentist' too.

Now, wherein lies the link between *civiltà* and Gramsci's category 'Past and Present', which is the focus of our attention? Evidently this 'lived culture' is also subject to the described tension between the two outlined meanings of 'Past and Present'. The short fourth paragraph of Notebook 21 quoted earlier, where this sentence is to be found, is then followed by a more vast analysis of the 'Concept of "National-Popular"'.[72] In fact, Gramsci deals with nothing else in these pages. He develops the concept in contrast to that used in an article published by the journal *Critica Fascista* (early August 1930), which laments the reprinting of French serialised novels of a century ago; again, *The Count of Monte Cristo* is amongst them. According to *Critica Fascista*, this expresses the newspapers' 'very poor idea of their readers', as they perceive them 'as if taste, interest and literary experience had not changed at all from then until now'.[73] *Au contraire*, says Gramsci. This lament not only fails to see the non-

---

68   Wolfgang Fritz Haug, one of the publishers of the German critical edition of the *Note-books*, argues that in German – otherwise than in English – '"culture" most likely gathers the adjacent semantic pathways' (2011, p. 136). This question already became controversial decades ago when it was necessary (and early Gramsci translations failed) to differentiate Gramsci's 'civil society' (*società civile*) from the Marxist term for 'bourgeois society'.

69   See Lauggas 2013, p. 71 ff.

70   See Seroni 1958.

71   Q17, § 29, p. 1934; Gramsci 1985, p. 376.

72   Q21, § 5, pp. 2113–20; Gramsci 1985, pp. 206–12; See Durante 2004; 2009.

73   Q21, § 5, p. 2114; Gramsci 1985, p. 206.

national-popular character of Italian literature, but it also – which is even more significant in this context – misses a simple insight: 'it is unable to draw the "realistic" conclusions from the fact that if people like the novels of a hundred years ago, it means that their taste and ideology are precisely those of a hundred years ago'.[74] The question of which needs are satisfied is also crucial for Gramsci here. Thus, he states: 'It is not by chance that this "commercial aspect" and a given public "taste" coincide'.[75] Or, as he elaborates: 'Indeed the serials written around 1848 had a specific socio-political line which still makes them sought after and read today by a public with the same feelings as in 1848'.[76]

6   Past and Present?

I conclude with the implicit question of my chapter: is there a logical reason, at the level of theory and content, for not anymore including the category of 'Past and Present' in the later Notebooks on popular literature? I do not think so. These last quotations in particular are directly connected to the definitional demand in Notebook 1, according to which the present has to become a criticism of the past. Gramsci says, 'we must stick closer to the present, which we ourselves have helped create'.[77] Our route takes us to Notebook 3, where the 'Influence of French Romantic Serials' is explicitly related to 'Past and Present' for the one and only time.[78] It is a B-text, one to which Gramsci does not return.[79] However, as I have shown, Gramsci does return to his discussion of Eugène Sue. 'Past and Present' therefore remains a category of the earlier miscellaneous Notebooks on questions of literature, too, because in the thematic ones, Gramsci no longer has any further need for it, and because it seems to have been increasingly difficult to demarcate its limits.

One characteristic instance is Gramsci's uncompleted attempt, in the spring of 1932, at constructing 'groupings of subjects' near the beginning of Note-

---

74   Q21, §5, p. 2114; Gramsci 1985, p. 207.

75   Q17, §29, p. 1934; Gramsci 1985, pp. 376–7.

76   Q17, §29, p. 1934; Gramsci 1985, p. 377.

77   Q1, §156, p. 137; Gramsci 2011, Vol. 1, p. 234.

78   Q3, §53, p. 334; Gramsci 1985, p. 345; although the editors of the *Selections from Cultural Writings* have erased the first part of the headline of the paragraph – 'Past and Present. Influence of French Romantic Serials'. Thus, it becomes evident that a reconstruction of the type that I attempt here can only be carried out successfully by deploying a critical edition of the *Prison Notebooks*.

79   For an explanation of Valentina Gerratana's terminology of A/B/C-texts, see footnote 4.

book 8,[80] which is, in a certain sense, quite mysterious. We are here on the threshold to the thematic notebooks and the 'groupings' seem to prepare them. Many signs indicate that Gramsci aims at a thematic reduction and furthermore begins to 'codify' certain topics,[81] also including the category of 'Past and Present'. Thus, the heading appears as the sixth item under *'A miscellany of various scholarly notes (Past and Present)'*.[82] In fact, as Fabio Frosini has shown,[83] it has already merged into the much more important item three by this time: *'Encyclopaedic notions and cultural topics'*.[84] These, in turn, are two headings which are brought together only at this point, starting with §125 of Notebook 8: 'This might serve as the general title for the survey that gathers together all the points and themes that have been noted thus far under different headings. Ideas for a dictionary of politics and criticism, encyclopaedic notions in the strict sense, themes of moral life, cultural topics, philosophical fables, etc.'[85]

The 'cultural themes', as we know, are strictly political, and how could literature, if it is about 'reaching' people, and especially the examinations of popular literature, be about anything but the *politics of the cultural*? The fragments of the thousands of pages of the *Prison Notebooks* are exposed to this integrated perspective. Gramsci's understanding of the term *politica culturale* expresses the essential political character of his concept of culture[86] while distinguishing it from pragmatic political action in the cultural field, and even more from the common understanding of 'cultural policy'.[87] Gramsci draws from the viewpoint of cultural history to the term of 'cultural "creation"', which is 'not to be confused with artistic creation, but to be related to political activities; and, indeed, it is in this sense that one can speak of a "cultural politics"'.[88] As one example among many, to illustrate Gramsci's distinction between art or literature in the narrower sense and 'culture' in the socio-political sense, we can single out his remarks on Luigi Pirandello. Gramsci recognises his importance, although he says that it is in fact 'Pirandello's critico-historical sense', which 'may have led him, in the cultural field, to overcome and dissolve the old tradi-

---

80   Q8, p. 936; Gramsci 2011, Vol. 3, p. 233.

81   Francioni 1984, p. 86.

82   Q8, p. 936; Gramsci 2011, Vol. 3, p. 233.

83   Liguori and Voza 2009, p. 627.

84   Q8, p. 936; Gramsci 2011, Vol. 3, p. 233.

85   Q8, §125, p. 1015; Gramsci 2011, Vol. 3, p. 306.

86   Another point of reference for the British Cultural Studies, in particular for Raymond Williams's sociology of culture, as I have recently elaborated (Pohn-Lauggas 2017).

87   See Haug 2011, p. 125ff. The term *politica culturale* is translated as 'cultural policy' in the English critical edition, see Gramsci 2011, Vol. 3, p. 99, p. 126.

88   Q23, §7, p. 2193; Gramsci 1985, p. 122.

tional, conventional theatre'.[89] Pirandello is thus an intellectual, who is making an active intervention. But, is this connected to his artistic significance? Gramsci asks, 'Is he not more a critic of theatre than a poet, more a critic of culture than a poet ...?'[90] For Gramsci, there are 'two sets of facts' at stake here, 'one aesthetic (to do with pure art), the other politico-cultural (that is, frankly political)'.[91] This is the basis for a political understanding of the cultural as a field of hegemonic struggles; its non-reductionist analysis being part of a political project.

The analysis makes evident that Gramsci does not discard this part of the perspective by subsuming 'Past and Present' under the 'Encyclopaedic notions and cultural topics', nor does he consider questions of popular literature in a detached way. His studies on literature, its effects, the reasons for its dissemination, and so on, stand in the uniform light of the theory of hegemony, as well as the phenomena associated with the heading of 'Past and Present'. These are connected to the twin aims of the 'explication' of the past and the strategic 'analysis' of the present.

---

89   Q14, §15, p. 1672; Gramsci 1985, p. 142.
90   Ibid.
91   Q15, §38, p. 1793; Gramsci 1985, p. 109. See Seroni 1958.

CHAPTER 18

The 'Mummification of Culture' in Gramsci's *Prison Notebooks*

Robert Jackson

1   Introduction

In his writings, Antonio Gramsci has recourse to a constellation of biological terms and metaphors that reflect the organic sphere in the broad sense. This 'language of life' refers to bodies, cells, germs, arteries, the molecular, fermentation, growth, decay and decomposition, to name but a few recurrent concepts and images.[1] In his *Prison Notebooks*, despite a significant modification of his earlier use of these terms, Gramsci continues to inscribe his project, the elaboration of a 'philosophy of praxis',[2] in the complexities of this semantic field. Gramsci uses the terms life and death not simply to discuss the corporeality of an individual organism, but as a means to explain the capillary processes of 'molecular' transformation in the movement of history.[3] Exploring the terminology associated with life and death illustrates the diagnostic function played by these concepts in Gramsci's assessment of the past. Thus, Gramsci's analysis of different historical traditions and cultural phenomena separates healthy elements from those that are putrefied and cadaverous. In particular, Gramsci illuminates the dangerous situation where a rotten past masquerades as one that is actually alive, obscuring the lines of real development. This distinction between the dead and the 'germ of new life to be developed' is an important part of unravelling the inherited nightmare that can entrap the social forces that are capable of acting 'as a fulcrum for creating new history'.[4]

---

1   For a detailed chronological reading of the development of Gramsci's use of the 'language of life' particularly in his pre-prison writings, see Ciliberto 1989.

2   Following Gramsci, Peter Thomas outlines its components as 'absolute "historicism"', 'absolute immanence' and 'absolute humanism' (Q11, §27, Gramsci 1975, p. 1437; Gramsci 1971a, p. 465). For an extensive account, see Thomas 2009a, pp. 243–439.

3   For a discussion of the methodological importance of the 'molecular', particularly in conditions of modernity, for Gramsci's conceptions of knowledge, transformation and history, see Forenza 2009, pp. 551–5.

4   Q10.II, §59ii, Gramsci 1975, p. 1354; Gramsci 1995, p. 416.

Investigating this life-death nexus, I suggest that Gramsci develops an innovative conception of the 'mummification of culture', in order to account for the stubborn persistence of certain traditions in the anachronistic form of the 'living dead'. This concept of mummification explains the embalming process through which cultural formations that are valuable and appropriate when created become fossilised and anachronistic when repeated in new conditions.[5] Gramsci's use of the concept of mummification plays a significant role in explaining the predominantly passive constitution of the subaltern groups through wider cultural processes.[6] Gramsci's conception of the mummification of culture is a process that takes place both from above and below. The former, mummification from above, is associated with the orchestrated efforts of dominant groups to interrupt any development towards coherence of the traces of autonomous action by the subaltern groups. The latter, mummification from below, manifests itself in the 'intellectual laziness' that Gramsci connects with the phenomenon of 'Lorianism', the 'lack of critical spirit' that characterises certain intellectuals who rely on a quasi-scientific sociology.[7] This original contribution is further evidence of the fertility of Gramsci's thought for developing a critical appreciation of the past in order to engage with the problems of our present.

2   Origins of Mummification

The 'language of life' manifests itself from Gramsci's early thought onwards in a multitude of concepts, metaphors and images. Focusing primarily on Gramsci's

---

5   There has been very little analysis of mummification and associated terms in the literature. For a further study towards the treatment of this concept, see Jackson 2016a.

6   The partial availability of Gramsci's writings on subalternity in anglophone anthologies of his *Prison Notebooks* has contributed to a restricted image of Gramsci's category, e.g. in academic contexts where it often denotes an 'undifferentiated mass combination' incapable of speaking for itself (see Liguori 2015a, p. 120). For a criticism of this usage, arguing instead for a conception of subalternity as a 'phased development' of diverse capacities belonging to a hegemonic-subaltern pairing, see Green 2002. The analysis of subalternity in its expansive relationship with the dominant classes (see also Liguori and Voza 2009, entry *Subalterno, subalterni* by J.A. Buttigieg, pp. 826–30) has been one of many fruits of the season of philological Gramscian scholarship, particularly in Italy (see, for example, Cospito 2011a, 2011b, Francioni 2009, 2016, Frosini 2010a, Gramsci 2009).

7   'Lorianism' is the term that Gramsci uses to describe the ethically indulgent mind-set of certain Italian intellectuals (and by extension national culture), exemplified by Achille Loria. For a more detailed examination of the phenomenon, see Imbornone 2009, pp. 487–9.

pre-prison writings, in particular from the newspaper *L'Ordine Nuovo*,[8] Michele Ciliberto organises his study of Gramsci's use of this language through the conceptual coupling of 'discipline' and 'spontaneity'.[9] These concepts relate, on the one hand, to the 'processes of disintegration, organic disorder, and decomposition of bourgeois-capitalist society', and on the other, to the 'identification of the structural characteristics of a new "order", of a new human community, by a strong, conscious will'.[10] Despite Gramsci's immersion in the language of some of his early influences (Sorel, Gentile, Croce, etc.), Ciliberto argues that, even at this stage, we should not elide his use of this network of concepts with the generic notion of life found in the matrices of Bergsonian or Gentilian thought in the years preceding the First World War.[11] Ciliberto stresses the originality of Gramsci's position, arguing that his analyses of processes of decomposition and of creation represent a dual concept of life, 'mutually reinforcing' but without ever merging into a 'definitive univocal synthesis'.[12]

While it is possible to identify notions associated with 'élan vital',[13] both positively and negatively, in the pages of *L'Ordine Nuovo*,[14] Gramsci is critical from the outset of any generic opposition between life and form. Gramsci's conception of society as an organism with a fundamental internal antagonism leads him beyond the purview of a general crisis of the notion of form itself, understood as inadequate to the task of comprehending the boundless and chaotic complexities of life. Gramsci analyses the decomposition of a particular form, the old bourgeois-capitalist society that has become 'detached from life'.[15] However, he is also concerned with the task of locating new forms and institutions that have the potential to develop into a new order.[16] In this sense, the new element of life represents its own generative organising principle. At this time, Gramsci's writings focus on the internal economic-productive life of the factory councils. He identifies the councils as potential cells of the new

---

8   The weekly newspaper published by Gramsci and his associates in Turin during 1919–22 and 1924–25.

9   Ciliberto 1989, p. 680, my translation (here and below where no English text given).

10   Ibid.

11   Ciliberto 1989, p. 681.

12   Ciliberto 1989, p. 680.

13   Deriving from the philosophy of Henri Bergson, 'élan vital' is the creative principle in living beings, 'an *original impetus* of life' (Bergson 1911, p. 87).

14   For example, using 'vital impulse' (*slancio vitale*) as a synonym for the 'rhythm of progress of communist society' in Gramsci 1987, p. 238, '*Sindicati e Consigli*' (11 October 1919); Gramsci 1977, p. 100, 'Unions and Councils'. Note that the synonym is indicated by a comma that is missing in the English translation. Thanks to Francesca Antonini for this observation.

15   Ciliberto 1989, p. 681.

16   Ibid.

institutions of a communist society.[17] In summary, we find a theory of revolution with a negative moment of decay and decomposition. However, the criticism of the old world is not able in and of itself to produce an alternative. Counterposed to this, we have the identification of a new 'principle of life',[18] capable of producing new institutions. Ciliberto argues that interpreters generally place insufficient emphasis on this second element of Gramsci's conception: of life as a 'disciplined organism, intimately organised, structured according to internal principles of cohesion, of solidarity, of the unity between the whole and the individual parts'.[19]

It is evident that this theoretical framework is closely bound to Gramsci's experiences during the struggles of the factory councils in Turin. We need not rehearse the subsequent defeat of this movement and the rise and consolidation of fascism in Italy. However, Ciliberto notes that the 'language of life' does not disappear from Gramsci's writings after this period, but persists into his *Prison Notebooks*.[20] In fact, this language undergoes a development that is set within a wider perspective, and 'continues to develop a significant political and theoretical function, above all on the delicate and crucial terrain of the criticism of "(party) bureaucracy", and of the uncritical and unconscious processes of "standardisation" of the masses'.[21] In this chapter, I will restrict myself to studying a concept from the language of life that has an intimate relation with these contested processes of 'conformism', namely Gramsci's innovative conception of the 'mummification' of culture. For Gramsci, mummification plays a fundamental role in the wider cultural processes that accompany and facilitate the creation of bureaucratic personnel in political organisations. It is also a concept lies at the intersection of these processes of growth and decay, at the intersection between the principles of life and death.[22]

I will begin by examining some origins of the term in Gramsci's pre-prison writings. The concept of mummification appears in one of Gramsci's journalistic pieces in *Avanti!* from 4 January 1917, entitled 'The Dead That Speaks' (*Morto che parla*).[23] Here Gramsci excoriates a Torinese politician, Donato

---

17 Gramsci 1987, p. 238, '*Sindicati e Consigli*', Gramsci 1977, p. 100, 'Unions and Councils'.
18 Ciliberto 1989, p. 687.
19 Ciliberto 1989, p. 681.
20 Ciliberto 1989, p. 692.
21 Ibid.
22 Ciliberto 1989, p. 687.
23 Gramsci 1980, p. 681. The title refers to a symbol from '*La Smorfia Napoletana*' which is a popular method in Italy, traditionally associated with Naples, for 'translating' symbols in dreams into numbers for playing the lottery.

Bachi,[24] who falls out of favour but fails to acquiesce to his new situation. According to Gramsci, despite being a useless 'instrument' lacking the authority of an earlier time, Bachi continues to hawk his 'mummified carcass' around town in order to gain a hearing from beneath his political 'tombstone': 'A corpse circulates in civic life. Stenches of pestiferous stink reach the nostrils of those unfortunate enough to have to remain in its vicinity; but the corpse imperturbably *continues to speak and to write*'.[25] Gramsci links this theme, of the politically 'dead' politician whose body continues to have a putrefied after-life and will not remain buried, to the postwar crisis. He argues that these periods can lend an air of contemporaneity to redundant politicians that continue to play a role in civic life.[26] At this point, we might consider this phenomenon to be a colourful metaphor through which Gramsci adds polemical flavour to his writings, e.g. by his allusions to the 'corpse-like smell' of certain publications or political groupings.

Nevertheless, in the same issue of *Avanti!*, in a text entitled 'On the Exhibition at the *Circolo degli artisti*' (*Sull'esposizione al circolo degli artisti*), Gramsci also refers to a similar phenomenon attaching itself to language. In the context of the exhibition, he warns against confusing its vocabulary with 'language': 'The vocabulary is a museum of embalmed corpses, language is the vital insight that gives new form to these corpses, new life because it creates new relations, new periods in which single words regain an exact and current meaning'.[27] Gramsci's early writings deploy these numerous allusions to tombs, putrefaction, embalming, etc. in a particular theoretical manner to denote the effects of anachronistic forces, detached from life and history. He writes of corpse-like forces attacking the living, and, as a consequence, of the 'corpses that need to be buried in the political cemetery'.[28] A few years later, in his famous letter to Leon Trotsky on the Futurist art movement (8 September 1922), Gramsci uses the term mummification, or a related term 'fossilisation', to describe

---

24   Donato Bachi (1866–1952) was an attorney and well-known socialist figure in Turin prior to fascism, later founding an anti-fascist review with Camillo Olivetti called '*Tempi Nuovi*'.

25   Gramsci 1980, p. 681, my translation.

26   The reader can undoubtedly conjure her own contemporary examples of this phenomenon.

27   Gramsci 1980, p. 683, my translation. Cf. Gramsci's well-known passage in Q11, § 28: 'language is at the same time a living thing and a museum of fossils of life and civilisations' (Gramsci 1975, p. 1438; Gramsci 1971a, p. 450). On the other hand, contrast with Q12, § 2, where Gramsci discusses the importance for children to learn the 'dead' language of Latin, 'which can be treated as a corpse which returns continually to life' (Gramsci 1975, p. 1545; Gramsci 1971a, p. 38).

28   Gramsci 1980, p. 227, 'The Altar-boy' (*Il chierichino*) in *Avanti!* (31 March 1916).

the outmoded academic culture of Italy, as 'fossilised/mummified and distant from the masses of the people'.[29]

In each situation, Gramsci uses this language of the 'living dead' to analyse the anachronistic character of an element of the political situation. Gramsci is exploring modes of illuminating the complex dialectic of restoration and innovation that will later come to occupy a prominent place in his *Prison Note-books*.[30] Yet, in his pre-prison writings, Gramsci does not appear to address the full complexity of the problem of burying these troublesome corpses. By contrast, in his later thought, Gramsci regards the stubborn persistence of the 'living dead' as an issue that requires more than simply verbal exposure. We continue to find the language of life, death and mummification prominently in his prison writings, but they suggest that a more variegated solution is required to lay these 'undead' traditions to rest. This question relates to the development of Gramsci's conception of subalternity,[31] and to the problem of the emergence of the subaltern groups from their predominantly passive condition. As Peter Thomas observes, the notion of passivity in the *Notebooks* is 'analysed as a social relation [that] we must actively construct, in relation to other equally active social relations'.[32] I will now examine how the process of mummification plays a useful role in helping us to understand this construction, and the relatedness to history of a certain type of passive activity, or the apparently 'living' role played by 'dead' traditions.

3   Mummification in the *Prison Notebooks*

In the *Prison Notebooks*, Gramsci deploys the concept of the 'mummification' across a broad array of topics, ranging from Americanism and Fordism, intel-

---

29   Gramsci 2014a, p. 123. As the original of this letter has not yet been found, we cannot be cer-tain of the exact metaphor deployed here (see Derek Boothman's editorial note in Gramsci 2014a, p. 54, n. 36). However, it is also worth noting Filippo Tommaso Marinetti's force-ful comparison between Italian 'museums' and 'cemeteries' in the *Manifesto of Futurism* (1909).

30   Boothman's recent edition of Gramsci's pre-prison letters illustrates Gramsci's interest for Egyptology and the related imagery of mummies, e.g. his drawings of a sphinx and pyram-ids on a postcard from Ivanovo-Voznesensk (Gramsci 2014a, p. 125).

31   As Joseph Buttigieg points out, Gramsci 'recognised rather late in the course of his work [in the *Prison Notebooks*] the importance of the study of the specific characteristics of subalternity in the social and political order' (Liguori and Voza 2009, entry *Subalterno, subalterni* by J.A. Buttigieg, p. 826, my translation).

32   Thomas 2009a, p. 305.

lectuals and political parties, Italian culture, the study of philosophy, Catholicism, Taylorism and the mechanisation of work, and the 'Lorianism' of the monarchist newspaper editor G.A. Fanelli, among others.[33] Before investigating Gramsci's conception of the 'mummification of culture' in the *Notebooks*, I note the caution required to read the term 'culture' in an expansive sense. Culture, as Kate Crehan points out, is central to understanding the lived experience of a reality divided by class conflict.[34] This means moving beyond a narrow notion of the products of artistic creation, towards a sense of a grouping of 'the social elements that share the same mode of thinking or acting'.[35] It also means criticising the predominant anthropological sense of a bounded, and sometimes romanticised, entity, in favour a more historically dynamic conception of cultural transformation.[36] For Gramsci, culture is a complex and articulated notion of a 'world', 'sphere', 'field' or 'structure' of activity associated with organisational functions of differing valences.[37] It is an 'expression of society',[38] understood through an interrelated network of concepts in Gramsci's thought. These include, in particular, the struggle for hegemony, and, among others, the notions of language and of 'common sense'. The latter is a sedimented document of a conception of life and of morality, relatively rigid but also somewhat diffuse and malleable, which is shared across social layers or spatial locations.[39] 'Moreover', as Gramsci says, 'common sense is a collective noun, like religion: there is not just one common sense, for that too is a product of history and a part of the historical process'.[40] With these precisions in mind, I will now trace the way Gramsci applies the concept of 'mummification' in different contexts: to workers, to political parties, to social groups, to the various manifestations of 'common sense', and to 'culture'. While these contexts vary quite significantly, I will suggest that they represent 'translatable' aspects of a unitary phenomenon.

---

33 For a full list of the 11 appearances of mummification in the *Notebooks*, and in the *Dizionario gramsciano* (under the entries for 'Arrogance of the party' (*Boria del partito*), 'Europe', 'Mechanicism', 'Internal politics', 'Psychology', 'Represented/representatives', and 'Weber, Max'), see Jackson 2016a, pp. 208–10.

34 Crehan 2002, p. 71.

35 Q11, § 12, Gramsci 1975, p. 1376; Gramsci 1971a, p. 324.

36 For an important confrontation of Gramsci's notion of culture with anthropological thought more generally, see Crehan 2002.

37 For a concise introduction to the concept of 'culture' in the *Prison Notebooks*, see Baratta 2009, pp. 190–4.

38 Q9, § 57, Gramsci 1975, p. 1130, my translation.

39 Q24, § 4, Gramsci 1975, p. 2271; Gramsci 1985, p. 421.

40 Q11, § 12, Gramsci 1975, p. 1378; Gramsci 1971a, pp. 325–6.

3.1   *Taylorism, Americanism and Fordism*

The first appearance of the term 'mummification' in the *Prison Notebooks*, in November 1930,[41] appears during Gramsci's discussion of the American industrialists' collective attempts to 'create, with unprecedented speed and a consciousness of purpose unique in history, a new type of worker and of man'.[42] Gramsci investigates the efforts of these industrialists to preserve a 'social passivity' among the workers by regulating their private lives, and thus their 'morality'. However, discussing the rationalisation of the work process under Taylorism, Gramsci says:

> Once the process of adaptation has been completed, the brain of the worker, in reality, does not become mummified but rather reaches a state of complete freedom. Physical movement becomes totally mechanical; the memory of the skill, reduced to simple gestures repeated with rhythmic intensity, 'makes its home' inside the bundles of muscles and nerves, leaving the brain free for other occupations.[43]

Thus, the concept of 'mummification' first appears in the *Notebooks* during a discussion of its absence.[44] Gramsci notes that the brains of workers do not succumb to mummification under the conditions of the mechanisation of manual labour. Quite the opposite, he argues that, having overcome the 'crisis of adaption' to these conditions, workers' brains tend towards a free state. Moreover, given the unsatisfying nature of their work, this situation raises the potential that they will reject the dominant modes of social conformism. Industrialists like Henry Ford were well aware of these social consequences. Gramsci's reflections indicate the important role that industrial labour plays in his conception of a new way of life in which culture does not suffer the blight of 'mummification'. The significance of the new industrial methods of Fordism and Taylorism was that they swept away 'the old that is not yet buried', albeit in the service of instituting 'wider margins of social passivity'.[45] However, for Gramsci, the coercive conformism associated with the methods of Fordism is not the

---

41   I use the chronology of notes in the *Notebooks* from recent scholarship in Cospito 2011b, p. 898.

42   Q4, §52, Gramsci 1975, p. 489; Gramsci 2011, Vol. 2, p. 215.

43   Q4, §52, Gramsci 1975, pp. 492–3; Gramsci 2011, Vol. 2, p. 219.

44   The passage quoted here is substantially unchanged in its second version (Q22, §12, Gramsci 1975, p. 2170; Gramsci 1971a, p. 309), which is also one of the final appearances of the term in the *Notebooks* (second half 1934 from July/August).

45   Q4, §52, Gramsci 1975, p. 491; Gramsci 2011, Vol. 2, p. 218.

only type available to us, as he intimates through his considerations of the early phases of the Soviet project.[46]

3.2   *Bureaucracy and Political Parties*

In the second appearance of the term, in December 1931, Gramsci turns his attention to the field of political parties, arguing: 'One of the most important questions regarding political parties is their "opportuneness" or "rightness for the times"; that is to say, the question of how they react against "habitude" and the tendency to become mummified and anachronistic'.[47] This is an example of the development of Gramsci's use of the 'language of life', identified earlier by Ciliberto, moving onto the 'delicate and crucial terrain of the criticism of "(party) bureaucracy"'.[48] The 'mummification' of a political party is the concrete expression of its separation from history. It is synonymous with the severing of the organic connection between the party and the social forces that provided it with its social base.[49] 'Mummification' is therefore a feature of parties that are incapable of adapting to 'new epochs or historical phases'.[50] As such, they are 'unable to develop in accordance with the ensemble of the relations of force [and therefore with congruous forces] in their particular country or in the international sphere'.[51] However, the phenomenon of mummification does not affect equally all elements of the 'collective organism' of the party:

> In this analysis, one must make distinctions: the social group; the mass of the party; the bureaucracy or general staff of the party. The latter is the most dangerous in terms of habitude: if it organizes itself as a separate body, compact and independent, the party will end up being anachronistic. This is what brings about the crises of parties that sometimes suddenly lose their historical social base and find the ground taken from under their feet.[52]

---

46   Interestingly, this is another example of Gramsci's reflections on mummification appearing in close proximity to his critical engagement with Leon Trotsky (Q4, §52, Gramsci 1975, p. 489; Q22, §11, Gramsci 1975, p. 2164).

47   Q7, §77, Gramsci 1975, p. 910; Gramsci 2011, Vol. 3, p. 209.

48   Ciliberto 1989, p. 692.

49   This process is related to Gramsci's notion of the 'arrogance of the party' (*boria del partito*), the substitution of conceit for 'concrete facts' developed from Giambattista Vico's 'conceit of nations' (*boria delle nazioni*) (Q14, §70, Gramsci 1975, p. 1732; Gramsci 1971a, p. 151). See also La Porta 2009, p. 79.

50   Q7, §77, Gramsci 1975, p. 910; Gramsci 2011, Vol. 3, p. 209.

51   Ibid.

52   Ibid.

In the second version of the note above, from Notebook 13 (May 1932–November 1933), Gramsci describes the bureaucracy as 'the most dangerous hidebound and conservative force', which, if allowed to solidify as a caste, voids the party of its social content.[53] In his own time, Gramsci found the political parties of France to be particularly ripe for this type of analysis. Having been 'spawned by the [17]89[54] revolution and subsequent movements',[55] Gramsci declares that the French parties 'are all mummified and anachronistic – historical-political documents of the various phases of French history'.[56] Thus, Gramsci does not simply address the issue of the creation of bureaucratic personnel, but uses the concept of mummification as a means of linking the processes of bureaucratisation to wider socio-cultural phenomena. Gramsci's use of the term in subsequent appearances fleshes out these internal connections in his conception of mummification by addressing questions of language, Italian culture, the philosophy of praxis, and religion.

3.3   Political Terminology

One particularly revealing appearance of the term mummification, in a note entitled 'Political terminology. Theorists, doctrinaires, abstractionists, etc.' (Q8, § 28, January/February 1932), illuminates the conservative aspect of Gramsci's concept of 'common sense'. Here, sandwiched between a discussion of 'Conservation and innovation' (Q8, § 27) and 'Good sense and common sense' (Q8, § 29), Gramsci describes the process by which certain terms acquire a negative aspect:

> In ordinary language, 'theorist' is used in a pejorative sense, like 'doctrinaire' or, better still, like 'abstractionist.' It has suffered the same fate as the technical-philosophical term 'idealist,' which has come to mean 'head in the clouds,' etc. It is no accident that certain words have acquired this pejorative connotation. It has to do with a reaction by common sense against certain cultural degenerations, etc. But 'common sense' in turn has been the agent of philistinism; it has mummified a justified reaction into a permanent attitude, into an intellectual laziness that is as degenerative and repulsive as the phenomenon it sought to combat. 'Good sense'

---

53   Q13, § 23, Gramsci 1975, p. 1604; Gramsci 1971a, p. 211.
54   The English translation appears to contain a misprint, reading '1889' (Gramsci 2011, Vol. 3, p. 209).
55   Q7, § 77, Gramsci 1975, p. 910; Gramsci 2011, Vol. 3, p. 209.
56   Q13, § 23, Gramsci 1975, p. 1604; Gramsci 1971a, p. 211.

has reacted, but 'common sense' has embalmed the reaction and made out of it a 'theoretical,' 'doctrinaire,' and 'idealistic' canon.[57]

In this context, the process of mummification is the degeneration of an initially healthy reaction of 'common sense'. It takes the form of a resistance to speculative intellectual abstraction, which sinks into a generic anti-intellectualism when repeated in changed circumstances. For Gramsci, the embalming process is stubborn, but does not appear to be inevitable. It relates to the introduction of a third term, 'good sense', into the process of reaction. Gramsci tends to associate 'good sense' with applying the 'power of rational concentration', even calling it 'the healthy nucleus that exists in "common sense"', the part of it which should be 'made more unitary and coherent'.[58] The reaction of 'common sense' can be 'justified', but, if allowed to embalm 'good sense', 'common sense' can also become an 'agent of philistinism', equally bad as the problem it sought to rectify.[59] It is therefore necessary to study the historical conditions that allow mummification to take hold and endure. This leads Gramsci to incorporate his conception of mummification as an element of his wider project of generating adequate criterion of historical analysis.

3.4   *Italy and Germany*

In December 1932 (Q14, § 47), Gramsci reflects on the distinctive characteristics of Italian culture, discussing the polemical debates on the interpretation of the history of the peninsula between Benedetto Croce, the dominant figure in Italian neo-idealism, and the fascist historian Gioacchino Vólpe.[60] Gramsci remarks that it is an important and typical characteristic of the Italian politico-cultural situation that such a diversity of interpretations of the facts are possible.[61] Gramsci identifies a number of aspects of this phenomenon:

---

57   Q8, § 28, Gramsci 1975, p. 958; Gramsci 2011, Vol. 3, p. 254. Here, Gramsci's concern with the creation of a 'canon' strikes some resonances with more recent sociological thought, such as Pierre Bourdieu's analysis of the confrontation between 'canonized' and 'non-canonized' texts in the literary field (Bourdieu 1993, p. 34).

58   Q11, § 12, Gramsci 1975, p. 1380; Gramsci 1971a, p. 328.

59   For an orientation in the complex issue of the relationship between 'good sense' and 'common sense', see Liguori 2009a, pp. 89–90.

60   Gioacchino Vólpe (1876–1971) was a nationalist historian who joined the fascist movement, writing, among others, the book *L'Italia in cammino* (1927) to which Gramsci refers in this note.

61   The Italian case is close to unique, Gramsci suggests, with the possible exception of Spain, whose position in relation to Europe and Africa was a matter of interpretative controversy (Q14, § 47, Gramsci 1975, p. 1704).

1) the fact that the intellectuals are disaggregated, without hierarchy, without a centre of ideological and intellectual unification and central-isation, which is the result of a lack of homogeneity, compactness and 'national' character of the ruling class; 2) the fact that these discussions are, in reality, the perspective and the foundation of implicit political pro-grammes, that remain implicit, rhetorical, because the analysis of the past is not made objectively, but according to literary prejudices or of literary nationalism ... .[62]

The 'theorisation' of national policy in abstract forms by these different writers, without a corresponding group that is able to put these political differences into terms of 'effectivity', argues Gramsci, leaves 'real affairs' in the hands of spe-cialist functionaries.[63] These functionaries, despite their 'undoubted technical-professional bureaucratic' capabilities, are 'without a continuing connection to "public opinion", that is, the national life'.[64] This is therefore a concrete example of the important relationship for Gramsci, identified above, between the creation of bureaucratic personnel and wider cultural phenomena. Gram-sci makes a comparison between the situation in Italy and Wilhelmine Ger-many, but identifies a significant difference between the 'national life' of the two:

> That in Wilhelmine Germany, behind the bureaucracy, were the Junkers, a social class that was mummified and mutilated, while in Italy no such force exists: the Italian bureaucracy can be compared to the Papal bur-eaucracy, or better still, to the Chinese bureaucracy of the Mandarins. It was certainly in the interests of very specific groups (primarily the agri-cultural interests, followed by protected industry, etc.), but without a plan and a system, without continuity, on the basis, briefly put, of the 'spirit of combination' that was necessary to 'harmonise' the many contradictions of national life, which it will never seek itself to resolve organically and with a consistent approach.[65]

This note (Q14, §47), previously unpublished in the English anthologies, adds complexity to Gramsci's use of the term 'mummification', deployed when describing national situations that involve a complex fusion of the old and

---

62   Q14, §47, Gramsci 1975, p. 1704, my translation.
63   Q14, §47, Gramsci 1975, p. 1705.
64   Ibid.
65   Ibid.

the new. Gramsci uses the 'mummified and mutilated' state of the Junkers to describe their specific role in the national life of Germany.[66]

On the one hand, the Junkers are an anachronistic element of the internal relations of Germany, a symptom arising from the 'universalistic and supranational institution and ideology' of the Holy Roman Empire.[67] Relating to the work of Max Weber,[68] Gramsci notes that German industry developed within a 'semi-feudal integument',[69] which impeded the development of the organic bureaucratic personnel of the bourgeoisie through the Junker's 'virtual monopoly' on the 'directive-organisational functions in political society'.[70] In turn, this led to 'continual parliamentary crises' and a 'fragmentation of the liberal and democratic parties'.[71] On the other hand, Gramsci later (July/August 1934–February 1935) takes up Antonio Labriola's argument explaining the durability of the Junkers (Q19, § 24), regardless of their anachronistic relation to the development of the power of industrial capitalism. For Labriola, the Junkers represent a kind of 'façade' that is useful for the bourgeoisie in order to disguise its own 'real domination'.[72]

Despite their declining economic power, the Junkers in Wilhelmine Germany retain a residual strength as a 'priestly-military caste'.[73] While incapable of turning back the clock to create a new German aristocracy, their mummified state gives them a strong sense of 'being an independent social group'.[74] In turn, this status makes them ripe for the crystallisation of bureaucratic cadre. By contrast, the configuration of national life in Italy, while sharing some historical similarities with Germany in terms of the cosmopolitan function of its intellectuals, results in a kind of 'bureaucratic monarchy', in which the King forms the 'first official' of a bureaucracy, which is 'the only "unitary" force in the country, permanently "unitary"'.[75] The concept of 'mummification' thus performs its

---

66   The Junkers, according to Gramsci, 'were the traditional intellectuals of the German industrialists, but retained special privileges and a strong consciousness of being an independent social group, based on the fact that they held considerable economic power over the land' (Q12, §1, Gramsci 1975, p. 1526; Gramsci 1971a, p. 19).

67   Q12, §1, Gramsci 1975, p. 1526; Gramsci 1971a, p. 18.

68   In particular, Weber's text, *Parliament and Government in Germany under a New Political Order* [*Parlament und Regierung im neugeordneten Deutschland*] (1918).

69   Note that there is another biological association here, in the sense of 'integument' as the durable outer layer of a plant or animal.

70   Q12, §1, Gramsci 1975, p. 1526; Gramsci 1971a, p. 19.

71   Q12, §1, Gramsci 1975, p. 1527; Gramsci 1971a, p. 19, n. *.

72   Q19, §24, Gramsci 1975, p. 2033; Gramsci 1971a, p. 83.

73   Q12, §1, Gramsci 1975, p. 1526; Gramsci 1971a, p. 19.

74   Ibid.

75   Q14, §47, Gramsci 1975, p. 1705.

part in illuminating the reciprocal relations between bureaucracy and wider culture in Gramsci's survey of different national configurations.

3.5   Philosophy and Popular Culture

It would be misleading to give the impression that, through his use of the term mummification, Gramsci's aim was to develop simply a more precise analysis of different historical situations. Throughout his entire body of writings, Gramsci is not content to describe the past (or the present) synchronically, but is interested in its transformation. In June/July 1933, at the beginning of the third phase of his prison writing,[76] under the thematic title of 'Introduction to the study of philosophy' (Q15, § 61), Gramsci discusses the 'process of "hierarchical" unification of world civilisation'.[77] Within this process, there is also a process of unification of European culture that, he says, 'has culminated in Hegel and the critique of Hegelianism'.[78] Gramsci addresses the personification of this cultural process in the intellectuals, contrasting it with popular culture, because, in this context, 'one cannot speak of critical elaboration and process of development'.[79]

According to Gramsci, however, the 'disintegration of Hegelianism' marks the opening of a 'new cultural process, different in character from its predecessors, a process in which practical movement and theoretical thought are united (or are trying to unite through a struggle that is both theoretical and practical)'.[80] The birth of this new cultural movement is not a discrete process, a smooth transition from one great work to another, but a passage and a transition, with all the complex disarray of the old and the experimental fumbling of new beginnings:

> It is not important that this movement had its origins in mediocre philosophical works, or at best, in works that were not philosophical masterpieces. What matters is that a new way of conceiving the world and man is born and that this conception is no longer reserved to the great intel-

---

76   See Frosini 2003a, pp. 23–9, and Thomas 2009a, pp. 113–16, for a discussion of the periodisation of the writing of Gramsci's Notebooks.

77   Q15, § 61, Gramsci 1975, p. 1825; Gramsci 1971a, p. 416.

78   Q15, § 61, Gramsci 1975, p. 1826; Gramsci 1971a, p. 416.

79   Q15, § 61, Gramsci 1975, p. 1826; Gramsci 1971a, p. 417. Except in the sense, as Gramsci notes, of the 'reciprocal translatability' between this 'theoretical and speculative' cultural process (classical German philosophy) and its '"practical" confirmation' in the 'real activity' of French politics. On this central thematic issue in Gramsci's writings, see also Frosini 2010b.

80   Q15, § 61, Gramsci 1975, p. 1826; Gramsci 1971a, p. 417.

lectuals, to professional philosophers, but tends rather to become a popular, mass phenomenon, with a concretely world-wide character, capable of modifying (even if the result includes hybrid combinations) popular thought and mummified popular culture.[81]

Here, the appearance of the term mummification takes on new dimensions in its association with the world-historical task of the philosophy of praxis, the elaboration of a new culture and, ultimately, a new form of civilisation. In this sense, Gramsci regards the philosophy of praxis as 'the result and the crowning point of all previous history'.[82] In contrast to the old and disintegrating cultural process, this new cultural movement is a 'mass phenomenon', which must elaborate its conception of the world, not only intellectually, but also as 'popular thought'. This returns us, via philosophy, to a whole series of interconnected problems, including those of 'common sense' and 'good sense' explored above, that Gramsci summarises here in his reference to the modification of 'mummified popular culture'.

Gramsci is attentive to the fact that the philosophy of praxis is not the only product of the critique of Hegelianism. Most significantly, the 'modern idealism' of Croce represents an alternative trajectory, albeit one that has assimilated elements of the philosophy of praxis, and which is an important interlocutor for the renovation of the philosophy of praxis itself.[83] However, according to Gramsci, it is only the philosophy of praxis, as 'absolute historicism or absolute humanism',[84] which can realise the aforementioned unity of theory and practice.[85] For Gramsci, this new character of concretely modifying popular thought cannot but be related to the phenomenon of religion (understood in a broad sense). As we shall see shortly, Gramsci's analysis of mummification also draws him towards the topic of religion more narrowly conceived, in his consideration of the Catholic Church. First, however, I will examine his use of

---

81   Ibid.

82   Ibid.

83   Gramsci's reflections on Croce's historicism form one part of the elaboration of his own distinctive understanding of historicism. These critical reflections constitute tentative sketches of a mooted wider project to produce an *anti-Croce* (Q8, §235, Gramsci 1975, p. 1088; Gramsci 2011, Vol. 3, p. 378). See also Liguori 2015b, p. 133.

84   'Absolute historicism' indicates Gramsci's inheritance and extension of prior historicist traditions, '"translating" their speculative claims' into a political form, self-aware of its own emergence, while also historicising the 'realm of conceptuality', locating it in an 'always active attempt … to modify social activity in general' (Thomas 2015b, p. 109).

85   By this means, Gramsci seeks to chart a course that is capable of avoiding both the pitfalls of speculative philosophy and the mechanistic and positivistic degenerations of Marxism.

the notion of mummification to assess the 'real content' of the ideology of the Jacobins, and their own concrete historical modification of culture.

3.6   The Philosophy of Praxis and Jacobinism

In his reflections in Q16, §9,[86] entitled *Some problems for the study of the development of the philosophy of praxis*, Gramsci considers the philosophy of praxis as 'a moment of modern culture',[87] or as he elaborates further, 'a diffuse atmosphere, which has modified old ways of thinking through actions and reactions which are neither apparent nor immediate'.[88] He takes up again the aforementioned theme of the philosophy of praxis's enrichment and rejuvenation of other cultural currents. On the one hand, various tendencies, represented by figures such as 'Croce, Gentile, Sorel, Bergson even, pragmatism', subsume, both explicitly and implicitly, elements of the philosophy of praxis.[89] This is one aspect of, what he calls, a 'double revision' of the philosophy of praxis.[90] On the other hand, Gramsci believes that the 'so-called orthodoxy' of Marxism, engaging with and reacting against the 'religious transcendentalism' that prevails among popular groups, has identified itself with 'traditional materialism'. This second revision leads towards a vulgarisation of Marxism, due to the suture of this 'orthodoxy' with certain positivist influences. From this discussion, Gramsci suggests a consistent development of the path pioneered by Antonio Labriola. This would enable the philosophy of praxis, which is an 'independent and original philosophy which contains in itself the element of a further development', to become 'from an interpretation of history, a general philosophy'.[91]

Towards the end of this note, Gramsci returns to the 'complex and delicate' question of the development of the philosophy of praxis, placing it within the context of the 'elaboration of all modern historicist doctrines', during the 'period of the Restoration' (circa 1815–48).[92] Gramsci traces in this period the

---

86   Written approximately between June/July 1932 and the second half of 1934 (from July/August).

87   Q16, §9, Gramsci 1975, p. 1854; Gramsci 1971a, p. 388. Gramsci's use of the term 'moment' is polysemic, combining the meanings of time, aspect, and force, as the editors of the latter have noted (Gramsci 1971a, p. 388, n. 17).

88   Q16, §9, Gramsci 1975, p. 1856; Gramsci 1971a, p. 391.

89   Q16, §9, Gramsci 1975, p. 1854; Gramsci 1971a, p. 389. Interestingly, Gramsci appears foremost to valorise the implicit influence. Thus, he says, 'the most important study, it seems to me, should be that of Bergsonian philosophy and of pragmatism, in order to find out to what extent certain of their positions would be inconceivable without the historical link of the philosophy of praxis' (Q16, §9, Gramsci 1975, p. 1856; Gramsci 1971a, p. 391).

90   Q16, §9, Gramsci 1975, p. 1854; Gramsci 1971a, p. 389.

91   Q16, §9, Gramsci 1975, p. 1855; Gramsci 1971a, p. 390.

92   Q16, §9, Gramsci 1975, p. 1863; Gramsci 1971a, p. 398. The latter is in fact a misnomer, since

formation of ideological currents that persist into his own time.[93] Moreover, he places the philosophy of praxis in its historical context:

> The historicist theories of the Restoration opposed the eighteenth century ideologies, abstract and utopistic, which remain alive as proletarian philosophy, ethics and politics, particularly widespread in France up to 1870. The philosophy of praxis was opposed to these eighteenth century popular conceptions as a mass philosophy in all their forms, from the most infantile to that of [Pierre-Joseph] Proudhon.[94]

Gramsci identifies the philosophy of praxis as an element within this historical situation, in which it acts and reacts against competing 'living' tendencies of thought. Nevertheless, he also shows how it is capable of moving beyond the limited and partial positions of other tendencies:

> If the conservative historicists, theorists of the old, are well placed to criticise the utopian character of the mummified Jacobin ideologies, philosophers of praxis are better placed to appreciate the real and not abstract value that Jacobinism had as an element in the creation of the new French nation (that is to say as a fact of circumscribed activity in specific circumstances and not as something ideologised) ... .[95]

The continuing importance of mummification in this context is notable, as a means of diagnosing the distance that has opened up between the 'real' and 'abstract' values of particular ideologies. The concept plays a role in determining the specificity of the absolute form of 'historicism', which is able to explain not only the past, but also 'to explain and justify historically itself as well'.[96] Elaborated through the philosophy of praxis, this 'total liberation from any form of abstract "ideologism"', according to Gramsci, portends 'the real conquest of the historical world, the beginnings of a new civilisation'.[97]

---

this period did not restore the old regime, but represented a temporary equilibrium of a new 'alignment of forces' that crumbled in the face of the 1848 revolutions.

93   For example, he analyses the waning of Papal power and the organisation of new forces, such as the Catholic Action. Elsewhere he describes this movement as a reaction to prevent 'mass apostasy' (Q20, §2, Gramsci 1975, p. 2086).

94   Q16, §9, Gramsci 1975, p. 1863; Gramsci 1971a, p. 398.

95   Q16, §9, Gramsci 1975, p. 1864; Gramsci 1971a, p. 399.

96   Ibid.

97   Ibid.

3.7   Adaptation and the Catholic Church

Gramsci returns to the concept of mummification in a note entitled *Integral Catholics, Jesuits, Modernists* (Q20, § 4),[98] in which he discusses the internal conflict within the Catholic Church between these three factions.[99] For Gramsci, this conflict had 'unbalanced' the church politically, because of a push to the right in its struggle against modernising tendencies. This over-reaction necessitated a re-alignment that could 're-endow it with a flexible political form, not constrained by doctrinally rigid positions, but allowing a wide-ranging freedom of manoeuvre'.[100] However, in view of the heterogeneous nature of these forces and their modes of organisation, steering such a course was not a simple question and required the deployment of variegated methods.

While these conflicts are of interest in their own right, Gramsci also develops an analysis of the adaptability of organisations that is of wider relevance. Thus, we find him interrogating the Catholic Church's oft-proclaimed possession of 'inexhaustible virtues of adaptation and development'.[101] Gramsci enumerates three 'decisive points' in the 'life of the Church': the schism in the Church 'between East and West', the Reformation and Counter-Reformation, and the impact of the French Revolution.[102] According to Gramsci, the first two represent, respectively, forms of territorial and cultural separation:

> [T]he third was that of the French Revolution (liberal-democratic Reform) which forced the Church to take up a yet more rigid stance and to assume the mummified shape of a formalistic and absolutist organism whose nominal head is the pope, with theoretically 'autocratic' powers, which in reality are very few because the whole system hangs together only by virtue of the rigidity typical of a paralytic.[103]

Through his analysis of the efforts of the Church to maintain its unity, waging internal and external struggles, Gramsci draws important lessons for the way in which collective organisms can enter a state of paralysis, taking the 'mum-

---

98   Written between July/August 1934 – first months (approx.) of 1935.

99   For an account of these groups, see the chapter by Takahiro Chino in the present volume.

100   Q20, § 4ii, Gramsci 1975, pp. 2092–3; Gramsci 1995, p. 81.

101   Q20, § 4ii, Gramsci 1975, p. 2093; Gramsci 1995, p. 82. In translation, we lose perhaps the Machiavellian overtones of the Italian 'virtù'.

102   Q20, § 4ii, Gramsci 1975, pp. 2093–4; Gramsci 1995, p. 82.

103   Q20, § 4ii, Gramsci 1975, p. 2094; Gramsci 1995, p. 83.

mified shape of a formalistic and absolutist organism'.[104] At the same time, Gramsci adopts a forensic approach in assessing the persistent efforts of the Church as an organism developing within the context of congruent forces. It is the third 'decisive point' of the French revolution that appears to pose the most serious challenge to Catholicism, driving it towards a mummified state. Overall, Gramsci gives a pessimistic prognosis of the opportunities for the Church to adapt itself, since, as he argues, the 'entire society in which the Church moves and is able to evolve has this tendency to become rigid'.[105] It is however, an important example from which the philosophy of praxis must learn if it is to be successful in its task of modifying 'popular thought and mummified popular culture'.

3.8   *Fascism and G.A. Fanelli*

The final appearance of the term 'mummification' in the Notebooks is found in Q28, §17, written during the first months of 1935. It occurs in the context of a discussion of G.A. Fanelli,[106] described by Joseph Buttigieg as 'a prominent voice of the traditionalist, anti-modern, and monarchist wing of the Fascist movement'.[107] Of significance here, as Buttigieg notes, is Fanelli's book *L'Artigianato: Sintesi di un'economia corporativa* (1929), which 'sets forth the notion that the system of small industries as operated by the Italian artisan class embodied the basic principles of corporative economics advocated by Fascist ideologues'.[108] Gramsci's reflections on Fanelli's book address the categories of 'Past and present', 'Americanism', and 'Lorianism'.[109] He undermines Fanelli's extreme provincial reaction against 'American' industrial production by pointing out that artisanal work in Italy is also a form of standardised mass production:

> Big industry seeks to standardise the taste of a continent or the whole world for a season or for a few years; handicrafts undergo an already exist-

---

104   It would be worth exploring this phenomenon further with reference to Gramsci's concept of 'phantasmagorical being' in his notes on fetishism as a cultural problem, see Q15, §13, Gramsci 1975, pp. 1769–71; Gramsci 1971a, p. 187, n. 83.

105   Ibid.

106   Giuseppe Attilio Fanelli (c. 1895–1985) – sources differ on his date of birth, which is listed as 1893, 1895, 1899, by the Italian Chamber of Deputies, English critical edition of the *Notebooks*, and Italian Central State Archives respectively – was an ultra-conservative editor-in-chief of *Il secolo fascista* (1931–35).

107   Gramsci 2011, Vol. 3, p. 555.

108   Gramsci 2011, Vol. 2, p. 693.

109   Q28, §17, Gramsci 1975, p. 2336.

ing and mummified standardisation in a valley or a corner of the world. A handicraft of arbitrary and constant 'individual creation' is so restricted that it only includes the artists in the strict sense of the word (and further: only the 'great' artists that become 'prototypes' for their pupils).[110]

Thus, for Gramsci, the attempted distinction by Fanelli between modern industry and handicraft production is, to a certain extent, simply a matter of scale. Moreover, the two systems are inter-linked, since the latter relies on the tools and materials produced by big industry. The difference, pointed out by Gramsci, is that the standardisation of handicrafts, far from being a model of 'pure' creativity, is in fact of a mummified form.

Of interest, for our purposes, is that 'mummification' applies here to the process of standardisation itself, and is associated with the creation of taste, of inclinations and dispositions. We can detect resonances here with the field of concerns of sociological thinkers like Pierre Bourdieu, in terms of the study of taste and dispositions.[111] For Gramsci's wider project, this is a problem related to the struggle between different historical types of conformism, and the normative assessment of them in terms of a critical notion of progress.[112] In the context of a conflict within the fascist movement between Fanelli and Gentile,[113] they also take on an added relevance by revealing fractures within the fascist project and its unstable hybrid of modernist and conservative tendencies.

4   Mummification from above and below

Building now on the above analysis, I would suggest that Gramsci's conception of mummification incorporates two elements. The first I will refer to as mummification from above, imposed by dominant groups in order to maintain their position. This includes the uses of the term involving conservative social milieux, such as the Junkers in Germany, from which a certain type of bureaucratic strata are crystallised. In the process of the bureaucratisation of an organisation, the mummification of culture appears to constitute a cultural phenomenon, a wider atmosphere, providing the conditions for the selection

---

110 Q28, §17, Gramsci 1975, p. 2336, my translation.
111 For a contribution to the comparative analysis of Gramsci and Bourdieu, see Jackson 2016b.
112 See Q11, §12, Gramsci 1975, p. 1376; Gramsci 1971a, p. 324.
113 For the scandal surrounding Fanelli's attack on Gentile's philosophy, see Q8, §16, Gramsci 1975, p. 947; Gramsci 2011, Vol. 3, p. 243.

of a priesthood-like caste of intellectuals.[114] It forms a field in which this caste is able to develop, what Gramsci refers to as, an 'esprit de corps'.[115] As we have seen above, the orchestration by the dominant groups of the interruption of the coherence of the autonomy of subaltern groups is a complex and variegated process. Mummification from above also refers to the processes of standardisation that take place in unhealthy forms. I would suggest that there is a close connection between the notion of mummification and that of passivity in Gramsci's thought. Gramsci sees this in the coercive imposition of a 'social passivity', such as that which is engendered by Americanism.[116] This cultural phenomenon forms a part of the complex puzzle by which the dominant social forces are able to obstruct the healthy development of new historical and political initiatives.

The second element of mummification, emerging from below, is associated with the 'mental' or 'intellectual laziness' of certain intellectuals that are associated with the subaltern groups. This is associated with the phenomenon of 'Lorianism', the 'lack of critical spirit' exemplified by Achille Loria. Loria displays, among other traits, a lack of coherence and a 'softness and ethical indulgence in the field of scientific-cultural activity'.[117] This represents for Gramsci some of the worst aspects 'of the mentality of a group of Italian intellectuals *and then* of the national culture'.[118] These intellectuals were, on the one hand, through their 'absence of restraint and criticism',[119] a cause of the poor formation of national culture, and, on the other hand, a reflection of the mummified state of Italian 'national life' itself. Despite making this analytical distinction, in actuality there is a constitutive interpenetration of these two forms of mummification. One conditions the other: the 'mental laziness' of Lorianism has been fomented by the dispersion wrought by the dominant groups, while the mummification of culture is able to achieve purchase on the life of the nation for as long as the subaltern groups are unable to develop a more coherent leadership.

As mentioned above, I have restricted myself in this chapter to examining the concept of mummification, but we can perhaps use this as a lens through which to comment on the development of the 'language of life' in Gramsci's

---

114   A further study might be possible considering the connection of this phenomenon to Gramsci's conception of 'organic centralism', see Q4, §33, Gramsci 1975, p. 452; Gramsci 2011, Vol. 2, p. 173.

115   Q12, §1, Gramsci 1975, p. 1515; Gramsci 1971a, p. 7.

116   Q4, §52, Gramsci 1975, p. 491; Gramsci 2011, Vol. 2, p. 218.

117   Q28, Gramsci 1975, p. 2321.

118   Ibid.

119   Q1, §25, Gramsci 1975, p. 22; Gramsci 2011, Vol. 1, p. 116.

thought. Previously, Gramsci appeared to combat the problem of the 'living dead' in terms of verbal exposure. We now have, as Ciliberto points out, a more developed critical analysis of mummification that addresses the formation of party bureaucracy and processes of standardisation. These considerations place many of Gramsci's most familiar passages in a new light. We might mention Gramsci's famous dictum in the *Notebooks*, referring to the modern 'crisis of authority' and the detachment of the masses 'from their traditional ideologies': 'The crisis consists precisely in the fact that the old is dying and the new cannot be born; in this interregnum a great variety of *morbid* symptoms appear'.[120] The 'language of life' provides key tools to understand this relationship between the past and the present, by explaining the past as a 'complex of the living and the dead'.[121]

5   De-mummification?

Gramsci's conception of the 'mummification of culture' may have a broader significance in relation to the important theme of 'translation' and 'translatability' within the *Prison Notebooks*.[122] It is plausible to conceive the process of mummification being connected to the blockage or seizing up of 'organic and thoroughgoing' processes of translation between different cultural paradigms,[123] which allows the philosophy of praxis to conduct a 'reciprocal "reduction," a passage from one to the other and vice versa'.[124] Reversing this logic, we might speculate, beyond the letter of Gramsci's texts, that the de-mummification of culture is a condition for the healthy development of historical initiative, described by Gramsci in terms of a cathartic movement.[125] In this process, the subaltern groups pass from their position as an 'object' in history to become a protagonist, or the authors of a new historical epoch.[126]

---

120   Q3, § 34, Gramsci 1975, p. 311; Gramsci 1971a, p. 275, my italics.

121   Q10.II, § 41xiv, Gramsci 1975, pp. 1325–6; Gramsci 1995, p. 374.

122   For Gramsci, 'translation' is a process that takes place between not only natural languages, or even different (national) cultural discourses, but through the 'interposition of the structural aspect of a society' that 'mediates, and maybe complicates, the task of translation' (Boothman 2010, pp. 122–3).

123   Q11, § 47, Gramsci 1975, p. 1468; Gramsci 1995, p. 307.

124   Q3, § 48, Gramsci 1975, p. 331; Gramsci 2011, Vol. 2, p. 51.

125   See Coutinho 2009, pp. 105–7. Note also that Gramsci's development of the term 'catharsis' is 'translated' from his analysis of Canto X of Dante's *Inferno*, wherein it is the life/death status of Cavalcante's son Guido that is the source of his torment, see Rosengarten 1986.

126   Q11, § 12, Gramsci 1975, p. 1388; Gramsci 1971a, p. 337.

Gramsci does not explicitly refer to such a concept, but if the philosophy of praxis is to be able to modify mummified forms of culture, this suggests that the desired product is a de-mummified form of culture and civilisation. Furthermore, the diagnosis performed by Gramsci's concept of mummification helps to renovate the philosophy of praxis through processes of 'translation', a precondition for unpacking the metaphors that are necessary for his critical project.[127] Rethinking these 'mythical' pathways to produce new critical categories requires the creation of a system of 'living philology' that can move towards embodying an organic relationship between theory and practice.[128]

Articulating such a collective complex requires, for Gramsci, the 'organic coalescence' of political parties 'with the intimate (economic-productive) life of the masses themselves' resulting in a standardisation of popular feeling which is no long 'mechanical and causal', but on that has become 'conscious and critical'.[129] We can think of the quality of this system in terms of 'plasticity': being rigid enough to be historically effective and yet sufficiently adaptable in order to resist ossification and anachronism. These constitute elements of a continuous criticism that Gramsci deems necessary for the successful elaboration of the philosophy of praxis. By these experimental means, Gramsci proposes to advance a new hegemony in the concrete organisational form of the collective 'organism' of the 'modern Prince'.[130]

6   Conclusion

Gramsci's analysis of the mummification of culture helps to advance a wider explanation of the largely passive condition of the subaltern groups within society. The concept of mummification plays an important role in articulating the intimate relationship between the dialectical poles of hegemony and subalternity. It plays a critical function by making an incision between forms of culture that are historically opportune and those that are anachronistic, the reactionary form of the 'living dead'. As Marcus Green has argued, 'Gramsci's investigation of subalternity is founded upon a transformative praxis that

---

127   In Gramsci's framework, the significance of metaphors is their ability to express previous research on practical political problems in summarised form.

128   Q11, § 25, Gramsci 1975, p. 1430; Gramsci 1971a, p. 429.

129   Ibid.

130   Q13, § 1, Gramsci 1975, p. 1558; Gramsci 1971a, p. 129.

attempts to understand the subaltern past and present in order to envision the political prospects of subaltern political struggle and the possibilities of a post-subaltern future'.[131]

Furthermore, the obstacles towards the emergence of the masses from their condition of subalternity, and the renovation of common sense, correspond to obstacles confronting the development of a new type of philosophy and its articulation through the philosophy of praxis. Gramsci's innovative ways of thinking through these problems continue to provide a fertile laboratory that helps us to confront our contemporary situation. While the term mummification appears in relatively few notes in Gramsci's prison writings, the resonance of this theme is highly significant for understanding the relevance that Gramsci's thought has today, and can open productive dialogues with wider debates in critical theory.[132] In a period that bears numerous 'undead' characteristics, from zombie-banks to vampire-capital,[133] it is also timely to consider the Sardinian thinker's contribution to these themes of political monstrosity.

---

131   Green 2011c, p. 400.
132   We might think here of recent debates in contemporary philosophy regarding 'conceptual corpses' and reinventions of the Hegelian notion of *plasticity* in dialogue with neuroscience, e.g. Catharine Malabou's discussion of this simultaneous capacity to take on and to give form (Malabou 2005).
133   For a broader discussion of these figures, from rebel-monsters to the corpse-economy and zombie-labourers, see McNally 2011. It is difficult to resist a parting note, in the context of Gramsci's reading of Machiavelli, of the proximity between the idea of a mummy and an 'undead' Prince.

PART 7

Historical Capitalism and World History

∵

CHAPTER 19

Gramsci and the Rise of Capitalism

Yohann Douet

1 Introduction

The problem of the origins of capitalism and of the transition from feudalism to capitalism is much debated among contemporary Marxists, particularly in relation to the works of Robert Brenner, Ellen Meiksins Wood and the tradition of 'Political Marxism'. But Gramsci's ideas on this question have been little studied. Of course, Gramsci does not give any systematic theory regarding this question; and he almost never uses the word 'capitalism'. Yet, several relevant elements may be found in the *Prison Notebooks*.

To better grasp the significance of these elements, we can use the theoretical framework of Ellen Meiksins Wood, which is summarised in *The Origin of Capitalism*.[1] She distinguishes between two main models for the rise of capitalism: the 'commercialisation' model (the most popular, even among Marxists), and the model of 'Political Marxism', to which she adheres. According to the commercialisation model, the rise of capitalism is explained by the gradual extension of markets, which outgrows feudal fetters, with at some point, eventually, a bourgeois revolution. Thus, the transition is supposed to be an urban phenomenon, and the urban bourgeoisie is the main agent of this process. Moreover, it is conceived as a linear process: there is no qualitative break between capitalism and the preceding mode of production, only a quantitative growth of trade, urban population, etc. This model is inspired by Adam Smith; it was proposed, for example, by the Belgian historian Henri Pirenne; and many Marxists, including Marx himself (at any rate before he started writing *Capital*), have used it. Brenner and Wood, however, have devised an alternative model, drawing particularly on Marx's conception of primitive accumulation. For them, the origin of capitalism is not just a quantitative extension of markets, but a qualitative modification of the social relations of production. Capitalism happened because English agrarian producers became, in the course of the sixteenth century, dependent on the market for their reproduction. Thus, subsistence economy was no longer possible, and the surplus extraction was

---

1 Wood 2002.

no longer direct (as it is under a feudalist mode of production, for example), but was carried out through market mechanisms. This process started in the countryside (the English countryside) and not in the cities, and the urban bourgeoisie was not at its centre. There is actually not a single class driving the process: on the contrary it can be explained by the class struggle between several actors – the landowners, the farmers, and the direct producers (the agrarian proletariat). Indeed, the producers became dependent on the market because of the result of class struggle: the producers were not completely victorious, so they did not get the ownership of their lands like in France; and they were not completely defeated, so they could escape serfdom, unlike in East Europe where a second phase of serfdom took place. That is why they had to sell 'freely' their labour force to capitalist farmers, in order to survive.

Gramsci's reflections about the transition from feudalism to capitalism have probably not influenced the dichotomy between these two models. But we can try to characterise his ideas in relation to them.[2] It seems that from a strictly economic point of view, Gramsci shares the main assumptions of the commercialisation model. But if we take into account other elements, such as politics and ideology, he obviously considers as well the idea of a qualitative break in social relations. To study these points in greater detail, I will briefly sketch Gramsci's conception of feudalism. Then, I will examine several dimensions of the transition: economic, political, and ideological. Finally, I will try to integrate these different elements into a whole. Indeed, for Gramsci, these different dimensions must be conceived in their 'organic unity'. Maybe that is why, in order to understand the transition, Gramsci favours the concept of 'historical bloc' (by which he refers to social totality) over the concept of 'mode of production'.

1.1 Gramsci's Conception of Feudalism

We can try to reconstruct Gramsci's conception of the Middle Ages and feudalism. In such a system, the economy is organised around agriculture. There are two main landowning social groups: the military aristocracy (which is characterised by its 'monopoly of military technical capacity')[3] and the clergy (which

---

2 A dialogue between Gramsci and Political Marxism can be found in Morton 2007a, chapter 3 (State Formation, Passive Revolution and International System). In particular, drawing on Gramsci, the author argues that in certain historical situations the rise of capitalism has to be understood as a process directed by the State, that is, as a passive revolution. We do not discuss this thesis here, mainly because it does not relate to the rise of capitalism in general, but to the entry into capitalist modernity of relatively belated countries, according to the theory of unequal and combined development.

3 Gramsci 1996b, Q4 § 49, p. 199.

'exercised the feudal ownership of land in the same way as the nobility, and which was economically on a par with the nobility'). Using Political Marxist vocabulary, we can say that 'economic exploitation' is implemented by 'extra-economic means': politico-military coercion and religious ideology.

In these conditions, the different social groups seem to lead separate lives, with different cultures, and relatively autonomous political institutions:

> ... in the ancient and medieval state, both territorial and social (the one is but a function of the other) centralization was minimal; in a certain sense, the state was a 'federation' of classes: the subaltern classes had a separate life, their own institutions, etc. (thus the phenomenon of 'two governments' became extremely conspicuous during times of crisis).[4]

A third important feature of medieval social organisation is the dialectical tension between particularism (localism) and universalism (cosmopolitanism). The political and cultural institutions are structured either at a universal (or rather European) level, such as the Holy Roman Empire and the Catholic Church, or at a local level (feudal fiefdom, medieval Communes, etc.). In most cases, the national level does not have any relevance.

Having said this, how are we to understand the transition from feudalism to capitalism?

2 The Elements Explaining the Rise of Capitalism

2.1 The Rise of Capitalism as a Transition from Feudalism
First of all, we have to say that Gramsci, agreeing with Wood's critique of the 'commercialisation model' on this point, refuses to understand capitalism as a natural phenomenon, or as doomed to appear in history.

Thus, Gramsci rejects the notion of 'ancient capitalism', the idea that capitalism existed in ancient times. He discusses the writings of Corrado Barbagallo on several occasions.[5] He says that Barbagallo 'set out to find in antiquity what is essentially modern, such as capitalism and the phenomena related to it'.[6] But, according to Gramsci, Barbagallo is wrong, because he mistakes 'cash economy' for 'capitalism'. Marx had raised the same objection against Theodor Mommsen. In other words, Gramsci accuses Barbagallo of falling into a tele-

---

4 Gramsci 1996b, Q3 § 18, pp. 24–5.
5 For instance, in Q4 § 60, and in a letter to Tania of 10 February 1930.
6 Gramsci 1996b, Q3 § 112, p. 101.

ological fallacy, which consists in projecting 'capitalism' backwards onto a time when this concept did not apply. Wood uses the same kind of argument against the 'commercialisation model' and its linear conception of the transition: she contends that this model projects capitalist social relations, especially market dependency, and its logic of production for profit, onto other periods. And the authors advocating this model fall into such an error precisely because they implicitly believe that capitalism is natural or necessary.

Gramsci also rejects Barbagallo's claim that machines were used in ancient times. In Q6, §156, he shows that the term 'machine' did not have the same meaning in ancient times (when machines were only something that helped manual workers) and under capitalist relations of production, where machines have replaced workers and where workers have to serve these machines (according to the logic of real subsumption).[7]

So, with these two points, Gramsci tells us that we must not overlook the historical specificity of capitalist relations of production. From this specificity we can infer that capitalism has a specific historical location, and then that its rise must be conceived as a transition from feudalism. Let us now try and find the reasons for this transition.[8]

2.2   *Economic Factors*

According to Gramsci, the 'reaction' against the feudal regime began after the year 1000.[9] For two or three centuries after that date, there was genu- ine economic prosperity and trade and agriculture expanded. Cities grew and the bourgeoisie, the 'new ruling class', developed, especially in Italy[10] and in Flanders. Consequently, mainly in these two regions, medieval Communes (autonomous city-states) flourished. These political entities were autonomous from feudal powers (the Empire, the Lords, the Church), and were ruled by the bourgeoisie.

---

7   Gramsci 2007a, pp. 117–18.

8   To deal with the problem of epochal changes in general terms, Gramsci uses on several occasions Marx's Preface to 'A Contribution to the Critique of Political Economy' and draws on this text to elaborate his own theoretical framework (for example in Q13 §17). It would be interesting to link this general theory to the specific question of the rise of capitalism. But we cannot do it in this paper, for reasons of space.

9   Gramsci 1996b, Q5 §123, p. 362.

10   According to Michele Ciliberto 1991 ('Rinascimento e riforma nei *Quaderni* di Gramsci'), Gramsci conceives this period of prosperity as the 'Renaissance' in a broad sense of the term ('spontaneous Renaissance') in contrast to a narrow sense of the term ('cultural Renaissance' in which Renaissance refers to the cultural movement of the fifteenth and sixteenth centuries). The first is a very progressive era, whereas the decline of Italy begins with the second.

When Gramsci refers to these different elements (economic prosperity, market expansion, growth of trade and of cities, rise of a new urban class), he seems to be very close to the 'commercialisation model'. This idea is supported by the fact that he mentions favourably the Belgian historian Henri Pirenne and his book *Medieval Cities: Their Origins and the Revival of Trade*,[11] which is precisely considered by Wood as a classic version of the commercialisation model.[12]

But the Communes did not transcend feudalism, even though they transferred power to the 'communal' bourgeoisie. As Gramsci writes,

> ... there was an organic transition from the Commune to a system that was no longer feudal in the Low Countries,[13] and there alone. In Italy, the Communes were unable to go beyond the corporative phase, feudal anarchy triumphed in a form appropriate to the new situation and then came the period of foreign domination.[14]

Then, the Communes declined, as well as the wealth of the cities.[15] There was no successful transition towards capitalism in Italy, although it was in Italy that cities, trade and the urban bourgeoisie developed the most. So, it is clear that the economic factor is not sufficient to explain the transition from feudalism to capitalism.

What other elements do we have to take into account to explain this failed transition to capitalism in Italy?

2.3   Political Factors

First of all, it seems that the Italian bourgeoisie did not transcend feudalism because it was not able to go beyond its immediate economic interests. Indeed, Gramsci conceives the Communes as the 'economic-corporative phase of the modern State'. This means that this kind of political entity was a tool directly in the service of the urban bourgeoisie and its interests, which prevented it from compromising with the interests of other classes. The lower urban classes were not represented, and they were hard-pressed by taxes and the public

---

11   Pirenne 1946 [1927].
12   Wood 2002, pp. 12–13.
13   In Flanders.
14   Gramsci 1996b, Q5 §123, p. 363.
15   In Gramsci's view, the Italian bourgeoisie was in decline from the fifteenth to the end of the eighteenth century. On this point, we can note that Gramsci says that Italian intellectuals retained up to the end of the eighteenth century a 'cosmopolitan function'.

debt.[16] Moreover, each Commune behaved towards the surrounding peasants as a collective landlord. For instance, in the '*contado*' system, the feudal rights previously owned by the count were now exercised by a corporative bourgeois committee: but it imposed on peasants the same kind of oppression and surplus extraction. As such, the Communes were just a new element in the same feudal logic. In this sense, the bourgeoisie did not establish its hegemony over the whole society. The bourgeois State did not have the 'consent of the governed', it was a dictatorship. Therefore, the bourgeoisie was not able to develop.[17]

Consequently, the cities were not hegemonic over the countryside. There was no territorial unity, and the feudal fragmentation of space (through local privileges, custom barriers, etc.) remained the rule. On this point, Gramsci does not think like Brenner and Wood that capitalist social relations come from the countryside. But he insists on the fact that capitalism cannot be an exclusively urban phenomenon: indeed, capitalism, if it wants to be stable, requires an organic relation between the city and the countryside. And such a relation was precisely missing in the Italy of the Communes.

That is probably a reason why the Communes were not able to go beyond a local level of political organisation: the bourgeoisie did not develop on a national scale and did not create a national political unity. Nor did it create cultural unity since Italy was still divided into many dialects and cultures. That is why Gramsci writes that the Communes did not transcend 'feudal anarchy'.

These two factors, corporatism (in relation to the lower classes and to the countryside) and localism, caused political instability, and hindered the expansion of capitalism. For capitalist social relations to develop, economic prosperity, commercialisation and urbanisation are not sufficient: an integral State seems to be required (to guarantee security), and the society has to be an 'integral society' (to guarantee stability).[18] For Gramsci, the medieval Communes

---

16   Gramsci 2007a, Q6 §13, p. 12: 'the dominant class (...) possessed the wealth and (...) was inclined to place the fiscal burden on the mass of the population by taxing consumption'.

17   Gramsci 2007a, Q6 §13, p. 13: 'the bourgeoisie of the commune was unable to move beyond the economic corporative phase – unable, in other words, to create a state based on "the consent of the governed" a state capable of further development'.

18   Cf. a letter to Tania of 7 September 1931 (Gramsci 1996a, p. 459): 'This conception of the role of intellectual clarifies, in my view, the reason or one of the reasons for the fall of the medieval Communes, that is to say of the rule of an economic class which was not able to create its own category of intellectuals and thus to exercise a hegemony rather than a mere dictatorship. Italian intellectuals did not have any national-popular character, but a cosmopolitan character derived from the model of the Church: Leonard did not scruple to sell the plans of the fortifications of Florence to the duke of Valentinois. The Communes were

were neither the one nor the other.[19] In medieval Italy, the bourgeoisie did not create the superstructures corresponding to its structural domination because, among other reasons, the bourgeoisie did not have any group of organic intellectuals who could have constructed such superstructures. Intellectuals did not have any national-popular feeling and could not create the superstructures of a national society (because, among other things, of 'the cosmopolitan function of Italian intellectuals').

Indeed, Italy was characterised by the double universalism or, more exactly, the double cosmopolitanism, of the Holy Roman Empire and of the Papacy. Such a cosmopolitanism was, as we pointed out earlier, a defining feature of feudalism. But it characterises Italy more than other regions of Europe: Italy was the centre of the Roman Empire; it was constantly torn by wars involving foreign powers and first of all the Holy Roman Empire; and most of all it was where the Church had its headquarters.[20] That is why Gramsci can write that 'the communal bourgeoisie was unable to go beyond the corporative phase and hence cannot be said to have created a state, whereas the Church and the Empire were really the state'.[21] So, in addition to corporatism and localism, a third factor, cosmopolitanism or universalism, was opposed to the creation of an 'integral society', which seems to be a significant condition for the development of capitalist social relations.

That is why absolute monarchy is a better frame for such a development than the direct political power of the Italian bourgeoisie.[22] Absolute national mon-

---

thus a corporative state which did not succeed in transcending this stage and becoming the kind of integral State which Machiavelli urged in vain' [my translation, YD].

19   Gramsci 2007a, Q6 §43, p. 35: 'By the beginning of the fifteenth century, the spirit of initiative of Italian merchants had declined; people preferred to invest the wealth they had acquired in landed property and to have a secure income from agriculture rather than risk their money again in foreign expeditions and investments. But how did this happen? There were several contributing factors: the extremely fierce class struggles in the communal cities, the bankruptcies caused by the insolvency of the royal debtors (...), the absence of a great state that could protect its citizens abroad – in other words, the fundamental cause resided in the very structure of the commune, which was incapable of developing into a great territorial state'.

20   Gramsci 2007a, Q8 §21, p. 248: 'The reason for the successive failures of the attempts to create a national-popular creative will is to be found in the existence of certain classes and in the particular character of other classes, conditioned by the international position of Italy (holy seat of the universal church). This position determined an internal situation that can be called "economic-corporative" that, politically, is a particular form of anarchic feudalism'.

21   Gramsci 1996b, Q5 §147, p. 395.

22   Gramsci 2007a, Q6 §52, p. 39: 'only an absolute monarchy could resolve the problems of the time'.

archy is the structure which enables bourgeois development and organisation. Indeed, under absolute monarchy, the political space is organised on a national scale. And, in its struggle against aristocracy, the bourgeoisie draws closer to the people, and has to construct its hegemony. That is why there has been a development of such a hegemony in France and not in Italy, even though the economic growth of the bourgeoisie was slower in France than in Italy.[23]

From all this, we can infer that a national-popular unity, an integral society and an integral State constitute an environment which fosters the expansion of capitalist relations of production, and that without such an environment, the bourgeoisie and its economic activity are doomed to decline. So, the formation of a kind of 'national-popular collective will' is a significant element in explaining the rise of capitalism. But such a formation does not only require political conditions (a national State). It also requires specific cultural conditions.

2.4   Cultural, Religious and Ideological Factors

I think that another significant element was missing in Italy:[24] The Reformation, which is part of another series of factors, that is, religious and cultural factors.

Gramsci discusses authors who deal with the historical link between religions and the rise of capitalism. In Q11, § 12, he refers to Bernard Groethuysen's book, *The Origins of Bourgeois Spirit in France*, which insists on the religious origins of bourgeois culture. And he also mentions, of course, Max Weber's *The Protestant Ethic and the Spirit of Capitalism*, which he had read in prison in 1931 and 1932.[25]

Gramsci, in agreement with Weber, considers that the Protestant Reformation is an important cause of the modernisation of European societies, and more precisely of the transition to capitalism.[26] In Q7, § 44 Gramsci writes that

---

23   Gramsci 1996b, Q5 § 123, p. 366: 'Another bundle of contradictions: in Italy, in fact, the innovative movement after 1000 was much more violent than in France, and in economic terms the class at the forefront of that movement expanded earlier and more powerfully than it did in France, and it also managed to overthrow the domination of its enemies; this did not occur in France'.

24   This element was, however, present in the Low Countries, which may explain why there was an 'organic transition' beyond feudalism there but not in Italy.

25   This work was published in the 'Nuovi Studi' from May 1931 to October 1932.

26   The idea that the Reformation promoted initiative and modernisation was very popular in Italy at the time of Gramsci. A movement called neo-Protestantism defended the view that Italy needed a religious Reform in order to modernise itself. Gramsci also thought that Italy needed a Reform, but not a religious one: an intellectual and moral Reform, provided by the philosophy of praxis. For more on this movement, see Frosini 2010a, pp. 251–2.

the Reformation shaped the 'ideology of nascent capitalism'.[27] And it seems to have been able to do so because of the rational character of Protestantism and because of the new conception of Grace it promotes, two things on which both Weber and Gramsci agree. Indeed, Gramsci writes that the Reformation determined 'a new attitude toward life, an active attitude of enterprise and initiative':[28] he seems to share with Weber the view that Calvinism acted as a psychological boost to economic activity. It is probably the case. Another aspect of Protestantism (of Protestantism as a whole, and not only of Calvinism) was probably even more decisive in Gramsci's view: the fact that Protestantism created a national-popular collective will – which, as we saw, plays a fundamental part in the transition.

Indeed, the main difference between Catholicism and Protestantism which is relevant here is the fact that the latter constituted a vast national-popular religious movement. The Reformation was a reaction against Catholic cosmopolitanism: it began with the translation of the Bible into German by Luther. It was also a reaction against the hierarchical organisation of religion which was the monopoly of the ruling class (at least of one of its parts, the Clergy).

In Q16, §9, Gramsci sums up these two elements (the Weberian one and the 'national-popular' one):[29]

> Calvinism, with its harsh conception of Grace and its harsh discipline, did not favour the free search for knowledge and the cult of beauty either, but it acquired the role, by interpreting, developing and adapting the concept of Grace into that of vocation, of energetically promoting economic life, production and the increase of wealth.[30]

---

27 Gramsci 2007a, Q7 §44, p. 193: 'The historic-cultural node that needs to be sorted out in the study of the Reformation is the transformation of the concept of grace from something that should "logically" result in the greatest fatalism and passivity into a real practice of enterprise and initiative on a world scale that was [instead] its dialectical consequence and that shaped the ideology of nascent capitalism. But now we are seeing the same thing happening with the concept of historical materialism. For many critics, its only "logical" outcome is fatalism and passivity, in reality, however, it gives rise to a blossoming of initiatives and enterprises that astonish many observers' (Gramsci notes in Q8 §231, Gramsci 2007a, p. 376, that 'Catholic mentality' prevents an understanding of such a phenomenon).

28 Ibid.

29 Gramsci 1971a, p. 394.

30 This first part of the quotation is an extract from Croce. But Gramsci seems to agree with him on this point.

DOUET

The Lutheran Reformation and Calvinism created a vast national-popular movement through which their influence spread: only in later periods did they create a higher culture. The Italian reformers were infertile of any major historical success.

But the phase of popular development enabled the protestant countries to resist the crusade of the Catholic armies tenaciously and victoriously. Thus there was born the German nation as one of the most vigorous in modern Europe.

So, the religious factor is significant in explaining the transition to capitalism.[31] But it is not only because Calvinism promoted individual initiative through psychological mechanisms, as Weber argues. It is also because the Reformation produced an ideological effect which caused the formation of national-popular blocs and of integral States and societies. The national-popular character of Protestantism is obviously opposed to the cosmopolitan character of Catholicism: and we have seen that such cosmopolitanism was partly responsible for the historical stagnation of Italy. Therefore, unlike what happened in Italy, the Reformation helped to create superstructures adequate to the development of capitalist relations of production.

We have thus three series of factors determining the rise of capitalism: economic, political and ideological. None of these factors is immediately determining (for example, capitalism did not rise in Spain in spite of the existence of an absolute monarchy); and they are not necessarily required (there was no absolute monarchy in the Low Countries). In other words, there is no direct nexus between national absolute monarchy, Reformation and the rise of capitalism, but only complex relationships that allow for different mediations and combinations: for example, in France, the Enlightenment played the role of the Reformation; in Germany, the Reformation did not directly cause the rise of capitalism: it established the ground on which it could take root, but only centuries later. That is why we now have to see how Gramsci conceives the interaction and the unity of the different factors.

---

31   Positively in the case of the Reformation, negatively in the case of the Catholic Church.

3 **Capitalist Society as a Complex Totality: The Concept of 'Historical Bloc'**

3.1 *Machiavelli as a Thinker of Capitalism?*

To conceive the articulation between the different dimensions we described (above), we can study what Gramsci says about Machiavelli's economic thought. Indeed, for Gramsci, Machiavelli is a theoretician of the modern State and culture. So, what he says about the economy in this context can perhaps teach us a little about the links between new political institutions and the new mode of production.

In Q8, §162,[32] Gramsci writes:

> If it is true that mercantilism is [merely] economic policy – insofar as it cannot presuppose a 'determinate market' or the existence of a prior 'economic automatism,' the elements of which emerge historically only at a certain stage of the development of a world market – it is obvious that economic thought cannot be blended into general political thought, that is, into the concept of the state and the forces that are supposed to be its components. If one can show that Machiavelli's goal was to create links between the city and the country and to broaden the role of the urban classes – to the point of asking them to divest themselves of certain feudal-corporative privileges with respect to the countryside, in order to incorporate the rural classes into the state – one will also be able to show that, in theory, Machiavelli had implicitly gone beyond the mercantilist phase and evinced traits of a 'physiocratic' nature. In other words, Machiavelli was thinking of the political social milieu presupposed by classical economics.

First of all, this extract teaches us that the laws of motion of capitalism ('economic automatism') can be fully efficient only if this mode of production has expanded on an international scale (if a 'world market' exists). Whether or not Gramsci considers that the Mediterranean economic system (in the case of Italy) and the transatlantic trade (in the case of Flanders) constitute such a 'world market' remains unclear. What is certain is that Gramsci brings up another prerequisite for a stable capitalist mode of production: the existence of a 'political-social milieu'. It is because Machiavelli advocated the elaboration of such a 'milieu' that Gramsci can compare him to the 'physiocrats' (the first

---

32   Gramsci 2007a, p. 327.

economists who favoured production over distribution). Indeed, Machiavelli has stressed the importance of unity between the cities and the countryside, and between the bourgeoisie and other classes. In other words, the 'milieu' required by capitalism is what Gramsci calls elsewhere an 'integral State' and an 'integral society'. That is to say, a system of superstructures (of political and cultural institutions) which would not be strictly 'economic-corporative', but would seek to obtain, to some extent, the 'consentment of the governed'.

This notion of 'milieu' indicates that Gramsci rejects any pluralist explanation of the rise of capitalism. Indeed, a 'milieu' has to be thought in its organic unity with what it conditions. We can therefore say that capitalism was not caused by a plurality of factors mutually independent from each other. On the contrary, the economic, ideological and political factors we distinguished analytically above must be grasped in their organic unity.

3.2   The Historical Bloc

The concept of 'historical bloc' is precisely used by Gramsci to refer to such a complex unity, in the perspective of a non-reductionist conception of social totality. In Q7, § 21, he introduces the concept of 'historical bloc' as follows:[33]

> Marx also stated that a popular conviction often has as much energy as a material force, or something similar, and it is very important. The analysis of these statements, in my view, lends support to the concept of 'historical bloc' in which in fact the material forces are the content and ideologies are the form. This distinction between form and content is just heuristic because material forces would be historically inconceivable without form and ideologies would be individual fantasies without material forces.

The distinction is only 'heuristic', analytical; it cannot be real, organic. We can apply this concept to the failure of capitalism to develop in medieval Italy. We could say that the Communes and the Catholic Church were forms which were not adequate to the economic content and were in contradiction with it. Consequently, the historical bloc was not stable: it was in perpetual crisis. Eventually, the Communes vanished, to be replaced by principalities; and the economy declined, replaced by investments in landed property. By contrast, absolute monarchy (in France for example) and the Protestant Reformation (in Germany or in the Low Countries) were 'forms' (superstructures) more suited to the growth of productive forces, and to the development of capital-

---

33   Gramsci 2007a, p. 172.

ism. That is why, even though the bourgeoisie rose in France later than in Italy, it developed more harmoniously in France: it was able to develop its own culture and cultural superstructures (the Enlightenment) and was finally able to create its own integral State and society at the time of the French Revolution and with the Jacobins.

Thus, with the concept of 'historical bloc', Gramsci insists on the 'necessary reciprocity between structure and superstructures (a reciprocity that is, precisely, the real dialectical process)'.[34] We have to think of capitalism and the transition from feudalism as a social totality, a complex and dialectical unity: as we cannot separate abstractly the different factors which played a role in the rise of capitalism. Another extract highlights this interdependence of the different spheres of social activity (culture, politics, economy). In Q8, § 21, Gramsci writes that:

> the modern Prince should focus entirely on these two basic points: the formation of a national popular collective will, of which the modern Prince is the acting and operative expression, and intellectual and moral reform. (...) Can there be cultural reform and a cultural improvement of the depressed members before there is an economic reform and a change in living standards? Intellectual and moral reform is therefore always tied to a program of economic reform; indeed, the program of economic reform is the concrete way in which intellectual and moral reform expresses itself.

Drawing on the analogy with Machiavelli and the epoch of the Reformation, Gramsci is here talking about his own time: the modern Prince is the Communist Party; the intellectual and moral reform is supposed to come from the diffusion of the philosophy of praxis; the formation of a national-popular collective will can only be achieved under the hegemony of the proletariat. But the interdependence between the three series of elements – political (the formation of a collective will), cultural (a necessary intellectual and moral reform) and economic – can be used to understand the sixteenth century. We could therefore say, using and reversing Gramsci's phrase, that the creation of a new kind of (integral) State and of a new culture (through the Reformation for instance) is the concrete way in which the new (capitalist) economy 'expresses itself'.

---

34   Gramsci 2007a, Q8 § 182, p. 340.

3.3 The Transition as Crisis

There is one last point we should emphasise: the idea of crisis. Indeed, for Gramsci, it seems that the transition from one epoch to another is linked to 'organic crises'. This idea is obviously present in one of his most famous statements: 'the crisis consists precisely in the fact that the old is dying and the new cannot be born'.[35] The transition from feudalism to capitalism can be conceived as a transition from one type of historical bloc to another. As such, it corresponds to a crisis (or, maybe more exactly, to a series of crises). Gramsci writes in Q6, §10:

> The medieval crisis lasted for several centuries, until the French Revolution, when the social grouping that had become the economic driving force in Europe after the year 1000[36] was able to present itself as an integral 'state' with all the intellectual and moral forces that were necessary and adequate to the task of organizing a complete and perfect society.[37]

Unfortunately, Gramsci tells us very little about the crisis of feudalism: we just know that it is linked to the loss of the 'monopoly of military technical capacity'[38] by the aristocracy, and to a detachment of clerical intellectuals from the people. But we can nevertheless say that the rise of capitalism can only be understood as a result of the crisis of feudalism.

4 Conclusion

We can now return to our discussion of Brenner, Wood and 'Political Marxism'. As we said, if we look at Gramsci's reflections on the economic aspect of the process, we could say that Gramsci anticipated a version of the 'commercialisation model'. By contrast, if we try to understand what he writes about the 'superstructural' aspects, we find more similarities between his approach and that of Brenner and Wood: all three insist on the importance of political conditions, on the significance of social relations in the countryside, the idea of a qualitative break and historical innovation, and reject a view of capitalist relations as natural. The difficulty in locating Gramsci's conception in Wood's dichotomy is probably linked to the concept of 'historical bloc'. Indeed, it seems

---

35   Gramsci 1996b, Q3 §34, pp. 32–3.
36   Namely, the bourgeoisie.
37   Gramsci 2007a, p. 9.
38   Gramsci 1996b, Q4 §49, p. 199.

that Gramsci favours this concept over the more traditional Marxist concept of 'mode of production'. This theoretical displacement has to be studied more precisely. The 'historical bloc' is not a 'fusion' of economy, politics, and ideology; it is not an undifferentiated unity. It is a complex unity, involving a multiplicity of elements; and the relations between structure and superstructures, between a mode of production, and the State, religion, culture pertaining to it must be analysed, both at an abstract level, and in particular historical situations[39] (and the transition from feudalism to capitalism is only one of these situations). But this difficult task lies well beyond the scope of this chapter.

---

39   On the importance of concrete historical analysis, see for example Gramsci 2007a, Q7 § 6, p. 159: 'The "experience" of historical materialism is history itself, the study of particular facts, "philology"'.

CHAPTER 20

The *Gramscian Moment* in International Political Economy

Lorenzo Fusaro

1   Introduction: The Organic Crisis of Contemporary Capitalism

Looking at present developments within the capitalist world economy suggests that Peter Thomas' idea of a *Gramscian Moment* is pertinent.[1] Hence two significant events, the Brexit vote and the election of Donald Trump as President of the United States, might probably be described using the Gramscian concept of the 'organic crisis' of contemporary capitalism. As also Giuseppe Vacca asserted commenting on the two events: 'we are witnessing phenomena that Gramsci categorised as an organic crisis of the system'.[2] Observing the *realisation* of the organic crisis at the time of the Great Depression of the 1930s Gramsci asserted that 'in every country the process is different, even if the content is the same. And the content is the crisis of the hegemony of the ruling class'.[3]

As if describing the present inability of the ruling classes, despite 'project fear' and their incessant efforts at trying to convince the masses to vote 'remain' in the case of the UK referendum, or to vote for Hillary Clinton in the US presidential election, Gramsci writes in Notebook 7: 'the old intellectual and moral leaders of society feel that the ground under their feet is fading away, they discover that their "sermons" have become exactly that, "sermons"'.[4] At a higher level of abstraction, Gramsci understands a crisis of hegemony as entailing the separation of elements (in this case: political society and civil society) which, as we shall see later, constitute what the author refers to as 'organic unities': 'Detachment of civil society from political society: there is a new problem of hegemony, that is the historical base of the State has moved'.[5] Alberto Burgio, paraphrasing Gramsci, eventually summarises the concept of crises of hegemony as follows: 'There is a "crisis of hegemony" when "civil society" stops

---

1   Thomas 2009a. The expression is reminiscent of Pococks' *The Machiavellian Moment*, 1975.
2   Vacca in *Il Mattino* 2016.
3   Gramsci 2001a, Q13 §23, p. 603.
4   Gramsci 2001a, Q7 §12, p. 863.
5   Gramsci 2001a, Q7 §28, p. 876.

providing the function of hegemonic apparatus of the dominants ... removing the normal support of direction, of the organisation of consensus ... from the "Government – State"'.[6]

Importantly, according to the reading of Gramsci adopted here 'organic crises' have their origins within the economic structure. The 'economic contradiction' for Gramsci 'becomes political contradiction'[7] as structural, economic contradictions *can* indeed become political and hence reach the level of the superstructures and induce a societal crisis or 'realise' the crisis. It is in fact only when the latter level is reached that it is possible to speak of an *organic crisis* of the 'State as a whole', which for Gramsci *is* a 'crisis of hegemony'. As he puts it in Notebook 13: 'One speaks of "crisis of authority" and this is exactly the crisis of hegemony, or crisis of the State as a whole'.[8]

Consistent with Gramsci's overall analysis, Burgio also reiterates the structural roots of the organic crisis, yet without identifying any particular 'contradiction' in the economy.[9] It is fair to suggest, I believe, that the structural, economic roots of the organic crisis, according to Gramsci, are to be found in production and are related to the tendency of the rate of profit to fall. Hence, in the *Notebooks*, Gramsci shows how many commentators looked at the crisis of the 1930s as originating in finance and saw the financial crack of 1929 as causing the crisis. Gramsci is critical of this and argues that the financial crack that happened in the US in 1929 is nothing but a 'clamorous manifestation'[10] of the crisis, arguing that the roots of the crisis need to be identified in production.

Hence, proposing a long term analysis of the evolution of capitalism from the early nineteenth century onwards, the *Notebooks* suggest how an initial phase of capitalist expansion where '[t]he economic base, due to industrial development is continually expanded and deepened'[11] is followed by a second period that stands in opposition to the first as 'the bourgeois class is "saturated": not only does it not assimilate new elements, but it rejects one part of itself'.[12] Gramsci identifies the turning point in 'the epoch of Imperialism',[13] or more precisely in '1870, with European colonial expansion'.[14] Incidentally, the latter is caused, according to Gramsci, by a decline in the rate of profit:

6   Burgio 2003, p. 157. Own translation.
7   Gramsci 2001a, Q10 § 33, p. 1279.
8   Gramsci 2001a, Q13 § 23, p. 1603.
9   Burgio 2003, pp. 161–2.
10   Gramsci 2001a, Q15 § 5, p. 1755.
11   Gramsci 2001a, Q13 § 37, p. 1637.
12   Gramsci 2001a, Q8 § 2, p. 937.
13   Gramsci 2001a, Q13 § 37, p. 1637.
14   Gramsci 2001a, Q13 § 37, p. 1562.

Capitalist Europe, rich in means and once it reached the point in which the rate of profit started to show the tendency to decline, had the necessity to widen the area of expansion of its profitable investments: hence the creation of colonial empires.[15]

Depicting the structural elements that eventually result in the 'organic crisis', Gramsci seems to articulate the relation between *The Law of the Tendency of the Rate of Profit to Fall* and *The General Law of Capitalist Accumulation.* What relates the two is the relative increase in constant capital (capital invested in machinery etc.) *vis-à-vis* variable capital (workers employed by capital), that *might* result, eventually,[16] in declining profitability *and* an expulsion of large layers of the proletariat from the direct production process. In general, the potential for an 'organic crisis' consists in the fact that the capitalist economy is increasingly unable to satisfy the aspirations of the subalterns, something that manifests itself, echoing Marx's *General Law*, also in their fall into 'permanent or semi-permanent unemployment'.[17]

While current economic and political developments are not equal to those Gramsci observed in the early 1930s, and while there are, of course, several other interpretations,[18] the author seems to offer, at least, valid analytical insights and useful concepts that might be helpful in comprehending important contemporary developments. These share present-day interpretations that see the current economic and political crisis as being eventually grounded (at least in the final analysis) in capitalist production and declining profitability.[19]

However, far more problematic is the deployment of Gramsci's thought (or so it appears) when attempting to understand further crucial trends that characterise the contemporary international political economy. For, as we shall see, the sort of intellectual path followed by neo-Gramscian scholars that posits

---

15   Gramsci 2001a, Q19 § 24, p. 2018.

16   Gramsci is, of course, aware of the powerful counter-tendencies to the decline in the rate of profit, arguing that whether the rate of profit declines or not is a historical matter. Importantly, according to Gramsci, the law of the tendency of the rate of profit to fall retains its validity independently from whether the rate of profit actually declines or not: capitalist development, even when profits rise, is characterised by an incessant struggle against downward pressure on profitability. See especially Gramsci 2001a, Q10 § 33, § 34, and Krätke and Thomas 2011 for a more general discussion on Gramsci's political economy.

17   Gramsci 2001a, Q1 § 127, p. 116.

18   For example, Nancy Fraser (2017) understands present developments in the 'western' world as a crisis of what she refers to as 'progressive neoliberalism', while Leo Panitch (see Gupta and Panitch 2016) speaks more generally of a 'crisis of neoliberalism' *tout court.*

19   See Roberts 2016 for a discussion of different Marxist approaches that attempt to analyse the current economic crisis.

the supersession of national divisions or the existence of a transnational ruling class, makes it difficult, I believe, to understand current geopolitical tensions, the possible return to nationalism, protectionist policies, bilateral trade agreements, imperialist disputes in critical regions such as the South China Sea, the Middle East, nor does the theory adequately address present divisions within the European Union, just to name a few examples. But as we shall argue in this chapter, taking a distance from neo-Gramscian analyses in important issues, Gramsci's understanding of international relations and hegemony at the international level, as developed in the *Prison Notebooks*, offers useful insights that might be helpful in comprehending present developments within the international political economy. In the following sections, I will hence return to the neo-Gramscian understanding of the contemporary world order (Section Two). Section Three will outline how Gramsci conceived hegemony at the international level and suggest ways by which the concept might be further elaborated. In my concluding remarks, I will briefly sketch out how these insights might apply to the understanding of the us in its effort to become hegemonic and maintain hegemony over its imperialist rivals.

2   The Great Deception?

As Theodore Cohn puts it in his *Global Political Economy*, 'Neo-Gramscian analysis is "the most influential Marxist theory in contemporary international relations"'.[20] One of the main references is, of course, Robert Cox's work. Criticising mainstream IR theories, Robert Cox originally proposed the differentiation between 'problem solving theory' and 'critical theory'.[21] While positivist problem solving theory, which characterises mainstream approaches, aims at maintaining the status quo, critical theory is critical, according to Cox, 'in the sense that it stands apart from the prevailing order of the world and asks how that order came about'.[22] Of course, and as further contributions in this volume demonstrate,[23] Gramsci's Philosophy of Praxis goes far beyond asking 'how that order came about'; nor does the philosopher of praxis 'stand apart from the prevailing order'.[24] After all, as Gramsci puts it, proposing a fundament-

---

20   Cohn 2012, p. 112.

21   Morton 2007a, p. 111.

22   Cox 1981, p. 129. See also Rupert's critique of mainstream approaches in Rupert 1995, Chapter 2. See also Gill 1993.

23   See Part III in this volume.

24   Gramsci 2001a, Q10 §62, p. 1487.

ally different epistemology compared to that of Cox, the philosopher of praxis, 'understood individually or understood as an entire social group', fully conscious of the contradictions 'poses itself as an element of the contradiction, elevates this element as a principle of knowledge and hence of action'.[25]

Notwithstanding this difference, neo-Gramscian analyses have made an important contribution by going beyond or deconstructing the reductionist understanding of the state that characterises mainstream IR theory, offering an analysis based on classes and class fractions resulting in the idea of the 'state–society complex'.[26] But, notably, Robert Cox's important theoretical addition centres on the concept of hegemony. In his seminal article 'Gramsci, Hegemony and International Relations: An Essay in Method',[27] Cox underlines the centrality of Machiavelli's legacy for comprehending Gramsci's understanding of power, exemplified in the comparison with a centaur: 'half man, half beast', and hence power as 'a necessary combination of consent and coercion'.[28] Accordingly, Cox argues that hegemony prevails when 'the consensual aspect of power is in the forefront'. Because hegemony is 'enough to ensure conformity of behavior in most people most of the time', coercion is mainly latent and used only in particular, deviant situations.[29] Robert Cox's concept of hegemony at the international level or the concept of a hegemonic world order is largely derived by *transposing* his interpretation of Gramsci's concepts such as 'hegemony', 'civil society', 'historic bloc' to the field of international relations. Following his argument to its logical extremes, as Germain and Kenny have indicated, the common (albeit imprecise) equation 'state = civil society + political society' takes the form of 'international state = global political society + global civil society'.[30] In fact, as Cox puts it, 'the hegemonic concept of world order is founded not only upon the regulation of interstate conflict but also upon a globally conceived civil society, i.e. a mode of production of global extent which brings about links among social classes of the countries encompassed by it'.[31] It should be noted that a 'hegemonic world order' rests on a coherent conjunction or 'fit' between 'production' or 'material capabilities', 'institutions' and 'ideas'.[32] Starting from the establishment of hegemony in a powerful state, the attainment of a hegemonic world order occurs when other states emulate the former by

25   Gramsci 2001a, Q10 § 62, p. 1487.
26   Cox 1981. See also Overbeek 2004.
27   Cox 1983.
28   Cox 1983, p. 164.
29   Cox 1983, p. 164.
30   Germain and Kenny 1998, p. 17.
31   Cox 1983, p. 171.
32   Cox 1981, p. 139.

adopting analogous productive, ideological and institutional forms:[33] Because eventually production determines the overall configuration of a world order, '[s]ocial forces may thus achieve hegemony within a national social order as well as through world order', as Bieler and Morton have put it, following Cox, 'by ensuring the promotion and expansion of a mode of production'.[34] By way of example we might mention the 'promotion and expansion' of the 'productivist ideology' that ensured, according to Mark Rupert, the adoption of Fordism in Europe and that, eventually, led to the constitution of a 'hegemonic world order'.[35]

The latter theory's difficulties in adequately addressing the current situation with regards to the previously mentioned developments rests, in my opinion, in the fact that when conceptualising contemporary capitalism and the contemporary world order, neo-Gramscian analyses largely abandoned the idea of competing national states as a fundamental feature of capitalist modernity by positing the overcoming of national division and the emergence of a transnational ruling class. In other words, they inscribe themselves in what Callinicos has characterised as theories for which 'geopolitical competition is obsolete',[36] or in what Radhika Desai has called the theory of 'cosmopolitan Marxists'.[37] Hence, anticipating similar understandings of contemporary capitalism put forward, amongst others, by Antonio Negri and Michael Hardt, the *sortie* from the crisis of the 1970s unleashed, according to these views, structural transformations in the realm of production that also translated to the superstructural level producing, as Hardt and Negri have put it, 'a *fundamentally* new situation and a significant historical shift'.[38] While not leading to *Empire*, characteristic of neo-Gramscian analyses is the internationalisation of production and the corresponding internationalisation of the state. As Bieler and Morton have put it, summarising Cox's argument,

> Since the erosion of *pax Americana* principles of world order in the 1970s, there has been an increasing internationalisation of production and finance driven, at the apex of an emerging global class structure, by a 'transnational managerial class.' ... Hence there has been a rise in

---

33 According to Cox, largely through processes of passive revolution. For a discussion of the latter concept see, for example, Callinicos 2010 and Morton 2010.
34 Bieler and Morton 2004, p. 93.
35 Rupert 1995.
36 Callinicos 2009, pp. 16–17.
37 Desai 2013.
38 Hardt and Negri 2000, p. 8, own emphasis.

the structural power of transnational capital supported and promoted by forms of elite interaction that have forged common perspectives, or an 'emulative uniformity', between business, state officials and representatives of international organisations favouring the logic of capitalist market relations.[39]

Notably, and giving rise to an important research agenda,[40] Robert Cox included, amongst others, the Trilateral Commission, the Bank of International Settlements, the G8, the Bilderberg conferences as constituting the central *loci* of influence within the global economy. Eventually, Cox labelled 'this global centralization of influence over policy ... the internationalizing of the state'.[41] While ultimately conceptually diluting these insights into a '*nebuleuse*',[42] Cox maintains that 'its common feature is to convert the state into an agency for adjusting national economic practices and policies to the perceived exigencies of the global economy. The state becomes a transmission belt from the global to the national economy, where heretofore it had acted as the bulwark defending domestic welfare from external disturbances'.[43]

As we shall see in the next section, the *Notebooks* present a quite different perspective. But what I wish to stress, already at this stage, is that Gramsci saw the existence of competing capitals and national states *not as conjunctural*, but as a *structural* or *organic* feature of capitalist modernity. Hence, again, as if depicting present developments within the international political economy, in 1933, Gramsci observed that states started to pursue protectionist policies, in terms of, for example, imposing tariffs, influencing currency exchange and instituting bilateral commerce agreements.[44] For Gramsci, this is the result of a *fundamental contradiction* that characterises capitalist modernity:

> One of the *fundamental contradictions* is this: that whereas economic life has internationalism, or better still cosmopolitanism, as a necessary premise, State life has always developed in the direction of 'nationalism', of 'self-sufficiency' and so on.[45]

39   Bieler and Morton 2004, p. 94. On the supposed emergence of a transnational state, see
      also Robinson 2001 and 2008.
40   See for example Gill 1991.
41   Cox 1992, p. 31.
42   Ibid.
43   Ibid.
44   Gramsci 2001a, Q15 §5, pp. 1757–8.
45   Gramsci 2001a, Q15 §5, p. 1757. Own emphasis.

While in his famous article 'The League of Nations' (January 1919) Gramsci reflects on liberalism's 'nice dream' that consists in the 'attempt to adapt international politics to the requirements of international trade',[46] and that might be seen as an invitation to conceive the possibility of the supersession of national divisions and the formation of transnational ruling class, already a few months later (and throughout the *Prison Notebooks*), he asserts that the liberal dream remained just that: a dream. Thus Gramsci writes already in July 1919: 'Liberals are unable to realise peace and the *International*, because private and national property generates divisions, borders, wars, national states in permanent conflict amongst themselves'.[47]

Notwithstanding the consideration of possible alliances and appreciating the transnational nature of capitalist accumulation, Gramsci is hence critical of the idea that this might lead to the formation of transnational ruling classes and a transnational state *under capitalist relations of production*. While Francesca Izzo understands Gramsci's notion of 'new cosmopolitism' as transcending national division *within* capitalist relations of production,[48] Gramsci, in my opinion, develops the idea that such supersession of national division is only possible when going beyond capitalism or by constructing an alternative to the capitalist mode of production. Were we to put it in 'hegelese' (using Žižek's expression),[49] we might argue that capitalism has negated a first form of 'cosmopolitanism', that characterised ancient Rome and Catholicism,[50] giving rise to national divisions. It is then the negation of capitalism that can give rise to a 'new cosmopolitanism'. As Gramsci puts it in Notebook 19, it is probably this second negation, or, in other words, the overcoming of capitalism at which the Italian working class (expansively understood) should aim. Hence, understanding the latter as the 'industrial reserve army of foreign capitals', Gramsci underscores that 'the "mission" of the Italian people is to resume roman and medieval cosmopolitanism, but in its most modern and advanced form'.[51] In doing so, Gramsci continues, it should 'insert itself in the modern front of struggle to reorganise also the non-Italian world'.[52]

---

46   Gramsci 2007c, p. 27, originally written in January 1919. See Domenico Losurdo on Gramsci's relation to Liberalism in Losurdo 1997.
47   Gramsci 1987, p. 117.
48   Izzo 2016. For a further interesting analysis of 'internationalism' and the 'national question', see Tinè 2012.
49   See, for example, Žižek 1997. Interestingly, concerning the conceptualisation of contemporary capitalism Žižek (1997, pp. 43–5) also adopts a view that is similar to that put forward by Hardt and Negri and the neo-Gramscians.
50   See for example Gramsci 2001a, Q17 § 21, p. 1924.
51   Gramsci 2001a, Q19 § 5, p. 1989.
52   Gramsci 2001a, Q19 § 5, p. 1989.

In contrast to neo-Gramscian analyses, and as will be evident when detailing Gramsci's take on International Relations and hegemony in the *Prison Notebooks*, Giovanni Arrighi's famous approach is more consistent with Gramsci's analysis. Hence, as with Gramsci, Arrighi retains the centrality of national states in his analysis. By also transposing Gramsci's concept of hegemony to the international level, Arrighi maintains that at the international level a state is hegemonic over the state system when it can credibly claim, thanks to its material and later financial supremacy, to be a motor force of a general expansion, thereby presenting its interests as being also those of subordinated states.[53] It should be noted that also here, hegemony, understood as an 'addendum' to domination, mainly relates to the consensual aspect of power. Important as Arrighi's insights are, the proposed theory, by neglecting the coercive moment when conceptualising hegemony, has difficulties in explaining how hegemony is constructed and maintained and risks being 'economistic'. The latter problem can be discerned, for example, when dwelling on Arrighi's conceptualisation of a 'crisis of hegemony'. In this case, the loss of economic supremacy (in the realm of production and later in finance) does *immediately* lead to a crisis of hegemony. This may be a 'signal crisis' (characterised by the loss of supremacy in production) or the subsequent 'terminal crisis' of a hegemonic power, associated with the collapse of what Arrighi refers to as the '*belle époque*', which has historically characterised a hegemonic power's financial expansion. As will be evident from the discussion of Gramsci's conception of hegemony at the international level, within the *Prison Notebooks*, the concept is developed in a way that avoids these problematics.

3   Towards a Classical Marxist Conceptualisation of Hegemony at the International Level

What the above discussion suggests is that, within Marxist international political economy, the concept of hegemony at the international level has been mainly developed by world-systems theory[54] and the neo-Gramscian school of thought. However, the concept remains largely under-theorised from what we might refer to as 'classical' Marxism, i.e. that school of thought within Marxist international political economy that takes Marx's *Capital* as its point of depar-

---

53   Arrighi 1994, p. 28.

54   This section of the chapter draws on Fusaro 2017. For a more exhaustive discussion see also Fusaro 2019. Apart from the aforementioned substantial contribution made by Arrighi, see also Wallerstein 1983 for a further conceptualisation of hegemony from the perspective of world-systems theory.

ture, counting, amongst others, the works of Lenin, Bukharin, Luxemburg, and most recently, works associated with the *New Imperialism*.[55] A return to the critical edition of Gramsci's *Quaderni* suggests that Gramsci not only developed the concept of hegemony at the international level, but also that the way in which he did so, is consistent with the overall framework developed by classical Marxists. He thereby builds a concept that contrasts with neo-Gramscian analyses and that might provide useful analytical tools for understanding the contemporary situation.

While an exhaustive elucidation of Gramsci's approach cannot be provided here, I wish to briefly point to three aspects in Gramsci's work that I consider to be crucial for understanding his conceptualisation of hegemony at the international level. Firstly, it seems necessary to consider Gramsci's approach and method to be found in Notebooks 10 and 11. A significant aspect relates to the fact that Gramsci's concepts should be understood as 'organic unities' composed of different contradictory parts. Thereby it is possible to distinguish methodologically (but not organically) between the two parts that constitute an organic unity.[56] Secondly, Gramsci's Marxism is further clarified when dwelling on Notebook 13, which contains a note of central importance: the 'Analysis of Situations'. Here we cannot but take notice that Gramsci's analytical starting point is the economic structure as indicated in Marx's *Preface* to the *Critique of Political Economy*,[57] which, according to Gramsci, represents 'the most important authentic source for the reconstruction of the philosophy of praxis'[58] and that Gramsci follows *ad litteram*, providing a non-determinist reading. Thirdly, the young Gramsci's famous 'Revolution against Capital',[59] a text from 1917, should not be read too literally: his critique of the 'stagist' and economistic interpretation of Marxism should not be understood as a departure from Marx's main work and approach that would legitimate the deployment of Gramsci's thought outside *Capital*. The *Prison Notebooks* remain permeated by the *law of value* and the *crisis tendencies* as analysed by Marx. With this in mind, we aim at presenting relevant aspects of Gramsci's conception of hegemony at the national level that might be useful to further elaborate on the author's conceptualisation of hegemony at the *international* level.

---

55   Harvey 2003, Callinicos 2009.
56   Gramsci 2001a, Q13 §18, p. 1590.
57   *MEW*, Bd. 13, p. 7.
58   Gramsci 2001a, Q11 §29, p. 1441.
59   Gramsci 2007c, p. 22.

3.1   *Hegemony at the National Level*

According to the above discussion, I believe that Marx's *Preface* represents a good starting point to address Gramsci's concept of hegemony at the national level. In particular, it is worth emphasising Marx's statement that when analysing epochal transformations,

> it is always necessary to distinguish between the material transformation of the economic conditions of production, which can be determined with the precision of natural science, and the legal, political, religious, artistic or philosophic – in short, ideological forms *in which men become conscious* of this conflict and fight it out.[60]

Paralleling Marx's *Preface*, Gramsci's 'Analysis of Situations' also starts from *objective changes* in the economic structure. What Gramsci seems to elaborate throughout the *Prison Notebooks* is Marx's idea that epochal change has the *potential* to occur within the structure *only* in cases in which 'men become conscious of this conflict'. By implication, a lack in the acquisition of consciousness that occurs at the level of ideologies (hence Gramsci's interest in ideology, intellectuals, etc.) changes, to put it crudely, absolutely nothing. Gramsci portrays how a social group related to the economic structure, going through different phases – 'different moments of the collective political consciousness'[61] – *might* become hegemonic. This can occur when the fundamental social group can supersede its narrow corporate interests, understanding that its interests, 'in their actual and future development', go beyond their corporate milieu and as such *can and must* become the interests of other subordinate groups.[62]

Crucially, the *realisation* of hegemony involves, eventually, the seizing of the state. Here the state 'is conceptualised as the organism of a group destined to create favourable conditions for the maximal expansion of the same group', underlining at the same time that 'this development and this expansion are conceptualised and presented as the motor force of a universal expansion, of the development of all national energies'.[63] Hence this reading of Gramsci's *Quaderni* suggests that the *full realisation of hegemony* occurs only when the fundamental social group is able to grasp power and take over the state. Conversely, hegemony 'at this side of possession of the state',[64] i.e. before taking

---

60   *MEW*, Bd. 13, p. 9, own emphasis.
61   Gramsci 2001a, Q13 §17, p. 1583.
62   Gramsci 2001a, Q13 §17, p. 1585.
63   Gramsci 2001a, Q13 §17, p. 1585.
64   Gramsci 2001a, Q16 §9, p. 1861.

political power, during the 'Sturm und Drang' or 'Romantic' phase of political struggle, as Gramsci calls it,[65] can 'only' be 'political hegemony' or 'hegemonic activity'. 'Hegemonic activity' is then a fundamental precondition for the full realisation of hegemony. In fact, as Gramsci asserts:

> A social group can, and indeed must be leading even before winning governmental power (this is one of the principal conditions for the same conquest of power); later, when it exercises power and even if it maintains it strongly in its hands, it becomes dominant but it needs to continue to be 'leading' as well. There must be *hegemonic activity* even before the rise to power and that one should not count only on material force which power gives in order to exercise an *efficient leadership*.[66]

Differently from Arrighi then who identifies 'domination' as being a precondition for hegemony, the contrary seems to be the case: a certain degree of hegemony ('political hegemony' or 'hegemonic activity') is a precondition for taking political power and hence for domination. In addition, once political power has been grasped and hence domination attained, the exercise of leadership continues to be a condition for its maintenance. Therefore, domination and hegemony are interrelated: the attainment of domination requires a *certain form* of hegemony ('political hegemony' or 'hegemonic activity' or 'leadership') and the realisation of hegemony requires political power and domination. Hence hegemony should be understood as the dialectical unity between 'leadership' (also referred as 'hegemonic activity' or 'political hegemony') and 'domination'.

The importance of both domination *and* leadership, coercion *and* consensus is further appreciated when considering Gramsci's concept of 'integral state' that should be understood as a further dialectical or organic unity: the one between civil society and political society. Significantly, the exercise of hegemony involves both spheres and cannot be reduced to civil society alone. Peter Thomas and Alberto Burgio go as far as to argue that this form of rule can be compared to the Foucauldian concept of 'biopolitics' emphasising, however, that in Gramsci it is based on class power.[67] Importantly, it is the relative stability of this form of class rule that eventuate in the fact that, according to

---

65   Gramsci 2001a, Q11 § 70, p. 1508.
66   Gramsci 2001a, Q19 § 24, pp. 2010–11, own emphasis.
67   Thomas 2009a, p. 225; Burgio 2009. See also recent work by Frosini 2016a. The author distinguishes between different ways in which hegemony is articulated and exercised, depending on different phases of capitalist development that correspond to those identified in section one of this chapter.

Gramsci, changes within the economy, as for example crises, *do not* immediately result in 'fundamental historical events' or crises of hegemony:

> It may be ruled out that immediate economic crises of themselves produce fundamental historical events; they can simply create a terrain more favorable to the dissemination of certain modes of thought, and certain ways of posing and resolving questions involving the entire subsequent development of national life.[68]

As I shall argue below when elaborating on the concept of hegemony at the international level this holds true also for the latter once hegemony is *fully realised*.

3.2   Hegemony at the International Level

As has been mentioned above, a transposition of Gramsci's concept does not seem pertinent, for, as also Adam Morton has in my opinion correctly emphasised, albeit reaching different conclusions compared to mine, international relations are not only *present* within the *Prison Notebooks*, they also retain crucial explanatory significance.[69] Moreover, as I wish to argue below, Gramsci's *Notebooks* provide clear elements of what hegemony at the international level entails. When addressing the latter, it should be emphasised that Gramsci provides a 'dialectical' understanding of the international. Hence, Gramsci compares the figure of the 'national personality' with the 'individual personality' thereby going beyond methodological individualism and methodological nationalism:

> ... the national personality (as the individual personality) is a mere abstraction if considered outside the international (or social) nexus. The national personality expresses a 'distinct' of an international complex, for this reason it is bound to international relations.[70]

At the same time, and as his theoretical reflections and historical examples suggest (e.g. his analysis of Italy), the influence that states are able to exercise over others varies. It is here that Gramsci explicitly introduces the concept of *hegemonic states*, typified by what I refer to as *relative geopolitical auto-*

---

68   Gramsci 2001a, Q13 §17, p. 1587.

69   Morton 2007a. For a further discussion on 'Gramsci and the international', see also Ives and Short 2013.

70   Gramsci 2001a, Q19 §2, p. 1962.

nomy. What characterises a hegemonic state then is 'its ability to impress upon state activity an autonomous direction, of which other states need to support the influence and repercussion'.[71] Thus elsewhere Gramsci writes: 'The line of a hegemonic state (hence of a great power) does not oscillate because it does determine the will of others and it is not determined by them'.[72] This line of reasoning is also already present within Gramsci's early writings as the author refers to Italy's subordinate position within the world economy as being exactly characterised by the country's lack of autonomy and sovereignty: 'after the instauration of British global hegemony the Italian people has become like the Chinese people: Italy has become a market of colonial exploitation, a sphere of influence, a dominion, everything aside from an independent and sovereign state'.[73]

The *Prison Notebooks* suggest that a nation state can be a world hegemonic power if it has 'the possibility to imprint upon its activities an absolutely autonomous direction, of which *all other powers*, great and minor, have to feel the influence'.[74] According to Gramsci, the status of a hegemonic power can be 'calculated' looking at 'the extension of territory', 'economic power' understood as 'productive capacity' and 'financial capacity' and finally, and very importantly, considering 'military power'.[75] Thus, according to this view, hegemony does not only rest on economic power as the latter needs to be realised as political and military power.

At the same time, also in the case of hegemony at the international level, the latter cannot be reduced to the consensual aspect of power only, for a state exercises hegemony using both leadership and domination, consensus and coercion. After all, as Gramsci puts it, 'war remains the decisive factor' for establishing whether a country became a hegemonic power.[76] Generally, according to Gramsci, 'the peripheral nation's economic life is subordinated to international relations'.[77] As his analysis of Italy reveals, hegemony is maintained through 'implacable repression' by the 'police system' as well as by 'political measures'.[78] One element amongst the latter, Gramsci elaborates later on, is the so-called 'party of the foreigner'.[79] This party does not represent the 'vital

71   Gramsci 2001a, Q13 §19, pp. 1597–8.
72   Gramsci 2001a, Q13 §32, p. 1629.
73   Gramsci 1987, p. 142.
74   Gramsci 2001a, Q2 §16, p. 166.
75   Gramsci 2001a, Q13 §19, p. 1598.
76   Gramsci 2001a, Q13 §32, p. 1628.
77   Gramsci 2001a, Q13 §2, p. 1562.
78   Gramsci 2001a, Q1 §43, p. 36.
79   Gramsci 2001a, Q13 §2, p. 1563.

forces of the country', nor is it part of a transnational ruling class; rather it represents 'the subordination and subservience to hegemonic nations or groups of hegemonic nations'.[80]

While not diminishing the consensual aspect of power as well as ideological and symbolic features, one should not confuse, I believe, hegemony at the international level with the *diktat of the law of value*. This is strongly manifest in Gramsci's discussion of *Americanism and Fordism*: In fact, Gramsci generally points out that Americanism – with its 'café life' and 'ideology of the Rotary Club'[81] – does not represent something particularly new, pointing to the fact that in the US the relation between classes has not changed. At the same time, according to Gramsci, Ford's method of production will spread. Generally, this occurs because this method is 'rational', and more immediately because of the 'implacable weight' of US production and because of 'American superpower', rather than through ideology and culture.[82] Forced by US competition, European states will have to develop new forms of states and life adequate to the new production methods, although by finding original combinations to do so:

> The problem is not whether in America a new civilisation and a new culture exists ... and if these are invading Europe: if the problematic is posed in this way, the answer would be easy: no it does not exist. The problem is rather this; whether America, through the implacable weight of its economic production (and therefore indirectly), will compel or is already compelling Europe to overturn its excessively antiquated economic and social basis. This would have happened anyway, though only slowly. In the immediate perspective it is presented as a repercussion of American super-power.[83]

Hence, Gramsci's argument strongly recalls Marx's analysis of relative surplus value production. In *Capital*, Volume one, Marx abstractly defines what Gramsci would later apply to the US and Europe. As Marx puts it in *Capital*, Volume one, when discussing the advantages that accrue to an innovative capital or 'first mover' (read: the US) within the market and the obligation that other

---

80   Gramsci 2001a, Q13 §2, p. 1563.
81   Gramsci 2001a, Q22 §15, p. 2180.
82   This argument thus contrasts with Rupert's, according to whom it is thanks to the spread of 'productivist ideology' that the US would secure hegemony over Europe. See Rupert 1995.
83   Gramsci 2001a, Q22 §15, p. 2178.

capitals (read: Europe) have to adopt similar production techniques or risk extinction as a result of the operation of the law of value: 'the law of the determination of value by labour-time ... acting as a coercive law of competition, forces his [the "first mover's"] competitors to adopt the new method [of production]' thereby emphasising that the advantages that accrued to the 'first mover' disappear 'so soon as the new method of production has become general'.[84] To be sure, and as evident from the above evocation of 'US superpower', Gramsci also considers how the *law of value* is *mediated* by introducing national states into the analysis. Moreover, he considers the superstructural transformations that the adaptation to the new production process would result in.

3.3   Expanding the Concept: 'Sturm und Drang' and 'Fully Realised' Hegemony

The *Prison Notebooks* suggest that hegemonic powers should be simultaneously understood as imperialist states, whereby Gramsci adopts a 'classical' understanding of imperialism that strongly recalls Lenin's.[85] What my analysis suggests is that imperialist states *must* become hegemonic in order to guarantee the accumulation of capital. This is based on a further implication of the law of value that *compels* capitals to grow and expand:

> [T]he development of capitalist production makes it constantly necessary to keep increasing the amount of the capital laid out in a given industrial undertaking, and competition makes the immanent laws of capitalist production to be felt by each individual capitalist, as external coercive laws. It compels him to keep constantly extending his capital, in order to preserve it, but extend it he cannot, except by means of progressive accumulation.[86]

The reproduction of capital and the related endless accumulation of capital cannot be confined within the borders of a national state. Being an international account, the accumulation of capital requires that states grant the necessary conditions for the accumulation of 'their' capitals thereby attempting to overcome the inherent contradictions that capitalist production entails. Subaltern states might hence be differently integrated in the hegemonic nation's

---

84   *MEW*, Bd. 23, pp. 337–8.
85   See for example Gramsci 2001a, Q19, §24, p. 2018.
86   *MEW*, Bd. 23, p. 618.

circuit of capital (and hence as providers of raw materials, labour power, production sites, markets for realisation, etc.), as *loci* for the externalisation of contradictions that arise within hegemonic states, and/or for geopolitical reasons necessary for the containment of rival states. It is therefore necessary to qualify Arrighi's claim that states become hegemonic by virtue of their ability to lead other states through a period of economic expansion. Following the above understanding of hegemony, states *must* become hegemonic and enforce the latter by means of both consensus and coercion if the accumulation of capital is to take place. This is reminiscent of Gramsci's theorisation, where, as we have seen, a fundamental social group *must* become hegemonic if it wants to expand and develop.[87]

Restricting the concept to hegemonic relations amongst 'core' or 'imperialist states', it refers to the hegemonic position of an imperialist state over other imperialist states. A regional hegemon is hegemonic at least in its respective region. A world hegemonic (imperialist) state prevents the construction of hegemonic relations by rival imperialist states. In fact, a crisis of world hegemony refers to the ability of rival (imperialist) states to become hegemonic at least in its respective region thereby challenging the position of the former world hegemon.

There is a further important refinement of the concept of hegemony at the international level I wish to propose. Drawing on Gramsci's discussion of hegemony at the national level and its distinction between 'hegemonic activity' (before the seizure of the state) and the effective realisation of hegemony that only occurs through the seizure of the state, I distinguish between two 'levels' of hegemony at the international level: 'Sturm und Drang hegemony' and 'fully realised hegemony'. Also at the international level, the construction of hegemony should therefore be understood as a process. In the first case – Sturm und Drang hegemony – the concept refers to a weak form of hegemony, as the latter includes mainly the economic moment. 'Fully realised hegemony', by contrast, represents a far more robust form of hegemony as it involves the economic, political and military moments. While in cases of Sturm und Drang hegemony the redistribution of economic power (usually associated with economic crises) might immediately lead to a crisis of hegemony, in cases of fully realised hegemony, hegemonic states can resort to battery of means in order to avoid crises of hegemony. These include their influence over currency exchange rates, but also political and military measures.

---

87   Gramsci 2001a, Q13 §17, p. 1585.

Finally, starting from Gramsci's notes, we might attempt to identify the organic roots that can lead to the rise of, borrowing Kees van der Pijl's expression, 'contender states'.[88] Notably, Gramsci asserted that structural or organic changes can modify the position of a state within the world economy:

> Do international relations precede or follow logically fundamental social relations? Without any doubt they follow. Any organic innovation in the social structure, through its technical military expressions, modifies organically the absolute and relative relations in the international field.[89]

In his work, the United States represents a clear example. The dramatic process of uneven development and amelioration of the US position within the world economy from the late nineteenth century onwards is associated with 'Fordism'[90] and the ability to counteract declining profitability. The latter was made possible by an increase in productivity derived from the introduction of new technology and the scientific managing of production accompanied by adequate or corresponding institutional and ideological arrangements.

But note that Gramsci also dwells on the precondition that enabled the US to *relatively autonomously shape* its development. Thus the primary conditions for 'the formation of the power of the United States' were, Gramsci outlines, first and foremost the revolutionary processes, from 'independence'[91] to the Civil War, the result of which posed the conditions for the US's subsequent development. Hence what are now referred to as the first and second American Revolution, by *breaking dependent relations* vis-à-vis the British Empire (independence) and establishing the modern liberal capitalist state under the leadership of the industrial north as a result of the Civil War, can be seen as having posed the *precondition* for both the astonishing results the US economy achieved and the creation of the potential to subsequently shape the world order. At the same time, it cannot be emphasised enough that these developments represent merely the potential to turn the country into a hegemonic power. For as the history of US hegemony reveals, and as we shall sketch out in our concluding remarks, the construction, full realisation and maintenance of hegemony is an arduous and long process.

---

88   Van der Pijl 1984.
89   Gramsci 2001a, Q13 §2, p. 1562.
90   Gramsci 2001a, Q22.
91   Gramsci 2001a, Q2 §16, pp. 166–8. Later, Dependency Theory advanced similar propositions. See, for example, Frank 1969.

4   Conclusion

This chapter argued that the concepts developed by Gramsci might be useful to address present problematics within the world economy, or in other words, that we might speak of a *Gramscian Moment* in International Political Economy. The *apparent* inability of Gramsci's thought to comprehend increasing geopolitical tensions, rivalries and divisions was mainly due to the peculiar way in which neo-Gramscian scholars have deployed Gramsci's thought. Hence, I attempted to show that while neo-Gramscian analyses largely transposed a particular interpretation of Gramsci's concepts (hegemony, civil society, historic bloc, etc.) to the international field, the *Prison Notebooks* already provide an understanding of hegemony at the international level. The latter, while interrelated, differs from hegemony at the national level. Hegemony at the international level is exercised by national states using both consensus and coercion. As a result of the law of value and capitalism's inherent drive to expand, imperialist states might attempt to become hegemonic over rival (imperialist) states in order to preserve the accumulation of 'their' capitals. Moreover, I maintained that the *full realisation* of hegemony involved the economic, political and military moments and that this form of hegemony should be differentiated from weaker forms, which I labelled 'Sturm und Drang hegemony'. Hence, following the analysis outlined in the previous paragraphs, I contend that the construction of US hegemony should be understood as a process going through different phases. Rather than leading to the emergence of a transnational ruling class, developments within the capitalist word economy were, and still are, characterised by the incessant efforts of imperialist states to attempt to construct and maintain hegemony over their imperialist rivals.

Hence, looking briefly at the history of US hegemony[92] from the analytical perspective developed in the previous paragraphs sustains recent historiographical works, as for example the one provided by Adam Tooze.[93] Differently from Arrighi, who maintained that the US was not hegemonic during the interwar period (and in stark contrast to the analysis put forward by Radhika Desai who maintains that the US has never been hegemonic[94]), I argue that the US became hegemonic already during the interwar period, with the qualification that the latter form of hegemony was deficient: while backed by the state *strictu sensu*, hegemony was exercised via private channels rather than public ones and took mainly an economic dimension. Political and military

---

92   For an exhaustive account, see Fusaro 2019.
93   Tooze 2014.
94   Desai 2013, p. 3.

involvement, while occurring, would be relatively restricted compared to the order that the US would establish after World War Two. This is why, relying on Gramsci's characterisation of a still incomplete form of hegemony, I refer to it as 'Sturm und Drang hegemony'. As a result of the 'endless accumulation of capital' and capital's drive to expand beyond its borders, nation-states are compelled to become hegemonic in order to secure the accumulation and reproduction of 'their' capitals. Thus, given the standing the US attained within the world economy already by the 1920s as confirmed by any important indicator (production, trade, finance), it was 'imperative', as Gilbert Ziebura has aptly underscored, that the US took control not only of the European but of the world economy as a whole.[95] The US would do so by launching the Dawes Plan (1924) in Europe, forcing most countries (including Britain) into the Gold Standard, the rules of which benefited the US and blocked Britain's attempt to revitalise its declining position. Moreover, through a series of agreements signed during the 1921/22 Washington Conference, the US was able to shape the balance of power in Asia as well as limit the military ambitions of its competitors. Hegemony was mainly exercised by private forces (analytically different from the state *strictu sensu*, but still part of the state integrally understood) and was prevalently economic, because direct political and military involvement, while existent, was limited.

It was exactly the relative weakness of this form of hegemony that meant that the Great Depression of the 1930s caused a crisis of US hegemony. Thus, rival imperialist states were able to start constructing hegemonic relations at the regional level (Germany and Japan), or attempting to reinvigorate their declining empire (Great Britain). Here, it can be argued that symbolically September 1931 was the point at which the foundation upon which US hegemony was constructed started to unravel. On 18 September, Japan invaded Manchuria thus breaking the status quo imposed in occasion of the Washington Conference; on 21 September, Britain abandoned the Gold Standard. In figurative and descriptive terms, we may characterise the Great Depression as bringing about the negation of a first, weak version of US hegemony, the further negation of which resulted in the postwar hegemonic order.

It is therefore only after World War Two that the United States became *fully hegemonic*, now involving the economic *cum* the political and military moment. US economic recovery was eventually brought about by rearmament worth around fifty times government expenditures under the New Deal and, eventually, through participation in World War Two in which the US was able to

---

95   Ziebura 1990.

create the conditions for re-launching its world hegemonic project by militarily defeating Germany and Japan and by forcing the opening up of the biggest
remaining closed trading block, i.e. Britain's Empire, through various means,
including the Lend Lease (starting in 1941). The full realisation of US hegemony
occurred only by circa 1950, and, reflecting the changes that occurred during
the Great Depression and during the war, it became increasingly *state-led, institutionalised, and eventually was cemented politically and militarily*. Through the
Marshall Plan in Europe and similar policies in Japan, the US set the conditions
for Germany and Japan to regain partially their former role as economic power-
houses in order to revive the respective economic areas under strict US control,
while Britain would retain a different role given the importance of the Empire
she still controlled. Yet in all cases, and differently from the 1920s, the US's grip
was secured militarily, through NATO for example.

Turning to the contemporary situation, we might argue that the objective and well-known redistribution of economic power did not lead, as world-
systems theory maintains, to a crisis of US hegemony. At the same time, the
developed framework of analysis also invites us to contrast the reading offered
by Panitch and Gindin, according to whom US hegemony continued because
former imperialist rivals and, later, rising powers such as China, were fully
integrated within and willingly reproduce the 'American Empire'.[96] Rather the
US would avoid a crisis of hegemony by countering the construction of hegemonic relations of its imperialist rivals in their respective regions (Germany
in Europe and Japan in Asia), exactly thanks to its hegemonic position. An
important element in the exercise of hegemony has been the use of the dollar and the control of exchange rates. At the same time, during the 1990s the US
would ensure that Japan's strengthening economic position would not translate into political, not to speak of military, leadership in East Asia.[97] Similarly,
the European project under Germany's direction was heavily influenced by
the US, who made sure that the EU's enlargement occurred under the guidance of the IMF while the continent still remains militarily dependent on the
US.[98] The position of China is different, and the country might indeed pose a
challenge to US hegemony, particularly so in East Asia. Following the framework outlined on the rise of contender states, the country, I argue, developed
largely outside US hegemonic relations and could do so thanks to the revolutionary processes that it underwent.[99] This enabled China to reach what I refer

---

96   Panitch and Gindin 2012.
97   See Gowan 1999.
98   See Carchedi 2001.
99   For example, see Meisner 1999 and Wei 2011.

to as 'relative geopolitical autonomy'. Thus, in East Asia at least, the country's economic expansion has been accompanied by significant steps towards the construction of hegemonic relations, involving economic, political and military features, which, however remain incomplete. Notably, under the presidency of Barack Obama, the US would again attempt to counter China's expansion in the region, for example, through the so-called 'Pivot to Asia'. At the time of writing, the new president's observations signalled an abrupt change of strategy. But, following the analysis presented in this chapter, we rather expect the pursuit of similar objectives, perhaps by other means.

CHAPTER 21

Rethinking Fordism

Bruno Settis

1 From Post-Fordism to Fordism

The present essay is not going to sum up the content of *Americanism and Fordism*, one of the densest among the *Prison Notebooks*. It is also today one of Gramsci's best-known and most quoted works:[1] he is thereby often invoked as the early interpreter of a new stage in the history of capitalist modernity, a stage that we are now used to calling 'Fordism', having identified its main feature in a social contract founded on the virtuous circle of mass production and mass consumption. Rather, the essay will follow the trajectory of Fordism in reverse, in order to find Gramsci's proper place in it – which will also be, I argue, to find the proper place of Fordism in Gramsci's thought. It must be noted in the first place that such a notion of Fordism as a stage of capitalism, or perhaps as a 'regime of accumulation', was a product of nothing less than ... the end of Fordism.

Gramsci's conception of Fordism was taken on by the Italian Left after the war, adapting it, in an often perfunctory way, to the context of the take-off of the Cold War and the Reconstruction 'politics of productivity'; and in this shape it arrived in workerist thought, i.e. the so-called *Operaismo*: one can think, for instance, of the section 'Marx in Detroit' in the second edition of Mario Tronti's *Workers and Capital*, or of the notion of Post-Fordism later elaborated by Toni Negri and Michael Hardt in *Empire*. Italian *Operaismo* transmitted the notion of 'Fordism' to the French regulationist school of Althusserian economists, whose main representatives were Michel Aglietta, Alain Lipietz and Robert Boyer: they made it the dominant feature of a 'regime of accumulation', and they baptised 'Post-Fordism' the historical stage that followed, from the 1980s onwards. The retrieval of Gramscian Fordism was therefore complementary to the diagnosis of the irreversible crisis of Fordism, overcome by Toyotism, flex-

---

1 Since secondary literature on these subjects – both on so-called Taylorism and Fordism themselves and on Gramsci's analyses of them – is as vast as it is uncontrollable, the bibliography shall be here reduced to a minimum. I have developed these arguments, with further reference to Gramscian literature, in Settis 2016.

ibility, and later neoliberalism. It can be noted, incidentally, that the notion of Post-Fordism sounds more adequate to spelling out a transition, rather than illustrating a period which is now longer than Fordism itself had been, if we make it coincide with the postwar boom and the 'Trente Glorieuses'. But that is another problem for the social sciences and contemporary Marxism to deal with.

We shall start our analysis by looking at the roots of the notion of Fordism. The regulationists' failure to recognise that they go much beyond Gramsci is a symptom of the fragility of their theoretical proposal. Some claim[2] that it was Gramsci himself who invented the very word 'Fordism'. This, as we shall see, is manifestly not true.

A deeper look into Gramsci's sources is necessary to have a better understanding of his writings (and hence, I argue, of our own present time). Starting with *My Life and Work* in 1922, Henry Ford published four books, co-written with (or probably written by) journalist Samuel Crowther. These books, it goes without saying, had the aim of creating the epic of the genius entrepreneur, and of providing a utopian aura around mass production, by the means of advertising and propaganda. They became instant classics in the United States, and they had an immediate impact on European intellectuals, the long-lasting influence of which is hard to overestimate. They were one of the main sources for the early works of Georges Friedmann, such as the essay on Taylorism published in the *Annales* and *La crise du progrès* (1935); they were widely read in Germany, not only by Hitler but also by entrepreneurs and executives, trade-unionists, social democrats, and communists; when *My Life and Work* was translated into Italian in 1925, both Piero Gobetti and Carlo Rosselli wrote long reviews, the former in particular being fascinated by Ford as a hero of industrial modernity.[3] Gobetti's article was a true inversion of Max Weber's paradigm: the impact of Fordist ethics on Italy would carry out, he wrote, the historical mission of the Reformation, which was stalled by the Church. Thanks to Gobetti's mediation, therefore, we can see how Gramsci's notes on the history of Italy, tracing back its incomplete modernity to the Renaissance and Counter-reformation, are directly connected to *Americanism and Fordism*.

In the Turi prison Gramsci owned three of Ford's books: *Moving Forward* in the Italian 1931 edition, *My Life and Work*, and *Today and Tomorrow* in French (with a preface by Victor Cambon he often quoted). While reading the latter

---

2   Lipietz 1993 is just one example among many.
3   Gobetti 1960, Rosselli 1973.

together with Alfred Marshall's and Luigi Einaudi's books, Gramsci wrote, in a letter to Tania on 23 May 1927, that 'Ford, though a great industrialist, is quite comical as a theorist'.[4] Various notes show that Gramsci himself was conscious that Ford's theories were wholly different from their application: he wrote, for instance, that 'high wages did not represent in Ford's industrial practice what Ford wanted them to represent in his theories'.[5]

Conversations with fellow prisoners must have helped renovate his interest in Fordism: Ezio Riboldi, a former member of the left wing of the Italian Socialist Party who had joined the Communist Party of Italy in 1924, had read Ford's books, concluded that Fordism was equal to Socialism, and planned on writing a book about it;[6] another Communist, Ercole Piacentini, recalled that in one of the courses he gave in prison, Gramsci had said that 'since the appearance of Americanism everything has changed', and that this should have been the starting point to build socialism in the West, which would necessarily require a process different from what happened in Russia.[7] This is wholly different from claiming that Gramsci's interest in Americanism implied a rediscovery of liberalism against Bolshevism.[8]

2   Americanism and Bolshevism

After all, there was in the 1920s and 1930s no outright opposition between Bolshevism and Americanism. In 1918, *The Immediate Tasks of the Soviet Government* was one of the first of Lenin's writings to become available in Italy.[9] Its influence on Gramsci has been often remarked upon, especially regarding the concepts of hegemony and revolution: it also contains an important passage on Taylorism, famous indeed, but that has not to my knowledge been directly connected to Gramsci. Earlier, in 1913, Lenin had condemned Taylorism and scientific management as mere means of exploitation; but after the revolution, confronted with the necessity of organising production (and especially of making the railways work), he decided himself to raise the question of labour discipline. 'We must raise the question of applying much of what is

---

4   Gramsci and Schucht 1997, p. 105.
5   Gramsci 2014b, Q6, §135, p. 799.
6   Lisa 1973, pp. 77–8, 100.
7   Baratta 2004, pp. 15–34.
8   Such is the position of Vacca 2012, pp. 133–7.
9   Paggi 1970, p. 225.

scientific and progressive in the Taylor system', Lenin wrote. Let me quote a long excerpt:[10]

> The Russian is a bad worker compared with people in advanced countries. It could not be otherwise under the tsarist regime and in view of the persistence of the hangover from serfdom. The task that the Soviet government must set the people in all its scope is – learn to work. The Taylor system, the *last word of capitalism* [or perhaps latest?] in this respect, like all capitalist progress, is a combination of the refined brutality of bourgeois exploitation and a number of the greatest scientific achievements in the field of analysing mechanical motions during work, the elimination of superfluous and awkward motions, the elaboration of correct methods of work, the introduction of the best system of accounting and control, etc. The Soviet Republic must at all costs adopt all that is valuable in the achievements of science and technology in this field. The possibility of building socialism depends exactly upon our success in combining the Soviet power and the Soviet organisation of administration with the up-to-date achievements of capitalism. We must organise in Russia the study and teaching of the Taylor system and systematically try it out and *adapt it to our own ends*. At the same time, in working to raise the productivity of labour, we must take into account the specific features of the transition period from capitalism to socialism, which, on the one hand, require that the foundations be laid of the socialist organisation of competition, and, on the other hand, require the use of compulsion, so that the slogan of the dictatorship of the proletariat shall not be desecrated by the practice of a lily-livered proletarian government.

Here, Lenin presented Taylorism as 'the last/latest word of capitalism': something the revolution should learn to master, nay, to integrate into the socialist economy in the making. Building socialism implied educating the Russian worker, also in the sense that such education involved searching for a new system of incentives, different from the capitalist ones. In this way, the Soviet revolution could 'fill the gap' separating backward Russia from advanced capitalist countries – just as the revolution itself had been possible, Gramsci had written in 1917, because 'Socialist thinking allowed the Russian people to reach

---

10   Lenin 1972.

the experiences of other proletariats' and their history of struggles.[11] The social character of techniques and technology was by no means a question only Marxist revolutionaries were dealing with: but one need only compare Lenin's writings with Carl Schmitt's *The Age of Neutralizations and Depoliticizations* (1929) to gauge the former's (and therefore the Leninists', and above all Gramsci's) distinct class and dialectical perspective, in order not to confuse it with interwar reflections on the 'spirit of technicity'.

Lenin formulated his discourse, in this and other writings, more or less 'coquetting' with Hegel, with a clear theoretical objective: first, the 'extraction' of rationality from the Taylor system, separating what was distinctly capitalist and exploitative from a technical core, supposedly politically neutral, that could (and should) be used by the revolution, in the transition from backwardness and capitalism to socialism; and, in pointing out the necessity of turning Taylorism upside-down (or right-side up), Lenin openly echoes the words of Marx, when he declared, in 1873, that dialectic had to be freed from the 'mystification [... it] suffers in Hegel's hands', 'if you would discover the rational core inside the mystical shell'.[12] In the second place, Lenin clearly states that Taylorised work could not but be hard in itself, but it would be compensated on two levels: upstream, because authority over the labour process would be political, thus implementing a self-discipline of the workers themselves – from a collective, not individual, point of view; downstream, because improvement in productivity would allow shorter working hours, and consequently it would give workers more time for leisure, education, participation in politics.

Lenin's were not mere philosophical meditations. Between War Communism and the NEP, the introduction of the Taylor system was the object of a long battle within the revolutionary front, opposing the Bolsheviks to the Trade Unions and the Socialist-Revolutionaries. The most aggressive role in this battle was played by Trotsky: the latter, renowned admirer of the Taylor system, enforced labour discipline in a framework of militarisation. A more properly Fordist turn in Soviet industrialisation would come later, with the Five Year Plans, based less on private automobiles than on heavy industry and Fordson tractors.

Gramsci would criticise Trotsky in *Notebook 22* because of his failure to realise the Taylor system had the potential to liberate work from coercion. On the other hand, though, in a stark critique of Labriola's historicist justification of

---

11   Gramsci 1982.
12   *MEW*, Bd. 23, p. 23; compare Harvey 2010, pp. 218–19.

slavery, Gramsci admitted that a backward social group or people could have the 'need of an exterior coercive discipline'. There is a coercion of the military kind, Gramsci continues, that can be applied also to the ruling class, because it is the adequate form of modern pedagogy, aimed at educating an immature element. We have here an explicit reference to the 'work army' created under War Communism and to Lenin's theories on Taylorism.[13]

Recalling Soviet Taylorism is not at all a diversion, since on one side it must be considered one of the main sources for Gramsci's understanding of Fordism while, on the other side, his knowledge of the 'original' Fordism must be put into perspective.

3   Gramsci's 'Periscope'

When Gramsci writes about the United States in his *Notebooks*, the scarcity of sources he had access to in prison is most evident. A sign of such distance is his appraisal of American literature and culture as arid and dull, in contrast with the discoveries and translations that in the very same years Elio Vittorini and Cesare Pavese were carrying out in Turin and Milan. Gramsci wrote that in the United States there was no proper superstructure, which meant that hegemony was not centred on the State: a void filled by direct engagement of economic power in the government of social relationships. Hegemonic structures were therefore somewhat transparent, creativity and rationality being directly and simultaneously engaged in the organisation of industrial production and organisation of society. Hence the famous quote, 'Hegemony was born in the factory'.[14]

This perspective on hegemony can be fruitfully compared to the Gramscian analysis of the fight between 'two conformisms', opposing the intellectuals and moral leaders of the old, dying civilisation, and the representatives

---

13   Gramsci 2014b, Q8, § 200, pp. 1060–1 and Q11, § 1, pp. 1366–8. In the second draft, the reference to the 'work army' is absent.

14   Gramsci 2014b, Q22, § 2, pp. 2145–6. In the terms of Laclau and Mouffe 2014, this would appear a textbook case of Marxist essentialism and homogenisation of the working class (which is a part of their argument against Marxist overdetermination: see for example pp. 68–72, in reference to Braverman's 'deskilling thesis' and Taylorism in general), while at the same time Gramsci acknowledges that the worker is being 'incorporat[ed] into a multitude of other social relations: culture, free time, illness, education, sex and even death' (see pp. 144–5, in reference to Aglietta). Whether this is an intrinsic ambiguity of Gramsci's analysis, or betrays a limit of Laclau and Mouffe's argument against classical Marxism goes beyond the scope of the present chapter.

of 'the new world in gestation'. The world of production, he wrote, will be the reference point of the old world:

> [T]he maximum degree of utilitarianism must inform every analysis of the moral and intellectual institutions to be created and of the principles to be disseminated; collective and individual life must be organized to maximize the yield of the productive apparatus. The development of economic forces on new foundations and of the new structure will heal the inevitable contradictions and, having created a 'new conformism' from below, will allow new possibilities for self-discipline – that is, new possibilities for freedom, including individual freedom.[15]

Is this an apology for utilitarianism? Ten years before, Gobetti had sketched a portrait of Gramsci as a 'cold utopist' who wanted to subdue society and historical reality as if it were a factory.[16] But such a portrait fails to show the scope of Gramsci's thought and its essentially dialectical nature, i.e. it conceived contradictions/conflicts not as accidents but as the *substance* of industrial society. In a note referring to Hyacinthe Dubreuil's *Standards*,[17] a copy of which he owned in Turi, Gramsci 'disassembled' the very concept of scientific management: scientific meant 'rationally adequate to the ends', which is the maximisation of efficiency; but we may assume that the rationality of the method does not imply the rationality of the ends, and that the ends of the capitalist and those of the worker can be divergent.

If science deals with 'the relationship between men and reality, mediated by technology' – as Gramsci emphasises in his reflections of science as a superstructure – it must have a deep connection to social relations and relations of production: 'science too – he argues – is a historical category, is a movement in constant development', and it is related to a conception of the world. It is not without reason that Gramsci, in describing the historical shift to a science of exact measurement, places side by side the scientist using the microscope and the specialist technician in the Ford factories.[18]

---

15   Gramsci 2014b, Q7, § 12, p. 863.
16   Gobetti 2008, pp. 95–8.
17   Dubreuil 1931.
18   Gramsci 2014b, Q6, § 165, pp. 817 and Q11, § 36–8, pp. 1451–8; compare Q6, § 10, p. 690: 'Only the struggle, by its result, and not by its immediate result but by that which becomes apparent in a permanent victory, will determine what is rational and what is irrational, what "deserves" to win because it continues, in its own way, and sublates the past'. As Thomas 2010, p. 394, points out, for Gramsci the 'human' is to be explained 'as an ensemble

Although Gramsci mentions him only in the aforementioned passage, the French unionist Hyacinthe Dubreuil should be considered a relevant source, too. His 1929 book *Standards* – translated in English as *Robots or Men?* – was a report of his voyage to the United States and of his short period working at Ford, River Rouge: he tried to debunk the myths about deskilling, dehumanisation of workers, excessive fatigue, and Ford's authoritarianism; he tried to detect something of the old craft, of the personal creativity of the artisan, inside the work on the assembly line. But this was also, indeed, an operation of propaganda, because Dubreuil admitted that his trip had been organised by the International Labor Organization and the Rockefeller Foundation. Gramsci was obviously aware of this, but nevertheless *Standards* could have had some influence on him: for instance, his notion that mechanisation might involve a liberation of mental faculties of the worker ('leaving the brain completely free', as in the act of walking) could be associated with Dubreuil's idea that the worker's mind could wander, while he performed his tasks. As mentioned earlier, Lenin held a different opinion: Taylorism would help the moral and cultural development of the worker by giving him more free time, not by lightening work itself, nor by renovating its creative side.[19]

Another fundamental source on Fordism for Gramsci was, of course, the factory itself, not in Detroit but in Turin. Giovanni Agnelli was the Italian pioneer of Fordism and during World War One he had started gradually importing scientific management and the conveyor belt in the Fiat factories: this was the context in which Gramsci became a socialist, a journalist, and finally a communist. Gramsci and his group, the socialists of *Ordine Nuovo*, became convinced that Taylorism and Fordism had a progressive potential during the period when they adhered to Leninism and its revolutionary perspective. One of the most curious, and still opaque, passages in *Notebook 22* recalls Agnelli himself trying to establish a dialogue with the *Ordine Nuovo* group because he understood that the workers were 'carrying the most modern needs of industry'.[20]

---

of historical relations *of class struggle*'. On Gramsci, scientific knowledge and science as a productive force, see Antonini 2014.

19   Lukács's 1923 position is also worth mentioning, since he, similarly to Lenin in 1913 but differing from Lenin in 1918, held that Taylorist rationalisation could provide nothing but a further, inescapable alienation and subjugation of the worker: 'With the modern "psychological" analysis of the work-process (in Taylorism) this rational mechanisation extends right into the worker's "soul": even his psychological attributes are separated from his total personality and placed in opposition to it so as to facilitate their integration into specialised rational systems and their reduction to statistically viable concepts' (Lukács 1972, p. 88).

20   Gramsci 2014b, Q22, § 2, p. 2146.

But in the 1920s Agnelli signed his deal with Fascism: this meant the progressive elements of Fordist organisation were overcome by the authoritarian
solution. In Italy, Fascism and Fordism subsumed each other. Both are defined
by Gramsci in the terms of passive revolutions, but with different connotations: the former is considered a surrogate of the latter, based on the alliance
between the avant-garde of modern industry and old parasite classes. To recall
what Marx said about the backwardness of Germany in 1842, Europe was, from
Gramsci's point of view, at the level of the decay of the West, without having
ever been at the level of the emancipation of the West. It suffered all the pain
of capitalist development, without benefiting from its advantages, because the
supremacy of fossil classes and their alliance with finance capital did not allow
it. This was especially true in Italy, where Fascism was the specific configuration of such a conservative bloc. Under Mussolini, Americanism and Anti-
americanism ('comical and stupid') were two sides of the same coin.[21]

The European capitalist ruling classes wanted to find an equilibrium
between the old and the new worlds, holding together the old, anachronistic
social structure and the ultra-modern form of production: 'to put it harshly,
Europe would like to have a full barrel and a drunken wife, to have all the benefits which Fordism brings to its competitive power while retaining its army of
parasites'.[22] In order to ensure and enforce this equilibrium, ruling classes were
willing to embrace an authoritarian solution. In the contradiction between the
'full barrel' and the 'drunken wife', the reader will recognise one of the main
political and theoretical problems of the *Prison Notebooks*, namely, the one
concerning the cosmopolitan character of economy and the national character of politics. The analysis of Fordism, in the context of American capitalism's
growing hegemony over the capitalist world, appears therefore as a necessary
part of the Gramscian analysis, testing the validity of its arguments and categories for advanced capitalism. Such an inquiry, therefore, is both necessary
to understand Italy's (and Fascism's) place in the capitalist world and economic
hierarchies, and to underline which aspects of Gramsci's analysis of hegemony
and power relations are valid not only for backward countries, but also for the
most advanced and developed ones. Had capitalism, as Ford claimed in his
books (and many socialists followed him), managed to overcome its limits, its
contradictions?

From the objective point of view (social and technical, not political), Fordism was following the road described by Marx in the first book of *Capital*,

---

21   Amongst the vast literature concerning the relationship between Fordism and Fascism in
      Gramsci's perspective, one can see Buci-Glucksmann 1975 and De Felice 1977.
22   Gramsci 2014b, Q22, § 2, pp. 2140–1.

from co-operation to machinery and modern industry: Gramsci wrote that, during the attempts of social stabilisation after the world war, 'the movement to develop the factory against professional organisation perfectly corresponded to the analysis of the factory system given by Marx in the first book of the *Critique of Political Economy*'.[23]

The outcome of this argument is that Fordism shall be seen as an attempt to avoid the tendency of the rate of profit to fall, both before and after the 1929 shock. A strong rise in productivity tried to overcome the problems of capitalism by amplifying capitalism itself, with an endeavour toward capitalist stabilisation: it was therefore a tentative solution to the social crisis that was an alternative to the fascist one, and a richer one, because it was more progressive. The term 'tendency' implied a dialectical logic, where progressive trends and catastrophic outcomes fostered each other: the attempt to avoid the catastrophe of the fall of the rate of profit through a new progressive boost, the conveyor belt technology and high salaries, the organisation of distribution and consumption,[24] was nevertheless doomed to fail, because – or, perhaps, as far as – the 'unceasing development of the social productive force of labor' will remain within the fences of capitalist relations of production.

Employing the category of 'passive revolution' in the understanding of Fordism as a historical process implies highlighting that this progressive and rationalist tendency was *inseparable* from the sharpening of the conflict between the development of productive forces and the relations of production. It is therefore improper to claim, as workerist intellectual Alberto Asor Rosa emphatically did in the early 1970s, that Gramsci established a '*comunanza di destini*', a 'commonality of destiny' (though partial, though temporary) between advanced capitalism and the 'advanced working class'.[25] Since Fordism is to be found at the crossroads of authoritarian practices in advanced capitalism, 'conservative modernisation' in a backward country such as Italy, and brave experiments in Socialist industrialisation, it is the *lieu* of manifestation of a contradiction, or rather of two fundamental principles of political science:

---

23 Gramsci 2014b, Q9, §67, pp. 1137–8; Roberto Finelli's claim that Gramsci's is a 'Marxism without *Capital*', and cast therefore a spiritualist shadow on the whole history of Italian Marxism, appears unsubstantiated or, to be more precise, once again underestimates Gramsci's peculiar conditions and limited sources in prison: see Finelli 2010 and 2016. The complexity of Gramsci's relationship to Marx cannot be dealt with in this context: further insights can be found in Frosini 2009 and Guzzone 2018.

24 See Gramsci's argument against Croce's notions of value and profit in Gramsci 2014b, Q10, §36, pp. 1281–4, where Ford's activity to avoid the tendency of the rate of profit to fall is mentioned.

25 Asor Rosa 1973, pp. 575–88.

1) that no social formation disappears until the productive forces that have been developed in it find a way to make an ulterior progressive movement; 2) that society does not pose itself tasks in the absence of the material conditions necessary for their solution.[26]

4   Conclusion

'All history [is] contemporary history', so wrote Benedetto Croce. 'All history is comparative history', recently added Carlo Ginzburg.[27] Gramsci's analysis of Fordism must be understood, first, as part of his own history and theory of modernity; and, second, inside this triangle, Fordism in Detroit, Fordism between late Liberalism and early Fascism in Italy, Taylorism in Soviet Russia. We could add, in a less relevant position, the French and Belgian debate, which he studied in Hyacinthe Dubreuil's and Henri De Man's books, and in Victor Cambon's introduction to Ford's.

It is a splendid moment of vivisection of the tendencies of the historical stage through which he was living, and that he tried to discern as best he could through the 'periscope' provided by the limited sources available in his confinement. Nevertheless, it must be stressed that Gramsci's Fordism no longer existed by the time he was writing about it: the Five Dollar Day had been eroded by massive inflation during the war and then dismantled in 1920; Ford factories underwent a deep restructuration in 1927 to catch up with General Motors; the 1929 crisis had crushed the whole model of consumption and exports; in the 1930s Ford was forced to face the increasing role of Big Labour in politics and Big Government in the economy – namely, the New Deal. Nor could Gramsci have observed the evolution of Fordism at Fiat, where Taylorist scientific management was substituted by the much simpler, and even more authoritarian, Bedaux system in 1927; later, towards the end of Gramsci's life, Agnelli started to build (and inaugurated, in the presence of Mussolini, in 1939) the factory that was to become the true symbol, temple, and battleground of Italian Fordism: Mirafiori.

Gramsci had seen Detroit in Turin: he hypostatised a moment of Ford's model, the one he knew mainly from Ford's autobiographies and 1920s Fiat.

One must not, therefore, overestimate Gramsci's knowledge of what was going on in Detroit. Nevertheless, his analysis was capable of understanding the

---

26   Gramsci 2014b, Q15, § 17, p. 1774, obviously echoing Marx's 1859 *Preface* to *A Contribution to the Critique of Political Economy*; compare Thomas 2010, pp. 155–6.

27   Croce 1938, p. 5, Ginzburg 2015, p. 461.

crisis of Italian civil society and the place of Fascist 'conservative modernisation' in the global economy; to debunk the idea of a 'structural' reconciliation of the interests of the capitalist with those of the workers, of a social harmony that could be guaranteed by improving capitalist productivity and prosperity; and to articulate the question of the possible socialist use of the productive forces born under capitalism, bending them in the context of the transition to Socialism. The assembly line-based industry appears to Gramsci, to recall Lenin's formula, the 'last/latest word of capitalism'. Fordism was ultimately a paradox of the structure: it was the capitalist realisation of Taylorism, and therefore its failure, because the progressive potentiality (*in itself*) of the Taylor system did not fully become actuality (*for itself*) in the American industrial regime. To Gramsci, as to Lenin, the true accomplishment of scientific management would be the scientific self-government of producers; the reconquest of science by the workers themselves, putting Fordism right-side up. By unveiling the class nature of Fordism, he pointed out what Adorno would call a 'false rationality'. The latter is itself a profoundly dialectical notion. Gramsci followed Lenin: the Taylor system was not a neutral technique, but it could be transferred to socialism, and therefore it should be transformed.

PART 8

Readings of Gramsci

∵

CHAPTER 22

Between Belonging and Originality: Norberto Bobbio's Interpretation of Gramsci

Alessio Panichi

1   Introduction

In his *Autobiografia*,[1] Norberto Bobbio reconstructs the main phases of his dialogue with a number of Italian Marxist scholars. In doing so, Bobbio asserts that during the first half of the 1950s he regarded these scholars as interlocutors rather than adversaries, remarking that 'the essays gathered in *Politica e cultura*' were the outcome of this judgement.[2] Actually, such an assertion does not exclusively concern that period of time or the topics tackled in these essays. The respectful and serene discussion, although it is not without polemical tones, characterises the whole history of the fifty year relationship between Bobbio and the Italian communists. This type of discussion reflects not only some of Bobbio's peculiar personality traits,[3] but also a clear historical and cultural awareness concerning the importance of the Marxist tradition within the context of political and intellectual history. In the last page of the essay entitled *Libertà e potere*, written in response to Palmiro Togliatti, Bobbio argues that

> if we had not learned from Marxism to look at history from the point of view of oppressed people, getting a new and immense perspective on the human world, we would not have saved ourselves. Either we would have searched for shelter on the island of our inner being or we would have put ourselves at the service of the old rulers.[4]

These words are neither a mere formal homage, imposed by the circumstances of the debate with Togliatti, nor an attempt to flatter him. Indeed, they are undoubtedly sincere, as shown by the fact that Bobbio reaffirms them even after many years have passed. For instance, in his *Autobiografia*, Bobbio, after

---

1   Bobbio 1999.
2   Bobbio 1999, p. 104.
3   Ibid.
4   Bobbio 2005, p. 240.

specifying that he has 'never been' and was 'never thought to be' a communist, acknowledges being aware that 'communism was an agent of great changes' as well as 'of a true revolution in the classical sense of the term'.[5] This awareness, which is frequent among the exponents of Italian liberal-socialism,[6] is coupled with occasional but long lasting interest in Marxian and Marxist thought, as shown by his several essays on Antonio Gramsci.

As a matter of fact, Bobbio was one of the main protagonists of the debate concerning Gramsci's ideas and their relationship to the Marxist tradition. After the publication of the *Letters from Prison* and the *Prison Notebooks*, Gramsci's theories not only influenced politics and culture in twentieth-century Italy. They also became the topic of different and opposed interpretations that, as shown by Guido Liguori in his book *Gramsci conteso*,[7] are helpful in throwing light on the history of Italian political culture. This is not the right place to reconstruct, even summarily, the root causes and consequences of this debate; instead, the important point is that it fosters and, at the same time, is fostered by Bobbio's interest in Gramsci, an interest that is sincere and long lasting, representing a strong *leitmotiv* that runs for a long time.

In the following pages, I will take into account the reasons for such an interest that, despite its sporadic nature, is continuous and manifests itself in several essays, quotations, and interviews. More specifically, I will focus on two of Bobbio's writings, that is, *Nota sulla dialettica di Gramsci* and *Gramsci e la concezione della società civile*,[8] which represent different but closely related features of his interpretation. As we shall see below, this interpretation stems from the belief that Gramsci fully belongs to the Marxist tradition, but in a rather peculiar way, which is rooted in his political commitment as well as in his organic connection with Italian history and culture. The analysis of those two writings will be flanked by the quotation and explanation of all of Gramsci's passages or concepts that are singled out by Bobbio, in order to contextualise their contents. Most importantly, it will be carried out through a careful narrative reading that aims to respect Gramsci's warning not 'to push the texts, that is, to make texts say more than they really say, just for the sake of supporting a thesis'.[9]

---

5   Bobbio 1999, p. 104; compare Bobbio 1974, p. 227.
6   Sbarberi 2005, p. xvi. See also Anderson 1988, and Greco 2000, pp. 112–15.
7   See Liguori 2012.
8   Published respectively in 1958 and 1969, see Bobbio 1958a (also Bobbio 1958b), and Bobbio 1969.
9   Gramsci 1975, Q6, § 198, p. 838.

2   On Gramsci: Admiration and Detachment

The reasons and nature of this interest are explained by Bobbio in the preface to *Saggi su Gramsci*, a volume which gathers together some of his most important writings on the Sardinian intellectual.[10] Bobbio admits to being attracted to the fact that Gramsci, while reflecting on Italian and European history, employed and reinterpreted the traditional categories of political thought in an original way. This attraction is then flanked by further reasons that are different but concomitant: Bobbio's 'intellectual sympathy' and 'deep admiration' for the 'very rare' example, set by Gramsci, of 'coherence between thought and action, and between professed ideas and political commitment'; his desire to understand and explain Gramsci; Bobbio's critical distancing from Gramsci's thought.[11] It is in light of these motivations that Bobbio, soon after the publication of the *Prison Notebooks* and incited by it, pays serious attention to the role and function of intellectuals in society,[12] a theme that is a nodal point of Gramsci's thinking as well as of Bobbio's research and scholarly activity. Bobbio mainly deals with four other topics by analysing numerous passages from the *Prison Notebooks*, and by following the same method, based on textual decomposition and recomposition, he applied to the study 'of some classics, such as Hobbes and Hegel'.[13]

2.1   *What Is Interesting and What Is Not*

The first three topics are the dialectic, civil society, and political theory. They are directly connected with episodes of the Italian debate on Gramsci's thought. I refer to the conferences that were held in Rome, Cagliari, and Turin, on the occasion of the second, third, and fifth decennial of Gramsci's death. The fourth topic arises from Bobbio's familiarity with Gramsci's cultural background, a familiarity due to the reading and rereading of his works. This topic is the problem concerning origin, sources, and the cultural boundaries of Gramscian ideas.[14]

The analysis of these themes, according to Bobbio, is counterbalanced by his lack of interest in the discussion of the relationship between Gramsci's theory and the Marxist-Leninist tradition. Indeed, Bobbio is fully convinced that the

---

10   Bobbio 1990b.
11   Bobbio 1990b, pp. 8–9; compare Bobbio 2006, p. 107.
12   Bobbio 1990b, p. 8. See Lanfranchi 1989, pp. 88–9, 94–5; D'Orsi and Chiarotto 2012, pp. 490–2.
13   Bobbio 1990b, p. 9.
14   Bobbio 1990b, pp. 9–11.

relevance of Gramsci's Marxism does not depend on its conceptual affinity to or distance from the classical texts of Marxism-Leninism.[15] Actually Bobbio, willingly or not, plays an important role in this discussion, because he casts light on the fact that there are some elements in Gramsci's thought which are unique and do not blindly mirror Marxian theories. Nevertheless, Bobbio speaks the truth when he claims – in step with his critically detached attitude – to respect this thought by refusing to exploit it and make it into an argument in favour of or against the communist movement.[16]

2.2   A 'Controversial' Quotation

Obviously, this does not mean that Bobbio never quotes Gramsci's passages in order to strengthen his own theses and counteract those put forward by some intellectuals belonging to the Italian Communist Party. Indeed, the first quotation from Gramsci appears in an essay entitled *Invito al colloquio*. It was published in 1951 in *Comprendre*, the journal of the European Society of Culture,[17] and four years later it was republished in the volume *Politica e cultura*.[18] In order to defend 'critical thinking' against 'dogmatic thinking',[19] Bobbio reminds his interlocutors, the Italian Marxists, that 'militant philosophy' is not at the service of political or ecclesiastical rulers, because it defends the 'freedom of illuminating reason' against the attacks launched by 'traditionalists' or 'innovators'. According to Bobbio, the intellectuals have not only the duty to be actively involved in the political struggle, but also the right to discuss and criticise or refuse features of the struggle.[20] In this regard, Bobbio quotes the following passage from Gramsci's notebook published in 1948 as *Il materialismo storico e la filosofia di Benedetto Croce*:

> To understand and to evaluate realistically one's adversary's position and his reasons (and sometimes one's adversary is the whole of past thought) means precisely to be liberated from the prison of ideologies in the bad sense of the word – that of blind ideological fanaticism. It means taking up a point of view that is 'critical', which for the purpose of scientific research is the only fertile one.[21]

---

15   Bobbio 1990b, p. 9.
16   Ibid.
17   See Bobbio 1951, pp. 102–3.
18   Bobbio 1990b, pp. 7–8.
19   Bobbio 1990b, p. 7.
20   Bobbio 2005, p. 5.
21   Gramsci 1948, p. 21. Compare Gramsci 1975, Q10, § 24, p. 1263.

Before examining Bobbio's interest in Gramsci further, I would like to make some clarifications about this passage that highlights only one side of Gramsci's concept of ideology. Indeed, the word ideology is given different meanings by Gramsci, who underlines the relevance and historical efficacy of ideological spheres by interpreting them in a way that presupposes and implies the refusal of the excess of economism, which 'overrates mechanical causes', as well as of the excess of ideologism, which overrates the "'voluntary' and individual element".[22]

More precisely, Gramsci distinguishes mainly, although not exclusively, two senses of that word.[23] On the one hand, ideologies 'are laughable' whenever they are 'pure rumour' and are meant 'to generate confusion', as well as 'to deceive and subjugate social energies' that are 'potentially antagonistic'.[24] To put it differently, the word ideology has a pejorative sense when it means, just to give a few examples, 'unilateral practical-political tendency',[25] 'arbitrary cogitations of some individuals',[26] and 'absolute and eternal truth'.[27] On the other hand, ideologies, instead of being 'arbitrary, rationalistic, and 'intended'', are 'historically organic' and 'necessary to a given structure'.[28] In this case, ideologies 'are anything but appearances and illusions', because they are 'an objective and operative reality', even though they are not 'the mainspring of history', meaning that it is not 'ideologies that create social reality but social reality, in its productive structure, that creates ideologies'.[29]

However, ideologies not only make possible the historical understanding of material forces, without which ideologies would be 'individual whims',[30] but also organise 'human masses' and 'shape the ground on which men move, acquire consciousness of their position, struggle etc.'.[31] For this reason, as Guido Liguori points out, 'the fight for hegemony is a fight between ideologies', since it is through ideology that 'a collective subject becomes conscious of itself and thus able to oppose itself to the rival hegemony'.[32] In short, ideology is

---

22   Gramsci 1975, Q4, § 38, p. 456. See Cospito 2004, pp. 232–3.
23   Liguori 2009c, p. 400; compare Liguori 2004a, pp. 135–6.
24   Gramsci 1984, p. 17.
25   Gramsci 1975, Q8, § 27, p. 958.
26   Gramsci 1975, Q7, § 19, p. 868.
27   Gramsci 1975, Q4, § 40, p. 466.
28   Gramsci 1975, Q7, § 19, pp. 868–9.
29   Gramsci 1975, Q4, § 15, p. 437.
30   Gramsci 1975, Q7, § 21, p. 869.
31   Gramsci 1975, Q7, § 19, p. 869.
32   Liguori 2009c, p. 401; compare Liguori 2004a, p. 143.

also something else and more than 'blind ideological fanaticism' or 'arbitrary cogitations of some individuals': it is the place where 'collective subjectivity' is born.[33]

3   Gramsci's Concept of Dialectic

On 11–13 January 1958, Bobbio attended the first Italian conference of Gramscian studies, organised by the Gramsci Institute in Rome. Originally expected to take place in 1957, twenty years after Gramsci's death, the congress was postponed because of the turbulent events of 1956. Thus, it came to represent 'an important stage' in the attempt made by Italian communists, 'to reopen the dialogue' with the 'non-communist democratic branches of the Italian culture'.[34] Bobbio was undoubtedly one of the main representatives of these branches. He gave a speech that, on his own account, 'was completely unnoticed'.[35] The speech, entitled *Nota sulla dialettica di Gramsci*, was published in the journal *Società* first and then in the conference proceedings.[36]

The starting point of the speech is that an adequate analysis of Marxist theory cannot neglect to consider the function performed by the dialectic. Nevertheless, the role played by this theme in Gramsci's thought has not received proper attention by scholars. Therefore, Bobbio decides to undertake research about the dialectic, in order to contribute to the 'detailed and organic' study of Gramsci's philosophy. He pays attention to three specific aspects: first, the importance that Gramsci gives to the concept of dialectic, second, the different meanings taken on by this word in Gramsci's reasoning, and third, the function performed by this concept in both the destructive and the constructive parts of his thought.[37]

3.1   *The Importance of the Dialectic*
In regard to the first aspect, Bobbio believes that Gramsci attaches 'fundamental importance to the dialectic', drawing on the thesis of Marx and Engels that the revolutionary feature of Hegel's philosophy lies in the dialectical method, which marks 'a turning point in the history of philosophy'.[38]

---

33   Liguori 2009c, p. 401; compare Liguori 2004a, pp. 139, 143.
34   Liguori 1996, p. 99.
35   Bobbio 1990b, p. 23.
36   See Bobbio 1958a and 1958b.
37   Bobbio 1990b, pp. 25–6.
38   Bobbio 1990b, p. 26.

Here Bobbio recalls the struggle waged by Gramsci against Bukharin, who is accused of demoting the dialectic to 'a sub-species of formal logic, an elementary scholastics'.[39] This allegation relies on the belief, clearly expressed by Gramsci, that the dialectic, besides being 'a technique', is as much 'a new way of thinking, a new philosophy',[40] as the 'doctrine of knowledge and the medullary substance of historiography and political science'.[41] Therefore, to think dialectically means to clash with 'vulgar common sense that is dogmatic, eager for imperious certainties, and has formal logic as its expression'.[42] Accordingly, Gramsci stresses how the anti-dialectical viewpoint, which marks those who lack 'historical sense in understanding the different moments of a process of cultural development', is 'dogmatic' and 'imprisoned in the abstract schemes of formal logic'.[43]

3.2   Meanings of the Dialectic

As for the second aspect, Bobbio writes that the term dialectic and its derivatives have, in the *Prison Notebooks*, the same three meanings given to them by Marx and Engels.

1. The first meaning is 'reciprocal action' and comes into view when Gramsci speaks about the reciprocal connection between intellectuals and masses, and more frequently about the relationships between structure and superstructure,[44] which Gramsci calls 'the crucial problem of historical materialism'.[45]

It is well known that Gramsci takes a stand against the economistic, deterministic and mechanistic interpretation of historical materialism, an interpretation that largely characterised the Second and Third International and is embodied in the *Prison Notebooks* by Bukharin.[46] In doing so, Gramsci critically rethinks the traditional dichotomy between structure and superstructure by arguing that the latter is neither a passive reflection nor an intentional distortion of the former.[47] The claim that every political and ideological fluctuation must be presented and explained 'as an immediate expression of the structure'

---

39   Gramsci 1975, Q11, § 22, p. 1425.
40   Gramsci 1975, Q4, § 18, p. 439.
41   Gramsci 1975, Q11, § 22, p. 1425.
42   Ibid.
43   Gramsci 1975, Q11, § 16, p. 1408.
44   Bobbio 1990b, pp. 29–30.
45   Gramsci 1975, Q4, § 38, p. 455.
46   Cospito 2009, p. 820.
47   Prestipino 2009, p. 214. See Prestipino 2004, p. 68.

is nothing else but 'primitive infantilism'.[48] On the contrary, Gramsci writes, if 'men acquire consciousness of their social position and tasks on the ground of the superstructures, this means that between structure and superstructure there is a necessary and vital nexus'.[49] More specifically, structure and super-structure are linked to each other through necessary 'reciprocity, which is the real dialectical process'.[50] Just as structure is the 'point of reference' and the 'dialectical, non-mechanical causation of the superstructures',[51] superstructure 'reacts dialectically on and modifies the structure'.[52] In other words, between structure and superstructure there is a distinction that is purely methodolo-gical, not organic,[53] and the same dialectical detachment existing 'between thesis and antithesis'.[54]

2. The second meaning of dialectic in Gramsci's *Prison Notebooks* is the 'pro-cess of thesis, antithesis, and synthesis'. According to Bobbio, it is 'the genuine Hegelian-Marxist meaning' and the most frequent and important in Gramsci's lexicon. This meaning expresses itself in the concept of history as a contradict-ory reality, whose course is not evolutionary, because it comes along 'through negation and negation of the negation',[55] or better, through the destruction of the thesis by the antithesis.

Gramsci argues, in fact, that in 'real history' the latter 'tends to destroy' the former and 'the synthesis will be a transcendence', even though no one can 'establish *a priori*' what element of the thesis 'will be 'conserved' in the synthesis'.[56] For this reason, Gramsci charges Proudhon (and Croce) with 'the mutilation of Hegelianism and of the dialectic', stressing that they make a philosophical mistake whose origin is practical and which turns out to be 'one of the many forms of anti-historicist rationalism'. The mistake lies in mechanic-ally presupposing that in the dialectical process 'the thesis must be 'conserved' by the antithesis in order not to destroy the historical process', which is thus foreseen 'as a mechanical, arbitrarily preordained repetition *ad infinitum*'.[57]

---

48   Gramsci 1975, Q7, § 24, p. 871.
49   Gramsci 1975, Q10, § 41, p. 1321.
50   Gramsci 1975, Q8, § 182, p. 1052.
51   Gramsci 1975, Q4, § 56, p. 503.
52   Gramsci 1975, Q7, § 1, p. 854; compare Gramsci 1975, Q8, § 37, p. 964; Q10, § 41, p. 1316 (where the expression 'dialectical, non-mechanical causation' is significantly substituted by 'dia-lectical impulse').
53   Liguori 2004b, p. 213.
54   Gramsci 1975, Q7, § 1, p. 854.
55   Bobbio 1990b, pp. 30–1.
56   Gramsci 1975, Q10, § 6, p. 1221.
57   Gramsci 1975, Q10, § 6, pp. 1220–1.

3. The third and last meaning underlined by Bobbio is the conversion of quantity into quality. It appears in Gramsci's polemic against (at least) three targets:[58] The first is Bukharin's materialism, which does not explain 'how the philosophy of praxis has 'concretised' the Hegelian law of quantity becoming quality'.[59] The second is vulgar evolutionary theory that 'is at the foundation of sociology which cannot know the dialectical principle with the passage from quantity to quality'.[60] The third is the thesis of the predictability of history, which stems from the erroneous idea that 'conflicting forces in continuous movement' are 'reducible to fixed quantities', whereas within these forces 'quantity continuously becomes quality'.[61]

3.3 The Constructive and Destructive Function of the Dialectic

With regard to the third aspect, Bobbio asserts that the concept of dialectic performs a very central function within Gramsci's thinking, a function that is 'almost exclusively linked to the second meaning illustrated above',[62] the process of thesis, antithesis, and synthesis, and allows Gramsci to carry out three conceptual operations.

1. The first of these operations is the characterisation of Marxism as a new philosophy that is better than others, since it is far more conscious of historical contradictions as well as being an active element within the framework of these contradictions.[63]

Indeed, Gramsci writes that the main difference between Marxism and 'other ideologies' lies in the fact that the latter 'are inorganic because they are contradictory' and 'directed at conciliating opposed and contradictory interests', whereas the former 'does not tend to resolve contradictions peacefully', but rather 'is the very theory of such contradictions'.[64] In this regard, Bobbio quotes another, famous passage where Gramsci asserts that the philosophy of praxis, besides being 'a reform and development of Hegelianism', as well as a philosophy that is 'set free (or attempts to set itself free) from any unilateral and fanatical ideological element',[65]

---

58   Bobbio 1990b, p. 31.
59   Gramsci 1975, Q11, §32, p. 1446.
60   Gramsci 1975, Q11, §26, p. 1432.
61   Gramsci 1975, Q11, §15, p. 1403.
62   Bobbio 1990b, p. 31.
63   Bobbio 1990b, pp. 31–2.
64   Gramsci 1975, Q10, §41, pp. 1319–20.
65   Gramsci 1975, Q11, §62, p. 1487.

is the full consciousness of contradictions, in which the philosopher him-self, either understood individually or understood as an entire social group, not only grasps the contradictions, but places himself as an ele-ment of the contradiction and raises this element to a principle of know-ledge and thus of action.[66]

2. The second conceptual operation is identifiable with the cultural battle fought by Gramsci against two theoretical enemies, according to the guidelines given by Marx and repeated many times by Engels.[67]

The first enemy, represented by a Hegelian idealism that is dialectical but employs the dialectic in a speculative way, is embodied by Croce,[68] who is one of the few thinkers to whom Gramsci 'devotes an almost systematic analysis and interest'.[69] Gramsci's battle against Croce, as Giuseppe Cacciatore observes, is generated not by an insignificant or merely propagandist polemic, 'but by a continuous and intense critical debate between materialist historicism and speculative historicism'.[70] For Gramsci, in fact, Croce's historicism 'still remains in the theological-speculative phase',[71] so that history becomes nothing more than 'a formal history, a history of concepts', and 'a history of intellectuals, indeed an autobiographical history of Croce's own thought, a history of coach-man flies'.[72] Similarly, Croce's philosophy contains not merely 'a trace of tran-scendence and theology', but 'all transcendence and theology, barely liberated from the more vulgar mythological exterior'.[73]

The second enemy is vulgar and traditional materialism, which is anti-idealistic but also non-dialectical. It is embodied by Bukharin[74] and repres-ented by his book *Theory of Historical Materialism*,[75] which was published in 1921 and republished 'in several editions and translations in the main European

---

66   Ibid. In quoting this passage, Bobbio does not accurately transcribe the last sentence, so that it loses its original and precise meaning. He writes 'pone se stesso come elemento e principio di conoscenza e quindi di azione' instead of 'pone se stesso come elemento della contraddizione, eleva questo elemento a principio di conoscenza e quindi di azione'. See Bobbio 1990b, p. 31.

67   Bobbio 1990b, p. 31.

68   Bobbio 1990b, p. 32. See Bobbio 1990b, p. 111; compare Bobbio 2014, pp. 35–6.

69   Cacciatore 2009, p. 188.

70   Ibid.

71   Gramsci 1975, Q10, §8, p. 1226.

72   Gramsci 1975, Q10, §1, p. 1241.

73   Gramsci 1975, Q10, §8, p. 1225.

74   Bobbio 1990b, p. 32.

75   Bukharin 1925.

languages', playing a very important role 'in the international communist move-ment'.[76] However, Gramsci attributes to Bukharin a vulgar and general under-standing of science that prevents him 'from acknowledging and valuing the concept of the dialectic and the essential function that it performs in historical materialism'.[77] Bukharin gives, then, an erroneous and dogmatic interpretation of historical materialism that is linked to the need, 'understood in a somewhat childish and naïve way', to resolve 'in peremptory fashion the practical problem of the predictability of historical events'.[78] For Gramsci, this need, along with the lack of understanding of the dialectic, leads Bukharin to identify historical materialism 'with the quest for the ultimate or single cause', without realising that 'the problem of ultimate causes is dispelled by the dialectic'.[79]

3. The third conceptual operation is the development of what Bobbio calls 'a nodal point for the interpretation of Gramscian philosophy', where this philo-sophy is understood as an inheritance and a continuation of the Marxist tradi-tion. This point concerns the dialectical mechanism, or better, the stages of the dialectical process and the transition from one stage to another. In short, this point concerns the relationship between thesis and antithesis.[80]

According to Bobbio, Gramsci, in his polemic against Croce, refers to a fam-ous passage of Marx's *Poverty of Philosophy* which asserts that the 'dialectical movement' is based on 'the coexistence of two contradictory sides, their con-flict and their fusion into a new category. The very setting of the problem of eliminating the bad side cuts short the dialectical movement'.[81] Consequently, Gramsci underlines how every antithesis 'must necessarily place itself as a radical antagonist of the thesis, up to the point of proposing to destroy it completely and to substitute it completely'.[82] To put it differently, Gramsci embraces the idea that dialectical thought has its own nucleus in the '*strength of negativity* in history', which means that the dialectic emphasises the anti-thesis and judges it to be the negation of the thesis, giving rise to the 'theoretical consciousness of the revolution'.[83]

---

76   Frosini 2009a, p. 85.
77   Frosini 2009a, p. 87.
78   Gramsci 1975, Q11, § 15, p. 1403.
79   Gramsci 1975, Q4, § 26, p. 445.
80   Bobbio 1990b, p. 34.
81   Marx 1976b [1847], p. 168.
82   Gramsci 1975, Q10, § 41, p. 1328.
83   Bobbio 1990b, pp. 35–6.

4   Between Belonging and Originality

As we can see, Bobbio's analysis comes to a clear and hardly equivocal conclusion. In his opinion, Gramsci's reflection on the dialectic follows faithfully the
teachings of Marx and Engels, without introducing new and original elements
into their conceptual framework. Indeed, Bobbio thinks that in the *Prison Notebooks* the meanings of dialectic are the same as those in the texts of Marx and
Engels, so much so that Gramsci's objections to Bukharin and Croce repeat
those that 'Marx and Engels made against mechanistic materialism and Hegel's
philosophy'.[84] After all, this conclusion is the logical and coherent consequence
of the two goals pursued by Bobbio in his essay: discerning the different meanings of the dialectic in compliance with the 'Marxian and Engelsian use', and
'showing the differences between Gramsci's use and that of Croce's'.[85]

Therefore, it is no exaggeration to say that Bobbio's *Nota sulla dialettica di
Gramsci* has a strong and important point and, at the same time, a characteristic that may explain why it was 'completely unnoticed'.[86] This writing, in light
of the observations made by Bobbio in the contemporaneous essay on Marx's
dialectic,[87] examines a feature of Gramsci's work which was little studied in
the 1950s, turning out to be pioneering from a historiographical point of view.
Nevertheless, such an examination comes to conclusions representing only one
part of Bobbio's reading of Gramsci, a part that was not debated or contested
by scholars. After all, it conveys and confirms the image of Gramsci as a faithful follower of Marx and Engels that, in the cultural climate of the Cold War,
could not displease Marxists and non-Marxists, although for different reasons.
Moreover, Bobbio's essay is based on a careful, prudent philological and terminological commentary on some of Gramsci's passages, so that not much room is
left for interpretative controversies. Anyway, Bobbio himself admits that the
theme of dialectic 'was quite neglected' and did not give rise 'to different and
controversial interpretations'.[88]

I say one part because Bobbio's reading swings between two polar opposites. On the one hand, Bobbio is aware that Gramsci was one of the chief
exponents of Marxism. On the other hand, his reading contends that Gramsci,
while developing a 'living' and 'coherent' Marxist theory,[89] was not a faith-

---

84   Bobbio 1990b, p. 56.
85   Bobbio 1990b, pp. 9–10.
86   Bobbio 1990b, p. 23.
87   See Bobbio 1958c, and 1965, p. 6; compare Violi 1997, p. xxxiv.
88   Bobbio 1990b, pp. 10–11.
89   Bobbio 2014, pp. 35–6.

ful imitator, because he made innovative and original contributions to both Marxist doctrine and the Italian political tradition. Bobbio never misses the chance to affirm and reaffirm that Gramsci, far from being a 'dead dog', was an original and 'lively thinker', who was so great that he is worth 'considering and judging in himself', regardless of the relationship between his thought and the 'almost sacralised' image of Marx and Lenin.[90] In short, Bobbio gives the reader a conception of Gramsci as a Marxist thinker who, with respect to the tradition in which he was fully situated, combined theoretical belonging and originality, which were not antithetical or juxtaposed, since they interacted and mutually completed each other, spawning an exceptional theoretical model.

So, it is hardly surprising that in 1967, at the Gramscian conference in Cagliari, Bobbio delivered a speech, *Gramsci e la concezione della società civile*,[91] where he clearly highlighted the peculiarities of Gramsci's Marxism. Actually, Bobbio begins by stressing the element of the belonging, or better, by explaining that the theory of state put forward by Gramsci in his *Prison Notebooks* has the same main features as those characterising the 'Marxian and Engelsian doctrine of state'.[92] These features can be summed up in the idea that the state

> is not an end in itself, but it is an apparatus, an instrument; it is the representative of interests that are not universal but particular; it is not an institution standing above society, but it is conditioned by and thus subject to society; it is not a permanent institution, but a particular one, which is meant to disappear with the transformation of the underlying society.[93]

However, Bobbio, soon after making this statement, shifts his own attention to the element of originality that, as stated above, is the main focus of his speech, taking a stand against misuse and abuse of some allegedly distinct and clear concepts. Indeed, Bobbio argues that anyone who is familiar with Gramsci's works knows that his thought has personal and original features, which forbid 'easy schematisations, almost always inspired by polemical political reasons', such as 'Gramsci is Marxist-Leninist', or 'he is more Leninist than Marxist', or 'he is more Marxist than Leninist', or 'he is neither Marxist nor Leninist',

---

90   Bobbio 1990b, pp. 16, 18, 20.
91   See Bobbio 1969.
92   Bobbio 1990b, p. 40.
93   Bobbio 1990b, p. 41.

as if 'Marxism', 'Leninism', 'Marxism-Leninism' were clear and distinct concepts, within which one can sum up this or that theory or group of theories without leaving margins of error, and one could employ them like a straight-edged ruler to measure the alignment of a wall.[94]

These remarks pave the way for a significant assertion that shows how Bobbio's interpretive perspective is not the same as that taken nine years earlier, when he focused on the lines of continuity existing between Marx, Engels, and Gramsci. Bobbio now comes to affirm that

> The first task of an enquiry on Gramsci's thought is to point out and ana-
> lyse these personal and original features, with no other concern than
> that of reconstructing the outlines of a theory that looks fragmentary,
> scattered, unsystematic, with some terminological oscillations, even
> though it is sustained, especially in the prison writings, by a fundamental
> unity of inspiration.[95]

5   The Nature of 'Civil Society'

5.1   *From the Philosophers of Natural Law to Hegel*

Driven by the idea that the reconstruction of Gramsci's political thought must take into account, first and foremost, its peculiar characteristics, Bobbio believes that such a reconstruction must begin by examining the 'key concept' of civil society. In Bobbio's view, in fact, Gramsci is 'the first Marxist writer' who employs this concept for analysing society, and, more importantly, his way of employing it differs as much from Hegel as from Marx and Engels.[96]

Bobbio highlights this difference with a brief explanation of the interpretation of civil society given by Hegel and Marx. Bobbio's first step is to point out the difference that exists between the philosophy of natural law and the Hegelian-Marxist tradition. Whereas in the former 'the expression *societas civilis*' indicates, 'according to the Latin use', political society and thus the state, in the latter it designates 'the pre-state society'. More specifically, Bobbio observes that Hegel makes a radical innovation 'with respect to the tradition of natural law'. In the 1821 edition of his *Philosophy of Right*,[97] he uses the

---

94   Bobbio 1990b, pp. 41–2.
95   Bobbio 1990b, p. 42.
96   Bobbio 1990b, pp. 42–3.
97   Hegel 1942.

term civil society to indicate not 'political society', unlike 'his immediate predecessors', but 'pre-political society', which 'until then had been called natural society'. Much more important, however, is the fact that Hegel, when describing pre-state relationships, 'abandons the mainly juridical analysis' carried out by the philosophers of natural law, who tend to identify 'economic relations' with 'their juridical forms (theory of property and of contracts)'. Since his youth, writes Bobbio, Hegel 'draws on the economists, especially the English ones',[98] in whose writings

> the economic relations constitute the fabric of pre-state society, and ... the distinction between pre-state and state is increasingly described as a distinction between the sphere of economic relations and the sphere of political institutions.[99]

5.2 *From Hegel to Marx*

The radical innovation made by Hegel is brought to completion by Marx, who, after all, explicitly refers to Hegel's civil society in a well known passage from the 1859 *Preface* to the *Contribution to the Critique of Political Economy*. Here Marx writes that his critical review of Hegel's *Philosophy of Right* led him to two conclusions. First, 'neither legal relations nor political forms could be comprehended whether by themselves or on the basis of a so-called general development of the human mind', because they are rooted 'in the material conditions of life', whose totality Hegel 'embraces within the term "civil society"'. Second, 'the anatomy of this civil society, however, has to be sought in political economy'.[100]

In light of this passage, Bobbio draws the conclusion that Marx makes civil society coincide with the structural level, establishing its meaning 'as a stage of the development of economic relations, which precedes and determines the political stage'. Bobbio strengthens this conclusion by quoting some famous passages from *The German Ideology*. These passages say that civil society 'is the true focus and theatre of all history', as it is the 'form of intercourse determined by the existing productive forces at all previous historical stages, and in its turn determining these'.[101] In other words,

> Civil society embraces the whole material intercourse of individuals within a definite stage of the development of productive forces. It embraces

---

98   Bobbio 1990b, pp. 44–5.
99   Bobbio 1990b, p. 45.
100   Marx 1987b [1859], p. 262.
101   Marx and Engels 1976a [1846], p. 50.

the whole commercial and industrial life of a given stage and, insofar, transcends the state and the nation, though … it must assert itself in its external relations as nationality and internally must organise itself as state.[102]

5.3   *From Marx Back to Hegel*

With these remarks Bobbio set the stage for his main thesis that, far from being ignored, has been harshly criticised by Marxist scholars. It ignited a lively debate both during the 1967 conference on Gramsci in Cagliari and in its aftermath. The core of this thesis is the belief that Marx's identification of civil society with the structural level is the starting point for analysing Gramsci's concept of civil society. In this regard 'Gramsci's theory introduces a deep innovation with respect to the whole Marxist tradition'.[103] This innovation lies in the fact that 'civil society in Gramsci does not belong to the structural moment, but to the superstructural one',[104] as shown in Bobbio's opinion by the following passage from the *Prison Notebooks*:

> What we can do, for the moment, is to fix two major superstructural 'levels': the one that can be called 'civil society', that is the ensemble of organisms commonly called 'private', and that of 'political society' or 'the State'. These two levels correspond on the one hand to the function of 'hegemony' which the dominant group exercises throughout society and on the other hand to that of 'direct dominion' or command exercised through the State and 'juridical' government.[105]

Behind Bobbio's main thesis there are two ideas related to each other. First, Hegel's concept of civil society is both wider and narrower than that accepted in the language of Marx and Engels. It is wider because Hegel's civil society includes not only 'the sphere of economic relations' and 'the development of classes', but also 'the administration of justice' and 'the administrative and corporate system'. It is narrower since civil society, 'in Hegel's trichotomic system', represents 'the intermediate stage between family and the state', and thus does not include 'all the pre-state relations and institutions, including family'. In short, Hegel's civil society is 'the sphere of economic relations' as well

---

102   Marx and Engels 1976a [1846], p. 89.
103   Bobbio 1990b, p. 48.
104   Ibid.
105   Gramsci 1975, Q12, § 1, pp. 1518–19.

as 'their external regulation according to the principles of the liberal state'.[106] Second, Gramsci, 'contrary to what is believed', draws his own concept of civil society not from Marx, but from Hegel, or better from an interpretation of Hegel's civil society that is 'a bit forced, or at least unilateral', as it focuses on only one of its features, that represented not by the economic relations, but by the institutions which regulate them.[107] Here Bobbio recalls and partly quotes the passage in which Gramsci stresses how one must distinguish civil society

> as Hegel understands it and in the sense it is often used in these notes (that is, in the sense of the political and cultural hegemony of a social group over the whole of society; as the ethical content of the State) from the sense given to it by Catholics, for whom civil society is, instead, political society or the State, as opposed to the society of the family and of the Church.[108]

5.4   Bobbio and Texier

Also in this case, it is necessary, or at least worthwhile, to make a short clarification about this passage in the wake of Jacques Texier, who rightly advises the readers that the adverb 'often' constitutes a warning, which clearly indicates 'how Gramsci employs the expression 'civil society' *also* in other senses'.[109]

One of them has been underlined by Texier himself, who calls it 'civil society-homo oeconomicus',[110] referring to the passage from the *Prison Notebooks* where Gramsci explains the concept of 'homo oeconomicus' by saying that it means 'the abstraction of the economic activity of a determinate form of society', that is, 'of a determinate economic structure'. Consequently, every 'social form has its 'homo oeconomicus', that is, its economic activity'. After giving this explanation, Gramsci declares, on the one hand, that civil society stands between 'the economic structure and the State with its legislation and its coercion'; and on the other hand, that civil society has to be 'radically transformed in concrete terms' by adjusting it to the economic structure. The instrument to make this adjustment possibile is the state,[111] although

---

106   Bobbio 1990b, pp. 46–7.
107   Bobbio 1990b, pp. 50–1.
108   Gramsci 1975, Q6, § 24, p. 703.
109   Texier 2009, p. 769.
110   Texier 2009, p. 770.
111   Gramsci 1975, Q10, § 15, pp. 1253–4.

it is necessary for the State to 'be willing' to do this; i.e. for the representatives of the change that has taken place in the economic structure to be in control of the State. To expect that civil society will conform to the new structure as a result of propaganda and persuasion, or that the old 'homo oeconomicus' will disappear without being buried with all the honours it deserves, is a new form of economic rhetoric, a new form of empty and inconclusive economic moralism.[112]

This passage and the other quoted above show that Gramsci's concept of civil society is complex and polysemous as well as linked to key features of his thought, such as hegemony and the entanglement between coercion and consent.[113] It is therefore not by chance that Bobbio and Texier write, respectively, that civil society is the 'essential point, upon which the whole of Gramsci's conceptual system is based'[114] and 'the sphere of political activity par excellence', since it is the place where the 'so called private organisations (syndicates, parties, every kind of organisation)' aim to transform 'men's way of thinking'.[115]

5.5   *Two Further Consequences*

As mentioned previously, Bobbio is led by two connected ideas to draw the conclusion that Gramsci, like Marx, consider civil society to be the active and positive moment of historical development. Nonetheless the former, unlike the latter, thinks that civil society is a superstructural level and includes all 'ideological-cultural relationships' as well as 'the whole [of] spiritual-intellectual life'.[116] This main difference, in Bobbio's view, that Gramsci shifts civil society from the structural level to the superstructural one, entails two further and equally significant differences.

The first consequence, according to Bobbio, is that Gramsci, in contrast to Marx, believes that the superstructure is the primary and dominating moment of history, whereas the structure is the subordinate and secondary moment, despite the reciprocal relation between these levels. Bobbio is well aware and explicitly states that Gramsci 'always had a very clear idea of the complexity of the relationships between structure and superstructure',[117] as shown by a famous passage taken from an early essay from 1918:

---

112   Gramsci 1975, Q10, § 15, p. 1254.
113   See Gramsci 1975, Q6, § 87, pp. 762–3.
114   Bobbio 1990b, pp. 48–9.
115   Texier 2009, p. 770.
116   Bobbio 1990b, pp. 10, 48–51.
117   Bobbio 1990b, p. 49.

Between the premise (economic structure) and the consequence (political constitution), relations are anything but simple and direct: and the history of a people is not documented only by economic facts. The twists and turns of the causation are complex and tangled, and in order to unravel them a deep and diffused study of all spiritual and practical activities is beneficial.[118]

The second consequence concerns the relationship between institutions and ideologies occurring within the superstructural level, rather than the fundamental relation between structure and superstructure. In this case, Bobbio's statements are also clear and unequivocal. Whereas Marx places institutions before ideologies, which are considered as 'posthumous and mystified-mystifying justification of class rule', Gramsci reverses the relation between them, it being understood that this relation is based on reciprocal action. Indeed, writes Bobbio, in Gramsci's thought 'ideologies become the primary moment of history, and the institutions the secondary one',[119] meaning that ideologies,

> are no longer seen just as a posthumous justification of power whose historical formation depends on material conditions, but are seen as forces capable of shaping and creating new history, and of collaborating in the formation of fledgling power, rather than to justify an already established power.[120]

6   Conclusion: A Fertile Link

Bobbio's main thesis provoked much debate among Gramscian scholars, whose reactions were not entirely surprising to him. Bobbio knew very well that such a thesis, which was an unusual position in the contemporary range of Gramscian studies, could be either misunderstood or polemically simplified. It is therefore not by chance that Bobbio, soon after putting forward his thesis, tried (unsuccessfully) to remove all doubts and misinterpretations by strongly asserting that he did not

---

118   Gramsci 1958, pp. 280–1. See Gramsci 1984, pp. 204–5.
119   Bobbio 1990b, p. 55.
120   Ibid.

intend to deny Gramsci's Marxism, but to call attention to the fact that the appreciation of civil society is not what relates him to Marx, as it may seem to the superficial reader, but, if anything, what distinguishes him.[121]

I say unsuccessfully, because some Marxist scholars, for instance Valentino Gerratana and Jacques Texier, were alarmed and worried not by Bobbio's intentions, but by the consequences, whether real or alleged, of his thesis, which would establish that Gramsci was not a Marxist at all. Texier – called by Bobbio 'the most ruthless' of his critics[122] – asserts that, if civil society identifies with the superstructural level and occupies centre stage in Gramsci's thought, then Gramsci becomes 'a pupil of left Hegelianism' and 'the theorist of an ideological concept of history' that subordinates historical development to the intellectuals, who are 'the protagonists of civil society'.[123] In his turn, Gerratana writes that, if one agrees with Bobbio, then

> it is just a euphemism to say that Gramsci places himself, with respect to Marx, beyond the dilemma of orthodoxy and heterodoxy. More simply, it should be said that he is quite another thing, and that he belongs to a completely different cultural sphere.[124]

Here I cannot reconstruct in detail these and other objections, to which Bobbio replies that his only goal has been to find the 'right place' for Gramsci's theory inside and not outside the Marxist tradition by highlighting its 'richness, complexity and fertility'.[125] I conclude my essay by making some brief remarks concerning the basic reasons both for Bobbio's thesis and his belief in Gramsci's originality.

These reasons refer to the link between biography, intellectual work, and national history that shapes the background of a large part of Bobbio's work, as well as of the Italian cultural tradition. A full understanding of Bobbio's essay on civil society in Gramsci cannot leave Bobbio's reflections on the main features of Italian Marxism out of consideration. In a manuscript contemporary with this essay (between 1966 and 1968), Bobbio writes that, among these features, are the 'appreciation of the superstructure' resulting from an 'opposition

---

121   Bobbio 1990b, p. 50.
122   Bobbio 1990b, p. 66.
123   Texier 1968, pp. 80–1, 87.
124   Gerratana 1969, pp. 170–1.
125   Bobbio 1990b, pp. 17–20.

to economic determinism', and the non-materialist interpretation of Marx. In this regard, Bobbio explicitly mentions Gramsci.[126]

Similarly, the singularity of Gramscian Marxism is due to two reasons. The first reason regards Gramsci's life, or better the fact that Gramsci, being a scholar as well as a man of action totally committed to the political struggle, deals with not only 'traditional philosophical problems', but also with the 'real problems of our time'. The second reason is the deep and organic connection between Gramsci's thought and the political and cultural history of Italy.[127] According to Bobbio, this connection, besides explaining the great success enjoyed by Gramsci in postwar Italy, is essential to understand Gramscian theory. On 13 May 1987, on the occasion of the fifth decennial of Gramsci's death, Bobbio delivered a speech in Rome where he asserted that 'Gramsci was Marxist and Leninist'. But, Gramsci re-elaborated his 'ideas by looking for fruitful and original relationships with Italian thought'.[128] Although Bobbio spoke these words on a very particular occasion, I think that they clearly express the overall meaning of Bobbio's interpretation of Gramsci's thought between originality and belonging.

---

126 Bobbio 2014, pp. 38–9.
127 Bobbio 1990b, pp. 102, 104.
128 Bobbio 1990b, p. 110.

CHAPTER 23

The Diffusion of Gramsci's Thought in the 'Peripheral West' of Latin America

Valentina Cuppi

1   Introduction

> Basically, there is no country in Latin America without publications or related comments on Gramsci. The editions of his works are or were widely spread especially in Argentina, Mexico and Brazil. His thought permeates Latin American culture to such an extent that several of his analytical categories are applied to the theoretical discourse of social scientists, historians, critics and intellectuals. These categories also penetrated, even though often misused, the common language of leftist groups and democrats. Who can think about big or small issues in our countries without resorting to words such as 'hegemony', 'historical block', 'organic intellectuals', 'organic crisis' and 'passive revolution', 'war of position' or 'of movement', 'civil society' and 'political society', 'extended state', 'transformism' and so on?[1]

José Maria Aricó wrote this in 1988. Gramsci's vocabulary became commonly used in a large part of Latin America, among scholars of social sciences, intellectuals, militants, and politicians. Every collection of data is partial, the spread of the politician's thought in these contexts can be neither outlined nor schematised in a precise manner as for the time, the places, the types, the branches of knowledge, and the reinterpretations of his work. This probably depends on the nature of Gramsci's work, which cannot be placed under a single label, but actually belongs to and involves various disciplines. His view became an important reference point for scholars of different disciplines such as philosophy, political science, international relations, literature, and cultural studies.

It is important to outline that, though Gramsci's thought permeated various fields of study since the beginning of the 1990s, its reception in Central and South America is marked by a special focus on politics. Latin America provides

---

1   Aricó 2005, p. 35. The translation is mine, unless otherwise indicated.

a breeding ground for the utilisation of Gramsci's ideas on the level of both theoretical analysis and political practice.

The Latin American left lacked some theoretical references and Gramsci was offering the tools to think about a methodology for a revolutionary action taking into account the specificities of each different national context. In this sense, his reflections on civil society, 'hegemony', education, and culture represented a reference point for those fighting against dogmatic Marxism in the 1960s, and, since the 1970s, they were central to the rethinking of a democratic and socialist society. In particular from 1975, the establishment of the dictatorial regime and the following necessity to create stable democratic systems led to the prevalence of a special focus on the Gramscian category of 'war of position' and his conception of 'western civil society', developed following the failed experience of the 'red biennium' and the fascist dictatorship. Those periods mirrored, in different shapes and times, the experiences of several leftist intellectuals who fled their countries after the advent of authoritarian regimes.[2] In addition to this, the success of the Cuban revolution – achieved by farm workers together with a group with bourgeois roots – proved that the way to socialism need not correspond to the Soviet paradigm of revolution guided by the Communist Party.

The most widely used reading of Gramsci in Latin America is that formulated by scholars who further deepened the study of his thought and were able to acknowledge its innovative aspects within the panorama of Marxism. These scholars used his reflections within a context of democratic politics, without turning him into a liberal thinker and capturing the elements of continuity between Gramsci's thought and that of Lenin. It can be said that there are different readings and interpretations regarding the Politician's thought. Those formulated by José Maria Aricó together with Juan Carlos Portantiero and by Carlos Nelson Coutinho are undoubtedly the most remarkable. What makes these readings stand out is the deep knowledge of the entirety of Gramsci's work and the loyalty to his thought and genesis; in other words, the methodologies they used to study his thought and the way they applied it to a different context, without changing its original meaning.

---

2 Even before the 1960s and the 1970s, many countries in Latin America were affected by the advent of several *coups d'état* and the establishment of dictatorial regimes such as the cases of Vargas in Brazil and Peron in Argentina. But the 1960s and the 1970s were characterised by a proliferation of coups and a climate of terror was created as a consequence of the guerrilla experiences. In the 1970s the 'Plan Condor' was implemented, which sought to mitigate or actually eliminate socialists and communists together with the help of the US, which played a leading role in supporting dictatorial regimes.

The aim of this chapter is to investigate the development of Gramscian studies in Latin America with a particular focus on the recovery of Gramsci's thought aimed at the renewal of theories and practices of the Latin American left. It will point out how Gramsci's thought had been used to renew the communist political culture, as early as the 1960s. Then it will analyse how, since the middle of the 1970s, Gramsci's work was reconsidered and became central in rethinking a new form of struggle – based on the concept of 'war of position' – which aimed at establishing a socialist society intertwined with the concept of democracy. In this context I will highlight the work of two Argentinian intellectuals, Portantiero and Aricó, and the Brazilian Coutinho, who used their studies on Gramsci to think of a new form of struggle, based on the concept of war of position.

2   The Diffusion of Gramsci's Thought in Latin America

At the beginning of the 1950s, some references to Gramsci's thought appeared in Latin America in a few articles. In that decade, the translation of his works and ideas began to spread. In the 1960s, Gramsci became one of the main reference points for leftists and those interested in Critical Marxism. It can be said that, starting from the mid-1970s, he was acknowledged not only as a source, but as the bearer of a revolutionary mode of thought within the context of Marxism.

Since the first appearances of his name, the focus was mainly on his political activity and he was considered as an 'anti-fascist martyr'. According to J. Massardo, the first reference to Gramsci in Latin America dates back to 1921 in Peru.[3] It belongs to a work by Mariategui and was written during the time he spent in Rome, where he discussed *L'Ordine Nuovo*.[4] After Mariategui, the next references can be dated to around the 1930s in Brazil, and in those texts Gramsci was portrayed as a heroic icon.

Though these references are not relevant from a political or philosophical point of view, they mark Gramsci's entrance into the Latin American world. It is interesting to note that these first mentions did not belong to communist environments: in Argentina for example the writer Ernesto Sabato

---

3   Massardo 1997.

4   José Carlos Mariátegui (1894–1930) was the most important Latin American socialist and Marxist thinker. He is considered the 'Gramsci of Latin America'. His most famous work is *Siete ensayos de interpretación de la Realidad Peruana* (1928).

was the first to talk about Gramsci in the journal *Realidad* in 1947.[5] After these initial cases, the dissemination of Gramsci's works was almost exclusively linked to the communist parties until the 1960s. The focus on the antifascist martyr figure continued to be dominant until then, despite the fact that some Argentinian studies of his texts had already crossed the heroic image.

It is difficult to give a well-defined picture of how different national realities perceived and approached Gramsci's thought. Unlike the Gramscian Argentinian case, other countries did not go through a gradual evolution of the spread of his ideas and works. Many factors and circumstances affected how his thought was interpreted and applied to different fields. Among those factors is the influence of Gramsci's interpretation elaborated by the Italian Communist Party after the war, besides the singular histories of each country, the establishment of dictatorial regimes and revolutions that occurred in the subcontinent. In the Latin American subcontinent especially until the 1980s, the utilisation of Gramsci's thought was exclusively linked to the political realm, to communism and to leftist environments, even as far as the intellectuals who spread his thought in the academic environment are concerned. For these reasons, the study of his texts was strongly connected to the historical and political events that characterised the history of Latin American countries. Gramsci's works were certainly not considered 'neutral'.

In Cuba, for instance, an interest in Gramsci started to grow during the post-revolutionary period.[6] In 1965 the Argentinian version of *Il materialismo storico e la filosofia di Benedetto Croce*, one of the volumes of the thematic edition of the *Prison Notebooks*, became available at the University of Havana and in 1966 it was fully published by the Edición Revolucionaria, the publishing house co-owned by Fernando Martinez Heredia.[7] The *Antología* of Antonio Gramsci by Sacristan,[8] edited for the first time in Mexico in 1970, was published in 1973 in Cuba and in 1975 some of the letters from prison were printed: those were

---

5 Burgos 2007.
6 In January 1959, Fulgencio Batista, Cuban dictator, was forced to escape by the revolutionary followers of Fidel Castro and Ernesto 'Che' Guevara. Since then, the issue of what type of socialism would have been established in Cuba started to be considered. Therefore, the 1960s were characterised by a great ferment and the thought of several Marxist authors started to be studied and debated.
7 Fernando Martinez Heredia was one of the first professors to introduce the study of the Italian politician to Cuban universities. See Martinez Heredia 2011, p. 80.
8 Manuel Sacristan was a Spanish Marxist philosopher who translated into Spanish various works of Gramsci, collected in the famous *Antologia*, published in Mexico in 1970 by the publishing house Siglo XXI.

the only works related to Gramsci during a period marked by the imposition of Marxism-Leninism. From the beginning of the 1970s until 1985 the government did not approve the study of authors belonging to 'Critical Marxism'. Only when Russian communism was on the verge of a crisis, did the diffusion of Gramsci's thought begin.[9]

In Chile, his works began to circulate during the Allende government, initially through the arrival of texts edited by the Argentinian publishing house Lautaro, and at a second stage edited by Osvaldo Fernandes. Some parts of the *Prison Notebooks* appeared in a Chilean version in 1971 and they were entitled *Maquiavelo y Lenis. Notas para una teoria politica Marxista*. During this period, Gramsci was looked at as an anti-fascist icon, and after the *coup d'état* the dissemination of his work became very limited, even though the Gramscian categories were utilised to investigate themes such as civil society, democracy and socialism. In 1987, thanks to the efforts of the Gramsci Institute in Rome, a seminar was organised. It was named *Vigencia y legado de Antonio Gramsci* and it marked a flourishing phase of studies on the Italian politician, nurtured with the anti-regime culture and continuing until the transition process towards democracy in 1990.[10]

Looking at these two national cases, it is evident how the international communist realm, the revolutions and the various putsches affected the study and the diffusion of Gramsci's texts.

The influence of the Italian Communist Party in its way of using and interpreting Gramsci's works should not be underrated. The Italian Communist Party (PCI) addressed its attention to Gramsci in the path that led to the creation of its 'new strategy'. The so-called Eurocommunism influenced the evolution of his retrieval among Latin American Marxist intellectuals. In the second half of the 1970s, thinkers interested in Gramsci's work started to focus their studies on the concepts of 'hegemony' and 'western civil society'. Both became the basis to rethink the strategies that would be implemented in order to achieve socialism in their countries.[11]

---

9   See Acanda Gonzales 2000, p. 111.

10   In 1970 in Chile, the coalition called Popular Unity (Unidad Popular – UP) came to power under Salvador Allende's presidency. Their purpose was to start a democratic revolution. On 11 September 1973, Augusto Pinochet Ugarte established a dictatorial regime with a *coup d'etat* that eliminated the political opponents through a system of the disappearance (desaparición) and torture. In 1987 a referendum was held to vote for the Presidency of the Republic; the only candidate was Pinochet. Following the victory of the 'No' campaign in December 1989, there were new elections and the Christian Democrat Aylwin became President of the Republic in March 1990.

11   See Liguori 2005, p. 121.

Raul Burgos, who tried to elaborate what he called a 'phenomenology' of the Italian communist in Latin America, defines a 'fourth figure' that confirms this trend. He pictured the re-utilisation of Gramsci's thought as a process made by different phases and represented by 'four figures': the 'political hero' (until the 1950s), the 'philosopher of praxis' (beginning of the 1960s), the 'thinker of Machiavellian-Jacobin observations' (1963–75), and the 'theorist of hegemony' (after 1975). According to the author, this subdivision can be generally applied to the whole of Latin America, even if each state has its own specificities, especially Brazil.[12] The division made by Burgos does not really correspond to the evolution of Gramscian studies in all the countries. As for the Argentinian case, the passages between one period and another were not so precise and for most of the nations, where it is possible to find an interest in Gramsci, the use of his categories has been discontinued.

It is true that until the 1950s Gramsci was mainly perceived just as an anti-fascist icon and a 'political hero'. But it is also true that already in the 1950s, the concept of organic intellectuals and the need to create a cultural hegemony could be found in prologues and texts by Argentinian translators of the author. However, these themes developed effectively in the second half of the 1970s. During the 1960s, a period defined by Burgos as Machiavellian/Jacobin, the excitement and hope aroused in the left world by the Cuban revolution led to a consideration of some aspects rather than others as far as Gramsci's thought is concerned. The 'spontaneity' of the masses, the relationship between workers and intellectuals and the 'national-popular' were all themes frequently discussed and often linked to the will to embrace change.

In Argentina, the Left strongly felt the theme of the 'historical bloc' between intellectuals and manual workers, especially since Peronism had been able to create a strong bond with the working classes, a bond that the Left had never been able to create. Despite Portantiero and Aricó having deepened the study of Gramsci, in that period of popular ferment the Sardinian Communist was only one of the references for the Left, like Che Guevara. In general, there was neither a focus on nor a systematic study of Gramsci. As Portantiero outlined: 'we were making a sort of cocktail, in which Gramsci was living together with Che Guevara and the Chinese Revolution. In this context we could see the possibility of articulating a historicist and voluntarist discourse'.[13] Basically, in the

---

12   The third figure coined by Burgos is further divided into three stages: the 'Gramscian-guevarist voluntarism' (1963–64), the Gramsci of 'national-popular' themes (1964–66), and the Gramsci 'councilist' (1966–73). See Burgos 2007.

13   Portantiero 1999.

1960s and in the first half of the 1970s the interest in Gramsci was mainly related to those themes that were considered useful in order to deal with the events of that period. Between the late 1960s and the beginning of the 1970s, the focus was on the works councils and *L'Ordine Nuovo*. The revolution starting from workplaces was raising hopes for an immediate change. Those periods were characterised by urban guerrilla and armed struggle and there was no space for a 'war of position'. Only in the second half of the 1970s were 'hegemony' and the 'war of position' placed at the centre of the recovery of Gramsci's work.

3   Gramsci in Brazil: The Role of Coutinho

As for the dissemination of Gramsci's thought in the subcontinent, the key countries are Argentina, Brazil and Mexico. Argentina can be seen as the cradle of Gramsci's ideas, Mexico can be considered as some sort of laboratory from the middle of the 1970s, and Brazil represents the outburst of Gramscian studies starting from the 1980s.[14]

In Brazil, the first appearance of Gramsci's name was not connected to the Brazilian Communist Party, and until the 1960s the politician from Sardinia was just perceived as the founder of the PCI or simply mentioned among the communist prisoners of the Fascist regime.

It was at the beginning of the 1960s that Gramsci's thought, perceived as theoretical reflection and philosophy of praxis, started to spread from Argentina to Brazil.

The reception of Gramsci in Brazil differs from the more general scheme formulated by Burgos; it has been divided into three periods by C.N. Coutinho. The first runs from the beginning of the 1960s to the middle of the 1970s. The second period starts from 1975 to 1980, where his theoretical and political reflections were finally taken into account. At last, there is the period that follows the reconstruction of democracy until the present day. The latter was marked by the spread of Gramsci's thought in the most various sectors: academic, cultural and political.

After the publication of Gramsci's works in Argentina in the 1960s, some Brazilians such as Antonio Cândido and Leandro Konder started to quote Gramsci in their works. However, the references to Gramsci were mainly philosophical rather than political. This first study did not utilise his thought as a

---

14   On Argentina see below, Section 3.

basis for political actions and his ideas were not considered revolutionary from a political point of view. In this regard, before the mid-1970s, the scholar Marcos Aurelio Nogueria states that 'all Gramscism has been an academic discipline, ignored by politicians it was forced within universities' walls'.[15]

Before the dictatorship established in 1964 led to the suppression of political rights and to the dissolution of Parliament in 1968, a translation of the Notebooks in the Togliatti and Platone edition was published. Between 1966 and 1968 the publishing house Civilizaçao Brasileira published for the first time in Portuguese all the works translated into Spanish and published by Lautaro in Argentina in the previous years.

Coutinho played a central role in this work since he made the translation, together with Leandro Konder, of *Il Materialismo Storico e la Filosofia di Benedetto Croce*. It was published in 1966 with the title *Concepção dialéctica da história*. In the same year the translation of the letters from prison, edited by N. Spinola, was printed. In 1968 *Note sul Machiavelli, la politica e lo Stato moderno* was translated by L.M. Gozzaneo and edited by Coutinho. In 1968, thanks to C.N. Coutinho, *Letteratura e vita nazionale*, and *Gli intellettuali e l'organizzazione della cultura* were translated and published.

As a member of the Partido Comunista Brasileiro (the Brazilian Communist Party, PCB), Coutinho became particularly close to Gramsci's thought. His aim was to utilise the politician's reflections and ideas to renew the political culture of his party. His study on Gramsci has always been connected to the possibility of using his ideas in political practice, but this happened when he became a member of Lula's Partido dos Trabalhadores (the Workers' Party, PT).[16]

Carlos Nelson Coutinho reinterpreted and took advantage of Gramsci's work in a very original and useful way. He utilised the category of 'passive revolution' to analyse contemporary history in his country. He claimed that it is through the application of this category that several crucial events of Brazilian history can be understood. Among these events he includes the process that led to the Independence of Brazil declared by King Pedro in 1822, the abolition of slavery in 1888 and the proclamation of the Republic in 1889 by republican movements. He identified the Vargas dictatorship as the most significant example of 'passive revolution'.[17]

---

15   Nogueira 2011, p. 120.
16   PT, the Workers' Party. The PT was founded in 1980 starting from action in the factories. Coutinho and Leandro Konder became members of the PT in 1989.
17   Vargas made a *coup d'ètat* in 1930 and in 1937 established an authoritarian regime called Estado Novo.

Coutinho initiated the utilisation of Gramsci's thought in order to create a theory that would orientate a political practice in the late 1970s. This happened also thanks to Berlinguer who, during the sixtieth anniversary of the October Revolution in Moscow, proclaimed in front of the PCUS that socialist change should be based on the union between socialism and democracy: 'democracy ... this is the universal value a socialist society should be based on'.[18]

The discussion about an original socialist society implied the abandonment of the modalities that were utilised by the Russian socialist system at the time. Berlinguer's quote travelled all over the world and it was taken as an example by those who wanted to build a new concept of socialism in Latin American countries. The PCI aroused the interest of several communist leaders and left wing intellectuals because it was the first European communist party to lay down the foundations to rethink the socialist strategy.

Coutinho edited the essay *A democracia como valor universal* in 1979.[19] In this text Gramsci's thought is the key element to rethink the bond between democracy and socialism. Gramsci also became a reference for the Partito dos Trabalhadores (PT), of which Coutinho could be considered an 'organic intellectual'. According to him, that party was a 'modern prince' who, starting from factories and breaking off from official trade unionism, could move the whole Brazilian society towards socialism. The innovation of the PT consisted in the proposal of a democratic socialism which was different from those already existing. The PT could represent the guide for the creation of a new 'historical bloc' able to compete with the hegemony of the dominant bloc.[20]

The relevant aspect is that Gramsci's thought was used to develop and guide political praxis within the hegemonic struggle of a political subject.

Like Coutinho for the Brazilian case, this reading was central for the works of the Argentinian Gramscians, José Maria Aricò and Juan Carlos Portantiero, exiled in Mexico in 1976 after the establishment of the dictatorial regime through the military coup in Argentina.

---

18   Della Torre and Mortimer 1978, p. 27. Berlinguer was the secretary of the Italian Communist Party from 1972 to 1984.

19   Coutinho 1980. From 1999 onwards Coutinho, with the collaboration of Nogueira, translated the *Prison Notebooks* into Portuguese, elaborating a thematic edition in six volumes. This edition took into consideration both the critical edition by Gerratana in 1975 and the previous one by Togliatti.

20   The PT won the elections in 2003. However, after a short time in government, Coutinho believed that Lula's politics were excessively reformist and therefore he left the party.

4   Gramsci in Argentina: The Essential Contribution of Aricó and Portantiero

In 1950, the publishing house Lautaro published for the first time in a foreign language the letters from prison in a book entitled *Letras desde la Carcel*. The Spanish and Portuguese translations in Argentina and Brazil preceded both Portugal and Spain; in this sense Latin America contributed to the initial diffusion of Gramsci's thought more than Europe did.

The translator of the letters from prison in Spanish was Héctor Pablo Agosti, one of the leaders of the communist party at that time. He had two collaborators assigned to the analysis of Gramsci's works which preceded the publication, José Maria Aricó and Juan Carlos Portantiero. Aricó was the secretary of the Federación Juvenil del Partido Comunista, the Communist Party Youth Federation, and Portantiero the secretary of *Cuadernos de cultura*, the communist party journal.

In 1953, two articles by Togliatti appeared on *Cuadernos de Cultura*; through these texts Agosti, director of the journal, began to spread Gramsci's view and ideas. The first one was *L'Antifascismo di Antonio Gramsci*,[21] and the second was *Problemi di cultura*.[22] Agosti used the first article to open up a debate on Peronism and wrote a prologue entitled *Noticias sobre Gramsci*, a brief biography of the Italian Communist. The article, which investigated culture, helped him to support his idea for the need to examine the relationship between intellectuals, culture and party. The purpose of building a strong union between the intellectuals and people was clear: Agosti's texts marked the intention of shaking the consciences of those opposing Perón, reconsidering the actions and positions of the Argentinian Communist Party (PCA), which has not been able to reconstruct the unity of the classes it was addressing. His translations and writings emphasised the importance of culture in the hegemonic battle against the ruling classes, placing it at the centre of the struggle for cultural hegemony, as Gramsci taught. This concept of culture was the same one that accompanied Aricó and Portantiero during their lives.

Agosti and his collaborators also translated the *Prison Notebooks* for the publishing house Lautaro. They came out in four volumes, two of which had an introduction by Agosti and Aricó. The first one, which appeared in 1958, had a prologue by Agosti and was entitled *El materialismo historico y la filosofia de Benedetto Croce*, the second one in 1960 was entitled *Los intelectuales*

---

21   Togliatti 1953a.
22   Togliatti 1953b.

y la organización de la cultura. The last two, translated by Aricó, were *Literatura y vida nacional* in 1961, with an introduction by Agosti, and *Notas sobre Maquiavelo, sobre la política y sobre el Estado moderno*, with an introduction by Aricó.

The translation of the *Prison Notebooks* represented the last chapter of Gramsci's existence within the PCA. His thought could not find space there. When the three intellectuals started to study the author, only a few members of the PCA seemed interested in the potential of change and renewal that his ideas represented. The majority looked at his work as a threat to their own cultural tradition.

Before that period the attention was focused on the figure of the opponent to fascism which Gramsci embodied. For this reason, making an easy parallel between Peronism and Fascism, the PCA initially had no trouble in welcoming the founder of the Italian Communist Party (PCI) as one of its heroes. This clearly shows that there was no deep understanding of the thought of Gramsci when it began to circulate within the communist environment. In fact, when the leaders of the PCA understood the revolutionary aim of his writings and his non-alignment with the dictates of the Communist Party of the Soviet Union, the group that continued to study his work resisted the devaluation of his thought and as a result was expelled from the Party. This happened to Aricó and Portantiero, both founders of the journal *Pasado y Presente*.

The work conducted by the *Pasado y Presente* group has been fundamental in the diffusion of Gramsci's thought in Latin America. Different factors determined the initial push in creating the journal. First of all the revolutionary events in Algeria and Cuba affected the will to change on the part of the Party's left wing. Then there was the need to avoid political positions that would exclude those who were not aligned to the official position of the PCA. This attitude precluded the possibility of creating unity among subaltern groups and would close the door to claims and struggles that were breaking out in universities, where student associations began to take left-wing positions. Those who were members of the editorial board of *Pasado y Presente* listened to these signals of hope and created a magazine that was open to every form of renewal. They aimed at putting into question the orthodox positions of the party in order to open it to a renovation and respond to the demands of the two social groups involved in the protests: workers and students.

When the first number of the magazine was printed, in 1963, it was clear that it was illicit within the PCA to take positions not aligned with the orthodox Marxism-Leninism. The group which founded *Pasado y Presente* was therefore expelled. However, the editorial unit did not dissolve, it left the party and kept publishing the journal. The foundational nucleus of the group worked in Córdoba and it was right in this new 'Turin of Argentina'[23] that the publication of the magazine started. Since the 1960s this city was at the centre of social struggles that followed the arrival of big foreign companies, such as Fiat. In Córdoba there were several factories that supplied the demand from the US and Europe for the production of military materials. In the same period, the influx of lower-middle-class students started to grow at the University of Córdoba, since then mainly attended by the Argentinian elites. These new realities, less wealthy students trying to make reforms at the university and workers and unionists fighting for workers' rights, led to the creation of Cordobazo in 1969.[24] It is for these reasons that the experience of *Pasado y Presente* took place in Córdoba. The members of the first editorial unit were in part militants expelled from the PCA and in part independent intellectuals. There is no specific group of people who constantly worked on this journal; various intellectuals were involved in it and not all of them could be considered 'Gramscians'. Only Aricó and Portantiero can be seen as authentic Argentinian Gramscians, since they studied the Italian Marxist in depth and took his thought as both a theoretical and political reference point. Both Aricó and Portantiero chose the Gramscian title of the journal at the same time, Aricó in Córdoba and Portantiero in Buenos Aires. As Aricó stated in an interview,[25] they both thought of the same title without previously agreeing on it, because the concept of the bond between past history and contemporary historical reality led them to question the guidelines of the Argentinian PC. Their way of dealing with the Gramscian categories has been neither instrumental nor superficial because it stemmed from a deep study of the author's works. Their contribution to the spreading of a political reading of Gramsci's texts and the understanding of the struggle for hegemony made them the most important Latin American Gramscists. They also made the first Latin Amer-

---

23   This is the definition Aricó gave in his text *La cola del Diablo* to describe Córdoba (Aricó 1988).

24   After the so-called 'noche de los bastones largos' on 29 June 1966, during which hundreds of professors and students protesting against repression at the University of Buenos Aires were brutally beaten in front of the media, a protest that opposed violence with violence began. In May 1969, following the death of a student during a protest at the University of the North East, the protests against the regime began to join nationwide and a series of demonstrations and strikes swept the country. There were three moments of occupation of the city and of the armed struggle that went down in history as the greatest moments of confrontation: the Rosariazo, the Cordobazo, and two years later the Viborazo. Of the three the most significant was the Cordobazo, which began on 30 May 1969, since in it the rioters were students and workers together.

25   Crespo 1999, p. 18.

ican analysis of Gramsci as the philosopher of praxis. The two scholars reacted to the repression of the dictatorship in the second half of the 1970s, elaborating their historical analysis and political proposals starting from the concept of hegemony.

5   Gramsci's Thought in Mexico

Portantiero and Aricó were forced into exile in Mexico and from 1976 to 1983 focused their theoretical-political analysis on the relation between the State, civil society, democracy and socialism, from a Gramscian perspective. The failure of what they considered a war of movement in Argentina, in the late 1960s and early '70s, led them to rethink the ways of transition to socialism by using the concept of hegemony.

In the 1970s, Mexico had become a political and cultural laboratory as it was the place to which many intellectuals moved because of the advent of dictatorial regimes in their own countries.[26] Before that period, the influence of the Italian Communist in Mexico was not that relevant, except within the communist environment. He was not unknown, thanks to the Argentinian works that arrived there, but during the '60s and at the beginning of the '70s the interest was mostly from some intellectuals linked to the PCM, such as Carlos Pereira, Luis Tapia and Arnaldo Córdova.[27] The PCM represents an exception among Latin American communist parties, strongly related to the Soviet orthodoxy, because Arnoldo Martinez Verdugo, Secretary of the Central Committee from 1963 to 1983, followed Gramsci's thought. The PCM opposed the invasion of Czechoslovakia and followed the Eurocommunist path of the French, Spanish and Italian communist parties.[28]

---

26   In Mexico since 1972 a period called the 'democratic opening' began, which created the opportunity to welcome intellectuals fleeing dictatorships. The work of the exiles was not addressed to actions in the Mexican context, but turned to their own and other countries, because, although the government pretended to give the country a democratic appearance, foreigners could not participate in national political life.

27   'In Mexico there is a history of Gramsci's thought before the late sixties when some intellectuals began to recover Gramsci. Luis Tapia, Arnaldo Cordova, Carlos Pereyra. From what I know they are the first Gramscians in Mexico and they were linked to the Mexican Communist Party'. Interview (5 June 2013) and translation by the author.

28   Kanoussi wrote: 'The PCM leadership, which went to jail because they took part in the 1968 movement, condemned the invasion of Czechoslovakia. The party, legalized in 1977, had always been very close to the PCM and PCI and followed a Eurocommunist policy marked as well by the frequent encounters with Enrico Berlinguer, Santiago Carrillo and

At the beginning of 1970s, Gramsci's view was introduced to the school of political education of the PCM by Javier Mena.[29]

As far as the academic environment is concerned, his thought was mainly spread by the Argentinian Gramscists exiled in Mexico; they represent in fact the heart of the dissemination of his view in the whole subcontinent.

Since 1975, Portantiero and Aricó addressed the utilisation of Gramsci's thought in the creation of a political theory for their Latin American 'peripheral West', which was characterised by the presence of a complex civil society, where it was necessary to fight wars of position instead of wars of movement.

This elaboration represents the climax of the process they began in the 1950s and continued with the publication of *Pasado y Presente* which occurred in two periods: from 1963 to 1965 and from 1973 to 1974. In 1968, they also created the series entitled *Cuadernos de Pasado y Presente*. This was the experience that most of all characterised their cultural work until 1983 and ended with the release of number 98 of *Cuadernos* in Mexico.

The most important of these notebooks is *Cuaderno 54*, a selection of writings from across the entire output of the politician from Sardinia, introduced in 1977 by the prologue *Los usos de Gramsci*. In this text, Portantiero describes the considerations, belonging to different periods, of Gramsci's activity as parts of a single 'theoretical system', in which the factory council, the role of the party in the revolution, and intellectual and moral reform were meant as different steps of a single theoretical system in the struggle for hegemony. Portantiero's interpretation is connected to the Gramscian approach of Aricó in his reconsideration of Marxism and socialism from a Latin American point of view in his works *Las Hipotesis de Justo, Marx y Latin America* and in a series of lectures held in 1977 at the Colegio de México.[30] Hegemony is also the foundation of the reflections of the two intellectuals elaborated in the articles of another review journal they founded in Mexico, *Controversia*, published between 1979 and 1981. It focused on the critique of 'real socialism' and on the request to reconsider socialism as a system based on the value of democracy. The experience of the Italian PCI, which had sought an alternative route to the one indicated by the Soviet Union, was to Aricó and Portantiero the prac-

---

Georges Marchais with Arnaldo Martínez Verdugo, Secretary of the PCM. Verdugo was indeed the promoter of a democratization of the political system in Mexico'. See Kanoussi 2011, pp. 315–16.

29   Javier Mena wrote two important texts dedicated to Gramsci (Mena 1996; Kanoussi-Mena 1985).

30   The classes were part of the course 'Economía y política en el análisis de las formaciones sociales'. See Aricó 2012.

tical example in creating strategies for the transition to socialism, developed for different specific national situations.

They attempted to apply Gramsci's analysis of the relationship between civil society and the State to the history of Argentina and Latin America, through the use and recontextualisation of the categories. Against the vision of the Third International, which perceived Latin America as part of the bloc of countries considered colonial or semi-colonial, they claimed the need to open a new perspective on the region, as Portantiero explained in *Los usos de Gramsci* and Aricó in several interviews:

> the sharp capitalist nature of the social-economic, political and cultural development of most of the countries, indicates the existence of different features that do not allow a simplistic identification with the Asian or African world that the Third International generically classified as 'colonial and semi-colonial countries'. Rather, they support an approach to Europe, the Europe of 'peripheral capitalism' that Gramsci exemplified by the cases of Italy, Spain, Poland and Portugal.[31]

They considered Latin America as the 'peripheral West', like Coutinho.[32] It was in Mexico that two important meetings took place, which represented the crucial moments that gave impetus to the penetration of Gramsci's thought in Latin America.

The meeting entitled *Gramsci y la Política* was organised at the UNAM (National Autonomous University of Mexico) from 5–9 September 1978, at the proposal of the two exiled Argentinian Gramscists. The lecturers were four researchers, two from Paris, Christine Buci-Glucksmann and Maria Antonietta Maciocchi, Giuseppe Vacca, who at the time was part of the Central Committee of the Italian Communist Party, as well as being a board member of the Gramsci Institute, and Juan Carlos Portantiero.

Giuseppe Vacca comments on the meeting:

> [T]hat conference and the following one marked the moment of impact of Gramsci's thought on Latin American intellectual and political elites and then marginalised on the one hand the Marxism-Leninism and on the other the influence of Althusser.[33]

---

31   Aricó 1991, p. 19.
32   See Coutinho 1999.
33   Interview (20 July 2013).

In 1975, Christine Buci-Glucksmann published the book *Gramsci et l'État*, where she first used the term 'expanded state' consolidating a new reading of Gramsci. The arrival of this view could be seen as a closure to the era of the dissemination of Gramsci's reflections through the filter of Althusser in Latin America and opened the door to the discussion of new forms of revolutionary change. The civil society became the place to fight the battle for 'hegemony' and to contest the organisation of society. It represented the dimension where a certain 'ideology', perceived as a 'world view' in Gramscian terms, could aim at preparing the soil to become dominant. Civil society in this sense can be seen as the realm where the masses organise themselves; it is also the place where the dominant ideology builds defences to protect its power and subaltern groups can fight for 'hegemony'. The transition to socialism was conceived of as the construction of 'democratic mass alternatives'. Buci-Glucksmann argued that Gramsci changed the conception of the transition to socialism, conceiving of it as an intellectual and moral reform, which would lead to the self-government of the masses.

The speech of Portantiero, *Gramsci para Latinoamericanos*, followed the one by the French philosopher. The speech recovered the themes discussed in *Los Usos de Gramsci*. First of all the definition of 'peripheral West' addressed to Latin American countries such as Argentina and Chile. Those countries represented an extremely receptive area for the utilisation of Gramsci's reflections. A second theme was the inability of the left parties to read the reality they had to deal with, remaining in fact entrapped in the concept of the 'instrumental State'. The aim of Portantiero was to provide the left parties with a clear way to build up a strategy, that was neither reformist nor insurgent. This position would be deepened in the following years, in the journal *Controversia*.

As Portantiero said, Gramsci's reading of the phenomenon of fascism as an example of passive revolution and reorganisation of the capitalist state could be applied to the analysis of the military neo-authoritarianism of South-American countries. In Argentina, for instance, the war of movement waged by the revolutionary groups, as in the case of the Montoneros and the Frente Popular, was won by the Army and this defeat demonstrated to Portantiero and Aricó the necessity of searching for a new strategy, changing completely the concept of revolution of the Latin American left wing. In order to achieve this it was necessary to take into consideration the proposal derived from Gramsci: the 'war of position'.

After the first seminar at UNAM, a second one took place at the University of Morelia in 1980. It represented the climax of the new utilisation of Gramsci's thought. The central topic of the meeting *Hegemonia y alternativas políticas en América Latina* was 'hegemony'. Aricó described the colloquium as a turning point for the debate on the relationship between Marxism and Latin America. It was meant to overcome the issue of the contextualisation of Marxism in the Latin American context – characterised by the lack of the proletariat as revolutionary class – by using the Gramscian concept of hegemony. This concept proposed a construction of social subjects through an intellectual and moral reform; this way the revolutionary subject was not conceived of as an *a priori* entity but as a historical bloc to be built.

The seminar in Morelia and the publication of *Controversia* can be seen as the most significant enterprises of the last period of exile of Aricó and Portantiero.

Controversia was a political project based on the notion of war of position and it outlined the possibility of a national path towards the restoration of democracy in Argentina.[34]

The lack of rule of law in their country led Aricó and Portantiero to a reading of Gramsci which initiates the use of the concept of hegemony in order to build, first, a solid democratic system and, second, a socialist society. They aimed at ending the division between governors and governed.

As Buci-Glucksmann said, in order to arrive at a socialist society, democracy would need to radicalise itself completely. This way, according the two Gramscians, the war of position would have been fought throughout all the components of the 'expanded state', within the 'casemates of power' but also through electoral battles. Because of this, they supported the political project of the radical Alfonsín once they returned from their exile in 1983.

In conclusion, both the proposal made by Aricó and Portantiero and that made by Coutinho at the end of the 1970s outlined the following points: the elaboration of a proposal for a new socialist strategy based on the utilisation of the Gramscian conceptions of hegemony, intellectual and moral reform, and war of position; the interpretation of the economic reality of their two countries as dominated by a new form of 'dependent capitalism'; the utilisation of the category of passive revolution as an instrument to analyse the history of the various countries and the revival of the theories elaborated by the PCI leaders which were the backbone of Eurocommunism in the 1970s. For what concerns 'the geography' of the diffusion of Gramsci's thought and the different ways in which his categories have been utilised and applied in the world, it is interesting to note their specific use of Gramsci's reflections. Their study of his thought is attributable to a context which is typical of the 'peripheral West' and it shows a

---

34   In Mexico, the Argentinian Gramscians founded in 1980 the 'group of socialist discussion' and then, back in Argentina, in 1984 they founded the 'club of Socialist Culture'.

real attempt to establish 'cultural hegemony' through action that would provide those who are governed with the necessary tools to develop their own critical, historical and political awareness. Aricó, Portantiero and Coutinho can be considered the most important Gramscian scholars to consider the totality of his work and to make it a reference point at the level of political practice.

CHAPTER 24

An Imaginary Gramscianism? Early French Gramscianism and the Quest for 'Marxist Humanism' (1947–65)

Anthony Crézégut

Marxism is, in a single movement and by virtue of the unique epistemological rupture which established it, an anti-humanism and an anti-historicism. Strictly speaking, I ought to say an a-humanism and an a-historicism.[1]

∙∙

1   Introduction

Althusser's well-known 1965 criticism of Gramsci is both severe and ambivalent. For over a decade, this analysis stood watch before the front gates of Gramscianism and presented to would-be initiates a straightforward message: 'no humanist may enter'. In his book on Gramsci and Althusser, Peter Thomas goes so far as to assert that it was the 'paradigm of *Gramsci ou Althusser* that defined the horizon of the French intellectual avant-garde', during an era which André Tosel considers the 'last great theoretical debate of Marxism'.[2] Althusser penned his 1965 criticism in a tense context, at a moment when a new generation of radical intellectuals was shifting from phenomenology to structuralism, or, as Foucault tendentiously described it, from 'a philosophy of experience, meaning, and subject to a philosophy of the concept, rationality and knowledge'.[3] In this polysemic text, Althusser had in mind the then current political and ideological struggles and his intent was to target specific intellectuals who made use of Gramsci to defend their own agenda. After 1945, Gramsci's thought

---

1   Althusser 1973 [1965], p. 150.
2   Thomas 2010, p. 8.
3   Foucault 1994, p. 764.

had no more than a spectral existence in France and his writings were almost entirely unknown. The conservative intellectual, Raymond Aron, described French readings of Marx, especially those of Sartre and Althusser, as 'imaginary Marxisms'.[4] An analogous expression could be used to characterise the widespread presence (and absence) of Gramsci's thought as 'imaginary Gramscianisms'. However, if one first takes into account the more rigorous consideration of Gramsci's works that followed Althusser's, one must understand that the roles played by imagination and political context in shaping the French readings of Gramsci were necessary preconditions for subsequent knowledge and action. In other words, the influence of Gramsci's shadow during this era should not be reduced to a case of 'false consciousness' or as a *'maîtresse d'erreur et de fausseté'* in the typical seventeenth-century conception of imagination, as expressed by Spinoza, Pascal, or Malebranche.

I would like to suggest in this chapter that there are three images of Gramsci, which crystallised around the middle of the century, and that these imaginary renderings relate directly to various social groups and political events. The first image is that of Gramsci as an anti-fascist martyr, the semblance consecrated by the Communist International (Comintern) after 1935 and through the 'Popular Front' era. Communist leaders and intellectuals were still referring to this image in the 1950s: for example, Louis Aragon and Georges Cogniot, contemporaries who campaigned with Romain Rolland and Henri Barbusse for Gramsci's liberation. The second image was Gramsci as a builder of the Workers' Councils in Turin in 1919–20. This version was the preference of the far-left transmitted by Alfred Rosmer, Pierre Monatte, Pierre Naville, and Alfonso Leonetti. It was a vision opposed to the fetishisation of the Communist party, at least in its Stalinist form. The third image emerged after the war. In this case, Gramsci was championed as a Marxist who paid attention to the *cultural* dimension of the revolution, to the role of the *intellectuals* in the Communist party, and to *history* as a test for Marxism. Merleau-Ponty used the term 'Western Marxism' to elicit this sort of association, although he does not explicitly refer to Gramsci.[5] This de-personalised vision of 'Western Marxism' appealed

---

4 Aron 1970. In his long-standing polemics on Marxism, Raymond Aron published a book after the events of May 1968 in which he identified two interpretations of Marxism. The first, in the wake of Sartre, was subjectivist-existentialist, while the other Althusserian interpretation was objectivist-structuralist. Both of them, Aron concluded, were very far from what a philological analysis of Marxian texts could call, and Aron had called, the 'Marxism of Marx' but were closer to an 'imaginary Marxism', a pure construction of their creative exegetes in France.

5 Merleau-Ponty 1955, p. 43.

to both the former generation of intellectuals ready to convert to Marxism and to young intellectuals who were willing to play a role in the reform of the French Communist Party (PCF).

During the 1960s, Gramsci's theoretical work was rescued from its obscurity: the prison letters were translated in 1953 and, significantly, a more complete anthology of the *Prison Notebooks* was published in 1959 by the PCF. Jean-Marie Vincent, the leading Marxist theoretician affiliated with Trotskyism, judged that the anthology was 'more than helpful', as the 'translation and the notes – although too blatantly orthodox – were generally excellent'.[6] He only regretted that 'the texts of the *Ordine Nuovo* were reduced to the smallest share'.[7]

In line with these three 'imaginary Gramscianisms', the reception after 1945 and the use of Gramsci's work afterwards took three different trajectories. At the philosophical level, his writings were used to promote a type of humanism that challenged the pairing of *existentialism/phenomenology*, which was the dominant academic and popular philosophy after 1945. Through the concept of *praxis*, this reading also promoted a western Marxism (*cultural-heretical*) that opposed Marxism-Leninism (*vulgar-official*). At the political level, Gramsci's work offered a way out of Stalinism and the hegemonic tendencies of the PCF, as the 'party of the working-class', with its long-lasting influence in the intellectual world, a party whose leadership was confused and sceptical towards the de-Stalinisation process initiated by Khrushchev and Togliatti. The aim was to reform the PCF from the inside and thereby to create a 'new left'. Finally, at a sociological level, intellectuals used Gramsci to redefine and enhance their role in the 'class struggle', through the merger of theory and practice. This move, in turn, signalled a new hegemonic formation within the working-class movement – one where the leaders and officials were mainly of blue-collar origin – also within the universities.

Given this theoretical and political context, I will explore the following question: did Gramsci's work develop an effective 'intellectual Marxism' – one which promoted an intellectual reform of Marxism as a de-Stalinised communism *as well* as a humanist Marxism – while promoting the social interests of intellectuals in the working-class movement? This exploration tests Althusser's challenge in 1965 to the trio of 'underground streams' of Gramscianism in France and does so in three stages: first through the question of humanism and of the 'third way'; second, through the issue of de-Stalinisation; and third, by examining the problematic role of intellectuals in the movement.

---

6   Vincent 1962, pp. 187–8.
7   Ibid.

2   Is Gramscianism a Humanism? (1947–56)

In 1947, Marxism corresponded to the spirit of the times, but the beginning of the Cold War soon forced intellectuals to choose between two camps: Stalinist communism or liberalism and capitalism. In this context, the leading figures of French intellectual life tried desperately to publish Gramsci in France, as well as to find a philosophical and political 'third way', one combining Marxism and humanism.

2.1   *Attending the Birth of French Gramscianism: Aragon, Mounier, and Sartre*

In 1949, the iconic poet of the PCF, Louis Aragon, became the first intellectual to express a wish to publish Gramsci's *Letters from Prison*. The directors of the *Istituto Gramsci* remembered Aragon as initially being delighted with the idea of publishing Gramsci's work with his PCF affiliated publishing house, *Editeurs français réunis*. They also recollect that Aragon then hesitated and finally abandoned the project due to the amount of work that it required. A series of hypotheses may account for the poet and novelist's initial curiosity. First, Aragon had an aesthetic passion for the letters, which were awarded a prestigious literary prize in 1947 in Italy. The second potential motivation concerns Aragon's own memories of the political fight against fascism waged alongside Romain Rolland and Henri Barbusse in the 1930s, during which time Aragon wrote a poem glorifying Gramsci and Matteotti. Third, his interest can be seen as a harbinger of the trend of 'Marxist humanism' that Aragon would promote after 1956 alongside Roger Garaudy.

A lesser-known leader of the French personalist movement, Emmanuel Mounier, was also the founder of *Esprit*, one of the two major papers of the non- and philo-communist left after 1945. Though emerging from a right-wing milieu and social Catholicism, under the guidance of Mounier, personalist circles became increasingly curious about Marxism. These groups searched for a 'third way' between communism and capitalism, one that would be based on respect for persons. Mounier perceived that orthodox Marxism scorned this sensitivity to persons while existentialists, for their part, neglected the way in which persons were inscribed in their social context. Mounier had heard of Gramsci through his discussions with Italian left-wing Christian-democrats and fellow travellers of the Italian Communist Party (PCI) at a Congress of the personalist movement, and he fell in love with the description they gave of this open-minded communist of whom he formerly knew only by hearsay (e.g. he wrote his name as 'Gramschi' at that time). In 1948, in a famous issue of *Esprit*, Mounier made of Gramsci the symbol of an '*Open* Marxism' and opposed this image to a '*scholastic* Marxism', the Marxism represented by the PCF and by Garaudy, the official philosopher of the party. At the same time, he pressed his Italian interlocutors to give him texts from Gramsci that promised to have a dramatic impact on French political life 'in the sense of a reaction towards a lively Marxism against a systematic Marxism'.[8] Mounier died prematurely in 1950, and his successors – who were closer to a non-Marxist new left – were soon to abandon his programme of personalist Marxism.

A more prominent initiative than that of Mounier was Jean-Paul Sartre's struggle to publish Gramsci's *Prison Notebooks* in France between 1955 and 1957. He did so after his friend and translator, Marc Soriano, along with the far-left editor Maurice Nadeau, gave him the manuscripts in the summer of 1955. Sartre drew up plans for an anthology with the publisher *Editions Julliard* and he [Besse] noted its expected 'accord with [the] audience of the collection (*Les Temps modernes*) he [Sartre] heads'.[9] In a prospectus for the anthology, Sartre envisioned a new preface (to be written by himself) and asked his friend Marc Soriano to translate 'other fragments of Gramsci's books that he wanted to include in his anthology'.[10] Sartre's interest in Gramsci lends some credence to Althusser's intuition in 1965 that Sartre's epistemological conceptions were close to Gramsci's on many points. However, Althusser conceded that 'we all know that Sartre's thought in no sense derives from Gramsci's interpretation of Marxism: it has quite different origins'.[11] Although an in-depth analysis of the conceptual transformations in Sartre's works would be needed to demonstrate this, Sartre's reading of Gramsci may have potential connections with the transition from his classical phenomenological work (and existentialist philosophy) to a form of active Marxism. This path was already outlined in *Questions de Méthode* in 1957 and it would culminate in the *Critique de la raison dialectique* from 1960. The concept of praxis came to occupy a central place in Sartre's philosophy. Fredric Jameson and Perry Anderson have indicated that praxis (or totalisation) came to more or less replace the concept of 'project' from *L'Etre et le Néant*.[12] However, these works make no reference to Gramsci, even though his name circulated positively among Sartre's entourage. In his journal, *Les Temps modernes*, an Italian special issue from 1948 praised Gramsci

---

8   Letter from Emmanuel Mounier to Giacomo Debenedetti, 27 January 1948, *Archives Mounier/Esprit*, IMEC – ESP 2. C1-02-02, Correspondance générale avec l'Italie 1946–53.
9   Note from Guy Besse to the Istituto Gramsci, 18 July 1956. *Archives Istituto Gramsci*, UA-47.
10   Ibid.
11   Althusser 1973 [1965], p. 173.
12   Jameson 1971, Chapter IV, and Anderson 1977, p. 82.

in the same vein as did *Esprit*. A second Italian issue in 1963, directed by André Gorz, initiated another critical encounter with Gramsci for a new generation of readers. Gramsci's potential influence on Sartre's circle illuminates Simone de Beauvoir's 1963 statement that 'in a brilliant synthesis, Gramsci, a Marxist, took up bourgeois humanism'.[13] More surprisingly, Maurice Merleau-Ponty – who never explicitly integrated Gramsci's thoughts into his philosophy – wrote a note for a handbook of philosophy in 1956, in which he incorporated the Italian political leader into the pantheon of famous philosophers. There, he praised Gramsci's 'considerable contribution' as well as his unique 'union of philosophy and politics'.[14] He also endorsed Gramsci's oft-quoted motto: 'To tell the truth is revolutionary'.[15]

2.2 *Insidious Censorship: Gramsci as a Prisoner of the Invisible Hand of the Market*

Why, we may ask, did all these projects end in failure? Why were they not picked up by Marxists and other intellectuals on the French left? The philosopher Georges Labica hypothesised that the PCF blocked them for political reasons.[16] Indeed, this theory helps to explain why the *Letters* and *Notebooks*, which were translated and ready for print in 1951 and 1955 respectively, were only published in 1953 and 1959. However, a level of complexity troubles Labica's theory because these surprising delays in the publication schedule of Gramsci's works were not tied to party presses but to the decisions of well-known 'bourgeois' publishing houses. The PCI preferred this type of outlet for Gramsci in France, as they also did with the publishing house Einaudi in Italy. The PCF, somewhat indifferent to Gramsci, agreed with this arrangement. Even if they demonstrated an interest,[17] the well-established publishers Flammarion in 1953, Seuil in 1954 and Gallimard in 1955, all declined to release Gramsci's works mostly for commercial reasons. At the same time, the *Istituto Gramsci* was sceptical about a number of houses, such as Plon, that proposed shorter anthologies, as these would have appeared without some of the most significant texts.[18] The *Istituto's* ideal of a 'total representation of the work of Gramsci' was also hobbled by the

---

13   De Beauvoir 1963, p. 117.
14   Merleau-Ponty 1956, p. 422.
15   Ibid.
16   Labica 1992, pp. 26–7.
17   Letter from the literary agent Odette Arnaud to Giuseppe Berti, 25 February 1957, *Archives Istituto Gramsci*, box UA-47.
18   Letter from Plon's Collection director Eric de Dampierre to Giuseppe Berti, 29 April 1957, Archives Istituto Gramsci, box UA-47.

commercial or 'pragmatic' reasoning of Gallimard, who desired that 'the selection [be] intended for ... French readers'.[19]

In 1954, Le Seuil also refused to print and release Gramsci's work, due to internal dissensions. According to the editor Maurice Nadeau, this was because the house had been established with clear Catholic affiliations and intentions. No doubt an awareness that their best seller during this time (with more than 1 million copies sold) was *Don Camillo*, the story of a priest who outsmarts a stubborn Italian communist mayor, also played a part. In 1956, Plon offered what appeared to be a way out of this publishing impasse. Eric de Dampierre, the young director of a human sciences collection was willing to support a more limited edition based on the volume *Note sul Machiavelli, sulla politica e sullo stato moderno*.[20] Dampierre was very close to the liberal-conservative intellectual Aron, and he would eventually translate classics of political science – such as those of Max Weber and Leo Strauss – that also took polemical aim against orthodox Marxism. Sartre, who wanted the contract on his own terms, denounced Plon as a 'notoriously reactionary publishing house'.[21] Nevertheless, Sartre's eleventh hour contract with Julliard in the summer of 1956 also failed, partially due to the colossal financial investment it demanded during what were particularly lean times for the publishing industry.

2.3   *The Canonical Image of Gramsci in the PCF: A Lifeline?*
The irony of all these abortive attempts to publish Gramsci's work in France with private publishers is that the PCF eventually took on the project in April of 1957. Under conditions stipulated by the *Istituto Gramsci*, the PCF agreed to double the volume of the abridged anthologies put forth by the commercial houses. The eventual PCF proposal included an incredible intellectual collective. It continued the work of Marc Soriano (who later became a specialist of popular literature, especially the tales of Charles Perrault) and Jean-Paul Sartre by adding to the team two skilled Italianists: Gilbert Moget and Armand Monjo as well as a philosopher of science, Jean-Toussaint Desanti. Georges Mounin, one of the most important linguists of the twentieth century, would serve as a supervisor and three historians would assist with historical notes. The first was Charles Parain, a specialist of Ancient History and contributor to the *Cambridge Economic History of Europe*. The second was Denis Richet, who was at

19   Letter from Odette Arnaud to the director of the *Istituto Gramsci*, 13 January 1955, *Archives Istituto Gramsci*, box UA-47.

20   Gramsci 1949.

21   Handwritten note on the letter from Plon's Collection director Eric de Dampierre to Giuseppe Berti, op cit.

that time a member of the PCF and specialist of the French Revolution (he later challenged the Marxist narrative of the Revolution with François Furet in the 1960s and 1970s). And finally, the third was the young Michel Vovelle, the renowned historian of modern history and explorer of the 'histoire des mentalités' in the *Nouvelles Annales*.[22] While it is a fact that no other French publishing house could have mobilised such forces, it should be noted that, at that time, the PCF held a mostly positive but still only partial vision of Gramsci. As one of the leading working-class intellectuals of the period, Léo Figuères confessed that many held an incomplete picture of Gramsci as 'a prisoner of Mussolini for whom we had campaigned … [and this image] remained prevalent until the end of the fifties'.[23] The translator Marc Soriano later pointed out that it was Louis Aragon and Georges Cogniot, the personal secretary of Maurice Thorez and a classical humanist intellectual, who encouraged his writings on Gramsci in the communist press. Another example of this enthusiastic, yet confused and partial, support for Gramsci can be seen in the way that Cogniot admonished George Mounin for having dared to pen a critical article on Gramsci's reading of Machiavelli, arguing that 'there are better things to do than quibbling over the conceptions of the great Italian revolutionary figure'.[24]

Most of the articles from this era defend a hagiographic and Stalinist version of Gramsci, one similar to the interpretation penned by Togliatti in an Italian communist review published in France in 1937.[25] For most of the French communist admirers of Gramsci, such as their translators Jean Noaro and Marc Soriano, he was 'the best disciple of Lenin and Stalin', the '*capo* of the working class', and the 'founder of the party'. This conception infuriated Alfred Rosmer and Pierre Monatte – both founders of the Communist party and former revolutionary syndicalists who were later close to Trotsky. They unambiguously denounced the work of Sartre's friend Soriano for trafficking in 'the worst Stalinist imaginary'.[26] For his part, Rosmer rediscovered Gramsci's writings in the newspaper *L'Ordine Nuovo* and encouraged Pierre Naville, a vanguard intellectual before the war in favour of surrealism and council communism, to read them. Naville perceived Gramsci as 'a danger to the Stalinists', because he accurately perceived 'the bureaucratic peril' of Stalinism.[27] Denis Richet, one of the

---

22   Interview by the author with Michel Vovelle, 6 December 2015, in Aix-en-Provence.
23   Interview by the author with Leo Figuères, 26 January 2011, in Malakoff. Figuères was the mayor of Malakoff from 1965 to 1996.
24   'Notes sur la fin de Machiavel', Georges Cogniot, 7 July 1954, *Archives Georges Cogniot*, in Archives départementales de Seine-Saint-Denis (archives of the PCF), 262 J 9, Bobigny.
25   Togliatti 1937.
26   Nadeau 1990, p. 269.
27   Letter from Pierre Naville to Alfred Rosmer, 29 December 1954, *Archives Pierre Naville*.

three historians assigned to the PCF project, provided a concise and pithy pré-
cis of Gramsci in two articles published in 1953–54.[28] In the first, he depicted
Gramsci as a son of the people and as a communist man, echoing the orthodox bestsellers of Thorez and Aragon. In the second, he addressed Gramsci's
interest in French history, especially Gramsci's praise for the 'special path' taken
by the French with Jacobinism, a path he recommended as educative for Italy
as well. Richet's point was that the PCF and Thorez embodied the vanguard of
the French people and the future of that tradition. Thus, Gramsci's historicism
would suggest that they had inherited and maintained the French special path.
So, following Gramsci's theory in France would mean following the political
line of Thorez.

3   Out of Stalinism? (1956–59)

In 1956, a great many intellectuals either left the party, broke with it, or began
to question it from within. For its part, the PCF refused the process of de-
Stalinisation then detectable in Italy under Togliatti's leadership. Instead, it
used Gramsci as a reservoir of ideas and symbols to justify change amid continuity, in particular to justify a commitment to a national path to socialism. In
1957, the PCI pressed the PCF to abandon the project of editing Gramsci (which
would have commemorated the twentieth anniversary of his death) as well as
organising the first *Convegno di studi gramsciani* in Rome (in fact delayed until
1958). What happened in the PCF during this period?

3.1   *The Reception of Gramsci by Those inside and outside the PCF*
Outside the Party, the periodical *Arguments*, directed by Edgar Morin, Kostas
Axelos and Pierre Fougeyrollas, explored Gramsci's work mostly in the writings
of the young Robert Paris, who sought to work out a perceived affinity between
Trotsky and conventional anti-Stalinism.[29] For *Arguments*, Gramsci, Lukács,
and Adorno were labelled Western Marxists, heretic communists, opposed to
official Marxism. Young intellectuals such as Alain Touraine, Gilles Deleuze,
and Michel Foucault published their first pieces of work in this pioneering
review. Another journal, *Les cahiers internationaux*, published half a dozen
other articles on Gramsci as early as 1949.[30] It was led by two left-wing anti-
Stalinist socialists: Lelio Basso (number two in the Italian Socialist Party (PSI))

---

28   Richet 1953 and 1954.
29   Paris 1962.
30   Bourgin 1949 and Terracini 1949.

and Gilles Martinet (founder of the Unified Socialist Party (PSU) in 1960), as well as by Konni Zilliacus (a British Labour MP). Prominent Marxist economists such as Paul Sweezy, Paul Baran, Oskar Lange and Charles Bettelheim, and historians ranging from Jean Bruhat to Maxime Rodinson, contributed to this oft-forgotten yet high-quality review. Effectively, the journal's editors were trying to position themselves as heterodox communists by publishing Gramsci's texts on *L'Ordine Nuovo* and *On Americanism and Fordism*.[31] The former communist Serge Mallet, the thinker of a New Left based upon the formation of a new working class, has certainly read Gramsci here.[32]

Inside the PCF, intellectuals were looking at the Italian model of de-Stalinisation and, particularly, at the alliances forged in Italy with a (new) socialist left. It was hoped that these alliances could give more space and freedom to intellectuals in the organisation while simultaneously loosening the party's bonds with the USSR. At least three dissenting bulletins invoked Gramsci, explicitly and implicitly, in this period. The first was *La Tribune du communisme*, directed by Serge Mallet (who had left the PCF to create the PSU). The second was Félix Guattari's *Tribune de discussion*, and the third, more insistently, was *l'Etincelle (the Spark)*, a dissenting bulletin whose contributors included Jean-Pierre Vernant, the famous historian of Greek myths, the philosopher Henri Lefebvre and Robert Brécy. Since 1955, and as the head of *Editions Sociales*, the latter had made a dramatic contribution to the publication of Gramsci's work. In 1958, Brécy was dismissed by the PCF for his divergences from the Party line. Now, as an iconoclastic figure, Gramsci was chosen as a symbol for *Voies nouvelles (New Pathways)*, a journal sponsored by Jean-Toussaint and Dominique Desanti, and supported by Georges Mounin and Henri Lefebvre. Desanti chose the title '*Voies nouvelles*' in reference to Gramsci, whose name was invoked during a debate with Henri Krasucki at a meeting of a local cell that was discussing the Hungarian events of 1956.[33] Krasucki was at that time a local communist leader but, by the 1980s, he would become the leader of the main trade union, the General Confederation of Labour (CGT). The bulletin *Le débat communiste (the Communist debate)* led by the zoologist Marcel Prenant, who fought against Lysenkoism in the PCF, chose as his motto the saying often associated with Gramsci: 'To tell the truth is revolutionary'.[34]

---

31   Dautry 1956 and Leonetti 1957.
32   Vincent 1973.
33   Desanti 2009, p. 823.
34   The exact quotation is 'To tell the truth, to arrive together at the truth, is a communist and
        revolutionary act', Gramsci 1977, p. 68. It is from an unsigned article written by Gramsci
        and Togliatti, *L'Ordine Nuovo*, 21 June 1919, Vol. 1, n. 7.

3.2   *The Instrumentalisation of Gramsci by the* PCF

Recognising the passion that Gramsci inspired among its members, the question of employing the Italian communist instrumentally was considered by some intellectuals in the higher echelons of the PCF's political apparatus, especially by Jean Kanapa and Roger Garaudy. Both had formerly been the French voices of cultural Zhdanovism: a socialist-realist metaphysics designed to challenge the activist philosophies of 'non-communist' thinkers, such as Sartre. Garaudy was the official philosopher of the party and a staunch Stalinist until 1956. He was also the 'master of ambiguity', as Henri Lefebvre nicknamed him.[35] Garaudy tried during this period to justify the unquestionable authority of the party and simultaneously to peddle a softer version of de-Stalinisation than the ones proffered by dissidents and by those who had left the party. Whereas Gramsci is never mentioned in Garaudy's works prior to 1956, his ideas appear in the first book that Garaudy published after the Khrushchev report, *Humanist Marxism* in 1957.[36] Garaudy, who knew Gramsci mainly through Togliatti's interpretation, introduced Gramsci to many readers in the communist press, when he began theorising the party as a 'collective intellectual'. This theoretical move corresponded perfectly to changes in the USSR and to the PCF after Stalin's death (even if this 'Gramscian' concept is hard to find in any of Gramsci's texts). Inspired by Gramsci, Garaudy devised a strategy for the PCF: conquer the 'traditional intellectuals' and form 'organic intellectuals'.[37] More concretely, Garaudy and Kanapa employed Gramsci in their polemics against the Marxist philosopher Henri Lefebvre, who was excluded from the party in 1958 for internal dissidence. Specifically, Garaudy and Kanapa opposed their own version of the 'organic intellectual' (obedient and faithful to the party, a collective intellectual) to the 'traditional intellectual' (an isolated, critical academic, without any sense of responsibility, who plays into the bourgeoisie's hands).[38] They associated the latter with Lefebvre. In Lefebvre's autobiography, he gives a caustic and disillusioned account of his clashes with Garaudy at this time, explaining how Garaudy seemed shocked that he criticised Gramsci's philosophy of praxis as well as how Garaudy wanted to force him to admit 'the dissolution of the conscious praxis in the revolutionary praxis, of the individual thinker in the collective thinker'.[39] Lefebvre's response was: 'You want to force me to accept Gramsci's stances – from what I understand of him, he makes of

---

35   Lefebvre, 1959, p. 79.
36   Garaudy 1957a, pp. 236 and 244.
37   Garaudy 1957b, pp. 97–107.
38   Kanapa 1957.
39   Lefebvre 1959, p. 103.

revolutionary Marxism a praxis and not an awareness, a scientific elaboration of universal praxis. I say: no! I contest, I refuse'.[40]

As late as 1959, Leo Figuères was considering a more rational use of intellectuals in the party. This deliberation inspired the creation of CERM, the *Centre d'études et de recherches marxistes* (*Center for Marxist study and research*), which took as its model the *Istituto Gramsci* in Italy as well as its motto: 'a seat for fruitful scientific activity with our best specialists'.[41] At the same time, the party's general secretary Maurice Thorez read Gramsci and, although sceptical of the concept of hegemony, he became interested in Gramsci's 'Notes on Machiavelli'.[42] In particular, Thorez was drawn to Gramsci's comments on the concept of Caesarism and parliamentary life in France, and especially the sentence implying the necessity of: 'a positive education – of those who have to recognise certain means as necessary, even if they are the means of tyrants, because they desire certain ends'.[43]

3.3 An a Posteriori Censorship by the PCF? (1959)

After years spent alternating between suspicion and attentiveness, by 1958–59, the PCF leadership was embarrassed by the slowly exploding 'time-bomb' represented by the writings of Gramsci. By that time, tension was also mounting between the PCF and the PCI on many political issues: from their differing assessments of the emerging European construction to the relationship with the international communist movement in general, and Moscow in particular. Gramsci's writings fell victim to the crossfire. As early as 1954, François Billoux, secretary for ideological issues and supervisor of the PCF presses, asked Soriano 'for what purpose' he intended to translate Gramsci. Soriano found it a very strange question: 'It was like asking why do we need to translate or spread Descartes, Spinoza or Kant! He is a great thinker, and a Marxist philosopher, with a lot of brio and humour, that's all!'[44] In 1956, Jean Kanapa sent reports of a growing revisionist threat, a danger fed by biased readings of Gramsci. He warned Laurent Casanova, then head of the PCF's intellectual section, that: 'Maybe we should be careful with the Italianist tendency, or the Gramscianists,

---

40   Ibid.

41   'Au sujet de l'organisation du travail parmi les intellectuels' (On the subject of the organisation of work among the intellectuals), note by Léo Figueres, 11 January 1959, *Archives Cogniot*, 292 J 67.

42   Handwritten notes of Maurice Thorez on the volume *Oeuvres choisies* published in 1959, Archives municipales d'Ivry-sur-Seine.

43   Q13, §10, Gramsci 1975, p. 1600; Gramsci 1971a, p. 135.

44   Soriano 1993, p. 468.

we will inevitably have troubles with them'.[45] After so many contradictory uses of Gramsci between 1957–1958, the leading intellectuals of the PCF at last began to read Gramsci carefully. Guy Besse, who supervised the process involved with the Gramsci volumes, gave the following assessment: While he found Gramsci's work 'very interesting and suggestive', he held serious reservations about their ambiguous formulations regarding the objectivity of the outside world, formulations which contradicted materialist doctrines.[46] Besse issued a contextual warning to Thorez: 'if, in 1959, we authorise the publication of such texts without a comment – in France – we would be guilty. The Fathers Calvez, Lefebvre and others would find ammunition there'.[47] Besse refused to censor the texts, however, he fashioned two notes correcting the 'errors' of Gramsci. Finally, Georges Cogniot wrote a superficially complimentary introduction that contained ambiguous undertones. On the one hand, he praised Gramsci as a 'great Marxist figure' and as a 'creative disciple of Lenin'.[48] He suggested that Gramsci remained faithful to the October Revolution and to the Communist party. On the other hand, he warned that while Gramsci elevated the organic intellectual, he was also too committed to criticising the traditional bourgeois intellectual. Thorez, for his part, pursued the Gramsci question at a Central Committee meeting in November 1959. There, he condemned those who took up historical materialism without dialectical materialism – a stance that the party had previously associated with Kautsky and Blum. For Thorez, Gramsci 'was a great communist leader', who had produced 'a considerable work', but 'he was isolated from the movement and did not know [of] Engels' work on the *Dialectics of Nature*'.[49] In a meeting of the Secretariat (6 November 1959), Gramsci was not praised as a 'great Marxist figure', and the Secretariat recommended that the spread of Gramsci's ideas in the intellectual world and among the party officials be discouraged.[50] After quickly selling out of its initial run, the *Anthology* would not be re-printed.

---

45 Letter from Jean Kanapa to Lauren Casanova, 5 November 1956, *Archives Maurice Thorez*, 626 AP/45.

46 Note written by Guy Besse for Maurice Thorez, 29 May 1959, *Archives Georges Cogniot*, 292 J 43/44.

47 Note written by Guy Besse for Maurice Thorez, op cit.

48 Cogniot 1959.

49 Intervention from Maurice Thorez at the Central Committee of Choisy-le-Roi, 2/3 November 1959, recordings at the Archives départementales de Seine-Saint-Denis, 4 AV/228 and 229.

50 Notes of the Secretariat of the PCF, file 2 NUM 4/12, Archives départementales de Seine-Saint-Denis.

4   Althusser's Challenge in Context (1960–65)

In the early 1960s, the PCF was nursing the wounds it had suffered from its engagements with the intellectuals. These intellectuals were looking to jump-start the growth of the Union of Communist Students (UEC), which the party had created in 1957. They saw in the UEC a new battlefield in their struggle for the reform of the PCF. The UEC resisted the Gaullist challenge from the PCF's social base among the workers. Simultaneously, in 1960, a new French left had emerged in response to the Algerian war with the creation of the Unified Socialist Party (PSU).

4.1   An 'Italian Party' Challenging the Authority of the PCF

From 1959 to 1965, the so-called 'Italian tendency' – those looking at the PCI and its process of de-Stalinisation as a model for the PCF – lead the student branch of communist organisation. They advocated for a greater autonomy of the UEC, as well as for a truly effective de-Stalinisation, following Togliatti, one that would further recognise the centrality of current and future intellectuals in society while also adopting structural reforms. The 'Italians' commonly referenced Gramsci in their texts, along with their mentor Jean-Toussaint Desanti – who proposed a special conference on phenomenology and praxis in 1963 that explored the question of shifting Husserlian phenomenology to a Gramscian philosophy of praxis.[51] The party elites already suspected the mentors of the UEC of heresy. Drawing on this inspiration, the students maintained that it was necessary to form a new 'historical bloc', one uniting budding intellectuals, technicians and 'practical' intellectuals.[52] The leadership of the PCF saw this call as an attempt to create a second, pro-Italian communist party that would oppose the official one. This assumption was not entirely wrong: without a doubt, the students wanted to define themselves as a unified social class with specific and legitimate interests. According to a secret report from a spy in a youth communist camp gathering Italian and French young activists, the French UEC officials were praising the PCI as a 'party of teachers', and as 'open-minded', while the PCF was viewed as the 'party of the working-class', as 'dogmatic', and as hostile to 'all intellectuals'. 'Gramschi' (sic) was the name on everybody's lips at this summer camp.[53]

---

51   Desanti 1963.
52   Bon and Burnier 1966.
53   Report from Michel Comerlatti to the Secretariat of the PCF, 11 September 1963, *Archives Roland Leroy*, 263 J/1.

4.2   *The New Left with Gramsci: What Is to Be Done with the*
   Intellectuals?

The central question of 1965 was, 'What is an intellectual?' More specifically, the question was posed of what the current intellectual transformations are, and how these changes could play a role in the new left. It is striking that it was only in 1965 that Sartre launched a significant discussion of Gramscian theses on these issues in Japan during two conferences. Sartre claimed that the golden age of the 'organic intellectuals' of the bourgeoisie expressing its objective spirit, was dead.[54] Contemporary intellectuals, he went on, are neither ideological clerks (builders of the dominant hegemony), nor practical experts (technicians, specific organic intellectuals), nor philosophers (old-fashioned organic intellectuals, now traditional intellectuals).[55] The intellectuals are the grandsons of philosophers, but have become technicians of practical knowledge, subordinated to the logic of profit, to specialisation. They are research specialists and servants of the hegemonic guardians of tradition, or, as Sartre says, 'subaltern government servants of the superstructures'.[56] They embody the contradiction, twisted between their own practical truth and the perpetuation of a dominant ideology. They cannot also be the organic intellectuals of the working-class, as logically they are distrustful of workers. These specialists cannot join the movement without annihilating their own critical vision, without being annihilated as intellectuals. These technicians are nothing but 'unhappy consciousnesses', the wretched men of a wretched society.[57]

Sartre's reflections were shared by others on the new left, especially in the periodical *Les Temps modernes*, directed by Sartre and Gorz, close to the new left party, the PSU. In 1964–65, everyone seemed to be writing on this crucial issue. Nicos Poulantzas, for instance, wrote his first Gramscian study in *Les Temps modernes* in 1965. In this article, he praised hegemony as the central concept necessary for a study of political power, a study based on a relational perspective of power between dominant and subaltern classes and which focused on the necessity of building ideological and political hegemony – even if this meant making economic concessions on the part of the subaltern classes. In his analysis, the intellectual played a central role as an organiser of hegemony. He welcomed as fact the shift in society from traditional

54   Sartre 1972, p. 24.
55   Sartre 1972, pp. 17–30.
56   Sartre 1972, p. 27.
57   Sartre 1972, pp. 40–1.

to organic intellectuals.[58] Another important figure in this debate over the role of the intellectual is André Gorz. In his response, he highlighted the repression of man's creative 'praxis' and its replacement by the mere reproduction of capital. As a solution, he insisted that only *'auto-gestion'* (self-management) can bring back 'praxis' into the factory.[59] Although Gorz admitted that socialism is 'the hegemony of the working-class', for him, the only way to fight against 'bourgeois hegemony' was to effect an alliance with, or even to rely on, the practical knowledge of practical intellectuals and the organizing skills of the 'technicians', to whom he conceded hegemony in the socialist movement.[60]

Surprisingly, the authors of the book that had the biggest influence on this discussion in 1966 were two pro-Italian students of the UEC, the 25-year-old Frédéric Bon and Michel-Antoine Burnier. This pair stressed the emergence of 'technicians' and 'executives': new organic intellectuals who were significant from a quantitative viewpoint, and whom they opposed to the 'traditional intellectual', to the 'great intellectual', by dint of their position in productive relations, and by their role in the diffusion of a practical hegemony.[61] This synthesis, along with the work of Roger Garaudy on the new 'historical bloc', constituted a breach in the defences of those arguing for the hegemony of intellectuals in the workers' movement against the conception of a PCF. By contrast, around 1968, the PCF was advancing a strategy of a union of intellectuals with the working-class under working-class hegemony.

4.3   Althusser: A Double Game for a Double Mind

If the publication of *For Marx*, and later *Reading Capital*, are seen in the context of this broader reception of Gramsci, a double-sided Althusser appears to the reader. In the chapter of *For Marx* entitled 'Contradiction and Overdetermination', originally published in 1962, he pays tribute to Gramsci in two footnotes.[62] According to Althusser, we find in Gramsci's *Prison Notebooks*:

> some completely original and in some cases genial insights into the problem, basic today, of the superstructures. Also, as always with true discoveries, there are *new concepts*, for example, *hegemony*: a remarkable example of a theoretical solution in outline to the problems of the interpenetration

---

58   Poulantzas 1965, pp. 862–96.
59   Gorz 1964, chapter I (*Au-delà des sous*) and Part V of chapter V (*La bataille culturelle*).
60   Gorz 1967, Part 4 of chapter III (*L'alternative globale. Le problème des alliances*).
61   Bon and Burnier 1966, pp. 34–5.
62   Althusser 2005 [1965], pp. 104 and 114.

of the economic and the political. Unfortunately, at least as far as France is concerned, who has taken up and followed through Gramsci's theoretical effort?[63]

However, in *Reading Capital*, Althusser dedicated considerable efforts to the refutation of Gramsci's philosophical theses, albeit with a number of reservations: 'I shall have to discuss Gramsci, therefore. I do not do so without profound misgivings, fearing not only that my necessarily schematic remarks may disfigure the spirit of this enormously delicate and subtle work of genius', namely 'Gramsci's fruitful discoveries in the field of *historical materialism*'.[64]

In Althusser's private collection of books, one can observe three readings of Gramsci, primarily based on the French anthology of 1959 but in every case deepened by the reading of the Italian thematic edition.[65] Althusser's first reading in 1962, focusing on the theme of politics in Gramsci's *Notes on Machiavelli*, is enthusiastic, not only with respect to the autonomy of the superstructures and the notion of hegemony, but also in respect to Gramsci's interpretation of Machiavelli.[66] For Gramsci, Machiavelli's Prince gives a form to a dispersed collective will by writing a 'political manifesto'. Althusser pays particular attention to the description of the Prince as a politically committed organism based on scientific grounds, passionate and rational.[67] In 1965, Althusser's second reading, consulting *The Philosophy of Croce and Historical Materialism*,[68] is entirely negative with regard to Gramsci's philosophy. However, it is striking that in 1967 Althusser re-read these texts, along with others on culture, in a contradictory way. This time, he found valuable ideas for the analysis of the various levels of philosophies, especially in the study of 'spontaneous' philosophies,[69] and for the analysis of hegemonic apparatuses (with texts that he may have read again in 1969–70). Nevertheless, in his conference in 1967 on the 'spontaneous' philosophies of scientists, Althusser never mentions Gramsci.[70]

Should we conceive Althusser's criticism of Gramsci as a cautious tactical move related to the troubles with the communist youth of the UEC? Althusser

---

63   Althusser 2005 [1965], p. 114.
64   Althusser 1973 [1965], p. 60.
65   Notes on the *Oeuvres choisies* of 1959 in private library of Louis Althusser, IMEC, Caen.
66   Notes called 'Notes sur Machiavel et Gramsci', early 1960s, file ALT2 A 31–05.06, based on the *Note sul Machiavelli*.
67   Ibid.
68   It is possible to find confirmation of this second reading in his notes of September 1967, 'Gramsci, philosophie et politique' file ALT2 A 10–05.05, IMEC, Caen.
69   Ibid.
70   Althusser 1974.

influenced the circle of Marxists at the Ecole normale supérieure (ENS), located in rue d'Ulm, who were close to Maoist positions. By condemning Gramscian historicism (in a manner that, in some respects, was very orthodox and close to the leadership of the PCF), he was sure not to be marginalised within the PCF, while maintaining an audience among leftist students, who were increasingly critical of the PCF leadership. Evidence for this hypothesis appears in Althusser's correspondence with his Italian translator, where Althusser says that:

> at the UEC, my young watchdogs, who are also young lions, have played a leading role, and that is just the beginning. This direct passage from theory to practice is absolutely logical, and they are very well prepared for that – only by giving weapons as a right conception of the things, in their true principles. We will have fun, believe me! And that is only the beginning.[71]

More broadly, in 1965 Althusser is leading a political assault on several fronts, both intellectual and political. Choosing Sartre as his main opponent is revealing. Sartre's prestige was fading, but he was still perceived as the embodiment of the 'classical' humanist intellectual, seeking to introduce historicity and praxis in his works. It is not a coincidence that Althusser highlights the points of convergence between Sartre and Gramsci in *Reading Capital*. However, Garaudy is the main target for practical reasons. These were the place of the dominant intellectual in the PCF, and the definition of the theoretical line of the party on the question of humanism. At this time in the mid-1960s, Garaudy's books began to be suspected within the PCF of revisionism. It was the perfect moment to challenge the hegemony of the almost untouchable Garaudy. It is interesting to see that the PCF general-secretary Waldeck Rochet remarked upon hidden references to Gramscian concepts in Garaudy's books in late 1965 – such as Marxism as a 'methodology of historical initiative' – and this reinforced Rochet's suspicion of Garaudy's revisionism.[72] In his archives, Althusser seems to have frowned upon the same formulation in Gramsci, and puts a note about it in *Reading Capital*.[73]

Was Althusser hoping for a new function for the 'intellectual' negotiated with the communist leadership? Althusser claims a new place for intellectuals

---

71   Letter from Louis Althusser to Franca Madonia, 18 March 1965, in Althusser 1998, p. 608.
72   *Critique du livre de Roger Garaudy, Le marxisme du 20e siècle*, in Archives Waldeck Rochet, 307 J 45.
73   Notes of September 1967 'Gramsci, philosophie et politique' file ALT2 A 10–05.05, IMEC, Caen. Althusser 1973 [1965], p. 175.

in the communist organisation, but on different grounds than the pro-Italian intellectuals. Marxism is a scientific doctrine opposed to its ideological versions (Garaudy), but as a science it is contaminated by a 'spontaneous philosophy' (empiricist) subordinated to dominant ideology. It needed the philosophers to enlighten scientific practice with a 'theory of theoretical practice', based primarily on 'dialectical materialism'. In 1965, Althusser wrote a note to Henri Krasucki, who was then responsible for the intellectuals in the PCF, to propose a complete reorganisation of the sector based on a rehabilitation of theoretical work in the PCF. This would attribute a new role to the intellectuals (and especially the 'philosophers') in the education of militants, while maintaining their own autonomy in the drafting of these lessons.[74] He also proposed to Krasucki the re-publication of some classic texts of Marxism, including works by Antonio Gramsci.

The most illustrative document is the exchange of letters between Louis Althusser and Guy Besse in July 1965, a model of negotiated censorship. Guy Besse noted two points that were unacceptable for the communist leadership and activists. First, he argued that Althusser had downgraded the role of self-taught workers and accentuated the importance of theoreticians. Second, he pointed to the relegation of Thorez from his position as a leading Marxist figure in France. For Besse, these points undermined the legitimacy of the political apparatus of the PCF, and their connection with the working-class. He even feared that having said that 'Thorez is not a theoretician', some intellectuals would further say, 'we, who are not dogmatic and know what is lively Marxism', we must now 'speak Italian'.[75] Althusser's answer was shrewd: he stepped back from a wider internal struggle within the PCF, avoiding pitting the theoreticians/intellectuals against the working-class officials, but remained firm on the non-inclusion of Thorez, giving specious justifications. Althusser reassured Besse by saying that 'the Italians will get what they deserve'. Althusser claimed that he had taken 'care of Gramsci and the Italian current at length', adding, 'I have dealt with Gramsci and the Italian "question" with a very particular care'.[76]

This straightforward and somewhat naïvely appealing attempt by Althusser may have influenced Krasucki or Besse. Althusser's veiled condemnation of Garaudy's historicism and humanism, with its own hidden references to Gram-

---

74   Note from Louis Althusser to Henri Krasucki, 25 February 1965, Georges Cogniot, 292 J 51, in *Fonds d'archives du PCF*: Bobigny.

75   Letter from Guy Besse to Louis Althusser, 18 July 1965, *Archives Louis Althusser*, ALT 2 C1–03.

76   Letter from Louis Althusser to Guy Besse, 25 July 1965, *Archives Louis Althusser*, ALT 2 C1–03.

sci, gave him an opportunity to intervene in the internal debates in the PCF during the years 1965–66. This was seen as a theoretical debate, but it was also a struggle for influence over the intellectuals. At stake was a sphere of autonomy in the organisation, concerning which the PCF leadership feared Althusser as much as Garaudy. Thus, Cogniot expresses his fear that the 'leftist Althusser' plots to take control of his review *La Pensée*.[77] On the Gramscians, Cogniot declares that 'theory is not the monopoly of the intellectuals; they tend to believe it too much! In particular, the admirers of Gramsci have this idea in mind!'[78] But, Cogniot has no illusions either on the motives of Althusser: 'the intention of Althusser is exactly what Garaudy indicates: an intellectualist tendency considering that in the Party only the philosophers are the custodians of scientific theory'.[79]

5   Conclusion

This chapter is not intended to judge the validity of Althusser's so-called refutation of Gramsci's 'philosophy of praxis', rather to contextualise this decisive moment within the genealogy of a specific French Gramscianism. Althusser, as well as the 'Italianists' that he tried to undermine, knew only a small portion of Gramsci's texts in 1965 – generally those reproduced in the anthology of 1959 – and they still had in mind an image of Gramsci that relied largely on their own imaginary production, a symbolic construction. While we cannot reduce Althusser's interventions to purely political manoeuvres, this context helps to explain his harsh criticism of Gramsci that led Étienne Balibar to view the chapter 'Marxism is not a Historicism' in *Reading Capital* 'with an absolute terror'. This chapter had 'an enormous influence for political reasons' that Balibar describes as 'a perfect example of the Stalinist method of criticising left-wing (Lukács) and right-wing deviations (Gramsci) based on the idea that they share a common ground: the ignorance of the scientific character of historical materialism'.[80] The necessity of a political and theoretical intervention that created a clear cleavage between what he perceived as a right and a false political and ideological line, as well as his partial knowledge of Gramsci at that time, certainly led Althusser to oversimplify Gramsci's conception of his-

---

77   In Archives Georges Cogniot, 292 J 51 (not classified yet).
78   Ibid.
79   Notes by Georges Cogniot written in 1966 on the dispute between Garaudy and Althusser for the general-secretary Waldeck Rochet, in Archives Waldeck Rochet, 307 J 38.
80   Balibar 2015.

tory and human action under the label of humanism and historicism. More precisely, these labels were inscribed in the French intellectual context of the mid-1960s. The double-sided, although evolving, perception that Althusser had of Gramsci, which Vittorio Morfino has recently traced with precision,[81] never distanced Althusser from the misgivings towards Gramsci that he formulated in 1965–66. As Pierre Macherey has underlined, Althusser was suspicious towards 'the (Gramscian) idea of a theoretical future of Praxis, that gives its basic principle to empiricism and pragmatism', against which Althusser argued that it was 'necessary to substitute a practical future of Theory'.[82]

---

81   Morfino 2015, pp. 62–81.
82   Macherey 2005, p. 151.

CHAPTER 25

Althusser, Gramsci, and Machiavelli: Encounters and Mis-encounters

Sebastian Neubauer

1 Introduction

Machiavelli's *Prince* has always been an enigmatic text and it has, in very different historical conjunctures, fascinated very different readers. And it is no accident that it continues to do so today. Among the most fascinating aspects of Machiavelli's *Prince* are, of course, the political emphasis displayed and the mysterious relationship between the text and its underlying political project, the new state.[1] These fascinating aspects find their most outstanding expression in chapter 26, *Exhortation to liberate Italy from the barbarian yoke*.[2] Regarding this chapter we might even speak of a revolutionary aspect to Machiavelli's work, an aspect that has provoked a variety of political appropriations in the course of the history of political thought. Whereas Hegel praised Machiavelli as the thinker of the French Revolution, Francesco De Sanctis and Benedetto Croce read him as the theorist of the consolidation of national unity.[3] To very different ends, Lenin thought of his own revolution in Machiavellian terms, whereas Gramsci (and a couple of other Marxist theorists in his vein) perceived Machiavelli as the theorist of revolutionary practice in the 'West'.[4]

Although Gramsci's account of Machiavelli is the most prominent milestone in the Marxist appropriation of the thinker, it is certainly not the last. Amongst others, Machiavelli reappears forcefully in the work of Louis Althusser, who developed his own very striking account of Machiavelli. Althusser devoted manifold writings to the Florentine secretary, and these have provoked remarkable discussions in the past years.[5] However, all but one of these writings saw daylight only after Althusser passed away. To this day, only a handful of them have been published, whereas the others continue to simmer in Althusser's

---

1 Machiavelli 1988.
2 Machiavelli 1988, p. 87.
3 Hegel 1983; De Sanctis 1941; Croce 1949.
4 Barthas 2010.
5 Del Lucchese 2010; Lahtinen 2009; Lahtinen 2013; Terray 1996; Vatter 2004.

archives. Regarding the Marxist appropriations of Machiavelli, it is noteworthy that Althusser elaborates his readings not only in an overarching Marxist context, but in explicit reference to Gramsci. In reading the Florentine, Althusser relies heavily on Gramsci's account: 'to my knowledge, Gramsci is the only one who went any distance on the road I am taking'.[6] However, it is interesting to note that at the very same time, Althusser almost aggressively turns against Gramsci and Gramsci's Machiavelli by stating: 'This is amateurism. This is adventurism'.[7] Thus, within Althusser's work we are confronted with a thought-provoking and problematic intersection of Marxism, Machiavelli and Gramsci that deserves a closer investigation.

In the following, I aim to map out the intriguing triangular relationship between Marxism, Gramsci and Machiavelli in terms of its productivity within the work of Althusser. I will thereby demonstrate how Althusser's thinking – a thinking that cannot be separated from a very specific given historical situation that saw Marxism at the brink of collapse – is structured from within by engaging this triangular relationship. Furthermore, I show how this engagement has significantly contributed to Althusser's famous theoretical interventions and thereby to the course of Marxism as such. Accordingly, what follows is focused entirely on Althusser's reading of Gramsci, of Machiavelli and of Gramsci's Machiavelli.

To this end, I will first provide a raw sketch of some aspects of Gramsci's reading of Machiavelli that Althusser impressively addresses. Second, I will examine how Althusser interprets Machiavelli in the tradition of Gramsci, and third, describe how he simultaneously develops an insightful critique of Gramsci's overall theoretical approach. Fourth, I argue that this fierce critique, articulated from within the Gramscian framework but motivated by a differing reading of Machiavelli, ultimately distinguishes Althusser's thought from that of Gramsci.

This Althusserian engagement with Gramsci's Machiavelli is far from a frivolous gymnastic act in the remote space of theory. On the contrary, it occurs in a very specific historical situation in which Althusser identifies – somewhat oddly – Gramsci with Eurocommunism, which he – again, somewhat oddly – blames for the ostensible collapse of Marxism. Althusser engages with this historico-political situation through his readings of Gramsci, of Machiavelli and of Gramsci's Machiavelli. Thus, in the material that is discussed in the following, we observe less the re-interpretation of past theories than the

---

6   Althusser 1969, p. 16.
7   ALT2. A26–05.07.

insertion and injection of the past theories of Gramsci and Machiavelli into the theoretical-political conjuncture of the present. In this regard, I hope to demonstrate that Althusser's treatment of Gramsci and Machiavelli is telling in respect not only to Althusser's views, but also 'in the last instance' to Marxist politics and theory as such. Despite the focus on Althusser, I hope to demonstrate how Althusser's engagement with Gramsci and Machiavelli might also be thought of as a very particular inquiry into the present significance of Gramsci and of Gramsci's Machiavelli.

2 Gramsci on Machiavelli

Gramsci, who devoted in-depth studies to the Florentine secretary, could not have been Gramsci without Machiavelli. Lengthy accounts on Machiavelli can be found in the Notebooks 1, 4, 5, 6, 7, 13, 14, 15 and 17; the most prominent of these is found in Notebook 13. Gramsci's readings of Machiavelli are well researched.[8] And it is not an accident that they continue to animate academic and political discourse. However, a deepened or even comprehensive analysis of Gramsci's Machiavelli is well beyond the scope of this article. Accordingly, in what follows I limit myself to a few very specific aspects of Gramsci's reading of Machiavelli.

In the same vein as Francesco De Sanctis and Benedetto Croce, Gramsci conceived of Machiavelli as the theorist of the autonomy of politics and somewhat of politics as such.[9] In the context of the Gramscian reading of Machiavelli, it is noteworthy that it was Croce who established the distinct relationship between Marx and Machiavelli by describing Marx as the 'Machiavelli of the proletariat'.[10] Following this Crocean line of thought, Gramsci reflects on the Marxist theory of politics and the State and on the (potential) forerunners of Marxism in early modern political thought. Thereby, Gramsci adopts Croce's challenge, attempting to demonstrate what it means to understand Marx as the Machiavelli of the proletariat; a phrase that already indicates the importance of the Florentine secretary (who could have been easily dubbed 'the Marx of the early modern epoch') vis-à-vis Marx.

In Gramsci's view there is a decisive theoretical and a political relationship between Marxism and Machiavelli. Hence, we find at the core of Gram-

---

8   Fontana 1993; Thomas 2009a.
9   Croce 1927; Croce 1924a; Barthas 2010, p. 259.
10   Croce 1927, p. 112.

sci's reading of Machiavelli the theorization of this presumed relationship, from which other core topics of his reading evolve. According to Gramsci, Machiavelli's thought possesses – as does Marx's – a specific and rare universal character. Gramsci argues that Machiavelli was the theorist of 'the revolutionary class of the time', the Italian 'people' or 'nation', whose education Machiavelli allegedly pursued.[11] Gramsci conceives of this presumed relationship between Marx and Machiavelli in the following terms, already indicating a circuit between Marxism and Machiavellianism: 'This position in which Machiavelli found himself politically ... is repeated today for the philosophy of praxis'.[12]

Against this backdrop, Gramsci thinks of Machiavelli's realistic theory of the political (and of his method to produce it) as the beginning of the future politics. Gramsci sees in Machiavelli – as in Marx – politics and theory inseparably intertwined, bridging into one another. Accordingly, he assigns himself the following task:

> This theme can be developed in a two-fold study: a study of the real relations between the two as theorists of militant politics, of action; and a book which would derive from Marxist doctrines an articulated system of contemporary politics of *the Prince* type. The theme would be the political party, in its relations with the classes and the State: not the party as a sociological category, but the party which seeks to found the State.[13]

Facing declining strength in prison, Gramsci was unfortunately prevented from accomplishing the task of overtly reworking Marxism as Machiavellianism. However, he provided a few sketches of this original and unfulfilled project. Conceiving of Machiavelli as an overall revolutionary thinker with a strong structural relationship to Marxism, Gramsci develops a conception of Machiavelli's *The Prince* as a 'revolutionary utopian Manifesto', that internally evolves into Marx and Engels's *Communist Manifesto*:[14]

> Machiavelli's style is not that of a systematic compiler of treatises, such as abounded during the Middle Ages and Humanism, quite the contrary; it is the style of a man of action, of a man urging action, the style of a party manifesto.[15]

---

11   Gramsci 1971a, p. 222 [Q13, §27].
12   Gramsci 1971a, p. 223 [Q13, §23].
13   Gramsci 1971a, p. 210 [Q13, §23].
14   Marx and Engels 1959 [1848].
15   Gramsci 1971a, p. 221 [Q13, §27].

Gramsci produces this hypothesis (that directly connects the foundation of the Marxist project with Machiavelli's thought) by analysing Machiavelli's method of theoretical production. Gramsci thinks of the latter's work as a successful mediation between Theory and Practice that simultaneously marks the beginning of Practice itself:

> The basic thing about *the Prince* is that it is not a systematic treatment, but a 'live' work, in which political ideology and political science are fused in the dramatic form of a 'myth'. Before Machiavelli, political science had taken the form either of the Utopia or of the scholarly treatise. Machiavelli, combining the two, gave imaginative and artistic form to his conception by embodying the doctrinal, rational element in the person of a condottiere, who represents plastically and 'anthropomorphically' the symbol of the 'collective will'.[16]

In sum, we might speak of Gramsci as having sought to rework Marxism as Machiavellianism and vice versa. However, Gramsci perceived of Machiavelli as – in the last instance – flawed by a certain utopian dimension:

> The utopian character of *the Prince* lies in the fact that the Prince had no real historical existence; he did not present himself immediately and objectively to the Italian people, but was a pure theoretical abstraction – a symbol of the leader and ideal condottiere. However, in a dramatic movement of great effect, the elements of passion and of myth which occur throughout the book are drawn together and brought to life in the conclusion, in the invocation of a prince who 'really exists'.[17]

Thus, in the framework of his project of the 'modern prince', Gramsci was very much preoccupied with overcoming this utopian dimension, that is replacing Machiavelli's presumed external relation between the Prince (as a single individual) and the people, by an internal and organic relation between the 'modern prince', that is the re-theorised Communist party, and the people. Gramsci states that 'the protagonist of the new Prince could in the modern epoch not be an individual hero, but only the political party'.[18] Therefore Gramsci argues: 'The modern prince, the myth-prince, cannot be a real person, a concrete indi-

---

16   Gramsci 1971a, p. 210 [Q13, §23].
17   Gramsci 1971a, p. 212 [Q13, §23].
18   Gramsci 1971a, p. 236 [Q7, §16].

vidual. It can only be an organism, a complex element of society in which a collective will, which has already been recognized and has to some extent asserted itself in action, begins to take concrete form'.[19]

3   Althusser with Gramsci on Machiavelli

Louis Althusser, for his part, was very much preoccupied with Gramsci. Althusser has, for a long time, been well-known as a reader of Gramsci – a topic that has been almost endlessly researched.[20] In the given context it is noteworthy (1) that Althusser crafted his approach to Machiavelli via his reading of Gramsci, and (2) that he read Gramsci through (his own very particular understanding of) Machiavelli.

In this regard, Althusser's recollection of his encounter with Machiavelli in 1961 proves quite instructive. In an autobiographical script, published only posthumously, Althusser provides telling insights into his 'discovery' of Machiavelli, indicating that for him Machiavelli outmanoeuvres Gramsci:

> For the first time, I discovered Machiavelli in August 1961 in Bertinoro, at an extraordinary, ancient and large estate, that was located on a hill dominating the entire Emilia-Romagna. ... One day, I was told that nearby Cesena was the small town from where Cesare Borgia took off for his great adventure. I was reading a little Gramsci (on the intellectuals), but I interrupted this reading very quickly in order to engage myself with Machiavelli.[21]

In the aftermath of this 'discovery', Althusser developed a sincere interest in Machiavelli that, as both unpublished materials and recent publications from his archives demonstrate, would last his entire life.[22] The earliest significant outcome of this interest was his first seminar (of many) held on the Florentine at the École Normale Supérieure in Paris in 1962.[23] Althusser's studies of Machiavelli reached – in terms of content and form – their peak with the book-length study *Machiavelli and us* from 1972.[24] However, Althusser con-

19   Gramsci 1971a, p. 215 [Q13, §23].
20   Thomas 2009a; Buci-Glucksmann 1981; Coassin-Spiegel 1983; Fontana 1993.
21   Althusser 2013, p. 487.
22   Althusser 1999; Althusser 1977c.
23   Althusser 1962.
24   Althusser 1999.

tinued this path until his very last theoretical writings in the mid-1980s.[25] These relentless efforts of reading and re-reading Machiavelli are well documented in innumerable manuscripts in his archives.[26] However, Althusser kept almost all of these texts in complete secrecy during his lifetime – apparently for political and strategic reasons. Facing this situation, it is well worth examining the traces of these 'hidden' works in Althusser's published contributions to Marxist theory; a project into which the present article provides an insight.

Regarding his enduring interest in the Florentine, it seems almost natural that Althusser terms Gramsci's reading of Machiavelli in 1962 as 'truly impressive' – without further explanation.[27] More than 15 years later, in his text 'Machiavelli's solitude', Althusser returns to precisely this point. He provides a more detailed account of why he finds Gramsci's reading of Machiavelli so impressive:

> Gramsci wrote that *the Prince* was a political manifesto ... But a manifesto that is political, and thus wishes to have historical effects, must inscribe itself in a field quite different from that of pure knowledge: it must inscribe itself in the political conjuncture on which it wishes to act and subordinate itself entirely to the political practice induced by that conjuncture.[28]

Althusser's manuscripts further suggest that he considers Machiavelli to be almost as important as Marx. He honours Machiavelli as 'the most important materialist philosopher of all ages', speaks of Machiavelli as the one and only theoretical witness of 'primitive political accumulation' and describes the Florentine as one of the very few actual 'political philosophers'.[29] Accordingly, he states: 'Since I first tried to read Machiavelli, to really conceive of Machiavelli, I kept returning to him without any interruption ... No doubt, Machiavelli is, much more than Marx, the author who has fascinated me the most'.[30]

---

25   Althusser 1982.
26   These texts include: Althusser 1962, Althusser 1972b, Althusser 2010, Althusser 1985, Althusser 2013, pp. 473–514, Althusser 1972a, and a manifold of resources from the IMEC Archives.
27   Althusser 1962, p. 196.
28   Althusser 1977c, p. 127.
29   Althusser 1982; Althusser 1977c.
30   Althusser 1985, p. 487.

From these short remarks it becomes evident that Althusser, following Gramsci, conceives of Machiavelli in a very special relationship with Marx. His writings further show that he elaborated, again in the vein of Gramsci, this very special relationship throughout his entire career.

However, Althusser's conception of this relationship changes over the course of the years, as does his comprehension of Gramsci and his theoretical path in general. In the 1960s Althusser became convinced that Machiavelli provided, within the realm of politics, the elements of a 'Marxist philosophy' that are – according to his famous claim in *Reading Capital* – so mysteriously absent in Marx. By contrast, in the 1970s he works on the reunification of Marx and Machiavelli into one single theoretical character (a process that increases in salience as Althusser confronts the *Crisis of Marxism*): 'The solution can only come from political practice, from the sudden appearance of an event, in such a place, under the name of such an individual, and in such a form at once necessary and unforeseeable'.[31] Finally, in his late works, Althusser inverts the roles he had assigned them earlier by presenting Marx as a component of a broader, mainly Machiavellian, schema: 'It was definitely my encounter with Machiavelli that turned out to be the fascination of all fascinations for me'.[32]

These three phases of Althusser's reading of Machiavelli can be seen to reflect the growing importance of Machiavelli for Althusser's Marxist thought under the perception of an escalating and ongoing internal crisis of Marxism. Althusser had on many occasions, most prominently in his essay on *The Crises of Marxism*, pointed to what he perceived as a deep political and theoretical crisis that touches the core of the Marxist project and that calls for a general theoretical overhaul.[33] Confronted with this situation, Althusser became more and more convinced that the Florentine secretary could provide the desired remedy to this crisis. For example, Althusser fosters a Machiavellian and aleatory account of the revolution that Marxism in his view lacks and presents it as a way out of the ailing economism:

> The foundation of a state ... in short, every absolute beginning requires the absolute solitude of the reformer or founder ... In order to derive a state from nothing, the founder must be alone ... before the vacuum of the conjuncture and its aleatory future.[34]

---

31   Althusser 1965; Althusser 1977a; ALT2. A31–04.05.
32   Althusser 1985, p. 487.
33   Althusser 1977a.
34   Althusser 1999, p. 64.

Given this course of Althusser's argument, it is not surprising that he admires Machiavelli so much that he even internalises the latter's hubris. Just as Machiavelli mistook himself for a commander on the battlefield (while he in fact was only producing theoretical writings that would not see daylight prior to his death), Althusser himself behaves like a general within the – militarily powerless – field of theory:

> Marxist-Leninist philosophy is therefore one of the two theoretical weapons indispensable to the class struggle of the proletariat. Communist militants must assimilate and use the principles of the theory: science and philosophy. The proletarian revolution needs militants who are both scientists (historical materialism) and philosophers (dialectical materialism) to assist in the defence and development of theory.[35]

However, in his admiration of and identification with Machiavelli, Althusser even went as far as directly identifying himself with Marx and Machiavelli:

> While I was lecturing, I had the impression that it wasn't me who lectured ... And eventually, when I think about this now ... I did not do anything else, while developing the contradictory demands of Machiavelli, then speaking of myself. The question I examined ... it was fully my own![36]

Leaving aside these complexities, the material on Althusser, Machiavelli, Gramsci and Marx suggests that Althusser regards Machiavelli – perfectly in line with Gramsci – as the one and only theorist who provides the tools for a proper Marxist account of the superstructures, of the State, and of politics, and therefore for revolutionary change:

> However, Machiavelli's discovery did not remain as he presented it to us: History has worked on it ... Marx borrowed from him ... We have known beginnings in politics other than *the Prince* and *the Discorsi*. In order to account for their continuing grip on us, there is need for a reason other than a theoretical discovery ...: a purchase on politics.[37]

---

35   Althusser 1971, p. 225.
36   Althusser 1998, p. 225.
37   ALT2. A31–04.03.

4   Althusser on Gramsci

By elaborating Gramsci's hypotheses on Machiavelli described above, Althusser follows the latter's work, though he does not completely absorb Gramsci's in-depth interpretation of Machiavelli. In sharp contrast to his apparent embrace of Gramsci's Machiavelli, Althusser's position on Gramsci's theoretical inter-ventions is thoroughly ambiguous. The most outspoken (and most intensively discussed) demonstration of this ambiguity is, of course, the comments on Gramsci in *Reading Capital* where Althusser accuses the latter of 'historicism'.[38] Balibar, recalling his life-long dialogue with Althusser, points out that Althusser had seen 'the necessity to read and to re-read Machiavelli in order to overcome the "historicism" that has – in Althusser's view – infected Gramsci's interpreta-tion of Machiavelli, without ignoring the question that Gramsci's reading had produced (the lack of an adequate Marxist concept of the political and the state)'.[39]

In regard to Machiavelli, the considerations on Gramsci that Althusser dis-plays in *Ideology and Ideological State Apparatuses* are most telling.[40] In this text, Althusser deploys the celebrated distinction between 'ideological' and 'repressive' state apparatuses (ISAs and RSAs), which is often regarded as a gloss on Gramsci's conception of hegemony as 'force and consent'.[41] Althusser himself strongly encourages this reading, since he states in a footnote: 'to my knowledge, Gramsci is the only one who went any distance on the road I am taking'.[42] This claim at first appears to be true, since Althusser's conceptions of the ISAs and the RSA comprise, like Gramsci's 'hegemony', the entire social life and since 'ideology' and 'repression' directly recall Gramsci's notions of 'con-sent' and 'force'.

However, this reading seems somewhat inadequate, if we regard how Althus-ser constructs the distinction between 'Ideology' and 'Repression'. He appar-ently follows Gramsci in his first statement: 'what distinguishes the ISAs from the RSA is the following basic difference: the RSA functions 'by violence', whereas the ISAs function "by ideology"'.[43] But, interestingly, only a few lines later, this seemingly clear-cut distinction is blurred and turns out to be not a matter of quality but a matter of quantity:

---

38   Althusser 1965.
39   Balibar 2009, p. 16.
40   Althusser 1969.
41   Lock 1996.
42   Althusser 1969, p. 16.
43   Althusser 1969, p. 196.

The RSA functions massively and predominantly by repression ... while functioning secondarily by ideology ... In the same way, but inversely, ... the ISA function massively and predominantly by ideology, but they also function secondarily by repression.[44]

Althusser thereby seems to elide the distinction between ideology and repression, and to focus on their relationship, perhaps on their identity, rather than elaborating on their differences. This becomes more evident as the essay continues, where ideology turns out to be subjection: 'The duplicate mirror-structure of ideology ensures simultaneously: 1. the interpellation of "individuals" as subjects; 2. their subjection to the Subject'.[45] This subjection is performed voluntarily, but without alternative, and is therefore ultimately produced by force. According to Althusser, the ISA's 'also function secondarily by repression, even if ultimately, but only ultimately, this is very attenuated and concealed, even symbolic. (There is no such thing as a purely ideological apparatus.)'[46]

Seen from this perspective, the conceptual difference between the ISAs and the RSA, between ideology and repression, between 'force' and 'consent' seems to vanish. Ideology is nothing other than a form of force and violence to which one (strangely enough) voluntarily submits. In other words, Althusser moves ideology from the realm of consciousness to the realm of the unconscious, hinting that consciousness itself is born out of force: 'I shall adopt Freud's expression word for word, and write [that] ideology is eternal, exactly like the unconscious'.[47]

This Althusserian re-conception of ideology is as telling in regard to the theory of ideology as it is telling in regard to Althusser's reading of Antonio Gramsci, since it marks a significant shift vis-à-vis the Gramscian conception. The notion of 'consent' that is so crucial for Gramsci, has disappeared from the scene. By eliminating the notion of 'consent' Althusser questions Gramsci's core concept, hegemony, as well. Seen from this perspective, Althusser's entire account of ideology seems to be an attack on Gramsci's overarching theoretical framework. However, Althusser elaborates this critique from within the Gramscian framework – it is internal to it and not external.

Althusser's approach to Gramsci remains thoroughly ambiguous throughout his life. This ambiguity is even more strongly displayed in Althusser's retro-

---

44 Althusser 1969, p. 20.
45 Althusser 1969, p. 181.
46 Althusser 1969, p. 146.
47 Althusser 1969, p. 146.

spective reflections on the theme of the ISAs, dating from the mid-70s, which I found in his archives. In one note, he states:

> I signalled in a footnote in my 'essay' that Gramsci was the first who had travelled any distance on the road toward a theory of the ISAs … But in fact, while writing my essay, I had completely ignored the entire theory of Gramsci and it was only a friend who brought the implicit references to my attention, so that I added the footnote. Since then, I asked myself often, whether I had, without having a clue as to what I was doing, done nothing other than repeat Gramsci by reformulating his theses in my own words, or whether I, despite my complete ignorance of Gramsci, had achieved something that effectively distinguishes me from him.[48]

I tend to think of these comments as a paradigmatic expression of Althusser's stance towards Gramsci. Accordingly, they call for a more detailed interpretation. When Althusser talks about being unable to determine the relationship of Gramsci's theory to his own, while simultaneously stating that there could be 'something' that 'effectively distinguishes' him from Gramsci, this 'something' could be thought as the Archimedean point in Althusser's reading of Gramsci. In this context, I inquire further: What is this 'something' that could effectively distinguish Althusser from Gramsci?

5   Machiavelli between Althusser and Gramsci

A solution can be found in the unpublished readings of Machiavelli simmering in Althusser's archives. These writings, most prominently the study *Marx in his limits* (published in 1994), show that Althusser is convinced that the flaws he sees in Gramsci, the points where Gramsci leaves – in his view – the Marxist-materialist path behind, are caused – again in Althusser's view – by a grave misunderstanding of Machiavelli.[49] Nevertheless, for Althusser this presumed misunderstanding has opened up the path for proper Marxist theory. It is therefore to be termed 'productive'. After explaining that it makes sense to speak of an 'ISA' as a machine that runs on 'ideology' (which is 'force'), Althusser accuses Gramsci in *Marx in his limits* of speaking incorrectly of 'hegemonic apparatuses': 'I do not know what they run on: a petrol engine runs on petrol;

---

48   ALT2. A18–03.11.
49   Althusser 2006.

an Ideological State Apparatus runs on ideology; but what does a hegemonic apparatus run on?'[50] With this question, Althusser claims that hegemony needs to be socially established. He further claims that Gramsci, falling into a circular argument, fails to think these social and material foundations. Leaving aside that Althusser for his part fails to ground his strongly-worded claims in a comprehensive analysis of Gramsci, it is telling that Althusser explains Gramsci's presumed failure to do so: 'He has read Machiavelli ... It is on this basis that ... Gramsci invites us into his problematic on the state'.[51]

In *Marx in his limits* Althusser unfortunately does not elaborate the Gramsci-Machiavelli relationship at length. However, a manuscript of about one hundred pages exists in his archives, dating from the mid-70s, that is entitled *Que Faire? – What is to be done?*[52] It is already instructive that the title recalls Lenin, of whom Althusser had always, as displayed in *For Marx*, thought of in Machiavellian terms: 'Lenin gave this metaphor above all a practical meaning ... So far there is no revelation here for readers of Machiavelli'.[53] *Que faire* begins with an analysis of the class struggle in contemporary Italy before shifting to Gramsci. Althusser's comments initially recall the arguments displayed in *Marx in his limits*, as quoted above.[54] However, in the course of *Que faire* Althusser displays an even stronger critique of Gramsci than in *Marx in his limits*. He states: 'There is a gigantic blind spot in the system of Gramsci in regard to everything that concerns the relations of production, exploitation and everything that constitutes their material condition'.[55] It is noteworthy that Althusser traces here, as he does in *Marx in his limits*, the apparent failure and the presumably non-Marxist aspect of Gramsci's thought back to Gramsci's Machiavelli: 'It is here that we fully understand the meaning of Gramsci's truly unconditional admiration for Machiavelli'.[56]

This is, again, not the place to judge on the validity of Althusser's devastating critique of Gramsci's theoretical endeavour; a critique that might well be called 'unfair'. To the contrary, what I find most interesting regarding this material is, how this very same critique structures Althusser's own theoretical interventions being performed in a very specific historico-political situation that cannot be separated from this reading of Gramsci. Following the outlined course of

50   Althusser 2006, p. 140.
51   Althusser 2006, p. 140.
52   ALT2. A26–05.07; ALT2.A26–05.06.
53   Althusser 1977b, p. 94.
54   Althusser 2006.
55   ALT2. A26–05.07.
56   ALT2. A26–05.07.

research, it is noteworthy that Althusser continues *Que faire* by making his own – from a historical point-of-view rather doubtful – claim that Machiavelli is the paradigmatic theorist of absolute monarchy – for Althusser, the seed of the bourgeois state.

> It suffices to know the history of the constitution of national states in broad outline to appreciate that Machiavelli does nothing but *think* the conditions of existence, and the class conditions, for that form of transition between feudalism and capitalism which is absolute Monarchy.[57]

From this point of departure, Althusser explains (as he does on several occasions) that Machiavelli developed a full account of social domination, of politics and the state, effectively rendering him Marx's predecessor. Althusser grounds this claim in a somewhat awkward reading of the eighteenth Chapter of *the Prince*, entitled *How rulers should keep their promises*, where Machiavelli argues that a prince has to be 'a man and a beast', while dividing the category of beast into 'the fox' and 'the lion':

> You must know there are two ways of contesting, the one by the law, the other by force; the first method is proper to men, the second to beasts; but because the first is frequently not sufficient, it is necessary to have recourse to the second ... A prince, therefore, being compelled knowingly to adopt the beast, ought to choose the fox and the lion.[58]

In this Machiavellian schema the figure of the man represents the ethical, conscious and rational being, whereas the figure of the lion represents force, violence and domination by subjection. The most interesting – and most mysterious – figure is the fox, which seems to represent a third way of domination, beyond force and consensus. The fox seems to represent ruse, fraud, trickery, which is neither ethical nor rational and therefore part of the animal world and which – at the very same time – engages the consciousness, the rationality, the humanity of the political actor. Accordingly, Althusser conceives of ruse, of the figure of the fox, as being the mediation between the lion and the man, between brute force and the existence of ethical and rational subjects:

---

57   Althusser 1999, p. 103.
58   Machiavelli 1988, p. 61.

Thus the political is at the same time haunted by the law and nevertheless rejects it most often by force. But this force is not blind ... Being a fox
means knowing how to dominate the usage of force by understanding
how to make it useful for one's own end.[59]

Althusser presents the fox/ruse as the element that points, within the Machiavellian schema, towards the reality of ideology, the reality of the state as constituted by the interplay of ideology and repression eventually grounded in force,
as is so crucial for Althusser's own theoretical architecture. Moreover, Althusser
perceives of all these insights as being very much alive in Machiavelli's overall account of the state, and its foundation, relying on the military. He even
describes the armed forces as 'the number 1, quintessential ideological state
apparatus'.[60] Accordingly, Althusser views Machiavelli as displaying a 'con-
science of the existence of ideology ... of an internal organic relationship
between the ideology and the essence of the political'.[61]

Returning to Gramsci, Althusser claims that the latter was right in arguing
that Machiavelli provides exactly the theory of politics that Marxism had
lacked. However, according to Althusser, Gramsci did not fully understand the
notion of the 'fox', of ruse, in Machiavelli and effectively limits himself to the
'man' and the 'lion', eventually leading to the conception of hegemony as 'consent plus force'. Althusser states:

One sees how much Gramsci, who adored Machiavelli, is poor in comparison to his master. Gramsci has, unlike Machiavelli, never acknowledged
the primacy of the 'moment' of force (the military) in the 'hegemony' in
the state ... Gramsci never had an inkling of the fact that force could be
productive, fertile, and proper in a strategy that allows it to produce the
effects of hegemony.[62]

In other words, and according to Althusser: having followed Machiavelli in
politics, but having not understood that for Machiavelli politics has the pair of
ideology and force, which means 'two modes' of force, at its very core, Gramsci fails theoretically. By relying on the duality of force and consent, Gramsci
proves unable, in Althusser's view, to produce a theory of the superstructures

---

59   Althusser 1962, p. 224.
60   Althusser 1999, p. 83.
61   Althusser 1962, p. 226.
62   ALT2. A26–05.07.

that takes the reality of ideology into account. Grounded in this theoretical mis-understanding Gramsci also fails, again only in Althusser's view, politically. This is because politics should not be thought of being the struggle for hegemony in civil society – a view Althusser somewhat awkwardly attributes to Gramsci – but are rather rooted only in the sphere of the two modes of force. Althusser even hints at the political failure of Gramsci's ideas through his followers in the Eurocommunist movement of the 1970s, who called for a democratisation of the state:

> Everything can be found in Machiavelli. The theory of the state and its two parts, the animal (the violence) and the human (the consent) ... From this point of departure Machiavelli advances much further than Gramsci in showing that ideology ... is constitutive for every power of the state ... whereas Gramsci never recognized, as Machiavelli had, the prerogative of the 'moment of force' (the army) for the hegemony in the state. Strongly displayed in Machiavelli, violence and force do not appear in Gramsci other than for preparing its pure and simple disappearance in the concept of the state as hegemony. Even if he invokes it, Gramsci never thought of force and violence other than as brute and naked force.[63]

However, instead of limiting his shattering critique of Gramsci to this point, Althusser further advances to a fundamental blow on the Gramscian school and on the supporters of a 'Gramscian' conception of politics as a whole. He moves from the assumption that the followers of Gramsci have misunderstood Machiavelli to the more radical position that this entire problematic renders Gramsci *de facto* non-Marxist. According to Althusser, Gramsci follows Machiavelli's politicism (that he even didn't understand properly) too far and therefore loses touch with the core of Marx's insights:

> Machiavelli offers Gramsci the occasion to find a father ... and to ana-chronistically bypass Marx. Machiavelli's theory is erected on a gigantic blind spot (the basis, the relations of production, the reproduction) ... For this, Machiavelli cannot be reproached. But, that the entire work of Gramsci, who thinks 300 years after Machiavelli and 70 years after a certain Marx, is also erected on the same gigantic blind spot is quite another thing.[64]

---

63   ALT2. A26–05.07.
64   ALT2. A26–05.07.

Despite all the outspoken praise and the theoretical loans discussed above, Althusser has nothing left for Gramsci other than pure contempt: 'This is amateurism. This is adventurism'.[65]

6   Conclusions

The material discussed demonstrates how ambiguous, but also how vigorous and challenging Althusser is in respect to Gramsci and to Gramsci's Machiavelli. Accordingly, Althusser's presumably Machiavellian critique of Gramsci poses, against the backdrop of a particular assessment of Eurocommunism, a very strong hypothesis on Gramsci and on Machiavelli. However, this Althusserian line of critique is, without any doubt, abridged. Althusser awkwardly elides Eurocommunism and Gramsci's thought and he dubiously claims that Gramsci thinks of politics as the 'struggle for hegemony in civil society' and that the latter forgets the Machiavellian moment of force.

Thus, we find ourselves confronted with a truly Althusserian dilemma. We find ourselves before a powerfully consistent yet inconsistent, albeit inspiring and thought-provoking, hypothesis that cannot be defended from a philological point-of-view. It can neither be justified in Gramsci's nor in Machiavelli's conceptual framework, but nevertheless forcefully engages Gramsci and Machiavelli in order to bridge their thought in a very specific historical situation. Althusser thereby succeeds in making Machiavelli and Gramsci speak to us in that very specific historical situation. Accordingly, I am tempted to conclude that the entire Althusserian endeavour concerning Gramsci and Machiavelli is not so much about critique, about interpreting past theorists. On the contrary, it is, I think, about the present, and it is about producing an intervention into the present: 'The conjuncture is ... no mere summary of its elements, or enumeration of diverse circumstances, but their contradictory system, which poses the political problem and indicates its historical solution, ipso facto rendering it a political objective, a practical task'.[66] Seen from this point-of-view, Althusser's effort, though it might be called unjust and outdated, is still ongoing.

---

65   ALT2. A26–05.07.
66   Althusser 1999, p. 19.

References

In the case of Thai authors, we follow Thai tradition, which normally notifies people with their first name, rather than family name. The format will show the first name and last name together.

[no author] 2014, 'Refugee Struggles from Hamburg to Europe: An Activist Travel-account', pamphlet.

Abdelrahman, Maja 2015, *Egypt's Long Revolution: Protest Movements and Uprisings*, London: Routledge.

Abud-Magd, Zeinab 2016, *Militarizing the Nation: The Army, Business, and Revolution in Egypt*, New York: Columbia University Press.

Acanda Gonzales, Jorge Luis 2000, 'La recepción de Gramsci en Cuba', in *Gramsci en América: II Conferencia Internacional de Estudios*, edited by Dora Kanoussi, Mexico D.F.: Plaza y Valdez.

Achcar, Gilbert 2013, *The People Want: A Radical Exploration of the Arab Uprisings*, London: Saqi.

Agamben, Giorgio 2014, 'What is a Destituent Power?', *Environment and Planning D: Space and Society*, 32, no. 1: 65–74.

Agosti, Héctor Pablo 1951, *Echeverría*, Buenos Aires: Futuro.

Agosti, Héctor Pablo 2002 [1958], *Nación y cultura*, Buenos Aires: Catálogos.

Agustín, Óscar García and Martin Bak Jørgensen (eds) 2016, *Solidarity without Borders. Gramscian Perspectives on Migration and Civil Society*, London: Pluto Press.

Ahmad, Aijaz 1992, *In Theory: Classes, Nations, Literatures*, London: Verso.

Alexander, Anne and Mostafa Bassiouny 2014, *Bread, Freedom and Social Justice: Workers and the Egyptian Revolution*, London: Zed Books.

Alicata, Mario 1954, 'Il meridionalismo non si può fermare ad Eboli', *Cronache Meridionali*, II, no. 9: 585–603.

Althusser, Louis 1962, 'Machiavel (1962)', in *Politique et histoire, de Machiavel à Marx: Cours à l'École normale supérieure de 1955 à 1972*, edited by François Matheron, Paris: Seuil.

Althusser, Louis 1965, *Lire Le Capital*, Paris: Maspero.

Althusser, Louis 1969, 'Ideology and Ideological State Apparatuses', in *On Ideology*, London: Verso.

Althusser, Louis 1971, *Lenin and Philosophy and Other Essays*, London: New Left Books.

Althusser, Louis 1972a, *Cours sur Rousseau*, Paris: Le Temps des cerises.

Althusser, Louis 1972b, 'Machiavel et nous', in *Écrits philosophiques et politiques*, Volume 2, Paris: Stock/IMEC.

Althusser, Louis 1974 [1967], *Philosophie et philosophie spontanée des savants*, Paris: Maspero.

Althusser, Louis 1977a, 'Enfin la crise du marxisme!', in *Solitude de Machiavel et autres textes*, edited by Yves Sintomer, Paris: PUF.

Althusser, Louis 1977b, *For Marx*, London: New Left Books.

Althusser, Louis 1977c, 'Machiavelli's Solitude', in *Machiavelli and Us*, London: Verso.

Althusser, Louis 1982, 'Le courant souterrain du matérialisme de la rencontre', in *Écrits philosophiques et politiques*, Volume 1, Paris: Stock/IMEC.

Althusser, Louis 1998, *Lettres à Franca (1961–1973)*, Paris: Stock.

Althusser, Louis 1999 [1994], *Machiavelli and Us*, London: Verso.

Althusser, Louis 2005 [1965], *Pour Marx*, Paris: Maspero/La Découverte.

Althusser, Louis 2006 [1994], 'Marx in his limits', in *Philosophy of the Encounter: Later Writings, 1978–87*, edited by Michael Goshgarian, London: Verso.

Althusser, Louis 2010, *Materialismus der Begegnung: Späte Schriften*, Zürich: Diaphanes.

Althusser, Louis 2013 [1996], *L'avenir dure longtemps: Autobiographie*, Paris: Flammarion.

Althusser, Louis and Etienne Balibar 1970, *Reading Capital*, London: New Left Books.

Althusser, Louis and Etienne Balibar 1973 [1965], *Lire le Capital*, Paris: Maspero.

Amin, Galal 1995, *Egypt's Economic Predicament: A Study in the Interaction of External Pressures, Political Folly, and Social Tension in Egypt, 1960–1990*, Leiden: Brill.

Anderson, Perry 1976, 'The Antinomies of Antonio Gramsci', *New Left Review*, I, no. 100: 5–78.

Anderson, Perry 1977, *Sur le marxisme occidental*, Paris: Maspero.

Anderson, Perry 1988, 'The Affinities of Norberto Bobbio', *New Left Review*, I, no. 170: 3–36.

Anderson, Perry 2017, *The Antinomies of Antonio Gramsci, with a new Preface*, London: Verso.

Antonini, Francesca 2014, 'Science, History and Ideology in Gramsci's *Prison Notebooks*', *HoST – Journal of History of Science and Technology*, 9: 64–80.

Antonini, Francesca forthcoming, *Caesarism and Bonapartism in Gramsci: Hegemony and the Crisis of Modernity*, Leiden: Brill.

Antonini, Francesca 2016, ' "Il vecchio muore e il nuovo non può nascere": cesarismo ed egemonia nel contesto della crisi organica', *International Gramsci Journal*, 2, no. 1: 167–84.

Apichai Pantasen (ed.) 2006, *Sangkroh Ongkwamru Keawkab Settakit Porpiang* [*Synthesising the knowledge of Sufficiency Economy*], Bangkok: Thailand Research Fund.

Apichai Pantasen (ed.) 2009, *Wikroh Nayobairat Nairadub Tangtang Ruamtang Pak Thurakit Lae Prachasaongkom Jak Settakit Porpiang B.E. 2540–2549* [*Analysing the State, Public, and Civil Society policies on the Sufficiency Economy*], Bangkok: Thailand Research Fund.

Apichat Sathitniramai 2007, *Weak State and Political Economy of Thailand: Ten Years after the Crisis*, Chiba: Institute of Developing Economies, Japan External Trade Organization.

Apichat Sathitniramai 2011, 'Sua Dang Kue Krai: Mob Term Ngern Prai Ruewa Chon Chanklang Mai Kab Tang Prang Sangkom Thai' ['Who are the Red Shirts? Money-Driven Movement, the Common or the New Middle Class: Prospect for Thai Society'], in *Red Why?*, edited by Pinyo Traisuriyatanma, Bangkok: Openbooks.

Apichat Sathitniramai 2013a, *Rat Thai Kab Karn Patiroop Setthakit* [*Thai State and Economic Reform*], Bangkok: Fah Deaw Kan.

Apichat Sathitniramai et al. 2013b, *Tobtuan Pumitat Karnmuang Thai* [*Rethinking Thailand Political Landscape*], Bangkok: TUHPP and Thai Health Promotion Foundation.

Apweiler, Arnold 1997, *Begründer der italienischen Komparatistik. Francesco de Sanctis und Arturo Graf*, Aachen: Shaker.

Arac, Jonathan 1998, 'Criticism Between Opposition and Counterpoint', *boundary 2*, 25, no. 2: 55–69.

Arendt, Hannah 1968 [1951], *The Origins of Totalitarianism*, New York: Harvest Book.

Aricó, José Maria 1957, '¿Marxismo vs leninismo?', *Cuadernos de Cultura*, 33: 90–6.

Aricó, José Maria 1963, 'Pasado y Presente', *Pasado y Presente*, I: 1–17.

Aricó, José Maria 1972, *Gramsci y las ciencias sociales. Cuadernos de Pasado y Presente*, Buenos Aires: Signos.

Aricó, José Maria 1982, *Marx y América Latina*, Lima: Cedep.

Aricó, José Maria 1985, 'Geografia di Gramsci in America Latina', *Critica marxista*, 5: 17–34.

Aricó, José Maria 1988, *La cola del diablo*, Buenos Aires: Puntosur.

Aricó, José Maria 1991 [1981], *Las hipótesis de Justo. Escritos sobre el socialismo en América Latina*, Buenos Aires: Editorial Sudamericana.

Aricó, José Maria 2012, *Nueve lecciones sobre economía política en el marxismo*, edited by H.A. Crespo, Argentina: Fondo de cultura económica.

Arnold, David 1984, 'Gramsci and the Peasant Subalternity in India', *The Journal of Peasant Studies*, 11, no. 4: 155–77.

Aron, Raymond 1970, *Marxismes imaginaires: d'une sainte famille à l'autre*, Paris: Gallimard.

Arrighi, Giovanni 1994, *The Long Twentieth Century: Money, Power, and the Origins of Our Times*, London: Verso.

Arrighi, Giovanni, Terence K. Hopkins and Immanuel Wallerstein 1989, *Antisystemic Movements*, London: Verso.

Asad, Talal (ed.) 1973, *Anthropology and the Colonial Encounter*, New York: Humanities Press.

Ashcroft, Bill and Edward W. Said 2004, 'Conversation with Edward Said', in *Interviews with Edward W. Said*, edited by Amritjit Singh and Bruce G. Johnson, Jackson, MS: University Press of Mississippi.

Asor Rosa, Alberto 1973, 'Note sul tema: intellettuali, coscienza di classe, partito, in *Intellettuali e classe operaia. Saggi sulle forme di uno storico conflitto e di una possibile alleanza*, Florence: La Nuova Italia.

Asor Rosa, Alberto 1988 [1965], *Scrittori e popolo: saggio sulla letteratura populista in Italia*, Turin: Einaudi.

Atabaki, Touraj 2008, *The State and the Subaltern: Modernization, Society and State in Turkey and Iran*, London: I.B. Tauris.

Atkin, Nicholas and Frank Tallett 2003, *Priests, Prelates and People: A History of European Catholicism since 1750*, Oxford: Oxford University Press.

Ayubi, Nazih 1995, *Over-Stating the Arab State: Politics and Society in the Middle East*, London: I.B. Tauris.

Badaloni, Nicola 1972, *Per il comunismo. Questioni di teoria*, Turin: Einaudi.

Badaloni, Nicola 1988, *Il problema dell'immanenza nella filosofia politica di Antonio Gramsci*, Venice: Arsenale Editrice.

Baehr, Peter and Melvin Richter (eds) 2004, *Dictatorship in History and Theory: Bonapartism, Caesarism and Totalitarianism*, Cambridge: Cambridge University Press.

Balibar, Étienne 2007 [1993], *The Philosophy of Marx*, translated by Chris Turner, London: Verso.

Balibar, Étienne 2009, 'Une rencontre en Romagne', in *Machiavel et nous*, by Louis Althusser, Paris: Tallandier.

Balibar, Étienne 2011, *Citoyen sujet et autres essais d'anthropologie philosophique*, Paris: PUF.

Balibar, Étienne 2014, 'Dall'antropologia filosofica all'ontologia sociale e ritorno: che fare con la sesta tesi di Marx su Feuerbach?', in *Il transindividuale. Soggetti, relazioni, mutazioni*, edited by Étienne Balibar and Vittorio Morfino, Milan: Mimesis.

Balibar, Étienne 2015, 'Althusser: une nouvelle pratique de la philosophie entre politique et idéologie. Conversation avec Étienne Balibar et Yves Duroux', *Cahiers du GRM*, 7. Available at: http://journals.openedition.org/grm/641.

Banti, Alberto M. 2000, *La nazione del Risorgimento. Parentela, santità e onore alle origini dell'Italia unita*, Turin: Einaudi.

Baratta, Giorgio 2000, *Le rose e i quaderni: saggio sul pensiero di Antonio Gramsci*, Rome: Gamberetti.

Baratta, Giorgio 2004, 'Americanismo e fordismo', in Frosini and Liguori (eds) 2004.

Baratta, Giorgio 2007, *Antonio Gramsci in contrappunto. Dialoghi col presente*, Rome: Carocci.

Baratta, Giorgio 2009, 'Cultura', in Liguori and Voza (eds) 2009.

Barthas, Jérémie 2010, 'Machiavelli in Political Thought from the Age of Revolutions to the Present', in *The Cambridge Companion to Machiavelli*, edited by John M. Najemy, Cambridge: Cambridge University Press.

Bartoli, Matteo G. 1912–13, *Glottologia*, unpublished manuscript, held at the Fondazione Istituto Gramsci (Rome).

Basile, Luca 2011, 'Gramsci e la costellazione idealistica tra il 1914 ed il 1917', in Di Bello (ed.) 2011.

Bassnett, Susan and André Lefevere 1990, *Translation, History, and Culture*, London: Pinter Publishers.

Baudrillard, Jean 1977, *Oublier Foucault*, Paris: Éditions Galilée.

Bauman, Zygmunt 1992, *Intimations of Postmodernity*, London: Routledge.

Bayart, Jean-François, Comi Toulabor and Achille Mbembe 1992, *La politique par le bas en Afrique Noire: Contributions à une problématique de la démocratie*, Paris: Karthala.

Beasley-Murray, John 2010, *Posthegemony: Political Theory and Latin America*, Minneapolis: University of Minnesota Press.

Beinin, Joel 1999, 'The Working Class and Peasantry in the Middle East: From Economic Nationalism to Neoliberalism', *Middle East Report*, 210: 18–22.

Beinin, Joel 2014a, 'History and Consequences', *Jadaliyya*, 19 March, available at: http://www.jadaliyya.com/pages/index/16966/history-and-consequences.

Beinin, Joel 2014b, 'On Revolutions and Defeated Revolutionary Movements: A Reply to Brecht De Smet', *Jadaliyya*, 11 June, available at: http://www.jadaliyya.com/pages/index/18109/on-revolutions-and-defeated-revolutionary-movement.

Bellamy, Richard 2001, 'A Crocean Critique of Gramsci on Historicism, Hegemony and Intellectuals', *Journal of Modern Italian Studies*, 6, no. 2: 209–29.

Bensaïd, Daniel 2009 [1995], *Marx for our Times: Adventures and Misadventures of a Critique*, London: Verso.

Berger, John 2013, 'How to Live with Stones', in Ekers et al. (eds) 2013.

Bergson, Henri 1911, *Creative Evolution*, translated by Arthur Mitchell, London: Macmillan.

Beverley, John 1999, *Subalternity and Representation*, Durham, NC: Duke University Press.

Bhatnagar, Rashmi 1986, 'Uses and Limits of Foucault: A Study of the Theme of Origins in Edward Said's "Orientalism"', *Social Scientist*, 14, no. 7: 3–22.

Bhattacharya, Baidik 2012, 'The Secular Alliance: Gramsci, Said and the Postcolonial Question', in Srivastava and Bhattacharya (eds) 2012.

Bhattacharya, Neeladri, Suvir Kaul, Ania Loomba and Edward W. Said 2004, 'An Interview with Edward W. Said', in *Interviews with Edward W. Said*, edited by Amritjit Singh and Bruce G. Johnson, Jackson, MS: University Press of Mississippi.

Bieler, Andreas and Adam David Morton 2004, 'A Critical Theory Route to Hegemony, World Order and Historical Change: Neo-Gramscian Perspectives in International Relations', *Capital and Class*, 28, no. 1: 85–113.

Biscione, Francesco M. 1995, 'Introduzione', in Antonio Gramsci, *Disgregazione sociale e rivoluzione. Scritti sul Mezzogiorno*, edited by Francesco M. Biscione, Naples: Liguori.

Bobbio, Norberto 1951, 'Invito al colloquio', *Comprendre*, II, no. 3: 102–13.

Bobbio, Norberto 1958a, 'Nota sulla dialettica di Gramsci', *Società*, XIV, no. 1: 21–34.

Bobbio, Norberto 1958b, 'Nota sulla dialettica di Gramsci', in *Studi gramsciani*, Rome: Editori Riuniti.

Bobbio, Norberto 1958c, 'La dialettica di Marx', *Rivista di filosofia*, XLIX, no. 2: 334–54.

Bobbio, Norberto 1965, *Da Hobbes a Marx. Saggi di storia della filosofia*, Naples: Morano.

Bobbio, Norberto 1969, 'Gramsci e la concezione della società civile', in *Gramsci e la cultura contemporanea*, Rome: Editori Riuniti.

Bobbio, Norberto 1974, 'L'attività di un intellettuale di sinistra', in *I comunisti a Torino 1919–1972. Lezioni e testimonianze*, Rome: Editori Riuniti.

Bobbio, Norberto 1979, 'Gramsci and the Conception of Civil Society', in *Gramsci and Marxist Theory*, edited by Chantal Mouffe, London: Routledge & Kegan Paul.

Bobbio, Norberto 1990a [1969], 'Gramsci e la concezione della società civile', in Bobbio 1990b. .

Bobbio, Norberto 1990b, *Saggi su Gramsci*, Milan: Feltrinelli.

Bobbio, Norberto 1999, *Autobiografia*, edited by Alberto Papuzzi, Rome-Bari: Laterza.

Bobbio, Norberto 2005 [1955], *Politica e cultura*, edited by Franco Sbarberi, Turin: Einaudi.

Bobbio, Norberto 2006, 'Postfazione', in Tommaso Campanella, *La città del Sole*, edited by Germana Ernst and Laura Salvetti Firpo, Rome-Bari: Laterza.

Bobbio, Norberto 2014, *Scritti su Marx. Dialettica, stato, società civile*, edited by Cesare Pianciola and Franco Sbarberi, Rome: Donzelli.

Bocock, Robert 1986, *Hegemony*, London: Tavistock.

Bon, Frédéric and Michel-Antoine Burnier 1966, *Les nouveaux intellectuels*, Paris: Cujas.

Bonefeld, Werner 2010, 'Free Economy and the Strong State: Some Notes on the State', *Capital & Class*, 34, no. 1: 15–24.

Bonefeld, Werner 2012, 'Freedom and the Strong State: On German Ordoliberalism', *New Political Economy*, 17, no. 5: 633–56.

Bonefeld, Werner 2014, *Critical Theory and the Critique of Political Economy: On Subversion and Negative Reason*, London: Bloomsbury.

Bonneuil, Christopher and Jean-Baptiste Fressoz 2016, *The Shock of the Anthropocene: The Earth, History and Us*, London: Verso Books.

Boothman, Derek 2004, *Traducibilità e processi traduttivi, un caso: A. Gramsci linguista*, Perugia: Guerra Edizioni.

Boothman, Derek 2010, 'Translation and Translatability: Renewal of the Marxist Paradigm', in Ives and Lacorte (eds) 2010.

Borghese, Lucia 2010, 'Aunt Alene on Her Bicycle: Antonio Gramsci as Translator from German and as Translation Theorist', in Ives and Lacorte (eds) 2010.

Bourdieu, Pierre 1993, *The Field of Cultural Production: Essays on Art and Literature*, New York: Columbia University Press.

Bourdieu, Pierre 2012 [1991], *Language and Symbolic Power*, Cambridge: Polity Press.

Bourgin, Georges 1949, 'A propos d' Antonio Gramsci', *Cahiers Internationaux*, 5.

Brandist, Craig 1996a, 'Gramsci, Bakhtin and the Semiotics of Hegemony', *New Left Review*, I, no. 216: 94–109.

Brandist, Craig 1996b, 'The Official and the Popular in Gramsci and Bakhtin', *Theory, Culture, Society*, 13: 59–74.

Brandist, Craig 2005, 'Marxism and the Philosophy of Language in Russia in the 1920s and 1930s', *Historical Materialism*, 13, no. 1: 63–84.

Bravo, Gian Mario 2003, '*Il fallimento della politica. Marx e gli altri. A proposito di Luigi Bonaparte*', in *Bonapartismo, cesarismo e crisi della società. Luigi Napoleone e il colpo di stato del 1851*, edited by Manuela Ceretta, Florence: Olschki.

Bréal, Michel 1982 [1900], *Semantics: A Study in the Science of Meaning*, translated by Nina Cust, Ann Arbor: University Microfilms International.

Brennan, Timothy 1992, 'Places of Mind, Occupied Lands: Edward Said and Philology', in *Edward Said: A Critical Reader*, edited by Michael Sprinker, Oxford: Blackwell.

Brennan, Timothy 2000, 'The Illusion of a Future: *Orientalism* as Traveling Theory', *Critical Inquiry*, 26, no. 3: 558–83.

Brennan, Timothy 2001a, 'Antonio Gramsci and Postcolonial Theory: "Southernism"', *Diaspora*, 10, no. 2: 143–87.

Brennan, Timothy 2001b, 'Angry Beauty and Literary Love: An *Orientalism* for All Time', in *Revising Culture Reinventing Peace: The Influence of Edward W. Said*, edited by Naseer Aruri and Muhammad A. Shuraydi, New York: Olive Branch Press.

Brennan, Timothy 2005, 'Resolution', in *Edward Said: Continuing the Conversation*, edited by W.J.T. Mitchell and Homi Bhabha, Chicago: University of Chicago Press.

Brennan, Timothy 2006, *Wars of Position: The Cultural Politics of Left and Right*, New York: Columbia University Press.

Brennan, Timothy 2013, 'Edward Said as a Lukácsian Critic: Modernism and Empire', *College Literature*, 40, no. 4: 14–32.

Buci-Glucksmann, Christine 1975, *Gramsci et l'État*, Paris: Fayard.

Buci-Glucksmann, Christine 1980, *Gramsci and the state*, translated by David Fernbach, London: Lawrence & Wishart.

Buci-Glucksmann, Christine 1981, *Gramsci und der Staat*, Köln: Pahl-Rugenstein.

Buckley, Michelle and Kendra Strauss 2016, 'With, against and beyond Lefebvre: Planetary urbanization and epistemic plurality', *Environment and Planning D: Society and Space* 34, no. 4: 617–636.

Bukharin, Nikolai 1925, *Historical Materialism: A System of Sociology*, authorised translation from the third Russian edition, New York: International Publishers.

Burawoy, Michael 1989, 'Two Methods in Search of Science: Skocpol versus Trotsky', *Theory and Society*, 18, no. 6: 759–805.

Burawoy, Michael 2003. 'For a Sociological Marxism: The Complementary Convergence of Antonio Gramsci and Karl Polanyi', *Politics & Society*, 31, no. 2: 193–261.

Burgio, Alberto 2003, *Gramsci storico: una lettura dei* Quaderni del carcere, Rome-Bari: Laterza.

Burgio, Alberto 2007, *Per Gramsci: crisi e potenza del moderno*, Rome: DeriveApprodi.

Burgio, Alberto 2009, *Senza democrazia. Per un'analisi della crisi*, Rome: DeriveApprodi.

Burgio, Alberto 2014, *Gramsci. Il sistema in movimento*, Rome: DeriveApprodi.

Burgio, Alberto 2016, 'Giudizi analogici e comparatistica storica nei *Quaderni del carcere*', in *Attualità del pensiero di Antonio Gramsci*, edited by Accademia nazionale dei Lincei, Rome: Bardi Edizioni.

Burgos, Raúl 1994, *As peripécias de Gramsci entre Gulliver e o pequeno Polegar (um estudio sobre os projetos políticos do PT e da FMLN)*, Campinas: UNICAMP.

Burgos, Raúl 2004, *Los Gramscianos argentinos: cultura y política en la experiencia de Pasado y Presente*, Buenos Aires: Siglo Veintiuno de Argentina.

Burgos, Raúl 2007, 'Los avatares de una herencia incómoda: el complicado diálogo entre Gramsci y la izquierda en América Latina', available at: www.acessa.com.

Burke, Seán 1998, *The Death and Return of the Author: Criticism and Subjectivity in Barthes, Foucault and Derrida*, Edinburgh: Edinburgh University Press.

Bush, Ray 1999, *Economic Crisis and the Politics of Reform in Egypt*, Boulder, CO: Westview Press.

Butler, Judith 1990, *Gender Trouble: Feminism and the Subversion of Identity*, New York: Routledge.

Buttigieg, Joseph A. 1990, 'Gramsci's Method', *boundary 2*, 17, no. 2: 60–81.

Buttigieg, Joseph A. 1992, 'Introduction', in Gramsci 1992–2007.

Buttigieg, Joseph A. 1994, 'Philology and Politics: Returning to the Text of Antonio Gramsci's *Prison Notebooks*', *boundary 2*, 21, no. 2: 98–138.

Buttigieg, Joseph A. 1999, 'Sulla categoria gramsciana di "subalterno"', in *Gramsci da un secolo all'altro*, edited by Giorgo Baratta and Guido Liguori, Rome: Editori Riuniti.

Buttigieg, Joseph A. 2001, 'Antonio Gramsci's "Return to De Sanctis"', in *Italian Cultural Studies*, edited by Graziella Parati and Ben Lawton, Lafayette, IN: Bordighera.

Buttigieg, Joseph A. 2002, 'Reading Gramsci', in *Gramsci, Culture and Anthropology*, edited by Kate Crehan, London: Pluto Press.

Buttigieg, Joseph A. 2009, 'Subalterno, subalterni', in Liguori and Voza (eds) 2009.

Buttigieg, Joseph A. 2013, 'Subaltern Social Groups in Antonio Gramsci's *Prison Notebooks*', in Zene (ed.) 2013.

Cacciatore, Giuseppe 2009, 'Croce, Benedetto', in Liguori and Voza (eds) 2009.

Cahill, Damien 2014, *The End of Laissez Faire? On the Durability of Embedded Neoliberalism*, Cheltenham: Edward Elgar.

Callinicos, Alex 2009, *Imperialism and Global Political Economy*, Cambridge: Polity Press.

Callinicos, Alex 2010, 'The Limits of Passive Revolution', *Capital & Class*, 34, no. 3: 491–507.

Campbell, Horace 2013, *Global NATO and the Catastrophic Failure in Libya*, New York: Monthly Review Press.

Canfora, Luciano 1999, *Giulio Cesare. Il dittatore democratico*, Rome-Bari: Laterza.

Canfora, Luciano 2010, *L'uso politico dei paradigmi storici*, Rome-Bari: Laterza.

Capone, Alfredo 1991, 'L'età liberale', in *Storia del Mezzogiorno. Volume XII. Il Mezzogiorno nell'Italia unita*, edited by Giuseppe Galasso and Rosario Romeo, Naples: Edizioni del Sole.

Capuzzo, Paolo and Sandro Mezzadra 2012, 'Provincializing the Italian Reading of Gramsci', in Srivastava and Bhattacharya (eds) 2012.

Carchedi, Guglielmo 2001, *For Another Europe: A Class Analysis of European Economic Integration*, New York: Verso.

Carlucci, Alessandro 2013a, *Gramsci and Languages. Unification, Diversity, Hegemony*, Leiden: Brill.

Carlucci, Alessandro 2013b, 'The Risorgimento and its Discontents: Gramsci's Reflections on Conflict and Control in the Aftermath of Italy's Unification', in Zene (ed.) 2013.

Caruso, Francesco 2015, *La politica dei subalterni*, Rome: Deriveapprodi.

Cervelli, Innocenzo 1996, 'Cesarismo: alcuni usi e significati della parola (secolo XIX)', *Annali dell'Istituto Storico Italo-Germanico in Trento*, XXII: 61–197.

Chakrabarty, Dipesh 2000, *Provincializing Europe: Postcolonial Thought and Historical Difference*, Princeton: Princeton University Press.

Chakrabarty, Dipesh 2002, *Habitations of Modernity: Essays in the Wake of Subaltern Studies*, Chicago: University of Chicago Press.

Chakrabarty, Dipesh 2008, *see* Chakrabarty 2000.

Chambers, Iain (ed.) 2010, *Esercizi di potere. Gramsci, Said e il postcoloniale*, Rome: Meltemi.

Chambers, Paul 2013, 'Economic Guidance and Contestation: An Analysis of Thailand's Evolving Trajectory of Development', *Journal of Current Southeast Asian Affairs*, 32: 81–109.

Chatterjee, Partha 2004, *The Politics of the Governed: Reflections on Popular Politics in Most of the World*, New York: Columbia University Press.

Chatterjee, Partha 2011, *Lineages of Political Society*, New York: Columbia University Press.

Chaturvedi, Vinayak (ed.) 2000, *Mapping Subaltern Studies and the Postcolonial*, London: Verso.

Chibber, Vivek 2013, *Postcolonial Theory and the Spectre of Capital*, London: Verso.

Chino, Takahiro 2018, 'Gramsci and Religion: An Overview', in *Gramsci on Religion: Text and Context*, edited by Cosimo Zene, Milan: Mimesis.

Christopher, Kommu William 2005, *Rethinking Cultural Studies: A Study of Raymond Williams and Edward Said*, Jaipur: Rawat Publications.

Chuaqui, Rubén 2005, 'Notes on Edward Said's View of Michel Foucault', *Alif: Journal of Comparative Poetics*, 25: 89–119.

Chuwas Rerksirisuk 2011, *Born to be Democracy*, Bangkok: Prachatai Book Club.

Ciavolella, Riccardo 2015, 'Un nouveau prince au-delà des antinomies. Lectures de Gramsci dans les mouvements sociaux contemporains', *Actuel Marx*, 57: 112–24.

Ciavolella, Riccardo forthcoming, 'Anthropology as a Science of the Political Subject', in *Cultural Hegemony in a Scientific World. Volume 1: Gramscian Concepts for the History of Science*, edited by Massimiliano Badino and Pietro Daniel Omodeo, Leiden: Brill.

Ciliberto, Michele 1989, 'Gramsci e il linguaggio della "vita"', *Studi storici*, 30, no. 3: 679–99.

Ciliberto, Michele 1991 'Rinascimento e riforma nei *Quaderni* di Gramsci', in *Filosofia e cultura. Per Eugenio Garin*, edited by Michele Ciliberto and Cesare Vasoli, Rome: Editori Riuniti.

Ciliberto, Michele 1999, 'Cosmopolitismo e Stato nazionale nei "Quaderni del carcere"', in *Gramsci e il Novecento*, Vol. I., edited by Giuseppe Vacca, Rome: Carocci.

Cirese, Alberto M. 1973, *Cultura egemonica e culture subalterne. Rassegna degli studi sul mondo popolare tradizionale*, Palermo: Palumbo.

Clifford, James 1988, *The Predicament of Culture: Twentieth-Century Ethnography, Literature, and Art*, Cambridge, MA: Harvard University Press.

Coassin-Spiegel, Hermes 1983, *Gramsci und Althusser: Eine Kritik der Althusserschen Rezeption von Gramscis Philosophie*, Berlin: Argument.

Cocks, Joan 1989, *The Oppositional Imagination: Feminism, Critique and Political Theory*, London: Routledge.

Cogniot, Georges 1959, 'Une grande figure marxiste', Introduction to the *Œuvres choisies*, Paris: Éditions sociales.

Cohn, Norman 1957, *The Pursuit of the Millennium: Revolutionary Millenarians and Mystical Anarchists of the Middle Ages*, Oxford: Oxford University Press.

Cohn, Norman 1962, 'Medieval Millenarism', in *Millennial Dreams in Action: Essays in Comparative Study*, edited by Sylvia L. Thrupp, London: Mouton.

Colliot-Thélène, Catherine 1992, *Le désenchantement de l'Etat. De Hegel à Max Weber*, Paris: Minuit.

Comaroff, John and Jean Comaroff 1991, *Of Revelation and Revolution*, Chicago: University of Chicago Press.

Concheiro Borquez, Elvira 2013, 'Arnoldo Martinez Verdugo: Comunista revolucionário', *La Jornada*, 4 June.

Connell, Raewyn 2007, *Southern Theory: The Global Dynamics of Knowledge in Social Science*, Cambridge: Polity Press.

Connors, Michael K. 2012, 'Notes Towards an Understanding of Thai Liberalism', in *Bangkok May 2010: Perspectives on a Divided Thailand*, edited by Michael J. Montesano et al. (eds), Singapore: Institute of Southeast Asian Studies.

Cooper, Mark 1982, *The Transformation of Egypt*, Baltimore, MD: Johns Hopkins University Press.

Copans, Jean 1975, *Anthropologie et impérialisme*, Paris: Maspero.

Córdova, Arnaldo 1985, 'Gramsci e l'America Latina: un contributo per spezzare il dogmatismo', *Rinascita*, XL: 36–7.

Córdova, Arnaldo 1987, 'Gramsci y la izquierda mexicana', *La Ciudad futura*, VI: 15–16.

Cospito, Giuseppe 2004, 'Struttura-superstruttura', in Frosini and Liguori (eds) 2004.

Cospito, Giuseppe 2009, 'Struttura', in Liguori and Voza (eds) 2009.

Cospito, Giuseppe 2011a, *Il ritmo del pensiero. Per una lettura diacronica dei 'Quaderni del carcere' di Gramsci*, Naples: Bibliopolis.

Cospito, Giuseppe 2011b, 'Verso l'edizione critica e integrale dei "*Quaderni del carcere*"', *Studi storici*, LII, no. 4: 896–904.

Cospito, Giuseppe 2016, *The Rhythm of Thought in Gramsci. A Diachronic Interpretation of Prison Notebooks*, Leiden: Brill.

Coutinho, Carlos Nelson 1984 [1979], *A democracia como valor universal e outros ensaios*, Rio de Janeiro: Salamandra.

Coutinho, Carlos Nelson 1985, 'Le categorie di Gramsci e la realtà brasiliana', *Critica marxista*, V: 35–55.

Coutinho, Carlos Nelson 1999 [1989], *Um estudo sobre seu pensamento político*, Rio de Janeiro: Civilização Brasileira.

Coutinho, Carlos Nelson 2006a, *Il pensiero politico di Gramsci*, Milan: Unicopoli.

Coutinho, Carlos Nelson 2006b, *Intervenções: o marxismo na batalha das idéias*, São Paulo: Cortez.

Coutinho, Carlos Nelson 2007, 'L'epoca neoliberale: rivoluzione passiva o controriforma?', *Critica marxista*, 22: 21–6.

Coutinho, Carlos Nelson 2009, 'Catarsi', in Liguori and Voza (eds) 2009.

Coutinho, Carlos Nelson 2013, *Gramsci's Political Thought*, Chicago: Haymarket Books.

Coutinho, Carlos Nelson and Marco Aurélio Nogueira (eds) 1988, *Gramsci e a América Latina*, Rio de Janeiro: Paz e Terra.

Cox, Robert 1981, 'Social Forces, States and World Orders: Beyond International Relations Theory', *Millennium: Journal of International Studies*, 10, no. 2: 126–55.

Cox, Robert 1983, 'Gramsci, Hegemony and International Relations: An Essay in Method', *Millennium: Journal of International Studies*, 12, no. 2: 162–75.

Cox, Robert 1987, *Production, Power, and World Order: Social Forces in the Making of History*, New York: Columbia University Press.

Cox, Robert 1992, 'Global Perestroika', *Socialist Register*, 28: 26–43.

Crehan, Kate 2002, *Gramsci, Culture, and Anthropology*, Berkeley: University of California Press.

Crehan, Kate 2016, *Gramsci's Common Sense*, Durham, NC: Duke University Press.

Crespo, Horacio (ed.) 1999, *José Aricó. Entrevistas 1974–1991*, Córdoba: Centro de Estudios Avanzados.

Croce, Benedetto 1900, *Materialismo storico ed economia marxistica*, Palermo: Remo Sandron.

Croce, Benedetto 1915, 'Religione e serenità', *La Critica*, 13: 153–5.

Croce, Benedetto 1924a, *Grundlagen der Politik*, München: Meyer & Jessen.

Croce, Benedetto 1924b, *The Conduct of Life*, translated by Arthur Livingston, New York: Harcourt, Bruce and World.

Croce, Benedetto 1927 [1900], *Materialismo storico ed economia marxistica*, Bari: Laterza.

Croce, Benedetto 1938, *La storia come pensiero e come azione*, Bari: Laterza.

Croce, Benedetto 1949, 'La questione del Machiavelli', *Quaderni della Critica*, 14.

Croce, Benedetto 1959, *Œuvres choisies*, Paris: Éditions sociales.

Croce, Benedetto 1963 [1932], *History of Europe in the Nineteenth Century*, translated by Henry Furst, London: Harcourt, Bruce and World.

Cronin, Stephanie (ed.) 2008, *Subalterns and Social Protest: History from Below in the Middle East and North Africa*, New York: Routledge.

D'Orsi, Angelo and Francesca Chiarotto 2012, 'Il Gramsci di Bobbio', in *Storia e critica della politica. Studi in memoria di Luciano Russi*, Soveria Mannelli: Rubbettino.

Dailynews 2015, 'Abhisit Cha Rabob Thaksin Ton Het Kwan Kadyaeng [Abhisit Claimed that the Thaksin Regime is the Real Root Cause of Conflicts]', 17 May, available at: http://www.dailynews.co.th/politics/321768.

Dal Pane, Luigi 1975, *Antonio Labriola nella politica e nella cultura italiana*, Turin: Einaudi.

Daldal, Asli 2014, 'Power and Ideology in Michel Foucault and Antonio Gramsci: A Comparative Analysis', *Review of Historical and Political Science*, 2, no. 2: 149–67.

Dautry, Jean 1956, 'Translation and Presentation of Gramsci's Texts of 1919–1920', *Cahiers internationaux*, 76.

Davidson, Alastair 1977, *Antonio Gramsci: Towards an intellectual biography*, Atlantic Highlands, NJ: Humanities Press.

Davis, John A. 2007, *Naples and Napoleon: Southern Italy and the European Revolutions (1780–1860)*, Oxford: Oxford University Press.

Day, Richard 2005, *Gramsci is Dead: Anarchist Currents in the Newest Social Movements*, London: Pluto Press.

De Beauvoir, Simone 1963, *La Force des choses*, Paris: Gallimard.

De Felice, Franco 1977, 'Rivoluzione passiva, fascismo, americanismo in Gramsci', in *Politica e storia in Gramsci*, Vol. 1, edited by Franco Ferri, Rome: Editori Riuniti.

De Genova, Nicholas 2015, 'Border Struggles in the Migrant Metropolis', *Nordic Journal of Migration Research*, 5, no. 1: 3–10.

De Giovanni, Biagio 1983, 'Sulle vie di Marx filosofo in Italia. Spunti provvisori', *Il centauro*, 9: 3–25.

De Martino, Ernesto 1949, 'Intorno a una storia del mondo popolare subalterno', *Società*, I, no. 3: 411–35.

De Martino, Ernesto 1951a, 'Il folklore progressivo emiliano', *Emilia*, 3: 251–4.

De Martino, Ernesto 1951b, 'Il folklore, un invito ai lettori del "calendario"', *Il Calendario del popolo*, 7: 989.

De Martino, Ernesto 1951c, 'Il folklore progressivo', *L'Unità*, 26 giugno.

De Martino, Ernesto 1953, 'Etnologia e cultura nazionale negli ultimi dieci anni', *Società*, XI, no. 3: 313–42.

De Martino, Ernesto 1961, *La terra del rimorso. Contributo a una storia religiosa del Sud*, Milan: Il Saggiatore.

De Martino, Ernesto 1992, 'Due inediti su Gramsci "Postille a Gramsci" e "Gramsci e il folklore"', *La Ricerca Folklorica*, 25: 73.

De Mauro, Tullio 1979, *L'Italia delle Italie*, Florence: Nuova Guaraldi.

De Rosa, Gabriele 1966, *Storia del movimento cattolico in Italia, Vol. 1: Dalla restaurazione all'età giolittiana*, Bari: Laterza.

De Sanctis, Francesco 1943 [1870], *Geschichte der italienischen Literatur. Band 2. Von der Spätrenaissance bis zur Romantik*, Stuttgart: Kröner.

De Saussure, Ferdinand 1959 [1916], *Course in General Linguistics*, New York: The Philosophical Library.

De Smet, Brecht 2014a, 'Revolution and Counter-Revolution in Egypt', *Science & Society*, 78, 1: 11–40.

De Smet, Brecht 2014b, 'Theory and Its Consequences: A Reply to Joel Beinin', *Jadaliyya*, 5 June, available at: http://www.jadaliyya.com/pages/index/18004/theory-and-its-consequences_a-reply-to-joel-beinin.

De Smet, Brecht 2014c, 'Once Again on Caesarism: Continuing the Debate with Joel Beinin', *Jadaliyya*, 30 July, available at: http://www.jadaliyya.com/pages/index/18719/once-again-on-caesarism_continuing-the-debate-with.

De Smet, Brecht 2016, *Gramsci on Tahrir: Revolution and Counter-Revolution in Egypt*, London: Pluto Press.

Del Lucchese, Filippo 2010, 'On the Emptiness of an Encounter: Althusser's Reading of Machiavelli', *Décalages*, 1, no. 1. Available at: https://scholar.oxy.edu/decalages/vol1/iss1/5/.

Derthick, Martha and Paul Quirk 1985, *The Politics of Deregulation*, Washington, DC: Brookings Institution.

Desai, Radhika 2013, *Geopolitical Economy: After US Hegemony, Globalization and Empire (The Future of World Capitalism)*, London: Pluto Press.

Desanti, Dominique 2009, *Ce que le siècle m'a dit: mémoires*, Paris: Hachette.

Desanti, Jean-Toussaint 1963, *Phénoménologie et praxis*, Paris: Éditions sociales.

Desidera, Bruno 2005, *La lotta delle egemonie: Movimento cattolico e Partito popolare nei Quaderni di Gramsci*, Padova: Il Poligrafo.

Destutt de Tracy, Antoine L.C. 1977 [1801–15], *Eléments d'Idéologie*, Frommann-Holzboog: Stuttgart-Bad Cannstatt.

Devoto, Giacomo 1974, *Il linguaggio d'Italia*, Milan: Rizzoli.

Di Bello, Anna (ed.) 2011, *Marx e Gramsci: Filologia, filosofia e politica allo specchio*, Naples: Liguori.

Di Meo, Antonio 2014, 'La "rivoluzione passiva" da Cuoco a Gramsci. Appunti per una interpretazione', *Filosofia italiana* [online].

Dickie, John 1999, *Darkest Italy: The Nation and the Stereotypes of the Mezzogiorno, 1860–1900*, New York: Palgrave Macmillan.

Dressel, Bjorn 2010, 'When Notions of Legitimacy Conflict: The Case of Thailand', *Politics & Policy*, 38, 3: 445–69.

Dubreuil, Hyacinthe 1931 [1929], *Standards: il lavoro americano veduto da un operaio francese*, translated by Alessandro Schiavi, Bari: Laterza.

Durante, Lea 2004, 'Nazionale-Popolare', in Frosini and Liguori (eds) 2004.

Durante, Lea 2009, 'Nazionale-Popolare', in Liguori and Voza (eds) 2009.

Ekers, Michael and Alex Loftus 2008, 'The Power of Water: Developing Dialogues Between Foucault and Gramsci', *Environment and Planning*, 26: 698–718.

Ekers, Michael and Alex Loftus 2013, 'Gramsci: Space, Nature, Politics', in Ekers et al. (eds) 2013.

Ekers, Michael and Gillian Hart, Stefan Kipfer, Alex Loftus (eds) 2013, *Gramsci: Space, Nature, Politics*, Oxford: Wiley-Blackwell.

Elden, Stuart 2004, *Understanding Henri Lefebvre*, London: Continuum.

Elden, Stuart and Neil Brenner 2009, 'Henri Lefebvre on State, Space, Territory', *International Political Sociology*, 3: 353–377.

Emig, Rainer 2012, 'Out of Place or Caught in the Middle: Edward Said's Thinking Between Humanism and Poststructuralism', in *Edward Said's Translocations: Essays in Secular Criticism*, edited by Tobias Döring and Mark Stein, London: Routledge.

Engels, Friedrich 1962 [1888], *Ludwig Feuerbach und der Ausgang der deutschen klassischen Philosophie*, in Marx-Engels-*Werke*, Vol. 21, Berlin: Dietz.

Epstein, Gerald 2005, *Financialization and the World Economy*, Cheltenham: Edward Elgar.

Eribon, Didier 2011, *Michel Foucault*, Paris: Flammarion.

Esping-Andersen, Gøsta 1990, *The Three Worlds of Welfare Capitalism*, Princeton, NJ: Princeton University Press.

Evans, Kate 2015, *Red Rosa: A Graphic Biography of Rosa Luxemburg*, London: Verso.

Featherstone, David 2013, '"Gramsci in Action": Space, Politics and the Making of Solidarities', in Ekers et al. (eds) 2013.

Feierman, Steven 1990, *Peasant Intellectuals: Anthropology and History in Tanzania*, Madison: University of Wisconsin Press.

Femia, Joseph 1981, *Gramsci's Political Thought*, Oxford: Oxford University Press.

Filippini, Michele 2011, *Gramsci globale: guida pratica alle interpretazioni di Gramsci nel mondo*, Bologna: Odoya.

Filo della Torre, Paolo, Edward Mortimer and Jonathan Story 1978, *Eurocomunismo, mito o realtà?*, Milan: Mondadori.

Finelli, Roberto 2010, 'Antonio Gramsci. La rifondazione di un marxismo "senza corpo"', in *L'altronovecento. Comunismi eretico e pensiero critico*, I. *L'età del Comunismo sovietico (Europa 1900–1945)*, edited by Pier Paolo Poggio, Milan: Jaca Book.

Finelli, Roberto 2016, *A Failed Parricide: Hegel and the Young Marx*, translated by Peter D. Thomas and Nicola Iannelli Popham, Leiden: Brill.

Fiori, Giuseppe 1990 [1970], *Antonio Gramsci: Life of a Revolutionary*, London: Verso.

Fiori, Giuseppe 1995 [1966], *Vita di Antonio Gramsci*, Rome-Bari: Laterza.

Fontana, Benedetto 1993, *Hegemony and Power: On the Relation between Gramsci and Machiavelli*, Minneapolis: University of Minnesota Press.

Fontana, Benedetto 2004, 'The Concept of Caesarism in Gramsci', in Baehr and Richter 2004.

Forenza, Eleonora 2009, 'Molecolare', in Liguori and Voza (eds) 2009.

Fortini, Franco 1950, 'Il diavolo sa vestirsi da primitivo', *Paese sera*, 23 February.

Foucault, Michel 1969, *L'Archéologie du savoir*, Paris: Gallimard.

Foucault, Michel 1970, *The Order of Things: An Archeology of the Human Sciences*, London: Tavistock.

Foucault, Michel 1975, *Surveiller et punir: naissance de la prison*, Paris: Gallimard.

Foucault, Michel 1976, *Histoire de la sexualité: la volonté de savoir*, Volume 1, Paris: Gallimard.

Foucault, Michel 1980 [1977], 'Truth and Power', in *Power/Knowledge: Selected Interviews and Other Writings 1972–1977*, edited by Colin Gordon, translated by Colin Gordon, Leo Marshall, John Mepham and Kate Soper, New York: Pantheon Books.

Foucault, Michel 1985, 'La Vie: l'expérience et la science', *Revue de métaphysique et de morale*, 90e année, 1: Canguilhem (janvier-mars), pp. 3–14, published in 1994, *Dits et écrits*, Vol. IV, Paris: Gallimard.

Foucault, Michel 1994 [1969], 'Qu'est-ce qu'un auteur?', in *Dits et écrits 1954–1988*, Volume 1, edited by Michel Foucault, Daniel Defert and François Ewald, Paris: Gallimard.

Francese, Joseph 2009, 'Thoughts on Gramsci's Need "To Do Something 'Für ewig'"', *Rethinking Marxism*, 21, no. 1: 54–66.

Francioni, Gianni 1984, *L'officina gramsciana. Ipotesi sulla struttura dei "Quaderni del carcere"*, Naples: Bibliopolis.

Francioni, Gianni 2009, 'Come lavorava Gramsci', in Gramsci 2009, Vol. 1.

Francioni, Gianni 2016, 'Un labirinto di carta (Introduzione alla filologia gramsciana)', *International Gramsci Journal*, 2, no. 1: 7–48.

Francioni, Gianni and Fabio Frosini 2009, 'Nota introduttiva al Quaderno 25', in Gramsci 2009, Vol. 18.

Frank, Andre Gunder 1969, *Underdevelopment or Revolution*, New York: Monthly Review Press.

Fraser, Nancy 2017, 'The End of Progressive Neoliberalism', *Dissent*, https://www .dissentmagazine.org/online_articles/progressive-neoliberalism-reactionary-populism-nancy-fraser.

Frosini, Fabio 2001, 'Il "ritorno a Marx" nei *Quaderni del Carcere* (1930)', in Paladini Musitelli and Petronio (eds) 2001.

Frosini, Fabio 2003a, *Gramsci e la filosofia. Saggio sui 'Quaderni del carcere'*, Rome: Carrocci.

Frosini, Fabio 2003b, 'Sulla "traducibilità" nei Quaderni di Gramsci', *Critica marxista*, 6: 1–10.

Frosini, Fabio 2004a, 'Filosofia della praxis', in Frosini and Liguori (eds) 2004.

Frosini, Fabio 2004b, 'L'immanenza nei *Quaderni del carcere* di Antonio Gramsci', «Isonomia. Rivista di Filosofia», 2004.

Frosini, Fabio 2008a, 'Il neoidealismo italiano e l'elaborazione della filosofia della praxis', in Giasi (ed.) 2008.

Frosini, Fabio 2008b, 'Beyond the Crisis of Marxism: Gramsci's Contested Legacy' in *Critical Companion to Contemporary Marxism*, edited by Jacques Bidet and Stathis Kouvelakis, Leiden: Brill.

Frosini, Fabio 2009a, 'Bucharin, Nikolaj Ivanovič', in Liguori and Voza (eds) 2009.

Frosini, Fabio 2009b, 'Immanenza', in Liguori and Voza (eds) 2009.

Frosini, Fabio 2009c, *Da Gramsci a Marx: Ideologia, verità e politica*, Rome: Derive-Approdi.

Frosini, Fabio 2010a, *La religione dell'uomo moderno. Politica e verità nei 'Quaderni del carcere' di Antonio Gramsci*, Rome: Carocci.

Frosini, Fabio 2010b, 'On "Translatability" in Gramsci's "Prison Notebooks"', in Ives and Lacorte (eds) 2010.

Frosini, Fabio 2011–12, 'Storicismo e storia nei *Quaderni del carcere* di Antonio Gramsci', *Bollettino Filosofico*, 27: 351–67.

Frosini, Fabio 2011, 'Dalla filosofia di Marx alla filosofia della praxis nei *Quaderni del Carcere*', in Di Bello (ed.) 2011.

Frosini, Fabio 2012a, 'Reformation, Renaissance and the State: The Hegemonic Fabric of Modern Sovereignty', *Journal of Romance Language Studies*, 12, no. 3: 63–77.

Frosini, Fabio 2012b, 'Politica e verità. Gramsci dopo Laclau', *Seminario 'Ideologia, verità e politica'*.

Frosini, Fabio 2013a, 'Spazio-tempo e potere alla luce della teoria dell'egemonia', in *Tempora multa. Il governo del tempo*, edited by Vittorio Morfino, Milan: Mimesis.

Frosini, Fabio 2013b, 'Quaderno 4. Appunti di filosofia. Materialismo e idealismo. Prima serie', International Gramsci Society Italia – Seminario sulla storia dei *Quaderni del carcere*, Rome, 8 March.

Frosini, Fabio 2014, 'Ideologia em Marx e em Gramsci', *Educação e Filosofia*, 23: 559–82.

Frosini, Fabio 2015, 'Hégémonie. Une approche génétique', *Actuel Marx*, 57: 27–42.

Frosini, Fabio 2016a, 'L'egemonia e i "subalterni". Utopia, religione, democrazia', *International Gramsci Journal*, 2, no. 1: 126–66.

Frosini, Fabio 2016b, 'L'eccidio di Roccagorga e la "settimana rossa": Gramsci, il "sovversivismo" e il fascismo', *Studi storici*, 1: 137–66.

Frosini, Fabio and Guido Liguori (eds) 2004, *Le parole di Gramsci. Per un lessico dei 'Quaderni del carcere'*, Rome: Carocci.

Fusaro, Lorenzo 2017, 'Why China is Different: Hegemony, Revolutions and the Rise of Contender States', *Research in Political Economy*, 32: 181–219.

Fusaro, Lorenzo 2019, *Crises and Hegemonic Transitions: From Gramsci's Quaderni to the Contemporary World Economy*, Leiden: Brill.

Gaboardi, Natalia 2015, 'Il concetto di "traducibilità" in Gramsci', *Gramsciana*, 1: 91–108.

Gandhi, Leela 1998, *Postcolonial Theory: A Critical Introduction*, New York: Columbia University Press.

Garaudy, Roger 1957a, *Humanisme marxiste*, Paris: Éditions sociales.

Garaudy, Roger 1957b, 'Introduction à l' œuvre d' Antonio Gramsci', *La Nouvelle Critique*, 87–8.

Garaudy, Roger 1965, *De l'anathème au dialogue*, Paris: Plon.

Garaudy, Roger 1966, *Marxisme du xxe siècle*, Paris: La Palatine.

Gentile, Giovanni 1923, *La riforma della dialettica hegeliana e altri scritti*, Messina: Principato.

Gentile, Giovanni 1987 [1916], *Teoria generale dello spirito come atto puro*, Florence: Le Lettere.

Gentile, Giovanni 2014 [1899], *La filosofia di Marx*, Pisa: Edizioni della Normale.

Germain, Randall and Michael Kenny 1998, 'Engaging Gramsci: International Relations Theory and the New Gramscians', *Review of International Studies*, 24, no. 1: 3–21.

Gerratana, Valentino 1969, 'Replica', in *Gramsci e la cultura contemporanea*, Rome: Editori Riuniti.

Gerratana, Valentino 1997, *Gramsci. Problemi di metodo*, Rome: Editori Riuniti.

Giarrizzo, Giovanni 1954, 'Moralità scientifica e folclore', *Lo spettatore italiano*, 7: 180–4.

Giasi, Francesco (ed.) 2008, *Gramsci nel suo tempo*, 2 Vols., Rome: Carocci.

Giasi, Francesco 2011, 'Marx nella biblioteca di Gramsci', in Di Bello (ed.) 2011.

Gide, Charles and Charles Rist 1926, *Histoire des doctrines économiques depuis le physiocrates jusqu'à nos jours*, 5th edn, Paris: Librairie du 'Recueil Sirey'.

Ginsborg, Paul 1984, 'The Communist Party and the Agrarian Question in Southern Italy, 1943–48', *History Workshop*, 17: 81–101.

Ginzburg, Carlo 2013, *The Night Battles: Witchcraft and Agrarian Cults in the Sixteenth and Seventeenth Centuries*, Baltimore: Johns Hopkins University Press.

Ginzburg, Carlo 2015, 'Microhistory and World History', in *The Cambridge World History Volume 6: The Construction of a Global World, 1400–1800 CE, Part 2: Patterns of Change*, edited by Jerry H. Bentley, Sanjay Subrahmanyam and Merry E. Wiesner-Hanks, Cambridge: Cambridge University Press.

Gledhill, John 2000, *Power and Its Disguises: Anthropological Perspectives on Politics*, London: Pluto Press.

Gobetti, Piero 1960 [1925], 'Ford', *La rivoluzione liberale* (8 March 1925), now in *Opere Complete, I. Scritti Politici*, edited by Paolo Spriano, Turin: Einaudi.

Gobetti, Piero 2008, *La Rivoluzione liberale. Saggio sulla lotta politica in Italia*, edited by Ersilia Alessandrone Perona, Turin: Einaudi.

Gorz, André 1964, *Classe ouvrière et néo-capitalisme*, Paris: Seuil.

Gowan, Peter 1999, *The Global Gamble: Washington's Faustian Bid for World Dominance*, London: Verso.

Graeber, David 2007, *Possibilities: Essays on Hierarchy, Rebellion, and Desire*, Oakland: AK Press.

Gramsci, Antonio 1948–51, *Quaderni del carcere*, 6 Vols., edited by Felice Platone, Turin: Einaudi.

Gramsci, Antonio 1948, *Il materialismo storico e la filosofia di Benedetto Croce*, Turin: Einaudi.

Gramsci, Antonio 1949, *Note sul Machiavelli, sulla politica e sullo Stato moderno*, Turin: Einaudi.

Gramsci, Antonio 1952 *see* Gramsci 1948.

Gramsci, Antonio 1957a, *The Modern Prince and Other Writings*, translated by Louis Marks, London: Lawrence and Wishart.

Gramsci, Antonio 1957b, *The Open Marxism of Antonio Gramsci*, translated and edited by Carl Marzani, New York: Cameron Associates.

Gramsci, Antonio 1958, *Scritti giovanili, 1914–1918*, Turin: Einaudi.

Gramsci, Antonio 1959, *Œuvres choisies*, Paris: Éditions sociales.

Gramsci, Antonio 1961, *Pisma wybrane*, translated by Barbara Sieroszewska, 2 Vols., Warszawa: Książka i Wiedza.

Gramsci, Antonio 1964, *2000 pagine di Gramsci, I: Nel tempo della lotta 1914–1926*, Milan: Il Saggiatore.

Gramsci, Antonio 1966, *La questione meridionale*, edited by Franco De Felice and Valentino Parlato, Rome: Editori Riuniti.

Gramsci, Antonio 1971a, *Selections from the Prison Notebooks*, edited by Quintin Hoare and Geoffrey Nowell Smith, London: Lawrence & Wishart.

Gramsci, Antonio 1971b, *La costruzione del partito comunista: 1923–1926*, Turin: Einaudi.

Gramsci, Antonio 1975, *Quaderni del carcere*, 4 Vols., edited by Valentino Gerratana, Turin: Einaudi.

Gramsci, Antonio 1977, *Selections from Political Writings 1910–1920*, edited by Quintin Hoare, London: Lawrence and Wishart.

Gramsci, Antonio 1979, *Letters from Prison*, translated and edited by Lynne Lawner, London: Quartet.

Gramsci, Antonio 1980, *Cronache torinesi 1913–17*, edited by Sergio Caprioglio, Turin: Einaudi.

Gramsci, Antonio 1982, *La città futura, 1917–1918*, edited by Sergio Caprioglio, Turin: Einaudi.

Gramsci, Antonio 1984, *Il nostro Marx, 1918–1919*, edited by Sergio Caprioglio, Turin: Einaudi.

Gramsci, Antonio 1985, *Selections from Cultural Writings*, edited by David Forgacs and George Nowell Smith, translated by W.Q. Boelhower, London: Lawrence and Wishart.

Gramsci, Antonio 1987, *L'Ordine Nuovo 1919–1920*, edited by Valentino Gerratana and Sergio Caprioglio, Turin: Einaudi.

Gramsci, Antonio 1988b, *An Antonio Gramsci Reader*, edited by David Forgacs, London: Lawrence & Wishart.

Gramsci, Antonio 1990, 'Some Aspects of the Southern Question' in *Selections from the Political Writings. 1921–1926*, with addictional texts by other Italian communist leaders, translated by Quintin Hoare, Minneapolis: University of Minnesota Press.

Gramsci, Antonio 1991, *Zeszyty filozoficzne*, translated by Barbara Sieroszewska and Joanna Szymanowska, edited by Sław Krzemień-Ojak Biblioteka Klasyków Filozofii, Warszawa: Wydawnictwo Naukowe PWN.

Gramsci, Antonio 1992–2007, *Prison Notebooks*, 3 Vols., edited by Joseph A. Buttigieg, New York: Columbia University Press.

Gramsci, Antonio 1992, *Prison Notebooks*, Vol. I (Notebook 1–2), edited by Joseph A. Buttigieg, translated by Joseph A. Buttigieg and Antonio Callari, New York: Columbia University Press.

Gramsci, Antonio 1994a, *Letters from Prison*, 2 Vols., translated by Raymond Rosenthal, edited by Frank Rosengarten, New York: Columbia University Press.

Gramsci, Antonio 1994b, *Pre-Prison Writings*, edited by Richard Bellamy, Cambridge: Cambridge University Press.

Gramsci, Antonio 1995, *Further Selections from the Prison Notebooks*, edited and translated by D. Boothman, London: Lawrence and Wishart.

Gramsci, Antonio 1996a, *Lettere dal carcere*, 2 Vols., edited by Antonio Santucci, Palermo: Sellerio.

Gramsci, Antonio 1996b, *Prison Notebooks*, Vol. II (Notebook 3–5), edited and translated by Joseph A. Buttigieg, New York: Columbia University Press.

Gramsci, Antonio 1999 [1971], *Selection from the Prison Notebooks*, edited by Quintin Hoare and Geoffrey Nowell Smith, London: ElecBook.

Gramsci, Antonio 1999–2002, *Cadernos do cárcere*, edited by Carlos Nelson Coutinho, Luiz Sérgio Henriques and Marco Aurélio Nogueira, Rio de Janeiro: Civilização Brasileira.

Gramsci, Antonio 2000, *The Gramsci Reader: Selected Writings. 1916–1935*, edited by David Forgacs, New York: New York University Press.

Gramsci, Antonio 2001a *see* Gramsci 1975.

Gramsci, Antonio 2001b, *Further Selections from the Prison Notebooks*, translated by Derek Boothman, London: ElecBook.

Gramsci, Antonio 2007a, *Prison Notebooks*, Vol. III (Notebook 6–8), edited and translated by Joseph A. Buttigieg, New York: Columbia University Press.

Gramsci, Antonio 2007b, *Quaderni del carcere, 1. Quaderni di traduzioni (1929–1932)*, edited by Giuseppe Cospito and Gianni Francioni, Rome: Istituto della Enciclopedia Italiana.

Gramsci, Antonio 2007c, *Nel mondo grande e terribile. Antologia degli scritti. 1914–1935*, Turin: Einaudi.

Gramsci, Antonio 2008a [1951], *Passato e presente, Opere di Antonio Gramsci*, edited by Felice Platone, Turin: Einaudi [electronic version: liberliber.it].

Gramsci, Antonio 2008b, *Favole di libertà. Le fiabe dei fratelli Grimm tradotte in carcere*, Rome: Robin.

Gramsci, Antonio 2009, *Quaderni del carcere. Edizione anastatica dei manoscritti*, 18 Vols., edited by Gianni Francioni, Rome-Cagliari: Istituto della Enciclopedia Italiana-L'Unione Sarda.

Gramsci, Antonio 2011, *see* Gramsci 1992–2007.

Gramsci, Antonio 2012a, *see* Gramsci 1985.

Gramsci, Antonio 2012b, *see* Gramsci 1971a.

Gramsci, Antonio 2013, *Nel tempo della lotta e lettere (1929–1937)*, edited by Aurelio Pino, Milan: Il Saggiatore.

Gramsci, Antonio 2014a, *A Great and Terrible World: the pre-prison letters 1908–1926*, edited and translated by Derek Boothman, London: Lawrence and Wishart.

Gramsci, Antonio 2014b, *see* Gramsci 1975.

Gramsci, Antonio and Tatiana Schucht 1997, *Lettere 1926–1935*, edited by Aldo Natoli and Chiara Daniele, Turin: Einaudi.

Greaves, Nigel M. 2009, *Gramsci's Marxism: Reclaiming a Philosophy of History and Politics*, Leicester: Matador.

Greco, Tommaso 2000, *Norberto Bobbio. Un itinerario intellettuale tra filosofia e politica*, Rome: Donzelli.

Green, Marcus E. 2002, 'Gramsci Cannot Speak: Presentations and Interpretations of Gramsci's Concept of the Subaltern', *Rethinking Marxism*, 14, no. 3: 1–24.

Green, Marcus E. 2006, *Gramsci's Concept of Subaltern Social Groups*, PhD thesis, Graduate Program in Political Science, York University, Toronto.

Green, Marcus E. (ed.) 2011a, *Rethinking Gramsci*, New York: Routledge.

Green, Marcus E. 2011b, 'Gramsci Cannot Speak', in Green (ed.) 2011a.

Green, Marcus E. 2011c, 'Rethinking the Subaltern and the Question of Censorship in Gramsci's *Prison Notebooks*', *Postcolonial Studies*, 14, no. 4: 387–404.

Green, Marcus E. 2013a, 'On the Postcolonial Image of Gramsci', *Postcolonial Studies*, 16, no. 1: 90–101.

Green, Marcus E. 2013b, 'Race, Class, and Religion: Gramsci's Conception of Subalternity', in Zene (ed.) 2013.

Green, Marcus E. and Peter Ives 2010, 'Subalternity and Language: Overcoming the Fragmentation of Common Sense', in Ives and Lacorte (eds) 2010.

Grigor'eva, Irina V. 1995, 'Presenza di Gramsci nella cultura sovietica', in *Gramsci nel mondo*, edited by Maria Luisa Righi, Rome: Fondazione Istituto Gramsci.

Groh, Dieter 1979, 'Cäsarismus, Napoleonismus, Bonapartismus, Führer, Chef, Imperialismus', in *Geschichtliche Grundbegriffe*, Vol. 1, edited by Otto Brunner, Werner Konze and Reinhardt Koselleck, Stuttgart: Klett-Cotta.

Gruppi, Luciano 1972, *Il concetto di egemonia in Gramsci*, Rome: Editori Riuniti.

Guglielmi, Guido 1976, *Da De Sanctis a Gramsci. Il linguaggio della critica*, Bologna: Il Mulino.

Guha, Ranajit 1982, 'On Some Aspects of the Historiography of Colonial India', in *Subaltern Studies I, Writings on South Asian History and Society*, Delhi: Oxford University Press.

Guha, Ranajit 1983, *Elementary Aspects of Peasant Insurgency in Colonial India*, New Dehli: Oxford University Press.

Guha, Ranajit 1988a, Preface to *Selected Subaltern Studies*, edited by Ranajit Guha and Gayatri Chakravorty Spivak, New York: Oxford University Press.

Guha, Ranajit 1988b [1982], 'On Some Aspects of the Historiography of Colonial India', in *Selected Subaltern Studies*, edited by Ranajit Guha and Gayatri Chakravorti Spivak, New York: Oxford University Press.

Guha, Ranajit 1997 [1989], *Dominance without Hegemony: History and Power in Colonial India*, Cambridge, MA: Harvard University Press.

Guha, Ranajit 1999 [1983], *Elementary Aspects of Peasant Insurgency in Colonial India*, Durham, NC: Duke University Press.

Guha, Ranajit 2011, 'Gramsci in India: Homage to a Teacher', *Journal of Modern Italian Studies*, 16, no. 2: 288–95.

Guha, Ranajit et al. (eds) 1982–99, *Subaltern Studies I–X*, New Delhi: Oxford University Press.

Gündogdu, Ayten 2015, *Rightlessness in an Age of Rights*, Oxford: Oxford University Press.

Gupta, Arun and Leo Panitch 2016, 'The Trump Way', *Jacobin*, https://www.jacobinmag.com/2016/12/donald-trump-workers-infrastructure-immigrants-jobs/.

Gutkind, Peter 1977, 'The View From Below: Political Consciousness of the Urban Poor in Ibadan', *International Journal of Sociology*, 15, no. 57: 40–83.

Guzzone, Giuliano 2018, *Gramsci e la critica dell'economia politica: dal dibattito sul liberismo al paradigma della traducibilità*, Roma, Viella.

Guzzone, Giuliano 2017, '"Distinto", "distinzione", "distinguere": un caso di traduzione nei "Quaderni del carcere" di Gramsci', *Annali della Scuola Normale Superiore di Pisa. Classe di Lettere e Filosofia*, 9, n. 2: 497–529.

Hall, Stuart 1986, 'Gramsci's Relevance for the Study of Race and Ethnicity', *Journal of Communication Inquiry*, 10, no. 2: 5–27.

Hall, Stuart 1987, 'Gramsci and Us', *Marxism Today*, June: 16–21, available at: https://www.versobooks.com/blogs/2448-stuart-hall-gramsci-and-us.

Hall, Stuart 1996, 'Gramsci's Relevance for the Study of Race and Ethnicity', in *Stuart Hall: Critical Dialogues in Cultural Studies*, edited by David Morley and Kuan-Hsing Chen, London: Routledge.

Handley, Paul M. 2006, *The King Never Smiles: A Biography of Thailand's Bhumibol Adujyadej*, New Haven: Yale University Press.

Hanieh, Adam 2013, *Lineages of Revolt: Issues of Contemporary Capitalism in the Middle East*, London: Haymarket.

Hardt, Michael and Antonio Negri 2000, *Empire*, Cambridge, MA: Harvard University Press.

Hardt, Michael and Antonio Negri 2004, *Multitude: War and Democracy in the Age of Empire*, London: Penguin.

Harman, Chris 1998, *Marxism and History*, London: Bookmarks.

Hart, Gillian 2002, *Disabling Globalisation*, Berkeley: University of California Press.

Hart, Gillian 2014, *Rethinking the South African Crisis*, Athens: University of Georgia Press.

Hart, Gillian 2015, 'Political Society and Its Discontents', *Economic & Political Weekly*, 50, 43: 43–51.

Hart, William D. 2000, *Edward Said and the Religious Effects of Culture*, Cambridge: Cambridge University Press.

Harvey, David 1973, *Social Justice and the City*, Oxford: Blackwell.

Harvey, David 1982, *Limits to Capital*, Oxford: Blackwell.

Harvey, David 1985, *The Urbanization of Capital*, Oxford: Blackwell.

Harvey, David 1996, *Justice, Nature and the Geography of Difference*, Oxford: Blackwell.

Harvey, David 2003, *The New Imperialism*, Oxford: Oxford University Press.

Harvey, David 2005, *A Brief History of Neoliberalism*, Oxford: Oxford University Press.

Harvey, David 2008, 'The Right to the City', *New Left Review*, II/53: 23–40.

Harvey, David 2010, *A Companion to Marx's Capital*, London: Verso.

Harvey, Graham and Robert J. Wallis 2007, *Historical Dictionary of Shamanism*, Lanham, MD: Rowman and Littlefield.

Haug, Wolfgang Fritz 1999, 'Rethinking Gramsci's Philosophy of Praxis from One Century to the Next', *boundary 2*, 26, no. 2: 101–17.

Haug, Wolfgang Fritz 2000, 'Gramsci's "Philosophy of Praxis"', *Socialism and Democracy*, 14, no. 1: 1–19.

Haug, Wolfgang Fritz 2001, 'Materialismo storico e filosofia della prassi', in Paladini Musitelli and Petronio (eds.) 2001.

Haug, Wolfgang Fritz 2006, *Philosophieren mit Brecht und Gramsci*, Erweiterte Ausgabe, Hamburg: Argument.

Haug, Wolfgang Fritz 2011, *Die kulturelle Unterscheidung. Elemente einer Philosophie des Kulturellen*, Hamburg: Argument.

Hegel, G.W.F. 1983 [1801], 'Die Verfassung Deutschlands', in *Frühe Schriften: Werke* (in zwanzig Bänden). Theorie-Werkausgabe, Vol. 1, 1832 edn, Frankfurt am Main: Suhrkamp.

Hegel, G.W.F. 1942 [1820], *Philosophy of Right*, translated by Thomas M. Knox, Oxford: Oxford University Press.

Hewison, Kevin 2014, 'Thailand: The Lessons of Protest', *Journal of Critical Perspectives on Asia*, 50, no. 1: 1–15.

Hobsbawm, Eric 1959, *Primitive Rebels: Studies in Archaic Forms of Social Movements in the 19th and 20th Centuries*, Manchester: Manchester University Press.

Hobsbawm, Eric 1960, 'Per lo studio delle classi subalterne', *Società*, 16, no. 3: 436–49.

Hobsbawm, Eric 1965 [1959], *Primitive Rebels: Studies in Archaic Forms of Social Movement in the 19th and 20th Century*, New York: Norton.

Hobsbawm, Eric 2013 [1975], *The Age of Capital*, London: Abacus.

Holub, Renate 1992, *Antonio Gramsci: Beyond Marxism and Postmodernism*, London: Routledge.

Hussein, Abdirahman A. 2002, *Edward Said: Criticism and Society*, London: Verso.

Hymes, Dell (ed.) 1974, *Rethinking Anthropology*, New York: Vintage.

Ikram, Khalid 2006, *The Egyptian Economy, 1952–2000: Performance, Policies, Issues*, London: Routledge.

Il Mattino 2016, 'Vacca: mondo eterogeneo e frammentato sinistra vittima dello scollamento politico', 9 November, http://www.ilmattino.it/pay/edicola/vacca_mondo_eterogeneo_e_frammentato_sinistra_vittima_dello_scollamento_politico-2070674.html.

Imbornone, Jole Silvia 2009, 'Lorianismo, loriani', in Liguori and Voza (eds.) 2009.

International Monetary Fund 1997, The Egyptian Stabilization Experience: An Analytical Retrospective, prepared by A. Subramanian, *IMF Working Papers*, WP/97/105, Washington, DC: The International Monetary Fund.

International Monetary Fund 1998, Egypt: Beyond Stabilization, Towards a Dynamic Market Economy, *IMF Occasional Paper*, 163, Washington, DC: The International Monetary Fund.

Isager, Lotte and Soren Ivarsson, 2010, 'Strengthening the Moral Fibre of the Nation: The King's Sufficiency Economy', in *Saying the Unsayable Monarchy and Democracy in Thailand*, edited by Soren Ivarsson and Lotte Isager, Copenhagen: NIAS.

Isin, F. Engin and Greg M. Nielsen 2008, *Acts of Citizenship*, London: Zed Books.

Ives, Peter 2004a, *Gramsci's Politics of Language: Engaging the Bakhtin Circle and the Frankfurt School*, Toronto: University of Toronto Press.

Ives, Peter 2004b, *Language and Hegemony in Gramsci*, London: Pluto Press.

Ives, Peter and Nicola Short 2013, 'On Gramsci and the International: A Textual Analysis', *Review of International Studies*, 39, no. 3: 621–42.

Ives, Peter and Rocco Lacorte (eds) 2010, *Gramsci, Language, and Translation*, Lanham, MD: Lexington Books.

Izzo, Francesca 2009, *Democrazia e cosmopolitismo in Antonio Gramsci*, Rome: Carocci.

Izzo, Francesca 2011, 'Marx dagli scritti giovanili ai *Quaderni*', in Di Bello (ed.) 2011.

Izzo, Francesca 2016, 'Il "cosmopolitismo di tipo nuovo" nei *Quaderni del carcere*', *Rivista di Studi Italiani*, 3: 185–98.

Jackson, Robert 2016a, 'Subalternity and the Mummification of Culture in Gramsci's "Prison Notebooks"', *International Gramsci Journal*, 2, no. 1: 201–25.

Jackson, Robert 2016b, 'On Bourdieu and Gramsci', *Gramsciana: Rivista internazionale di studi su Antonio Gramsci*, 2: 141–76.

Jakob, Christian 2016, *Die Bleibenden. Wie Flüchtlinge Deutschland seit 20 Jahren verändern*, Berlin: Ch. Links Verlag.

Jameson, Fredric 1971, *Marxism and Form: Twentieth-Century Dialectical Theories of Literature*, Princeton: Princeton University Press.

Janya Yimprasert 2011, 'Political Prisoners', available at: http://hirvikatu10.net/timeupthailand/?p=1097&lang=th.

Jessop, Bob 2005, 'Gramsci as a spatial theorist', *Critical Review of International Social and Political Philosophy*, 8, no. 4: 421–437.

Ji Ungpakorn 2007, *A Coup for the Rich: Thailand's Political Crisis*, Bangkok: Workers Democracy Publishers.

Ji Ungpakorn 2010, *Thailand's Crisis and the Fight for Democracy*, n.p.: WD Press.

Jones, Steve 2006, *Antonio Gramsci*, London: Routledge.

Jory, Patrick 2003, 'Problems in Contemporary Thai Nationalist Historiography', *Kyoto Review of Southeast Asia*, available at: http://kyotoreview.org/issue-3-nations-and-stories/problems-in-contemporary-thai-nationalist-historiography/.

Kaiwar, Vasant 2014, *The Postcolonial Orient: The Politics of Difference and the Project of Provincialising Europe*, Leiden: Brill.

Kanapa, Jean 1957, 'Le marxisme est-il malade?', *France Nouvelle*, 4 July.

Kandil, Hazem 2012, *Soldiers, Spies, and Statesmen: Egypt's Road to Revolt*, London: Verso.

Kanoussi, Dora (ed.) 2004, *Poder y hegemonia hoy: Gramsci en la era global*, Mexico: Plaza y Valdes.

Kanoussi, Dora 2000 *Una introducción a Los cuadernos de la cárcel de Antonio Gramsci*, México D.F.: Plaza y Valdès.

Kanoussi, Dora and Javier Mena 1985, *El concepto de revolución pasiva: una lectura de los* Cuadernos de la cárcel, Puebla: Universidad Autonoma de Puebla.

Kanoussi, Dora, Giancarlo Schirru and Giuseppe Vacca (eds) 2011, *Studi gramsciani nel mondo: Gramsci in America Latina*, Bologna: Il Mulino.

Karawane [Für die Rechte der Flüchtlinge und MigrantInnen] 2011, *The Caravan for the Rights of Refugees and Migrants to the Second Assembly of the International Migrants Alliance.*

Kasian Tejapira 2006, 'Toppling Thaksin' *New Left Review*, 39: 5–37.

Kassem, Maye 2004, *Egyptian Politics: The Dynamics of Authoritarian Rule*, Boulder, CO: Lynne Rienner.

Kennedy, Valerie 2000, *Edward Said: A Critical Introduction*, Cambridge: Polity Press.

Kiely, Ray 2007, 'Poverty Reduction through Liberalisation? Neoliberalism and the Myth of Global Convergence', *Review of International Studies*, 33, no. 3: 415–34.

Kienle, Eberhard 2001, *A Grand Delusion: Democracy and Economic Reform in Egypt*, London: I.B. Tauris.

Kienle, Eberhard 2003, 'Domesticating Economic Liberalization: Controlled Market-Building in Contemporary Egypt', in *Politics from Above, Politics from Below: The Middle East in the Age of Economic Reform*, edited by E. Kienle, London: Saqi.

Kipfer, Stefan 2008, 'How Lefebvre urbanized Gramsci: hegemony, everyday life, and difference' in *Space, Difference, Everyday Life: Reading Henri Lefebvre* edited by Kanishka Goonewardena, Stefan Kipfer, Richard Milgrom and Christian Schmid, London: Routledge.

Kipfer, Stefan 2013, 'City, Country, Hegemony', in Ekers et al. (eds) 2013.

Kipfer, Stefan and Gillian Hart 2013, 'Translating Gramsci in the Current Conjuncture' in Ekers et al. (eds) 2013.

Konings, Martijn 2011, *The Development of American Finance*, Cambridge: Cambridge University Press.

Kouvelakis, Stathis 2003, *Philosophy and Revolution: From Kant to Marx*, London: Verso.

Kozłowski, Michał 2015, 'Youngsters and Refugees, or How Exile Changes Eastern Europe', *Open Democracy*, available at: https://www.opendemocracy.net/can-europe-make-it/michal-kozlowski/youngsters-and-refugees-or-how-exile-changes-eastern-europe.

Krätke, Michael and Peter Thomas 2011 'Antonio Gramsci's Contribution to a Critical Economics', *Historical Materialism*, 19, no. 3: 63–105.

Kreps, David (ed.) 2015, *Gramsci and Foucault: A Reassessment*, Farnham: Ashgate.

Krippner, Greta 2005, 'The Financialization of the American Economy', *Socio-Economic Review*, 3, 2: 173–208.

Krippner, Greta 2011, *Capitalizing on Crisis: The Political Origins of the Rise of Finance*, Harvard: Harvard University Press.

Krzemień-Ojak, Sław 1983, *Antonio Gramsci. Filozofia, teoria kultury, estetyka*, Warszawa: Państwowe Wydawnictwo Naukowe (PWN).

Krzemień-Ojak, Sław 1991, 'Wprowadzenie', in Antonio Gramsci, *Zeszyty filozoficzne*, Warszawa: Państwowe Wydawnictwo Naukowe (PWN), VII–XXXVII.

Kurtz, Donald 1996, 'Hegemony and Anthropology: Gramsci, Exegesis, Reinterpretations', *Critique of Anthropology*, 16, no. 2: 103–35.

La Porta, Lelio 2009, 'Boria del partito', in Liguori and Voza (eds) 2009.

La Rocca, Tommaso 1991, *Gramsci e la religione*, Brescia: Queriniana.

Labastida del Campo Martin, Julio (ed.) 1998, *Hegemonía y alternativas políticas en América Latina*, México D.F.: Siglo Veintiuno.

Labica, Georges 1992, 'La reception de Gramsci en France: Gramsci et le PCF', in *Modernité de Gramsci?*, edited by André Tosel, Paris: Diffusion Les belles lettres.

Labriola, Antonio 1908, *Essays on the Materialistic Conception of History*, Chicago: Charles H. Kerr & Company.

Labriola, Antonio 1912, *Socialism and Philosophy*, Chicago: Charles H. Kerr & Company.

Laclau, Ernesto 1977, *Politics and Ideology in Marxist Theory: Capitalism, Fascism, Populism*, London: New Left Books.

Laclau, Ernesto 2005, *On Populist Reason*, London: Verso.

Laclau, Ernesto and Chantal Mouffe 1985, *Hegemony and Socialist Strategy: Towards a Radical Democratic Politics*, London: Verso.

Laclau, Ernesto and Chantal Mouffe 2014 *see* Laclau and Mouffe 1985.

Lacorte, Rocco 2010, 'Translatability, Language and Freedom in Gramsci's "Prison Notebooks"', in Ives and Lacorte (eds) 2010.

Lacorte, Rocco 2012, '"Espressione" e "traducibilità" nei "Quaderni del carcere"', in *Domande dal presente: studi su Gramsci*, edited by Lea Durante and Guido Liguori, Rome: Carocci.

Lahtinen, Mikko 2009, *Politics and Philosophy: Niccolò Machiavelli and Louis Althusser's Aleatory Materialism*, Leiden: Brill.

Lahtinen, Mikko 2013, 'Althusser, Machiavelli and Us: Between Philosophy and Politics', in *Encountering Althusser: Politics and Materialism in Contemporary Radical Thought*, edited by Katja Diefenbach et al., New York: Bloomsbury.

Lanfranchi, Enrico 1989, *Un filosofo militante. Politica e cultura nel pensiero di Norberto Bobbio*, Turin: Bollati Boringhieri.

Lanternari, Vittorio 1954, 'Religione popolare e storicismo', *Belfagor*, 9: 675.

Lanternari, Vittorio 1963 [1960], *The Religions of the Oppressed: A Study of Modern Messianic Cults*, New York: Knopf.

Lanternari, Vittorio 1972, *Occidente e Terzo Mondo*, Bari: Dedalo.

Lanternari, Vittorio 1974, *Antropologia e imperialismo*, Turin: Einaudi.

Lapavitsas, Costas 2013, *Profiting Without Producing: How Finance Exploits Us All*, London: Verso.

Latin American Subaltern Studies Group 1993, 'Founding Statement', *boundary 2*, 20, no. 3: 110–21.

Lauridsen, Laurids 2009, 'The Policies and Politics of Industrial Upgrading in Thailand during the Thaksin Era (2001–2006)', *Asian Politics & Policy*, 1, no. 3: 409–34.

Lazarus, Neil 2011, *The Postcolonial Unconscious*, Cambridge: Cambridge University Press.

Lecercle, Jean-Jacques 2006, *A Marxist Philosophy of Language*, Leiden: Brill.

Lecercle, Jean-Jacques 2009 [2005], *A Marxist Philosophy of Language*, Chicago: Haymarket Books.

Lefebvre, Henri 1959, *La Somme et le reste*, Paris: La Nef de Paris.

Lefebvre, Henri 1974, *The Survival of Capitalism*, London: Allen and Busby.

Lefebvre, Henri 1991, *The Production of Space*, Oxford: Blackwell.

Lenin, V.I. 1972 [1918], 'The Immediate Tasks of the Soviet Government', now in *Collected Works*, Volume 27, Moscow: Progress Publishers.

Leonetti, Alfonso 1957, 'Presentation of *Americanisme et fordisme*', *Cahiers internationaux*, 89.

Liguori, Guido 1996, *Gramsci conteso. Storia di un dibattito 1922–1996*, Rome: Editori Riuniti.

Liguori, Guido 2004a, 'Ideologia', in Frosini and Liguori (eds) 2004.

Liguori, Guido 2004b, 'Stato-società civile', in Frosini and Liguori (eds) 2004.

Liguori, Guido 2005, 'Note sulla fortuna di Gramsci in Brasile', in *Filosofia e politica in America Latina*, edited by Pio Colonnello, Rome: Armando.

Liguori, Guido 2006, *Sentieri gramsciani*, Rome: Carocci.

Liguori, Guido 2009a, 'Buon senso', in Liguori and Voza (eds) 2009.

Liguori, Guido 2009b, 'Common Sense in Gramsci', in *Perspective on Gramsci. Politics, Culture and Social Theory*, edited by Joseph Francese, London: Routledge.

Liguori, Guido 2009c, 'Ideologia', in Liguori and Voza (eds) 2009.

Liguori, Guido 2011, 'Tre accezioni di "subalterno" in Gramsci', *Critica marxista*, 6: 33–41.

Liguori, Guido 2012, *Gramsci conteso. Interpretazioni, dibattiti e polemiche. 1922–2012*, Rome: Editori Riuniti University Press.

Liguori, Guido 2015a, 'Conceptions of Subalternity in Gramsci', in McNally (ed.) 2015.

Liguori, Guido 2015b, *Gramsci's Pathways*, Leiden: Brill.

Liguori, Guido 2015c, '"Classi subalterne" marginali e "classi subalterne" fondamentali in Gramsci', *Critica marxista*, 4: 41–48.

Liguori, Guido 2016, 'Subalterno e subalterni nei "Quaderni del carcere"', *International Gramsci Journal*, 2, no. 1: 89–125.

Liguori, Guido and Pasquale Voza (eds) 2009, *Dizionario gramsciano 1926–1937*, Rome: Carocci.

Lipietz, Alain 1993, 'Fordism and Post-Fordism', in *The Blackwell Dictionary of Twentieth Century Social Thought*, edited by William Outhwaite and Tom Bottomore, Oxford: Blackwell.

Lisa, Athos 1973, *Memorie. Dall'ergastolo di Santo Stefano alla Casa penale di Turi di Bari*, Milan: Feltrinelli.

Lloyd, David 1993, *Anomalous States: Irish Writing and the Post-Colonial Moment*, Durham, NC: Duke University Press.

Lo Piparo, Franco 1979, *Lingua, intellettuali, egemonia in Gramsci*, Bari: Laterza.

Lo Piparo, Franco 2010, 'The Linguistic Roots of Gramsci's Non-Marxism', in Ives and Lacorte (eds) 2010.

Lo Piparo, Franco 2014, *Il professor Gramsci e Wittgenstein. Il linguaggio e il potere*, Rome: Donzelli.

Lock, Grahame 1996, 'Subject, Interpellation, and Ideology', in *Postmodern Materialism and the Future of Marxist Theory: Essays in the Althusserian Tradition*, edited by Antonio Callari and David F. Ruccio, Hanover: Wesleyan University Press.

Loomba, Ania 2005, *Colonialism/Postcolonialism*, London: Routledge.

Losurdo, Domenico 1997, *Antonio Gramsci, dal liberalismo al comunismo critico*, Rome: Gamberetti.

Ludden, David (ed.) 2001, *Reading Subaltern Studies: Critical History, Contested Meaning and the Globalization of South Asia*, London: Anthem Press.

Lukács, Georg 1972, *History and Class Consciousness: Studies in Marxist Dialectics*, translated by Rodney Livingstone, Cambridge, MA: MIT Press.

Luporini, Cesare 1950a, 'Intorno alla storia del "mondo popolare subalterno"', *Società*, VI, no. 1: 95–106.

Luporini, Cesare 1950b, 'Ancora sulla "storia del mondo popolare subalterno"', *Società*, VI, no. 2: 309–12.

Luporini, Cesare 1967, 'Introduzione', in Karl Marx and Friedrich Engels, *L'ideologia tedesca*, edited and translated by Fausto Codino, Rome: Editori Riuniti.

Luporini, Cesare 1974, *Dialettica e materialismo*, Rome: Editori Riuniti.

Lutz, Helma et al. (eds) 2011, *Framing Intersectionality: Debates on a Multi-Faceted Concept in Gender Studies*, Farnham: Ashgate.

MacDiarmid, Hugh 1967 [1955], 'Let us arise', in *Collected Poems*, London: Macmillan.

Macherey, Pierre 2005, 'Verum est factum: les enjeux d'une philosophie de la praxis et le débat Althusser-Gramsci', in *Sartre, Lukács, Althusser, des marxistes en philosophie*, by Stathis Kouvelakis and Vincent Charbonnier, Paris: PUF.

Macherey, Pierre 2008, *Marx 1845. Les 'thèses' sur Feuerbach*, Paris: Éditions Amsterdam.

Machiavelli, Niccolò 1988 [1513], *The Prince*, Cambridge: Cambridge University Press.

Maciocchi, Maria Antonietta 1974, *Per Gramsci*, Bologna: Il Mulino.

Makram-Ebeid, Dina 2015, '"Old People Are Not Revolutionaries!" Labor Struggles between Precarity and Istiqrar in a Factory Occupation in Egypt', *Jadaliyya*, 25 January, available at: http://www.jadaliyya.com/pages/index/20632/%E2%80%9Cold-people-are-not-revolutionaries%E2%80%9D-labor-struggl.

Malabou, Catherine 2005, *The Future of Hegel: Plasticity, Temporality and Dialectic*, translated by Lisabeth During, London: Routledge.

Manacorda, Giuliano 1975, 'Introduzione', in *Antonio Gramsci: Marxismo e letteratura*, edited by Giuliano Manacorda, Rome: Editori Riuniti.

Manager 2014, 'Thaksin Shinawatra Kab Ton Het Kan Taek Yaek Kong Kon Nai Chat [Thaksin Shinawatra is the Cause of National Disharmony', 13 February, available at: http://www.manager.co.th/Daily/ViewNews.aspx?NewsID=9570000017483.

Mangoni, Luisa 1979, 'Per una definizione del fascismo: i concetti di bonapartismo e cesarismo', *Italia contemporanea*, 135: 17–52.

Mansfield, Becky 2008, *Privatization: Property and the Remaking of Nature-Society Relations*, Oxford: Blackwell.

Manzoni, Alessandro 1956 [1827], *The Betrothed*, translated by Archibald Colquhoun, London: J.M. Dent and Sons/E.P. Dutton.

Marshall, Andrew M. 2014, *A Kingdom in Crisis*, London: Zed Books.

Marshall, Shana and Joshua Stacher 2012, 'Egypt's Generals and Transnational Capital', *Middle East Report*, 262, available at: http://www.merip.org/mer/mer262/egypts-generals-transnational-capital.

Marx, Karl 1958 [1845], *Thesen über Feuerbach*, in *Marx-Engels-Werke*, Vol. 3, Berlin: Dietz.

Marx, Karl 1961 [1859], *Zur Kritik der politischen Ökonomie*, in *Marx-Engels-Werke*, Vol. 13, Berlin: Dietz.

Marx, Karl 1976a [1845], *Theses on Feuerbach*, in *Marx and Engels Collected Works*, Vol. 5, London: Lawrence & Wishart.

Marx, Karl 1976b [1847], *The Poverty of Philosophy. Answer to the Philosophy of Poverty by M. Proudhon*, in *Marx and Engels Collected Works*, Vol. 6, London: Lawrence & Wishart.

Marx, Karl 1979 [1852], *The Eighteenth Brumaire of Louis Bonaparte*, in *Marx and Engels Collected Works*, Vol. 11, London: Lawrence & Wishart.

Marx, Karl 1985 [1869] *Preface* to the second edition of *The Eighteenth Brumaire of Louis Bonaparte*, in *Marx and Engels Collected Works*, Vol. 21, London: Lawrence & Wishart.

Marx, Karl 1987a [1857–58], *Grundrisse* (second part), in *Marx and Engels Collected Works*, Vol. 29, London: Lawrence and Wishart.

Marx, Karl 1987b [1859], *A Contribution to the Critique of Political Economy. Part One*, in *Marx and Engels Collected Works*, Vol. 29, London: Lawrence and Wishart.

Marx, Karl and Frederick Engels 1976a [1846], *The German Ideology*, in *Marx and Engels Collected Works*, Vol. 5, London: Lawrence and Wishart.

Marx, Karl and Friedrich Engels 1956–90, *Marx-Engels-Werke* (*MEW*), 43 Vols., Berlin: Dietz.

Marx, Karl and Friedrich Engels 1959 [1848], *Manifest der Kommunistischen Partei*, in *Marx-Engels Werke*, Vol. 4, Berlin: Dietz.

Mastroianni, Giovanni 2003, 'Gramsci, il *für ewig* e la questione dei "Quaderni"', *Giornale di storia contemporanea*, 6, no. 1: 206–31.

Mayo, Peter (ed.) 2010, *Gramsci and Educational Thought*, Oxford: Wiley-Blackwell.

McCargo, Duncan 2005, 'Network Monarchy and Legitimacy Crises in Thailand', *The Pacific Review*, 18, no. 4: 499–519.

McNally, David 2001, *Bodies of Meaning: Studies on Language, Labor, and Liberation*, Albany, NY: SUNY Press.

McNally, David 2011, *Monsters of the Market: Zombies, Vampires and Global Capitalism*, Leiden: Brill.

McNally, Mark (ed.) 2015, *Antonio Gramsci*, Basingstoke: Palgrave Macmillan.

Medhi Krongkaew 2003, 'The Philosophy of Sufficiency Economy', *Kyoto Review of Southeast Asia*, available at: http://kyotoreview.org/issue-4/the-philosophy-of-sufficiency-economy/.

Meisner, Maurice 1999, *Mao's China and After: A History of the People's Republic*, New York: The Free Press.

Mellino, Miguel 2016, 'Gramsci in Slices: Race, Colonialism, Migration and the Postcolonial Gramsci', in García Agustín and Bak Jørgensen (eds) 2016.

Mena, Javier 1996 [1981], *Gramsci y la revolución francesa*, Mexico D.F.: Plaza y Valdés.

Menchú, Rigoberta 1984, *I, Rigoberta Menchú: An Indian Woman in Guatemala*, edited and introduced by Elisabeth Burgos-Debrai, translated by Ann Wright, London-New York: Verso.

Meret, Susi and Elisabetta Della Corte 2016, 'Spaces of Resistance and Re-Actuality of Gramsci in Refugees' Struggles for Rights? The "Lampedua in Hamburg" between Exit and Voice', in García Agustín and Bak Jørgensen (eds) 2016.

Merleau-Ponty, Maurice 1955, *Les Aventures de la dialectique*, Paris: Gallimard.

Merleau-Ponty, Maurice 1956, *Les Philosophes célèbres*, Lausanne: Citadelles et Mazenod.

Merrifield, Andy 2002, *Metromarxism*, London: Routledge.

Mignolo, Walter 1995, *The Darker Side of the Renaissance: Literacy, Territoriality and Colonization*, Ann Arbor: University of Michigan Press.

Mignolo, Walter 2000, *Local Histories/Global Designs: Coloniality, Subaltern Knowledges, and Border Thinking*, Princeton: Princeton University Press.

Mills, Sara 2003, *Michel Foucault*, London: Routledge.

Mitchell, Timothy 2002, *Rule of Experts: Egypt, Techno-politics, Modernity*, Berkeley, CA: University of California Press.

Modonesi, Massimo 2010, *Subalternidad, antagonismo, autonomia. Marxismo y subjetivación política*, Buenos Aires: Clacso/Prometeo Libros.

Modonesi, Massimo 2014, *Subalternity, Antagonism, Autonomy: Constructing the Political Subject*, London: Pluto Press.

Modonesi, Massimo 2015, 'Pasividad y subalternidad. Sobre el concepto de revolución pasiva de Antonio Gramsci', *Gramsciana*, 1: 35–60.

Moe, Nelson 2002, *The View from Vesuvius: Italian Culture and the Southern Question*, Berkeley, CA: University of California Press.

Mohamed Mahmoud, Yasser 2009, *A Political Economy of Egyptian Foreign Policy: State, Ideology and Modernisation since 1970*, PhD dissertation, Department of International Relations, London School of Economics and Political Science.

Molony, John 1977, *The Emergence of Political Catholicism in Italy: Partito Popolare 1919–1926*, London: Croom Helm.

Momani, Bessma 2005, 'IMF-Egyptian Debt Negotiations', *Cairo Papers in Social Science*, 263, Cairo: American University in Cairo Press.

Monforte, Pierre 2014, *Europeanizing Contention: The Protest Against 'Fortress Europe' in France and Germany*, New York: Berghahn Books.

Moore, Jason W. 2015, *Capitalism in the Web of Life: Ecology and the Accumulation of Capital* London: Verso.

Morfino, Vittorio 2015, 'Althusser lecteur de Gramsci', *Actuel Marx*, 57: 62–81.

Morris, Rosalind (ed.) 2010, *Can the Subaltern Speak: Reflections on the History of an Idea*, New York: Columbia University Press.

Morton, Adam D. 2007a, *Unravelling Gramsci: Hegemony and Passive Revolution in the Global Political Economy*, London: Pluto Press.

Morton, Adam D. 2007b, 'Waiting for Gramsci: State Formation, Passive Revolution and the International', *Millennium: Journal of International Studies*, 35, no. 3: 597–621.

Morton, Adam D. 2010, 'The Continuum of Passive Revolution', *Capital & Class*, 34, no. 3: 315–42.

Morton, Adam D. 2011, *Revolution and State in Modern Mexico: The Political Economy of Uneven Development*, Lanham, MD: Rowman & Littlefield.

Morton, Adam D. 2013, 'Traveling with Gramsci: The Spatiality of Passive Revolution', in Ekers et al. (eds) 2013.

Mouffe, Chantal 1979, 'Hegemony and Ideology in Gramsci', in *Gramsci and Marxist Theory*, edited by Chantal Mouffe, London: Routledge & Kegan Paul.

Muscetta, Carlo 1991, 'Gramsci e De Sanctis', in *Gramsci e la modernità. Letteratura e politica tra Ottocento e Novecento*, edited by Valerio Calzolaio, Naples: CUEN.

Musolino, Rocco 1977, *Marxismus und Ästhetik in Italien*, Dresden: VEB Verlag der Kunst.

Nadeau, Maurice 1990, *Grâce leurs soient rendues*, Paris: Albin Michel.

Nation TV 2015, 'Prayuth Chee Thaksin Pen Ton Het Rattapaharn [Prayuth Claimed that Thaksin was the Real Reason Behind the Coup]', 23 May, available at: http://www.nationtv.tv/main/content/politics/378456900/.

Negri, Antonio 1999, *Insurgencies: Constituent Power and the Modern State*, translated by Maurizia Boscagli, Minneapolis: University of Minnesota Press.

Nichols, Robert 2010, 'Postcolonial Studies and the Discourse of Foucault: Survey of a Field of Problematization', *Foucault Studies*, 9: 111–44.

Nietzsche, Friedrich 2002 [1886], *Beyond Good and Evil*, Cambridge: Cambridge University Press.

Nilsen, Alf Gunvald and Srila Roy (eds) 2015, *New Subaltern Politics. Reconceptualizing Hegemony and Resistance in Contemporary India*, New Delhi: Oxford University Press.

Niyogi, Chandreyee 2006, 'Orientalism and its Other(s): Re-reading Marx on India', in *Reorienting Orientalism*, edited by Chandreyee Niyogi, New Delhi: Sage.

Nyers, Peter 2008, 'No One Is Illegal Between City and Nation', in *Acts of Citizenship*, edited by Engin F. Isin and Greg M. Nielsen, London: Zed Books.

O'Hanlon, Rosalind and David Washbrook 1992, 'After Orientalism: Culture, Criticism, and Politics in the Third World', *Comparative Studies in Society and History*, 34, no. 1: 141–68.

Ochoa, John 2006, 'Said's Foucault, or the Places of the Critic', in *Paradoxical Citizenship: Essays on Edward Said*, edited by Silvia Nagy-Zekmi, Lanham, MD: Lexington Books.

Olsen, Kevin 2015, 'Epistemologies of Rebellion: The Tricolor Cockade and the Problem of Subaltern Speech', *Political Theory*, 43, no. 6: 730–52.

Orizzonti Meridiani (ed.) 2014, *Briganti o emigranti. Sud e movimenti tra conricerca e studi subalterni*, Verona: Ombre Corte.

Ortner, Sherry 1995, 'Resistance and the Problem of Ethnographic Refusal', *Comparative Studies in Society and History*, 37, no. 1: 173–93.

Osman, Tarek 2010, *Egypt on the Brink: From Nasser to Mubarak*, New Haven, CT: Yale University Press.

Overbeek, Henk 2004, 'Transnational Class Formation and Concepts of Control: Towards a Genealogy of the Amsterdam Project in International Political Economy', *Journal of International Relations and Development*, 7, no. 2: 113–41.

Paggi, Leonardo 1970, *Antonio Gramsci e il moderno principe. I. Nella crisi del socialismo italiano*, Rome: Editori Riuniti.

Paggi, Leonardo 1984, *Le strategie del potere in Gramsci. Tra fascismo e socialismo in un solo paese. 1923–1926*, Rome: Editori Riuniti.

Pala, Mauro (ed.) 2014, *Narrazioni egemoniche: Gramsci, letteratura e società civile*, Bologna: Il Mulino.

Paladini Musitelli, Marina 2004, 'Brescianesimo', in Frosini and Liguori (eds) 2004.

Paladini Musitelli, Marina 2009, 'Letteratura Popolare', in Liguori and Voza (eds) 2009.

Paladini Musitelli, Marina and Giuseppe Petronio (eds.) 2001, *Marx e Gramsci: Memoria e attualità*, Rome: Manifestolibri.

Pandey, Gyanendra (ed.) 2010, *Subaltern Citizen and Their Histories: Investigations from India and the USA*, New York: Routledge.

Pandey, Gyanendra 2006, 'The Subaltern as Subaltern Citizen', *Economic and Political Weekly*, 41, no. 46: 4735–41.

Panitch, Leo and Sam Gindin 2012, *The Making of Global Capitalism*, London: Verso.

Paris, Robert 1962, 'Le socratisme de Gramsci', *Arguments*, 6: 25–6.

Pasquinelli, Carla (ed.) 1977, *Antropologia culturale e questione meridionale. Ernesto De Martino e il dibattito sul mondo popolare subalterno negli anni 1948–1955*, Florence: La Nuova Italia.

Petrusewicz, Marta 1998, *Come il Meridione divenne una questione. Rappresentazioni del Sud prima e dopo il Quarantotto*, Soveria Mannelli: Rubbettino.

Piotte, Jean-Marc 1970, *La pensée politique de Gramsci*, Ottawa: Parti pris.

Pirenne, Henri 1946 [1927], *Medieval Cities: Their Origins and the Revival of Trade*, Princeton: Princeton University Press.

Pitch Pongsawas 2004, 'Thaksiniyom Eek Tee [Thaksinism as Hegemonic Project (again)]', in *Piss Thaksin [Toxinomics]*, edited by Pinyo Traisuriyathanma, Bangkok: Open.

Pizza, Giovanni 2013, 'Gramsci e De Martino. Appunti per una riflessione', *Quaderni di teoria sociale*, 13: 77–121.

Pocock, John G.A. 1975, *The Machiavellian Moment: Florentine Political Thought and the Atlantic Republican Tradition*, Princeton: Princeton University Press.

(Pohn-)Lauggas, Ingo 2013, *Hegemonie, Kunst und Literatur: Ästhetik und Politik bei Gramsci und Williams*, Wien: Löcker.

(Pohn-)Lauggas, Ingo 2015a, 'Lorianismus', in *Historisch-Kritisches Wörterbuch des Marxismus (HKWM)*, Vol. 8/II, edited by Wolfgang Fritz Haug, Frigga Haug, Peter Jehle and Wolfgang Küttler, Hamburg: Argument.

Pohn-Lauggas, Ingo 2015b, 'Kulturwissenschaftliche Literaturwissenschaft und das Problem der ästhetischen Autonomie: Lehren aus der Kunsttheorie des frühen Novecento', in *Literatur als Herausforderung. Zwischen ästhetischem Autonomiestreben, kontextueller Fremdbestimmung und dem Gestaltungsanspruch gesellschaftlicher Zukunft*, edited by Henning Hufnagel and Barbara Ventarola, Würzburg: Königshausen & Neumann.

Pohn-Lauggas, Ingo 2017, 'Die Politik des Kulturellen in Raymond Williams' Soziologie der Kultur', in *Über Raymond Williams: Annäherungen, Positionen, Ausblicke*, edited by Ingo Pohn-Lauggas, Roman Horak and Monika Seidl, Hamburg: Argument.

Pollard, John 2008, *Catholicism in Modern Italy: Religion, Society and Politics since 1861*, London: Routledge.

Portantiero, Juan Carlos 1961, *Realismo y realidad en la narrativa argentina*, Buenos Aires: Procyon.

Portantiero, Juan Carlos 1963, 'Política y clases sociales en la Argentina actual', *Pasado y Presente*, I: 18–23.

Portantiero, Juan Carlos 1964, 'Un análisis "marxista" de la argentina', *Pasado y Presente*, V/VI: 82–6.

Portantiero, Juan Carlos 1973a, 'Clases dominantes y crisis política en la Argentina actual', *Pasado y Presente*, I (2°): 31–64.

Portantiero, Juan Carlos 1973b, 'Introducción a un inédito de Cooke', *Pasado y Presente*, II/III (2°): 369–72.

Portantiero, Juan Carlos 1977, *Antonio Gramsci, Escritos Políticos (1917–1933)*. *Cuadernos de Pasado y Presente*, 54, México: Pasado y Presente.

Portantiero, Juan Carlos 1978, *Estudiantes y política en América Latina*, Mexico: Siglo XXI.

Portantiero, Juan Carlos 1979, 'Transformación social y crisis de la política', *Controversia*, II/III: 1–4.

Portantiero, Juan Carlos 1988, *La producción de un orden*, Buenos Aires: Ediciones Nueva Visión.

Portantiero, Juan Carlos 1999 [1971], *Los usos de Gramsci*, Buenos Aires: Grijalbo.

Portantiero, Juan Carlos and Miguel Murmis 2004 [1977], *Estudios sobre los orígenes del peronismo*, Buenos Aires: Siglo XXI.

Portelli, Hugues 1976, *Gramsci e la questione religiosa*, translated by Giangiacomo Cantoni, Milan: Mazzotta.

Poulantzas, Nicos 1965, 'Préliminaires à l'étude de l'hégémonie dans l'état', *Les Temps modernes*, 234: 862–96 and 235: 1048–69.

Poulantzas, Nicos 1968, *Pouvoir politique et classes sociales*, Paris: Maspero.

Poulantzas, Nicos 1978, *State, Power, Socialism*, translated by Patrick Camiller, London: New Left Books.

Prachatai 2015, 'Kadee Min Laew Set 239 Kadee Jak Kang Pee Kon 443 Kadee [Lese majesté Cases were cleared for 239 cases as derived from the last year for 443 cases]', 25 April, available at: http://prachatai.org/journal/2015/04/58968.

Pravit Rojanaphruk 2015, 'How Thailand's Military Junta Tried to "Adjust My Attitude" in Detention', 23 September, available at: http://thediplomat.com/2015/09/how-thailands-military-junta-tried-to-adjust-my-attitude-in-detention/.

Prestipino, Giuseppe 2004, 'Dialettica', in Frosini and Liguori (eds) 2004.

Prestipino, Giuseppe 2009, 'Dialettica', in Liguori and Voza (eds) 2009.

Quijano, Anibal 2000, 'Coloniality of Power, Eurocentrism, and Latin America', *Nepantla: Views from South*, 1, no. 3: 533–80.

Rabasa, José 2010, *Without History: Subaltern Studies, the Zapatista Insurgency, and the Specter of History*, Pittsburgh: University of Pittsburgh Press.

Racevskis, Karlis 2005, 'Edward Said and Michel Foucault: Affinities and Dissonances', *Research in African Literatures*, 36, no. 3: 83–97.

Radhakrishnan, Rajagopalan 1990, 'Toward an Effective Intellectual: Foucault or Gramsci?', in *Intellectuals: Aesthetics, Politics, Academics*, edited by Bruce Robbins, Minneapolis: University of Minnesota Press.

Ragazzini, Dario 2002, *Leonardo nella società di massa. Teoria della personalità in Gramsci*, Bergamo: Moretti Honegger.

Reed, Jean-Pierre 2012, 'Theorist of Subaltern Subjectivity: Antonio Gramsci, Popular Beliefs, Political Passion, and Reciprocal Learning', *Critical Sociology*, 39, no. 4: 561–91.

Rehmann, Jan 2013, *Theories of Ideology. The Powers of Alienation and Subjection*, Leiden: Brill.

Richards, Alan 1991, 'The Political Economy of Dilatory Reform: Egypt in the 1980s', *World Development*, 19, no. 12: 1721–30.

Richet, Denis 1953, 'Gramsci, le géant', *La Nouvelle Critique*, 50.

Richet, Denis 1954, 'Gramsci et l'histoire de France', *La Pensée*, 55.

Richter, Melvin 2005, 'A Family of Political Concepts: Tyranny, Despotism, Bonapartism, Caesarism, Dictatorship, 1750–1917', *European Journal of Political Theory*, 4, no. 3: 221–48.

Riechers, Christian 1970, *Antonio Gramsci: Marxismus in Italien*, Frankfurt: Europäische Verlagsanstalt.

Rivera, Annamaria 2007, 'Storie etnografiche e "culture subalterne"', in *Culture planetarie? Prospettive e limiti della teoria e della critica culturale*, edited by Sergia Adamo, Rome: Meltemi.

Roberts, David D. 2011, 'Reconsidering Gramsci's Interpretation of Fascism', *Journal of Modern Italian Studies*, 16, no. 2: 239–55.

Roberts, Michael 2016, *The Long Depression: Marxism and the Global Crisis of Capitalism*, Chicago: Haymarket Books.

Robinson, Andrew 2005, 'Towards an Intellectual Reformation: The Critique of Common Sense and the Forgotten Revolutionary Project of Gramscian Theory', *Critical Review of International Social and Political Philosophy*, 8, no. 4: 469–81.

Robinson, William I. 2001, 'Social Theory and Globalisation: The Rise of a Transnational State', *Theory and Society*, 30, no. 2: 157–200.

Robinson, William I. 2008, *Latin America and Global Capitalism*, Baltimore: Johns Hopkins University Press.

Roccu, Roberto 2013, *The Political Economy of the Egyptian Revolution: Mubarak, Economic Reforms and Failed Hegemony*, Basingstoke: Palgrave Macmillan.

Roccu, Roberto 2017, 'Passive revolution revisited: From the *Prison Notebooks* to our "great and terrible world"', *Capital & Class*, 41, no. 3: 537–59.

Rodríguez, Ileana and María Milagros López (eds) 2001, *The Latin American Subaltern Studies Reader*, Durham, NC: Duke University Press.

Roll, Stephan 2010, '"Finance Matters!" The Influence of Financial Sector Reforms on the Development of the Entrepreneurial Elite in Egypt', *Mediterranean Politics*, 15, no. 3: 349–70.

Roseberry, William 1994, 'Hegemony and the Language of Contention', in *Everyday Forms of State Formation*, edited by Gilbert Joseph and David Nugent, Durham, NC: Duke University Press.

Rosengarten, Frank 1986, 'Gramsci's "Little Discovery": Gramsci's Interpretation of Canto X of Dante's Inferno', *boundary 2*, 14, no. 3: 71–90.

Rosselli, Carlo 1973 [1925], 'Le memorie di Henry Ford', *La riforma sociale* (Fall 1925), now in *Socialismo liberale e altri scritti, 1919–1930*, edited by John Rosselli, Turin: Einaudi.

Ruggiero, Raffaele 2015, *Machiavelli e la crisi dell'analogia*, Bologna: Il Mulino.

Rupert, Mark 1993, 'Alienation, Capitalism and the Inter-state System: Toward a Marxian/Gramscian Critique', in *Gramsci, Historical Materialism and International Relations*, edited by Stephen Gill, New York: Cambridge University Press.

Rupert, Mark 1995, *Producing Hegemony: The Politics of Mass Production and American Global Power*, Cambridge: Cambridge University Press.

Saad, Reem 2002, 'Egyptian Politics and the Tenancy Law', in *Counter-Revolution in Egypt's Countryside: Land and Farmers in the Era of Economic Reform*, edited by Ray Bush, London: Zed Books.

Sadiki, Larbi 2000, 'Popular Uprisings and Arab Democratization', *International Journal of Middle East Studies*, 32, no. 1: 72–95.

Said, Edward W. 1966, *Joseph Conrad and the Fiction of Autobiography*, Cambridge, MA: Harvard University Press.

Said, Edward W. 1970, 'The Arab Portrayed', in *The Arab-Israeli Confrontation of June 1967: An Arab Perspective*, edited by Ibrahim Abu-Lughod, Evanston: Northwestern University Press.

Said, Edward W. 1975, *Beginnings: Intention and Method*, New York: Columbia University Press.

Said, Edward W. 1978, *Orientalism: Western Conceptions of the Orient*, New York: Pantheon Books.

Said, Edward W. 1979, *The Question of Palestine*, New York: Times Books.

Said, Edward W. 1981, *Covering Islam: How the Media and the Experts Determine how We See the Rest of the World*, New York: Pantheon Books.

Said, Edward W. 1983a, 'Criticism Between Culture and System', in Edward W. Said, *The World, the Text, and the Critic*, London: Vintage.

Said, Edward W. 1983b, 'Reflections on American "Left" Literary Criticism', in Edward W. Said, *The World, the Text, and the Critic*, London: Vintage.

Said, Edward W. 1983c, 'Traveling Theory', in Edward W. Said, *The World, the Text, and the Critic*, London: Vintage.

Said, Edward W. 1986, 'Intellectuals in the Post-Colonial World', *Salmagundi*, 70/71: 44–64.

Said, Edward W. 1992, 'Interview with Edward Said', in *Edward Said: A Critical Reader*, edited by Jennifer Wicke and Michael Sprinker, Oxford: Blackwell.

Said, Edward W. 1993, *Culture and Imperialism*, London: Chatto & Windus.

Said, Edward W. 1994, *Representations of the Intellectual: The 1993 Reith Lectures*, London: Vintage.

Said, Edward W. 2000a, 'Foucault and the Imagination of Power', in Edward W. Said, *Reflections on Exile and Other Essays*, Cambridge, MA: Harvard University Press.

Said, Edward W. 2000b, 'Traveling Theory Reconsidered', in Edward Said, *Reflections on Exile and Other Essays*, Cambridge, MA: Harvard University Press.

Said, Edward W. 2001a, 'History, Literature and Geography', in Edward W. Said, *Reflections on Exile and Other Literary and Cultural Essays*, London: Granta.

Said, Edward W. 2001b, 'Traveling Theory Reconsidered', in Edward W. Said, *Reflections on Exile and other Literary and Cultural Essays*, London: Granta.

Said, Edward W. 2003 [1978], *Orientalism*, London: Penguin.

Said, Edward W. 2004, *Humanism and Democratic Criticism*, New York: Columbia.

Salamini, Leonardo 1981, *The Sociology of Political Praxis: An Introduction to Gramsci's Theory*, London: Routledge & Kegan Paul.

Sanguineti, Edoardo 2000, 'Letteratura e vita nazionale', in *Il chierico organico. Scritture e intellettuali*, edited by Erminio Risso, Milan: Feltrinelli.

Santucci, Antonio 2010, *Antonio Gramsci*, New York: Monthly Review Press.

Sartre, Jean-Paul 1960, *Critique de la raison dialectique*, Paris: Gallimard (with *Questions de méthode* as an introduction, originally published in *Les Temps modernes*, 139 and 140, September and October 1957).

Sartre, Jean-Paul 1966, 'Jean-Paul Sartre répond', in *L'Arc*, 30.

Sartre, Jean-Paul 1972, *Plaidoyer pour les intellectuels*, Paris: Gallimard.

Sassen, Saskia 1991, *The Global City: New York, London, Tokyo*. Princeton: Princeton University Press.

Sawatri Suksri 2011, 'Kod Mai Computer Tong Mee Pua Kamnod Kobket Kwam Rabpid [Computer Crime Act is Needed in order to Scope the Quilt]', in *Born to be Democracy*, edited by Chuwas Rerksirisuk, Bangkok: Prachatai Book Club.

Sawatri Suksri 2012, *Kwam Mued Klang Saeng Daed [Darkness in the Sunshine]*, interviewed by Worapot Panpong and Thiti Meetam, Bangkok: Banglumpoo.

Sbarberi, Franco 2005, 'Introduzione', in Norberto Bobbio, *Politica e cultura*, edited by Franco Sbarberi, Turin: Einaudi.

Schirru, Giancarlo and Giuseppe Vacca (eds) 2007, *Studi gramsciani nel mondo 2000–2005*, Bologna: Il Mulino.

Schlumberger, Oliver 2008, 'Structural Reforms, Economic Order, and Development: Patrimonial Capitalism', *Review of International Political Economy*, 15, no. 4: 622–45.

Schneider, Jane (ed.) 1998, *Italy's Southern Question: Orientalism in One Country*, Oxford and New York: Berg.

Schwartzmantel, John 2009, 'Gramsci in His Time and in Ours', in *Gramsci and Global Politics: Hegemony and Resistance*, edited by Mark Mcnally and John Schwartzmantel, New York: Routledge.

Scott, James C. 1985, *Weapons of the Weak: Everyday Forms of Peasant Resistance*, New Haven, CT: Yale University Press.

Scott, James C. 1990, *Domination and the Arts of Resistance: Hidden Transcripts*, New Haven, CT: Yale University Press.

Sen, Amartya 2003, 'Sraffa, Wittgenstein, and Gramsci', *Journal of Economic Literature* 41, no. 4: 1240–55.

Seroni, Adriano 1958, 'La distinzione fra "critica d'arte" (estetica) e "critica politica" in Gramsci, il concetto di "lotta culturale" e le indicazioni metodiche per un nuovo storicismo critico', in *Studi gramsciani. Atti del convegno tenuto a Roma nei giorni 11–13 gennaio 1958*, Rome: Editori Riuniti.

Settis, Bruno 2016, *Fordismi. Storia politica della produzione di massa*, Bologna: Il Mulino.

Sewell, William 1988, 'Le Citoyen/la Citoyenne: Activity, Passivity, and the Revolutionary Concept of Citizenship', in *The Political Culture of the French Revolution*, edited by Colin Lucas, Oxford: Pergamon Press.

Shepperson, George 1962, 'The Comparative Study of Millenarian Movements', in *Millennial Dreams in Action: Essays in Comparative Study*, edited by Sylvia L. Thrupp, London: Mouton.

Short, Nicola 2013, 'Difference and Inequality in World Affairs: A Gramscian Analysis', in Ekers et al. 2013.

Smith, Gavin 2004, 'Hegemony: Critical Interpretations in Anthropology and Beyond', *Focaal*, 43: 99–120.

Smith, Gavin 2014, *Intellectuals and (Counter-)Politics: Essays in Historical Realism*, London: Berghahn Books.

Smith, Neil 1984, *Uneven Development: Nature, Capital and the Production of Space*, Oxford: Blackwell.

Soja, Edward 1989, *Postmodern Geographies*, London: Verso.

Soliman, Samer 2011, *The Autumn of Dictatorship: Fiscal Crisis and Political Change in Egypt under Mubarak*, Princeton, NJ: Princeton University Press.

Somchai Preechasilpakul and David Streckfuss 2008, 'Ramification and Re-sacralization of the Lèse Majesté Law in Thailand', in *10th International Conference on Thai Studies, Bangkok, Thailand*.

Soriano, Marc 1993, 'In Francia con Gramsci', *Belfagor*, 48, no. 4: 465–474.

Śpiewak, Paweł 1977, *Gramsci*, Warszawa: Wiedza Powszechna.

Spivak, Gayatri C. 1985, 'Subaltern Studies: Deconstructing Historiography', in *Subaltern Studies IV*, edited by Ranajit Guha, Delhi: Oxford University Press.

Spivak, Gayatri C. 1988a, 'Can the Subaltern Speak?', in *Marxism and the Interpretation of Culture*, edited by Lawrence Grossberg and Cary Nelson, Urbana, IL: University of Illinois Press.

Spivak, Gayatri C. 1988b, 'Deconstructing Historiography', in *Selected Subaltern Studies*, edited by Ranajit Guha and Gayatri Chakravorty Spivak, Oxford: Oxford University Press.

Spivak, Gayatri C. 1990, *The Postcolonial Critic: Interviews, Strategies, Dialogues*, New York: Routledge.

Spivak, Gayatri C. 2000, 'The New Subaltern: A Silent Interview', in *Mapping Subaltern Studies and the Postcolonial*, edited by Vinayak Chaturvedi, London: Verso.

Spivak, Gayatri C. 2005, 'Scattered Speculations on the Subaltern and the Popular', *Postcolonial Studies* 8, no. 4: 475–86.

Spivak, Gayatri C. 2012, 'Scattered Speculations on the Subaltern and the Popular', in *An Aesthetic Education in the Era of Globalization*, Cambridge, MA: Harvard University Press.

Springborg, Robert 1989, *Mubarak's Egypt: Fragmentation of the Political Order*, Boulder, CO: Westview Press.

Srivastava, Neelam and Baidik Bhattacharya (eds) 2012, *The Postcolonial Gramsci*, New York: Routledge.

Stalin, Joseph S. 1954 [1925], *Works*, Vol. 7, Moscow: Foreign Languages Publishing House.

Storper, Michael and Richard Walker 1989, *The Capitalist Imperative*, Oxford: Blackwell.

Streckfuss, David 2010, 'The Intricacies of Lese-Majesty: A Comparative Study of Imperial Germany and Modern Thailand', in *Saying the Unsayable Monarchy and Democracy in Thailand*, edited by Soren Ivarsson and Lotte Isager, Copenhagen: NIAS.

Streckfuss, David 2011, *Truth on Trial in Thailand: Defamation, Treason, and Lèse-Majesté*, London: Routledge.

Swyngedouw, Erik 1996, 'The city as a hybrid: on nature, society and cyborg urbanization', *Capitalism Nature Socialism*, 7, no. 2: 65–80.

Swyngedouw, Erik 2015, 'Depoliticized environments and the promises of the Anthropocene' in *The International Handbook of Political Ecology*, edited by Raymond Bryant, Cheltenham: Edward Elgar.

Szacki, Jerzy 1962, 'Gramsci: filozofia "czlowieka zbiorowego"', *Filozofia i socjologia XX wieku* 1: 179–203.

Tagliavini, Carlo 1965, *La stratificazione del lessico albanese*, Bologna: Pàtron.

TCIJ 2014, 'Karn Chai Lae Satiti Kadee Matra 112 [Usages and Statistics of the Article 112]', 14 April, available at: http://www.tcijthai.com/tcijthainews/view.php?ids=4217.

Terracini, Umberto 1949, 'Antonio Gramsci ou la restauration idéologique du mouvement ouvrier italien', *Cahiers intrernationaux*, I.

Terray, Emmanuel 1996, 'An Encounter: Althusser and Machiavelli', in *Postmodern*

Materialism and the Future of Marxist Theory: Essays in the Althusserian Tradition, edited by Antonio Callari and David F. Ruccio, Hanover: Wesleyan University Press.

Teti, Andrea 2014, 'Orientalism as a Form of Confession', *Foucault Studies*, 17: 193–212.

Texier, Jacques 1968, 'Gramsci teorico delle sovrastrutture e il concetto di società civile', *Critica marxista*, VI, no. 3: 71–99.

Texier, Jacques 1979, 'Gramsci, Theoretician of the Superstructures', in *Gramsci and Marxist Theory*, edited by Chantal Mouffe, London: Routledge and Kegan Paul.

Texier, Jacques 2009, 'Società civile', in Liguori and Voza (eds) 2009.

Thak Chaloemtiarana 2007, *Thailand: The Politics of Despotic Paternalism*, Cornell: South East Asia Program Publications.

The Lampedusa in Hamburg 2013, 'Erklärung an die Politik und die Öffentlichkeit "Lampedusa in Hamburg II"', 20 May, at http://lampedusa-hamburg.info//page/21/.

The Lampedusa in Hamburg 2016, *International Conference of Refugees & Migrants. The Struggle of Refugees. How to Go On? Stop War on Migrants*, Hamburg, 26–28 February, printed flyer.

The VOICE Refugee Forum 2014, *1994–2014: 20 Years are Not Enough*, printed flyer.

Thomas, Peter D. 2006, 'Modernity as "Passive Revolution": Gramsci and the Fundamental Concepts of Historical Materialism', *Journal of the Canadian Historical Association / Revue de la Société historique du Canada*, 17: 61–78.

Thomas, Peter D. 2008, 'Katharsis', in *Das historisch-kritische Wörterbuch des Marxismus* 7/I, Berlin: InkriT.

Thomas, Peter D. 2009a, *The Gramscian Moment: Philosophy, Hegemony and Marxism*, Leiden: Brill.

Thomas, Peter D. 2009b, 'Catharsis', *Historical Materialism*, 17, no. 3: 259–64.

Thomas, Peter D. 2010, *The Gramscian Moment: Philosophy, Hegemony and Marxism*, Chicago: Haymarket.

Thomas, Peter D. 2013a, 'The Communist Hypothesis and the Question of Organization', *Theory & Event*, 16, no. 4. Available at: muse.jhu.edu/article/530491.

Thomas, Peter D. 2013b, 'Hegemony, Passive Revolution and the Modern Prince', *Thesis Eleven* 117, no. 1: 20–39.

Thomas, Peter D. 2015a, 'Cosa rimane dei subalterni alla luce dello "Stato integrale"?', *International Gramsci Journal*, 1, no. 4: 83–93.

Thomas, Peter D. 2015b, 'Gramsci's Marxism: the "Philosophy of Praxis"', in McNally (ed.) 2015.

Thompson, Edward P. 1977, 'Folklore, Anthropology and Social History', *Indian Historical Review*, III, no. 2: 247–66.

Thompson, Edward P. 1991, *Customs in Common*, New York: New Press.

Thongchai Winichakul 2014, 'The Monarchy and Anti-Monarchy: Two Elephants in the Room of Thai Politics and the State of Denial', in *Good Coup Gone Bad: Thailand's*

Political Developments Since Thaksin's Downfall, edited by Pavin Chachavalpongpun, Singapore: Institute of Southeast Asian Studies.

Timpanaro, Sebastiano 1969, *Classicismo e illuminismo nell'Ottocento italiano*, Pisa: Nistri-Lischi.

Tiné, Salvatore 2012, 'Internazionalismo e questione nazionale nel pensiero di Gramsci', *Associazione Politico-Culturale Marx XXI*, http://www.marx21.it/storia-teoria-e -scienza/marxismo/1228-internazionalismo-e-questione-nazionale-nel-pensiero- di-gramsci.html.

Togliatti, Palmiro 1937, 'Antonio Gramsci, capo della classe operaia', *Lo Stato operaio* (Paris), 5–6 (May–June).

Tomba, Massimiliano 2013, *Marx's Temporalities*, Leiden: Brill.

Tooze, Adam 2014, *The Deluge: The Great War and the Remaking of Global Order, 1916– 1931*, London: Penguin.

Torfing, Jacob 1999, *New Theories of Discourse: Laclau, Mouffe and Žižek*, Oxford: Blackwell.

Tosel, André 1995, 'In Francia' in *Gramsci in Europa e in America*, edited by Antonio A. Santucci, Rome-Bari: Laterza.

Trotsky, Leon 2007, *History of the Russian Revolution*, London: Pluto Press.

Tuğal, Cihan 2012, 'Egypt's Emergent Passive Revolution', *Jadaliyya*, 20 June, available at: http://www.jadaliyya.com/pages/index/6095/egypts-emergent-passive- revolution.

Turner, Victor 1974, *Dramas, Fields, and Metaphors: Symbolic Action in Human Society*, Ithaca: Cornell University Press.

Tylor, Edward Burnett 1920 [1871[1]], *Primitive Culture*, New York: Putnam.

Unger, Daniel 2009, 'Sufficiency Economy and the Bourgeois Virtues', *Asian Affairs: An American Review*, 36, no. 3: 139–56.

Vacca, Giuseppe (ed.) 1999, *Gramsci e il Novecento*, Rome: Carocci.

Vacca, Giuseppe 2011, 'Gramsci studies since 1989', *Journal of Modern Italian Studies*, 16, no. 2: 179–94.

Vacca, Giuseppe 2012, *Vita e pensieri di Antonio Gramsci, 1926–1937*, Turin: Einaudi.

Vacca, Giuseppe, Paolo Capuzzo and Giancarlo Schirru (eds) 2008, *Studi gramsciani nel mondo: gli studi culturali*, Bologna: Il mulino.

Van der Pijl, Kees 1984, *The Making of the Atlantic Ruling Class*, London: Verso.

Vanzulli, Marco 2013, *Il marxismo e l'idealismo: Studi su Labriola, Croce, Gentile, Gramsci*, Rome: Aracne Editrice.

Vatter, Miguel 2005, 'Machiavelli After Marx: The Self-Overcoming of Marxism in the Late Althusser', *Theory and Event*, 7, no. 4. Available at: https://muse.jhu.edu/article/ 244122.

Venuti, Lawrence 2012, *The Translator's Invisibility: A History of Translation*, Hoboken, NJ: Taylor and Francis.

Verucci, Guido 2006, *Idealisti all'indice: Croce, Gentile e la condanna del Sant'Uffizio*, Bari: Laterza.

Vincent, Jean-Marie 1962, 'Report on Oeuvres choisies', *Revue française de science politique*, 12, no. 1.

Vincent, Jean-Marie 1973, 'Hommage à Serge Mallet', *L'Homme et la société* (Paris), 29, no. 1.

Violi, Carlo 1997, 'Introduzione', in Norberto Bobbio, *Né con Marx né contro Marx*, edited by Carlo Violi, Rome: Editori Riuniti.

Vološinov, V.N. 1973 [1929], *Marxism and the Philosophy of Language*, translated by L. Matejka and I.R. Titunik, New York: Seminar Press.

Voza, Pasquale 2004, 'Rivoluzione passiva', in Frosini and Liguori (eds) 2004.

Wagner, Birgit 1999, 'Argomenti di cultura. I 'Quaderni' alla luce delle scienze culturali', in *Gramsci. Il linguaggio della politica*, edited by Rita Medici, Bologna: CLUEB.

Wagner, Birgit 2011, 'Cultural Translation: A Value or a Tool? Let's Start with Gramsci!', *Goethezeitportal*, available at: http://publikationen.ub.uni-frankfurt.de/frontdoor/index/index/docId/23347.

Wagner, Birgit 2012, 'Gramsci heute lesen', in *Antonio Gramsci: Literatur und Kultur*, edited by Ingo (Pohn-)Lauggas, Hamburg: Argument.

Wainwright, Joel 2013, 'On the Nature of Gramsci's Conception of the World', in Ekers et al. (eds) 2013.

Walker, Andrew 2010, 'Royal Sufficiency and Elite Misrepresentation of Rural Livelihoods', in *Saying the Unsayable: Monarchy and Democracy in Thailand*, edited by Soren Ivarsson and Lotte Isager, Copenhagen: NIAS.

Walker, Andrew 2012, *Thailand Political Peasants: Power in the Rural Economy*, Madison: University of Wisconsin Press.

Wallerstein, Immanuel 1983, 'The Three Instances of Hegemony in the History of the Capitalist World-Economy', *International Journal of Comparative Sociology*, 24, no. 1–2: 100–8.

Watcharabon Buddharaksa 2014a, *The Old is Dying and the New Cannot Be Born: Organic Crisis, Social Forces, and the Thai State, 1997–2010*, PhD thesis, University of York.

Watcharabon Buddharaksa 2014b, *A Survey of Gramsci's Political Thought* [in Thai], Bangkok: Sommadhi.

Wei, George 2011, 'Mao's Legacy Revisited: Its Lasting Impact on China and Post-Mao Era', *Asian Politics and Policy*, 3, no. 11: 3–27.

Williams, Gareth 2002, *The Other Side of the Popular: Neoliberalism and Subalternity in Latin America*, Durham, NC: Duke University Press.

Williams, Raymond 1958, *Culture and Society 1780–1950*, New York: Columbia University Press.

Williams, Raymond 1977, *Marxism and Literature*, Oxford: Oxford University Press.

Williams, Raymond 2005 [1980], *Culture and Materialism*, London: Verso.

Wood, Ellen Meiksins 2002 [1999] *The Origin of Capitalism: A Longer View*, London: Verso.

World Bank GINI Index (World Bank Estimate), available at: http://data.worldbank.org/indicator/SI.POV.GINI?page=1.

Worsley, Peter 1957, *The Trumpet Shall Sound: A Study of 'Cargo' Cults in Melanesia*, London: MacGibbon & Kee.

Worsley, Peter 1964, *The Third World*, London: Weidenfeld and Nicolson.

Worsley, Peter 1969, 'The Concept of Populism', in *Populism: Its Meanings and National Characteristics*, edited by Ghita Ionescu and Ernest Gellner, London: Weidenfeld & Nicolson.

Worsley, Peter 1997, *Knowledges: Culture, Counterculture, Subculture*, New York: New Press.

Wu Ming 2014, *L'armata dei sonnambuli*, Milan: Bompiani.

Wurzel, Ulrich 2009, 'The Political Economy of Authoritarianism in Egypt: Insufficient Structural Reforms, Limited Outcomes and a Lack of New Actors', in *The Arab State and Neo-Liberal Globalization: The Restructuring of State Power in the Middle East*, edited by Laura Guazzone and Daniela Pioppi, Reading: Ithaca Press.

Young, Robert 1990, *White Mythologies: Writing History and the West*, London: Routledge.

Young, Robert 2001, *Postcolonialism: An Historical Introduction*, Oxford: Blackwell.

Young, Robert 2012, 'Il Gramsci meridionale', in Srivastava and Bhattacharya (eds) 2012.

Yovel, Yirmiyahu 1989, *Spinoza and other Heretics: The Adventures of Immanence*, Princeton, NJ: Princeton University Press.

Zaalouk, Malak 1989, *Power, Class and Foreign Capital in Egypt: The Rise of the New Bourgeoisie*, London: Zed Books.

Zene, Cosimo (ed.) 2013, *The Political Philosophies of Antonio Gramsci and B.R. Ambedkar: Itineraries of Dalits and Subalterns*, New York: Routledge.

Zene, Cosimo 2011, 'Self-Consciousness of the Dalits as "Subalterns": Reflections on Gramsci in South Asia', *Rethinking Marxism*, 23, no. 1: 83–99.

Ziebura, Gilbert 1990, *World Economy and World Politics, 1924–1931: From Reconstruction to Collapse*, New York: Berg.

Žižek, Slavoj 1997, 'Multiculturalism, Or, The Cultural Logic of Multinational Capitalism', *New Left Review*, I/225.

Archival Sources

Louis Althusser, in Fonds de l'IMEC: Abbaye d'Ardenne.

Georges Cogniot, in Fonds d'archives du Parti communiste français (PCF): Bobigny.

Edizioni e traduzioni di Gramsci all'estero, UA-47, in Fondo Istituto Gramsci: Roma.

Roland Leroy, in Archives départementales de Seine-Saint-Denis, Fonds d'archives du Parti communiste français (PCF): Bobigny.

Emmanuel Mounier/Esprit, in Fonds de l'IMEC: Abbaye d'Ardenne.

Pierre Naville, in Fonds du Musée Social/CEDIAS: Paris.

Waldeck Rochet, in Archives départementales de Seine-Saint-Denis, Fonds d'archives du Parti communiste français (PCF): Bobigny.

Alfred Rosmer, in Fonds du Musée Social/CEDIAS: Paris. Maurice Thorez, in Archives nationales: Paris.

Maurice Thorez, in Bibliothèque privée de M. Thorez: Ivry-sur-Seine.

Sources from Althusser's Archives

All taken from the IMEC Archives (IMEC 2013) and translated by the author from the French. See: http://www.imec-archives.com/fonds/althusser-louis/

ALT2. A18–03.11: Appareils Idéologiques d'État. Fragments.

ALT2. A26–05.06: Que faire?, 1978.

ALT2. A26–05.07: Que faire? (suite), 1978.

ALT2. A31–04.03: Machiavel et nous. Projet de début du texte.

ALT2. A31–04.05: Fragments du cours sur Machiavel.

Index of Names

Index of Subjects

CPSIA information can be obtained
at www.ICGtesting.com
Printed in the USA
JSHW041454031120
9286JS00007B/101